Cognitive Assessment

The Guilford Clinical Psychology and Psychotherapy Series
Michael J. Mahoney, Editor

Agoraphobia: Nature and Treatment
Andrew M. Mathews, Michael G. Gelder, and Derek W. Johnston

Cognitive Assessment
Thomas V. Merluzzi, Carol R. Glass, and Myles Genest, Editors

Cognitive Therapy of Depression
Aaron T. Beck, A. John Rush, Brian F. Shaw, and Gary Emery

In Preparation
Relapse Prevention
G. Alan Marlatt and Judith Gordon

Cognitive Therapy of Pain
Dennis Turk, Donald Meichenbaum, and Myles Genest

Insomnia
Richard Bootzin, Thomas Borkovec, and Peter Hauri

Knowledge Organization and Emotional Disorders
V. F. Guidano and G. Liotti

Attributional Processes in Clinical Psychology
Lyn Abramson, Editor

Cognitive Assessment

Edited by

Thomas V. Merluzzi
University of Notre Dame

Carol R. Glass
The Catholic University of America

and

Myles Genest
University of Saskatchewan

The Guilford Press • *New York   London*

©1981 The Guilford Press, New York
A Division of Guilford Publications, Inc.
200 Park Avenue South, New York, N.Y. 10003

Printed in the United States of America

Library of Congress Cataloging in Publication Data
Main entry under title:

Cognitive assessment.

 (The Guilford clinical psychology and psychotherapy series)
 Bibliography: p.
 Includes indexes.
 1. Cognition—Testing.   2.   Personality assessment.
I.   Merluzzi, Thomas V.   II.   Glass, Carol R.
III.   Genest, Myles.   IV.   Series: Guilford clinical psychology
and psychotherapy series.   [DNLM: 1.   Cognition.
2.   Psychotherapy BF 311   C6774]
BF698.4.C63   153.9′3   80-24870
ISBN 0-89862-001-5

Contributors

Merrill P. Anderson, PhD, Department of Psychology, Houston Cardiovascular Rehabilitation Center, Houston, Texas

John T. Cacioppo, PhD, Department of Psychology, The University of Iowa, Iowa City, Iowa

Roy Cameron, PhD, Department of Psychology, University of Saskatchewan, Saskatoon, Saskatchewan, Canada

Keith S. Dobson, PhD, Department of Psychiatry, The University of Western Ontario, London, Ontario, Canada

Martha L. Epstein, MS, Department of Psychology, The Pennsylvania State University, University Park, Pennsylvania

K. Anders Ericsson, PhD, Department of Psychology, University of Colorado at Boulder, Boulder, Colorado

Myles Genest, MA, Department of Psychology, University of Saskatchewan, Saskatoon, Saskatchewan, Canada

Carol R. Glass, PhD, Department of Psychology, The Catholic University of America, Washington, D.C.

Linda Rose Krasnor, MASc, Department of Psychology, University of Waterloo, Waterloo, Ontario, Canada

Michael J. Mahoney, PhD, Department of Psychology, The Pennsylvania State University, University Park, Pennsylvania

F. J. McGuigan, PhD, Performance Research Laboratory, University of Louisville, Louisville, Kentucky

Donald Meichenbaum, PhD, Department of Psychology, University of Waterloo, Waterloo, Ontario, Canada

Thomas V. Merluzzi, PhD, Department of Psychology, University of Notre Dame, Notre Dame, Indiana

Walter Mischel, PhD, Department of Psychology, Stanford University, Stanford, California

Greg J. Neimeyer, PhD, Counseling Center, University of California, Irvine, California

Robert A. Neimeyer, PhD, Department of Psychology, University of Nebraska, Lincoln, Nebraska

Clifford I. Notarius, PhD, Department of Psychology, The Catholic University of America, Washington, D.C.

Richard E. Petty, PhD, Department of Psychology, University of Missouri, Columbia, Missouri

Kenneth H. Rubin, PhD, Department of Psychology, University of Waterloo, Waterloo, Ontario, Canada

Thomas E. Rudy, MA, Department of Psychology, University of Notre Dame, Notre Dame, Indiana

Brian F. Shaw, PhD, Departments of Psychiatry and Psychology, University Hospital and The University of Western Ontario, London, Ontario, Canada

Herbert A. Simon, PhD, Department of Psychology, Carnegie–Mellon University, Pittsburgh, Pennsylvania

Harry J. Sobel, PhD, Department of Psychiatry, Harvard Medical School and Massachusetts General Hospital, Boston, Massachusetts

Norman D. Sundberg, PhD, Department of Psychology, University of Oregon, Eugene, Oregon

Dennis C. Turk, PhD, Department of Psychology, Yale University, New Haven, Connecticut

Preface

The recent surge of cognitivism in the science of psychology has been termed "revolutionary" by some, "reactionary" by others. The mere presence of the dialectic indicates change. The clinical sciences are experiencing the impact of an increasing cognitive emphasis, particularly in cognitively oriented treatment interventions.

With the increased attention to cognitions in clinical treatment, the need arises to document cognitive changes that occur. Moreover, in studies that compare cognitive treatments with other therapies, it is important to look at comparative changes in cognitive measures. Only in this way can we investigate the potential role of cognitive change in mediating or contributing to behavior change. It is erroneous to assume that cognitive change is the exclusive domain of cognitive therapies. Further, our understanding of the *process* of change in psychotherapy can be expanded through the study of the nature of cognitive change and how it occurs. Therefore, reliable and valid cognitive measures are essential to the growth and development of all therapies.

There is, however, a disparity between our current knowledge of the efficacy and procedures of cognitive therapy and the development and validation of cognitive assessment methodology. The imminent danger is that the immediate need for cognitive assessment methods will foster inadequate ones for the sake of expediency. Adequate measures develop in the context of sound methodology and clear conceptualization. Such development occurred in behavior therapy. However, there is much more consensus concerning what behavior is than what cognition is.

Our goal in this book is to present a broad review of the growing field of cognitive assessment. We hope that this volume will contribute to the development, validation, and progression of cognitive assessment methods and will stimulate future research in this area. Clear methods and concepts can only help to ensure the utility of this material for researchers concerned with the etiology and maintenance of psychological problems, outcome and process research in psychotherapy, and the interrelationships among cognition, psychophysiology, emotion, and behavior. In addition, the practicing clinician may find the methods provocative and useful in the applied setting. In many chapters, methods are explicitly presented or aviable in the primary references cited. This volume should also be appropriate as a text or as additional reading in courses in cognitive therapy or assessment, behavioral assessment, and the even more traditional personality assessment.

The methods described in this book are clearly distinct from traditional "cognitive" assessment methods that focused mainly on cognitive abilities and cognitive styles. In Part I, Meichenbaum and Cameron (Chapter 1) and Sundberg (Chapter 3) provide an introduction to the field of cognitive assessment and place such methods in context relative to traditional and behavioral assessment. In addition, Ericsson and Simon (Chapter 2) and Merluzzi, Rudy, and Glass (Chapter 4) explore the potential connection between cognitive assessment and cognitive psychology, which could provide a link to an area of research that is replete with well-developed methods and theoretical perspectives. A potential outcome of that union could be a more unified cognitive science.

Methods, issues, and approaches to cognitive assessment are presented in Part II. Sobel (Chapter 5) details the innovative use of projective methods for cognitive assessment. Anderson (Chapter 6) and Neimeyer and Neimeyer (Chapter 7) have contributed comprehensive accounts of approaches to the assessment of imagery and personal constructs, respectively. Also detailed are think-aloud and thought-sampling approaches (Genest & Turk, Chapter 8), the technology and research concerning the electrophysiological measurement of cognitive activity (McGuigan, Chapter 9), and thought-listing techniques derived from social psychological research (Cacioppo & Petty, Chapter 10). The section ends with Notarius's (Chapter 11) speculations on the use of sequential analysis in evaluating the patterning and the process of thought.

Part III is devoted to more applied issues and focuses on clinical applications of cognitive assessment in four important areas of study. Shaw and Dobson (Chapter 12) discuss the various cognitive assessment methods that have evolved in the area of depression. Glass and Merluzzi (Chapter 13) examine the literature on assertiveness and on social, test, and speech anxiety and review methods of assessing irrational beliefs, self-statements, expectations, problem-solving strategies, and self-evaluations. In Chapter 14, Mahoney and Epstein consider the thoughts and coping strategies of top athletes. The section concludes with a review and an original methodology for studying children's interpersonal problem-solving skills (Krasnor & Rubin, Chapter 15).

In Part IV, Mischel (Chapter 16) summarizes and evaluates the current status of cognitive assessment and discusses future directions. He presents an approach to unifying the efforts in cognitive assessment research by framing the research in social learning theory.

This volume represents the end product of much work, stimulating collaboration, and numerous long-distance telephone calls. The three of us shared equally in all chapter planning, author contact, and editorial decisions. We would like to thank Michael Mahoney (the editor of this series) and Donald Meichenbaum for their support, suggestions, and encouragement. Thanks are also extended to Seymour Weingarten, editor-in-chief of The Guilford Press, for pursuing the original ideas that led to this volume, and to John Cacioppo, whose input helped shape those ideas. Finally, we would like to thank the contributors themselves for the thoughtful and original work that made this book possible.

Thomas V. Merluzzi
Carol R. Glass
Myles Genest

Notre Dame, Indiana
Washington, D.C.
Saskatoon, Saskatchewan
July 1980

Contents

Part I · Cognition and Cognitive Assessment

1. Issues in Cognitive Assessment: An Overview 3
   Donald Meichenbaum and Roy Cameron

   Introduction 3
   Process of Assessment 5
   Targets of Assessment 9
   Reference Notes 13
   References 13

2. Sources of Evidence on Cognition: A Historical Overview 16
   K. Anders Ericsson and Herbert A. Simon

   Introduction 16
   Structuralism 22
   Behaviorism 28
   Gestalt Psychology 34
   Direct and Indirect Assessment of Cognitive Structures 39
   Conclusion and Summary 46
   Acknowledgments 48
   Reference Notes 48
   References 49

3. Historical and Traditional Approaches to Cognitive Assessment ... 52
   Norman D. Sundberg

   Historical Domains and Landmarks in Cognitive Assessment 53
   Cognitive Aspects of Widely Used Tests and Traditional
       Approaches to Clinical Testing 56

Critique of Traditional Testing 71
Final Words—The Psychologist's Cognitions, Too 72
Acknowledgments 73
Reference Notes 73
References 74

4. *The Information-Processing Paradigm:*
Implications for Clinical Science **77**
Thomas V. Merluzzi, Thomas E. Rudy, and Carol R. Glass

Introduction 77
The Information-Processing Paradigm 79
Illustrative Lines of Research 90
Conclusion 117
Acknowledgment 117
Reference Notes 117
References 118

Part II • Methods, Issues, and Approaches

5. *Projective Methods of Cognitive Analysis* **127**
Harry J. Sobel

Introduction 127
Background and Historical Context 128
Projective Analysis: Definition and Redefinition 131
Projective Test Design and Construction 135
Cognitive Variables and the Projective Assessment 139
Conclusion and Summary 144
Acknowledgment 146
References 146

6. *Assessment of Imaginal Processes: Approaches and Issues* **149**
Merrill P. Anderson

Issues in Imagery Assessment 149
Selected Approaches to Imagery Assessment in Clinically
    Oriented Research 155
Imagery Assessment by Content Analysis of Narrative Reports 162

A Content Analysis System for Assessing Imaginal Detail 172
Acknowledgments 183
Reference Notes 183
References 184

7. *Personal Construct Perspectives on Cognitive Assessment* **188**
   Greg J. Neimeyer and Robert A. Neimeyer

   Introduction 188
   Illustrative Assessment Techniques 193
   Illustrative Lines of Investigation 217
   Conclusion 226
   Reference Notes 228
   References 228

8. *Think-Aloud Approaches to Cognitive Assessment* **233**
   Myles Genest and Dennis C. Turk

   Introduction 233
   A Perspective on Self-Report Strategies 234
   Access to Cognitive Antecedents of Behavior 237
   Think-Aloud Methods 247
   Conclusion 263
   Reference Notes 263
   References 264

9. *Issues in Electrophysiology and Cognition* **270**
   F. J. McGuigan

   Sources of Electrophysiological Signals 270
   Electropsychology: Covert Behavior Electrophysiologically
      Measured 271
   The Evolution of Electrophysiology 272
   The Nature of Bioelectrical Phenomena 274
   The Taxonomy of Covert Processes 275
   Electrophysiological Methods for Studying Cognitive Processes ... 280
   Theoretical Integration of Electrically Measured
      Cognitive Processes 287
   Consequences of a Science of Covert Behavior for
      Clinical Practice 296
   Reference Notes 305
   References 305

10. *Social Psychological Procedures for Cognitive Response*
    Assessment: The Thought-Listing Technique 309
    John T. Cacioppo and Richard E. Petty

    Measures of Cognitive Responses: An Overview 310
    The Thought-Listing Technique 315
    Some Final Considerations 331
    Acknowledgments 337
    Reference Notes 337
    References 337

11. *Assessing Sequential Dependency in*
    Cognitive Performance Data 343
    Clifford I. Notarius

    Types of Data 343
    Describing Sequences 345
    Sackett's Lag Sequential Analysis 349
    Stability of Event Sequences 352
    Methodological Considerations 354
    Summary 355
    Reference Note 356
    References 356

Part III · Clinical Implications

12. *Cognitive Assessment of Depression* 361
    Brian F. Shaw and Keith S. Dobson

    Introduction 361
    Characteristic Cognitions and Cognitive Processes in Depression .. 363
    Current Strategies in the Cognitive Assessment of Depression 375
    Future Studies 379
    Reference Notes 382
    References 383

13. *Cognitive Assessment of Social-Evaluative Anxiety* 388
    Carol R. Glass and Thomas V. Merluzzi

    A Cognitive Model of Social-Evaluative Concerns 388

Cognitive Therapy Approaches for Social-Evaluative Anxiety 391
Cognitive Assessment of Social-Evaluative Anxiety 398
Conclusion: Crucial Issues in Cognitive Assessment 425
Acknowledgments 431
Reference Notes 431
References 432

14. *The Assessment of Cognition in Athletes* 439
    Michael J. Mahoney and Martha L. Epstein

Introduction 439
Sport Personology: The Search for Athletic Traits 441
Skillpower: The Search for Athletic Psychological Skills 443
Summary and Implications 449
Reference Notes 450
References 450

15. *The Assessment of Social Problem-Solving Skills
    in Young Children* 452
    Linda Rose Krasnor and Kenneth H. Rubin

Introduction 452
Definition and Varying Theoretical Concerns 453
Assessing Social Problem Solving:
    The Hypothetical–Reflective Method 455
Social Problem Solving: An Observational Perspective 462
Social Problem Solving in the Natural Setting: A Brief Review 466
Hypothetical–Reflective and Behavioral Assessment
    Reconsidered 467
A Model for Assessing Social Problem-Solving Skills
    in Young Children...................................... 468
Reference Notes 473
References 474

Part IV · Future Directions

16. *A Cognitive–Social Learning Approach to Assessment* 479
    Walter Mischel

Some Preliminary Issues 479

Person Variables in the Cognitive–Social Learning Approach 483
Some Cautions for Cognitive Assessors 496
Acknowledgment 498
Reference Notes 498
References 499

Author Index 503

Subject Index 519

Part I

Cognition and Cognitive Assessment

Issues in Cognitive Assessment: An Overview

Donald Meichenbaum and Roy Cameron

Introduction

Although psychology has been concerned since its inception with assessing cognition (see Chapter 2, this volume), interest in the role of cognition in the field of behavior modification has been quite recent (e.g., Bandura, 1974; Mahoney, 1974; Meichenbaum, 1977). Social learning theorists and cognitively oriented behavior therapists have only recently developed an appreciation of the reciprocal relationships among cognition, affect, behavior, and environmental consequences. Although these various streams of experience are viewed as concurrent and interdependent, there is a need to develop independent assessment techniques and procedures for each.

Thus, in the same manner in which Ekman, Freisen, and Ellsworth (1972) and Izard (1977) attempted to develop procedures to assess facial expressions of emotion, in which Mason (1974) developed bioassay procedures to measure biochemical changes, or in which the ethologist describes overt behavior, this book will map the cognitive domain. The book is offered in the recognition that this is a first attempt and that there is much to learn. Moreover, even though cognitions are highlighted, the authors are aware of the other concurrent streams of experience. We expect that, as assessment procedures for the respective streams are developed, we will be able to integrate them into a comprehensive theory of behavior.

A host of cognitive assessment procedures already has been employed to

Donald Meichenbaum • Department of Psychology, University of Waterloo, Waterloo, Ontario, Canada.
Roy Cameron • Department of Psychology, University of Saskatchewan, Saskatoon, Saskatchewan, Canada.

study a wide variety of populations. The populations assessed range from athletes (e.g., see Chapter 14, this volume) to persons presenting with anxiety (Sarason, 1980; Wine, 1980; Chapter 13, this volume), depression (see Chapter 12, this volume), anger (Novaco, 1979), sexual deviations (Rook & Hammen, 1977), pain (Turk, Meichenbaum, & Genest, 1981), and alcohol problems (Marlatt, 1979). The assessment procedures that have been used include interviews, think-aloud protocols, self-report scales, postperformance videotape reconstructions, thought listing, thought sampling, spontaneous private speech, and projective techniques. There is clearly a ground swell of interest in cognitive assessment, and as the reader of this volume will discover, exciting work is being done.

At a time when there appears to be much enthusiasm for cognitively oriented assessment, we believe it is important to remain cognizant of the profound challenges that face us. The study of cognitive experience is fraught with difficulty and potential pitfalls. We are unable to observe directly the object of our study (cognition); we rely heavily upon our subjects' self-reports; and in some cases we may infer cognitive processes from nonverbal behaviors and performance. Thus we must think creatively in order to develop assessment strategies that will yield useful, credible data. We must also think critically and remain aware of the limitations of our data and the extent to which the data may be shaped by the procedures used to collect them.

Given the complexity of the field, we believe it is extremely important to begin by conducting methodological studies to determine how best to conduct cognitive assessments. Until we have established some principles to guide us, it would seem rash to plunge hastily into studies aimed at explicating cognitive factors in various populations. Those of us who are more interested in human processes than in psychometric investigation seem to have a penchant for putting the cart before the horse, rushing into content-oriented studies before establishing the reliability and validity of our procedures. In our view, it would be most unfortunate if we became prematurely enamored of particular approaches to assessment that subsequently proved to yield dubious data. We hope to concentrate on focusing our lenses before beginning to describe what we think we see.

This introductory chapter will highlight and discuss some of the challenges that face us as we contemplate how to conduct cognitive assessments. In attempting to assess cognition, the investigator is confronted with several important questions concerning what to assess, where and how to assess the subject's cognition, how to score the thought processes in terms of the units and levels of analyses, and most important, how to interpret the data collected. Only a few of these issues will be covered here, because several of them have been discussed at length elsewhere (e.g., Butler & Meichenbaum, 1980; Meichenbaum & Goodman, 1980; Meichenbaum, Henshaw, & Himel, 1980; Meichenbaum, Burland, Gruson, & Cameron, Note 1). The other contributors to this book also discuss several of these issues, as do the authors who have contributed to a volume on cognitive assessment edited by Kendall and Hollon (1980).

Process of Assessment

Self-Reports

Cognitive assessment depends primarily upon the subject's self-report. The collection and interpretation of self-reports is an extremely delicate process. The major difficulties are readily apparent. Meichenbaum *et al.* (Note 1) have summarized some of these difficulties as follows:

> Some subject populations (e.g., children, retarded persons) have limited ability to comprehend questions, and the investigator faces the challenge of developing an appropriate interview schedule or questionnaire which is comprehensible to subjects. Given that the subject comprehends, he must also be able to express his experiences verbally, and be *motivated* to do so. If a subject reports no . . . [cognitive] activity, the investigator is confronted with the difficult problem of deciding whether this indicates an absence of . . . [cognitive] activity, the operation of implicit ("unconscious") . . . rules, failure to comprehend questions, inability to verbally describe the subjective experience, or lack of motivation to offer a report. Conversely, if the subject does report . . . [cognitive experiences], we must decide whether he is reporting something he actually experiences, or whether he has confabulated his report (perhaps by inferring from his behavior what he "must have been thinking"). (p. 26)

It seems to us that these are problems that cannot be surmounted completely. The most reasonable objective would be to specify the conditions under which self-reports will have maximum credibility and to collect data under such conditions insofar as this is possible.

What, then, are the conditions under which such cognitive assessments might reasonably be expected to yield the most credible data? Interest in this question is reflected in the controversial paper by Nisbett and Wilson (1977) entitled "Telling More Than We Can Know: Verbal Reports on Mental Processes." Several authors have commented on or rebutted Nisbett and Wilson (e.g., Bainbridge, 1979; Genest & Turk, Chapter 8, this volume; Meichenbaum & Butler, 1980; Smith & Miller, 1978; White, 1980; Meichenbaum *et al.*, Note 1; Adair & Spinner, Note 2; Bowers, Note 3; Ericsson & Simon, Note 4). These authors suggest a number of guidelines for conducting cognitive assessments, which we will review.

In general, two self-report formats have been used for conducting cognitive assessments. Subjects or clients can be asked to describe their cognitive experience in an *open-ended* way. Alternatively, *self-report inventories* listing cognitive themes that are likely to occur in the target situation can be administered, and respondents can be asked to endorse items and themes they experience. Each format has both advantages and disadvantages.

The inventory approach is attractive in that it is economical to administer, its scoring is straightforward, and it provides a basis for standardization across studies. Such inventories, however, may increase the likelihood of fabricated responses. Also, it is likely that much information will be lost when inventories are used. For instance, one may fail to tape the sequencing and evolution of cognitive themes, nonverbal cognitive experience (e.g., images), qualitative differences in the ways in which a given theme may be experienced across individuals, and idiosyncratic themes that are experienced but not included on the inventory.

The open-ended format may be more difficult to standardize and is likely to yield data that are more difficult to score for purposes of quantitative analysis. However, open-ended interviews potentially offer richer data, and, relative to self-report inventories, there appears to be less danger of fabricated responses. Most of our work (reviewed in Meichenbaum *et al.,* Note 1) has involved open-ended self-reports. It seems to us that the scoring problems associated with this approach are not insurmountable (see Meichenbaum *et al.,* Note 1, for examples of scoring strategies) and that the richness of the data more than compensates for the logistical difficulties. Moreover, we believe that work in the area must begin with studies involving open-ended questions in order to establish the content of any inventory that may be developed subsequently. The guidelines that follow are most pertinent to assessments involving open-ended self-reports. (We note in passing that there is no reason that the two formats cannot be used to complement each other in the same study; this hybrid approach might eventually prove to be most desirable.)

Guidelines for Conducting Self-Reports

There are several steps that a researcher or clinician can take to increase the richness and credibility of cognitive self-report data. Ericsson and Simon (Note 4) have developed an information-processing model of verbal self-reports. Their model suggests that the following guidelines be followed:

1. The inquiry should be conducted as soon as possible following the cognitive events of interest, assessing directly for information in short-term memory whenever possible.
2. The amount of probing should be minimized in order to decrease the likelihood that subjects will engage in inferential processes about their own cognitive experience or about the expectancies of the experimenter.
3. Analysis of the internal consistency of such reports should be included in order to assess the validity of the verbal data.

4. Subjects should be asked to describe verbally their cognitive experience. They should not be asked to explain why they behaved as they did or to provide motives for their behavior.

Further guidelines have been suggested by Adair and Spinner (Note 2). In general, their recommendations complement those of Ericsson and Simon, so they have been integrated into the same list:

5. Subjects should be given a set that motivates them to provide honest and full accounts. In providing such a set, the assessor might emphasize that his or her ability to study the target experience depends entirely upon honest, careful reporting.
6. It may be helpful to provide a set that legitimizes disclosure of cognitions. For example, subjects might be asked to provide their "impressions" or descriptions of their experience during the experimental task, as opposed to being asked to "recollect" what occurred or to tell what they "did."
7. Providing the subject with retrieval cues immediately after performance may also foster full and veridical reporting.

At first glance, Ericsson and Simon's recommendation to avoid probing (guideline 2) appears to contradict Adair and Spinner's suggestion that retrieval cues be provided (guideline 7). These are not necessarily contradictory suggestions. It may be possible to provide retrieval cues (thereby reducing cue-dependent forgetting) without using probes that would be leading. For instance, Meichenbaum and Butler (1980) have described a videotape reconstruction strategy for providing nonleading retrieval cues. The strategy involves videotaping persons performing a task and subsequently asking them to watch themselves on the tape as they recount their cognitive and affective experiences. As Meichenbaum and Butler caution, the videotape reconstruction does not eliminate the possibility of fabricated reports. However, it may be a particularly valuable approach to providing retrieval cues because many nonverbal as well as verbal cues are available by means of the videotape. Moreover, because the retrieval cues are self-generated (the subject observes himself or herself on the videotape), the difficult problem of experimenter bias in providing retrieval cues is minimized.

The value and meaning of verbal reports may be clarified if asessors adopt a "converging operations" or multimethod approach to cognitive assessment in the tradition of Garner, Hake, and Eriksen (1956) and Campbell and Fiske (1959). If, for instance, behavioral data are consistent with the subject's self-report data, the credibility of the self-report is enhanced. If, on the other hand, behavioral data are not consistent with the self-report, the investigator might have to do some detective work to account for the discrepancy. Although the discrepancy may point to a fabricated report, it would be rash to draw this conclusion without entertaining other possible explanations. For instance, a child who indicates the use of a particular problem-solving strategy but who makes moves inconsistent with the strategy may be giving a veridical account of his or her cognitive experience even though the child's verbal report is discrepant with his or her behavior. It is conceivable that the child's self-regulating cognitive activity is failing to regulate his or her behavior. It would be intriguing to investigate this possibility more fully. Although the discrepancy between behavior and self-report may signify a fabricated self-report, the investigator might miss an excellent opportunity to learn something important if he or she rushed to this conclusion uncritically.

In short, the validity of the self-report data emerges from the questions and phenomena one is studying. As with any other aspect of assessment, whether one is measuring heart rate or recording nonverbal behavior, the value of the assessment must be repeatedly demonstrated. Given the tortuous history of cognitive assessment, from the classical introspectionism à la Titchener to the resulting attacks on introspection à la Watson, psychologists have been reluctant to employ it formally.

One rarely hears from the subjects of psychological investigations. A quick perusal of any psychological journal illustrates the void in assessing how subjects viewed the experiment and their performance in it. There seems to be an inherent distrust of the data obtained by interviews, think-aloud techniques, postperformance questionnaires, thought sampling, or other such methods. We believe that this distrust is misguided and that it has limited psychological investigations. Clearly, there are problems in conducting, using, and interpreting such self-report data, but this is true of other modes of assessment. This volume attests to the fact that the field is now beginning to explicate and deal with these problems.

There is an increasing appreciation that each cognitive assessment approach has strengths and weaknesses and that several techniques must be used concurrently. Meichenbaum *et al.* (Note 1) have reviewed several complementary cognitive assessment strategies (including postperformance interviews and questionnaires, think-aloud data gathered as subjects perform target tasks, utilization of behavioral observation to draw inferences about cognition, observation of spontaneous private speech, peer teaching, and performance component analysis) that may be blended to provide the sort of converging operations that appear to be called for at present. Although investigators may always have to be critical of self-reports of cognitive experience, the likelihood of their being misled will be minimized if they check the consistency of data across assessment methods. Such cross-method comparisons should also assist investigators in evaluating the validity of the various methods.

In setting out to study cognitive experience and its relationship to affect, behavior, and consequences, it might be advantageous to remember that some situations may call for deliberate, conscious self-regulation, whereas others may elicit behavior that is "scripted" (Abelson, Note 5) or "mindless" (Langer, 1978; Thorngate, 1976, Note 6). Undoubtedly, both consciously regulated and automatically regulated behaviors are of theoretical and clinical interest. However, cognitive self-reports are most likely to be of use in studying those behaviors that are consciously self-regulated. Conscious self-regulation appears to occur most often in situations that call for difficult, unrehearsed responses, in which decisions are required in order to establish a path of action (Borkowski, Note 7). Such situations include those calling for performance on complex, novel tasks; those calling for choices and judgments; and those in which habitual ways of acting fail or in which there is an interruption of behavioral acts and thought processes as described by Mandler (1978). As clinicians become more sophisticated, they will learn how to set up assessment situations that maximize production of relevant cognitive processes so that their clients have rich and pertinent cognitive experience to report. No doubt they also will develop a clearer idea of the situations in which cognitive assessment is of little value.

Targets of Assessment

So far, we have discussed some of the issues that arise in collecting and interpreting data pertaining to cognitive experience. The focus has been on the process of assessment, and the objective has been to underscore some of the difficulties facing us. We have argued for the need to be creative in the attempt to develop assessment strategies that will result in rich and credible data. We have outlined some of the guidelines proposed to facilitate collection of such data. We have further argued for the need to maintain a self-critical, self-correcting attitude while developing strategies; the need to evaluate the validity of the strategies; and the need to employ multimethod assessments, which may enhance our ability to interpret the findings.

We turn now from the process of assessment to the targets of assessment. "Ecological validity" must be retained in our research and tunnel vision must be avoided. Our research will have the most meaning if we can avoid restricting it to observations made in contrived, artificial laboratory situations, because such situations may not elicit the central, recurrent cognitive themes and processes that are typical of the individual. We also believe that it is crucial to avoid studying cognition in isolation. As indicated at the beginning of this chapter, cognitive processes are probably at once both causes and effects, and it will be important, as cognitive processes are studied, to keep in mind the interplay between cognition, affect, behavior, and environmental consequences. In this section, we will comment on these two concerns, namely, the issue of ecological validity and the need to relate cognitive assessment to other ongoing streams of behavior.

Person-Focused Approach

Much of the research on cognitive assessment has involved conducting assessments in specific situations. Without denying that situational analyses are valuable, we suggest that it is also important to adopt a strategy of studying individuals across situations in order to identify cognitive processes that are central to the person versus those that are situation-specific. This concern may be illustrated by Allport's work. Allport (1955) suggested that "the possession of long-range goals, regarded as central to one's personal existence, distinguishes the human being from the animal" (p. 51). To illustrate the extent to which goals, plans, and aspirations may influence a person over a lifetime, Allport (1955) presented a synopsis of Raold Amundsen's autobiography:

> In his autobiography, Raold Amundsen tells how from the age of fifteen he had one dominant passion—to become a polar explorer. The obstacles seemed insurmountable, and all through his life the temptations to reduce the tensions engendered were great. But the striving persisted. While he welcomed each success, it acted to raise his level of aspiration, to maintain an over-all commitment. Having sailed the Northwest Passage, he embarked upon the painful project that led to the discovery of the South Pole. Having discovered the South Pole, he planned for years, against extreme discouragement, to fly over the North Pole, to a task he finally accomplished. But his commitment never wavered until at the end he lost his life in attempting to rescue a less gifted explorer, Nobile, from death in the Arctic. Not only did he maintain his style of life, without ceasing, but this central commitment enabled him to withstand the temptation to reduce the segmental tensions continually engendered by fatigue, hunger, ridicule, and danger. (p. 49)

If we brought Amundsen into our laboratory and asked him about his cognitive processes as he solved some task, we might collect some interesting data but would also come away with a limited and somewhat narrow view of the man's cognitive functioning. Investigators must not become so focused on studying cognitive processes in specific situations that they forget to inquire about those central themes and processes that are characteristic of the individual across situations and over time and that, in fact, may influence which situations the individual approaches or avoids in his or her day-to-day affairs.

An illustrative study of this person-focused approach has been offered by Csikszentimihalyi and Beattie (1979), who have explored "life themes" (defined as affective and cognitive representations of existential problems that a person wishes to resolve) by means of a retrospective interview study. The investigators were able to distinguish professionally "successful" and "unsuccessful" individuals in terms of whether they viewed their lives and professions in problem-solving terms. Although such retrospective assessment procedures are fraught with dangers, the consistent findings offered by Csikszentimihalyi and Beattie are indeed provocative. (It would be interesting to verify their findings in a prospective, rather than another retrospective, study.) Their results are consistent with the finding summarized by Meichenbaum *et al.* (1980) that one useful way of coping with stress (whether it be pain, social evaluation, an interpersonal provocation, or professional striving) is to view it as a problem to be solved rather than as a personal threat. Psychologists have much to learn about the life themes or set-inducing cognitive processes that are central to an individual's functioning.

Recent work on metacognition suggests another target of assessment that warrants attention. Following from an information-processing view, cognition usually has been conceptualized as a set of relatively discrete cognitive abilities or thought processes. More recent literature has stressed the importance of a different level of analysis, that is, analysis at the level of metacognition, which may substantially influence the ongoing cognitive processes observed in think-aloud protocols, postperformance interviews, and so on (e.g., see Brown & DeLoache, 1978; Flavell & Wellman, 1977; Meichenbaum *et al.,* Note 1). "Metacognition" refers to the person's awareness of the variables that affect the efficient use of cognitive skills, including knowledge about cognitive rules, awareness of one's own cognitive abilities, and active monitoring and regulation of cognitive processes. Metacognition thus includes a complex set of variables related to person (i.e., self-appraisal of abilities, attribution of outcome), task (perception of task difficulty and purpose), and strategy (strategy knowledge and recognition of the need to apply strategies). Cognitive assessment thus needs to go beyond the assessment of only directly accessible self-reports to a consideration of the higher-order variables that affect how (and whether) "on-line" cognitive processes will be employed.

Integrative Approach

If attempts at cognitive assessment are to pay off, investigators must also avoid the temptation to study cognition in isolation. Concurrent collection of both self-report and behavioral data, for instance, may lead to a much richer assessment protocol than collection of either set of data in isolation. For instance, Gruson (1980) found that some pianists behaviorally evidenced practice straegies that they did not report consciously using. Reliance upon cognitive self-report alone to identify practice strategies would have resulted in incomplete data in this case. Interestingly, Gruson's pianists varied in level of competence, ranging from novices to concert pianists (cross-sectional comparison), and were studied over a dozen sessions as they learned a new piece (developmental or longitudinal comparison). Gruson not only used the pianists' self-reports on how they went about learning the piece (e.g., the strategies involved) but also conducted an observational study of how they learned the piece, recording errors, section repeats, note repeats, and so forth.

The collection of both self-report and observational data makes it possible to juxtapose the subject's verbal self-report (e.g., "I was just trying to avoid errors" vs. "I was trying to get a feel for the piece and experiment with it") with the behavioral pattern of performance. A crucial issue for assessment is how the respective streams of piano playing and self-report change with the development of proficiency. Are there points in the development of a skill, or in the development of automaticity of an act, at which particular aspects of behavior are described differently or not even reported? It is possible that the same behavioral sequence may be described quite differently depending upon the level of competence or the stage of development of a skill. In the context of this chapter, the important point is that simultaneous monitoring of the behavioral and cognitive streams may be most helpful in understanding how someone acquires a skill and develops proficiency and expertise.

Meichenbaum and Butler (1980) have discussed in some detail an approach to assessment that they have termed "cognitive ethology." The approach is integrative and has as its objective the tracking of the interactions between cognition and the streams of emotional experience and behavior. This integrative approach to assessment is dynamic rather than static. There is less emphasis upon discrete reponses and more upon the patterning and sequencing of responses.

Like the behavioral ethologist, the cognitive ethologist searches for any common fixed action pattern of ideation and the accompanying releasing stimuli that contribute to performance across tasks and situations and over time. That such patterns may indeed be evident is reported by Meichenbaum and Butler (1980), who describe the role of "negative self-referent ideation" as a correlate of stress-related performance deficits, no matter what the nature of the stressor. Some of the characteristics of this negative self-referent ideation include the subject's (1) being self-oriented rather than task-oriented, (2) engaging in negative "catastrophizing" ideation, and (3) having thinking processes that have a run-on quality such that negative ideation is followed by emotional reactions, which, in turn, contribute to further negative ideation and so forth. This pattern of negative thinking has been evident in many different populations—including athletes, hospitalized patients, low-creative individuals, and pain patients—examined in a host of studies by means of a variety of cognitive assessment techniques, including think-aloud procedures, postperformance questionnaires, interviews, and so on (see Meichenbaum & Butler, 1980, for a summary of these studies).

In short, what is being suggested is the provocative hypothesis that a common pattern of ideation (a fixed action pattern, if one wishes to use the ethology analogy) may be an important correlate of inadequate performance. At this point, the data are seen as only provocative. A clear causal relationship cannot be drawn between this negative thinking pattern and inadequate performance without further research. These preliminary findings have been described in order to indicate the potentially exciting direction that may emerge as cognitive assessment procedures are developed as described in this book.

However, a caveat must be given concerning the use of the term "cognitive ethology." We are not suggesting that the patterns of ideation that emerge are in any way genetically or predispositionally based. There are indeed limitations as to how far one can extend the analogy of ethology. Rather, cognitive ethology reflects our concern with the need to search for consistent patterns across response modes. The comprehensive perspective introduced by this integrative approach appears to hold considerable promise for providing a context in which to place data pertaining to cognitive experience.

In this chapter we have tried to highlight some of the difficulties and challenges that must be dealt with if psychologists are to expand their understanding of the cognitive processes of their clients and subjects. Although the problems are substantial, we firmly believe that the field will move forward dramatically if we are equal to the challenges. We believe that we are on the threshold of exciting research developments.

Reference Notes

1. Meichenbaum, D., Burland, S., Gruson, L., & Cameron, R. *Metacognitive assessment.* Paper presented at the University of Wisconsin conference on the growth of insight, Madison, October 1979.
2. Adair, J., & Spinner, B. *Subjects' access to cognitive processes: Demand characteristics and verbal report.* Unpublished manuscript, University of Manitoba, 1979.
3. Bowers, K. *Saying more than we can know permits knowing more than we can say: On being informed.* Paper presented at the Stockholm conference on environmental effects on behavior, June 1979.
4. Ericsson, K., & Simon, H. *Protocols as data: Effects of verbalizations.* Unpublished manuscript, Carnegie–Mellon University, 1978.
5. Abelson, R. *Scripts.* Paper presented at the meeting of the Midwestern Psychological Association, Chicago, May 1978.
6. Thorngate, W. *Memory, cognition and social performance.* Unpublished manuscript, University of Alberta, 1977.
7. Borkowski, J. *Signs of intelligence: Strategy generalization and metacognition.* Paper presented at the University of Wisconsin conference on the growth of insight, Madison, October 1979.

References

Allport, G. *Becoming: Basic considerations for a psychology of personality.* New Haven: Yale University Press, 1955.
Bandura, A. Behavior theory and models of man. *American Psychologist,* 1974, *29,* 859–869.
Bainbridge, L. Verbal reports as evidence of the process operator's knowledge. *International Journal of Man–Machine Studies,* 1979, *11,* 411–436.
Brown, A., & DeLoache, J. Skills, plans and self-regulation. In R. Siegler (Ed.), *Children's thinking: What develops?* Hillsdale, N.J.: Erlbaum, 1978.
Butler, L., & Meichenbaum, D. The assessment of interpersonal problem-solving skills. In P.

Kendall & S. Hollon (Eds.), *Cognitive–behavioral interventions: Assessment methods.* New York: Academic Press, 1980.

Campbell, D., & Fiske, D. Convergent and discriminant validation by the multitrait–multimethod matrix. *Psychological Bulletin,* 1959, *56,* 81–105.

Csikszentimihalyi, M., & Beattie, O. Life themes: A theoretical and empirical explanation of their origins and effects. *Journal of Humanistic Psychology,* 1979, *19,* 45–63.

Ekman, P., Freisen, W., & Ellsworth, P. *Emotion in the human face.* Oxford, England: Pergamon Press, 1972.

Flavell, J., & Wellman, H. Metamemory. In R. Kail & J. Hagen (Eds.), *Perspectives on the development of memory and cognition.* Hillsdale, N.J.: Erlbaum, 1977.

Garner, W., Hake, H., & Eriksen, C. Operationism and the concept of perception. *Psychological Review,* 1956, *63,* 149–159.

Gruson, L. *Piano practicing skills: What distinguishes competence?* Unpublished doctoral dissertation, University of Waterloo, Waterloo, Ontario, 1980.

Izard, C. *The face of emotion.* New York: Appleton-Century-Crofts, 1977.

Kendall, P., & Hollon, S. (Eds.). *Cognitive–behavioral interventions: Assessment methods.* New York: Academic Press, 1980.

Langer, E. Rethinking the role of thought in social interaction. In J. Harvey, W. Ickes, & R. Ridel (Eds.), *New directions in attribution research* (Vol. 2). Hillsdale, N.J.: Erlbaum, 1978.

Mahoney, M. *Cognition and behavior modification.* Cambridge, Mass.: Ballinger, 1974.

Mandler, G. Thought processes, consciousness and stress. In V. Hamilton & D. Warburton (Eds.), *Human stress and cognition: An information processing.* London: Wiley, 1979.

Marlatt, G. Alcohol use and problem drinking: A cognitive behavioral analysis. In P. Kendall & S. Hollon (Eds.), *Cognitive–behavioral interventions: Theory, research and procedures.* New York: Academic Press, 1979.

Mason, J. Specificity in the organization of neuroendocrine response profiles. In P. Seeman & J. Brown (Eds.), *Frontiers in neurology and neuroscience research.* Toronto, Ontario: University of Toronto Press, 1974.

Meichenbaum, D. *Cognitive-behavior modification: An integrative approach.* New York: Plenum Press, 1977.

Meichenbaum, D., & Butler, L. Cognitive ethology: Assessing the streams of cognition and emotion. In K. Blankstein, P. Pliner, & J. Polivy (Eds.), *Advances in the study of communication and affect: Assessment and modification of emotional behavior* (Vol. 6). New York: Plenum Press, 1980.

Meichenbaum, D., & Goodman, S. Critical questions and methodological problems in studying children's private speech. In G. Zivin (Ed.), *Development of self-regulation through speech.* New York: Wiley, 1980.

Meichenbaum, D., Henshaw, D., & Himel, N. Coping with stress as a problem-solving process. In W. Krohne & L. Laux (Eds.), *Achievement, stress and anxiety.* Washington, D.C.: Hemisphere, 1980.

Nisbett, R., & Wilson, T. Telling more than we can know: Verbal reports on mental processes. *Psychological Review,* 1979, *84,* 613–624.

Novaco, R. The cognitive regulation of anger and stress. In P. Kendall & S. Hollon (Eds.), *Cognitive–behavioral interventions: Theory, research and procedures.* New York: Academic Press, 1979.

Rook, R., & Hammen, C. A cognitive perspective on the experience of sexual arousal. *Journal of Social Issues,* 1977, *33,* 7–29.

Sarason, I. (Ed.). *Test anxiety: Theory, research and application.* Hillsdale, N.J.: Erlbaum, 1980.

Smith, E., & Miller, F. Limits on perception of cognitive processes: A reply to Nisbett and Wilson. *Psychological Review,* 1978, *85,* 355–362.

Thorngate, W. Must we always think before we act? *Personality and Social Psychology Bulletin,* 1976, *2,* 31–35.

Turk, D., Meichenbaum, D., & Genest, M. *Cognitive therapy of pain.* New York: Guilford Press, 1981.

White, P. Limitations on verbal reports on internal events: A refutation of Nisbett and Wilson and of Bem. *Psychological Review,* 1980, *87,* 105–112.

Wine, J. Cognitive–attentional theory of test anxiety. In I. Sarason (Ed.), *Test anxiety: Theory, research and application.* Hillsdale, N.J.: Erlbaum, 1980.

2

Sources of Evidence on Cognition: A Historical Overview

K. Anders Ericsson and Herbert A. Simon

Introduction

From the beginnings of civilization, people have been intrigued by their subjective experiences and their own thinking, a fascination that has led to considerable speculation and theorizing. Within the past 100 years (we may take Wundt's laboratory as our starting point), this speculation has been subjected to the critique of scientific and experimental methods in the psychological laboratory. A major theme in this critique has been the question of what constitutes evidence in psychology—of the nature of psychological data and their interpretation.

The nature of data, and of admissible procedures for gathering and interpreting them, cannot be discussed very long in theory-free terms. The epistemological question (how the experimenter gains reliable information about the subject) is closely interwoven with the psychological question (how the subject gains and retains reliable information about the world). As a result, psychologists who have held different theoretical positions with respect to the substantive laws of psychology have also generally held different methodological positions with respect to the validity of various kinds of psychological evidence, and vice versa.

It is the purpose of this chapter to discuss this interaction between substance and method in psychology, with particular reference to the status that has been accorded to verbal data by different schools of psychology, and with

K. Anders Ericsson • Department of Psychology, University of Colorado at Boulder, Boulder, Colorado.
Herbert A. Simon • Department of Psychology, Carnegie–Mellon University, Pittsburgh, Pennsylvania.

special application, in the last section, to the assessment of individual differences. We will not try to duplicate the many excellent overviews of the different schools of psychology that are already available. Our task is different and in some ways more difficult. It is not enough to describe each school in terms of its own concepts and the data it has used for testing those concepts. One of the curious and important consequences of the interdependence of theory and methodology is that each school of psychology tended to develop its own characteristic kinds of data and to test its theories, as well as criticize its opponents' theories, almost exclusively with the help of these data. At the same time, each school tended to ignore the "illegitimate" or "irrelevant" data used by its competitors.

Schools may legitimately differ in their theoretical interpretations of evidence about psychological phenomena. However, surely it is necessary that psychological facts and data be explained by and incorporated into succeeding theoretical proposals rather than discarded as irrelevant. One test of a new theory is that it give a satisfactory account (in its own terms, of course) of the data produced by investigators working in other theoretical frameworks.

With the advent of human information-processing theory, detailed models of memory and problem solving (e.g., Anderson & Bower, 1973; Newell & Simon, 1972) have been put forward that give us tools with which to analyze more precisely the mediating processes that generate behavior, including verbal behavior, and hence provide us with new means for investigating the processes of data production in the psychological laboratory. Thus our strategy will be to review the methodological issues raised by the main classical schools of psychology in light of our current understanding of the system and processes that produced the recorded behavior.

Although we have long known about limits of human mental activity, few attempts were made until recently to relate this knowledge to analyses of cognitive processes. An intriguing exception is the early criticism of analytic introspection, which was called into question by opponents who doubted that such a cognitive activity was compatible with the known limits on attention and short-term memory. (We will discuss these arguments in more detail later.)

We have also long known, both from experiments and from everyday experience, how subjects' behaviors are affected by expectation, context, and measurement procedures. The notion that there can be "neutral" methods for gathering data has been refuted decisively. Hence, if a theory of data gathering and analysis is to be satisfactory, it must incorporate a theory of the effects of the data-gathering procedures. There appear to be two compatible approaches to the problem of dealing with the impact of observation upon behavior. One is to use new experimental paradigms and methods that enable us to manipulate systematically and to control for the effects of expectations and of measurement procedures. The other approach, which will be emphasized in this chapter, is to give a detailed account of the underlying mechanisms—the cognitive processes and structures—that give rise to these effects.

After some further introductory material, the analysis of this chapter will be carried out in three main sections devoted to structuralism, behaviorism, and Gestalt psychology, respectively. These are followed by a section in which we discuss, from a contemporary standpoint, the direct and indirect assessment of cognitive structures. Each of these sections, is divided into three parts: (1) a brief outline of key theoretical ideas associated with the school under discussion and their relationship to previous research and theorizing; (2) a review of the principal kinds of data that were considered relevant by adherents of the school and that were used in their research; and (3) a discussion of issues and controversies relating to the uses of these data— a discussion carried out in light of current knowledge about cognitive mechanisms and structure.

This chapter aims at being selective rather than comprehensive. In all sections, we will focus especially on the uses of verbal reports as data (in the case of structuralism, upon introspective methods). Before starting the main part of our discussion, we will present some of the core elements of our view of cognition and will then discuss briefly some different types of observations that can be made of cognitive processes and cognitive structures.

Conceptual Framework

Currently, the most influential and complete conceptual framework for human cognition is the human information-processing model, a general model that covers all important aspects of cognition and cognitive processes and that requires, or at least allows, detailed analyses of cognitive phenomena. The model makes contact with and has implications for a wide range of observable behavior and data.

For the purposes of this chapter, a presentation of the core ideas of information-processing psychology is sufficient. (For fuller discussion, see Newell & Simon, 1972, and Ericsson & Simon, 1980, Note 1.) According to the human information-processing model, a cognitive process can be seen as a sequence of internal states successively transformed by a series of information processes. Information is stored in several memories, with different accessing characteristics and capacities: a sensory store of short duration, a short-term memory with limited capacity and/or intermediate duration, and a long-term memory with large capacity and relatively permanent storage but with slow fixation and access times compared with the other types of memories.

A main assumption is that information recently acquired is heeded[1] by the central processor and kept in short-term memory, where it is accessible

---

[1]Because the phrase "attended to" is often stylistically awkward, we will sometimes use "heeded" instead. Thus we will say, more or less synonymously, that information was "attended to," was "heeded," or was "stored in short-term memory."

for further processing (e.g., for producing verbal reports). Of the wealth of information coming into the sensory stores, the central processor actively selects a subset for attention, determining what information will be heeded by directing, for example, eye movements. The activity of the central processor leaves a trace of the heeded information in long-term memory automatically, provided that the information resides in short-term memory for a sufficiently long time. Information from long-term memory must be accessed by attending to retrieval cues, which need to be sufficiently unique to evoke the particular memory structure that is sought. This means that information in long-term memory often is very incompletely retrieved, for it is difficult to regenerate the necessary retrieval cues. Only after information has been retrieved from long-term memory, that is, transferred to short-term memory, can it be processed further (e.g., reported).

Data on Cognitive Processes and Structures

There are considerable discrepancies with respect to what the different schools and research approaches consider to be facts or data about cognitive processes and structures. Because we believe in a single description of the cognitive process that will account for all recordable information about it, we will be particularly concerned about claims from different schools that certain types of recordable information are useless or invalid.

The following kinds of information can be observed and recorded for a cognitive process elicited by a task instruction in a laboratory experiment:

1. The *latency,* or the time taken between the beginning and the end of the cognitive process.
2. The *result* of the cognitive process, which in most cases can be evaluated with respect to correctness and accuracy.
3. The *observable behavior* and *physiological activity* occurring during the cognitive process, such as eye movement, spontaneous verbal activity, galvanic skin response (GSR), and so forth.
4. *Concurrent verbalizations,* obtained by instructing the subject to verbalize his or her ongoing thoughts by "thinking aloud." (For a discussion of different types of instructions, see Ericsson & Simon, Note 2.)
5. *Retrospective reports* and other behavior elicited after the end of the process, reflecting memory of the cognitive process in question.

All these types of information are legitimate observations relating to the process, yet, depending on the particular hypotheses under consideration and on the theoretical bias of the investigator, usually only a small part of this potentially available information is recorded and further analyzed.

We will now describe briefly what it means to account for or explain data in the information-processing framework. Basically, to account for data, one must specify one or more mechanisms that, given the same information as was presented to the subjects, would be able to regenerate the recorded pattern of observations. Considerable research in cognitive science has been directed toward specifying mechanisms (often described as computer programs) that would be able to generate the correct results to presented tasks in a given domain. To claim psychological relevance for such a mechanism, one has to show that the information it uses observes the limits of the three different types of human memories described previously and that the mechanism has access only to knowledge that the human subjects can be supposed to have available. Furthermore, it is necessary that the postulated mechanisms account for all of the other types of data observed for the human cognitive process in the same task. For example, one can claim that, in order for a human subject to attend to visually presented information, this information has to be within the range of his or her visual gaze at least once; one can assume a rough correspondence between the direction of the gaze and attended information. Similarly, if a subject produces aloud a series of partial results in a mental multiplication task, the model must generate these same results to account for the fact that they can be verbalized.

Data vary greatly in terms of how informative they are or how much information they represent. A "yes" response to the question "Is Einstein's law relating mass and energy $E = mc^2$?" can be generated by a simple, even random, mechanism, whereas the response "$E = mc^2$" to the question "What is Einstein's law relating mass and energy?" would require a much more complex mechanism involving long-term memory. In general, verbal reports—either concurrent or retrospective—represent much more information than other types of data and hence constrain more closely the possible ways in which a cognitive process can be realized. We will therefore be particularly interested in our historical overview in discussing claims that such data are irrelevant and epiphenomenal to the cognitive processes generating the results. Data of such great potential value are not to be abandoned lightly.

Some research approaches instruct subjects to give direct descriptions of cognitive structures, general solution procedures, and so forth, and claim that these data should be conceived of, as holding a special status, that is, as being error-free descriptions. The notion of regeneration can be applied to such data as well, relieving us of any disturbing assumption that these reports have special status (Anderson, Note 3).

Historical Background

Early speculations about the human mind and human subjective experiences were closely related to religious and philosophical questions about the nature of man. The human mind was predominantly viewed as divine and therefore beyond understanding in other terms. However, individual philosophers did attempt to inquire about what mechanisms were responsible for acquiring new knowledge and how the external world corresponded to the subjective experience.

The basic source of information for these inquiries was observation of the philosophers' own cognitive processes, that is, introspection. These analyses were directed toward very general issues and questions regarding the mechanisms and structure of the human mind and were primarily speculative, with little concern for establishing empirical support for the proposed ideas. Speculations and self-observations were inextricably mixed and interrelated, for they were all the products of the same individual. Although many of the proposed ideas for mechanisms became very influential in subsequent theorizing, this type of inquiry gradually became suspect because it did not conform to scientific methods.

One could observe a similar pattern of speculation for extending our knowledge about the physical environment before the emergence of a distinctive scientific approach to the analysis of physical phenomena. The scientific approach specifies a difference between facts and theory, regarding as facts only "indisputable" observations that should be accounted for and predicted by a corresponding theory. Methods of controlled observation and experimental manipulation are essential components of the scientific method. It was several centuries after the emergence of the natural sciences that scientific methods began to be applied to the study of the mind and human behavior.

Considerable effort has been devoted in psychology, as in the natural sciences, to specifying what constitutes indisputable evidence. Because all observations are made by humans, it was important to secure general agreement on what kind of observations reflected the external world rather than the individual observer. Complex assessments were disputed constituting as empirical evidence or were even discarded, for they were judged to require inferences and knowledge that were not shared by all observers. Complex assessments were also thought to be sensitive to the expectations and subjective bias of the observer. However, simple perceptual judgments based on sensory qualities, such as distinguishing colors, were found to be invariant over different observers and, in principle, independent of such biasing factors as differences in knowledge and earlier experience.

In the early years of psychology, the direct observation of mind in operation was taken as the primary method of obtaining information about the mind and its contents. William James (1890), one of the pioneers of modern psychology, used introspection (in a broad sense of the term) naturally and unselfconsciously as a major tool of investigation.

> *Introspective Observation is what we have to rely on first and foremost and always.* The word introspection need hardly be defined—it means, of course, the looking into our own minds and reporting what we there discover. (p. 185)

Another pioneer, Binet, went so far as to make the definition of psychology contingent on the use of the introspective method.

> Introspection is the basis of psychology; it characterizes psychology in so precise a way that every study which is made by introspection deserves to be called psychological, while every study which is made by another method belongs to some other science. (cited in Titchener, 1912*b*, p. 429)

At the turn of the century there was a consensus about the value of naive introspection.

> We need not hesitate to admit, on the other hand, that a roughly phenomenological account, a description of consciousness, as it shows itself to common sense, may be useful or even necessary as a starting-point of a truly psychological description. (Titchener, 1912*c*, p. 490)

However, as we will see, naive introspection was deemed to be as unscientific as casual observation of natural events would be for the natural sciences. To provide facts about the mind, more rigorous and systematic methods of introspection were required.

Structuralism

The main aim of Titchener's research was to gather facts about consciousness (the content of mind) and in the process to uncover its structure. The facts consisted of subjects' direct descriptions of consciousness; inferences and generalizations based on conscious experiences were not accepted.

> But the data of introspection are never themselves explanatory; they tell us nothing of mental causation, or of physiological dependence, or of genetic derivation. The ideal introspective report is an accurate description, made in the interest of psychology, of some conscious process. Causation, dependence, development are then matters of inference. (Titchener, 1912*c*, p. 486)

Titchener proposed to separate theory and facts by letting the subjects describe only their experienced conscious content, leaving the inferential process to the experimenter.

In response to the question of how the contents of consciousness should be reported, Titchener proposed a description in terms of the sensory components of thought. There appear to be at least two somewhat different reasons for this choice, which we will review briefly. The first one is theoretically based and should be seen as a hypothesis. Titchener, like Wundt, held the hypothesis that all mental states and experiences could be described in terms of their sensory and imaginal components. Wundt's thesis was that human experience of external stimulation had two phases. First, the invariant sensory attributes of the stimulation were immediately experienced. Second, mediating processes occurred, relating the sensory stimulation to existing general knowledge and prior experiences. According to Wundt, it was the result of the second phase that constitued the cognitive phenomena we call consciousness. Wundt assumed that people were born with the sensory components of the first stage already fixed and that they remained unchanged throughout life. Changes in the way in which people experienced the same sensory stimulation were atributable to changes in the associations evoked by the stimulation; that is, they were the result of the second stage. Assuming that all knowledge was ultimately derived from experience (the assumption of Locke's empiricism), and that all experience corresponded to a conglomerate of sensations, then the structure of mind and consciousness, including thought, could be described in terms of sensory components. In the search for intersubjective invariants and general psychological laws it was therefore natural to concentrate on the structure of the immediate sensations.

The second reason for Titchener's choice of a vocabulary of consciousness is basically methodological and concerns the difficulty of transmitting the conscious experience without contaminating it through words with imprecise meanings.

> I quote an illustration from Titchener; a half-trained student reports in an experiment a feeling of "perplexity." Now perplexity is clearly a complex experience. A group of processes is present, some of which we can experience in other contexts, disjoined from each other. True, I have a fair idea of what he has experienced. But only a *fair* idea. The description should be so full and complete that one can imaginatively or sympathetically reconstruct the experience. (English, 1921, p. 406)

Titchener's proposal was that consciousness should be described in terms of its elementary components.

> By the "description" of an object we mean an account so full and so definite that one to whom the object itself is unfamiliar can nevertheless, given skill and materials, reconstruct it from the verbal formula. Every discriminable part or feature of the object is unambiguously named; there is a one-to-one correlation of symbols and the empirical items symbolised; and the logical order of the specifications is the order of easiest reconstruction. This, then, is what we mean by "description" in psychology. (Titchener, 1912*a*, p. 165)

This procedure is analogous to transmitting a picture as a pattern of dots (e.g., a television picture) where no biasing semantic descriptors are required. This analogy may be considered a fair approximation of Titchener's idea, for he says "the record must be photographically accurate" (Titchener, 1909, p. 24). This view harmonizes well with the conservative criteria for simple perceptual observations used in the natural sciences and with the notion that introspection is analogous to inspection in physics, but with consciousness as its observational target.

In their efforts to find the elementary units of thinking, the structuralists searched not only for the elements of thought content but also for the elementary processes involved in thinking. Relatively early, Wundt started to pursue research along the lines of Donders, who is seen as the pioneer in the analysis of cognitive processes by means of observed latencies. (See Woodworth, 1938, for a fuller discussion of Donders's work.) Donders's central idea was that more complex processes could be viewed as compounded additively from simple reactions and the other cognitive processes. Three different tasks were proposed by Donders to allow estimation of the durations of the most basic cognitive processes, that is, stimulus discrimination and response selection. The most basic task was simple reaction in which the subject responded with a given single response, such as a button press, as soon as a stimulus was presented (a-reaction). In the c-reaction the subject responded only to a certain type of stimuli with a given single response. The c-reaction was assumed to differ from the a-reaction by requiring an initial discrimination of the stimulus. For the b-reaction the subject responded for each stimulus with a different response and thus was required not only to discriminate but also to select the correct response. Wundt extended this method by proposing an additional reaction, which will be discussed in the following section.

Principal Data

Titchener relied primarily on introspective reports given after the completion of the processes, but the latencies of the cognitive processes were also used in his analyses. The introspective reports requested by Titchener were very different from the phenomenal accounts provided by naive introspection. Subjects required extensive practice to break away from their habits of giving phenomenal accounts. Subjects had an initial tendency to commit the "stimulus error," which was to report information reflecting previous experience and knowledge from the second stage (e.g., to report "seeing a book") instead of reporting the sensory and imaginal components of the thought or presented stimulation. The extent of training that was required is indicated by Boring (1953), who mentions that Wundt required his subjects to have 10,000 supervised practice trials before they could participate in any real experiments.

One crucial aspect of these introspections was that, in the structuralist view, the contents of the self-observations, or introspections, were considered to be facts or data. From an information-processing point of view, on the other hand, the fact or datum is that a subject said or reported "X." In the former interpretation, one is obliged to trust that the subject is honest and that the words and the sentences are understood in the same way by the subject and the experimenter. In the latter interpretation, it is sufficient to reproduce or account for the report or aspects of it. Taking it literally as an observation is just one of many alternative interpretations.

Another crucial aspect of classical introspection was that, in the direct description of the sensory components, it was not obvious what were to be taken as the elementary units of sensation. Much introspective research activity was devoted, therefore, to determining the characteristics of these units. In this kind of analysis, the observers made decisions about which of several proposals for sensory units was correct and thus reported direct judgments and evaluation of hypotheses. This kind of introspective analysis was very different from the direct description advocated by Titchener and was also particularly plagued by extensive disagreements among different laboratories.

Latencies of cognitive processes were considered intersting as a separate source of data on the structure of thought processes. Donders's proposal for three types of reactions (a, b, c) was extended by Wundt, who suggested that the c-reaction, in which the subject gave a fixed response to only a certain type of stimulus, involved not only a discrimination but also a choice of whether to respond or not. As a consequence of this criticism, Wundt proposed the d-reaction, in which the subjects would respond as soon as they had made a cognitive discrimination of the stimulus. As the subjects did not have to make a choice to respond or not—they always responded because discrimination of a stimulus invariably occurred—this d-reaction would be a pure measure of the time taken to discriminate or to cognize the stimulus.

Issues

Titchener's type of introspection was severely criticized on at least two major accounts. The Wurzburgers and the Gestalt psychologists claimed that many aspects of consciousness could not be reduced to sensory and imaginal components and that consequently the method of analytic introspection was inadequate and should be replaced with the phenomenal reports. In addition, the researchers at Wurzburg collected phenomenal evidence rejecting the assumptions underlying the subtraction method to measure the duration of cognitive processes.

The behaviorists, with Watson, reacted against the direct observation of consciousness and claimed that only observable behavior (see discussion in the section on data) could be used as facts or data. Watson pointed out the lack of reproducibility of analytic introspections from different laboratories, that is, disagreements on issues such as the existence of imageless thought, whether there are three or four primary colors and what the fundamental attributes of visual sensation are. At the same time he acknowledged the reliable and robust results obtained by introspection in psychophysics. These two lines of critique suggested other methods of study, which will be considered later. First, we will discuss why the difficulties with analytic introspection of thought did not prevent reliable results from being obtained in psychophysical studies. Then we will briefly review the unsuccessful attempts of the structuralists to measure the speed and duration of the basic cognitive processes.

Analytic Introspections. We wish to describe and reinterpret in information-processing terms the cognitive processes involved in making analytic introspections and observations of the sensory and imaginal components of thought. Unfortunately, there is very little explicit discussion of these processes by the introspectionists themselves; our explication therefore will be in part inferred and hypothesized.

The first phase, involving the sensory attributes, appears to be very similar to the processes attributed to the sensory stores in the human information-processing model. Classical introspection was aimed at describing the contents of these sensory stores at discrete time intervals, which was like taking photographic snapshots (to be interpreted generally to include nonvisual sensations and imagery) corresponding to the complex thoughts.

> Observation, as we have said above, implies two things: attention to the phenomena, and record of the phenomena. The attention must be held at the highest possible degree of concentration; the record must be photographically accurate. (Titchener, 1909, p. 24)

From the point of view of attention, this means that the subject has to redirect attention intentionally from the spontaneously emerging thought content of short-term memory to a single sensory store in order to register rapidly the active sensory components. Let us assume for the moment that this is possible. Each recognized pattern in short-term memory would correspond to a very large number of independent sensory components, which would all have to be retained in short-term memory or stored in long-term memory until they could be reported. However, storage of information in long-term memory, with usable retrieval cues, requires considerable time— estimated at 8 seconds for each chunk by Simon (1979)—which would basically exclude the possibility of storage in long-term memory in this case.

Span of attention was known by contemporary research to be limited to a small number of elements (see Woodworth, 1938). It was possible to retain much more information if familiar patterns or organizations were recognized, but encoding in such patterns would violate the notion of a description directly in terms of sensory and imaginal components. This raised the question of how all these sensory components could be registered and then stored while awaiting their reporting, because reporting was known to take considerable time: "Strange to say, a ten-second period of thinking sometimes required as many minutes to recount and make clear to E" (Woodworth, 1938, p. 783).

There are some methodological problems inherent in evaluating the completeness, objectivity, and verdicality of the psychological description of thought contents, because the experimenter lacks external control of or independent access to the thought content described. One answer to the problem of the brief availability of thought content is tachistoscopic representation of visual stimuli. This technique provides experimental control over the visual stimuli that are presented and allows assessment of the veridicality and accuracy of the psychological descriptions. In a noted study in 1904, Külpe (cited in Chapman, 1932) found that, with tachistoscopic presentations of colored letters, an instruction to report certain aspects first, such as the colors of the letters, led to a serious decrement in the subsequent reportability of other aspects of the stimulus, for example, the positions of the letters.

Külpe's study does not discriminate between an incomplete encoding of the presented visual stimulus and a decay of memory for the information that was not initially reported. In a later study, Chapman (1932) demonstrated that informing the subjects about the aspect to be reported prior to the tachistoscopic presentation led to more accurate reports than informing the subjects about this immediately after the presentation. Still more recently, Sperling (1960) measured the duration of these initial "iconic" recordings of sensory stimuli and demonstrated that their content, though enduring only a fraction of a second, exceeded the capacity of short-term memory. However, it is notable that the units of reporting in Sperling's studies were not elementary sensory components, but letters or digits.

The important conclusion is that reportability depends on what information is focally heeded, which, in turn, is influenced by the task ("Aufgaben"). The findings suggest not only that the capacity to retain information is limited but also that the reported information can be affected by an initial bias to search for certain information. There are several possible sources of bias associated with introspective reports, including theoretically biased training of observers, uncontrolled use of questions (Humphrey, 1951), and the fact that many of the subjects (often faculty and graduate students) are not naive to the hypotheses addressed in these studies (Comstock, 1921). Taking these possible sources of bias into account, the differential reportability of certain aspects becomes hard to accept as scientifically valid evidence. In fact, it was proposed in the case of imageless thought that the observers simply overlooked the actual images and kinesthetic sensations, "so quick is the process of thought and so completely is the attention of the subject likely to be concentrated on meaning. We have a parallel case in the neglect of after-images and double images . . . in everyday experience when other things are in the focus of attention" (Comstock, 1921, p. 211).

Psychophysical Judgments. Having discussed some of the sources of problems and bias associated with analytic introspection of thought, we will now remark on the reliable results obtained from introspective analysis of psychophysical relations. We think the explanation is simple. The experimental situation for making psychophysical judgments of sensory stimulation is very different from the one described previously. The observer is instructed in advance when to attend and what to attend to, and the stimulus is simple and presented over an extended period. Moreover, the judgments, generally comparative, involve highly encoded stimuli and say nothing about subjects' ability to report raw sensory components. Essentially no additional memory is required for the observation before it can be reported. On the basis of these differences, we can readily accept psychophysical introspections, but not analytic introspections, as reliable.

Latencies. The structuralists' research on latencies was, interestingly enough, critiziced on basically the same grounds as was Titchener's analytic introspection of thought. Some initial research with Wundt's d-reaction, in which the subjects responded as soon as they had recognized the stimulus, gave very reasonable estimates for the time taken to cognize stimuli. Then a series of studies (See Woodworth, 1938) showed the d-reaction to take as much time as the simple reaction. Berger (cited in Woodworth, 1938) explained these results by pointing out that the response in the d-reaction was independent of which stimulus was recognized, in that the subject always responded regardless of the characteristics of the presented stimuli, as in simple reactions. Hence there was no objective criterion that could be used to ascertain that the subject waited until the stimulus was discriminated. In fact, unless the subject was to make his or her motor response contingent on the result of the discrimination, there seemed to be no way to ensure that the motor response was not initiated earlier and was not parallel with the perceptual processes. Again it appears that subjects were asked to do an impossible task.

These analyses of latencies were discarded on more general grounds when evidence was found against Donders's crucial assumption that the stages of discrimination and response selection in the b-reaction and c-reaction were simply inserted additively in the simple reaction (a-reaction). Ach and Watt from the Wurzburg laboratory found from retrospective reports that the processes of preparing for these several reactions were very different in terms of what was attended to prior to the presentation of the stimuli (Woodworth, 1938). These different types of reactions should thus be seen as wholly distinct procedures, and the differences in duration among them could not be used as estimates of the durations of unique cognitive processes. In current research using chronometric analysis of cognitive processes, this criticism does not generally apply, for the subjects are doing the same task in all conditions, and only the stimuli are varied.

Behaviorism

In his famous *Psychological Review* article, Watson (1913) opposed nearly all the attributes of structuralism and analytic introspection. The only acceptable facts or data were behavior and recordable events that could be observed by an independent observer, as opposed to direct introspective analysis. The emphasis was on collecting and analyzing such facts, and theorizing was a subordinate activity.

> [Behaviorism] may never make a pretense of being a *system*. Indeed systems in every scientific field are out of date. We collect our facts from observation. Now and then we select a group of facts and draw certain general conclusions about them. In a few years as new experimental data are gathered by better methods,

even these tentative general conclusions have to be qualified. (Watson, 1930, p. 18).

Even more recent behaviorists have argued that their scientific activity was theory-free (Turner, 1965), but we will later argue that this claim must be modified.

Watson (1925) wanted to use this methodology "to predict and to control human activity" p. 11). Unlike the structuralists, who were content with an accurate description of the structure of consciousness without implications for behavior and real-life applications, Watson (1913) was very concerned with finding results with social implications for modifying and changing behavior. It was therefore natural for Watson and the behaviorists to focus their research on learning and on the development of methods for eliminating undesirable behavior effectively and for acquiring new skills efficiently.

Of particular interest here is Watson's view of cognition. He opposed the structuralists' attempts to study cognitions directly and questioned the need for postulating cognitive structures and mechanisms beyond describing them in terms of stimulus–response (S-R) connections. Watson wanted very strongly to eliminate the magic surrounding unobservable cognitive structures by showing that they could be understood in terms of observable events or at least potentially observable events. Rigor and conceptual precision are not qualities to be associated with Watson's account of how memory and thinking can be described in terms of observable S-R connections. Because this account represents an extreme, yet important, viewpoint, we will briefly describe it without critical comments.

Watson (1925) proposed that memory could be accounted for adequately by old established S-R bonds, which could have been observed at the time of acquisition. He explicitly refuted the need for memory as a cognitive structure.

> The behaviorist never uses the term "memory." He believes that it has no place in an objective psychology. (p. 177)

> By "memory," then, we mean nothing except the fact that when we meet a stimulus again after an absence, we do the old habitual thing (say the old words and show the old visceral-emotional behavior) that we learned to do when we were in the presence of that stimulus in the first place. (p. 190)

Watson proposed that thinking could be seen as sequences of S-R connections that are primarily verbal. These covert verbal responses could be observed either by asking the subject to think aloud or by sensitive registration of the muscular activity of the larynx and the speech organs.

> The behaviorist advances the view that *what the psychologists have hitherto called thought is in short nothing but talking to ourselves.* (Watson, 1925, p. 191)

> If then, you grant that *you have the whole story of thinking when he thinks aloud, why make a mystery out of it when he thinks to himself.* (Watson, 1924, p. 198)

To explain productive thinking, Watson proposed the mechanism of trail and error, which will be discussed briefly along with Duncker's harsh critique in the section on Gestalt psychology.

Principal Data

There are basically no restrictions on the kinds of observable behavior or events that Watson and the behaviorists accepted as data beyond that of requiring that, to be scientifically interesting, they should be reproducible in a given experimental situation. However, although the behaviorists claimed independence of theories and data, it is clear that certain types of data were discounted on grounds that we would regard as theory-based.

The behaviorist, emphasizing that concern with cognitive mechanisms was basically unnecessary, was led to disregard data concerning the process by which observed behavior was produced. Because S-R psychology viewed the elicitation of responses from stimuli as being immediate, there are essentially no studies collecting and analyzing latencies for simple responses. In contrast, such latencies were for the structuralists, and have been in more recent research, a major data source for examining cognitive structures and processes.

In discussing Watson's view of verbalizations as data, it is important to distinguish two generating mechanisms. The first type of verbalization produces the covert language responses that Watson proposed as an integrated part of the sequence of S-R units. For some people and/or in some circumstances, the language responses are overt and directly observable, but it is also possible to identify the covert language responses by sensitive registration of the muscles in the larynx. In an attempt to study these language responses, Watson (1920) was the first investigator to request a subject to think aloud while thinking and solving a problem. In this case the observed behavior is simply vocalized covert language responses and hence completely legitimate from a behaviorist viewpoint. However, hardly any S-R psychologists collected this kind of data after Watson's pioneering effort (for an exception, see Mayzner, Tresselt, & Helbock, 1964).

The second type of verbalization is the report of internal stimulation. Analogous to our ability to report verbally the activity and emotional states of other people (e.g., when they are blushing), we are able, according to Watson, to report concurrent stimuli, such as the feeling of coldness, the feeling of pain, and so on. Until such time that it would be possible to register internal neural activity directly and objectively with sensitive instruments, Watson (1924) proposed that verbal reports could be considered a crude and inexact source of information about this stimulation. Watson also accepted the reliable verbal reports obtained for psychophysical relationships. These reports not only were reproducible but could also be verified by their consistent relationships to the presented stimuli. Furthermore, Watson (1913) suggested that the same results (for example, regarding discriminability) could have been obtained in experiments requesting the subjects to give nonverbal responses. There were, however, clear limits on what information could be reported.

> The subject can observe that he is using words in thinking. But how much word material is used, how much his final formulation is influenced by implicit factors which are not put in words and which he cannot himself observe, cannot be stated by the subject himself. (Watson, 1924, pp. 353–354)

Observe that both of the mechanisms for generating overt verbalizations operate on concurrently activated responses or stimuli. In anecdotal form, Watson (1920) pointed to instances of incorrectly reported information, when it had to be retrieved from long-term memory. More important is Watson's observation that the language behavior associated with many activities, such as playing golf, is totally detached from the subjects' actual behavior— hence it is possible to talk about playing golf, and even to describe verbally how one should do it, without actually being able to play. Verbal reports on behavior can therefore be generated without any relation to actual behavior.

The most important behaviorist constraints on what observable behavior is to be analyzed appear to be methodologically based. Watson was very permissive in his view of the types of behavior that could be considered observable responses (including complex behavior, such as building skyscrapers, and verbal behavior). However, only simple behaviors that could be assessed unambiguously and reliably, relying on simple perceptual judgments such as button presses, were acceptable for scientific purposes; complex behavior, which required intermediate processing and thus subjective interpretation, was not. This fact has resulted in behaviorism's providing hardly any means for describing and analyzing motor and other complex behavior. Instead, considerable effort has gone into designing experimental procedures that constrain the subjects' interesting responses to a small number of discrete alternatives. For example, in memory experiments, recognition by yes or no responses is preferred over uncontrained recall. Often the subject is instructed as to what responses are acceptable and how they are to be interpreted. It seems hard to reconcile such elaborate instructions, requiring transformations of responses into experimenter-determined categories, with skepticism about cognitive structures.

Issues

The following discussion will concentrate on the crucial behaviorist assertion that an analysis of consciousness and cognitive structures is unnecessary for understanding behavior. Watson and the behaviorists insisted that reports about cognitive structures be verified before being admitted as scientific evidence. Many investigators verified reported information by finding direct correspondence with the observed behavior (Patton, 1933; Eindhoven & Vinacke, 1952), at which point the information could be assessed directly from behavior without the reports. With this criterion for the admissability of data, it is difficult to see how one could ever refute the assertion that cognitive structures are unnecessary for understanding behavior.

The behaviorists assume that different types of behavior are generated separately rather than being different expressions of common cognitive structures and processes. It was even proposed that verbal reports could be conditioned independently of other behavior (Verplanck, 1962). Empirical evidence for this extreme view is discussed in Ericsson and Simon (1980). We will now turn to three different research efforts that have been widely cited as evidence that there is little correspondence between observed task-directed behavior and behavior assumed to reflect consciousness. The absence of such correspondence would, of course, refute the hypothesis of a common cognitive basis.

The first line of research demonstrated that subjects may differ considerably in the relevant information they report yet show no discernable differences in performance. In a classical study on concept formation, or abstraction, Hull (1920) presented Chinese characters that had one of several simple signs (radicals) embedded in them. In one experiment Hull investigated whether learning was facilitated by presenting the pure signs (radicals) in association with their correct responses, thus eliminating the process of abstracting these from the compound characters. At the end of the learning trials, there was no reliable difference in correct assignment of concepts for the condition in which the pure sign was presented as compared with controls. However, when half of the subjects were asked to draw a picture of crucial features corresponding to the concept names, the concepts presented with the pure sign were described twice as well as the others, as assessed by independent judges. Hull (1920) concluded that "the power to define is thus in some cases at least a very inadequate index of the functional value of a concept" (p. 84).

This study has frequently been cited, we think incorrectly, as evidence that inaccessible cognitive structures generate the observable behavior. We will argue that in this experiment the information that allowed subjects to draw a picture of the crucial features of the concepts was accessed only partially, if at all, in actually generating the behavior. In analyzing Hull's data further, we find that only between 7% and 14% of the variability of the subjects' performance can be accounted for by the differences in their ability to define, which is not statistically significant with this small number of subjects (five). It is abundantly clear that the knowledge resulting from the presentation of component signs was insufficient for the subjects' learning the complex concepts. Identifying these radicals as components of the corresponding characters was not an obvious matter. Hull (1920) showed that an initial red marking of the radical in the character led to considerable improvements in performance.

A second important related argument against verbal reports was based on contemporary work on concept formation showing that subjects, contrary to the normative logical view, relied largely on memorizing exemplars or sets of correlated discriminating features rather than on abstracting the common features of exemplars. The subjects were often unable to verbalize the concept as defined by the experimenter, yet they were fully able to differentiate instances from noninstances. These results have been cited in support of a dissociation of reported information from behavior. In our view the only conclusion that can legitimately be drawn from this research is that concept formation is a much more complex cognitive process, as shown by concurrent and retrospective reports, than just a search for the experimenter's definition of the concept.

A third line of research has claimed to show that changes in behavior and learning can occur without awareness as assessed by verbal reports. An often-cited study by Greenspoon may serve as an example of this line of research. (For an extensive review, see Brewer, 1974.) Greenspoon (1955) asked his subjects to generate single words in a free association type of experiment. Some kinds of words (e.g., concrete nouns in the plural form) were reinforced by the experimenter's saying "mmm-hum," and subjects produced these responses more and more frequently in later trials. After the experiment, the subjects were asked general questions—for example, what they thought the experiment was about and whether they noticed any changes in the kinds of words in their responses. All subjects who reported noticing a relationship between the verbal response of the experimenter and their uttered words were eliminated from further analysis. For the remaining subjects, marked increases in frequency of the reinforced words were found. It was proposed that these changes occurred without awareness.

What it actually means to stress awareness is rarely explicated within the behaviorist tradition, but Ericsson and Simon (1980, Note 1) have proposed an information-processing description of such assessment. According to this account, for learning to take place, the information to be learned must be heeded by the central processor, and this will be available in short-term memory for further processing. However, many factors decrease the probability that the information would still remain in short-term memory at the time subjects were questioned about it. Experiments of the type just described often included overlearning or extinction trials, and it is not clear that the questioning took place immediately after the experiment. Critics of the research (e.g., Brewer, 1974) have pointed to the lax questioning of the subjects and have demonstrated that, with more detailed and thorough questioning, many more subjects report awareness, and the effects of reinforcement for the remaining subjects disappear.

Assuming that the subjects have to retrieve the information from long-term memory in these postexperimental interviews, more detailed questioning will provide subjects with useful retrieval cues to facilitate access to long-term memory. Under the general questioning of Greenspoon's (1955) study, it is not even clear that the subjects attempted to search long-term memory for relevant information. In a more detailed review, Ericsson and Simon (1980, Note 1) have found that research using detailed questioning to obtain information from long-term memory or research using concurrent probing and reporting from short-term memory in this type of learning experiment showed a consistent relationship between awareness and observed behavior.

Finally, there may be considerable difficulty in tapping attended information and cognitive structures with a fixed set of predetermined responses. A study by Lazarus and McCleary (1951) found that tachistoscopically presented nonsense syllables that had earlier been conditioned in subjects by an electric shock gave, on the average, higher GSRs than unconditioned syllables, even when the subjects were unable to identify the presented stimulus correctly in a forced-choice recognition from 10 different alternatives. This result was interpreted as evidence for an automatic discrimination of the conditioned syllables without reportable awareness.

Several other accounts of this result have been proposed that do not resort to the hypothesis of automatic discrimination (Eriksen, 1956). The most interesting account concerns awareness of partial information. Bricker and Chapanis (1953) showed that, even when subjects were unable to identify the tachistoscopically presented stimuli on their first guess, subsequent guesses were far more accurate than chance. In restricting subjects to a single guess, the conscious discrimination would be underestimated. The result of Lazarus and McCleary (1951) could be explained by assuming stimulus generalization of the GSR elicited by the partial information attended, as revealed by a free report of the subject (Eriksen, 1956). In a large number of studies, the notions of partial information and partially related stimulus contingencies adequately account for subjects' behaviors. Because these behaviors often differ between situations and between individuals, they require a free-report methodology for their assessment.

Gestalt Psychology

Gestalt psychology is probably best seen as a reaction against the postulates of structuralism—that awareness and thought could be described and represented in terms of sensory components. In fact, the Gestalt psychology program is sometimes characterized as a series of criticisms of, and counter-examples to, the sensory elements of structuralism and the simplisitic mechanisms proposed by S-R psychology. Wertheimer's demonstration of the phi-phenomenon, where turning two lamps on or off at a certain rate produced a perception of movement, is generally taken as the founding of Gestalt psychology.

Gestalt psychologists emphasized the structure and internal relations of the stimulation and rejected the view that our perceptions are a result of a summation of stimuli or that similarity is a function of the number of common stimulus elements. One of their favorite examples was the striking similarity of a melody played in two different keys, where the two realizations of the melody may completely lack common stimulus elements.

Gestalt psychology made its major contributions in the study of perception, but it also contained many important individual contributions to the study of cognition. For example, Katona (1940) and Wertheimer (1945) opposed the simple notion of rote learning and pointed to the efficacy of conceptual understanding for retention and transfer. Wulf opposed the simple decay theory of memory and proposed a process of autonomic memory change (Woodworth, 1938). Duncker (1926, 1945) opposed the simple S-R and associative accounts of problem solving and proposed an internal representation or understanding of the problem and general problem-solving methods. Köhler (1925) opposed the notion of trial-and-error and incremental learning and proposed a process of insight and understanding.

Principal Data

The basic source of data for Gestalt psychology was immediate reports of the experiences of naive subjects. These verbal reports depended on already existing reporting skills of the subjects and hence did not require any training that might, as in the case of analytic introspection, induce bias.

A major portion of Gestalt psychology research was oriented toward perception of specially prepared stimuli. The data in these experiments were direct descriptions of the corresponding experiences. For processes of considerable duration, subjects were asked to give concurrent expression to their thinking, that is, to "think aloud." Duncker (1945) was careful to point out the differences between this type of verbalization and the unsuccessful introspection.

> While the introspecter makes himself as thinking the object of his attention, the subject who is thinking aloud remains immediately directed to the problem, so to speak allowing his activity to become verbal. When someone, while thinking, says to himself, "One ought to see if this isn't . . ." or "It would be nice if one could show that, . . ." one would hardly call this introspection. (p. 2)

In other studies a variety of measures of performance was used, and there appears to be little difference between the behaviorists and the Gestaltists as to what type of data they accepted (cf. Marx & Hillix, 1973).

Because the Gestaltists explored new areas and wanted to demonstrate and illustrate mechanisms and effects, their analyses of data and experimental design were sometimes less rigorous than those of the methodologically oriented behaviorists (Marx & Hillix, 1973). Nevertheless, if the actual analysis, especially of their collected reports, was intuitive and less rigorous, it was clearly sufficient to demonstrate the general effects in which they were interested.

Issues

The complex mental structures and processes proposed by the Gestaltists constitute a challenge for any theory. We will discuss three aspects of their position in some detail and will evaluate whether they can be, or whether they already have been, reasonably explicated. First, we will discuss the Gestalt theory of forgetting and its contemporary reinterpretation by Woodworth. Second, we will discuss Duncker's theory of problem solving and its relation to the theory of problem solving proposed by Newell and Simon (1972). Finally, we will discuss the processes associated with generating immediate phenomenal reports and offer some proposals for the underlying mechanisms. Other aspects of Gestalt psychology that have been discussed in information-processing terms include perceptual phenomena of reversible and impossible figures (Simon, 1967) and insight (Ericsson & Simon, 1980, Note 1).

Forgetting. The Gestalt psychologists proposed that memory traces were autonomically transformed over time to "better figures" (defined in terms of the laws of perceptual organization) rather than simply being reduced in distinctiveness by loss of attributes through decay of the memory trace. By having subjects reproduce originally presented figures repeatedly at different time intervals, Wulf (cited in Woodworth, 1938) found that the reproduced figures became more pregnant with "better form" and that these changes increased with the passage of time.

Woodworth (1938) was able to explain this rather magical process through which memories appear to be transformed rather than forgotten. The subjects' initial perception (not memory), as measured by immediate reproduction, could account for an important portion of the observed differences or changes. Furthermore, subjects had a tendency to make symmetrical—"good"—figures when not contradicted by specific memory, as shown by studies in which subjects were asked to complete incomplete figures. A more complete discussion of the empirical evidence of autonomous change in the memory trace is given in Baddeley (1976).

The systematic changes over time from one reproduction to subsequent ones was shown by Hanawalt (1937) to most likely result from using the inappropriate method of successive reproductions. Each new reproduction appeared to tap memory from earlier reproductions (which, of course, also left a memory trace) rather than just the original stimulus, for the amount recalled was drastically reduced by having subjects make a single reproduction at a given time delay (Hanawalt, 1937). The systematic changes observed in repeated reproduction could thus be explained by the subjects' remembering primarily their last reproduction, including the erroneous inferences for missing details discussed previously. It is not obvious that we can retrieve information from long-term memory without subsequent effects of that retrieval. Reminiscence, in which a subjects' memory improves with time after repeated reproductions, can also be given a natural explanation on the basis of this effect (Woodworth, 1938).

Problem Solving. In his attempt to understand the underlying mechanisms of productive thinking—the solution of problems not previously encountered—Duncker (1926) carefully discussed earlier explanatory proposals. He characterized a problem in terms of a given situation (S) and a desired situation (P); solving it consisted of finding an aspect (M) that was associated with a method for attaining P, given S. After careful examination and presentation of counterexamples, Duncker (1926) rejected the associative theory that aspect M could be evoked by finding separate associations between M and S and between M and P. Contrary to the empirical evidence, mechanisms operating on associations between specific situations would yield blind searches and generation of "stupid" solution attempts, some of which would be highly improbable. Duncker (1926) harshly rejected an account in terms of the behavioristic principles of frequency, recency, and intensity.

> Such statements as are to be found in Watson's tenth lecture before the People's Institute might at the most impress a credulous audience. Theoretical nonentities as "bring to bear your previous manual (or verbal) organization upon the present problem," or still more profound, "by manipulating words . . . as also the poet does shifting them about until a new pattern is hit upon" are not worth serious consideration. (pp. 662–663)

Duncker (1926) concluded that more general mental structures were required to account for the directed generation of solution attempts. By understanding the conflict between S and P, it was possible to evoke a general method for how it must work, (functional value) and then select the particular concrete means by which to attain the specific solution. As Duncker (1945) stated, "*the general or 'essential' properties of a* solution *genetically precede the specific properties; the latter are developed out of the* former" (p. 8).

In his main paper, "On Problem Solving," Duncker (1945) explicates the general processes and methods that either evoke solutions directly or constitute the necessary steps for evoking them. These general principles can then be made into specific solution attempts that can be tested and evaluated. Examples of these general methods are analysis of the goal, analysis of the situation, and analysis of the "situation as analysis of conflict," that is, identifying conflict elements. These ideas were partly rediscovered and explicated in the work of Newell, Shaw, and Simon (1958) in their information-processing model and computer simulation of problem solving. In a recent American Psychological Association (APA) address on the history of cognition, Newell

(Note 4) shows, in a detailed examination of Duncker's work, that many of Duncker's proposals and ideas have been explicated and integrated in the current information-processing theory of cognition.

Phenomenal Reports. A core assumption of the Gestalt psychologists is that the phenomenal verbal report reflects a heeded cognitive structure. The verbal reports should be seen as verbal expressions of these structures, for the latter largely are not originally encoded in verbal form. If one is interested in searching for invariances involving the same or similar phenomenal experiences in different subjects, there is the problem of identifying these experiences, because the same heeded cognitive structure would not necessarily be recoded into the same sequence of words. To relate the verbal reports to the hypothesized underlying cognitive structures, a model is needed for the processes governing the translation or expression of those structures into verbal form.

The Gestaltists used the verbal reports to discriminate between markedly different phenomena rather than to attempt to describe a given experience uniquely (cf. Titchener's attempt to attain a complete description). Under these circumstances, the verbal report can be viewed as a communication link to be used for assessing to which set of cognitive structures the report best conforms.

This view of the verbal report as a means of communicating or transferring information is apparent in the research of Werner and Kaplan (1963). They were interested in finding the attributes of the subjects' internal representations by comparing verbal descriptions of perceived stimuli made by the subjects for their own use with descriptions of the same stimuli made for the use of other people. They presented subjects with odors and nonfigurative drawings and asked them to describe these stimuli verbally so that they themselves or some other persons, respectively, would be able to identify the stimuli among a set of distractors from the descriptions.

Unfortunately, the information value of the verbal descriptions was never tested in these studies. In a concept formation experiment, Wilson (1974, 1975) asked subjects to write down their rules for positive instances at each trial and then to sort a series of test instances. To assess the information transmitted in these verbal descriptions of rules, Wilson had the same subjects, as well as subjects who had not earlier participated in the experiment, re-sort the test series on the basis of the verbal rules. He found a high general agreement among all the sorts, including the original ones.

In more recent analyses, attempts have been made to extract from the reported information specific information that is relevant to hypotheses about the cognitive process. The most important general method for specifying relevant information is the task analysis proposed by Newell and Simon (1972), in which relations and knowledge required for the problems' solutions are isolated, and problem spaces are postulated in which possible states of knowledge can be represented. These explicit knowledge states are then identified from the verbally reported information by coding assessments. Here, transforming the verbally reported information into categories defined a priori is the predominant technique.

There have been some successful attempts to go further in the analysis and regeneration of verbalizations. Ericsson and Simon (1980, Note 2), proposed different processes for overt verbalization of heeded information in short-term memory, depending on whether the information was verbally coded or coded in some other way. For information in verbal code, as in tasks such as mental arithmetic and multiplication, the overt verbalization is achieved by simple vocalization, and overt verbalization can occur in these cases without any observable decrement in speed of the original processes (Ericsson & Simon, 1980, Note 2). For nonverbal information, there is a growing body of evidence suggesting that, among the logically possible ways of expressing some information, subjects tend to select a verbal realization that reflects the underlying internal representation of that information. Clark and Chase (1972) found that, when subjects described a picture of two different symbols with a simple sentence, they reliably described the relationship in terms of above and below, depending on characteristics of the presented symbols. These encoding preferences were validated by an analysis of latencies from an associated experiment with sentence verification, where shorter latencies were observed when the relation term in the subjects' encoding matched the relation term in the sentence to be verified.

In a study of verbal descriptions of the layouts of apartments, Linde and Labov (1975) found that major rooms (independently assessed) were introduced in subject–noun phrases and with definite articles, whereas minor rooms were not. Osgood (1971) has shown that the form and content of verbalized descriptions of presented events reflect the structure of the perceived situation and the subjects' presuppositions based on earlier presented events. We believe that the processes underlying verbal reporting are no more mysterious than those underlying other types of behavior and that they can be modeled and understood at the same level of detail.

Direct and Indirect Assessment of Cognitive Structures

The research approaches described in previous studies of this chapter were directed toward isolating general relationships averaged over subjects. However, there has also been considerable research aimed at measuring and describing individual differences—in particular, differences in cognitive structure. This research has adopted many of the ideas advocated by Watson. The approach has been to search for aspects of behavior that remain invariant over some class of situations yet that discriminate one individual from another. Collecting observations and discovering behavioral regularities (especially with the help of correlational techniques) have been emphasized over theoretical analysis. Much of the research has been directed toward useful, "real-world" applications: selecting people for education, jobs, and various forms of clinical treatment.

It has been customary to interpret invariant aspects of behavior that are found by assessment in terms of postulated internal states or traits. General abilities, such as numerical skill, are associated with traits, as are many stable aspects of personality, such as aggressiveness. In the approach described previously, which we will term "indirect assessment," the invariant structures are induced from many specific observations.

Within the same framework, attempts have been made to gain information about these general invariant structures more directly. Instead of time-consuming observation of subjects' behavior in concrete situations (e.g., while selecting food dishes), one could ask for their reactions to a verbal description of a general class of situations (e.g., "Do you like to eat fish?") and thus access general preferences directly. Alternatively, one can ask subjects after they have exhibited some behavior why they did it, hoping to receive a report of a general motive that could explain or predict their behavior over a wide range of situations. This research has taken a basically empirical approach to finding behavioral regularities and has not attempted to specify the cognitive mechanisms that generate behavior and that are accessible for verbal questioning. Implicit reference is made to the commonsense notion that people are aware and rational and therefore able to answer questions about the cognitive structures responsible for their overt behavior.

Data: Types of Assessment Methods

Consistent with the behaviorist viewpoint, the research on both indirect and direct assessment has not collected observations and data about the processes underlying the generation of the targeted behavior. Concurrent verbalizations, retrospective reports, and latencies have been collected and analyzed only very sparingly and recently.

Indirect assessment of cognitive structures or traits has been used primarily and most successfully for cognitive abilities. In ability tests a sample of representative tasks for the ability in question is generated, and the subjects' reponses are evaluated as to correctness. An assessment of a given subject's ability is then made in terms of his or her pattern of success on the various items. But here, again, the cognitive structures are inferred indirectly.

To create representative situations that will elicit behavior reflecting hypothesized traits, such as preferences, aggressiveness, and other personality-based characteristics, is much harder. Some research has employed observers to record subjects' behavior in natural environments or in semicontrolled group interactions. However, most of the research has been directed to other more direct assessment procedures. We have distinguished four types of methods and corresponding data for assessing traits. Some of these distinctions have been proposed by Olson (1976).

In the first type of assessment procedure, observers who study the subjects' behavior in one or several types of situations make direct estimates afterward of the levels of certain traits for the subjects. These ratings by the observers constitute the data.

In the second type of procedure, the subjects' memories are probed for their previous behavior or covert reactions in particular classes of situations. The subjects are generally asked to respond with one alternative from a predetermined set, which asks about the degree of regularity (e.g., "never," "occasionally," "often") of the behavior.

A third type of procedure obtains subjects' reactions to verbal stimuli describing their opinions or predicted actions in general situations verbally described. To gain a better understanding of what is actually asked of the subject when this method is used, we will give an example of a stimulus and an excerpt from an instruction given to subjects (Mischel, 1968).

> I enjoy social gatherings just to be with people. [Item from California Psychological Inventory.] (p. 61)

> Your first impression is generally the best so work quickly and don't be concerned about duplications, contradictions or being exact. [Item from instructions to the Leary Checklist.] (p. 62)

The data in this case are the categories (e.g., "very much," "not at all") that the subject selects, and the responses are not conceptualized as introspective reports about the associated traits.

In the fourth type of procedure, subjects are asked for explanations of, or motives for, their observed behavior. When the subjects are asked how they were thinking throughout the experiment or why they elicited particular behavior, the experimenter seeks to learn directly from them about the underlying cognitive structure that produced the overt behavior.

Issues

Indirect assessment of cognitive abilities has been found to be very successful in reliably predicting behavioral differences in real-life situations. This stands in rather stark contrast to the controversies surrounding assessment (direct or indirect) of personality-based traits and direct assessment of cognitive structures in general. Correlations between different methods and tests for assessing the same personality traits are very often unsatisfactorily low (e.g., Campbell & Fiske, 1959). Reported reasons for behavior are unrelated to experimentally induced variations in behavior (e.g., Nisbett & Wilson, 1977). Reported attitudes do not correspond to actual behavior (e.g., Calder & Ross, 1973; Schuman & Johnson, 1976; Wicker, 1969).

In discussing the relative success of indirect assessment of cognitive abilities as compared with other types of assessment, we will again try to suggest explications in terms of differences in the cognitive processes involved and the cognitive structures assessed. Unfortunately, there has been little research directed toward uncovering processes, most analyses having been made on data representing the final result of the processes. Lacking extensive data on the relevant processes, we will proceed by making assumptions derived from other areas of cognition where more of such data has been gathered. We will first note some general differences between the kinds of cognitive processes evoked by ability tests and the kinds evoked by personality tests and direct assessments and then turn to a discussion based on a more detailed explication of the cognitive processes underlying probes to assess cognitive structures directly.

Processes Evoked by Assessment. There are at least three marked differences between the cognitive processes evoked by items in an ability test and those evoked by items in a test to assess traits by self-reports. The first difference concerns the degree of confidence that the experimenter can have that the relevant cognitive processes and structures are actually evoked or accessed. The "first impression" requested by the instruction for self-reports and the emphasis that responses are neither right nor wrong stand in stark contrast to the instructions for ability tests, where responses are carefully considered and are either correct or incorrect. To generate the correct answer or response in an ability test, the information has to be carefully processed by the relevant sequence of operations. The probability that a subject could generate the answer by guessing or by some short-circuiting procedure, such as first impression, is very small. Thus there is much more experimental control for ability items than for self-report items over the cognitive processes and structures that need to be activated in order to generate a valid response. For self-report items, uninteresting response processes, such as always agreeing with the statement or simply selecting the socially desirable alternative, often appear to account for an impressive fraction of the variance. However, by careful selection of questionnaire items, more recent studies have reduced the extent to which subjects can rely on, for instance, social desirability of the statements.

The second difference between ability tests and other tests concerns the relationship between the test item and the "real" situation in which the actual nontest behavior occurs. Many symbolic tasks, such as arithmetic, occurring in the real situation are rather accurately represented by a verbal description in the form of a test item. By contrast, verbal description of a social interactive situation is usually a rather poor representation of the situation and does not communicate many essential aspects that would influence the actual nontest behavior. We will return to this issue later.

Third, direct assessment, as contrasted with indirect assessment, often requires subjects to make inferences in order to generate the answers from the information available to them.

Memories versus Inferences. The frequent low correlations between different assessment tests of the same trait provide grounds for skepticism about verbal reports.

> Inaccuracy has been attributed mainly to a variety of distorting motivational forces, including deliberate faking, lack of insight, and unconscious defensive reactions, all of which presumably produce inaccurate self-descriptions. (Mischel, 1968, p. 69)

However, Mischel (1968) points to research supporting other possibilities that are consistent with the notion that subjects are able to describe and predict specific behavior with minimal interpretation of its meaning. The self-reports in response to the stimuli described so far require the subjects' global interpretations of their own general behavior patterns rather than descriptions of specific behavior. Likewise, the attributes assessed by observers are mostly high-level traits and involve considerable inferential activity of the observer. Correlations could be low between different assessments because they elicited different inferences and not because of any conflict in evidence at the level of description of specific behavior. In support of this view, Mischel (1968) cites research showing that intercoder reliabilities decrease rapidly as the necessity for complex inference increases. For further discussion of the special problems involved in assessments by observers, see Fiske (1978) and Mischel (1968).

In a more detailed analysis of the cognitive processes involved in assessment procedures, we need to distinguish probing subjects' memories for past processes and occurrences of acts and reactions from probing for subjects' anticipated responses in verbally described situations or to described classes of objects or people.

In addressing the probing for subjects' memories, we will assume that information about specific past behavior and covert reactions is generally stored in episodic form in long-term memory. This assumption implies that a statement about occurrences of a certain kind will require access to the memory of all relevant specific occurrences. For simplicity, we will not discuss the exceptions, in which subjects have been asked similar questions before or have, by their own reflective activity, already generated the corresponding general information, which then can be directly accessed.

From general research on recall, we know that ability to recall specific events—especially with detailed information—deteriorates rapidly with time (see Cannell & Kahn, 1968). Recall depends very much on the availability of retrieval cues. Because general verbal descriptions of classes of events most often will be insufficient as cues for retrieving specific events, subjects will have to supply additional information in order to generate more specific cues, such as the relevant time period and specific situations in which the activity might have occurred. If the experimenter specifies the relevant time period and the particular type of event to be recalled, recall increases considerably (e.g., Biderman, 1967). This type of recall is very time consuming and can hardly take place in the time allotted for filling out a questionnaire, unless the relevant episodes were few and easily retrieved because of recency.

If the subjects were able and motivated to retrieve all relevant episodes, they would face the problem of converting the information into fixed alternatives, such as "often," "frequently," and so on. Mischel (1968) cites a study by Simpson, who demonstrated that a wide range of percentages was cited for such words when presented out of context. For example, one fourth of Simpson's subjects associated "frequently" with events occurring more than 80% of the time, whereas another fourth associated it with events occurring less than 40% of the time. The processing activity that would be needed for accurate responses to questions about past overt and covert behavior—given the limits of recallability—appears to be incompatible with the relatively fast responses requested.

Let us now turn to the questioning of subjects about the reasons or causes of their behavior. A recent review (Nisbett & Wilson, 1977) has suggested that these reports are inaccurate and, furthermore, that they are not based on introspective access to memory. In terms of our model, legitimate probes for reasons and motives for observed behavior in a given process are just one kind of cue for retrieving information selectively from the memory trace of that process. From studies of current verbalization of heeded information, we know that subjects often generate goals in solving problems, hypotheses in concept-formation experiments, and evaluations in decision making. These should be easily elicited by probes of *why* a specific overt behavior was elicited. (One should not assume that the subjects can directly assess that specific responses were "caused" indirectly by more general goals or hypotheses, as noted by Titchener, 1912c.) As shown in our discussion of behaviorism, cognitive processes often involve attention to specific information that is *not* a specification of heeded general structures, such as goals. In other cases information is heeded as a result of direct recognition, without any intermediate states entering consciousness (Ericsson & Simon, 1980, Note 1). In these cases the subject cannot answer a why question by direct retrieval from memory.

Much of the research cited by Nisbett and Wilson (1977) concerns experiments in which the subjects have been questioned about a long series of experimental trials. When subjects are asked about their average behavior or motives, they obviously cannot answer questions by retrieving a single motive or episodic memory. The behavior on different trials may correspond to very different cognitive processes and it may, in any event, be difficult to retrieve them all from memory. Therefore it is reasonable to assume that the subject either infers general motives or processes from retrieved selected episodic memories or tries to rationalize his or her behavior using sources of information other than the memory of the processes.

Smith and Miller (1978) noted that, in many of the experiments cited by Nisbett and Wilson, the subjects were asked why their behavior in one condition of the experiment differed from other subjects' behavior in other conditions of the experiment. In such a situation it is not clear to subjects that their memory is relevant to answering the question, as shown by the following initial step of a "typical" dialogue:

> Question: "I notice that you took more shock than average. Why do you suppose you did?"

> Typical answer: "Gee, I don't really know . . . Well, I used to build radios and stuff when I was 13 or 14, and maybe I got used to electric shock." (Nisbett & Wilson, 1977, p. 237)

The subject appears to understand the assertion to mean that more shock was received than other subjects in the *same* condition and therefore tried to remember explanations that would be independent of the situation and hence of the processing activity.

If the subject, to give a valid report, has to rely on memory for earlier processing, it would be necessary for him or her to have experienced *both* experimental conditions in order to explain any differences in behavior between them. Inferring what one would do in a new situation should not be confounded with reporting actual memory of completed processes.

In the case of asking subjects for their reactions to classes of persons or objects, or for their expectations of their behavior in verbally described situations, few data exist on what cognitive processes and structures are evoked. It is most plausible to assume that the subject forms some kind of representation or "image" of what is verbally described and uses this to determine hypothetical reaction or behavior. La Piere (1934) questioned the extent to which subjects in many situations were able to represent internally the crucial aspects of the verbally described situations. Any such failure would make their conceived behavior different from actual nontest behavior.

> Thus from a hundred or a thousand responses to the question "Would you get up to give an Armenian woman your seat in a street car?" the investigator derives the "attitude" of non-Armenian males towards Armenian females. Now the question may be constructed with elaborate skill and hidden with consummate cunning in a maze of supplementary or even irrelevant questions yet all that has been obtained is a symbolic response to a symbolic situation. The words "Armenian woman" do not constitute an Armenian woman of flesh and blood, who might be tall or squat, fat or thin, old or young, well or poorly dressed—who might, in fact, be a goddess or just another old and dirty hag. And the questionnaire response, whether it be "yes" or "no," is but a verbal reaction and

this does not involve rising from the seat or stolidly avoiding the hurt eyes of the hypothetical woman and the derogatory stares of other street-car occupants. (La Piere, 1934, p. 230)

In a classic study, La Piere (1934) studied attitudes and behavior toward Orientals. Six months after a large number of hotels and restaurants had been visited by an Oriental couple, the same places were sent a questionnaire with the question "Will you accept members of the Chinese race as guests in your establishment?" The overwhelming majority of the places visited answered "no," with a smaller number saying "under some circumstances." Similar disassociation between verbal reports in response to symbolic situations and real behavior has been found by Kutner, Wilkins, and Yarrow (1952).

In information-processing terms, La Piere's hypothesis is that, in the case in which the generated internal representation contains all relevant aspects appropriately portrayed as in the real situation, the behavior and verbally reported behavior will be consistent. When the real situation is more or less symbolic, as in the case of voting, very accurate predictions can be made for actual behavior on an aggregate level from verbal reactions to questions (see Schuman & Johnson, 1976). Similarly, Katona (1975, 1979) has found that sampled subjects' reports of the expectations of future prices, future income, and so on, give valid information for predicting changes in purchasing behavior for the general population to which they belong. Ajzen and Fishbein (1977) showed in a recent review that when the attitude measurement situation corresponds closely to the situation in which the behavior to be predicted occurs, high agreement between attitudes and behavior is found. Fazio and Zanna (1978) have found that extended direct experience with specific entities leads to better-defined attitudes (and stable internal representations evoked by the questionnaire items), which can better predict subsequent behavior. When the information in focus of attention is taken into account, attitudes appear to be consistent with each other and with behavior (Taylor & Fiske, 1978).

Our general conclusion from this brief overview of controversies concerning direct assessment by verbal probing and questioning is that a detailed model of cognitive processes and cognitive structures is needed for making decisions concerning when and how to use this type of assessment procedure.

Conclusion and Summary

In our selective overview of various approaches to identifying cognitive processes and structures, we have focused on the kinds of observations that have been made. We have found basically no disagreement concerning what kinds of raw observations of behavior (latencies, verbal behavior, etc.) are legitimate sources of scientific evidence. The disagreements concern the evaluation of the usefulness of some types of observations and the interpretation or mapping of raw observations onto the proposed cognitive structures.

The first type of disagreement arises from the decisions of investigators with different theoretical backgrounds to record and analyze only selected portions of the potentially recordable behavior. The most direct instance of this is probably the failure of the behaviorists to record and analyze latencies. As pointed out previously, this omission was theoretically based. Similarly, the structuralists were constrained by their definition of psychology to observations (e.g., verbal reports and latencies) that would reveal the structure of consciousness. In omitting various form of verbal reports and behavior, the exclusion practiced by the behaviorists was deliberate and was dictated not only by theoretical but also by methodological considerations; they found complex—not just verbal—behavior difficult to analyze and encode into well-defined objective categories.

More fundamental disagreements arise at the step in which the raw observations are interpreted as evidence for theoretically proposed cognitive structures or processes. This step is often inconspicuous and the source of many arguments. In classical introspection it was assumed that the observations made by the observers were direct assessments of cognitive structure that could not be in error—if made by a sufficiently skilled observer. This is, however, a theoretical interpretation, and the only raw observation is the observed verbal report.

It is essential that a theory of human cognition be explicit about how the theoretically proposed cognitive structures are related to the observed behavior. However, the early proposals and even later ones (cf. direct assessment) relied on commonsense and loosely defined models of processes and structures. The need to be explicit about the relationship between cognitive structures and observed behavior is particularly important when we want to demonstrate converging support for a given cognitive structure from different kinds of data, or when we want to disprove that two sources of data reflect the same cognitive structure (cf. the relationship between postexperimental questionnaires and behavior during the experiment),

Within the information-processing model, we are able to specify the relationships between very different types of overt behavior and cognitive structures—for example, by attributing to various types of memories specific access and storage characteristics. We have tried to demonstrate the advantages of analyzing the cognitive processes in terms of information-processing models when addressing old controversies.

Let us summarize briefly some of the methods used in our overview. Information-processing analysis allows one to evaluate critically the *feasibility* of proposed mechanisms and processes. Complete analytic introspection was found to be incompatible with accepted limits of attention and the known capacities of memories. Some of the controversial differences in reported content of consciousness can be attributed to implicit bias of selective attention due to expectations. The varying estimates for time to cognize stimuli can also be resolved by finding that the assumed cognitive processes underlying the d-reaction are incompatible with the information-processing models. Information-processing analysis forces us to explicate the type of memory accessed in generating observed behavior.

Some evidence proposed by behaviorists to demonstrate a dissociation of consciousness and behavior was reviewed. The assumption that consciousness during an experiment can be assessed after the experiment, thus by access of long-term memory of the process, was questioned. Reports of information in short-term memory have been found to be valid and related to behavior (Ericsson & Simon, 1980, Note 1). The information conveyed in fixed alternative responses was shown to underrepresent severely the attended information.

Information-processing analysis allows explication of informal ideas into detailed models and permits computer simulation. For most of the cognitive mechanisms proposed by the Gestaltists, we were able to report recent research demonstrating the feasibility of detailed interpretations of these mechanisms in terms of explicit information-processing models.

In the final section we applied our information-processing account to verbal reports as a means of making direct and indirect assessments of cognitive structures and subjects' personal characteristics. Information-processing models of human thinking allow us to discover the underlying consistencies in a mass of experimental literature that has been the basis for much past controversy and to provide information-processing interpretations that make the continuation of the controversy unnecessary.

ACKNOWLEDGMENTS

This research was supported by Research Grant MD-07722 from the National Institute of Mental Health. We are grateful to Susan Fiske and Carl-Martin Allwood for their constructive criticisms of an earlier draft of this chapter.

Reference Notes

1. Ericsson, K. A., & Simon, H. A. *Retrospective verbal reports as data* (C.I.P. Working Paper No. 388). Unpublished manuscript, Department of Psychology, Carnegie–Mellon University, 1978.
2. Ericsson, K. A., & Simon, H. A. *Thinking-aloud protocols as data: Effects of verbalization* (C.I.P. Working Paper No. 397). Unpublished manuscript, Department of Psychology, Carnegie–Mellon University, 1979.
3. Anderson, J. R. Personal communication, 1978.
4. Newell, A. *Duncker on thinking: An inquiry into progress in cognition.* Paper presented at the annual meeting of the American Psychological Association, New York, September 1979.

References

Ajzen, I., & Fishbein, M. Attitude-behavior relations: A theoretical analysis and review of empirical research. *Psychological Bulletin,* 1977, *84,* 888–918.

Anderson, J. R., & Bower, G. H. *Human associative memory.* Washington, D.C.: Winston, 1973.

Baddeley, A. D. *The psychology of memory.* New York: Basic Books, 1976.

Biderman, A. D. Surveys of population samples for estimating crime incidence. *The Annals of the American Academy of Political and Social Science,* 1967, *4374,* 16–33.

Boring, E. G. A history of introspection. *Psychological Bulletin,* 1953, *50,* 169–189.

Brewer, W. F. There is no convincing evidence for operant or classical conditioning in adult humans. In W. B. Weimer & D. S. Palermo (Eds.), *Cognition and symbolic processes.* Hillsdale, N.J.: Erlbaum, 1974.

Bricker, P. D., & Chapanis, A. Do incorrectly perceived tachistoscopic stimuli convey some information? *Psychological Review,* 1953, *60,* 181–188.

Calder, B. J., & Ross, M. *Attitudes and behavior.* Morristown, N.J.: General Learning Press, 1973.

Campbell, D. T., & Fiske, D. W. Convergent and discriminant validation by the multitrait-multimethod matrix. *Psychological Bulletin,* 1959, *56,* 81–105.

Cannell, C. F., & Kahn, R. L. Interviewing. In G. Lindzey & E. Aronson (Eds.), *The handbook of social psychology* (Vol. 2). Reading, Mass.: Addison-Wesley, 1968.

Chapman, D. W. Relative effects of determinate and indeterminate "Aufgaben." *American Journal of Psychology,* 1932, *44,* 163–174.

Clark, H. H., & Chase, W. G. On the process of comparing sentences against pictures. *Cognitive Psychology,* 1972, *3,* 472–517.

Comstock, C. On the relevancy of imagery to the processes of thought. *American Journal of Psychology,* 1921, *32,* 196–230.

Duncker, K. A qualitative (experimental and theoretical) study of productive thinking (solving of comprehensible problems). *Pedagogical Seminary,* 1926, *33,* 642–708.

Duncker, K. On problem solving. *Psychological Monographs,* 1945, *58* (1, Whole No. 270).

Eindhoven, J. E., & Vinacke, W. E. Creative processes in painting. *Journal of General Psychology,* 1952, *47,* 139–164.

English, H. B. In aid of introspection. *American Journal of Psychology,* 1921, *32,* 404–414.

Ericsson, K. A., & Simon, H. A. Verbal reports as data. *Psychological Review,* 1980, *87,* 215–251.

Eriksen, C. W. Subception: Fact or artifact. *Psychological Review,* 1956, *63,* 79–80.

Fazio, R. H., & Zanna, M. P. Attitudinal qualities relating to the strength of the attitude-behavior relationship. *Journal of Experimental Social Psychology,* 1978, *14,* 398–408.

Fiske, D. W. *Strategies for personality research: The observation versus interpretation of behavior.* San Francisco: Jossey-Bass, 1978.

Greenspoon, J. The reinforcing effect of two spoken sounds on the frequency of two responses. *American Journal of Psychology,* 1955, *68,* 409–416.

Hanawalt, N. G. Memory trace for figures in recall and recognition. *Archives of Psychology,* 1937, No. 216, 1–89.

Hull, C. L. Quantitative aspects of the evolution of concepts: An experimental study. *Psychological Monographs,* 1920, 28 (1 Whole No. 123).

Humphrey, G. *Thinking: An introduction to its experimental psychology.* London: Methuen & Co. Ltd., 1951.

James, W. *The principles of psychology* (Vol. 1). New York: Holt, 1890.

Katona, G. *Organizing and memory.* New York: Columbia University Press, 1940.

Katona, G. *Psychological economics.* New York: Elsevier, 1975.

Katona, G. Toward a macro psychology. *American Psychologist,* 1979, *34,* 118–126.

Köhler, W. *The mentality of apes.* New York: Harcourt Brace, 1925.

Kutner, B., Wilkins, C., & Yarrow, P. R. Verbal attitudes and overt behavior involving racial prejudice. *Journal of Abnormal Social Psychology,* 1952, *47,* 649–652.

La Piere, R. T. Attitudes vs. actions. *Social Forces,* 1934, *13,* 230–237.

Lazarus, R. S., & McCleary, R. A. Autonomic discrimination without awareness: A study of subception. *Psychological Review,* 1951, *58,* 113–122.

Linde, C., & Labov, W. Spatial networks as a site for the study of language and thought. *Language,* 1975, *51,* 924–939.

Marx, M. H., & Hillix, W. A. *Systems and theories in psychology.* New York: McGraw-Hill, 1973.

Mayzner, M. S., Tresselt, M. E., & Helbock, H. An exploratory study of mediational responses in anagram problem solving. *Journal of Psychology,* 1964, *57,* 263–274.

Mischel, W. *Personality and assessment.* New York: Wiley, 1968.

Newell, A., Shaw, J. C., & Simon, H. A. Elements of a theory of human problem solving. *Psychological Review,* 1958, *65,* 151–166.

Newell, A., & Simon, H. A. *Human problem solving.* Englewood Cliffs, N.J.: Prentice-Hall, 1972.

Nisbett, R. E., & Wilson, T. D. Telling more than we can know: Verbal reports on mental processes. *Psychological Review,* 1977, *84,* 231–259.

Olson, S. R. *Ideas and data: The process and practice of social research.* Homewood, Ill.: The Dorsey Press, 1976.

Osgood, C. E. Where do sentences come from? In D. D. Steinberg & L. A. Jakobovitz (Eds.), *Semantics: An interdisciplinary reader in philosophy, linguistics and psychology.* Cambridge: Cambridge University Press, 1971.

Patton, E. F. The problem of insightful behavior. *Psychological Monographs,* 1933, *44* (98, Whole No. 197).

Schuman, H., & Johnson, M. P. Attitudes and behavior. In A. Inkles (Ed.), *Annual Review of Sociology,* 1976, *2,* 161–207.

Simon, H. A. An information-processing explanation of some perceptual phenomena. *British Journal of Psychology,* 1967, *58,* 1–12.

Simon, H. A. How big is a chunk? In H. A. Simon (Ed.), *Models of thought.* New Haven: Yale University Press, 1979.

Smith, E. R., & Miller, F. S. Limits on perception of cognitive processes: A reply to Nisbett and Wilson. *Psychological Review,* 1978, *85,* 355–362.

Sperling, G. The information available in brief visual presentations. *Psychological Monographs,* 1960, *74* (1 Whole No. 498).

Taylor, S. E., & Fiske, S. T. Salience, attention, and attribution. In L. Berkowitz (Ed.), *Advances in experimental social psychology.* New York: Academic Press, 1978.

Titchener, E. B. *A text-book of psychology* (Vol. 1). New York: Macmillan, 1909.

Titchener, E. B. Description vs. statement of meaning. *American Journal of Psychology,* 1912, *23,* 165–182. (*a*)

Titchener, E. B. Prolegomena to a study of introspection. *American Journal of Psychology,* 1912, *23,* 427–448. (*b*)

Titchener, E. B. The schema of introspection. *American Journal of Psychology,* 1912, *23,* 485–508. *(c)*

Turner, M. B. *Philosophy and the science of behavior.* New York: Appleton-Century-Crofts, 1965.

Verplanck, W. S. Unaware of where's awareness: Some verbal operants—notates, monents and notants. In C. W. Eriksen (Ed.), *Behavior and awareness—A symposium of research and interpretation.* Durham, N.C.: Duke University Press, 1962.

Watson, J. B. Psychology as the behaviorist views it. *Psychological Review,* 1913, *20,* 158–177.

Watson, J. B. Is thinking merely the action of language mechanisms? *British Journal of Psychology,* 1920, *11,* 87–104.

Watson, J. B. *Psychology: From the standpoint of a behaviorist* (2nd ed.). Philadelphia: J. B. Lippincott, 1924.

Watson, J. B. *Behaviorism.* New York: W. W. Norton, 1925.

Watson, J. B. *Behaviorism.* Chicago: The University of Chicago Press, 1930.

Werner, H., & Kaplan, B. *Symbol formation.* New York: Wiley, 1963.

Wertheimer, M. *Productive thinking.* New York: Harper & Row, 1945.

Wicker, A. W. Attitudes vs. actions: The relationship of verbal and overt behavioral responses to attitude objects. *Journal of Social Issues,* 1969, *25,* 41–78.

Wilson, A. The verbal report of the concept in concept-learning research (Doctoral dissertation, University of Victoria, 1973). *Dissertation Abstracts International,* 1974, *35,* 1097B.

Wilson, A. The inference of covert hypotheses by verbal reports in concept-learning research. *Quarterly Journal of Experimental Psychology,* 1975, *27,* 313–322.

Woodworth, R. S. *Experimental psychology.* New York: Holt, 1938.

3

Historical and Traditional Approaches to Cognitive Assessment

Norman D. Sundberg

Cogito, ergo sum.

Descartes

Die Gedanken sind frei.

German saying

Descartes found the essence of human nature in thinking. These days, psychologists are fascinated again by thoughts and brain activities as cognitive science and neuroscience have become dominant areas of research. *Homo* is *sapiens,* and glories in discernment, reason, analysis, and judgment. Computerized prostheses for the mind provide both method and analog for human mental function. But—*die Gedanken sind frei*—free and elusive thoughts warn that some day the cognitive explosion may become boring and frustrating, and creative effort will turn elsewhere, perhaps to overlooked possibilities in old issues. As we become involved in cognitive assessment, we need perspective.

A hundred years after Wundt's first laboratory, we are coming back to a concern for consciousness and the functioning of "the mind" (Hilgard, 1980). Psychology is young, but there is considerable evidence for the recycling of its dominating issues. One thinks of the emphasis on observable actions—behaviorism—the initial flurry in the second and third decades of the century with Watson and the second behavioral revolution in the '60s and '70s, especially affecting clinical psychology. The emotional–motivational side of humankind in the form of psychoanalysis was of great interest to both

---

Norman D. Sundberg • Department of Psychology, University of Oregon, Eugene, Oregon.

clinicians and experimentalists in the '40s and '50s but has been on the decline recently and has partially become an amalgamation with cognitive–perceptual features by way of ego psychology (cf. Breger, 1969). In the early '80s, it looks as if cognitive aspects of human functioning will be permeating both the behavioral and psychoanalytic wings of clinical psychology. The humanistic psychologists, too, have always emphasized perception, personal views of the world, and the concept of self. Thus seeds from the discoveries and inventions of those who study cognitive processes and brain function seem to have fertile ground on which to fall in the last two decades of this century.

Historical Domains and Landmarks in Cognitive Assessment

In the hoary tripartite division of psychology into cognition (thinking), affect (feeling, emotion), and conation (willing, acting), "cognition" refers to such processes as sensing, attending, perceiving, remembering, differentiating, abstracting, imagining, conceptualizing, judging, deciding, planning, and reasoning. These mental activities are, of course, only inferable in others, because there is yet no way to connect directly with another's brain.

Psychologists, as most people must, assume similarities between their own conscious processes and those of others. They also observe the results of tasks given others and make inferences about the internal activities from contrived or naturalistic observations. Any given observation will be a composite of cognitive, affective, and conative attributes of the person; in studying cognition, however, psychologists attend particularly to certain aspects that they classify as thought-related. Very commonly, they exclude the following: reflexes and motoric behavior (though the import of mental imagery for sports is significant, as another chapter in this book demonstrates); highly emotional behavior (though thoughts about one's likely success or failure relate closely to depression and sexual performance, as is pointed out elsewhere); and social interaction (though cognition is part and parcel of attitudes and assumptions about other people). In sum, cognition is related to all human behavior because the higher mental processes are always involved. Psychologists, however, are accustomed to abstracting those aspects of behavior that relate to what they experience as awareness, memory, reasoning, and so on.

Psychologists can get away from the rampant subjectivity by simply measuring variations in timing and products of internal processes, such as is exemplified by chronometric studies (cf. Posner, 1978). The experimenter varies stimuli on a computer-connected oscilloscope. He or she records exactly the time taken to carry out the instructions and the correctness of the response. Thus the chronometry of the operations of that mysterious "black box" inside the skull is data for the psychologist's manipulations in testing a theory. However, such objectification is fairly recent (within the past two decades), and as yet there are few developed procedures for practical use in assessment, which will be the focus of this chapter. Posner and Rothbart (1981) review some ways in which to measure individual differences in attention and other information-processing variables that will be important as the field develops, and several other chapters in this book demonstrate other possibilities. The discovered components of cognition promise some day to be connected with clearly defined interventions to aid in education and rehabilitation.

For clinical assessment or personality research in cognition, one may focus on individuality and differences in three ways—on the products of thought, the process of thinking, or the conditions surrounding cognitive activity. Take creativity as an example. *Product-oriented* psychologists may use Guilford's tests (such as a test asking for a listing of all the uses of a brick that one can think of) to study individual differences in produced quantity, variability, and originality of responses. As another example of product orientation, one might do a content analysis of objects in paintings by Picasso and Pollock and relate the content to their personal life histories. The latter study would emphasize the intrapersonal aspect of assessment—that is, a concern for individuality—such as is often required in clinical studies. (See Tyler, 1978, for an extensive examination of research, much of it related to cognitive assessment and to what she calls "possibility theory.") Most of the assessment procedures to be covered in this chapter are product-oriented. The traditional tests of clinical and personality psychology have tried to measure current status, not process.

Other assessment procedures may be *process-oriented*. For instance, with a creative person, one may study the different stages in the development of a painting or a piece of music. I once had the pleasure (and pain) of observing an artist at work for 88 hours, going without sleep. (That is, the artist attempted to stay awake; I took turns with colleagues.) We took pictures of paintings as they progressed and interviewed and tested the artist from time to time as well as observing his behavior. The question was whether sleeplessness might generate creativity or at least bizarre artistic expressions, but the findings were to the contrary; at the end, the poor fellow became too tired to lift a brush or to give original answers and began to have sensory illusions (Sundberg & McCabe, Note 1). Beethoven's processes of composing, as revealed in successive copies of his scores, showed that he often started out with quite a banal idea and revised and revised before arriving at the final magnificent product; in contrast, it is reputed that a whole musical composition might flash into Mozart's mind as he stepped from a carriage. In a rigorous fashion, psychologists may study problem-solving or memorizing processes (not end products) by obtaining results on successive trials or by interviewing the person about his or her ways of thinking about the task. Other chapters in this book present many examples of this focus on cognitive processes.

The third and last possibility to be mentioned is the concern for the conditions of cognitive activity. Again using the example of creativity, the *condition-oriented* psychologist may study either the external or internal conditions of the person. It is interesting that many writers seek to be alone when they write at a beach cabin or in a library and that some can write only in the morning and some only late at night. Are these conditions related to environmental distractions or to internal clocks? Some musicians feel that certain drugs help them to perform or improvise well: What are the relationships between physiological conditions and performance? Think tanks, research and development organizations, and academic departments need to be concerned about the proper care and feeding of creative talent; why are some physical and social surroundings better than others? The new field of environmental psychology might well take on the task of identifying the settings fostering creative thinking.

Scattered here and there in other chapters of this book, one will find illustrations of the conditions for facilitating cognitive activities such as remembering and learning; assessment as a field, however, has yet done very little to integrate environmental, organizational, and sociocultural principles and procedures with the study of individual differences. There are some interesting beginning attempts, particularly with retarded children, to study conditions for learning as well as learning processes (cf. reviews by Anderson, 1980, and Haywood, Filler, Shifman, & Chatelanat, 1975), but these are few and far between. The two disciplines of psychology—the experimental and the naturalistic–correlational—as Cronbach (1957, 1975*a*) has noted, have separate histories, and the courtship, let alone the consummation, is slow in coming. Clinical and counseling psychologists should have excellent opportunities for a successful union because they are interested not only in individual differences and natural correlation (assessment and related research) but also in conditions and process (counseling, psychotherapy, consulting in the community, etc.). Grand syntheses take time and serendipity, and that integrative history has yet to be written.

The history of concern with the assessment of human cognition is outlined in many of the events listed in Table 1. This compilation was gleaned from several other listings (Goldberg, 1971; McReynolds, 1975; Jackson & Paunonen, 1980; Matarazzo & Pankratz, 1980) and my own judgments. Some readers may think I have included too much. Perhaps so, but it is difficult to draw an exact cutoff of assessment devices according to whether they include or emphasize cognition. It is clear that intelligence and cognitive style measures should be included. Some projective techniques, such as the Rorschach, have been concerned with cognitive variables from the beginning; others are mainly concerned with emotional expression. Some personality inventories, as will be seen later, display an interest in cognitive assessment, though one would not think so at a superficial glance. In a sense, many traditional psychological assessment procedures, including interviews and observations, can be seen as cognitive; they require thinking, and the thinking elements can be the focus of the analysis of any behavior produced. What I have tried to do in Table 1 is to give a sample of the variety and content of the major devices that have been used to assess cognitive products or to infer cognition.

What can be generalized from this list of 75 events? First, concern for assessment of mental abilities and activities goes back a long way. (Incidentally, those wishing a more thorough discussion of the early entries should read McReynolds, 1975.) Second, assessment is interwoven with governmental and sociopolitical considerations, dating from the civil service examinations in China, through Binet's identification of retarded children for the Parisian schools and the Soviet Union's ban on testing, to the recent court decisions in the United States. Assessment is used for making hard choices about and by individuals and classes of individuals. It must relate to societal values and agency policies dictating who is to receive what kinds of jobs or treatments. Third, a large industry has grown up to meet the increasing need for assistance in decision making, which is a major purpose of testing and assessment, and in the understanding of people for clinical treatment. Fourth, the psychological profession has produced important concepts and methods for examining and judging the adequacy of assessment procedures, especially validity and prediction. These may be too often ignored by psychologists eager to explore with new cognitive and personality tests. Finally, there is great variety in theories and methods of how to approach traditional cognitive assessment. This point will be examined in the next section.

Cognitive Aspects of Widely Used Tests and Traditional Approaches to Clinical Testing

The purpose of this chapter is to point out that the history of assessment is rich with information. There are many useful ideas and methods to be found in traditional approaches as the new concerns for cognitive processes develop. As some subsequent remarks will indicate, I am very much in sympathy with the information-processing and learning potential movements, which emphasize the analysis of processes and conditions for cognitive behaviors, and with a competence orientation as outlined by several authors (e.g., Resnick, 1976; Sundberg, Snowden, & Reynolds, 1978; Tyler, 1978). However, I want to caution the new wave of cognitive assessors that there are many useful ideas from the past that need to be considered if we are to accomplish the tasks of clinical and applied psychology.

This section will particularly emphasize in quick survey the major principles related to cognitive aspects of both the commonly used tests and the widely researched testing areas of the past few decades. Surveys of clinical usage (Brown & McGuire, 1976; Lubin, Wallis, & Paine, 1971; Piotrowski & Keller, 1978; Sundberg, 1961) reveal convincingly that, in the last quarter

Table 1. Seventy-Five Significant Events in the History of Assessment of Cognition and Personality

Date	Event
2000 B.C.–200 A.D.	Early uses of examinations for official positions in China develop during the Han dynasty (260 B.C.–220 A.D.) into competitive examinations of knowledge of Confucianism (the forerunners of civil service tests).
529 B.C.	Pythagorus founds his center at Crotonia, Greece, and probably conducts personality assessments in connection with physiognomic interpretations, which he originated.
1219 A.D.	Probably the first formal academic examinations are held, beginning at the University of Bologna.
1575	The Spanish physician Juan Huarte publishes *Examen de Ingenios* (translated into English in 1698 as *The Tryal of Wits*)—"the first book on assessment" (McReynolds, 1971, preface).
1692	The German philosopher, Thomasius, publishes books on the first use of quantitative data for "obtaining knowledge of men's minds."
1810–1819	Gall and Spurzheim of Austria describe the use of phrenology to reveal individual psychological differences.
1816	Bessel of the Greenwich observatory invents the "personal equation" for astronomers, a first measure of reaction time in recording observations; he discovered this when reading about an astronomer's firing his young assistant for reporting the transit of stars across the telescope's hairline one second later than he did.
1835	The Belgian mathematician, Quetelet, founds psychological and social statistics through analysis of demographic characteristics.
1869	Galton publishes "Classification of Men According to Their Natural Gifts," initiating scientific psychological study of individual differences.
1886	U.S. legislation, the Idiot's Act, identifies idiocy and imbecility and requires institutional care.
1888	Cattell inaugurates his testing laboratory at the University of Pennsylvania and later (1890) introduces the term "mental tests."
1898	Ebbinghaus originates the completion test to measure children's mental abilities.
1898	The Torres Straits Expedition off Australia (by Rivers, McDougall, and others) is the first study of preliterate people that uses psychological instruments.

(continued)

Table 1. (continued)

Date	Event
1900	Freud publishes *The Interpretation of Dreams,* building on his techniques of free association.
1904	Spearman introduces the two-factor theory of intelligence (general and specific) and proposes statistical procedures.
1905	Jung presents the word association test for uncovering unconscious complexes.
1905	Binet and Simon develop the intelligence test for screening school children in Paris.
1911	Freud publishes ''Formulations of the Principles of Mental Functioning,'' postulating primary and secondary processes of thinking.
1916	The first edition of the Stanford–Binet intelligence test is published by Terman; it is revised in 1937, 1960, and 1972.
1917	Psychologists, led by Yerkes, use the Army Alpha and Beta tests for mass intelligence screening of recruits and draftees in the United States.
1918	Woodworth develops the first major personality inventory, the Personal Data Sheet, for U.S. Army screening for maladjustment; the invention of the standardized test item was one of the most important in psychology (Jackson & Paunonen, 1980).
1921	Rorschach publishes *Psychodiagnostics,* initiating use of the ten inkblots for assessment of mental disorders.
1922	Cattell establishes the Psychological Corporation, the first major test-publishing and consulting business.
1923	The publication of the Stanford Achievement Test initiates achievement batteries for school subjects.
1926	Goodenough publishes the Draw-A-Man Test.
1927	Strong publishes the Strong Vocational Interest Blank (men's form).
1928	The English language version of Piaget's *Judgment and Reasoning in the Child* is published.
1928	Hartshorne and May publish first reports on *Studies in Deceit,* raising questions about the situational generalizability of traits.
1935	Thurstone, building on earlier work, develops factor analysis techniques and uses them to determine primary mental abilities.
1936	The influential journal *Psychometrika* is established.

Table 1. (continued)

Date	Event
1936	The Soviet Union abolishes standardized psychological testing.
1937	Allport publishes *Personality,* supporting a wide array of assessment approaches.
1938	Bender introduces the Bender Visual–Motor Gestalt Test for assessing maturation, brain damage, and personality.
1938	Murray and associates at Harvard publish *Explorations in Personality,* reporting extensive assessment and theoretical work, including the Thematic Apperception Test (which first appeared in 1935).
1938	Buros initiates the series of mental measurements yearbooks, providing bibliographies and critiques of all tests published in English.
1939	Wechsler publishes the Bellevue Intelligence Scale, which was revised in 1955 as the Wechsler Adult Intelligence Scale.
1939	Frank introduces the term "projective techniques" for ambiguous stimuli on which the subject "projects" inner needs and conflicts.
1942	Hathaway and McKinley publish the Minnesota Multiphasic Personality Inventory.
1946	Cattell publishes *Description and Measurement of Personality* as an early effort in a long career in factor analysis; his most widely used test is the 16PF.
1947	The Educational Testing Service is formed by a merger of the College Entrance Examination Board and other testing programs and goes on to become a leading research and development organization and publisher in psychological assessment.
1947	Halstead publishes *Brain and Intelligence* and goes on to produce the Halstead–Indiana, from which Reitan develops further neuropsychological assessment.
1947–1948	The U.S. Army Air Force psychology section publishes extensive reports on pilot selection using many innovative procedures.
1948	The Office of Strategic Services reports on "the assessment method," using a living-in setting and applying many tests and situational techniques and many observers to select service people for dangerous missions and special assignments; this process arose from earlier German and British assessment centers.
1949	The Wechsler Intelligence Scale for Children is published; it is revised in 1974.

(continued)

Table 1. (continued)

Date	Event
1949	Davis contends that intelligence tests are biased against lower-socio-economic-level children.
1950	*The Authoritarian Personality* is published, showing that ethnocentric and prejudiced people show cognitive rigidity and intolerance of ambiguity.
1950	Gulliksen publishes *The Theory of Mental Tests.*
1951	Rapaport edits *Organization and Pathology of Thought,* which, together with his book with colleagues, *Diagnostic Psychological Testing,* are definitive expressions of psychodynamically oriented asessment.
1954	Meehl, in *Clinical vs. Statistical Prediction,* shows that formulas equal or improve on expert's judgments.
1954	Rogers, with Dymond, publishes research on self-perceptual changes in therapy using Q sorts.
1954	Witkin and colleagues publish *Personality through Perception,* an early report on a long series of studies of field dependence–independence, also reported on in *Psychological Differentiation* in 1962 and later.
1955	Kelly publishes *The Psychology of Personal Constructs,* which includes the Role Construct Repertory Test.
1955	Cronbach and Meehl propose the concept of construct validity.
1955	Cronbach publishes "Processes Affecting Scores on 'Understanding of Others' and 'Assumed Similarity,' " which was influential for research on clinical judgment.
1957	Gough publishes the California Psychological Inventory.
1957	Cronbach and Gleser's book extends test theory to include decision making; the book is revised in 1965.
1957	Osgood and colleagues publish *The Measurement of Meaning,* presenting extensive research with the semantic differential technique.
1959	Campbell and Fiske propose convergent and discriminant validation and multitrait–multimethod procedures for test development.
1959	Eysenck publishes the Maudsley Personality Inventory and in many studies relates introversion–extroversion to mental disorders.
1959	Guilford introduces a three-dimensional "structure of intellect" model comprising 120 abilities.

Table 1. (continued)

Date	Event
1963	Glaser propounds criterion-referenced testing as opposed to norm-referenced testing.
1963	Cattell postulates fluid versus crystallized intelligence.
1963	Tomkins and Messick publish *Computer Simulation of Personality,* one of the first such efforts in a field barely begun.
1964	The use of group intelligence tests is discontinued in New York City schools.
1965	Kanfer and Saslow publish one of the first articles applying behavioral techniques to psychological and psychiatric assessment.
1966	The American Psychological Association publishes *Standards for Educational and Psychological Tests and Manuals;* the book is revised in 1974.
1966	Endler and Hunt publish "Sources of Behavioral Variance as Measured by the S-R Inventory of Anxiousness," inaugurating a series of studies and debates on personal, situational, and interactional influences on responses.
1968	McReynolds edits the first in a series of volumes, *Advances in Psychological Assessment.*
1968	Feuerstein introduces the Learning Potential Assessment Device at the first international conference on mental deficiency; the measurement of learning and training provides an alternative to IQ testing.
1969	Interpretation of tests is automated, as represented by reports in Butcher's book on MMPI developments.
1971	In the case of *Griggs v. Duke Power,* a U.S. federal court decides that tests used in personnel selection must demonstrate manifest relationships to the job being considered.
1972	In the case of *Larry P. v. Riles,* a California judge condemns the use of IQ tests for placing black children in special classes.
1973	Mischel publishes "Toward a Cognitive Social Learning Reconceptualization of Personality," which outlines needed assessment concepts building on his attack on trait psychology in his 1968 *Personality and Assessment.*
1975	U.S. Public Law 94-142 passes, proclaiming the right to education for all handicapped children, spurring the need to assess learning skills.
1976–1977	The first major works on behavioral assessment are published.

century, clinical psychologists faced with practical decisions have found a rather limited number of tests highly useful. They include tests of intelligence, such as the Wechsler Intelligence Scale for Children (WISC), the Wechsler Adult Intelligence Scale (WAIS), and Stanford–Binet; projective techniques, such as the Rorschach, the Bender–Gestalt, figure drawings, the Thematic Apperception Test (TAT), and sentence completions; and objective personality inventories, especially the Minnesota Multiphasic Personality Inventory (MMPI).

These tests not only are widely used but have also received much attention from research, as evidenced by the number of publications. The MMPI and the Rorschach are the most widely published tests of all time, each totaling approximately 5000 entries (extrapolating from the latest Buros yearbook, 1978). The correlation between popularity and publication rate is low, and academic clinicians often rate some tests, especially projective techniques, low in psychometric quality (Reynolds, 1979). However, these tests' widespread usage cannot be ignored. In addition to the widely used intelligence, projective, and personality tests, this brief overview will cover special areas of testing and research, such as creativity, cognitive style, and intellectual deficit, that have been associated with traditional approaches to cognitive assessment.

Intelligence Testing

Three lessons—or at least questions—need to be noted in reviewing the cognitive aspects of traditional intelligence tests.

1. *Are simple processes useful?* History shows that the early attempts by J. M. Cattell to measure reaction times and other basic processes did not work for the practical tasks of judging which children would profit from regular schooling and which would not. As Resnick (1976) points out, "the great successes of intelligence testing came, after all, when pretenses of measuring 'basic' or 'underlying' processes were dropped. Binet's essentially atheoretical work succeeded" (pp. 4–5). This history raises questions about the practical utility of the chronometric and other experimental approaches being used today. Further, Resnick indicates that the information-processing studies are now moving into the investigation of more complex processes than those covered in Cattell's and Galton's time. If this new approach to cognitive assessment is to prove itself of value in applied situations and not just in the laboratory, it must deal with the complex forms of reasoning, analysis, and memory revealed in the complex and "impure" mixtures of the tasks of everyday living and of schooling.

2. *Is there a pervasive general factor?* In the history of intelligence testing a major battle has been waged between those emphasizing a single dominant component and those believing in many basic abilities. With a multitudinous variety of procedures, investigators have shown a persistent unity in divers-

ity. That is, the general ability factor, *G,* appears repeatedly as a correlation between many different intellectual tasks. Others contend that there are many components to intellectual activity and find only low correlations among them. For practical purposes, anyone doing research or clinical studies, one element of a task to consider is the degree to which individual differences variance is accounted for by general intelligence measures such as IQ. One suspects that many a study of personality differences, cognitive styles, field dependence, learning potential, and psychotherapy would fail to gain significance if IQ were controlled statistically. Listing the correlates of IQ would be an enormous task. Jensen (1980) summarizes the findings as follows:

> A review of the correlates of highly G-loaded tests, such as standard IQ tests, reveals that G has many correlates with variables outside the realm of the tests themselves, probably more correlates with more far-reaching personal and social significance than any other psychological construct. IQ alone predicts scholastic performance better than any other single variable or combination of variables that psychologists can measure. . . . The high predictive validity . . . is not at all due to common learned content between the tests and the school subjects, but to essential mental processes common to both spheres. (p. 363)

He states that IQ is correlated only slightly with certain simple cognitive processes, such as rote learning and memory, but shows high correlations with organization of complex material, perception of relationships, and the like. Also, IQ has important nonscholastic correlates, such as occupational level in adulthood, and there is an IQ threshold for success in many occupations. Some psychologists would take issue with some of Jensen's conclusions, but few would deny that *G* is a major component in current intelligence tests.

3. *Is there a great variety of specific intellectual tasks?* Despite the prominence of *G* in intelligence tests, intelligence is far from a simple, monolithic ability. Commonly used tests, such as the Wechsler scales, consist of several different tasks, and countless factor analytic studies on intelligence tests or tasks produce proposals ranging from 2 to 120 factors. Horn's (1976) review of human abilities notes that crystallized and fluid intelligence are frequently found. "Crystallized intelligence" is knowledge of concepts and terms related to vocabulary and general information; and "fluid intelligence" is facility in reasoning, often on nonverbal tasks. In studies of creativity, these two factors are often found, along with what Horn calls "verbal productive thinking," which is facility in producing lists of consequences, alternate uses, or improvements—what Guilford calls "divergent thinking." Though verbal productive thinking and *G* are positively correlated, they are not highly so. Guilford's (1959, 1967) theoretical contributions of the structure of intellect model, giving 120 intersections on a cube of operations, content, and products, has, of course, been highly generative of variety in intelligence testing and of some criticisms (e.g., Undheim & Horn, 1977). Like many others,

Bouchard (1968) sees the assessment task as one of devising measures that specify the important parameters of cognitive structure, with Guilford's model as a useful illustration of the complexity of that task.

In discussing the variety of thinking tasks, mention should be made of an old (1942) test of an important ability, the Watson–Glaser Critical Thinking Appraisal. This test covers tasks of inference, deduction, and evaluation of argument—important topics for cognitive psychology. Like most of the tests in this section, it is reviewed in the recent Buros yearbooks (1972, 1978). Given the importance of logical and evaluative judgments in the "real world," it is surprising that there is so little assessment research in this field.

To add to the variety of considerations within the domain of intellectual tasks, one should note that cross-cultural and cross-ethnic studies show developmental variance across various groups in the nature of the tasks, familiarity with test materials, kinds of instructions, exposure to schooling, and even geographical environment (Goodnow, 1976). One way to look at cultural effects is in terms of the demands culture places on mastery of different kinds of cognitive skills and content. On the basis of analyses of American and African childrens' performances, Olson (1970) concludes that "we may infer that the . . . culture determines which elaborated cognitive structures will develop. . . . The lack of some such structure says more about the requirements of the culture than it does about the structure of the primitive mind" (p. 115). Much more detailed understanding is needed about the assumptions made about tasks, what a "good" performance would be, and their test-taking attitudes in general. (For a review of cross-cultural assessment, see Sundberg & Gonzales, 1981.)

Creativity

Much research energy in the past 30 years has gone into trying to assess creativity and to distinguish "traditional" intelligence test results from those of creative tasks. As mentioned previously, some intellectual activities are called more creative than others—namely, those that result in original or innovative ideas or problem solving. Several reviews (e.g., Horn, 1976; Tyler, 1978; Wallach, 1971) point to a general conclusion that distinctions can be made between what is called "intelligence" and what is called "creativity" and that, above a certain basic level of intelligence for a given task or profession, there is little correlation between the two. A retarded youngster, or even one of ordinary verbal ability, will never be a great poet, but among great poets there would be a considerable range of measured intelligence. Barron's report (1968) on his extensive studies of creativity adds another interesting psychophysiological conjecture about intelligence: "The more energy a person has at his disposal, the more fully will he become committed to the most complex possible integration. In this connection, I think it is important to remember that intelligence is a form of energy" (p. 5).

The Guilford and Torrance tests have been extensively used in research on creativity, but reviews of these and other tests are disappointing in terms of evidence of predictive validity and reliability (Anastasi, 1976; Noppe, 1980; Tryk, 1968). Horn's review suggests that a playful, relaxed atmosphere in the testing situation probably contributes to the reliability and validity of measures of creativity. His conclusion is supported by a recent clinical study (Keefe & Magaro, 1980) showing better creative performance among schizophrenics who are not suspicious and paranoid compared with those who are. Keefe and Magaro come to the interesting conclusion that patterns of creative and schizophrenic thinking are very similar; both processes involve sampling from a wide range of stimuli, free expression of imagery, pictorial thinking, and the combining of multiple cues into rare combinations. The social criteria for judging which kind of thinking is to be valued form the crux of the problem.

Cognitive Style

"Cognitive style" refers to "how individuals conceptually organize the environment" or "the way an individual filters and processes stimuli so that the environment takes on psychological meaning" (Goldstein & Blackman, 1978, pp. 462–463). Assessment of cognitive style has proceeded along several lines. Probably the most widely known and extensive work is that of the late Herman Witkin and his associates. Using the Rod-and-Frame Test, the Embedded Figures Test, and a number of other measures, they identified differences in the way people were able to disassociate their perceptions from the surroundings of the specified stimulus, or on the other hand, in the degree to which they were influenced by the surroundings. They called this characteristic "field dependence–independence," or psychological differentiation. More differentiated, or field-independent, people seem to be more active in dealing with their environments, more in control of impulses, and more aware of their inner experience.

Another widely known relevant approach is George Kelly's personal construct theory (1955), especially his notion of "cognitive complexity." Typically using the Role Construct Repertory Test, the experimenter ascertains the number and kinds of ways in which the subject differentiates among people representing important roles in his or her life; the more constructs used, the higher the cognitive complexity and the more differentiated the person. Several studies of this concept suggest that it relates to accuracy in perception of others and to one's ability to tolerate inconsistency (Goldstein & Blackman, 1978).

Another interesting variation on the personal construct approach is that of Brian Little (Note 2). He asks subjects to reveal their constructs about their projects or plans rather than the roles of others around them, thus getting at ways of conceptualizing and differentiating the intentions and goals of living.

There are many other variations to Kelly's personal construct approach (see Chapter 7, this volume).

Goldstein and Blackman (1978) review in some detail several other approaches to assessing cognitive style, including tolerance for unrealistic experiences, constricted–flexible control, leveling and sharpening, scanning, category width, reflection–impulsivity, intolerance of ambiguity, and integrative complexity. They indicate that there are not high correlations among these measures, though most of them are satisfactorily stable over short periods. One problem is contamination with general intelligence (or *G*). Positive correlations as high as .40 or .60 between field independence and intelligence have been found. In general, it seems important that these many studies of cognitive style over the past 30 or 40 years be analyzed and taken into account by today's students of cognition. In general, these assessment instruments, as well as those for creativity, have not been used for clinical purposes but mainly for research.

Cognitive Dysfunction

In contrast to the previous two categories, this category has received a great deal of clinical attention. Clinicians frequently are asked to assess cognitive dysfunction or intellectual impairment in cases of brain injury. This field is often called "neuropsychological assessment." Available to the practitioner is a wide variety of instruments. Some assess memory, such as the Wechsler Memory Scale and the Benton Visual Retention Test. Some, such as the widely used Bender Visual–Motor Gestalt Test, involve figure copying to reveal difficulties in perception and motoric coordination, which are indicators of brain malfunction; the Bender also is used with children to evaluate maturation or retardation. The Goldstein–Scheerer Tests of Abstract and Concrete Thinking were at one time widely used procedures for studying the overly concrete and rigid thinking displayed by people with brain injuries; subjectivity in evaluation and susceptibility to effects from schizophrenia and depression may be why they are little used nowadays.

The most widely used procedures now are those in the Halstead–Indiana or Halstead–Reitan battery. Various structured tasks assess both receptive and expressive problems in many modes, including the visual, aural, oral, motoric, and speech modes. This is no place to review these in detail; the interested reader is referred to the Buros yearbooks and to such reviews as those by Boll (1977), Golden (1980), and Reitan (1975, 1976). A more clinical approach is represented by Lezak's book (1976), now being revised. The person interested in cognitive science would do well to study the history of attempts to measure disorders of functioning, such as those found in aphasia, minimal brain damage, and various kinds of lesions. One interesting conjecture is that the new developments in brain scans (i.e., the computerized axial tomographic scanner) will probably reduce the requests to clinicians for diagnosis and location of brain lesions but will lead, instead, to an emphasis on the measurement of related behavioral dysfunction in order to make recommendations for rehabilitation (Wedding & Gudeman, 1980). Assessors (perhaps with the aid of information-processing researchers) need to develop batteries for measuring component cognitive skills in much more detail and then relate these to clinical, educative, and rehabilitative strategies. The finer details of assessment must be balanced by more global clinical sensitivities. Hirt and Genshaft (1980) discuss information-processing deficiencies, with particular concern for attentional problems and minimal brain damage; they bemoan the lack of correspondence between existing tests and specific clinical needs. They suggest that the clinician be alert to problems in all the information-processing components, such as perception, memory, and motor responses, and be aware of the base rates in establishing a differential diagnosis. They believe careful history taking and observation of behavior are the most important sources of information.

Projective Techniques

Cognitive aspects have long been prominent in many projective procedures. Jung in 1905 started the use of word associations to reveal inner complexes; he particularly noted delayed reaction times in response to the presented words and the degree of strangeness and symbolic meaning of the content of the responses. Since the Rorschach's first appearance in 1921, users of that technique have developed many scores related to thinking tendencies—for example, the disposition to perceive wholes rather than details, the ability to integrate diverse features and details (the Z score), the use of human movement as an indicator of active imagination, and the similarity of the subject's reported percepts to the actual configurations of the blots (i.e., the scoring of good or bad form, providing the very important index, $F+\%$). Goldfried, Stricker, and Weiner (1971), in a systematic review of Rorschach literature, are very critical of Rorschach scores for clinical use, but they conclude that the test is promising as a direct measure of cognitive style and perceptual organization or as a structured interview conducted by a skilled clinician. They warn against high levels of theoretical interpretation, including the psychoanalytic use of symbols.

As one illustration of the application of an important psychoanalytic approach to cognition, let us look at ways in which primary process thinking is assessed. "Primary process thinking . . . is defined as a mode of thinking that disregards time and logical and realistic considerations and is dominated by instinctual drives" (Lazar & Harrow, 1980, p. 497). Moreover, as Dudek (1980) indicates in her review, primary process thinking can be seen as a childish, immature, and impulsive expression, lacking in reasoning and having a poor relation to reality. The psychoanalytic assumptions formulated by Freud as the cornerstone of this model of thinking are that primary process thoughts are expressions of drive gratification through hallucinatory perceptions in the absense of the original object for drive reduction. In other words, ideation or fantasy affords some degree of discharge for id impulses. When secondary process thinking develops in the child, reality and reason are more prominent, and thinking is not dominated directly by the pleasure principle.

The measurement of primitive, drive-dominated thinking has been formulated by Holt (e.g., 1956, 1977). His scoring system for the Rorschach (which can be extrapolated to other projective records) includes content representing aggressive and libidinal drives (such as perceptions of murder, mutilation, sexual acts, nursing, and excretory organs) and deviations from orderly and realistic thinking (e.g., "people flying through the air" or neologisms). Studies reviewed by Lazar and Harrow (1980) and Dudek (1980) have shown that drive-dominated thinking can be increased by inducing artificial hostility or by hypnosis. There is also a positive relationship between creativity in artists and primary process ideation. The authors note the relationship of creativity to the ego analytic idea of regression in service of the ego. Holt's system seems complex and time consuming and not practical for clinical work, though interesting for research.

Frequent criticisms of the Rorschach are its questionable reliability and interpretive validity, which are attributed to the use of only 10 inkblots and to the great variability of subjects in their productivity (number of responses). The Holtzman Inkblot Technique (HIT) controls for these problems because it has 45 stimuli and because only one response is permitted per card. In addition, the HIT has two well-matched forms, thus providing opportunities for investigations of change. Most of the Rorschach scores, plus some additional ones such as barrier and penetration, which seem to relate to body image, may be obtained on the HIT. Holtzman himself (1975) provides a good review of findings based on more than 300 studies. In general, correlations with self-report personality inventories are low, but there are many striking differences among such groups as normals, retardates, chronic schizophrenics, and depressives in directions expected by Rorschach theory. Of special interest to cognitive assessors is the finding in many studies of significant correlations between movement scores and intelligence; Holtzman (1975) concludes that movement denotes only a particular kind of intelligence, namely, "lively, active imagination and ability to project outward from one's fantasies . . . rather than factual information, word meanings and analytical problem-solving" (p. 255). Possibly, movement responses relate to the right hemispheric activity rather than the left.

In the interests of space, and in fear of the enormous job it would be even to scan the whole literature on projective techniques, I will stop at this point. Readers should know, however, that many other techniques have actual or potential relationships to cognitive assessment, including sentence completions, drawings (such as the Goodenough Draw-A-Man, which has shown clear and reliable relationships to intellectual maturity in children, and drawings of persons that are used by Witkin and colleagues to indicate psychological differentiation), the TAT and its variations, and word association. In other chapters of this book (particularly Chapter 5), readers will find other illustrations of the use of TAT-like stories and other techniques for studying cognitions.

Personality Inventories

Surprising as it may seem at first thought, even paper-and-pencil responses to questions about personal preferences and self-concepts have proven useful in studying thinking. The MMPI, being the most published test of all time, is a good candidate for use in finding scales relating to cognitive functioning. (There are now more scales and subscales than the 550 items on the test!) Readers will find the two volumes of the MMPI handbook (Dahlstrom, Welsh, & Dahlstrom, 1972, 1975) to be major resources for finding relevant information. Of most interest to cognitive assessors are the following: assessment of control (such as the F-to-K relationship, the Ego Strength scale, the Control scale, and the Hostility scales), assessment of certain pathological symptoms in which thought disorders are prominent (e.g., the Psychasthenia, Paranoid, and Schizophrenia scales and studies of fears and phobias), various measures and studies of self-attitudes and creativity, and studies of the role of anxiety in learning.

For a more detailed illustration, let us take Gough's California Psychological Inventory (CPI), which was first published in 1957. Like the MMPI, it was developed largely by the contrasting groups method, that is, by selecting from a large item pool the items that discriminate between a selected set of individuals and a general normative group. For instance, the Socialization scale was originally developed by comparing delinquent youngsters with nondelinquents; subsequently, many studies have shown it to differentiate between many groups varying in obedience to social rules in several different cultures. Of most interest to us here are certain scales that appear to be getting at cognitive activity: *Ac* (Achievement via Conformance), *Ai* (Achievement via Independence), *Ie* (Intellectual Efficiency), *Py* (Psychological Mindedness), and *Fx* (Flexibility). Gough (1968) describes each of these and lists adjectives that have been found through research with raters to characterize high and low scorers on the scales. For instance, the 52-item *Ie* scale was developed by correlating personality items in the large pool with measures of intelligence to produce a subtle kind of measure of intellectual ability. The *Ie* correlates about + .50 with intelligence tests in many samples. The word "efficiency"in the name of the scale emphasizes the implication of skill in directing efforts and applying abilities with ease and efficiency. In college samples, Gough (1968, p. 71) reports that high-scoring males are described by raters as "capable, confident, efficient, foresighted, independent, intelligent, reasonable," and high-scoring females as "capable, clear-thinking, confident, efficient, informal, intelligent.'' Low scorers for both sexes receive such ratings as "awkward" and "interests narrow." It is likely that cognitive researchers would find such characteristics of interest in a number of studies, and the CPI now has a rich literature of application not only in research but also in clinical and counseling work.

There are, of course, many other personality inventories that could be mentioned here as having applications or potential applications to cognitive assessment, but this brief mention will, I hope, suffice to encourage readers to investigate further on their own. There are also many verbal self-report scales that might be resources in addition to personality inventories. For instance, some attitude scales, such as the California *F* scale for measuring authoritarianism and the Rokeach dogmatism scale for studying open- and closed-mindedness, have been shown to relate to assessments of cognitive styles by Goldstein and Blackman (1978). Some interest tests, such as the Strong–Campbell Interest Inventory and the Holland Self-Directed Search, have confirmed relationships between choice of careers and life styles on the one hand and scientific investigation and artistic creativity on the other. One of the important clinical features of interest inventories such as the Strong is that the results can be discussed *with* clients, unlike results of many more pathology-oriented procedures. Thus the client's thinking about interests can be directly used.

Miscellaneous Assessment Procedures

The remaining chapters of this book will give other examples of relevant assessment procedures. Such well-researched cognitive measures as Rotter's locus of control, Jane Loevinger's levels of ego development, and Kohlberg's stages of moral development could very well be topics of relevance for cognitive studies. Simple techniques such as word listing ("write down the first 25 words that come to mind") have been found useful for investigating internal versus external orientation, cross-cultural differences in content of thought, and ways in which people organize content and "chunk" sequences of thought (Chartier & Sundberg, 1969; Shaffer, Sundberg, & Tyler, 1969).

The reader still interested in further possibilities will find many chapter titles whose topics are related to cognitive assessment in Woody's *Encyclopedia of Clinical Assessment* (1980): ego development, ego delay, moral reasoning, decisiveness, risk taking, self-disclosure, tolerance for ambiguity, disturbed thinking, information-processing, deficit, primary process ideation, daydreaming, sexual fantasy, creative thinking, integration of perceptual and conceptual processes, object relations, body image creativity, associative elaboration, visual search ability, mnemonic organization, and expectancy behavior in hypnosis. It is a big field—and much in want of theory and organization to help in the assessor's constant battle with confusion.

Critique of Traditional Testing

The preceding overview has suggested that cognitive features are important in many existing traditional tests of intelligence, creativity, cognitive style, cognitive dysfunction, and personality. These tests should still provide a useful pool of tasks and resources for further research and practice in cognitive psychology. The creative efforts of psychologists in the past have produced a great variety of possibilities for examining mental activity. Young researchers do not have to reinvent thinking wheels, if they know some eager person years ago has also produced useful ways of seeing "how the wheels go around."

Furthermore, the long history of psychometrics is relevant to the new cognitive assessment enterprise. All new instruments produced, like the traditional tests, must be subjected to questions about reliability, validity, norms, social desirability, and test-taking attitudes. They also should be scrutinized for their incremental utility; that is, such questions as the following should be asked: Do new cognitive measures add any validity to predictions and other operations beyond that provided by old procedures? If they do, are they more efficient, less time consuming, or easier to administer?

The kinds of tests commonly used by applied clinical psychologists so far in this century have largely had severe limitations. It is not surprising, given the wide use and social impact of these tests, that there have been many criticisms. (See Cronbach, 1975*b*, for an excellent review and commentary on the history of criticism.) For one thing, the way in which most tests are constructed and used implies static traits or characteristics. The one-time product orientation of most intelligence and personality tests encourages interpretation of human activity as fixed in time. In contrast, many clinical and educational tasks require information for intervention, that is, for the processes of therapy and teaching.

What is needed is what the new cognitive assessment approach is attempting—the measurement of processes of change. Cognitive–behavioral approaches (e.g., Kendall & Korgeski, 1979; Meichenbaum, Chapter 1, this volume) and some work in the earlier clinical–cognitive, ego-oriented psychology (e.g., Breger, 1969) offer examples of clinical attempts at assessing process. The learning potential movement (e.g., Budoff & Hamilton, 1976; Feuerstein, 1979; Haywood *et al.,* 1975) provides examples of work in education, especially with the retarded. The latter approach, building on Piagetian and behavioral principles, essentially offers tryouts of various kinds of learning situations or work samples. The ability of the person to modify behavioral output or reported thought is thus directly measured. Still another approach is represented by the aptitude-treatment interaction studies (Cronbach, 1975*a*). This work asks which personality characteristics of individuals (e.g., cognitive or learning styles), when matched with which learning conditions (e.g., different teaching modes), result in the most effective learning.

New concern with individual differences and development on the part of information-processing researchers also promises to provide important contributions (Posner & Rothbart, 1981).

Another problem with traditional testing is relevance to environments of importance. This criticism relates partly to improper or misleading use of tests. For instance, industries and schools in the past have used IQ measures to screen people, even though IQ beyond a low minimal level may be of no importance in terms of the tasks involved. United States' laws, promoting equal opportunity for all people, especially women and minorities, are putting the burden of proof of relevance on the test users now. In addition, this criticism of questionable relevance to the environment can be applied to clinical situations and everyday life (Sundberg *et al.,* 1978). Traditionally, clinical assessment has made little or no connection with environmental factors and the adaptability of individuals to different situations. The new cognitive measures also need to demonstrate ecological validity and to incorporate ecological principles (cf. Bronfenbrenner, 1979; Wicker, 1981).

Finally, many of the traditional tests, especially personality procedures, have a pathological bias. The terminology and traditional lore surrounding the Rorschach and MMPI emphasize psychiatric disorders and labels. A count of positive and negative terms on typical clinical reports would very likely show that the balance is heavily weighted toward what is wrong with the person. However, to treat, rehabilitate, or educate patients or clients, we need an understanding of what strengths the person has to build on; we need an assessment of positive potentialities and interests. A new start with cognitive processing procedures offers an opportunity to discover and stress the resources of the person for learning and for coping with daily needs.

Final Words—The Psychologist's Cognitions, Too

The interaction between theory and practice has always seemed to me to be a primary fascination in clinical and other applied psychology. The generation of ideas and the testing of them go both ways. I hope that, as cognitive assessment develops its principles and methods, it will keep this vital interaction going. There is much to be exchanged between cognitive and theoreticians in information-processing, ego psychology, social learning, and cognitive–behavioral research. Clinicians need not only a general knowledge base from theory but also, for their daily activities, they must have at hand a theory of practice. All decisions, predictions, and descriptive elaborations are based on assumptions about how people think, act, and feel in the real world. As Argyris and Schön (1974) point out, there is often a large and unseen disparity between one's espoused theory and one's theory in use.

For an understanding and a theorizing about clinician's activities, we need to apply our growing knowledge of cognitive science to the functioning mind of the clinician as well. After all, clinical assessment is a prime example of cognitive process—in assessment the clinician searches for information; collects, organizes, and interprets information; extracts the essences from a mass of data; and evaluates, communicates, follows up on, and modifies information. A number of theories, research approaches, and methods with cognitive components could guide us in this important effort: the lens model, attribution theory, decision research, person perception, and information-processing principles. (For elaborations, see Hirt & Genshaft, 1980; Jackson & Paunonen, 1980; Meehl, 1973; Mischel, 1973; Slovic, Fischhoff, & Lichtenstein, 1977; Wiggins, 1973). Schwartz and Lazar (1979) analyzed the clinician's interpretive activity with the Rorschach and other clinical information; they concluded that the diagnosing clinician is mapping observations against a nosological scheme and that he or she uses tests like an ethnologist or historian, discerning meaning and describing a person, not using ordinary causal relations and inference. Meehl (1979), in a different way, calls for a thorough search for what is meaningful in clinical work—the underlying "taxons," or etiology-based types for classifying clinical disorders. The debates about the cognitive activities of clinicians—art versus science, clinical versus statistical, taxonomic sorting versus emerging synthesis (Sundberg & Tyler, 1962)—are far from dead.

Furthermore, if, as Zajonc (1980) concludes, affect and cognition are under the control of separate and partially independent systems in the individual, then cognitive approaches are limited. Behavioral, cognitive, and emotional–motivational approaches are all just parts of the whole reality of human beings interacting in their environments. Cognitive assessors need to be aware that understanding thinking is only part of their goal. We have selected for analysis the thinking parts of what is taking place in the larger interpersonal and community ecology in which we live and from which we take our sustenance and significance. Building on an impressive history, cognitive psychologists may decide to seek a larger synthesis.

ACKNOWLEDGMENTS

The author appreciates very much the contributions to his thinking about cognitive assessment from the following people who have read earlier drafts of this chapter: Ida Pacheco, Michael Posner, and Leona Tyler.

Reference Notes

1. Sundberg, N. D., & McCabe, S. P. *Sleep deprivation and creativity: An intensive study of an artist.* Paper presented at the meeting of the American Psychological Association, St. Louis, September 1962. *American Psychologist,* 1962, *17,* 369. (Abstract)
2. Little, B. Personal communication, 1980.

74   *Norman D. Sundberg*

References

Anastasi, A. *Psychological testing* (4th ed.). New York: Macmillan, 1976.

Anderson, R. L. Mental retardation. In R. H. Woody (Ed.), *Encyclopedia of clinical assessment* (Vol. 1). San Francisco: Jossey-Bass, 1980.

Argyris, C., & Schön, D. A. *Theory in practice: Increasing professional effectiveness.* San Francisco: Jossey-Bass, 1974.

Barron, F. X. *Creativity and personal freedom.* New York: Van Nostrand, 1968.

Boll, T. J. A rationale for neuropsychological evaluation. *Professional Psychology,* 1977, *8,* 65-71.

Bouchard, T. J. Current conceptions of intelligence and their implications for assessment. In P. McReynolds (Ed.), *Advances in psychological assessment* (Vol. 1). Palo Alto, Calif.: Science & Behavior Books, 1968.

Breger, L. (Ed.). *Clinical–cognitive psychology: Models and integrations.* Englewood Cliffs, N.J.: Prentice-Hall, 1969.

Bronfenbrenner, U. *The ecology of human development.* Cambridge, Mass.: Harvard University Press, 1979.

Brown, W. R., & McGuire, J. M. Current assessment practices. *Professional Psychology,* 1976, *7,* 475–484.

Budoff, J., & Hamilton, J. L. Optimizing test performance of moderately and severely mentally retarded adolescents and adults. *American Journal of Mental Deficiency,* 1976, *81,* 49–57.

Buros, O. K. (Ed.). *The seventh mental measurements yearbook* (Vols. 1 & 2). Highland Park, N.J.: Gryphon Press, 1972.

Buros, O. K. (Ed). *The eighth mental measurements yearbook* (Vols. 1 & 2). Highland Park, N.J.: Gryphon Press, 1978.

Chartier, G. M., & Sundberg, N. D. Commonality of word listing, predictability, originality, and chunking: An analysis of American and Indian ninth-graders. *International Journal of Psychology,* 1969, *4,* 195–205.

Cronbach, L. J. The two disciplines of scientific psychology. *American Psychologist,* 1957, *12,* 671–684.

Cronbach, L. J. Beyond the two disciplines of scientific psychology. *American Psychologist,* 1975, *30,* 116–127. *(a)*

Cronbach, L. J. Five decades of public controversy over mental testing. *American Psychologist,* 1975, *30,* 1–14. *(b)*

Dahlstrom, W. G., Welsh, G. S., & Dahlstrom, L. E. *An MMPI handbook* (Vol. I): *Clinical interpretation.* Minneapolis: University of Minnesota Press, 1972.

Dahlstrom, W. G., Welsh, G. S., & Dahlstrom, L. E. *An MMPI handbook* (Vol. II): *Research developments and applications.* Minneapolis: University of Minnesota Press, 1975.

Dudek, S. Z. Primary process ideation. In R. H. Woody (Ed.), *Encyclopedia of clinical assessment* (Vol. 1). San Francisco: Jossey-Bass, 1980.

Feuerstein, R. *The dynamic assessment of retarded performance: The Learning Potential Assessment Device: Theory, instruments, techniques.* Baltimore: University Park Press, 1979.

Goldberg, L. R. A historical survey of personality scales and inventories. In P. McReynolds (Ed.), *Advances in psychological assessment* (Vol. 2). Palo Alto, Calif.: Science & Behavior Books, 1971.

Golden, C. J. Organic brain syndromes. In R. H. Woody (Ed.), *Encyclopedia of clinical assessment* (Vol. 1). San Francisco: Jossey-Bass, 1980.

Goldfried, M. R., Stricker, G., & Weiner, I. R. *Rorschach handbook of clinical and research applications.* Englewood Cliffs, N.J.: Prentice-Hall, 1971.

Goldstein, K. M., & Blackman, S. Assessment of cognitive style. In P. McReynolds (Ed.), *Advances in psychological assessment* (Vol. 4). San Francisco: Jossey-Bass, 1978.

Goodnow, J. J. The nature of intelligent behavior: Questions raised by cross-cultural studies. In L. B. Resnick (Ed.), *The nature of intelligence.* Hillsdale, N.J.: Erlbaum, 1976.

Gough, H. G. An interpreter's syllabus for the California Psychological Inventory. In P. Mc-Reynolds (Ed.), *Advances in psychological assessment* (Vol. 1). Palo Alto, Calif.: Science & Behavior Books, 1968.

Guilford, J. P. Three faces of intellect. *American Psychologist,* 1959, *14,* 469–479.

Guilford, J. P. *The nature of human intelligence.* New York: McGraw-Hill, 1967.

Haywood, H. C., Filler, J. W., Shifman, M. A., & Chatelanat, G. Behavioral assessment in mental retardation. In P. McReynolds (Ed.), *Advances in psychological assessment.* San Francisco: Jossey-Bass, 1975.

Hilgard, E. R. Consciousness in contemporary psychology. *Annual Review of Psychology,* 1980, *31,* 1–26.

Hirt, M., & Genshaft, J. Information-processing deficit. In R. H. Woody (Ed.), *Encyclopedia of clinical assessment* (Vol. 1). San Francisco: Jossey-Bass, 1980.

Holt, R. R. Gauging primary and secondary processes in Rorschach responses. *Journal of Projective Techniques,* 1956, *20,* 14–25.

Holt, R. R. A method for assessing primary process manifestations and their control in Rorschach responses. In M. A. Rickers-Ovsiankina (Ed.), *Rorschach psychology* (2nd ed.). New York: Krieger, 1977.

Holtzman, W. H. New developments in the Holtzman Inkblot Technique. In P. McReynolds (Ed.), *Advances in psychological assessment* (Vol. 3). San Francisco: Jossey-Bass, 1975.

Horn, J. L. Human abilities: A review of research and theory in the early 1970's. *Annual Review of Psychology,* 1976, *27,* 437–486.

Jackson, D. N., & Paunonen, S. V. Personality structure and assessment. *Annual Review of Psychology,* 1980, *31,* 503–552.

Jensen, A. R. *Bias in mental testing.* New York: Free Press, 1980.

Keefe, J. A., & Magaro, P. A. Creativity and schizophrenia: An equivalence of cognitive processing. *Journal of Abnormal Psychology,* 1980, *89,* 390–398.

Kelly, G. A. *The psychology of personal constructs.* Vol. 1: *A theory of personality;* Vol. 2: *Clinical diagnosis and therapy.* New York: Norton, 1955.

Kendall, P. C., & Korgeski, G. P. Assessment and cognitive–behavioral interventions. *Cognitive Therapy and Research,* 1979, *3,* 1–21.

Lazar, B. S., & Harrow, M. Primitive drive-dominated thinking. In R. H. Woody (Ed.), *Encyclopedia of clinical assessment* (Vol. 1). San Francisco: Jossey-Bass, 1980.

Lezak, M. D. *Neuropsychological assessment.* New York: Oxford University Press, 1976.

Lubin, B., Wallis, R. R., & Paine, C. Patterns of psychological test usage in the United States: 1935–1969. *Professional Psychology,* 1971, *2,* 70–74.

Matarazzo, J. D., & Pankratz, L. D. Intelligence. In R. H. Woody (Ed.), *Encyclopedia of clinical assessment* (Vol. 2). San Francisco: Jossey-Bass, 1980.

McReynolds, P. (Ed.). *Advances in psychological assessment.* Vol. 1, Palo Alto, Calif.: Science & Behavior Books, 1968; Vol. 2, Science & Behavior Books, 1971; Vol. 3, San Francisco: Jossey-Bass, 1975; Vol. 4, Jossey-Bass, 1978.

Meehl, P. E. *Psychodiagnosis: Selected papers.* Minneapolis: University of Minnesota Press, 1973.

Meehl, P. E. A funny thing happened to us on the way to the latent entities. *Journal of Personality Assessment,* 1979, *43,* 563–581.

Mischel, W. Toward a cognitive social learning reconceptualization of personality. *Psychological Review,* 1973, *80,* 252–283.

Noppe, L. D. Creative thinking. In R. H. Woody (Ed.), *Encyclopedia of clinical assessment* (Vol. 2). San Francisco: Jossey-Bass, 1980.

Olson, D. *Cognitive development: The acquisition of diagonality.* New York: Academic Press, 1970.

Piotrowski, C., & Keller, J. W. Psychological test usage in Southeastern outpatient mental health facilities in 1975. *Professional Psychology,* 1978, *9,* 63–67.

Posner, M. I. *Chronometric explorations of mind.* Hillsdale, N.J.: Erlbaum, 1978.
Posner, M. I., & Rothbart, M. K. *The development of attentional mechanisms.* In J. H. Flowers
    & H. E. Howe (Eds.), *1980 Nebraska symposium on motivation.* Lincoln: University of
    Nebraska Press, 1981.
Reitan, R. M. Assessment of brain–behavior relationships. In P. McReynolds (Ed.), *Advances
    in psychological assessment* (Vol. 3). San Francisco: Jossey-Bass, 1975.
Reitan, R. M. Neurological and physiological bases of psychopathology. *Annual Review of Psy-
    chology,* 1976, *27,* 189–216.
Resnick, L. B. (Ed.). *The nature of intelligence.* Hillsdale, N.J.: Erlbaum, 1976.
Reynolds, W. M. Psychological tests: Clinical usage versus psychometric quality. *Professional
    Psychology,* 1979, *10,* 324–339.
Schwartz, F., & Lazar, Z. The scientific status of the Rorschach. *Journal of Personality Assess-
    ment,* 1979, *43,* 3–11.
Shaffer, M., Sundberg, N. D., & Tyler, L. E. Content differences on word listings by American,
    Dutch and Indian adolescents. *Journal of Social Psychology,* 1969, *79,* 139–140.
Slovic, P., Fischhoff, B., & Lichtenstein, S. Behavioral decision theory. *Annual Review of Psy-
    chology,* 1977, *28,* 1–40.
Sundberg, N. D. The practice of psychological testing in clinical services in the United States.
    American Psychologist, 1961, *16,* 79–83.
Sundberg, N. D., & Gonzales, L. R. Cross-cultural and cross-ethnic assessment: Overview and
    issues for clinical and community psychology. In P. McReynolds (Ed.), *Advances in psy-
    chological assessment* (Vol. 5). San Francisco: Jossey-Bass, 1981.
Sundberg, N. D., Snowden, L. R., & Reynolds, W. M. Toward assessment of personal compe-
    tence and incompetence in life situations. *Annual Review of Psychology,* 1978; *29,* 179–221.
Sundberg, N. D., & Tyler, L. E. *Clinical psychology.* New York: Appleton-Century-Crofts,
    1962.
Tryk, H. E. Assessment in the study of creativity. In P. McReynolds (Ed.), *Advances in psycho-
    logical assessment* (Vol. 1). Palo Alto, Calif.: Science & Behavior Books, 1968.
Tyler, L. E. *Individuality: Human possibilities and personal choice in the psychological develop-
    ment of men and women.* San Francisco: Jossey-Bass, 1978.
Undheim, J. O., & Horn, J. L. Critical evaluation of Guilford's S-I Theory. *Intelligence,* 1977,
    1, 65–81.
Wallach, M. A. *The intelligence/creativity distinction.* New York: General Learning Press, 1971.
Wedding, D., & Gudeman, H. Implications of computerized axial tomography for clinical neuro-
    psychology. *Professional Psychology,* 1980, *11,* 31–35.
Wicker, A. W. Assessing the settings of human behavior: Recent contributions from the ecologi-
    cal perspective. In P. McReynolds (Ed.), *Advances in psychological assessment* (Vol. 5).
    San Francisco: Jossey-Bass, 1981.
Wiggins, J. S. *Personality and prediction: Principles of personality assessment.* Reading, Mass.:
    Addison-Wesley, 1973.
Woody, R. H. (Ed.). *Encyclopedia of clinical assessment* (Vols. 1 & 2). San Francisco: Jossey-
    Bass, 1980.
Zajonc, R. B. Feeling and thinking: Preferences need no inferences. *American Psychologist,*
    1980, *35,* 151–175.

4

The Information-Processing
Paradigm: Implications
for Clinical Science

Thomas V. Merluzzi, Thomas E. Rudy, and Carol R. Glass

Introduction

The relatively recent pervasive emergence (or reemergence) of cognition in the science of psychology has been characterized by some as revolutionary science in the Kuhnian sense (Lachman, Lachman, & Butterfield, 1979). According to Kuhn's (1962) paradigmatic perspective, normal science (i.e., commonly accepted paradigms and concomitant methods) may be challenged because of problems and unaccounted-for anomalies in the prevailing paradigms(s). When a new paradigmatic perspective is proposed to challenge the prevailing paradigm(s), a state of revolutionary science emerges. The impact of the new paradigm can be twofold: first, new methods of inquiry may develop, and second, a new community of scientists may come to endorse the new paradigm. With the acceptance and promulgation of the new paradigm, a state of normal science once again prevails. If we may borrow a term of Mike Mahoney's, the preceding process is referred to as "science friction."

It may be somewhat grandiose to conceive of the shift from behavioral to cognitive perspectives as a paradigmatic shift. As a science, psychology is perhaps too young and immature to enter a revolutionary cycle. Yet, if we

Thomas V. Merluzzi and Thomas E. Rudy • Department of Psychology, University of Notre Dame, Notre Dame, Indiana.
Carol R. Glass • Department of Psychology, The Catholic University of America, Washington, D.C.

adopt the Kuhnian perspective, it may goad us into being more skeptical of merely reinterpreting cognitive theory in terms of learning theory. At the same time, we must remember that the precise definition of "paradigm" is elusive and that documenting a paradigmatic shift is a process that is based more on opinion than on objective evidence.

In the clinical sciences, cognitive approaches largely grew out of the behavioral perspective. The term "cognitive-behavior modification" indicates that the cognitive approach in clinical science is perhaps a test of the elasticity of the parameters of behavior modification. It is easier to see a paradigmatic distinction when one contrasts Freudian ideas and research methods with those of behaviorism. Yet, there are substantial efforts to integrate the two (Wachtel, 1977). Likewise, there are attempts to blur the distinctions between cognitive and psychoanalytic perspectives (Sarason, 1979).

Moreover, it must be noted that there may be a distinction between paradigmatic revolutions shared by a community of scientists and those that have a more pervasive impact. For example, although we have no hard evidence to support this assertion, it appears that the Freudian paradigm is still better known to the community at large than is the behavioral paradigm. Also, witness the expression on your neighbor's face when you indicate that you use behavior modification (B-mod) with your child (student, spouse). On the other hand, the discrimination between cognitive and behavioral perspectives within the scientific community may be a cause of controversy but is certainly not as obvious a distinction in the clinical sciences as in experimental cognitive psychology (cf. Lachman *et al.,* 1979).

Recent articles (Mahoney, 1977; Wolpe, 1978), as well as critical reviews of and rejoinders to outcome literature, have illustrated the point that cognitive and behavioral perspectives have not been clearly distinguishable from a paradigmatic perspective (Ledwidge, 1978, 1979*a*, 1979*b*; Mahoney & Kazdin, 1979; Meichenbaum, 1979; Locke, 1979). The paradigmatic lines are being drawn, however, as the following statement illustrates: "Cognitivism constitutes a counterrevolution to the behavioristic revolution that promised to promote psychology to a scientific status" (Observer, 1978, p. 157).

Scope of the Chapter

An elaboration on the controversy between behaviorism (behavior therapy) and cognitivism (cognitive therapy) is beyond the scope of this chapter. The reader is directed to an excellent review by Gordon Bower (Note 1). Suffice it to say that the emphasis on cognitivism has the potential for constituting a paradigmatic shift; however, it is not clear that that shift will be experienced in the clinical sciences. The clarity and elaboration of the cognitive perspective may be enhanced by investigating other areas of psychology that have experienced similar transformations. It is obvious that the revolutionary science cycle will not manifest itself in identical fashion across scientific disciplines. Moreover, within various areas of psycholgy, the notion of cognition or higher order mental processes receives a mixed endorsement. Thus, one certainly would not expect a Copernican revolution in psychology as a function of cognitivism.

One alternative, which we have taken, is to investigate a paradigm that has developed in an area that has a rich scientific history in psychology. In doing so we follow the lead of Bower (1978), who skillfully presented how the information-processing view might interface with social learning theory and cognitive therapy. There are several hazards to this approach, which we will confront in presenting the paradigm. However, information processing from a paradigmatic perspective has potential for organizing and unifying a cognitive science within psychology.

As mentioned previously, paradigmatic differences may be unclear and difficult to evaluate. In presenting the information-processing paradigm (IPP), we do not assert that it is the only paradigm that may encompass the clinical–cognitive perspective, nor do we assert that it is the right and only way to proceed. Our assumptions are more basic and pragmatic. The IPP has provided a framework for the study of higher human mental processes and a model of humankind that is potentially applicable to many areas of psychology. In fact, it is the synthesis of many disciplines within and outside the field of psychology.

After presenting the IPP, we will review its major historical roots and some representative literature in the experimental, clinical, and social areas that may illuminate the direction of information-processing research in the clinical sciences. The reader must bear in mind that we are discussing a paradigm, *not* a theory. Also, the information is offered under the assumption that many clinical scientists (even those who espouse a cognitive perspective) may be relatively uninformed concerning the dominant paradigm in cognitive psychology.

The Information-Processing Paradigm

Currently, the IPP is the dominant and most comprehensive approach to human cognition. Cognitive psychologists who are information-processing-oriented are principally interested in the study of higher mental processes, including learning, memory, language, thinking, and understanding. From the IPP perspective, the study of human cognition becomes basically the investigation of the ways in which humans collect, store, modify, interpret, understand, and use environmental or internal information.

After some brief historical background, the focus of the present section will be devoted to major theoretical and conceptual frameworks as well as specific content areas of study within the IPP. Certainly, our treatment of this enormous and rapidly burgeoning area of psychology is at best cursory and skeletal. We strongly recommend that the reader interested in pursuing the IPP in more depth consult Lachman *et al.* (1979) or Bransford (1979). Both works are well-written and comprehensive treatments of cognitive psychology from an IPP perspective. Our basic purpose here is to acquaint the unfamiliar reader with the IPP and to highlight areas of theoretical or methodological relevance to clinical psychology. It is our belief that human information-processing research not only can aid in understanding other human characteristics, such as social interaction, personality, emotions, and psychopathology, but can also provide direction for future investigations in these areas. We will begin discussing IPP with a brief exposition of each of the concepts of "information," "processing," and "paradigm."

Information

In 1948, Claude Shannon, a mathematician at Bell Laboratories, demonstrated that information could be quantified exactly (Shannon & Weaver, 1949). Central to his description of a general communications system were the concepts of information and uncertainty—that is, information is only communicated when uncertainty is present. Uncertainty, in turn, is related to the number of alternatives. The more alternatives available, the more uncertainty, and thus the greater potential for information transmission. Information in this system becomes quantified in terms of the number of alternatives that can be measured in a metric, called a "bit" *(A)*. Whenever the number of alternatives is doubled, uncertainty is increased by one bit. To summarize, uncertainty *(H)* is conventionally defined by the following equation:

$$H\,(A) \,=\, \log_2 A_j$$

where A_j refers to the number of alternative events. Furthermore, because uncertainty depends not only on the number of alternatives but also on the probability of each, Shannon derived a measure of the average amount of uncertainty to correct for unequal probabilities:

$$\mathrm{H}\,(A) \,=\, -\Sigma p\,(A_j)\,\log_2 p\,(A_j)$$

In the revised equation, $p\,(A_j)$ represents the probability of the alternatives.

The honeymoon between psychology and formal information theory was short lived. Shannon's theory of information required that information be measured with reference to the entire set of available alternatives. That is, the amount of information was not a function of a specific message but, rather, depended on the total set of messages that might have been sent. Thus the measure of *H* applied only to situations in which the possible set of alternative events could be specified and the probability of each known. This type of precision is rarely obtained in studying the cognitive life of human beings.

A second major difficulty of formal information theory is that the measure of H tells us nothing about the value of the information received. A bit of information may have very different value to people in different circumstances (Brody, 1971).

In general, although the idea of uncertainty and the structure of the situation as key psychological concepts evolved primarily from information theory (Garner, 1962) and stimulated important research in the areas of perception, concept formation, and memory, contemporary research in the information theory tradition is no longer concerned with quantity of information but with the nature of psychological information and its structure (Garner, 1974). Nevertheless, information theory has provided psychology with the basic concept of information itself, has provided an important normative model for the IPP approach (Garner, 1974), and has led psychologists to compare various human capabilities to communication channels. A profoundly important conclusion has resulted: although human capacities are limited, their limitations are often not fixed like those of passive communication channels. Humans actively increase their capacities by recoding the material in accordance with information or knowledge stored in their permanent memories (Lachman *et al.,* 1979). We shall present, in subsequent sections of this chapter, some germinal literature that illustrates the utility of this last statement (see also Ericsson & Simon, Chapter 2, this volume; Shaw & Dobson, Chapter 12).

Processing

The IPP views humans as active seekers and users of information. The cognitive system is seen as constantly active, adding to its environmental input and essentially constructing the mind's view of reality. For example, rather than being viewed as experiencing a negatively or positively rewarding event, the human learner is conceptualized as an active processor in an information feedback chain (Borkowski, 1979).

The work of Newell and Simon has been a major impetus toward viewing the mind as a general symbol manipulating system (Newell & Simon, 1972, 1976; Newell, Shaw, & Simon, 1958). They were among the first to conceptualize the computer as a general-purpose symbol manipulator and to suggest that some of the capabilities of the computer parallel those of the human mind. As the computer analogy of the mind increased in popularity, cognitive psychologists become increasingly dissatisfied with rote associative approaches to learning and began to ask questions regarding how people take in information, how they transform their internal knowledge states, and how they translate these states into behavioral outputs.

The concepts borrowed from computer science, such as input, output, storage, buffer, executive processor, and system architecture, are all used to highlight the fact that the flow of information through the human cognitive system proceeds though active stages that take time. The end result, as with the computer, is the creation of new knowledge. Thus, referring to cognitive behavior as a response implies something very different from calling it an output.

In sum, from the information-processing viewpoint, the essence of interaction with the world is embodied in our capacity to identify and acquire potentially useful stimuli, to translate and transform the information received into meaningful patterns, and to use those patterns in choosing an optimal response (Suedfeld, 1971).

Paradigm

As mentioned in the introduction to this chapter, it has been argued that a scientific revolution is under way in psychology (Lachman *et al.,* 1979; Segal & Lachman, 1972). In cognitive psychology, scientists began to question the conventional commitments of the learning (S-R) theorists. These cognitively oriented researchers challenged the dominant paradigm, which emphasized learning as an association between stimuli and responses, and proposed to study the structure and function of mental life, such as language, memory, and information processing.

The Kuhnian usage of "paradigm" refers to the role of research conventions in guiding progress, or lack of it, in any science. Kuhn asserts that every scientist operates within two sets of rules—rational and conventional. When scientific revolution occurs, the conventional rules are affected most, that is, what observations are worth making and how they are interpreted. Thus the revolution affects not only the methods of scientific inquiry but also the basic assumptions, beliefs, and analogies associated with a particular perspective.

Although psychology has always been, and still is, multiparadigmatic, Lachman *et al.* (1979) assert that, currently, the dominant paradigm in cognitive psychology is the information-processing approach. Their belief is that more and more cognitive psychologists have found the IPP more helpful in their daily decision making and thus have abandoned neobehaviorism, with its emphasis on conditioning, as the central form of learning. It is not that associations are viewed as unimportant or nonexistent, but that the focus has shifted to the active strategies used by the learner to make learning and problem-solving tasks easier (Borkowski, 1979).

Historical Background

With the rejection of behavioristic approaches to learning and cognition, there came a search for ideas not only from other areas of psychology but also from other disciplines. This borrowing of concepts and language from other sciences is not uncommon, especially during a paradigmatic revolution. We will present a brief overview of the major areas that substantially influenced the IPP. This presentation is gleaned from the excellent review of this area by Lachman *et al.* (1979). The reader is also referred to Ericsson and Simon (Chapter 2, this volume) for a historical perspective on sources of cognitive information from various theoretical formulations. The five major contributions to the IPP that we will review are verbal learning, human engineering, communications engineering, linguistics, and computer science.

Verbal Learning. The area within psychology that was most influential in shaping the IPP was verbal learning. Although it shared many common theoretical ideas with neobehaviorism, verbal learning had a flavor all its own. With a firm commitment to the empiricist tradition, verbal learning set out to study "the acquisition, retention, and transfer of associations of verbal units found under controlled laboratory situations" (Jung, 1968, p. 3). Memory quickly became a key research area and has retained its importance in the IPP. Perhaps the most important contribution was the development of many laboratory procedures and measurement techniques. The standard research tactics in verbal learning (serial, paired associate, free recall) have provided important insights into learning strategies and organizational processing. The paired-associate design appears to have been the most popular and reflects the tie of verbal learning to neobehaviorism and the concept of associationism.

By the 1950s, some difficult and major issues began to develop. Researchers began to raise the following questions: What was the stimulus in serial learning? Was paired-associated learning all-or-none or incremental? Did subjects use strategies to help them learn? How might the serial position curve, as well as the phenomena of forgetting, be explained? Also, many verbal learning researchers became dissatisfied with the low generalizability of their results.

In 1956, George Miller brought a new and refreshing perspective to verbal learning. His perspective, which came from information theory, was that humans need to "chunk" (combine) information because of a limited capacity to remember. This idea of human capacity limitations stimulated verbal learners to study how people reorganize material to overcome the limitations of their immediate memories (e.g., Tulving, 1962, 1968). The method of free recall became the major tool by which to study subjective organization (e.g., how we idiosyncratically cluster stimuli or events). Increasingly, the focus moved from the impact of external variables to the internal activities of the person. Recently, clinical and social cognitive research has begun to draw upon these methods to make inferences about social and psychopathological processes.

Another major force that changed the focus of verbal learning was the work of Peterson and Peterson (1959). Using a technique developed by Brown (1958), they addressed the issue of forgetting. By incorporating elements of both interference and decay, Peterson and Peterson (1959) concluded that rehearsal was needed to keep material alive in primary memory in order to process it further and transfer it to a secondary, more permanent memory store. Thus they addressed forgetting from the perspective of an active process rather than through the traditional notions of trace decay or interference.

Human Engineering. The conceptualization of the human organism as an information transmitter has its roots in military psychology, which came to be called "human engineering." By World War II, weaponry had become highly sophisticated and technical, resulting in heavy demands on human operators. Learning no longer was the central problem; rather, the focus shifted to performance. An important concept, the "man–machine system," emerged. Thus the human being and the machine came to be viewed, in terms of functioning, as similar operating units.

Subsequent research increasingly began to focus on divided attention, or perception and decision making, which eventually emerged into the theory of signal detectability. The difficulties experienced by a radar operator, for example, were conceptualized as a perception-plus-decision-making problem. The challenge became how to obtain a pure measure of sensory sensitivity, uncontaminated by response bias. In this regard, perhaps the most important contribution human engineering made to the IPP was the precise quantification of the consequences of mental events, which helped to legitimize the investigation of cognitive processes.

Communications Engineering. Utilizing Shannon's (1948) mathematical theory of information, communications engineers have developed general principles applicable to communications systems. In viewing human beings as communication channels, cognitive psychologists have borrowed two basic concepts from communications engineering—coding and channel capacity. "Coding," a very general concept, has been defined as "a set of specific rules or transformations where messages, codes, signals, or states of the world are converted from one representation to another, one medium of energy to another or one physical state to another" (Lachman *et al.,* 1979, p. 68).

"Channel capacity" generally refers to how many signals a communication channel can carry in a fixed period, no matter how efficient the code. Before the concept of channel capacity, psychologists had not seriously concerned themselves with the significance of human capacity limits. They soon began to realize, however, that humans draw from a large repertoire of processes in order to overcome their capacity limitations. Concepts related to information transmission efficiency, such as serial and parallel processing, began to emerge. Researchers began to look for ways in which capacities of biological systems are enhanced and made more efficient.

The fundamental question of whether cognitive processs are performed parallel or serially has become an important issue in the IPP and owes its advent to communications engineering, which stimulated the view that a person could be conceived as an information-handling channel.

Linguistics. Human language became an area of major debate between behaviorists and linguists. Linguists maintained that behavioristic psychology underrated the novelty, productivity, and complexity of human language use. In sum, linguists asserted that behaviorism ignored the structural nature of language. To the linguist, the central questions that needed answers were related to competence, not performance. Specifically, linguists were primarily interested in researching and understanding "the rules in the user's head" that enable an individual to deal with the structure of language.

With Chomsky's (1959) review of Skinner's book *Verbal Behavior* (1957), many cognitive psychologists found the arguments against a behavioristic approach to language compelling. That an individual has the capability of inventing and understanding a potentially infinite number of sentences "poses an insuperable difficulty for any explanation of language that relies on repetition and practice, as S-R conditioning theories ultimately do" (Lachman *et al.,* 1979, p. 82).

The dialogue between psychology and linguistics gave substantial support and impetus to information-processing psycholinguists who adopted the sentence as the unit of analysis and focused on language as a central human behavior. They did not, however, reject performance as a legitimate area of study but shared with linguists a concern for competence and the understanding of an individual's knowledge and use of grammatical rules.

Computer Science. Computer science has suggested to psychologists the appropriateness of describing rational mental processes at the "program level" (Lachman *et al.,* 1979), that is, at the level of the computer analogy. In the computer analogy, human capacities are likened to computer processes. Thus information-processing psychologists began to put cognitive processes between people's "input" and "output," just as computer scientists put programs and flowcharts between the computer's input and output. They became more and more interested in the codes used for storing information; whether there were several kinds of memory stores; how people know where to find specific items in their memory; whether the human system, like the computer, has a buffer that holds inputs until a central processor can work on it; and other similar questions from the perspective of computer science.

It is essential to understand that the computer analogy has provided new ways for the cognitive psychologist to theorize in terms of the individual's ability to transfer and manipulate symbols. The analogy does not refer to parts of the brain (i.e., the system's hardware), but rather to human competence and the capacities of the mind. In sum, computer science has provided the IPP with new ideas regarding symbolic processes, a new way to view memory, and a new way of expressing and testing theories through computer simulation. However, as Stone (1971) warns "there is always a tempting delight in fabricating models of the mind's processes in much the same manner as utopian writers use everyday knowledge to envision the operation of an ideal society" (p. 42).

It is our position that the computer analogy does not represent what must be the processes of the mind, but rather is a useful construct to aid our theorizing regarding the mechanisms by which the transmission or organization of information takes place.

Major Tenets

According to Kuhn (1970), any scientific paradigm can be identified by its intellectual antecedents, by its pretheoretical ideas, by its subject matter, by the concepts and language that its adherents use, by their preferred analogies, or by the methods and procedures that its scientists employ. In this section we will look paradigmatically at the information-processing approach, highlight its major commitments, and compare these with its major psychological antecedent—neobehaviorism.

The IPP makes several metascientific assumptions about human beings and their mental structures and processing capacities: (1) mind itself is a real event acceptable for scientific study; (2) cognitive systems add to stimulus input and actively reconstruct the mind's view of reality; and (3) innate capabilities combine with experience to produce cognitive phenomena (Borkowski, 1979).

Information-processing psychologists generally view cognition as emerging from the interactions among a system of components. They believe that these components or processing stages take time and that they can be isolated and studied. The concepts of symbol representation and manipulation are essential to the IPP and help create the image of humans as information processors, decision makers, and mental executors. Meaning, comprehensive, and knowledge have become tractable problems from the IPP perspective. In general, the IPP makes inferences regarding underlying mental processing mechanisms by using convergent validation techniques.

Table 1 highlights some of the basic paradigmatic differences between associationism and the information-processing approach. It should be emphasized that, although we are stressing "sources of rebellion," neobehaviorism has made substantial contributions to information-processing cognitive psychology. Most notable among those contributions have been nomothetic explanation as the goal of the IPP, empiricism as its method of proof, laboratory experiments as its mode of operation, and operationism as a way of describing experimental procedures and the rational canons of science (Lachman *et al.,* 1979).

Decomposing Mental Processing

Within IPP there are some core assumptions that have contributed to the illumination of certain mental processes. One central assumption is that cognitive processes are noninstantaneous. It is assumed that, because these processes take time, their duration is informative and can be used to decouple

Table 1. Paradigmatic Assumptions of Associationism and Information Processing

	Associationism	Information processing
Metascientific assumptions	Mind is passive Behavior is a product of the environment Tabula rasa Behavior is modifiable	Mind is dynamic and active Behavior is a product of mental acts Innate properties Mind is modifiable
Subject matter	Performance Conditioning Testing learning theory	Mental processes Thought and language Comprehension and knowledge
Methodologies	Reversal and multiple-baseline designs Classical and operant research paradigms	Convergent validation techniques Use of reaction time to decouple cognitive processes Computer simulations
Concepts	Stimulus, response, associations, reinforcement, incentives, and so forth	Input, output, encoding, storage, retrieval, competence, executive processor, primary and secondary memory, and so forth
Theories	Mechanistic: S-r-s-R	Computerlike: mind, as a rule governs learning

mental processes from one another. Reaction time has become a major dependent variable and has been used to study topics such as sensory coding and selective attention, the retrieval of information from long- and short-term memory, psychological refractoriness, parallel and serial information processing, the psychological representation of semantic and logical relations, and the selection and execution of responses. In these investigations, however, reaction time measures may sometimes be used as much for convenience as for any particular theoretical purpose.

Pachella (1974) asserted that, without the explicit statement of how reaction time is related to the ongoing process, it is often difficult to relate the observed variation in the obtained reaction times to the information transformations and manipulations that are supposed to be going on in the hypothesized processing network. Basically, it may not always be obvious how knowledge of process duration is psychologically meaningful.

Smith (1968), utilizing basic facts from information theory experiments, contributed significantly to the IPP by conceptualizing a sequence of mental events occuring between stimulus presentation and response. The basic stages of that sequence are presented in Figure 1. This hypothetical sequences illustrates the computer analogy in that the mind is represented as a computer executing a program. No matter how rapidly this execution occurs, an orderly sequence of operations is utilized.

Consistent with the Smith model, Sternberg (1966, 1969, 1975) developed

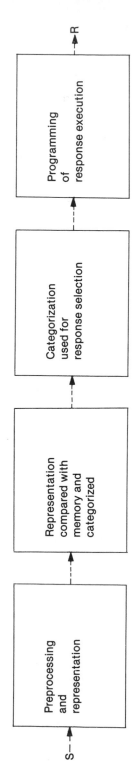

Figure 1. Smith's sequence of mental events.

an additive factor method to study high-speed memory scanning, which assumes that the reaction time interval is filled with a sequence of independent stages or processes. A major tenet of the additive factor method is that the nature of the information transformation produced by a stage is taken to be independent of the duration of the stages that have preceded it. As a general rule, therefore, when two variables have additive effects, they are acting on different stages of processing. Thus mental processes may be decomposed.

For example, Checkosky (see Sternberg, 1975) provided a demonstration of the decomposition assumption and the applicability of the additive factor logic to clinical populations. He found that, although mean reaction time is slowed in hospitalized schizophrenics and alcoholics, high-speed memory scanning is evidently not one of the cognitive processes that is adversely affected. Finally, although there is need for caution in using reaction time to decompose mental processes (Pachella, 1974), Sternberg's research represented a radical departure from the behavioristic presuppositions.

The Information-Processing Paradigm and the Clinical Sciences

As mentioned previously, the recent surge in cognitivism in clinical science has raised much dust. The struggle has illustrated that there are those who patently reject cognitivism (Observer, 1978) as the "wrong way" to proceed and those who see no incompatibility between behaviorism and cognitivism and thus no paradigmatic shift (Wilson, 1978). Interestingly, there has been little dialogue or interface between the clinical sciences and information-processing-oriented cognitive psychologists. A notable exception is social learning theory (Bandura, 1977b). In social learning theory there may be a possible common ground (see Bower, 1978; Rosenthal & Zimmerman, 1978). Recent developments in information processing have made the integration of areas a distinct possibility.

The IPP has many implications for clinical sciences. First, the IPP may provide pretheoretical assumptions and a rich scientific history, which is now virtually ignored or given terse recognition. Second, there may be methods and theories available that may help illuminate the cognitive components of psychopathology. Third, there may be opportunities for collaborative efforts in that commonalities among various areas of psychology would increase. Evidence of this is already apparent in the area of children's learning strategies (Borkowski & Cavanaugh, 1978; Meichenbaum & Asarnow, 1979), in remediating reading deficiencies (Ryan, 1981), and in social interaction (Flavell, Note 2; Merluzzi & Rudy, Note 3). This direction in clinical research has recently been endorsed by Goldfried (1979): "The conceptualization of maladaptive cognitions within the broader context of cognitive psychology and semantics has the potential of providing us with a more thorough understanding of the cognitive structure that may be mediating emotional arousal'' (p. 147).

Goldfried's view is consistent with our approach in this chapter. He presents information-processing approaches (particularly language processes) as contributing to the understanding of psychopathology. We emphasize Goldfried's perspective because it may help counter the impression that the IPP is totally mechanistic and unable to deal with emotion (Rosenthal & Zimmerman, 1978). In the same breath we recognize the deficiency in the IPP approach in accounting for the development of personality and psychopathology.

Illustrative Lines of Research

In the remainder of the chapter, we will review literature that has an information-processing perspective. Our intention is to be brief and suggestive, rather than definitive.

Early Stages of Information Processing

There is a developing literature in the area of early information processing that has sought to establish characteristic and transient dysfunctions in information processing among various groups diagnosed as having emotional problems and between those groups and controls. This literature has had two focuses: (1) to document differences as just noted and (2) to develop "at risk" or "vulnerability–sensitivity" measures.

In research exemplified by Miller, Saccuzzo, and Braff (1979), Saccuzzo and Braff (in press), and Steronko and Woods (1978), early information-processing deficits have been found in schizophrenics. In these studies a backward-masking task is used. Subjects were exposed to a stimulus (e.g., a letter) for a brief period, followed by a masking stimulus, which disrupted poststimulatory processing. Consistent findings indicated that schizophrenic or nonpsychotic schizotypic individuals required a significantly longer critital interstimulus interval (ISI) to recognize target letters adequately. That is, they required more time to elapse between the presentation of the target stimulus and the masking stimulus than nonpsychotic individuals or manic controls. In addition, Saccuzzo and Braff (in press) found that schizophrenics with good prognosis (as defined by Taylor & Abrams, 1975) improved over trials to the levels of ISI exhibited by controls. Those results were obtained after the exposure time of the target stimulus was adjusted to ensure that criterion accuracy was equated across groups. It is interesting to note that schizophrenics with poor prognosis required significantly longer stimulus durations to achieve criterion accuracy than both schizophrenics with good prognosis and controls.

Although schizophrenics with poor prognosis were affected by backward masking, they were not different from other groups and controls in a forward-masking task (in which the masking stimulus is presented before the target stimulus). The authors concluded that slow processing is a stable characteristic and may be a central factor in the cognitive disorganization found in schizophrenics with poor prognosis.

This area of research and related research efforts (e.g., Steffy, Mac-Crimmon, & Bellissimo, Note 4) have taken a microanalytic approach and in general have assumed that early information-processing deficits may contribute to an understanding of schizophrenia. Although theorizing in this area is in its infancy, the research appears to emphasize processes that occur prior to higher order processing of information. In fact, Saccuzzo and Braff (in press) note that gross pathology observed in schizophrenia may be secondary to early information-processing deficits. Although that assertion may be quite sweeping, the role of attentive (or preattentive) skills or abilities is critical in getting information into the system. Efficient attentive abilities are important determinants of subsequent processing (Smith, 1968).

The Role of Attention

The literature briefly reviewed in the previous section alludes to the importance of attention in information processing. Increasingly, information-processing theorists have come to view attention as processing capacity (Lachman *et al.,* 1979). Additionally, it is generally believed that people can attend without awareness and thus have the ability to process information "unconsciously."

One prevalent model of attention in cognitive psychology is Kahneman's (1973) model, in which he proposes flexible attentional deployment. That is, people change their "allocation policy" from moment to moment, and the amount of "central processing units" allocated is determined largely by the demands of the task at hand. For example, Underwood (1974) demonstrated that, with practice with simultaneous complex tasks, subjects can change the allocation of attention. Similarly, Shiffrin and Grantham (1974) showed that people could be as accurate when they divided their attention among three modalities as when they focused on one. Spelke, Hirst, and Neisser (1976) trained two people to read and take dictation at the same time. Thus parallel processing might occur whenever the combined processing capacity of several tasks is less than a person's total attentional supply.

In sum, the ability to focus our attention on some things and ignore others is extremely important, because without it, we would be overwhelmed by many extraneous events. The ability to control or focus our attention can contribute to our understanding of differences in learning abilities. Problems of focusing our attention, for example, because of anxiety, depression, fear, and so on, set up a condition of attentional competition and impede learning.

In an intriguing study by Oltmanns (1978), schizophrenics, manics, and normals were provided with lists of neutral and distraction words. They were to recall the neutral words (read by a female) while ignoring the distractions (read by a male). In general, schizophrenics were more distractable (i.e., performance was more deficient) than manics or normals. Results of analysis of serial position curves (i.e., looking at the items recalled as a function of the presentation order) indicated that schizophrenics were deficient in remembering early items, whereas all groups were similar for late items. More intriguing findings were that (1) schizophrenics did not benefit from slower presentation rates, whereas normals did, and (2) more intrusion errors occurred in the end of the list for schizophrenics. The latter two findings may indicate that normals code and rehearse relevant items that have been stored in echoic (short-term auditory) memory, whereas schizophrenics do not use that strategy. Instead, schizophrenics may rely more heavily on the sensory store in which both relevant and distracting information is equally represented. Oltmanns concluded that active processing operations are disrupted in schizophrenia.

It is not difficult to see that attention, encoding, memory, control processes, and retrieval do not function independently. In Oltmanns's study, attending was followed by various encoding and rehearsal strategies. Attention, that is, the ability to heed relevant information, is one process in a chain of processes that determines the course of information processing.

The findings reported by Oltmanns (1978) illustrate how differences in attention strategies may affect subsequent processing. Kahneman's attention deployment model appears to be a reliable model for conceptualizing problems in the attentional skills of schizophrenics. However, as noted previously, attention cannot be divorced easily from other cognitive processes. In a subsequent section we will review research that has focused on attention and memory.

Attention and Anxiety

The literature in the previous sections used traditional methods frequently employed in memory research. However, there is a body of clinical literature that has construed anxiety as a problem in controlling attention. Reviews of this literature are offered by Sarason and Stoops (1978) and Wine (1980a, 1980b). Briefly stated, the direction-of-attention hypothesis states that the explanation for performance differences between high- and low-test-anxious individuals lies in the different attentional focuses of these persons. In evaluative situations the text-anxious individual divides attention between self-preoccupied worry and task cues, and the less anxious person focuses more fully on task-relevant variables (Wine, 1980a). Thus high levels of emotionality experienced by anxious people may reflect an increased attention to themselves and their internal states and less attention to task.

The direction-of-attention theory of anxiety draws heavily on Easterbrooks's (1959) cue utilization hypothesis, which states that relevant task cues will be used more by low-anxious than high-anxious individuals. In terms of Kahneman's attention deployment model, critical components that determine our attention allocation policy are (1) the evaluation of demands on attentional capacity and (2) arousal. Thus, if we are susceptible to evaluation (i.e., test anxious), and if the material is sufficiently difficult, our attention capacity may be minimized. If we are also allocating a portion of the attention to ourselves, then our attention to the task is consequently reduced. Therefore, relevant cues to maximize performance may not be heeded. Although Kahneman's model is helpful in conceptualizing the attentional theory of anxiety, research by Mueller and his colleagues exemplifies an information-processing perspective. In the next section we will briefly review that research as an example of the linkage between the general attentional theories presented by Wine and Sarason (Wine, 1980a; Sarason, 1975, 1976) and general memory research.

Levels of Processing: Encoding Information

In 1972, Craik and Lockhart published what is now a classic paper. Their basic contention, which was the first substantial criticism of multistore models of episodic memory, was that information can be processed and rehearsed at various levels and that deeper levels of analysis result in superior long-term retention. Important to its many adherents is the fact that Craik and Lockhart advanced their theory "as a conceptual orientation that emphasized the role of memory processes instead of the multistore models' emphasis on structure" (Lachman *et al.,* 1979, p. 274).

Thus, with the emphasis on the dynamic aspects of memory, the input operations performed on incoming information were viewed as a sort of perceptual–conceptual analysis determined by the individual's intentions. Therefore, the type and depth of encoding utilized was used to explain forgetting phenomena rather than a series of transformations that occurred to information as it moved from store to store in the memory system. In addition, rehearsal can be utilized to maintain stimulus processing at the same level. That type of rehearsal is viewed as "shallow" or "superficial" and as not sufficient for long-term retention. A "deep" or "elaborative" level of encoding occurs when semantic features are analyzed and stored. Memory improves when more rehearsal time is devoted to the latter type of processing. In the words of Craik and Tulving (1975), "depth implies that encoding operations are carried out in a fixed sequence but spread (elaboration) leads to the more flexible notion that the basic perceptual core of the event can be elaborated in many different ways" (pp. 290–291). Paradigmatically, the challenge Craik and Lockhart posed to the associationistic perspective is clear. Items are remembered, not as presented stimuli acting on the organism, but as components of mental activity.

Before concluding the presentation of the levels-of-processing approach to memory, we should note that this approach has not been without criticism (Baddeley, 1978; Eysenck, 1978). For example, results reported by Morris, Bransford, and Franks (1977) seriously question whether "deeper" processing always is necessarily better. Bransford, Franks, Morris, and Stein (1978) suggest that the notion of transfer-appropriate processing is a more valid idea than levels of processing. That is, different encodings are better for different retrieval tasks. However, as Bransford (1979) states, "the levels of processing framework is valuable because it suggests that poor learners and rememberers, far from suffering some inherent storage or capacity deficit, may simply need help in selecting learning activities that involve deeper levels of processing" (p. 53).

In summary, the view of encoding information presented by Craik and Lockhart is an attribute model of memory. Although the initial encoding is probably representational and quite transient, it is generally held that no representation of an item per se is stored; rather, certain features are selected or abstracted, and these features or attributes represent the stored information. Thus the mere presentation of stimulus information is not sufficient for making predictions about the degree of learning and subsequent memory performance.

Levels of Processing and Test Anxiety. It is obvious from this discussion that anxiety, or arousal in general, was not presented as a component of the levels of processing. Indeed, in the experimental cognitive psychology literature, there is little mention of the role of emotion in the processing of information. In the work to be reviewed in this section, we will present primarily the ideas of Mueller and his colleagues (Mueller, 1979; Mueller, Carlmusto, & Marler, 1978), who have integrated memory and personality research.

In his analysis of the role of anxiety in terms of both drive theory (Spence & Spence, 1966) and information processing, Mueller (1979) points out that drive theory ignored encoding processes while primarily concentrating on retrieval or performance. Subsequent theories have provided a more adequate explanation of encoding processes as they relate to anxiety or arousal. In particular, Easterbrook's (1959) cue utilization hypothesis is gaining in its explanatory power. The levels-of-processing analysis of anxiety as presented by Mueller is highly consistent with the cue utilization approach of Easterbrook.

In a typical experiment using the levels-of-processing analysis, Mueller (1978) presents triads such as table–chair–share to high- and low-anxious subjects. This triad allows for encoding at a superficial (rhyming) level and at a deep (semantic) level. Retrieval is a free recall task, while three orienting tasks were used for encoding. For each word, subjects are asked whether it was pleasant (or unpleasant) or whether it began with a vowel (or consonant) or are given no task. In general, the deep task (e.g., pleasantness) helps, and the shallow task hinders, anxious subjects compared to the no-task conditions. However, for low-anxious subjects, no facilitation is derived from the orienting tasks. Although these results seem to support the levels analysis of memory as a function of anxiety, several other studies do not provide similar support (Mueller, 1977; Mueller *et al.,* 1978). In the latter two studies, differences were found in recall for both rhyming words and semantically associated words.

Mueller (1979) has recently presented an elaboration of the initial levels-of-processing analysis that is consistent with current reformulations of the levels of processing (Klein & Saltz, 1976). In this reformulation, Mueller suggests that, in addition to depth of processing, elaboration of encoding may be a critical aspect of memory. Thus encoding for high- and low-anxious subjects may be equally deep, but high-anxious subjects may not use as many features of the stimulus as low-anxious subjects. Although the utility of this notion is yet to be fully tested, initial evidence (Mueller, 1980) is consistent with this interpretation. However, based on an analysis of several experiments, Mueller has concluded that high-anxious subjects to approach tasks with more rigidity than do low-anxious subjects. We will elaborate more on this in the section on metacognition and strategic learning.

Levels of Processing and Depression. Rogers, Kuiper, and Kirker (1977) extended the traditional levels-of-processing paradigm to include a self-reference level or dimension. They tested the notion of the importance of the self-system in the processing of information by having subjects perform structural, phonemic, semantic, and self-reference-orienting tasks, followed by a measure of incidental recall. The results indicated that adjectives rated under the self-reference task were recalled the best. It was concluded that, as an aspect of the human information-processing system, the self appears to function as a superordinate schema.

In view of this evidence confirming the importance of the self-system in cognitive processing and Beck's (1972) theory of cognitive distortion in depression, Davis (1979a) attempted to extend theorizing into the realm of psychopathology and to evaluate the self-schema of depressives. Davis (1979a) provided clinically depressed and normal control subjects with lists of words preceded by structural, phonemic, semantic, and self-reference-orienting tasks. The encoding task was then followed by an incidental recall task. The depressives failed to show the enhanced recall for adjectives rated under the self-reference task (as compared to other semantic and nonsemantic tasks) shown by the nondepressives. Davis (1979a) concluded that the self is not well organized in depression and thus "a self-schema is not an active agent in the encoding of information in depression as it is with normal individuals" (p. 107). Davis's conclusions are in marked contrast to Beck's theory (1976) and earlier supporting evidence (DeMonbreun & Craighead, 1977; Nelson & Craighead, 1977; Wener & Rehm, 1975) that suggests that depressives possess a negative self-concept.

However, one variable that Davis neglected to consider was the affective nature of the stimulus words. Evidence indicates that the processing of affective stimuli and feedback appears to be important in differentiating depressed and nondepressed individuals (cf. DeMonbreun & Craighead, 1977; Finkel, Glass, & Merluzzi, Note 5). Depressives seem to estimate less exposure to positive stimuli and also to rate affective stimuli less extremely than nondepressives. There are also indications that the effects noted are not merely a result of the affective nature of the stimuli, but an interaction of the affective quality with the degree of personal reference. For example, the task used by DeMonbreun and Craighead (1977) of requiring judgments of stimulus slides of varying shades of gray was likely not interpreted by subjects as being personally relevant, and thus no differences in processing, as measured by ratings, were noted between depressed and nondepressed individuals.

A dissertation by Greene (1977), investigating affective learning and mood, had subjects rate nonsense trigrams on an affective dimension. Using a free recall procedure, he found no difference in memory of positive and negative trigrams between elation-induced and depression-induced subjects. Again, no difference in processing was noted, most likely because of the impersonal nature of the stimuli. Similar results also occurred in Finkel *et al.*'s study (Note 5), in which no differences were found between depressives and nondepressives in the ratings of non-self-referent statements, although ratings varied significantly between groups for self-referent statements. This study also pointed out the importance of the affective nature of the stimuli, as no differences in ratings were noted between depressed and nondepressed subjects for neutral self-referent statements. Therefore, the generally non-pathological adjectives used by Davis (1979a) may have been inappropriate for assessing the self-concept in depressives.

In view of this, Kuiper and Derry (1981) have proposed a "content specificity" hypothesis in regard to information processing in depression. This hypothesis states that, if depressives possess an integrated *negative* self-concept that is specific for depressively toned stimuli, then in depressives, enhanced recall of self-referent encodings would occur only for depressively toned stimuli. Similarly, nondepressives would be expected to recall nondepressively toned self-referent stimuli better. The authors tested this idea using the orienting tasks in which depressive and nondepressive adjectives were rated under structural and self-referent conditions, followed by an incidental recall tests. Results for nondepressives indicated that self-referent enhancement of recall occurred only with nondepressive content, which is consistent with the content specificity hypothesis. However, for depressives, severity of the disorder seemed to be important. "Mild" depressives did not benefit from self-referent instructions in either content condition, whereas "moderate" depressives showed enhanced recall for both depressive and nondepressive adjectives with the self-referent instructions.

Kuiper and Derry (1981) thus suggested that not only content but also cohesiveness of the self-schema is important in information processing and depression. That is, for nonpathological individuals, the self-schema seems to be a well-organized and highly stable structure. However, with increasing severity of depression, the cognitive structure may change. Thus the authors suggest that nondepressives possess a positive self-schema, but that with the occurrence of mild depression, the self-schema is in a state of confusion, and as the depression worsens, negative information is incorporated with the positive information until a negative self-schema emerges in severe depression. These conclusions have received some convincing validation recently by Davis (1979*b*, Note 6). Using a measure of subjective organization (i.e., the extent to which subjects impose structure on the stimuli to aid recall), Davis (Note 6) found higher subjective organization of self-descriptive adjectives for long-term depressives and nondepressives than for short-term depressives. He concluded that the self-schema of long-term depressives and nondepressives may be well developed and stable. However, short-term depressives may not have developed a stable self-schema.

This conceptual framework is helpful in explaining the results of Nelson and Craighead (1977) and DeMonbreun and Craighead (1977), in which both mildly depressed and severely depressed subjects recalled receiving less positive feedback. In other words, neither of these types of subjects possessed an adequate positive schema. Furthermore, the indications that depressives are more "accurate" in their self-perceptions (see Lewinsohn, Mischel, Chaplin, & Barton, 1980; Finkel *et al.*, Note 5) may result from using mild to moderately depressed subjects in whom the self-schema is more flexible in processing both positive and negative information. Recent studies (Bower & Gilligan, 1979; Kuiper & Rogers, 1979) will likely lead to a revision in interpreting this new body of literature. However, the prospects for elaborating upon existing theories and for a more complete understanding of cognitive processes in psychopathology seem to be improving.

The next section will present issues related to the retrieval of information. A subsequent section will prevent a converging line of research that has potential for exacting the nature or function of schemata about the self and social situations. That work will be summarized in a subsequent section on schemata and information processing.

Retrieval Processes

Obviously, the storage of information is of little value unless we can retrieve stored information. Different memory measures (e.g., recognition, recall, relearning) provide varying amounts of information at the time of testing. Therefore, different retrieval environments are involved, and the assessment of learning depends, in part, on the nature of the testing context.

Earlier, in our presentation of Craik and Lockhart's (1972) concept of levels of processing, we introduced the notion of transfer-appropriate processing. Morris, Bransford, and Franks (1977), in addition to replicating

Craik and Tulving's (1975) findings that semantic processing resulted in better recognition performance than did more superficial processing, demonstrated significant differences between groups of subjects who experienced identical acquisition situations but who received different types of retrieval tests. Therefore, the value of particular levels of analysis seems to be relative to the type of test situations encountered at the time of retrieval. An important implication, in light of our present discussion, is that people must learn to perform learning activities appropriate to subsequent tasks they will perform.

A study by Bower, Clark, Lesgold, and Winzenz (1969) illustrates the importance of organized retrieval schemes. In that study, the development of hierarchical organizing structures had a powerful effect on retention. These structures likely guide retrieval at the time of recall. Experiments by Tulving (1962) similarly suggest that effective learners impose their own subjective organizational structure on a list of items with seemingly no inherent structure or relationship.

The principle of encoding specificity (Tulving, 1978) appears to offer the most plausible account of retrieval cue effectiveness. Basically, remembering is easier when there is greater overlap between the information acquired at the time of acquisition and the retrieval information available at the time of recall. It still remains unclear, however, what determines which cues are encoded during acquisition and used during recognition and recall. Salzberg (1975) has suggested that it is the cue's concreteness, Spryopoulos and Ceraso (1977) have emphasized the stimulus classification, and Stein (1977) believes that the uniqueness of the relationship between an event and the contextual cue determines that cue's effectiveness as a retrieval prompt. All of these hypotheses, in one way or another, imply the activation of some sort of knowledge base, which is also an emphasis in elaborative encoding approaches during acquisition (Anderson & Reder, 1978; Bransford *et al.,* 1978; Craik & Tulving, 1975).

In summary, retrieval processes certainly have major implications for understanding learning activities. In fact, some forgetting may be due to retrieval rather than encoding failures (Tulving & Psotka, 1971). It appears that "deeper" processing is not always better in learning situations; rather, the effective learner also needs to have the ability to interrelate items and form effective retrieval schemes.

Retrieval Processes in Test Anxiety and Laboratory-Induced Mood States. Consistent with Mueller's (1979) analysis of test anxiety, we can readily see, from the perspective of memory research, that retrieval cues in test anxiety are as critical as encoding cues. On an important test item, for instance, a highly anxious subject may be less able to perceive or utilize cues provided by the instructor in the test item unless specifically directed to attend to the cues.

Mueller (1978, Experiment 1) reported that, on a delayed recall test (48-hour delay), compared to no cues, shallow (letters) cues negatively affected recall for both high- and low-anxiety subjects, as if those cues had not been used (or were not useful after 48 hours). Semantic cues, on the other hand, improved recall for high-anxiety subjects more than for low-anxiety subjects. This may indicate that low-anxiety subjects routinely encoded more deep cues.

Although this is only preliminary evidence, it directs attention to the broader issue of the role of *emotional* states in cognitive processes. Could retrieval be hindered (or facilitated) by a contextual cue such as emotional arousal? For example, Sarason (1978) allowed high-anxious subjects to retake exams under nonevaluative conditions and found that performance markedly improved.

Two recent studies (Teasdale & Fogarty, 1979; Teasdale, Taylor, & Fogarty, Note 7) have examined the effects of induced elated and depressed moods on the accessibility of memories of real-life experiences. In both studies, mood differentially affected the retrieval of memories of happy or unhappy experiences. The authors concluded "that mood states modify the accessibility of different types of cognitions" (Teasdale *et al.,* Note 7, p. 11).

Those results suggest that, for example, because of the similarity of the initial context (e.g., pleasant) of the memory and the retrieval state (e.g., elation), pleasant events are more accessible in the state of elation than unpleasant ones (and vice versa). Thus emotional state may be construed as a critical variable in the encoding and retrieval of real-life information. In terms of depression, the persistent depressed mood makes certain unpleasant cognitions more available. These results are consistent with the findings of Isen, Shalker, Clark, and Karp (1978), in which the authors viewed positive events (i.e., positive mood) as cuing other positive material in memory, which, in turn, establishes a cognitive loop that mediates the experience of feeling good.

In the sections that follow, we will be making a transition from the relatively microscopic approach in memory research to more molar issues, such as comprehension, schema theory, metacognition, and strategic behavior.

Comprehension

Traditionally, investigators in verbal learning employed nonsense syllables or words as the principal stimulus materials. Consequently, the study of comprehension, the ability to understand and remember, has only recently begun to assume more of a central role in the research on cognitive processes.

The early work on comprehension by Buhler (1908) and later by Bartlett (1932) appears to have been ignored until the information-processing approach became popular in cognitive psychology. Perhaps more important, early work on comprehension and memory was hampered by the lack of a theory for the representation of meaning (Kintsch, 1978). Recently, several investigators have proposed models for the representation of memory that have subsequently guided research in language comprehension and communication. Although some emphasize the structure and nature of semantic memory, whereas others are more psycholinguistically oriented, all attempt to answer the central question of how permanently stored knowledge is activated and used to interpret new inputs.

Bransford (1979), in his review of basic cognitive prerequisites for comprehension, asserts that effective learning always appears to be a function of relationships between the materials to be learned and the learner's currently activated skills and knowledge. Therefore, the ability to activate appropriate knowledge effectively has a powerful effect not only on comprehension and memory but also on areas such as interpersonal communication and problem solving.

In the next section, we will address comprehension from a psycholinguistic perspective, including the relationship between previous knowledge and comprehension, as well as comprehension and communication.

Psycholinguistic Perspective on Comprehension. As information-processing psychologists turned from the more syntactically oriented theories of Chomsky toward more semantic issues, psycholinguistically oriented research began to focus on how linguistic input is converted with a semantically analyzed mental representation of the ideas expressed by the input (Lachman *et al.,* 1979). Comprehension undoubtedly involves a large and unknown number of unobservable events that occur between input and observable response. Many of these events are even unobservable by the person in whose mind they occur. The majority of research in this area appears to focus either on the form of a message when it has been understood or on the content of the understood message. In addition, theories regarding the unseen events that produce comprehension have generally been in the form of subdivisions between linguistic input and output.

Although the possibility of parallel processing may be more descriptive under certain conditions (e.g., as in the levels-of-processing approach), comprehension can be viewed as a sequence of processes. Lachman *et al.* (1979), in their summarization of how information-processing psychologists in general view the events between linguistic input and output, present an early, middle, and late model.

Early comprehension processes presumably yield a phonological representation of the input, which feeds later syntactic analysis and word meaning determinations. Linguistic knowledge about phonemes, words, morphemes, and possibly phrases is assumed to be utilized at this stage. The middle comprehension processes, utilizing linguistic knowledge about syntax and word meanings, process the phonological representation of input further to reach determinations regarding word classes and to begin to establish meaning. The output of the middle processes is believed to be a surface structural representation of the input. The late comprehension processes process this product further by employing previous knowledge and by considering the context. The end result of this process is the extracting of the semantic content.

Completing these comprehension processes produces understanding of an input sentence or utterance. Lachman *et al.* (1979) do not appear to overemphasize the temporal aspects of these processes, but rather stress that these "groups of processes might be better viewed as differing in their depth, where depth is the extent to which the processes draw on permanent knowledge" (p. 413). It should be emphasized that the resulting meaning derived from the various processes of input synthesis is by no means identical to the linguistic input that began the process. Lachman *et al.* (1979) refer to the end product or meaning representation as the "synthesized code" and suggest that this code sometimes gives rise to action plans, which organize immediate responses, whereas on other occasions the synthesized code is integrated with the permanent knowledge system, thereby modifying it. From Tulving's (1978) perspective, although the code may well be an episodic memory for the meaning of an input, it may also become a permanent representation in semantic memory of the input's meaning. Thus the synthesized code can be viewed as bridging immediate and permanent memory.

Although the necessity of some type of synthesized code is rather obvious, its form is not. Herbert Clark (Clark, 1969, 1974; Clark & Chase, 1972; Haviland & Clark, 1974), a major contributor in the area of psycholinguistic research, claims that the form can best be described as a recorded linguistic string; that is, the synthesized code is propositional. Basically, the comprehension process is conceived of as the recoding of the literal input into an abstract propositional format. Clark attempts to test his representational ideas by building models to predict subject latencies and errors in various comprehension tasks. His principal concern has been with representing the meaning of a single sentence and how this meaning representation is synthesized and then utilized. In fact, his propositional theory might be better described as a theory about the utilization of sentence representations rather than as a theory of comprehension (Anderson, 1976). Nonetheless, Clark's analyses have made a significant contribution to the understanding of language comprehension, especially the comprehension of literal content. Additionally, Carpenter and Just (1975, 1976) have continued to develop Clark's sentence–picture comparison model and appear to account adequately for verification latencies in a wide variety of psychological experiments.

Previous Knowledge and Comprehension. Input synthesis is a constructive process; that is, other knowledge than that contained in a sentence itself is used to comprehend the sentence. In fact, most sentences or other forms of communication do not explicitly contain all the information necessary for effective comprehension. People therefore fill in the gaps by making inferences and assumptions based on their general knowledge of the world. The inferential process is so intimately tied into comprehension that, in an experiment by Bransford, Barclay, and Franks (1972), subjects were unable to distinguish the presented sentences from inferences made in the process of their comprehending the sentences. Baggett (1975) reports similar results when picture stories, rather than sentences, are used. It appears that constructive inferences are part of extracting meaning and are an essential component in the process of comprehension.

The inferential process, however, does not refer to a unitary entity. Anderson (1976) makes a distinction between natural inferential process and strategic inferential processes. Natural inferences are believed to operate in situations in which there is little constraint on the inferences, whereas strategic inferences operate in situations in which sufficient constraints exist on the possible inferences that special strategies can be employed to make the inferential processes more efficient. Thus the difference between the two depends on the context in which the inferences are made.

Experiments by Anderson and Ortony (1975) demonstrate that identical words are interpreted differently, depending on the linguistic context. For example, the word "basket" was a much more effective retrieval cue for recall of the sentence "The container held the apples" than was the word "bottle." However, "bottle" was more effective than "basket" in the recall of the sentence "The container held the cola." These results suggest that people's interpretations of the word "container" varied as a function of context and that their interpretations also were guided by their general knowledge. Bransford and McCarrell (1974) have found similar flexibility of interpretation for identical visual entities.

Effective comprehension, however, involves much more than simply the use of prior knowledge to form more specific interpretations of the presented information. Comprehension also involves active contributions by the listener or reader. The various types of activities involved in constructive inferential processes include making inferences about spatial relationships (Bransford *et al.,* 1972), inferring the consequences of events (Johnson, Bransford, & Solomon, 1973), and creating situations that justify the relationships among events (Lakoff, 1971; Bransford & Johnson, 1973; Rumelhart, 1975, 1977). These active inferential processes, however, have both positive and negative implications. A major positive aspect lies in the fact that speakers and writers do not need to give a multitude of explicit details. That is, it is assumed that the comprehender will bridge existing gaps, as long as those gaps are not too wide or complex. We have all experienced occasions, however, when these constructive processes create misinterpretations and hence misunderstandings of our intended message. Part of the difficulty appears to be related to the role played by presuppositions. The speaker or writer has to assess how much information the listener or reader already knows and what may be new. Presuppositions are like background conditions in that they must be true for meaning to result. Frequently, if an individual is not previously aware of presupposed information, he or she will infer it.

For example, if one were to overhear the sentence "Have you stopped dating your secretary?," it would likely be inferred that the individual being addressed has been dating his or her secretary. If this presupposition were false, the question would be meaningless. Experiments conducted by Hornby (1974) suggest that the normal comprehension strategy is to evaluate assertions actively (in the preceding example, the assertion about stopping) but to take presuppositions as true (the dating).

Another major source of misunderstanding arises when the contributions of the listener entirely transcend the literal content of a message (Lachman *et al.*, 1979). Frequently, even though the message may be oblique or distorted, the listener may extract the intended message. Although cognitive psychology only recently has begun to study the nonliteral comprehension of linguistic inputs, psychotherapists for some time have addressed the issue of "hidden communications," that is, what people, especially intimates, extract from each other's nonliteral messages. Clark and Lucy (1975) proposed that people, in processing distorted sentences, first attempt to compute the literal meaning and then test it against the context to check its plausibility. If the meaning is not plausible, listeners then employ the rules of conversation and their prior knowledge to compute the conveyed or intended meaning.

Comprehension and Communication. The process of understanding even simple sentences involves assumptions and inferences based on general knowledge. Apparently, we use linguistic knowledge in conjunction with general knowledge to understand effectively (Schank, 1972). That effective comprehension involves more than merely linguistic knowledge has important implications for understanding interpersonal communication.

Clark (1976) has proposed a model of conversational comprehension that suggests that speakers and listeners work within the confines of a type of unspoken contract. A major assumption of the model is that comprehension occurs by adding new information to information already known. Thus, if the speaker adheres to the contract, a presupposition will be used to communicate the material that should already be known and, in addition, will include an assertion that is geared to convey the new component of the message. Clark and Haviland (1977) have described this as the "given–new contract." In order to maintain the listener's part of the "contract," he or she needs to follow a comprehension strategy that first makes the assumption that the "given" information is contained in linguistic presuppositions and that it will correspond to an entity in memory. If the listener is told too much or too little, the assumption then is that the message must be a nonliteral type. Thus both speaker and listener, at least to some extent, engage in reading each other's mind and draw inferences regarding what is known, what is new, and what is intended. Naturally, previous linguistic contexts or interactions often increase the accuracy and depth of this "mind-reading" process.

Lachman *et al.* (1979), however, point out that, if a speaker underestimates the listener's knowledge, the latter will feel that the "new" part of the contract has been violated and will become bored or feel patronized. On the other hand, an overestimation results in leaving the listener confused and uninformed.

Clark (Note 8) has suggested several ways in which listeners can cope with being overloaded and when the assumed given information is not in their memory. If, as listeners, we are unable to locate the antecedent information in memory, we frequently (probably many times without conscious awareness) construct it by inference. This construction process may occur by addition, bridging, or restructuring. Clark views both addition and bridging inferences as a type of implicature. His assumption is that people usually construct the shortest bridge or make the smallest addition sufficient to provide a necessary antecedent. The new information can then be integrated into the memory structure by attaching it to the constructed antecedent. Restructuring is less frequently used and appears necessary only when speakers violate the given–new contract by putting given information in the assertion and new information in the presupposition.

Clark's (Note 8) theory also addresses certain general rules that speakers must follow for an effective conversation. Appropriateness, relevance, uniqueness, and computability are of central importance. "Appropriateness" refers to the syntactic constructions used by the speaker to facilitate the listener's separation of given and new information. "Relevance" refers to the contextual cues provided to listeners, which allow them to make the intended inferences. The third requirement, "uniqueness," is defined as having only one antecedent designated by the given information. The fourth and final rule, "computability," states that the listener must not be asked to do too much bridging. As Lachman *et al.* (1979) point out, this rule is frequently violated by authors of statistics textbooks who follow lists of formulas with a remark such as "Obviously therefore. . . ." Thus, to keep from violating the requirement of computability, a speaker must accurately estimate the listener's skill in bridging.

Clinical Implications. Although Clark's theory of conversational comprehension is quite new, the emphasis on constructive synthesis, nonliteral comprehension, and presuppositions offers the necessary breadth and depth needed for an adequate theory of conversation. Additionally, the given–new model is spelled out in sufficient detail to suggest and facilitate experimentation. For example, the types of additions and bridgings constructed when the given information cannot be located seem especially clinically relevant. The inferences created may reflect underlying schemata (to be discussed later). In part, if the inferences created are "unauthorized," an understanding of the basis for them could be helpful in the treatment of communication problems, especially between intimates. Because bridging, addition, and restructuring should take time, it may well be that certain clinical populations take significantly longer to complete these cognitive operations. Similarly, from the speaker's standpoint, it may be that certain clinical populations have difficulty carrying out the four rules suggested by Clark (Note 8). This may be particularly true with regard to the rule of computability. For example, psychotic patients may, in some sense, be asking the listener to do too much bridging and to reach very unobvious conclusions. In sum, the given–new model is likely to spawn much research because it effectively treats communication as a two-way street and provides understanding of both sides.

Schemata and Information Processing

In the section on comprehension, we mentioned schemata theories of comprehension. The general notion of schemata theory is that certain "sets" of information help guide constructive comprehension or reconstructive processes. There has been a recent emergence of schemata in social psychology in the areas of person perception (Wyer & Srull, 1981; Wyer, Note 9) and self-perception (Markus, 1977, 1980).

The basic assumption of schemata theories is that information we have about people or ourselves is represented in an organized fashion. Thus, much in the way George Kelly (Kelly, 1955; Neimeyer & Neimeyer, Chapter 7, this volume) envisioned the role of constructs as an organizing, interpretive tool, schemata theorists (Taylor & Crocker, 1981; Wyer, Note 9) assert that a schema can be used (1) to interpret and organize new information; (2) to make inferences about missing or unavailable information about a stimulus, person, or event; and (3) to aid in retrieval by supplying cues for recalling or reconstructing information.

It is apparent from the section on comprehension and the points enumerated here that different schemata can be involved in the same situations. Thus one critical question may be whether selection, organization, and invocation of schemata may be related to psychopathology.

If schemata do in fact (1) determine what information will be encoded or retrieved from memory and (2) affect processing time, speed of information flow, and speed of problem solving, then the research tools of cognitive psychology provide a basis for empirically deriving the nature and form of the schemata. Recognition memory tasks, with related measures such as false positives and sensitivity measures, may help recover the types of schemata employed by systematically varying the distraction (or filler materials). Current research is focusing on the interpretive and inferential functions of schemata. That is, schemata may add information that compliments the incoming information in order to provide a basis for interpreting, planning, problem solving, and so on. However, faulty inferences may develop when the wrong schema is used to process information, when the right schema is used but is exaggerated, or if we process new information as consistent with the schema when it is neutral or even inconsistent. For an elaboration of the liabilities of schemata and the resulting faulty inferences, the reader is directed to Taylor and Crocker (1981).

Suffice it to state that schemata theory has potential for looking at the social cognitive processes involved in clinical problems. For example, little work has been done to relate schemata theory to social-evaluative anxiety (see Glass & Merluzzi, Chapter 13, this volume).

In a similar vein, Markus (1977, 1980) has presented an approach to schemata in which the self is conceived of as a system of self-schemata or knowledge structures that integrate information about the self into a systematic framework. Markus asserts that individuals may or may not develop schemata about certain aspects of their self. For example, Markus, Sentis, and Hamill (Note 10) found that people who had self-schemata for body weight consistently processed verbal and pictorial information differently than aschematics (people who had no definitive body weight schemata).

Schemata about Social Situations. One alternative approach to studying schemata in complex social situations might include the use of multidimensional scaling techniques. We have recently conducted a series of studies (Rudy, Merluzzi, & Henehan, Note 11) to investigate how people construe social situations in which the type of behavior, type of person, and type of environmental context are systematically varied. The primary objectives of these studies have been (1) to quantify and interpret the structure of individuals' cognitive representations of social situations; (2) to identify the relative contributions of types of behavior, target persons, and environmental contexts to these cognitive representations, especially when determining the level of difficulty in responding to specific situations; (3) to isolate and measure individual or subgroup differences in these cognitive representations with respect to level of social skill; and (4) to construct a domain of specific social situations by first systematically analyzing the individual components and tailoring the situations to a unique population. These situations can then be used in a factorial design. Toward these ends, two studies have been conducted to date.

The primary objective of our first experiment was to gain a plenary understanding of the three major components of social situations—the type of behavior, target persons, and environmental contexts—before combining these components into complete specific, complex social situations.

A total of 20 undergraduate males (aged 18–21) first scaled 29 target persons and then 26 environmental contexts into categories of equal similarity. They were instructed to base their similarity judgments on an imagined interaction either with these people or in these environments. Multidimensional scaling (KYST; Kruskal, Young, & Seery, Note 12) and hierarchical clustering using a diameter method (Johnson, 1967) were applied to the scaled items. Two major dimensions and four significant clusters adequately explained both targets and contexts. The target dimensions were described as intimate/open versus nonintimate/cautious and high status versus low status. The four clusters were interpreted as intimates, friends and acquaintances, service workers, and status people. The context dimensions appear to be informal/comfortable versus formal/uncomfortable and on-campus versus off-campus. The four clusters seem to represent formal, informal, public, and medical environments.

In addition to the sorting tasks, subjects were asked to rate 17 types of social (assertion) situations on five 7-point scales measuring frequency, familiarity, ego involvement, difficulty, and uncomfortableness. They were instructed to imagine themselves in each situation as they made their ratings. Of the nine "positive" types of social situations (e.g., paying compliments or expressing opinions despite, perhaps, some risk), four were chosen (defending someone being verbally abused, complaining about someone's behavior that is an annoyance to you, expressing an adverse opinion to someone who expects the opposite, and paying a compliment to someone) that demonstrated the following patterns: (1) a strong, significant negative correlation between frequency/familiarity and difficulty/uncomfortableness, whether or not the level of ego involvement was controlled for, and (2) nearby equal ratings on the five bipolar ratings. (The exception was paying a compliment, which was seen as both more familiar and easier.)

Of the eight "negative" types of social situations rated (e.g., unreasonable requests), three were chosen (someone asking to borrow $25, someone asking you to change tables, and someone cutting in front of you while you are waiting in line) that demonstrated the following patterns: (1) a strong, significant positive correlation between ego involvement and difficulty/uncomfortableness, whether or not the level of frequency/familiarity was controlled for, and (2) nearby equal ratings on the five bipolar ratings.

In general, subjects seemed more comfortable and familiar with what we termed "positive" types of social situations than with "negative" ones. The overall level of ego involvement, however, was not significantly different between these two types of social situations. Thus, assuming that some difficulty and anxiety is associated with all types of social (assertion) situations, these two different types seem qualitatively different; that is, the level of familiarity seems to be the most salient feature to study in the positive assertive instances, whereas the level of ego involvement appears to be the most salient feature in the negative instances. Because of these findings as well as size considerations, our research program has studied these two basic types of social situations separately.

The stimulus material used in the second study resulted from combining target and context items from the significant clusters in the first study with the seven selected situations. All four target clusters were used; however, because of the small number of items in the medical environment cluster, it was eliminated from further analysis. Using a full factorial arrangement resulted in 36 negative and 48 positive vignettes, although the same stimulus from each target or environmental cluster was not used. The compositional rule applied favored realistic combinations, as well as maintaining a full factorial. Thirty-two male subjects sorted the 36 negative vignettes, and another 32 sorted the 48 positive vignettes into categories of equal difficulty. There were no restrictions placed on the number of piles of cards or on the number of cards per pile. Subjects also rated their respective situations on 21 bipolar scales and completed a social skills questionnaire (Levenson & Gottman, 1978).

The data analysis was conducted in the following manner: Subjects were divided into high, medium, and low groups, based on their scores on the social skills questionnaire. Three proportion matrices of similarity were computed from subjects' sorting data for both positive and negative social situations. The three similarity matrices were submitted to "individual differences multidimensional scaling" (INDSCAL), a three-way, multidimensional scaling analysis of proximity data by means that retain individual or subgroup differences, while at the same time computing a common group space (Carroll & Chang, 1970). A Monte Carlo procedure was conducted to determine if subgroup weighting differences on the INDSCAL dimensions were statistically significant. Using the actual data from subjects, subgroups of randomly selected individuals from the sample were formed. Dimensional weights were then determined for these random subgroups, and sampling distributions were derived. The mean ratings on the bipolar scales were used to aid dimensional interpretations by using the linear regression option in property fitting (PROFIT), a computer algorithm developed by Chang and Carroll (Note 13) for fitting outside property vectors into stimulus spaces. Analysis of variance was performed on the stimulus coordinates resulting from the group INDSCAL solution to aid in dimensional interpretations, especially to determine the relative contributions of types of behaviors, targets, and contexts to each dimension.

Although an in-depth discussion of these analyses is beyond the scope of this chapter, several results need to be highlighted. First, despite the amount and complexity of stimuli, both 2-way and 3-way multidimensional scaling of the similarity matrices indicated that subjects used some common and generally consistent patterns in their sorts. The INDSCAL analyses of the positive situations indicated that 70% of the variance was accounted for by a three-dimensional solution. Three dimensions were both necessary (7% more variance than two dimensions) and sufficient (only 2% less variance than four dimensions). Similarly, 44% of the variance was accounted for in the negative situations by using a four-dimensional solution. Additionally, all six data matrices were scaled separately, using KYST, and had residual stress values (SFORM 1; Kruskal, 1964) less than 10%. Thus, although high-, medium-, and low-skilled subjects used similar dimensions in construing complex social situations, the importance of those dimensions appears to vary as a function of their level of skill (Table 2).

Table 2. Dimension Weights for Level of Social Skill from an INDSCAL Analysis of Negative Situations

Group	Dimension			
	1	2	3	4
High	.378*	.178	.358*	.203
Middle	.196	.297	.414*	.432*
Low	.364*	.433*	.079*	.222
Random sampling mean	.189	.183	.203	.228
Standard deviation	.088	.065	.058	.090

*$p < .05$

A second major result of this study indicated that the INDSCAL dimensions were indeed psychologically meaningful and unique and could generally be recovered and interpreted in an objective manner. This was accomplished by using a multiple regression procedure (PROFIT; Chang & Carroll, Note 13) to regress mean ratings of stimuli on each of the 21 bipolar scales over the three dimensions in the positive solution or over the four dimensions in the negative condition. Inspection of Table 3 reveals that most of the multiple correlations for the scales are highly significant and that most of the dimensions have a high regression weight for at least a few of the bipolar scales.

A third and final major finding resulted when the INDSCAL group coordinates were analyzed using analysis of variance. It will be recalled that the positive and negative stimuli represented a full factorial arrangement, that is, positive—4 (behavior) × 3 (environment) × 3 (person)—and negative—3 (behavior) × 3 (environment) × 4 (person). Main effects in each dimension were tested separately using one-way analyses of variance. Interactions, unfortunately, could not legitimately be tested for significance because only one score existed per cell and thus an error term was not available.

For the sake of brevity, we will discuss only the results of the negative situations. Taking into account the analysis of variance and bipolar solutions, Dimension 1 appears to focus primarily on the target person. This dimension may represent assertion with persons exactly equal in power versus those unequal in power. More specifically, this particular dimension could be important in construing those social situations in which one is called upon to behave assertively with individuals who are higher in status. The dimension weightings generated by INDSCAL indicate that this dimension is significantly important for high and low socially skilled individuals, but not for those who fall in the middle range.

The second dimension appears to focus on the type of social situation. This dimension could well represent the irritation aroused when social

Table 3. Multiple Regression of Bipolar Scale Ratings on INDSCAL Dimensions
(Negative Situations)

Bipolar scales	Dim. 1	Dim. 2	Dim. 3	Dim. 4	R
1. Exactly equal power vs. very unequal power	−.803	−.399	.263	−.357	.698**
2. Similar roles and behaviors vs. different roles and behaviors	−.792	−.551	.257	−.057	.786**
3. Personal vs. impersonal	−.671	−.612	−.181	.378	.767**
4. Involved vs. detached	.156	−.870	.290	−.367	.889**
5. Cooperative vs. competitive	−.138	−.782	−.200	.574	.813**
6. Irritating vs. nonirritating	.365	.769	.001	−.526	.801**
7. Socially appropriate vs. socially inappropriate	−.303	−.768	.202	.527	.817**
8. Positive consequences vs. negative consequences	−.311	−.743	−.031	.591	.813**
9. Expected vs. unexpected	−.406	−.721	.378	.415	.742**
10. Fair vs. unfair	−.414	−.709	−.309	.480	.850**
11. Friendly vs. hostile	−.421	−.708	−.325	.464	.788**
12. Informal vs. formal	−.744	−.362	.556	−.074	.814**
13. High anxiety vs. low anxiety	.417	.549	−.419	−.591	.825**
14. Unfamiliar vs. familiar	.331	.672	−.378	−.544	.736**
15. Accidental vs. intentional	−.299	−.631	.083	.721	.561
16. Intense vs. superficial	.502	.439	−.231	−.708	.609*
17. Threatening vs. nonthreatening	.276	.717	−.269	−.583	.760**
18. Predictable vs. unpredictable	−.526	−.619	.166	.588	.738**
19. Easy vs. difficult	−.514	−.585	.299	.552	.732**
20. Comfortable vs. uncomfortable	−.448	−.694	.189	.532	.816**
21. Tense vs. relaxed	.482	.617	−.334	−.526	.819**

Regression weights (direction cosines)

*$F(4,31), p < .01$
**$F(4,31), p < .001$

norms and customs are not followed. One pole of the dimension contains situations in which people politely ask to borrow $25, whereas the opposite pole contains situations in which people rudely make you change tables or cut in front of you in line. The request for $25 is done in a socially appropriate manner (in the form of a polite request); however, the other situations seem to represent blatant violation of social propriety. This dimension could well account for the anxiety aroused when such a violation occurs. The weightings here show that Dimension 2 is significant only for low socially skilled individuals.

Dimension 3 deals also with varying types of social situations and, in fact, has items at its poles similar to those in Dimension 2. However, there appears to be a noticeably different element in the Dimension 3 situations. One pole deals with formal, unfamiliar, unexpected types of situations, such as the secretary of a top university official asking for $25, whereas the second pole contains informal, expected, and familiar situations, such as watching a campus movie. Interestingly, Dimension 3 was viewed as significantly important for high- and medium-skilled individuals, and significantly unimportant for low-skilled individuals.

The analysis of variance and bipolar solutions indicate the importance of target and type of assertion in describing Dimension 4. The distinguishing factor between the poles of this dimension appears to lie in the intensity of the situation. One pole deals with situations in which intrusion by another person is precipitous. Furthermore, the intruder is generally an unfamiliar target. The other pole concentrates on relatively relaxed conditions with more familiar targets. Dimension 4 could possibly represent the contrast between situations in which action is precipitous and situations that occur in a relaxed or unaroused situation. The weightings for this dimension indicate that it is significant for members of the medium-skilled group.

In summarizing these results, it must be noted that high-, medium-, and low-assertive individuals all implement the same dimensions in construing negative assertion situations. The INDSCAL analysis indicates, however, that, although individuals share the same dimensions, some of the dimensions are more significant to some individuals than to others. One can infer from the fact that more value is placed on some dimensions than on others that information is represented differently psychologically for some individuals than for others. The status level of the target in negative situations was generally important to all groups. Additionally, social appropriateness was a more important construct for the low-assertive group than for the medium- or high-assertive groups. For medium- and high-assertive individuals, however, the plausibility or familiarity with the situation is a more important schema by which to evaluate negative assertion situations. Finally, hostility versus cooperativeness seems to be a particularly useful evaluative construct for the average assertive individual.

The goal of this research was to determine how people construe complex assertion situations. The multidimensional scaling techniques aided in the recovery of the schemata (cognitive representations) that people used to represent the information contained in the complex social situations. Those schemata are the social–cognitive maps that people used to "read" social situations. By documenting those schemata, we can determine the importance of certain types of information for people who vary in their level of social skill. Thus we can gain a more complete assessment of social skill problems. These techniques have also been used to study the comprehension of prose (LaPorte & Voss, 1979) and stressful life events (Weinberg & Lief, Note 14) and therefore may be of value to experimental and clinical researchers.

There are several clinical uses for the results of these studies. First, we may begin to develop assessment instruments that systematically include the major components of assertion. The dimensions obtained through INDSCAL may allow us to choose items that are psychologically meaningful and that vary in importance as a function of the individual's level of social skill. Further, the technology of item construction can be replicated at different sites, and, assuming that the dimensions derived are similar, we may be able to achieve content specificity without sacrificing reliability. The INDSCAL procedures that we have used seem especially useful in this regard, because the judgmental tasks required of subjects are simple, nonreactive, and natural. Furthermore, important attributes of assertion situations, ones that might not be assessible to direct judgment methods, are tapped by using similarity judgments.

A second use of the results may be that social skill training may be devised in ways that reflect the information-processing perspective. The results clearly document that low-assertive individuals use certain dimensions and not others. Thus those individuals may be extracting information that may be less useful or valuable in their social decision making. Our research (Rudy & Merluzzi, Note 15) at present is focusing on decision modeling of assertiveness and the possibility that individuals may, in fact, combine and utilize the information regarding type of assertion, targets, and environmental contexts differently, depending on their present level of assertiveness. Additionally, the information they extract may, in fact, perpetuate social skill deficits. For example, low-assertive individuals do not seem to use the more subtle dimensions and are more prone to dimensionalize a situation with anxiety and arousal constructs.

Finally, the value of the information presented here may be that it departs from traditional cognitive and behavioral formulations of assertion. In fact, the information-processing approach presented here was not derived from a treatment theory. That is, previous conceptualizations of assertion have relied on treatment intervention to explain the clinical problem. The approach offered here has no preferred treatment, although as noted previously, there are treatment implications. Thus the model of assertion that may develop from an information processing perspective may be a model based more on the study of social–cognitive behavior than the treatment of nonassertiveness.

In the next section we will discuss metacognition, another molar approach to information processing. The utility of metacognition as an educational tool has been firmly established. However, the clinical utility of metacognition has yet to be systematically explored.

Metacognition

Metacognition is an area that has distinct potential for unifying ideas from a diversity of areas in psychology and education. Even in the early stages of research and conceptualization of metacognition, the number of diverse areas that are discovering the utility of the construct is remarkable.

Metacognition has had an impact on social cognition (Flavell, Note 2), intelligence theory (Sternberg, 1979; Campione & Brown, Note 16) education and instruction (Meichenbaum & Asarnow, 1979; Borkowski & Cavanaugh, 1978), reading abilities (Brown, 1977; Ryan, 1981), and playing musical instruments (Gruson, 1980). It is safe to assert that these promising research and theoretical developments have emerged from this widespread interest in metacognitive processes. The potential for use in the clinical sciences will be presented after a brief description of metacognition. The reader is also referred to Chapter 1, this volume, for a brief synopsis of work conducted by Meichenbaum and his colleagues.

Description. "Metacognition" refers to the ability to monitor a wide variety of cognitive enterprises. It has been variously defined as the ability to monitor one's memory and comprehension, or knowing about knowing or an awareness of one's own cognitive machinery and the way it operates (see, e.g., Brown, 1977; Meichenbaum & Asarnow, 1979; Flavell, Note 2). In our explication of metacognition, we have drawn heavily from Flavell (1979, Note 2) because he has skillfully articulated, from the perspective of memory research, the potential relationship between metacognition and social cognition and personality. Flavell describes four classes of events that might constitute metacognitive processes: metacognitive knowledge, metacognitive experiences, goals (tasks), and actions (strategies).

From the perspective of memory research, metacognition refers to the ability to know and plan strategically in cognitive tasks. Moreover, the knowing and the planning are monitored so that performance may be evaluated and the subsequent experience used to modify future performance. Thus metacognition has two central components: knowledge about cognition and self-regulation of cognition (Brown & Campione, Note 17).

Therefore metacognitive knowledge constitutes an awareness of one's cognitive resources (e.g., the knowledge that the best way for me to solve this problem is to break it down into two parts), and metacognitive experience is a thought, attitude, judgment, or feeling that leads to an increased awareness, which may, in fact, invoke metacognitive knowledge. However, not all metacognitive experiences result in the retrieval of metacognitive knowledge: there may be instances in which no metacognitive knowledge directly applies. Also, metacognitive experiences may modify or revise metacognitive knowledge. Finally, metacognitive experiences may activate strategies aimed at metacognitive and cognitive goals.

Potential for Use in the Clinical Sciences. In his intriguing paper extending metacognitive principles to the area of social cognition, Flavell (Note 2) proposes an area of research that has great clinical potential. For example, with respect to metacognitive knowledge, Flavell presents three factors that may contribute to such knowledge of social–cognitive enterprises: person, task, and strategy variables.

The *person* variable can include all that you "know" about yourself and others. Perhaps a more euphemistic term would be "social understanding," that is, knowledge of yourself and others that you assume has some impact on understanding social behavior. For example, one may think of oneself as an astute judge of deceitful behavior.

Task variables concern our knowledge of the quality and quantity of information available and the implications of that information for how we proceed. For example, we may determine that to judge someone harshly may be inappropriate until we have more information about a particular incident. Another task variable may be our ability to know when our social-cognitive monitoring should be turned on or off. There may be situations in which we need to learn more because the outcome of the social situation may be critically determined by our gathering more information.

Finally, we may choose *strategies* that will help us achieve some goal or help us monitor whether we are on track toward our goal. An example of the latter may be that we ask a potential friend how he or she perceives our friendship or that we intuit the other person's feelings by trying to imagine how he or she feels.

Metacognitive experiences may be minimal, fleeting thoughts about a social situation or elaborate routines about the situation before, during, or after the experience (Flavell, Note 2). In the former situation there may be little opportunity for a metacognitive experience (e.g., having a beer in a familiar bar with an old friend). In contrast, recall your first date, a recent job interview, or situations in which you did not trust your judgment. In such situations, we may slow down our stream of thoughts, generate hypotheses concerning what is going, and so forth, all stimulated by metacognitive experience. In these situations, we can also invoke cognitive or metacognitive strategies. For example, a social-cognitive strategy in a job interview may be to find out more about the prospective employer. However, if you realize after a few minutes that the interviewer is put off by your taking too much control of the interview (social metacognition), you then become less dominant and ask fewer questions.

The value of metacognitive processes for the study of personality and psychopathology is derived from Flavell's inclusion of the affective domain. The experience of certain affective states may be a metacognitive experience, which, in turn, may invoke or establish metacognitive knowledge that has an impact on task demands and choice of strategy.

The utility of metacognition for theory development is evident in its relationship to self-regulation (see Bandura, 1977a). Mischel (1979) has demonstrated that children are very capable of articulating plans for self-regulation and of increasing control over their environment. Mischel (1979) also notes the following:

> With greater age there also may be increasing reliance on a kind of cognitive shorthand in which the formulation and implementation of many complex

plans may become more automatic, abbreviated, and rapid without requiring extensive or explicit self-instructions for each step in an increasingly complex organization hierarchy. (p. 749)

Mischel (1979) concludes that children are very aware of their own "information processing strategies and other features of cognition" (p. 749). Mischel and Mischel (Note 18) illustrate these principles by noting that, by the third grade, children are active in generating strategies to delay gratification and clearly understand how those strategies relate to resisting temptation.

These findings have potential value for elaborating theoretical bases for self-control strategies, for alleviating behavior problems, and for establishing the role of strategic behavior and metacognition in that process. Thus self-control, self-regulation, and self-efficacy, which are integral aspects of social learning theory, may be natural points of intersection with metacognition.

Although we have presumptuously suggested the significance of the role of metacognition in research on personality and behavior problems, several studies have already accomplished that interface. For example, Borkowski and Peck (Note 19) have investigated the relationship between impulsivity–reflectivity in children and the comparative use of strategic behavior and metamemory. They found that acquistion, maintenance, and generalization of strategies was greater for reflective than for impulsive children. Further, the authors found that an index of metamemory correlated better with strategic behavior than the measure of impulsivity. Borkowski and Peck concluded that metamemorial awareness may be a more critical determinant of strategy utilization than traditional measures of cognitive style.

Although the main thrust of Mueller's work (reviewed previously) was not metacognitive, he reported some intriguing findings that may lead to more work on metacognition in the area of test anxiety. These results are only suggestive, in that the strategies are indirectly inferred from the overt productions of subjects in Mueller's test anxiety research. In general, Mueller (1979) reports that test-anxious subjects tend to use inefficient strategies and, in fact, display those strategies in an inflexible fashion (see also Brown & Campione, Note 17). We must caution the reader that, without direct tests of strategy usage or assessments of metacognitive processes, Mueller's speculations on differential strategy usage and differential awareness are just that.

A final study by Steffen and Lucas (Note 20) had high and low socially competent males and females participate in a 10-minute role play, which was videotaped. Subjects viewed the videotape, recalled their thoughts, and finally were asked a standard set of probing questions about "mental processes" used in the interaction. The experimenter asked 29 open and closed questions that tapped the subject's understanding of what transpired during the interaction. Strategies were either original (i.e., offered by the subjects) or suggested (i.e., following a prompt from the experimenter). Both original and suggested strategies were rated as positive (effective) or negative (ineffective). Results indicated that the high-competent subjects mentioned twice as many original–positive strategies as the low-competent subjects. Thus the former may have a wider range of strategies to employ in social situations. Also, there is some indirect evidence that high-competent subjects were more aware of their partner's feelings. Again, although the metacognitive analysis is not an integral part of Steffen and Lucas's study, there are indications, based on the strategy assessment, that social understanding may be a critical component of competent social behavior.

One hazard inherent in the whole notion of metacognition is the question of causality. With socially competent people, there may be some reciprocal relationships between the self and the social context (Bandura, 1978) that modify the self, which, in turn, modifies the experience of the environment, and so on. In reference to this causal inference problem in metamemory, Brown and Campione (Note 17) hypothesized a bidirectional chain wherein metamemory may be necessary for the development and use of strategic behavior, which, in turn, enhances metamemory, and so on. The challenge, therefore, is to look at deficits in, and the development of, metacognitive abilities.

Finally, of particular interest to clinicians may be the extent to which metacognitive abilities may enhance treatment maintenance and generalization. This issue has been reviewed by Meichenbaum and Asarnow (1979) and thoroughly explicated by Borkowski and Cavanaugh (1978). From the perspective of maintaining and generalizing the effects of treatment gains, there are definite parallels to the existing literature in metamemory. Based on the recommendation of Borkowski and Cavanaugh (1978) and of Campione and Brown (Note 16), maintenance and generalization are enhanced by (1) training the individual in depth on strategies and concomitantly enhancing the individual's awareness of the need for, and the usefulness of, the strategy or techniques; (2) teaching the individual to evaluate a variety of situations in order to extract relevant information that may lead to the appropriate selection of a strategy; and (3) giving feedback about the usefulness of the chosen strategy. Thus, in our therapeutic interventions, we may, by adhering to the recommendations concerning generalization, ensure that clients develop metacognitive skills.

It is evident from the discussion of metacognition that research, from a clinical perspective, is in its infancy. Conceptual problems are apparent in the looseness of the basic terminology. That problem is exacerbated by the deficiencies in adequate assessment of metacognitive and strategic behavior. Despite the conceptual and methodological problems, the potential contribution of this area for a clinical cognitive science is abundantly evident.

Conclusion

We have attempted to present the dominant paradigm of experimental cognitive psychology, as well as its major components, and to review briefly the literature in the clinical area that has an information-processing perspective. We acknowledge the limitations of such a broad-based approach but also recognize the need for more interface between clinical cognitive research and experimental cognitive research.

As the germinal work reported in this chapter progresses, there are at least two potential benefits of the IPP for clinical science. First, the methods associated with the IPP may allow for more elaborate, yet more precise, descriptions of clinical problems from a cognitive perspective. Second, as the methods are used and adapted for clinical assessment, they may be used as outcome measures to assess the impact of treatment on cognitive processes.

ACKNOWLEDGMENT

The authors wish to thank Carol B. Finkel for her contribution to the section in this chapter on levels of processing and depression.

Reference Notes

1. Bower, G. *Critique of S-R conditioning theory.* Unpublished manuscript, Stanford University, 1979.
2. Flavell, J. H. *Monitoring social cognitive enterprises: Something else that may develop in the area of social cognition.* Paper prepared for the Social Science Research Council Committee on Social and Affective Development during Childhood, January 1979.
3. Merluzzi, T. V., & Rudy, T. E. *Toward an information processing decision making analysis of assertive behavior.* In J. P. Galassi (Chair), Current issues and research in cognitive assessment and cognitive behavioral counseling. Symposium presented at the meeting of the American Psychological Association, Montreal, 1980.
4. Steffy, R. A., MacCrimmon, D. J., & Bellissimo, A. *Reaction time indices reflecting changes in the clinical state of chronic schizophrenic patients.* Unpublished manuscript, University of Waterloo, 1979.
5. Finkel, C. B., Glass, C. R., & Merluzzi, T. V. *Differential discrimination of self-referent statements by depressives and nondepressives.* Manuscript submitted for publication, 1980.
6. Davis, H. *The development of the self-schema in adult depression.* Manuscript submitted for publication, 1980.
7. Teasdale, J. D., Taylor, R., & Fogarty, S. J. *Effects of induced elation–depression on the accessibility of memories of happy and unhappy experiences.* Manuscript submitted for publication, 1979.
8. Clark, H. H. *Bridging* (Working Paper). Unpublished manuscript, Stanford University, 1977.
9. Wyer, R. S. *The nature and use of schemata about persons.* Paper presented at the meeting of the Midwestern Psychological Association, Chicago, May 1979.
10. Markus, H., Sentis, K. P., & Hamill, R. *Thinking fat: Self-schemas for body weight and*

the processing of weight relevant information. Manuscript submitted for publication, 1980.

11. Rudy, T. E., Merluzzi, T. V., & Henehan, P. *Construal of complex social situations: A multidimensional analysis.* Manuscript submitted for publication, 1980.

12. Kruskal, J. B., Young, F. W., & Seery, J. B. *How to use KYST, a very flexible program to do multidimensional scaling and unfolding.* Unpublished manuscript, Bell Laboratories, 1973.

13. Chang, J. J., & Carroll, J. D. *How to use PROFIT, a computer program for property fitting by optimizing nonlinear or linear correlation.* Unpublished manuscript, Bell Laboratories, 1968.

14. Weinberg, S. L., & Lief, J. *Measurement of stressful life events associated with transition to parenthood.* Paper presented at the meeting of the American Psychological Association, New York, September 1979.

15. Rudy, T. E., & Merluzzi, T. V. *Decision modeling of assertion: An application of conjoint measurement analysis.* Manuscript in preparation, 1980.

16. Campione, J. C., & Brown, A. L. *Toward a theory of intelligence: Contributions from research with retarded children.* Paper presented at the meeting of the American Educational Research Association, Toronto, 1978.

17. Brown, A. L., & Campione, J. C. *Inducing flexible thinking: The problem of access.* Paper presented at the NATO International Conference on Intelligence and Learning, York, England, July 1979.

18. Mischel, W., & Mischel, H. N. *The development of children's knowledge of self-control.* Paper presented at the meeting of the Society for Research in Child Development, San Francisco, March 1979.

19. Borkowski, J. G., & Peck, V. *Children's strategy transfer: Influences of impulsivity and metamemory.* Paper presented at the meeting of the Psychonomic Society, Phoenix, November, 1979.

20. Steffen, J. J., & Lucas, J. *Social strategies and expectations as components of social competence.* Manuscript submitted for publication, 1980.

References

Anderson, J. R. *Language, memory, and thought.* Hillsdale, N. J.: Erlbaum, 1976.

Anderson, J. R., & Reder, L. M. An elaborative processing explanation of depth of processing. In L. S. Cermak & F. I. M. Craik (Eds.), *Levels of processing and human memory.* Hillsdale, N.J.: Erlbaum, 1978.

Anderson, R. C., & Ortony, A. On putting apples into bottles—A problem of polysemy. *Cognitive Psychology,* 1975, *7,* 167–180.

Baddeley, A. D. The trouble with levels: A reexamination of Craik and Lockhart's framework for memory research. *Psychological Review,* 1978, *85,* 139–152.

Baggett, P. Memory for explicit and implicit information in picture stories. *Journal of Verbal Learning and Verbal Behavior,* 1975, *14,* 538–548.

Bandura, A. Self-efficacy: Toward a unifying theory of behavior change. *Psychological Review,* 1977, *84,* 191–215. (*a*)

Bandura, A. *Social learning theory.* Englewood Cliffs, N. J.: Prentice-Hall 1977. (*b*)

Bandura, A. The self in reciprocal determinism. *American Psychologist,* 1978, *33,* 344–358.

Bartlett, F. C. *Remembering: A study in experimental and social psychology.* London: Cambridge University Press, 1932.

Beck, A. T. *Depression: Causes and treatment.* Philadelphia: University of Pennsylvania Press, 1972.

Beck, A. T. *Cognitive therapy and the emotional disorders.* New York: International Universities Press, 1976.

Borkowski, J. G. Research tactics in complex learning, memory, and cognition. In D. C. Anderson & J. G. Borkowski (Eds.), *Experimental psychology: Research tactics and their applications.* Glenview, Ill.: Scott-Foresman, 1979.

Borkowski, J. G., & Cavanaugh, J. C. Maintenance and generalization of skills and strategies by the retarded. In N. Ellis (Ed.), *Handbook of mental deficiency: Psychological theory and research* (2nd ed.). Hillsdale, N.J.: Erlbaum, 1978.

Bower, G. Contacts of cognitive psychology with social learning theory. *Cognitive Therapy and Research,* 1978, *2,* 123-146.

Bower, G. H., Clark, M. C., Lesgold, H. M., & Winzenz, D. Hierarchical retrieval schemes in recall of categorized word lists. *Journal of Verbal Learning and Verbal Behavior,* 1969, *8,* 323-343.

Bower, G. H., & Gilligan, S. G. Remembering information related to one's self. *Journal of Research in Personality,* 1979, *13,* 420-432.

Bransford, J. D. *Human cognition: Learning understanding and remembering.* Belmont, Calif.: Wadsworth Publishing Company, 1979.

Bransford, J. D., Barclay, J. R., & Franks, J. J. Sentence memory: A constructive versus interpretive approach. *Cognitive Psychology,* 1972, *3,* 193-209.

Brandsford, J. D., Franks, J. J., Morris, C. D., & Stein, B. S. An analysis of memory theory from the perspective of problems of learning. In L. S. Cermak & F. I. M. Craik (Eds.), *Levels of processing and human memory.* Hillsdale, N.J.: Erlbaum, 1978.

Bransford, J. D., and Johnson, M. K. Considerations of some problems of comprehension. In W. G. Chase (Ed.), *Visual information processing.* New York: Academic Press, 1973.

Bransford, J. D., and McCarrell, N. S. A sketch of a cognitive approach to comprehension. In W. Weimer & D. S. Palermo (Eds.), *Cognition and the symbolic processes.* Hillsdale, N.J.: Erlbaum, 1974.

Brody, N. Information theory, motivation, and personality. In H. M. Schroder & P. Suedfeld (Eds.), *Personality theory and information processing.* New York: Ronald Press, 1971.

Brown, A. L. Development, schooling, and the acquisition of knowledge about knowledge. In R. Anderson, R. Spiro, & W. Montague (Eds.), *Schooling and the acquisition of knowledge.* Hillsdale, N.J.: Erlbaum, 1977.

Brown, J. A. Some tests of the decay theory of immediate memory. *Quarterly Journal of Experimental Psychology,* 1958, *10,* 12-21.

Buhler, K. Tatschen und Probleme zu einer Psychologie der Denkuorgange, III. Ueber Gedankenerinnerungen. *Archives f.d. Gestalt Psychologie,* 1908.

Carpenter, P. A., & Just, M. A. Sentence comprehension: A psycholinguistic processing model of verification. *Psychological Review,* 1975, *82,* 45-73.

Carpenter, P. A., & Just M. A. Models of sentence verification and linguistic comprehension. *Psychological Review,* 1976, *83,* 318-322.

Carroll, J. D., & Chang, J. J. Analysis of individual differences in multidimensional scaling via an *N*-way generalization of "Eckart-Young" decomposition. *Psychometrika,* 1970, *35,* 283-319.

Chomsky, N. A review of Skinner's *Verbal Behavior. Language,* 1959, *35,* 26-58.

Clark, H. H. Linguistic processes in deductive reasoning. *Psychological Review,* 1969, *76,* 387-404.

Clark, H. H. Semantics and comprehension. In R. A. Sebcok (Ed.), *Current trends in linguistics* (Vol. 12). The Hague: Mouton, 1974.

Clark, H. H. Inferences in comprehension. In D. LaBerge & S. J. Samuels (Eds.), *Perception and comprehension.* Hillsdale, N.J.: Erlbaum, 1976.

Clark, H. H., & Chase, W. G. On the process of comparing sentences against pictures. *Cognitive Psychology,* 1972, *3,* 472-517.

Clark, H. H., & Haviland, S. E. Comprehension and the given–new contract. In R. O. Freedle (Ed.), *Discourse, production, and comprehension.* Norwood, N.J.: Ablex Publishing, 1977.

Clark, H. H., & Lucy, P. Understanding what is meant from what is said: A study in conversationally conveyed requests. *Journal of Verbal Learning and Verbal Behavior,* 1975, *14,* 56–72.

Craik, F. I. M., & Lockhart, R. S. Levels of processing: A framework for memory research. *Journal of Verbal Learning and Verbal Behavior,* 1972, *11,* 671–684.

Craik, F. I. M., & Tulving, E. Depth of procesing and the retention of words in episodic memory. *Journal of Experimental Psychology: General,* 1975, *104,* 268–294.

Davis, H. Self-reference and the encoding of personal information in depression. *Cognitive Therapy and Research,* 1979, *3,* 97–110. (*a*)

Davis, H. The self-schema and subjective organization of personal information in depression. *Cognitive Therapy and Research,* 1979, *3,* 415–425. (*b*)

DeMonbruen, B. G., & Craighead, W. E. Distortion of perception and recall of positive and neutral feedback in depression. *Cognitive Therapy and Research,* 1977, *1,* 311–329.

Easterbrook, J. A. The effect of emotion on cue utilization and the organization of behavior. *Psychological Review,* 1959, *69,* 183–201.

Eysenck, M. W. Levels of processing: A critique. *British Journal of Psychology,* 1978, *69,* 157–169.

Flavell, J. H. Metacognition and cognitive monitoring: A new area of cognitive–developmental inquiry. *American Psychologist,* 1979, *34,* 906–911.

Garner, W. R. *Uncertainty and structure as psychological concepts.* New York: Wiley, 1962.

Garner, W. R. *The processing of information and structure.* Potomac, Md.: Erlbaum, 1974.

Goldfried, M. R. Anxiety reduction through cognitive–behavioral intervention. In P. C. Kendall & S. D. Hollon (Eds.), *Cognitive–behavioral interventions: Theory, research, and procedures.* New York: Academic Press, 1979.

Greene, P. A. *Affective learning and mood induction.* Unpublished doctorial dissertation, Long Island University, 1977.

Gruson, L. *Piano practicing skills: What distinguishes competence?* Unpublished doctorial dissertation, University of Waterloo, 1980.

Haviland, S. E., & Clark, H. H. What's new? Acquiring new information as a process in comprehension. *Journal of Verbal Learning and Verbal Behavior,* 1974, *13,* 512–521.

Hornby, P. A. Surface structure and presupposition. *Journal of Verbal Learning and Verbal Behavior,* 1974, *13,* 530–538.

Isen, A. M., Shalker, T. E., Clark, M., & Karp, L. Affect, accessibility of material in memory, and behavior: A cognitive loop? *Journal of Personality and Social Psychology,* 1978, *36,* 1–12.

Johnson, M. K., Bransford, J. D., & Solomon, S. Memory for tacit implication of sentences. *Journal of Experimental Psychology,* 1973, *98,* 203–205.

Johnson, S. C. Hierarchical clustering schemes. *Psychometrika,* 1967, *32,* 241–254.

Jung, J. *Verbal learning.* Toronto: Holt, Rinehart & Winston, 1968.

Kahneman, D. *Attention and effort.* Englewood Cliffs, N.J.: Prentice-Hall, 1973.

Kelly, G. A. *The psychology of personal constructs.* New York: Norton, 1955.

Kintsch, W. Comprehension and memory of text. In W. K. Estes (Ed.), *Handbook of learning and cognitive processes: Linguistic functions in cognitive theory* (Vol. 6). Hillsdale, N.J.: Erlbaum, 1978.

Klein, K., & Saltz, E. Specifying the mechanisms in a levels-of-processing approach to memory. *Journal of Experimental Psychology: Human Learning and Memory,* 1976, *2,* 671–679.

Kruskal, J. B. Multidimensional scaling: A numerical method. *Psychometrika,* 1964, *29,* 1–27.

Kuhn, T. S. *The structure of scientific revolutions.* Chicago: University of Chicago Press, 1962.

Kuhn, T. S. *The structure of scientific revolutions* (2nd ed.). Chicago: University of Chicago Press, 1970.

Kuiper, N. A., & Derry, P. A. The self as a cognitive prototype: An application to person perception and depression. In N. Cantor & J. Kihlstrom (Eds.), *Cognition, social, interaction, and personality.* Hillsdale, N.J.: Erlbaum, 1981.

Kuiper, N. A., & Rogers, T. B. Encoding of personal information: Self-other differences. *Journal of Personality and Social Psychology,* 1979, *37,* 499–514.

Lachman, R., Lachman, J. L., & Butterfield, E. C. *Cognitive psychology and information processing: An introduction.* Hillsdale, N.J.: Erlbaum, 1979.

Lakoff, R. If's, and's, and but's about conjunction. In C. J. Fillmore & D. T. Langendoen (Eds.), *Studies in linguistic semantics.* New York: Holt, Rinehart & Winston, 1971.

LaPorte, R. E., & Voss, J. F. Prose representation: A multidimensional scaling approach. *Multivariate Behavioral Research,* 1979, *14,* 39–56.

Ledwidge, B. Cognitive behavior modification: A step in the wrong direction? *Psychological Bulletin,* 1978, *85,* 353–375.

Ledwidge, B. Cognitive behavior modification: A rejoinder to Locke and to Meichenbaum. *Cognitive Therapy and Research,* 1979, *3,* 133–139. (*a*)

Ledwidge, B. Cognitive behavior modification or new ways to change minds: Reply to Mahoney and Kazdin. *Psychological Bulletin,* 1979, *86,* 1050–1053. (*b*)

Levenson, R. W., & Gottman, J. M. Toward the assessment of social competence. *Journal of Consulting and Clinical Psychology,* 1978, *46,* 453–462.

Lewinsohn, P. M., Mischel, W., Chaplin, W., & Barton, R. Social competence and depression: The role of illusory self-perception? *Journal of Abnormal Psychology,* 1980, *89,* 203–212.

Locke, E. A. Behavior modification is not cognitive—and other myths: A reply to Ledwidge. *Cognitive Therapy and Research,* 1979, *3,* 119–125.

Mahoney, M. J. Reflections on the cognitive-learning trend in psychotherapy. *American Psychologist,* 1977, *32,* 5–13.

Mahoney, M. J., & Kazdin, A. E. Cognitive behavior modification. Misconceptions and premature evacuation. *Psychological Bulletin,* 1979, *86,* 1044–1049.

Markus, H. Self-schemata and processing information about the self. *Journal of Personality and Social Psychology,* 1977, *35,* 63–78.

Markus, H. The self in thought and memory. In D. M. Wegner & R. R. Vallacher (Eds.), *The self in social psychology.* New York: Oxford University Press, 1980.

Meichenbaum, D. Cognitive behavior modification: The need for a fairer assessment. *Cognitive Therapy and Research,* 1979, *3,* 127–132.

Meichenbaum, D., & Asarnow, J. Cognitive-behavior modification and metacognitive development: Implications for the classroom. In P. C. Kendall & S. D. Hollon (Eds.), *Cognitive-behavioral interventions: Theory, research, and procedures.* New York: Academic Press, 1979.

Miller G. A. The magical number seven, plus or minus two: Some limits on our capacity for processing information. *Psychological Review,* 1956, *63,* 81–97.

Miller, S., Saccuzzo, D., & Braff, D. Information processing deficits in remitted schizophrenics. *Journal of Abnormal Psychology,* 1979, *88,* 446–449.

Mischel, W. On the interface of cognition and personality. *American Psychologist,* 1979, *34,* 740–754.

Morris, C. D., Bransford, J. D., & Franks, J. J. Levels of processing versus transfer appropriate processing. *Journal of Verbal Learning and Verbal Behavior,* 1977, *16,* 519–534.

Mueller, J. H. Test anxiety, input modality, and levels of organization in free recall. *Bulletin of the Psychonomic Society,* 1977, *9,* 67–69.

Mueller, J. H. The effects of individual differences in test anxiety and type of orienting task on levels of organization in free recall. *Journal of Research in Personality,* 1978, *12,* 100–116.

Mueller, J. H. Anxiety and encoding processes in memory. *Personality and Social Psychology Bulletin,* 1979, *5,* 288–294.

Mueller, J. H. Test anxiety and the encoding and retrieval of information. In I.G. Sarason (Ed.), *Text anxiety: Theory, research, and applications.* Hillsdale, N.J.: Erlbaum, 1980.

Mueller, J. H., Carlmusto, M., & Marler, M. Recall and organization in memory as a function of rate of presentation and individual differences in test anxiety. *Bulletin of Psychonomic Society,* 1978, *12,* 133–136.

Nelson, R. E., & Craighead, W. E. Selective recall of positive and negative feedback, self-control behaviors, and depression. *Journal of Abnormal Psychology,* 1977, *36,* 379–388.

Newell, A., Shaw, J. C., & Simon, H. A. Elements of a theory of human problem solving. *Psychological Review,* 1958, *65,* 151–166.

Newell, A., & Simon, H. A. *Human problem solving.* Englewood Cliffs, N.J.: Prentice-Hall, 1972.

Newell, A., & Simon, H. A. Computer science as empirical inquiry: Symbols and search. *Communications of the ACM,* 1976, *19,* 113–126.

Observer. The recycling of cognition in psychology. *Psychological Record,* 1978, *28,* 157–160.

Oltmanns, T. Selective attention in schizophrenia and manic psychoses: The effects of distraction on information processing. *Journal of Abnormal Psychology,* 1978, *87,* 212–225.

Pachella, R. G. The interpretation of reaction time in information processing research. In B. H. Kantowitz (Ed.), *Human information processing: Tutorials in performance and cognition.* Hillsdale, N.J.: Erlbaum, 1974.

Peterson, L. R., & Peterson, M. J. Short-term retention of individual verbal items. *Journal of Experimental Psychology,* 1959, *58,* 193–198.

Rogers, T. B., Kuiper, N. A., & Kirker, W. S. Self-reference and the encoding of personal information. *Journal of Personality and Social Psychology,* 1977, *35,* 677–688.

Rosenthal, T. L., & Zimmerman, B. J. *Social learning and cognition.* New York: Academic Press, 1978.

Rumelhart, D. E. Notes on a schema for stories. In D. G. Bobrow & A. M. Collins (Eds.), *Representation and understanding: Studies in cognitive science.* New York: Academic Press, 1975.

Rumelhart, D. E. Understanding and summarizing brief stories. In D. LaBarge & S. J. Samuels (Eds.), *Basic processes in reading: Perception and comprehension.* Hillsdale, N.J.: Erlbaum, 1977.

Ryan, E. B. Identifying and remediating failures in reading comprehension: Toward an instructional approach for poor comprehenders. In T. G. Waller & G. E. MacKinnon (Eds.), *Advances in reading research* (Vol. 2). New York: Academic Press, 1981.

Saccuzzo, D. P., & Braff, D. L. Early information processing deficit in schizophrenia: New findings using schizophrenic sub-groups and manic controls. *Archives of General Psychiatry,* in press.

Salzberg, P. M. On the generality of encoding specificity. *Journal of Experimental Psychology: Human Learning and Memory,* 1975, *2,* 586–596.

Sarason, I. G. Test anxiety, attention, and the general problem of anxiety. In C. D. Spielberger & I. G. Sarason (Eds.), *Stress and anxiety* (Vol. 1). Washington, D.C.: Hemisphere, 1975.

Sarason, I. G. Anxiety and self-preoccupation. In I. G. Sarason & C. D. Spielberger (Eds.), *Stress and anxiety* (Vol. 2). Washington, D.C.: Hemisphere, 1976.

Sarason, I. G. The test anxiety scale: Concept and research. In C. D. Spielberger & I. G. Sarason (Eds.), *Stress and anxiety* (Vol. 5). Washington, D.C.: Hemisphere, 1978.

Sarason, I. G. Three lucunae of cognitive therapy. *Cognitive Therapy and Research,* 1979, *3,* 223–235.

Sarason, I. G., & Stoops, R. Test anxiety and the passage of time. *Journal of Consulting and Clinical Psychology,* 1978, *46,* 102–109.

Schank, R. C. Conceptual dependency: A theory of natural language understanding. *Cognitive Psychology,* 1972, *3,* 552–631.

Segal, E. M., & Lachman, R. Complex behavior or higher mental process: Is there a paradigm shift? *American Psychologist,* 1972, *27,* 46–55.

Shannon, C. E. A mathematical theory of communication. *Bell System Technical Journal,* 1948, *27,* 379–423; 623–659.

Shannon, C. E., & Weaver, W. *The mathematical theory of communication.* Urbana: University of Illinois Press, 1949.

Shriffin, R. M., & Grantham, D. W. Can attention be allocated to sensory modalities? *Perception and Psychophysics,* 1974, *15,* 460–474.

Skinner, B. F. *Verbal behavior.* New York: Appleton-Century-Crofts, 1957.

Smith, E. E. Choice reaction time: An analysis of the major theoretical positions. *Psychological Bulletin,* 1968, *69,* 77–110.

Spelke, E., Hirst, W., & Neisser, U. Skills of divided attention. *Cognition,* 1976, *4,* 215–230.

Spence, J. T., & Spence, K. W. The motivational components of manifest anxiety: Drive and drive stimuli. In C. D. Spielberger (Ed.), *Anxiety and behavior.* New York: Academic Press, 1966.

Spyropoulos, T., & Ceraso, J. Categorized and uncategorized attributes of recall cues: The phenomenon of limited access. *Cognitive Psychology,* 1977, *9,* 384–402.

Stein, B. The effects of cue-target uniqueness on cued recall performance. *Memory and Cognition,* 1977, *5,* 319–322.

Sternberg, R. J. The nature of mental abilities. *American Psychologist,* 1979, *34,* 214–230.

Sternberg, S. High-speed scanning in human memory. *Science,* 1966, *153,* 652–654.

Sternberg, S. Memory scanning: Mental processes revealed by reaction time experiments. *American Scientist,* 1969, *57,* 421–457.

Sternberg, S. Memory scanning: New findings and current controversies. *Quarterly Journal of Experimental Psychology,* 1975, *27,* 1–32.

Steronko, R. J., & Woods, D. J. Impairment in early stages of visual information processing in nonpsychotic schizotypic individuals. *Journal of Abnormal Psychology,* 1978, *87,* 481–490.

Stone, P. J. Computer models of information processing. In H. M. Schroder & P. Suedfeld (Eds.), *Personality theory and information processing.* New York: Ronald Press, 1971.

Suedfeld, P. Information processing as a personality model. In H. M. Schroder & P. Suedfeld (Eds.), *Personality theory and information processing.* New York: Ronald Press, 1971.

Taylor, M. A., & Abrams, R. Manic–depressive illness and good prognosis in schizophrenia. *American Journal of Psychiatry,* 1975, *132,* 741–742.

Taylor, S. E., & Crocker, J. Schematic bases of social information processing. In E. T. Higgins, C. P. Herman, & M. P. Zanna (Eds.), *Social cognition: The Ontario symposium on personality and psychology.* Hillsdale, N.J.: Erlbaum, 1981.

Teasdale, J. D., & Fogarty, S. J. Differential effects of induced mood on retrieval of pleasant events from episodic memory. *Journal of Abnormal Psychology,* 1979, *88,* 248–257.

Tulving, E. Subjective organization in free recall of "unrelated" words. *Psychological Review,* 1962, *69,* 344–354.

Tulving, E. Theoretical issues in free recall. In T. R. Dixon & D. L. Horton (Eds.), *Verbal behavior and general behavior therapy.* Englewood Cliffs. N. J.: Prentice-Hall, 1968.

Tulving, E. Relation between encoding specificity and levels of processing. In L. S. Cermak & F. I. M. Craik (Eds.), *Levels of processing and human memory.* Hillsdale, N.J.: Erlbaum, 1978.

Tulving, E., & Psotka, J. Retroactive inhibition in free recall: Inaccessibility of information available in the memory store. *Journal of Experimental Psychology,* 1971, *87,* 1–8.

Underwood, G. Moray vs. the rest: The effects of extended practice on shadowing. *Quarterly Journal of Experimental Psychology,* 1974, *26,* 368–373.

Wachtel, P. L. *Psychoanalysis and behavior theory.* New York: Basic Books, 1977.

Wener, A. E., & Rehm, L. P. Depressive affect: A test of behavioral hypotheses. *Journal of Abnormal Psychology,* 1975, *84,* 221–227.

Wilson, G. T. Cognitive behavior therapy: Paradigm shift or passing phase? In J. P. Foreyt & D. P. Rathjen (Eds.), *Cognitive behavior therapy.* New York: Plenum Press, 1978.

Wine, J. D. Cognitive–attentional therapy of test anxiety. In I. G. Sarason (Ed.), *Test anxiety: Theory, research, and application.* Hillsdale, N.J.: Erlbaum, 1980. (*a*)

Wine, J. D. Evaluative anxiety: A cognitive attentional construct. In H. W. Krohne & L. C. Laux (Eds.), *Achievement, stress and anxiety.* Washington, D. C.: Hemisphere, 1980. (*b*)

Wolpe, J. Cognition and causation in human behavior and its therapy. *American Psychologist,* 1978, *33,* 437–446.

Wyer, R. S., & Srull, T. K. Category accessibility. Some theoretical and empirical issues concerning the processing of social stimulus information. In E. T. Higgins, C. P. Herman, & M. P. Zanna (Eds.), *Social cognition: The Ontario symposium on personality and social psychology.* Hillsdale, N.J.: Erlbaum, 1981.

Part II
Methods, Issues, and Approaches

5

Projective Methods of Cognitive Analysis

Harry J. Sobel

Introduction

There is a large segment of the behavioral community for which the title of
this chapter will promptly cause an inexorable quandary about whether an
editorial error has been made. The notion of a projective analysis, or indeed
the label itself, has come to serve as a stimulus for our habitual Freudophobic responses. The term "projective," or "projective test," often elicits imagery of our prior bondage within the psychoanalytic pyramids: days
when the exodus into the promised cognitive–behavioral homeland was but
a wishful self-instruction! Throughout the past 10 years, as behavioral and
cognitive–behavioral models have proliferated and changed the course of
clinical psychology, projective analysis has generally been viewed as an im-
practical avenue for the *science* of assessment.

In many respects such an outright rejection was necessary as an initial
act of housecleaning. Behavior modification and behavioral assessment had
clear-cut goals concerning a learning-theory-based therapeutic approach,
and there did not seem to be a place for instruments or inkblots that made
trait, characterological, or nonenvironmental assumptions about human
functioning. Now that behavior modification has survived its adolescence,
resolving the expected confusion in professional identity and entering young
adulthood with the parenting of a hybrid cognitive offspring (Mahoney,
1974), paradigm development need not preclude an awareness of ancestral
roots (Sobel, 1978). As we move toward the development of a clinical cog-

Harry J. Sobel • Department of Psychiatry, Harvard Medical School and Massachusetts General Hospital, Boston, Massachusetts.

nitive model, and as we revise the more global behavioral paradigm, it is necessary to reconsider and to redefine concepts, models, and actual diagnostic techniques. An integrative, or dialectical, model for cognitive therapy will be determined by our willingness to examine prior foundations and innovative future possibilities. In effect, a paradigm cannot emerge if we merely insist on the design of one technique of assessment or intervention after another (Deitz, 1978). Technical innovation requires support and foresight from theoretical integration (Sarason, 1979; Wachtel, 1977).

The purpose of this chapter is to redefine projective analysis for a theoretically relevant application within cognitive–behavioral assessment and modification. At present, there is little use of the technique, and there are perhaps even fewer attempts at reconceptualization. Therefore, this chapter does not purport to review the literature, but rather aims at giving a theoretical and historical context to a technique that now has mainly heuristic potential. I have chosen this goal in order to reiterate the need for theoretical speculation before technical prescription. This chapter will attempt to bridge the gap that separates cognitive assessment from cognitive–developmental psychology and the ego-analytic tradition by using the projective test as an example of how integration and application might proceed. The space limitations imposed by a chapter do not permit a comprehensive review of the many traditional projective concepts and how they have been described under such headings as unconscious and conscious externalizations, fantasy attributions, or motivational needs. For a historical overview of this perspective and the many scoring systems, see Murstein's (1963) book on research in projective techniques.

Background and Historical Context

Certainly there has not been a paucity of criticism aimed at projective analysis. As behavioral therapy matured, it was an accepted premise that a precise A-B-C assessment could not rely on the type of "analytic" information that had emanated from projective instruments. The behavioral clinician was neither willing to assume the presence of indirect clues to personality nor able to justify a one-to-one correspondence between projective diagnosis and treatment management. As early as 1968, Mischel discussed the seemingly inevitable constraints imposed on a science of assessment by traditional assumptions:

> The most important barrier to behavior assessment is the prevalence of the psychodynamic dictum that the proper foci of assessments are inferences about presumed underlying processes rather than behavior itself. This reflects the psychodynamic belief that behavior is merely the surface manifestation of underlying causes and should be used only as a clue to detect underlying deep-rooted problems. Indeed, this view holds that indirect assessment has the important advantage of bypassing the assessee's defensive distortions. To justify

that belief, however, would require compelling evidence that inferences to these hypothesized underlying states can be made reliably and that they have utility. (Mischel, 1968, p. 142)

For most behaviorists, this "compelling evidence" has never been realized, and therefore projective analysis has remained under the so-called rubric of unempirical psychodynamic methodology.

The primary purpose of clinical assessment and diagnosis is to provide information for the planning of an effective treatment intervention. Undoubtedly, early psychometricians specializing in projective methods intended to reach these goals. The use of normative data was seen as basic to diagnostic success. Its consistent application over time seemed to be a feasible procedure. Unfortunately, the link between psychological information and treatment management was lost in the midst of a preoccupation with the instruments per se. This link might have appeared had projective methods been seen as just one vehicle within a broader, clinical problem-solving process (Sloves, Docherty, & Schneider, 1979). Traditional projective methods were unable to fill a place in the behaviorist's armamentarium for additional reasons even beyond the typical sign–sample or "underlying trait" assumptions.

The psychotherapy literature continues to be replete with uniform prescriptions (Kiesler, 1966). In many respects it was the behavioral school that gradually prodded traditional disciplines, urging them to reconsider the lack of specificity in most psychotherapeutic processes. Assessment practices were no exception to their companion psychotherapies. Projective testing was indiscriminately utilized, promoted in a uniform manner, and generally unable to uncover precise patient–environment interactions. A given patient's $F+$ % of 50 on the Rorschach was not qualitatively or practically differentiated from another individual's $F+$ % of 50. This pseudo empiricism was but a disguise for diagnostic uniformity, a trend that orthodox behaviorists were attempting to alter.

A significant characteristic of both behavioral and cognitive procedures is the willingness to accept a self-control and patient-participatory model. In traditional projective analysis the patient remains, for the most part, in a passive, nonparticipatory role. Typically, the examiner views the patient as someone "to be found out," "uncovered," or skillfully led down an intricate maze, hoping that lacunae in defensive operations will arise, hence permitting a transparent glance into psychological functioning. As such, the relationship is seen as a delicate dynamic, one that the clinician must balance with great interpretive acumen (Schaefer, 1954).

The medical model perspective rarely assumes that the patient himself or herself has the capacity to function as a participating member of the diagnostic evaluation team. The construction of the traditional projective test negates a patient-participatory role, for it postulates that the projective instrument exists to "tease" the patient into disclosing material that would otherwise be withheld. For the behaviorist committed to the specifics of environmental contingencies and eventual self-control, these ambiguous and indirect test stimuli are untenable. If the patient is to be accepted as a colleague, coevaluator, or apprentice (Fischer, 1970; Meichenbaum, 1977; Mischel, 1977), then traditional projectives breach the initial conjoint therapeutic contract.

> The client should be maximally involved in the process of assessment. This reduces the likelihood of inaccurate judgment, provides the client with a reasonable opportunity to have the satisfaction of being heard, and increases the probability that the therapist and client will agree and be equally committed to treatment goals. (Stuart & Stuart, 1976, p. 150)

Integration of Basic Assumptions

Assessment as an ongoing functional analysis, or contextual "psycho-situational assessment" (Bersoff, 1973), has been widely discussed in the behavioral literature (Cone & Hawkins, 1977; Goldfried & Kent, 1972; Mash & Terdal, 1976; Mischel, 1968). There is no need to review the basic assumptions of a behavioral personality assessment (Goldfried & Sprafkin, 1974). It is advantageous to list briefly the primary assumptions of a traditional projective test so that a redefinition for a cognitive–behavioral paradigm is clarified. What I hope to suggest is that functional behavioral assumptions can be integrated into a projective methodology without totally discarding the method. Despite our Freudophobic behaviors, it may not be necessary, or dialectically appropriate, to throw the baby out with the bathwater—or the cigar with the man!

The basic assumptions in a psychodynamic application of projective analysis are as follows:

1. Interpersonal differences on a given trait determine the quantity of that existing trait. Each individual has a certain amount of a specific resource.

2. The traits, behaviors, affects, or cognitions of primary interest require a subtle extraction from behind the multiple layers of psychological insulation. The projective method therefore allows the clinician to examine levels of consciousness, including those which the patient cannot perceive himself or herself.

3. Broad personality characteristics of individuals will appear as perceptual projections on ambiguous stimuli, regardless of the situation or ecological variance.

4. Variability through time and situation is generally the exception, not the rule.

5. Environmental contingencies during the testing process do not exert a great deal of influence upon the projective data.

6. Projective data will yield a relatively fixed diagnosis, which will signal the end of formal evaluation and the beginning of treatment.

7. Defensive operations, accepted as structural mechanisms of personality adaptation, are more important to uncover during the diagnostic projective analysis than are active coping strategies, personal preferences, or problem-solving behaviors.

8. The more dissimilar the projective stimuli are to the patient's problem behaviors or environmental conditions, the more information will be elicited on psychological functioning and motivational determinants.

9. The course and stages of human development are significant forces in determining future vulnerability and adaptation. The projective instrument is capable of inferring developmental sequences as well as past foundations for current developmental processes.

10. Projective data permit inferences and judgments about global personality functioning in the social environment.

11. Mediational or cognitive activities are guiding events and are uncovered indirectly through common, consistent, and often symbolic projections.

For most behavioral and cognitive therapists, most of these assumptions are untenable and obviously not in synchrony with our standard clinical modus operandi. Historically, we have rejected these concepts, preferring a working model with significantly fewer inferences about causal traits, psychogenetic predispositions, or unconscious energizing forces. However, in totally rejecting much of the psychoanalytic and ego-analytic discipline, we have hindered the development of an integrative paradigm, a paradigm that draws upon and alters prior theory and techniques (Sarason, 1979; Wachtel, 1977).

Cognitive therapy, as Mahoney (1974, 1977) and others have noted, represents the early phase of an integrated paradigm. With this emergence, mediational constructs embedded within the ego-analytic tradition no longer seem so alien. In fact, careful investigation of the neo-Freudian school shows that it has marked similarities to the cognitive–behavioral model and that it can illustrate adjuncts to the further design of the model. The indirect projective instrument, despite its psychoanalytically laden genealogy, can be redefined for cognitive assessment without reverting to the assumptions listed previously (Knutson, 1973). Such a process preserves a valuable vehicle for the refinement of behavioral assessment.

Projective Analysis: Definition and Redefinition

A "projective-cognitive instrument" can be defined as a sequentially derived method[1] for sampling an individual's problem-solving behavior, coping repertoire, and self-instructional style as applied to a specific, situationally bound life task or concern. "Projection" implies that the patient is

[1]See Goldfried and D'Zurilla (1969) for a discussion of the sequential method.

asked to engage in a sample of covert behavior overtly, in relation to structured pictorial stimuli representing some particular and relevant dilemma. Let me redefine the 11 traditional projective assumptions within a cognitive frame of reference, so that it becomes clear how certain key behavioral and analytic notions are retained:

1. Intraindividual differences are of primary interest and do not signify a set quantity of a given psychological resource. In other words, normative comparison of the projected covert behavior is not seen as the first step of assessment interpretation.

2. The existence of multiple layers of consciousness is not denied, but these layers are not the crucial elements in diagnostic evaluation or treatment. What the patient perceives and concomitantly produces in the act of coping with the simulated task is of major importance and a likely predictor of future adaptation. Present awareness and projected self-instructions are not necessarily supported by underlying motivational patterns.

3. Ecological variation and situational contexts will inevitably modify the projected sample of cognitive coping strategies.

4. In general, variability over time is the rule, not an exception.

5. The testing environment and the test itself exert a strong pull on the projective data.

6. A projected mediational structure, such as problem-solving style, is an *in-process* variable signaling the beginning of treatment. Cognitive diagnosis is ongoing and is a salient dimension of the overall treatment program.

7. Understanding coping behavior, and not defenses, is a major goal for the clinician when he or she analyzes the projected stories, preferences, or self-instructions.

8. The more similar the projective stimuli are to the patient's problem behaviors or life tasks, the more information will be obtained for treatment and the prediction of coping.

9. Developmental progression and regression occur continuously in the cognitive and behavioral realm. The projective–cognitive instrument should be capable of evaluating the rapid shifts in development and psychological functioning as they occur from one stimulus to another. Previous cognitive patterns, occurring during various periods of development, cannot be reliably sampled.

10. Projective data permit an observation about specific behavioral and cognitive coping responses made to a particular life task at a particular time and facilitate inferences about eventual adaptation in the social environment.

11. Cognitive or covert activities are significant guiding behaviors and are observed *directly* by the specific, "uncommon" projections to a specific, "nonsymbolic" task.

These assumptions, or tentative principles for a redefinition of projective analysis, delineate dimensions of a more integrated cognitive psycho-therapy and assessment model, a model drawing upon both behavioral and nonbehavioral disciplines. What are some of the key assumptions running through these tentative principles?

Key Assumptions Underlying Redefinition

In adopting an ecological perspective, I am reiterating the necessity of Bersoff's (1973) "psychosituational" viewpoint. In his indictment of tradi-tional assessment practices as "psychological alchemy," Bersoff noted, quite appropriately, how projective analyses have always viewed "behavior as relatively independent of the situation in which the person is immersed" (p. 893). To ignore the patient's context or to disavow the stimulus proper-ties of the projective card is to accept a static model of ongoing cognition while ignoring the import of information theory (Fulkerson, 1965; Mischel, 1977). If we were to utilize a projective instrument in this static fashion, then both the behavioral and ego-analytic models would be rejected, be-cause the former urges more specificity and environmental observation, and the latter acknowledges developmental changes, process, and constant shifts in psychological functioning. In fact, one is hard pressed to accept a traditional projective instrument as based on anything more than a very orthodox Freudian model.

A redefined instrument capable of eliciting a fairly reliable sample of cognitive behavior will aim at "contextualizing" (Bersoff, 1973) the testee and the examiner as well as describing the test stimuli themselves. Basically, there are multiple contexts accounting for the variance in cognitive data. Thus idiographic, rather than normative, analysis becomes the first line of data interpretation, especially given a sequential design of the projective test, which will be described later.

An idiographic approach, coupled with an acceptance of contextual de-terminants, should not deter us from a cognitive–developmental perspec-tive. Psychosituational assumptions capture the needed developmental structures, which are often forgotten by the behavioral tradition and mis-directed by analytic approaches. The Freudian school saw the concept of developmental lines as vital to the understanding of psychopathology and change. Nonmediational behaviorists, and in fact most cognitive therapists, incorporate some developmental notions into their assessment practices by accepting the usefulness of constant monitoring and observation over time. However, monitoring a patient's responses does not imply that we have a structural understanding of that patient's developmental processes.

A developmentally based projective–cognitive test, derived from an in-tegrated paradigm, will have to (1) see larger structures than just a self-instruction or an irrational belief; (2) accept response specificity within the framework of constant shifting and more global self-instructional patterns;

(3) recognize that an assessment of global self-instructional styles does not mean a return to static state–trait models; (4) accept the premise that self-instructions fall into various cognitive structures that respond under different environmental conditions; and (5) acknowledge that an empirical cognitive–behavioral assessment is not synonymous with a reductionistic method. In our earnest desire to avoid trait assessments, we must be cautious not to miss the complexity and orderliness of human development.

A self-instruction is more than just a self-instruction made in response to specific projective card stimuli or a real-life event. It is part of a cognitive process and is not a cognitive trait; thus a vital part of assessment is to contextualize a self-instructional response within the individual's broader cognitive structures. I do not believe it is contradictory to accept ego-analytic or organismic (Werner, 1948) notions of development along with response specificity assumptions from traditional behaviorism. They complement one another, allowing for a projective test that contextualizes in the widest possible sense of the word. So long as cognitive processes and structures are not equated with traits or fixed resources, we will not be returning to a static Freudian model.

Although Wapner and his associates (Wapner, Kaplan, & Cohen, 1973) at Clark University are not focusing on cognitive therapy per se, their current methodology is an excellent example of an integrated organismic–developmental model that simultaneously considers ecological variables and cognitive organization. In studying person–environment transactions, they have formulated a systems perspective that incorporates significant cognitive assumptions but that does not reject the interdependence of cognitive and affective modes as they interact with life tasks. This view can be summarized by noting these investigators' procedural principles:

> (1) Focus on everyday life, (2) Interdependence of psychological processes, (3) Importance of basic attitudes, (4) Agent-dependence of structuralization, (5) Multiple worlds of agents, (6) Structurization as historical process, (7) Varied units and levels of analysis, and (8) Developmental ordering. (Wapner *et al.,* 1973, p. 262)

Utilizing semiprojective map sketch tests in which subjects are asked to organize their environment, the Clark studies have significant relevance for the cognitive behaviorist in that thoughts or self-instructions are seen as processes that unfold in definite, but changing, developmental sequences. By relying on developmental principles (Werner & Kaplan, 1963), Wapner and his associates assume that cognitions progress from a relatively global and undifferentiated pattern toward a well-articulated, integrated, and differentiated process.

These ecological variables provide us with valuable cognitive assessment tools, for they facilitate an analysis of projected self-instructions within more meaningful structures, such as styles or developmental characteristics. It seems feasible, moreover, to conceptualize a sequence of self-instructions made in response to a simulated life task as having a "content dimension" (What is said?), a "structural dimension" (How, and in what format, is it said?), and a "developmental dimension" (Does it change? Is it similar to productions by other age groups? Is it situation-specific?). By adopting a developmental and psychosituational model of self-instructions, we will be much closer to gaining access to a patient's process of coping, coping elasticity, and probable adjustment in the face of future stress. Without such redefinitions in our working paradigm, our instruments are bound to resemble the same unilevel scales against which the behavioral heritage reacted. Cognitive self-instructions have a context in development, in cognitive structure, in transactions with the environment, and in sequence with prior self-instructions (Sarason, 1979). A series of projective cards, designed to match a specific life task, will lead, I hope, to this type of contextual analysis as it concomitantly supports an integrated paradigm.

Projective Test Design and Construction

Most behaviorists have been unable to use traditional projective tests because of their nonspecific and ambiguous quality. Although it has been assumed that such global ambiguity facilitates diagnostic assessment, little can be found in the literature to support this original claim. On the contrary, ambiguity in card stimuli has precluded precise assessment, leading to indiscriminate matching between instruments, patients, and the presenting symptoms or disorders.

Applying the TAT, for example, to all types of patients manifesting all forms of psychopathology, is analogous to a blind application of X rays to all patients appearing with a sore throat. Although the sore throat might indeed represent an early sign of malignant growth, it could also be the effect of many other conditions. Clinical psychology, especially in its support of traditional psychodiagnostic assessment procedures, has failed to take into account the myths of nonspecificity (Kiesler, 1966).

The design and construction of a cognitive–behavioral projective test should be conducted by applying a sequential method (Turk, Sobel, Follick, & Youkilis, 1980). This approach makes it possible to devise an instrument that will be reliable, valid for a specific group of patients manifesting a specific disorder, and theoretically linked to current views on coping that are oriented toward process and problem solving (Lazarus, 1978; Meichenbaum, 1977; Weisman & Sobel, 1979).

Goldfried and D'Zurilla's (1969) original behavioral–analytic model serves as a good example of a sequential or functional model leading to the design of a useful projective–cognitive instrument. Basically, their procedure permits a way in which to sample certain behaviors, to derive an empirical instrument, and to establish specific and relevant scoring criteria. The first stage of this a priori model—the criterion analysis—involves three phases: (1) problem identification, (2) response enumeration, and (3) response evaluation.

Rather than assume, post hoc, that one understands the significant problems, concerns, or tasks related to a certain patient population or syndrome, the criterion analysis utilizes a problem identification phase to sample the range of these potential tasks. Therefore, right from the outset, we are making an empirical decision to collect situation-specific data for eventual use as a projective cue.

The next phase, response enumeration, requires a sampling of the various responses that are made as the subject confronts the tasks presented during problem identification. If one is to generate a sequentially derived projective–cognitive instrument, then the response enumeration phase must elicit covert as well as overt behaviors (Turk *et al.*, 1980). In collecting this type of information, the researcher is attempting to gain a perspective on how, what, or when covert behaviors facilitate or inhibit the implementation of adaptive cognitive or behavioral coping strategies.

Furthermore, these self-instructions require a cluster analysis for compiling common cognitive pathways or personal styles operating within the various situations and tasks. In this fashion, the derived projective instrument will tap not only the coping strategies but also the metacognitive activity interacting with the production of coping behavior and the probable course or cognitive pathway that a self-instruction might take, depending on the simulated adjustive demand (i.e., card stimuli). Thus one patient's self-instructional style might, for example, be self-devaluing and externally directed only in response to interpersonal demands or illness-related tasks, but this may not be a characteristic pattern when confronting vocational concerns.

During the third phase of the criterion analysis, a response evaluation is completed. Here the goal is to assess the relative effectiveness of the responses collected previously. To ensure a multidimensional assessment or scaling of probable efficacy, it is feasible to use both patient and professional rating groups. This increases the predictive validity of scoring criteria, a factor most often criticized in traditional projective methods. As is apparent, a sequential process in designing situation-specific tests cannot be developmentally relevant unless the following conditions are met:

1. A range of problems or tasks for any given adjustive demand must be examined.
2. This range of problems must be followed longitudinally (implying follow-ups and multiple assessments).
3. Ipsative as well as normative analyses are required.
4. Assessment must be accepted as an ongoing component of therapy, not just as a temporary diagnostic probe.

The growing role that psychologists are asked to play in medical consultation, evaluation, and treatment planning increases the need for precise and specific assessment instruments. Although behaviorists have made sophisticated advances in the science of assessment, their future role in behavioral medicine, for example, will require an even further refinement in diagnostic measures. Although projective methods may not be the techniques of choice, they do seem to hold some clinical promise, especially in their capacity for integration within the ongoing therapy process. Furthermore, if behaviorists are to meet the demand for precision and specificity in their instruments, then following a sequential method of test development is a necessity.

In many medical institutions, consultation testing and evaluation operate through a confounded application of traditional projective methods in combination with the Minnesota Multiphasic Personality Inventory. Excluding the MMPI, which has some specificity built into it by way of diverse comparison samples, the traditional testing approach is not based on a priori knowledge of the various syndromes encountered. This fact severely limits predictive validity and efficiency. Invariably, we are also unable to continue using the test when the patient is referred for therapy. A problem-specific projective test would significantly add to the clinical armamentarium within behavioral medicine and thus enhance the value of behaviorists' presence within the general hospital setting. Obviously, this is true for many other settings as well.

The Cancer Problem-Solving Projective Test: An Example

Let me describe one component of the ongoing behavioral medicine research at Project Omega, a multidisciplinary group based at the Massachusetts General Hospital (Sobel & Worden, 1979; Weisman & Sobel, 1979; Weisman & Worden, 1976; Worden & Sobel, 1978). As part of our overall goal to identify the highly distressed cancer patient early in the course of the illness and then to administer structured cognitive–behavioral interventions, we recognized the need for a sequential research model. Such a model was required for the actual design of an intervention and for an instrument that could provide information on cognition and coping as opposed to general personality functioning.

The Cancer Problem-Solving Projective (CPSP) Test, which is still in the process of development and empirical study, was designed as a test and therapeutic instrument for use with newly diagnosed cancer patients, all of whom would have at least a 3-month life expectancy. We wanted an instrument that would:

1. Elicit coping behavior and not focus solely upon defense mechanisms or pathological responses (Haan, 1977).
2. Simultaneously provide a clinician with a picture of a patient's self-

instructional patterns, metacognitive activity, and typical behavioral strategies when faced with cancer-specific tasks.
3. Be useful for initial diagnostic impressions as well as for ongoing therapy.
4. Assess problem solving as a significant cognitive activity.
5. Appear as educational and not as psychologically intrusive or ambiguous.
6. Be designed in a projective pictorial format so as to involve the examiner during the examination, therefore reducing the social distance with the patient.

To meet these criteria, a sequential model was applied. This meant that an initial sample of 163 cancer patients be followed over time in order to obtain basic descriptive data on such things as current concerns, patterns of adjustment, typical and predominant life tasks during cancer, successful and maladaptive coping strategies, and whether or not high-risk psychosocial groups could be identified early on in the course of the disease. A 3-year longitudinal effort was required before it was possible to design a tentative instrument and to conceptualize a practical course of psychosocial intervention. In analyzing our data, we used a sequential method, uncovering the life tasks and dilemmas facing newly diagnosed cancer patients, and then we created a projective instrument that could confront patients with specific and relevant issues.

As a cognitive instrument, the CPSP test assesses problem-solving strategies, self-instructions as they operate on the decision-making process, and shifts in cognitions relative to a developmental perspective. Each cancer dilemma is portrayed on two cards, the first of which has an accompanying vignette to structure the patient's task even further. In all cases, the first card depicts the problematic situation (e.g., fear or inability to confront a physician) and briefly discusses some of the important contingencies (e.g,. that Jane has just had a mastectomy and is receiving regular chemotherapy).

The second card is presented to the patient as a resolution card, but no one coping strategy is suggested. The resolution card just shows that the problem has been solved. The patient is asked to work on the presented task by "thinking or talking out loud," sharing perceptions, spontaneous imagery, alternative solutions, potential consequences of solutions, ways of redefining the initial problem, and probable obstacles in getting from the first card to the second. The second card helps the patient perceive that a resolution is at least possible (e.g., patient is now speaking with her physician).

Because each card was derived, in part, by the sequential method, we are able to evaluate coping effectiveness by comparing the patient's strategies to our original response evaluations and to knowledge of cancer adaptation patterns (Sobel & Worden, 1979; Weisman & Worden, 1976). Ipsative evaluation becomes more important when the CPSP test is used for an individual cognitive therapy program.

In the case of therapy, the test can serve as a vehicle for teaching problem solving and for evaluating coping (Spivack, Platt, & Shure, 1976). As a projective instrument, the CPSP test has many innovative applications within a therapy context because patients will respond differently, making use of the stimuli in their own creative way. However, the freedom that the projective test allows in this respect does not detract from the fact that each patient is responding to an empirically derived item that poses issues relevant to the cancer plight at very precise points in the course of the disease. In effect, the structured empirical basis for the instrument has not interfered with a flexibility in application, as traditional views might have predicted. If anything, patients appreciate the individual tailoring of assessment and therapeutic intervention.

The sequential method for designing projective instruments requires a programmatic research model in which problems are first identified, not assumed, on pilot samples. Responses are then enumerated and evaluated for long-term coping efficiency, and finally an instrument is integrated into the course of treatment from initial assessment to follow-up evaluations. The projective approach, as exemplified by the CPSP test, does not hinder behavioral methodology, but rather builds on the behavioral tradition by treating cognitions as developmentally based, interacting, and multidimensional processes that can be sampled in a semistructured manner (Sarason, 1979). Specificity of stimuli, and not random ambiguity (Epstein, 1966), is a prerequisite for ensuring reliability and validity in projective instruments.

Cognitive Variables and the Projective Assessment

The future of cognitive-behavior modification lies in its willingness to explore the psychological constructs of other disciplines and in its ability to avoid a dogmatic absolutism in theoretical speculation. There are positive signs that the field is aware of potential roadblocks and is attempting to match a commitment to clinical technique with an openness in paradigm integration. As I suggested previously, cognitive and developmental psychology are rich resources for such an integration. There is evidence in the recent literature that cognitive behaviorists are indeed heading in this direction, recognizing the utility of multiple perspectives (Arnkoff, 1980; Bower, 1978; Mahoney, 1977; Meichenbaum & Asarnow, 1978; Sarason, 1979). Sarason (1979) appropriately noted the "lacunae" in cognitive therapy, calling for an extension of the "clinical scope of cognitive behavioral methods" (p. 234).

The theory and practice of psychological assessment offer an ideal arena for considering the feasibility of alternative hypotheses and dialectical changes. Because projective assessment has received attention from a multifaceted array of disciplines, it is advantageous that the cognitive therapist consider projective instruments as available techniques when experimenting with paradigm refinement.

For the purpose of illustration, I would like to present a few examples of how a cognitive assessment of a patient's internal dialogue can be combined with an assessment of other cognitive variables by means of the projective test. The basic assumption being made is that our internal dialogues, or self-instructions, are part of a more global, interacting, and developmentally based set of cognitive processes. The word "process" implies a dynamic model of cognitions, which constantly change through time. Therefore, it is irrelevant to speak of a patient's field dependence in the traditional trait sense of the variable. What is more useful is a discussion of a field-dependent cognitive response made by a patient to a specific life task at a specific time, as manifested through a projected internal dialogue. In Wallace's (1966, 1967) sense, we would be assessing a cognitive "response capability," a so-called unit of skill, which is field-dependent in relation to one specific interaction of cognition and a life task. The field-dependent response could then be scored for effectiveness, based on a preexisting normative sequential analysis, and for likelihood of being produced, on an idiographic basis.

Assuming that a projective instrument has been derived sequentially, it will elicit a pool of data relative to a given patient's cognitive coping repertoire. Patients are requested to respond to the task stimuli and then typically produce a series of projected self-statements, problem solutions, situational inferences, metacognitions, evaluations, and so forth. All of these constitute the problem-specific internal dialogue, and not an X ray of personality functioning.

From a purely content point of view, the productions can be scored on such dimensions as probable effectiveness in solving the particular task, number of positive self-references, omission of pictorial information, or, for example, the predominant affects perceived and projected onto the structured task. Until just recently, such a content approach has prevailed in cognitive-behavior therapies and assessment. Rational–emotive assessment, with its major emphasis on irrational beliefs, represents a content methodology. A more sophisticated and broader spectrum cognitive analysis is inhibited, which, in turn, generates further diagnostic reductionism. On the other hand, I am suggesting that we redirect cognitive-behavior assessment into a *structured* channel that integrates field theory, the Clark tradition initiated by Werner, Piagetian notions, operant theory, and many of the ego-psychological approaches to adaptive and self-determined coping. The recent volume by Forgus and Schulman (1979) lays an excellent foundation for this redirection in clinical assessment.

Diagnostic Questions

There is a plethora of cognitive variables under exploration, many of which incorporate developmental and process notions without absorbing orthodox psychoanalytic views (Arnkoff, 1980; Forgus & Schulman, 1979; Goldstein & Blackman, 1978; Mahoney, 1974; Santostefano, 1978; Wachtel, 1977; Wapner *et al.*, 1973). The following diagnostic questions are examples of cognitive structural inquiries that can be made in relation to projective data and that seem to follow the basic assumptions discussed previously in this chapter. Again, one should keep in mind that the goal is to move away from viewing a self-instruction as just a self-instruction. Our purpose is to obtain both a cognitive and psychosituational context for the patient's covert dialogue and therefore to understand the fluctuating and interacting patterns of cognitive controls that lead to coping behavior. The diagnostic questions are:

1. Does the patient's internal dialogue shift attention from one stimulus to another (Feffer, 1967) or does it remain fixed (i.e., decentering)?

2. What style or course does the decentering process take during the projective assessment?

3. Is there a certain content of projected thoughts that never permits adequate decentering and information seeking?

4. Do the patient's self-instructions and metacognitions reinforce conceptual differentiation (cognitive control) and therefore lead to an awareness of multiple categories of the task stimuli (Gardner, 1962)?

5. Does the projected internal dialogue show signs of scanning? For example, does the patient self-instruct himself or herself to check what has been solved or perceived (Santostefano, 1978)?

6. Does the self-instructional style demonstrate field articulation as the projective card increases in stimulus complexity and simulated adjustive demands?

7. Is a projected, self-instructional sequence of thoughts cognitively complex (Crockett, 1965), and does it facilitate multiple inferences for one set of pictorial information?

8. Does the projected story succeed in solving the problem or task? If so, are potential obstacles analyzed concomitantly, with a recognition of means–end behavior (Spivack *et al.*, 1976)?

9. Does the patient project a story that acknowledges the need for further information and assimilation (Schroder, Driver, & Streufert, 1967)?

10. How selective are the self-instructions? Are they overly precise in their attentional nature (Flavell, 1977)?

11. Is there a linguistic pattern to the projected internal dialogue that leads to arbitrary inferences, overgeneralizations, or magnifications of the pictorial data (Beck, 1976)?

12. What changes occur in various cognitive structures as the patient continues his or her projected internal dialogue in response to pictorial tasks of increasing stress? Does the patient's style become more or less complex, and is the complexity correlated with a shift in positive or negative self-instructions?

13. Is effective problem solving on the card task inhibited when we vary the level of informational complexity (Schroder *et al.,* 1967)?

14. What is the most prevalent locus of control in the projected dialogue? How does it shift as tasks change?

15. Are there problem-solving deficits that are reinforced by a particular self-instructional style?

16. If a projective card is employed solely as a problem-solving test, then where does the projected internal dialogue interfere with the processing of information?

17. Do the task-specific self-instructions consider prior self-instructions and outcome?

18. Does the projected story show cognitive flexibility and elasticity in terms of recognizing the feasibility of redefining an initial problem (Weisman & Sobel, 1979)?

19. To what degree does the internal dialogue acknowledge environmental contingencies and interactional influences that could occur?

20. Are certain self-instructional patterns suggestive of earlier developmental cognitive processes? For example, does a particular projected story to a particular task show signs of concrete thinking in a Piagetian sense? Are there rapid shifts from one phase-appropriate style to another?

As directly implied by many of these questions, there is much heuristic utility for integrating Piagetian notions into a projective–cognitive analysis (Moos, 1974). Although he did not employ a sequentially structured projective technique, Feffer (1967; Feffer & Suchotliff, 1966) attempted to apply Piaget's concept of cognitive decentering in a study of interpersonal behavior. The primary purpose was to evaluate a subject's capacity to shift cognitive focus from one perspective to another. A role-taking task was used, which required the subject to project a story onto an ambiguous picture and then to retell the story as if he or she were another TAT figure within the picture. The decentering skill—or the ability to consider multiple perspectives simultaneously and to remain cognitively "elastic"—manifests itself quite readily in a patient's self-instructional style as we increase the complexity of the viewpoints depicted on the projective card. The inability to decenter represents a form of developmentally primitive cognition.

Thus our test protocol can observe a patient's cognitive maturational shifts from one task to another and how these correlate with changes in the internal dialogue or metacognitions. This type of developmental perspective does not make inferences about the past, but rather studies how a current self-instructed cognitive style recapitulates in the present a less adaptive structure, strategy, or method of problem solving. The projective card facilitates an observation of these fluctuations while controlling the environmental stimuli through simulation.

By accepting a cognitive–developmental perspective for self-instructional behavior, we are inexorably led to acknowledge that adults, like children, progress and regress through various information-processing phases, each setting limits on the processes of perceptual selectivity (Gibson, 1969), complexity integration, inference generation, environment scanning, or reversibility. We cannot assume that, once a certain self-instructional style or hierarchy is reached in relation to a task, fluctuations or shifts will not occur. It is more likely that the developmental characteristics of an internal dialogue will show many shifts, which in time will affect adaptation and problem-solving effectiveness.

For example, on certain similar task cards, a patient may demonstrate a self-instructional process that consistently is unable to balance assimilation and accommodation. The internal dialogue and subsequent coping behavior could proceed by a rigid insistence on not recognizing new card data and instead focus on the simulated dilemma through prior schemata only. Many behavioral disorders as well as traditional personality diagnoses can be understood from a continuum of hypo–hyper assimilation versus hypo–hyper accommodation, as reflected in the patient's projected covert processes. We are then able to ask questions such as the following: (1) Can the patient adopt a personally untested self-instruction and then assimilate or attend to novel task data? (2) Can he or she recover developmentally after a period of cognitive regression? or (3) What task solutions are derived when assimilation of information is inhibited by a rigid metacognitive pattern, and how does this correlate with self-efficacy, affect, self-control, and overall coping? In approaching these assessment and clinical issues, it is essential that we reexamine some of the basic child cognitive research (Flavell, 1977; Harter, 1977).

Indeed, there are many additional diagnostic questions that could be asked during a projective–cognitive analysis. My intention has been to demonstrate the possible interactions of cognitive variables, developmental notions, and cognitive-behavior modification when analyzing task-specific projective material. Therefore, when a patient responds to a card with a statement such as "I'm not sure what she is feeling, but I suppose she is concerned about telling her family what is happening and is telling herself to seek out information" and so forth, it is important that we view the production on both a content and a structural level. Structurally, our goal is to understand the cognitive pathways and how a given dialogue functions within a larger cognitive system.

A typical section from a structurally oriented diagnostic report might read as follows:

> Mrs. CBM approached the simulated projective task of confronting the physician in a very focused, step-by-step manner. She sought out information, clearly defined the presented problem, generated a number of alternative solutions, and then carefully evaluated the pros and cons of each solution. Her internal dialogue manifested many positive self-statements, especially when she would succeed in recognizing potential obstacles to solving the task. The tasks were appropriately and effectively scanned for perceptual accuracy, enabling the pa-

tient to organize and reorganize, to differentiate and articulate relationships among the data she worked upon. Global-like conclusions and inferences did not appear until the patient had examined the specifics in each dimension of the task. In no way did she have difficulty decentering from her own perspectives or the task information, and her ongoing self-instructions consistently reinforced such a pattern. Problem solving was not undertaken at the expense of precluding a recognition of affect. Mrs. CBM's approach to each step of the task always considered probable emotions occurring in the characters portrayed on the projective card. Developmentally speaking, the patient integrated prior steps and was capable of self-controlled cognitive shifting. Flexibility in cognitive style seems to be a prominent skill for Mrs. CBM when she is requested to confront the specific task of how to assert oneself in the presence of a physician. Future and regular assessments will monitor any changes in the patient's cognitive processes. At present, there is no evidence to suggest significant coping deficits when approaching this particular task.

This type of report has the advantage of specificity without totally ignoring some implications for generalization. However, its main purpose is to circumvent trait inferences while describing, in depth, a patient's cognitive behavior toward a structured life task. Taken over a period, the clinician is able to obtain a cognitive–developmental picture of the patient and to monitor any therapeutic changes. It is important to reemphasize the need for multiple assessments if we are to maintain the developmental and process point of view. Self-instructions change, and, subsequently, each interaction between cognition and the environment leads to a new process influencing adaptation and coping.

Conclusion and Summary

Throughout this chapter I have tried to communicate the basic point that useful innovations in assessment techniques go hand in hand with theoretical integration and paradigm refinement. Cognitive therapy and assessment are relative newcomers to clinical psychology and the behavior modification tradition. In order to inhibit a unidimensional and hence self-limiting model from evolving, it seems necessary to explore our psychological neighbors housed in the developmental, cognitive, and ego-analytic spheres. Before too long, it may be quite possible to view cognitive therapy as the clinical *Australopithecus* (i.e., the missing link) of ego-psychoanalytic–developmental theory. In many respects, cognitive therapy and the type of projective–cognitive assessment presented here are logical clinical extensions of the neo-Freudian school.

As redefined in this chapter, projective–cognitive analysis is one among many new emerging techniques (Kendall & Korgeski, 1979; Meichenbaum, 1977) for assesssing a patient's internal dialogue. It is one dimension of a complete behavioral assessment; it is not a psychohistological sample of per-

is true for the entire cognitive theory discipline (Kendall & Korgeski, 1979). Cognitions and the structural properties of human information processing pose immense challenges for the researcher and the psychometrician. Sequential and functional assessment models are not panaceas, but they do offer tentative outlines for continuing our investigation of innovative assessment methods. The empirical sophistication of cognitive assessment also lies in its willingness, as I have highlighted, to assimilate and integrate ideas from other psychological disciplines, including those traditionally associated with psychoanalysis (Sarason, 1979; Wachtel, 1977). The projective instrument serves as one medium from which to attempt such paradigm integration.

Ultimately, it is our professional self-instructions and metacognitions that will determine the success of this venture. The theoretical flexibility of hypotheses relies heavily on a multilevel, process sequence in our own internal dialogue. Reliable cognitive instrumentation cannot but recapitulate our ongoing cognitive self-instructions as we function as clinical psychologists and researchers. By permitting paradigmatic shifts in our daily scientific perspectives, we will inevitably increase the chances of construct redefinition and discovery.

ACKNOWLEDGMENT

Gratitude and appreciation is extended to Melvin D. Rosenthal, PhD, for teaching me to cope creatively with my own cognitive projections, regressions, and progressions.

References

Arnkoff, D. Psychotherapy from the perspective of cognitive theory. In M. J. Mahoney (Ed.), *Cognition and clinical science.* New York: Plenum Press, 1980.

Beck, A. *Cognitive therapy and the emotional disorders.* New York: International Universities Press, 1976.

Bersoff, D. Silk purses into sow's ears: The decline of psychological testing and a suggestion for its redemption. *American Psychologist,* 1973, *28,* 892–899.

Bower, G. H. Contacts of cognitive psychology with social learning theory. *Cognitive Therapy and Research,* 1978, *2,* 123–146.

Cone, J., & Hawkins, R. *Behavioral assessment: New directions in clinical psychology.* New York: Brunner/Mazel, 1977.

Crockett, W. Cognitive complexity and impression formation. In B. A. Maher (Ed.), *Progress in experimental personality research* (Vol. 2). New York: Academic Press, 1965.

Deitz, S. Current status of applied behavior analysis: Science versus technology. *American Psychologist,* 1978, *33,* 805–814.

Epstein, S. Some theoretical considerations on the nature of ambiguity and the use of stimulus dimensions in projective techniques. *Journal of Consulting Psychology,* 1966, *30,* 183–192.

Feffer, M. Symptom expression as a form of primitive decentering. *Psychological Review,* 1967, *74,* 16–28.

Feffer, M., & Suchotliff, L. Decentering implications of social interaction. *Journal of Personality and Social Psychology,* 1966, *4,* 415–423.

Fischer, C. T. The testee as co-evaluator. *Journal of Counseling Psychology,* 1970, *17,* 30–36.

Flavell, J. *Cognitive development*. Englewood Cliffs, N.J.: Prentice-Hall, 1977.

Forgus, R., & Shulman, B. *Personality: A cognitive view*. Englewood Cliffs, N.J.: Prentice-Hall, 1979.

Fulkerson, S. Some implications of the new cognitive theory of projective tests. *Journal of Consulting Psychology*, 1965, *29*, 191–197.

Gardner, R. W. Cognitive controls in adaptation: Research and measurement. In S. Messick & J. Ross (Eds.), *Measurement in personality and cognition*. New York: Wiley, 1962.

Gibson, E. J. *Principles of perceptual learning and development*. New York: Appleton-Century-Crofts, 1969.

Goldfried, M. R., & D'Zurilla, T. J. A behavioral-analytic model for assessing competence. In C. D. Spielberger (Ed.), *Current topics in clinical and community psychology*. New York: Academic Press, 1969.

Goldfried, M. R., & Kent, R. Traditional versus behavioral personality assessment: A comparison of methodological and theoretical assumptions. *Psychological Bulletin*, 1972, *77*, 409–420.

Goldfried, M. R., & Sprafkin, J. N. *Behavioral personality assessment*. Morristown, N.J.: General Learning Press, 1974.

Goldstein, K. M., & Blackman, S. Assessment of cognitive style. In P. McReynolds (Ed.), *Advances in psychological assessment*. San Francisco: Jossey-Bass, 1978.

Haan, N. *Coping and defending*. New York: Academic Press, 1977.

Harter. S. A cognitive–developmental approach to children's expression of conflicting feelings and a technique to facilitate such expression in play therapy. *Journal of Consulting and Clinical Psychology*, 1977, *45*, 417–432.

Kendall, P., & Korgeski, G. Assessment and cognitive–behavioral intervention. *Cognitive Therapy and Research*, 1979, *3*, 1–21.

Kiesler, D. Some myths of psychotherapy research and the search for a paradigm. *Psychological Record*, 1966, *65*, 110–136.

Knutson, J. The new frontier of projective techniques. In J. Knutson (Ed.), *Handbook of political psychology*. San Francisco: Jossey-Bass, 1973.

Lazarus, R. Strategy for research in hypertension. *Journal of Human Stress*, 1978, *4*, 34–39.

Mahoney, M. *Cognitive and behavior modification*. Cambridge, Mass.: Ballinger, 1974.

Mahoney, M. J. Reflections on the cognitive-learning trend in psychotherapy. *American Psychologist*, 1977, *32*, 5–13.

Mash, E., & Terdal, L. (Eds). *Behavior-therapy assessment: Diagnosis, design, and evaluation*. New York: Springer, 1976.

Meichenbaum, D. *Cognitive-behavior modification: An integrative approach*. New York: Plenum Press, 1977.

Meichenbaum, D., & Asarnow, J. Cognitive-behavior modification and metacognitive development: Implications for the classroom. In P. Kendall & S. Hollon (Eds.), *Cognitive–behavioral intervention: Theory, research and procedure*. New York: Academic Press, 1978.

Mischel, W. *Personality and assessment*. New York: Wiley, 1968.

Mischel, W. Direct versus indirect personality assessment: Evidence and implication. *Journal of Consulting and Clinical Psychology*, 1972, *38*, 319–324.

Mischel, W. On the future of personality assessment. *American Psychologist*, 1977, *4*, 246–254.

Moos, R. Psychological techniques in the assessment of adaptive behavior. In G. Coelho, D. Hamburg, & J. Adams (Eds.), *Coping and adaptation*. New York: Basic Books, 1974.

Murstein, B. *Theory and research in projective techniques*. New York: Wiley, 1963.

Santostefano, S. *A biodevelopmental approach to clinical child psychology: Cognitive controls and cognitive control therapy*. New York: Wiley, 1978.

Sarason, I. G. Three lacunae of cognitive therapy. *Cognitive Therapy and Research*, 1979, *3*, 223–235.

Schaefer, R. *Psychoanalytic interpretation in Rorschach testing*. New York: Grune & Stratton, 1954.

Scope of the Imagery Construct

Almost all references to imagery include the idea of a conscious experience that has some visual qualities but that occurs in the absence of the external stimulus that would normally give rise to such an experience. Most formal definitions of imagery do not restrict the term to exclusively visual experiences, however, but enlarge its range to include all conscious experiences with sensory qualities that occur in the absence of their normal empirical precursors. Thus references are made to auditory imagery, tactile imagery, olfactory imagery, and kinesthetic imagery, in addition to visual imagery. Imagery then becomes more broadly defined as quasi-sensory conscious experiences (Holt, 1972) or as quasi-perceptual experiences (Neisser, 1972). Because in everyday usage the word "image" strongly connotes the visual modality—a mental picture—the use of "image" in conjunction with the nonvisual senses sometimes leads to mild confusion, reflected by questions such as "How can I have a picture of an odor?" This type of confusion can be alleviated somewhat by thinking in terms of imaginery experiences rather than imagery experiences, the connotation for "imaginary" being less strongly visual.

Various conscious experiences have at one time or another been termed imaginal (see McKellar, 1972, for a discussion). Most of them have in common the awareness of sensory qualities in the absence of appropriate external stimuli, but beyond that common core, they differ in a host of other respects, some of which will be mentioned.

Imagery can be either static in the sense of a photograph or dynamic in the sense of a motion picture. Imaginal rehearsals or mental practice efforts represent deliberate attempts to use imaginal processes in the pursuit of goals, whereas imaginal experiences such as dreams, hallucinations, and fantasies seem to occur without any volitional effort at all. Klinger (1971) has referred to this distinction as the "operantness" or "respondentness" of the experience. Imaginal experiences can be from a phenomenological perspective, in which the imaginer is a participant in the imagined activity, or from an objective perspective, in which the imaginer is more of an observer, detached from the imagined scene. This brief list of kinds of imaginary experiences is doubtlessly incomplete, but it should serve to illustrate the point that there is a wide variety of conscious experiences that have been termed imaginal. The interested reader could probably enlist his or her own imaginary skills to expand the list.

A Working Definition

This chapter is about the assessment of imagery from the standpoint of the clinical psychologist, both the practitioner and the investigator. Thus the working definition will be at the level of the previously discussed general meaning of imagery in order to encompass the different imaginal processes that are of interest to the clinician. "Imaginary experiences" will refer, at a minimum, to awareness of sensorylike qualities in the absence of environmental stimuli appropriate to the sensation. This will usually involve awareness of visual qualities, but not always. Along with the minimum requirement of sensory awareness, imaginary experiences may also include thought segments that are part of, or that occur within the context of, the imaginal sensory awareness. Thoughts that are *about* the imaginary experience, or that are evaluative of it as an experience, are excluded from the definition.

For example, suppose that I imagine myself lecturing to a large audience in a large auditorium and, as part of that imaginary scene, experience thoughts such as "Why aren't they listening? I must be boring." Under the proposed definition these thoughts would be included as part of the imaginary experience because they are thoughts that would be appropriate to the imaginal context and are, in a sense, a component of the total imaginary experience rather than a response to it. Assume that, while imagining this scene, I also experience thoughts of the following type: "Boy, that's really a vivid image I'm having. I must be more anxious about that lecture than I thought." These would not be considered imaginal because they are about the imaginary experience rather than part of it. With respect to imagery assessment, it is important to remember that, because a wide range of conscious activity is included in this broadly defined realm, there is probably not a single, all-purpose assessment procedure.

This working definition is based on an assumption about the nature of imaginal experiences, and of cognition generally, that should be made explicit. Imagining is assumed to be a constructive act, something that a person actively does. This view is opposed to the historical conception according to which imagery is a mental entity or product that a person has inside his or her mind and which is perceived with the mind's eye. The position taken here is consistent with that of several recent theorists (Klinger, 1971; Lang, 1977; Neisser, 1976; Sarbin, 1972; Lang, Note 1). It is important to make this assumption explicit, because in spite of relatively widespread agreement on this point at the theoretical level, many of us are still prone to adopt the older metaphor in our more relaxed thinking about the subject. Failure to keep the distinction clear can lead to problems in designing and choosing assessment procedures for imaginal experiences.

Goals of Imagery Assessment

The dimensions of a person's imaginal processes that are assessed and the approach used are partly determined by the goals of the assessment. Imagery assessments are usually undertaken to obtain information about one of three general areas: naturally occurring imaginal processes, therapeutic imagery, or individual differences in imagery ability.

Assessment of Naturally Occurring Imaginal Processes. A clinician may

investigator. The particular dimensions of imagery that are assessed depend on the purposes of the assessment and on hypotheses about associations between dimensions of imagery and behavioral outcomes.

Qualitative Dimensions. The most commonly assessed qualitative dimension is vividness of imagery. The rationale for assessing vividness is usually of the form that the more vivid the imagery, the better the performance on the imagery-mediated task or treatment. In fact, vividness is often almost equated with imagery ability—that is, good imagers equal vivid imagers. "Vividness" generally refers to the verisimilitude of the imaginal representations. Beyond this general sense of the term, however, there are several specific meanings of imagery vividness. For example, it can refer to a quality of visual clarity, sharpness, or resolution similar to the quality controlled by the focusing mechanism on a camera. Vividness can also refer to the sensory richness or sensory impact of the imaginary experience. Klinger (1978*a*) uses the term "sensory saturation" to describe this meaning of vividness and presents data suggesting that the qualities of clarity and sensory saturation may jointly define vividness. Sarbin (1972) proposes that vividness reflects degree of involvement in imaginal activity. Lang (Note 1) defines vividness as the degree to which perceptual response operations and other response systems are engaged by the imaginary activity.

This brief list of meanings of vividness demonstrates that it is not always clear what is meant by the term. The implication of this state of affairs for the assessment of vividness is that assessment techniques should be geared to the meaning one assigns to the term. If vividness is thought of as degree of involvement in imaginings, then ratings of vividness defined as visual clarity may not be appropriate.

The other most frequently researched qualitative dimension of imaginary experience is controllability. "Controllability" refers to the degree to which a person can intentionally guide his or her imaginary experience in desired directions. Hypotheses regarding this dimension have usually suggested that the ability to use imagery in a deliberate and controlled manner should be associated with improved performance on imagery-mediated tasks and treatments (Richardson, 1972). By far the most commonly used assessment instrument for controllability is the Gordon Test of Visual Imagery Control (Richardson, 1969), a 12-item questionnaire about subjects' ability to generate and manipulate specific images.

Vividness and controllability are easily the most commonly assessed qualitative dimensions of imaginary experiences. Additional qualitative dimensions that have been investigated include absorption in imagery (Singer & Antrobus, 1972), auditoriness (Klinger, 1978*b*; Singer & Antrobus, 1972), and detailedness and directedness (Klinger, 1978*b*). There are other qualitative dimensions that have been investigated, but the ones mentioned here account for most of the published research.

Content Dimensions. Imaginary experiences can also be assessed on a wide variety of content dimensions. By far the most frequently investigated group of content dimensions is that characterizing the affective tone of imaginary experiences. In particular, investigators have been interested in assessing the amount of negative emotions, such as anxiety, depression, guilt, and hostility, that is suggested by the content of daydreams, fantasies, and dreams. Content analysis has been the most frequently used means of assessing these dimensions, though questionnaires such as Singer's Imaginal Processes Inventory also index these kinds of dimensions. For an expanded list of these types of dimensions, the reader is referred to some of the content analysis systems used for assessing dream reports (Gottschalk & Gleser, 1969; Hall & Van de Castle, 1966).

A large group of content dimensions is defined simply by the thematic topics of the imaginal experience. For example, imaginary experiences can be about sexual, heroic, or achievement-related topics. The list of potential topical dimensions is limited only by the particular reasons for conducting the assessment.

Finally, imaginal content can be characterized according to its relationship to the imager's concurrent environmental situation or to potentially realizable external situations. Included in this group would be stimulus independence–dependence (Singer, 1974), and fancifulness and bizarreness versus realism (Klinger, 1978a, 1978b).

Selected Approaches to Imagery Assessment in Clinically Oriented Research

This section catalogs the different kinds of approaches to imagery assessment, mentions the best known examples of each kind, and indicates the typical uses to which information obtained from each approach has been put. Occasional reference is made to empirical data relevant to a particular assessment procedure, but no attempt is made to review the empirical literature comprehensively. Important reviews of this literature are referenced for the interested reader.

Self-Reports

Imaginary experiences are subjective phenomena directly observable by a population of one. As such, subjects' self-reports about aspects of their imaginary experiences represent an important source of data around which several assessment approaches have been designed.

Subjective Ratings. Asking subjects to rate dimensions of their imaginal productions on anchored scales is the most frequently used approach to imagery assessment, and vividness of imagery is the dimension most often assessed by this method. The Betts Questionnaire on Mental Imagery (QMI) is

according to whether or not they successfully formed the requested image. The TVIC is largely used as an ability measure to predict performance on imagery-mediated tasks. In a factor analytic study both the QMI and the TVIC loaded on the same factor (DiVesta *et al.,* 1971). Hiscock (1978) found significant correlations between the two measures. White *et al.* (1977) concluded that the evidence for a correlation between the two tests is variable and interpreted this to mean that the two tests tap different aspects of the same basic process. In one clinically oriented study the TVIC did not successfully predict success with desensitization therapy (McLemore, 1972). There is some evidence that TVIC scores successfully predict performance on motor tasks following mental practice sessions (Rawlings & Rawlings, 1974) and on mental rotation and mental comparison tasks (see review by Ernest, 1977). The Gordon test loaded on the same social desirability factor as the QMI in the DiVesta *et al.* (1971) factor analytic study, but other evidence suggests that the TVIC is relatively free of such bias (Ernest, 1977).

Two major imagery questionnaires besides the TVIC are Singer's Imaginal Processes Inventory (IPI) (Singer & Antrobus, 1972) and Paivio's Individual Differences Questionnaire (IDQ) (Paivio, 1971). These instruments differ from both the QMI and the TVIC in that they consist of questions about subjects' normal thinking habits and styles rather than about images subjects are asked to generate. The IPI is an extensive inventory that probes a wide variety of dimensions of subjects' normal daydreaming patterns. Singer and Antrobus (1972) factor analyzed responses to this inventory and were able to identify some basic daydreaming patterns. Some investigators have chosen to use only those scales specifically relevant to imagery (e.g., visual imagery in daydreams, auditory imagery in daydreams) rather than the entire inventory (Fusella, 1973; Starker, 1974*a*, 1974*b*).

The IDQ is a 86-item true–false instrument that inquires about normal thinking patterns and preferences. Both an imagery score and a verbal score are derived from it. The scales are usually used to classify people as visualizers or verbalizers according to their preferred thinking styles. Paivio developed the scale as part of an imagery ability test battery that he used in some verbal learning studies (Ernest & Paivio, 1971). The imagery scale of the IDQ has been shown to correlate with QMI imagery scores, and some investigators have recommended its use as a measure of imagery vividness (Hiscock, 1978; Richardson, 1977). Hiscock (1978) has revised the questionnaire by eliminating a few items on the basis of an item analysis and by changing the response format to a Likert scale.

Performance Tests

The assessment approaches grouped in this category involve tasks that either intuitively seem to require some kind of imagery mediation or on which subjects are instructed to use an imaginal mediation strategy. Performance differences are assumed to reflect differences in skill at using imaginal processes. The appeal of this approach is that it provides more objective measures of imagery ability and avoids some of the problems inherent in self-report approaches. In spite of several attempts to find a performance measure of imaginal ability that would show some clinical utility (Anderson, 1975; Danaher & Thoresen, 1972; McLemore, 1976; Rehm, 1973; Rimm & Bottrell, 1969), no clear candidate has emerged. Nevertheless, these types of measures have been used in imagery studies in other areas of psychology (Ernest, 1977), and, as reflected by the preceding citations, they have generated interest among clinically oriented investigators.

Spatial Reasoning Tests. This group of performance tests generally requires mental or imaginal manipulation of geometric forms. Space Relations from the Differential Aptitudes Test (Bennett, Seashore, & Wesman, 1959), the Minnesota Paper Form Board (Likert & Quasha, 1941), and Flags (Thurstone & Jeffrey, 1956) are examples of three frequently used tests of this type. Ernest (1977) reviewed their use in studies on verbal learning, memory, and perception and concluded that there is some relationship between the abilities assessed by these tests and the imaginal abilities involved in these aspects of cognitive functioning.

Memory Tests. Imagery has been used as a mnemonic aid at least since the time of ancient Greene (e.g., the method of loci). Performance tests of imagery ability based on this phenomenon are generally of two types: memory for verbal materials and memory for visual materials. The first type is based on portions of Paivio's (1971) extensive research program on the role of imagery mediation in verbal learning. His research suggests that, especially for concrete nouns, imagery mediation is associated with improved recognition memory and free recall. Three separate clinically oriented investigations of relationships among potential imagery measures included a measure of performance on paired-associate learning tasks under imagery instructions (Danaher & Thoresen, 1972; Rehm, 1973; Rimm & Bottrell, 1969). The conclusion from all three is that this approach does not hold much promise as a generally useful objective measure of imagery ability.

Memory for briefly presented visual stimuli has also been used as a measure of imagery ability. For example, Danaher and Thoresen (1972) used a pattern reconstruction task originally developed by Sheehan (1966). Matrices of geometric forms are briefly presented on a screen, and, after working on a delay task, subjects are asked to reconstruct the pattern using blocks. No significant results were obtained with the measure in this study. Rimm and Bottrell (1969) used a similar approach that involved memory for the location of items in a domestic scene. Low, but significant, correlations were obtained between this measure and recall improvement and measures of respiratory change during imagery.

A more developed measure of the same type was reported by Marks (1972). Subjects are presented slides of sets of either unrelated objects or

of information useful for answering different questions, and that methods appropriate to each type of datum should be developed and refined.

Imagery Assessment by Content Analysis of Narrative Reports

The approach to imagery assessment presented in this chapter involves the content analysis of descriptive reports of imaginal activity. Content analysis has a long history as a research methodology in the social sciences in general (Holsti, 1969), and in psychotherapy research in particular (Marsden, 1971). Used in conjunction with psychophysiological indexes of rapid eye movements (REMs), it has been a major tool in the exploration of an important category of imaginal activity, dreams (Gottschalk & Gleser, 1969; Hall & Van de Castle, 1966; Rechtschaffen, 1967). The theoretical perspective and supporting data that led to the approach presented here are given first.

Theoretical Perspective

Conceptions of Imagery from Cognitive Psychology. The content analysis system presented here was developed in an effort to explore the hypothesis that the amount of detail included in narrative reports of imaginal experiences might be a useful index of the quality of imaginal activity. This hypothesis was prompted by two recent theoretical thrusts in cognitive psychology: the propositional interpretation of imaginal activity and Ulric Neisser's recent theorizing on the nature of perception and cognition.

In cognitive psychology circles, the key issue toward which the propositional interpretation of imaginal activity is directed is the question of the form in which knowledge is stored or represented. (This discussion is based on the articles by Pylyshyn, 1973, and Kieras, 1978.) Stated simply, the argument is whether information is stored in quasi-sensory formats such as imaginal and verbal codes or in a single, more abstract, common format. Neither position denies the existence of the conscious experience of imagery. Rather, there is disagreement about whether the information that one is aware of while imagining is stored in an imaginal form or in some alternate form.

The alternative that has been proposed is that the information is stored in a propositional format. "Propositions" are thought of as informational units containing knowledge about meanings, relations, concepts, and properties. Simple propositions can be thought of as consisting of two concepts or properties linked by a relationship. For example, the statement "The man is fat" consists of the concept "man" and the property "fat" linked by the relationship *"is."* A group of simple propositions can be joined in network fashion to represent all of the information contained in an image or imaginary experience. The proponents of the propositional position explicitly emphasize that propositional representations should not be thought of as semantic in nature, despite the similarity of their model to the idea of semantic networks and the fact that words must be used to communicate the idea. According to the propositional interpretation, it is knowledge of the *meanings* and the *relationships* communicated by words and pictures that is stored.

The propositional representations underlying imaginal experiences are thought of as being more analogous to descriptions of the original stimulus situations than to pictures of them, in that a description contains information *about* the objects and relationships in a picture. This implies that images of different quality ("quality" referring here to degree of concordance between an image and its external counterpart) would be generated by propositional networks that differed in the amount of descriptive detail or information they contained. One way of assessing the quality of imaginal experiences would be to follow this line of reasoning in reverse. That is, use the relative amount of detail that people can report from their imaginal experience as an index of the quality of the underlying representation. (Lang, 1977, made the same suggestion on the basis of this literature.) Although this is a self-report approach and is prey to all of the problems inherent in them, it might represent a more direct means of assessing a functionally important dimension of imaginal activity (i.e., ability to include detail) than self-report approaches such as ratings and questionnaires about general thinking habits.

The second source of ideas for the present approach is the conception of imaginal activity contained in Neisser's recent theorizing about the nature of perceptual processes (Neisser, 1976). He proposes that perception involves an interaction of cognitive, behavioral, and environmental feedback factors. The cognitive factors are thought of as schemata that "anticipate" the general form of the information to be perceived. Within this model, imaginal activity is conceptualized as the manipulation of anticipatory schemata in the absence of new perceptual information appropriate to the manipulated schemata. As Neisser (1976) states,

> The experience of having an image is just the inner aspect of a readiness to perceive the imagined object, and differences in the nature and quality of people's images reflect differences in the kind of information they are prepared to pick up. (p. 131)

Even more directly relevant to the present approach, Neisser (1976) states that "a description of a visual image is a description of what one is ready to see" (p. 168).

The implications of Neisser's view of imaginal activity for the assessment of that activity are similar to those derived from the propositional approach: imaginal constructions may be qualitatively differentiated according to the information people can report from them. The principal difference between the two is that Neisser's conceptualization seems to underline the importance of the *kind* of information represented in the imaginal activity, and

detail that is of interest varies according to the specific clinical or research purposes, but the amount of detail reported seems to be a widely used index of quality. One reason for this may be that the number of variables available to the clinician and researcher for influencing the quality of clients' imagery is limited. Techniques such as relaxation, reduction of extraneous stimulation, assumption of a supine or reclining position, and adoption of a first-person participant attitude are other widely used aids, but none of these provides as direct a means of assessing and manipulating the imaginal activity as the descriptive report of the imager and the amount of detail he or she includes.

Data from four widely dispersed areas of research on imaginal processes provide even further support for the assumption of a close relationship between descriptive detail and quality of imaginal activity. Haber and Haber (1964) used the amount and accuracy of detail that children could report from memory images as a criterion for differentiating eidetic from noneidetic children. Visual stimuli were presented for 30 seconds each; after their removal, subjects were asked if they could still see the stimulus and to describe what they saw as completely as possible. The reports of 8% of the children were qualitatively discontinuous with those of the others on several measures, indicating the presence of eidetic imagery.

As part of a large-scale project investigating the determinants and dimensions of naturalistic thought content, Klinger (1978b) obtained thought samples from subjects both in and out of the laboratory by having them report their mental contents at random intervals and then rate them on a number of dimensions. Reporting only on the variables of interest here, subjective ratings of detailedness of imaginal thought content were significantly correlated with both visualness and controllability of thought content. Detailedness also was the only imagery variable from the thought sample ratings that correlated significantly with Betts's QMI imagery scores.

Antrobus, Fein, Jordan, Ellman, and Arkin (1978) reported that visual imagery ratings of dreams by subjects were significantly related to a visual imagery score based on the total number of concrete nouns, visual modifiers, action verbs, and spatial prepositions that were included in subjects' reports of dream content.

Finally, Kazdin (1979) investigated the influence of elaborations of imaginal scenes on the efficacy of covert modeling in the treatment of nonassertive behavior. (This study was based on earlier post hoc findings obtained from narrative reports of imagery!) Subjects instructed to elaborate scenes beyond the script (i.e., add their own detail) demonstrated greater improvement on self-report and role-playing tests than either a group of yoked controls or a group who imagined only the scripted scenes. Yoked controls received the elaborated scenes of the scene elaboration group. Kazdin concluded that *active* elaborating of scenes containing basic elements appropriate to the behaviors being learned was the best treatment combination. With respect to the present argument, this report suggests that encouraging construction of more detailed and personalized imaginal productions is associated with improved treatment outcome. The mechanism through which this effect is achieved is, of course, left unspecified by Kazdin's results, but he speculates that involvement on the part of the subject may be one possibility.

The information presented in this section from theoretical papers, empirical studies, and clinical techniques provides tentative support for the idea that descriptive detail may be a useful index of quality of imaginal activity. Content analysis of verbal reports of the content of imaginal activity is the most appropriate methodological approach for assessing the amount of detail included. In the following section, I shall examine some of the problems inherent in using verbal reports of conscious experiences as data and some of the issues that must be confronted in using content analysis as a methodology.

Issues in the Use of Verbal Reports of Conscious Experience as Data

There are undeniable problems with accepting verbal reports of cognitive activity as data in scientific investigations. However, there is almost no substitute for relying on verbal reports to some extent because of the kinds of information about mental content that are available through them. Nonetheless, I do not propose that verbal reports should constitute the only form of data about cognitive activity in general, or about imaginal activity in particular. Physiological data, especially, can be extremely valuable, as Lang's research and that of others has shown (McGuigan & Schoonover, 1972; Lang *et al.,* Note 2) and as the dream literature indicates. Stoyva and Kamiya (1968) provide an excellent discussion of the value and logic of the combined use of physiological data and verbal report for the study of conscious activity. With respect to verbal reports, therefore, it behooves cognitively oriented investigators to develop methods for obtaining and quantifying verbal reports that take into account the problems inherent in them.

Before discussing the real-world problems involved with using verbal reports, it may be instructive to think about what the ideal verbal report of imaginal activity would contain. Rather simply, the ideal verbal report would provide a perfectly accurate and comprehensive account of the content of imaginal activity. Nothing would be omitted, added, or distorted. Of course, such a perfect report is unobtainable when the object of the report is conscious content. Interestingly, however, it is probable that such a perfect report is unobtainable even when the report concerns an external object or event. As the cognitive psychologists have demonstrated, perception is selective (Neisser, 1967), and reports of perception are likely to be even more so. The particular difficulty for the investigator using verbal reports of imaginal processes is that he or she cannot monitor or evaluate the selection process. As a result, the investigator can never know for sure what has been omitted and what may have been added. The following sections provide an overview

involves a "second look" at the imaginary experience, during which additional information may be processed. Separating what was processed originally from what was added can be difficult.

Additional content information is also likely to be reported if the request for a report occurs after the imaginal experience and if it specifies the types of information desired (e.g., some of the more ineffable aspects). The request for specific types of information can constitute a demand for such, and then during the "second look" that type of information is added to the original experience. A solution to this type of contamination is to make the original instructions about giving verbal reports as complete as possible regarding the types of awarenesses that are to be reported and to make the later specific postimagination requests as simple and general as possible.

The second form of this type of contamination consists of the inclusion in the verbal report of comments that are *about* the content that was actually processed rather than part of it. For example, comments about the clarity or difficulty of the imaginal activity are properly treated as the reporter's evaluation of that activity as a cognitive act rather than as part of its content. Verbal reports also may contain passages that serve to explain a portion of the content that was imagined but that are not part of the content. These latter forms of addition are usually relatively easy to identify, whereas the former are, on the basis of verbal report alone, very difficult to determine.

Some methods for controlling the tendency of subjects to add information in their reports include the following: careful instructions to limit the report to what was experienced, specific cautions to be aware of and to resist the temptation to add to the report, training experiences focused on limiting the report to what was experienced, and postexperimental questionnaire items designed to assess the extent to which subjects believe they may have unwittingly supplemented their reports.

Verbal Ability. A final factor that may diminish confidence in the scientific utility of verbal reports of imaginal activity is the potentially confounding role of individual differences in verbal ability and, in particular, in verbal productivity. In other words, some people talk more than others. This factor could be especially troublesome when the measures one wishes to derive from the verbal report are based on word counts. In the present case these measures may reflect the loquaciousness of the individuals as much as the quality of their imaginal experiences.

Foulkes and Rechtschaffen (1964) provide some data indicating that the extent of the confounding may not be serious. Word counts from TAT protocols correlated $r = +.47 (p = .02)$ with word counts from dream reports obtained during REM periods but only $r = +.08$ with reports from non-REM periods. If verbal productivity were a confounding factor, it should have affected reports from both sleep periods rather than only one. Because one would expect more vivid and detailed dreams during the REM periods, this result is consistent with the idea that the word count measure reflects qualitative differences in the imaginal activities underlying them. In spite of this encouraging result, more research in this area is needed, especially some that focuses on word counts obtained from verbal reports of waking imaginal activity rather than from dreams.

Types of Content Analysis Systems

The investigator interested in adopting content analysis as an assessment approach must make decisions about a number of issues, the most fundamental of which is discussed here. More extensive discussions of this and related issues may be found in the following sources: Arkin, Antrobus, and Ellman (1978), Berelson (1952), Gottschalk and Gleser (1969), Hall and Van de Castle (1966), Holsti (1969), and Marsden (1971).

Following Holsti's definition (1969), "content analysis" is a research method designed for use when the content of communication is the basis of inference for the variables of interest. A content analysis system is a clearly articulated, systematic set of rules and procedures for classifying the contents of communication in a manner calculated to shed light on those variables.

Systems of classification or of coding can be differentiated according to the amount of inference required in the actual coding of the communication. "Classical" and "pragmatic" are terms that have been used to describe content analysis systems at opposite ends of this dimension (Berelson, 1952). Classical content analysis refers to more objective, low-inference systems in which content is coded into categories that are descriptive of its semantic or syntactic features. Higher reliability of coding is usually obtainable with these systems, probably because of the low levels of inference involved. The principal difficulty with classical content analysis systems is devising a procedure for collapsing the precise, easily coded categories into larger, more theoretically relevant categories, which can serve as the basis for inference. Failure to accomplish this may lead to more trivial and less theoretically interesting results than might be obtained with a more inferential system.

With pragmatic content analysis systems, content is coded into categories designed to reflect attributes of the communicator rather than of the communication. Coding involves making inferences about the psychological, instead of the semantic, meanings of the communication. Intercoder reliability is typically lower with these systems than with classical systems, though not necessarily prohibitively low, because of the greater probability of intercoder disagreement due to the amount of inference required. Lower reliabilities, of course, make it more difficult to obtain results in the first place and threaten the validity of any results that are obtained. Compared to classical systems, pragmatic systems may require more extensive training of coders and/or more psychologically sophisticated coders to achieve satisfactory reliabilities. As a result, these systems may be more expensive and more cumbersome to work with. On the other hand, the effort put into a carefully developed prag-

Table 2. (continued)

	Response propositions
Outcome of own behavior	References to outcomes of one's own behavior.
Posture	References to one's postural position (e.g., "I was sitting on . . . "). Excludes active forms such as "I sat down."
Sense organ adjustment	References to deliberate attending behavior or orienting of sense organs (e.g., watching, listening). Excludes introductory phrases such as "I saw . . . ."
Processor characteristics	References to properties of perception or cognitive processing during the imagined activity. Includes references to quality of perception (e.g., "The audience was a blur") and to characterizations of processing such as concentrating, forgetting, trying to remember.
Body parts	References to external parts of the body when they are involved in movement or are in a state of arousal.
Verbal behavior	Reports of verbalizations. Coded in same fashion as "verbal behavior of people."
Thoughts	References to the content of covertly experienced images or thoughts without the implication of its being spoken aloud in the imagined scene. Includes self-instructional phrases and evaluative phrases about people and events.
Emotions	References to emotions clearly labeled as such. No inference of emotion allowed.
Visceral parts	References to internal organs.
Bodily states	References to awarenesses of any type of bodily condition. May be either positive or negative (e.g., sweating, flushing, feeling good, feeling cool or hot).

some covering clauses or sentences. Coding is limited to information that is clearly descriptive of the content of the person's imaginal activity and excludes segments that either evaluate or explain that content, as well as a variety of phrases and references that are more a function of the way in which the subject communicates the information verbally than of the content of the imaginal activity.

The present system is very similar in concept and procedures to a content analysis system reported by Antrobus, Schnee, Lynne, Silverman, Offer, and Boback (1977). In spite of their similarities, the two systems were developed independently. Interestingly, Antrobus *et al.* reported that an index of the amount of information contained in reports of sleep experiences based on a count of content-related words discriminated REM and non-REM states as well as any other variable associated with that distinction.

Development of the System

Initially I drew up a list of categories that seemed sufficient to cover the types of stimulus and/or reponse information that might be included in verbal reports. The categories were developed on the basis of intuition and of the set of categories suggested by Lang (1977). This initial set of categories was applied to descriptions of imaginary scenes from pilot subjects, and categories were refined, added, or eliminated according to the coding situations encountered.

After an intermediate version of the system was developed, a group of content analysts was trained in its use. Training began with an introduction to the purposes of the coding and to the categories, followed by a discussion of sample transcripts that I had precoded. Trainees coded a different set of transcripts on their own, and their coding was compared to my independent coding of the same transcripts.

Discussions about discrepancies and disagreements led to further refinement of categories. At this point it became apparent that the system could easily become more complex and unwieldy than was warranted for such an exploratory effort. Because the measures to be derived from the coding were at the level of the larger categories of stimulus and response propositions, no particular advantage was to be gained by proliferating the subcategories, as long as reliable coding could be achieved with the present set by way of more precise category definitions and coding conventions. The set of coding categories for the system are presented in Table 2. In a final round of pilot testing with this set of categories, intercoder reliabilities in the + .90s were achieved.

Coding Guidelines

Most coding situations can be resolved by the definitions provided in Table 2. A supplementary set of guidelines and conventions has evolved for handling problem situations. The complete set of these is not reproduced here, but the most important guidelines include the following:

1. Explanatory or associational clauses or sentences that represent neither stimulus objects and events nor an individual's behavior or experience are excluded. Typically these explain some aspect of what was imagined but are not part of the content.
2. The general rule with verbalizations and thoughts is that each complete thought segment is coded as one unit. Thus simple sentences are coded as one unit, compound or run-on sentences are subdivided, and complex sentences are divided at the level of major and subordinate

After you've imagined a scene, you'll be asked to describe out loud as completely as you can what you imagined. When you do this, try to include in your description everything that you can remember about the scene, including the setting, the objects and other people in the scene, and your own behaviors, feelings, thoughts and other sensory awarenesses while imagining the scene. You might find that you're tempted to add things to your description that weren't actually in the scene as you imagined it. It's important that you resist this temptation and limit your description to only those things you know you were aware of while you were imagining the scene. There will be plenty of time for you to describe the scene and to have a rest period before the next scene is presented. Remember to be as complete as you can in your description.

Postimagery Instructions. The report of imaginal content should be given as quickly as possible after the imaginal activity is terminated. The request for report should be limited to a simple instruction, such as "Describe your scene." The request should be brief and nonspecific about content areas in order to minimize the lag between experience and report and to minimize the amount of demand placed on the subject to include features that were not actually part of his or her imagery. A balance must be achieved between the preimagery and postimagery instructions such that subjects know the range of content areas that is of interest (the initial instructions) but do not feel compelled to include all of them in their report, regardless of their actual occurrence. Nonspecific postimagery requests offer the best chance for the primary determinant of the content of the report to be the content actually imagined rather than the request for the report.

Subjective Ratings. If subjective ratings are to be taken of imagery variables such as vividness, controllability, clarity, fear, and so forth, these should be obtained after the imaginal activity and before the verbal report. If the ratings follow the report, they may be affected as much by the act of reporting as by the experience itself. It seems unlikely that the confounding would be as serious if the ratings preceded the report. Subjects should know that ratings will be requested and ideally should be familiar with the scale points so that they can quickly rate their experience and proceed to the verbal report.

Preserving the Verbal Report. There is no substitute for tape-recording verbal reports. If possible, the subject or client should not be required to operate the tape recorder. In research situations the tape recorders should be remotely controlled or should operate continuously, and in clinical situations they should be controlled by the therapist. This minimizes any memory loss due to the distracting effects of having to attend to the tape recorder.

Reports can be coded directly from tapes, but this practice is not recommended, especially when the data are being used for research purposes. The preferred method is to have typed transcripts made from the taped reports and to have the coding done on the transcripts themselves. This provides the researcher with a written record of the actual coding, which then can be referred to easily later. With coding done directly from tapes, it is very difficult to reconstruct the coding decisions that were made. The disadvantage of using typed transcripts is that producing them is a tedious, time-consuming, and potentially expensive process. The possibility of errors in transcription is also ever present.

Coding. The coding procedure is relatively straightforward, as it should be with a low-inference system of this type. Coders are instructed to read completely through the transcript of a single report before attempting to code it. A coder then works through the transcript from beginning to end, dividing the content into units and assigning the units to coding categories. Frequency counts are made of each coding category, and these are transferred to summary sheets. An example of a coded transcript from a speech phobic's report of a public-speaking scene is presented in Table 3 (Anderson & Borkovec, 1980). A specific category notation system has not been developed at this time, so the category names are abbreviated above the units.

Measures. The measures derived from this coding procedure are designed to reflect the amount and kind of detail included in the imagery report. Measures for stimulus and response propositions consist of sums of the coding categories subsumed under each. The measures reported here were designed for use in answering specific research questions. Other measures could be obtained from the system according to the purposes of a particular clinician or investigator.

Reliability of Coding. Intercoder reliability has been determined by correlating the measures for stimulus detail, response detail, and total detail from two separate coder's scoring of the same set of transcripts. In one study the correlations obtained on transcripts of 80 individual scenes were as follows: $r = +.94$ for stimulus detail, $r = +.91$ for response detail, and $r = +.95$ for total detail (Anderson & Borkovec, 1980).

Process Assessment of Therapeutic Imagery by Content Analysis: An Exploratory Study

Borkovec and I used the content analysis system described here in a study on the effects of repeated imagination of two types of anxiety-arousing scenes with speech-anxious college students (Anderson & Borkovec, 1980). This study is reported here as an example of how the content analysis procedure can be used as a research tool. It represented an exploratory application of the content analysis procedure, designed to test its technical feasibility for research and to obtain initial data on its utility and validity as a means of assessing therapeutic imagery.

In a $2 \times 4 \times 5$ repeated-measures design, half of the subjects imagined four scenes presented only in terms of stimulus propositions, and half imagined the same four scenes described in terms of both stimulus and response propositions. Each scene was presented a total of five times. The scene descriptions used in each condition are presented in Table 4. Heart rate was

Table 3. Sample Coded Transcript

spatial	object	body part	motor behavior of self	object

I'm still at / the podium, / and my hands / are kind of clutching /   the side,

people   spatial   spatial   object   processor characteristic
and there are people / behind me / in / chairs, / but again I can't see any faces, /

       setting   people   motor behavior of people
and it seems like there's a whole auditorium / filled with people /   that are listening. /

      verbal behavior   temporal   bodily state
I start to read or to give my speech, / and again / my hands / are getting sweaty, /

property of own behavior   body part   bodily state   bodily state
and I find it hard to talk. / My mouth / is dry, /   and I get a queasy feeling /

   visceral part   thought
in my stomach, / and it seems like the whole place is like really big.

recorded continuously, with samples taken from the 10 seconds immediately preceding presentation of each scene and from the first 10 seconds of each 20-second scene visualization. Subjects verbally rated each scene visualization on vividness, detail, and fear. They described their imaginal contents on the first and last presentation of each scene. Descriptions were tape-recorded, transcribed, and coded according to the procedures previously outlined.

Each subject was placed in an experimental room equipped with a bed, a pillow, and a microphone suspended from the ceiling above the head of the bed. Instructions were tape-recorded and presented through speakers mounted on the wall. Subjects were given 5 minutes to prepare and 3 minutes to give a speech on a current campus issue. They were told that their speech was being tape-recorded, though it actually was not. They were then instructed in an abbreviated progressive relaxation procedure.

Next, they received general instructions about the course of the experiment and specific instructions regarding the ratings and the imagery descriptions (see the initial instructions presented previously). Because of the potentially disruptive effects of the scene descriptions on the physiological data, the scenes were presented in two phases. During Phase 1, each scene was presented for one 20-second visualization. Each scene was rated in the 30 seconds immediately following its visualization and was then described. Two minutes were allowed for scene descriptions.

Phase 2 consisted of four consecutive 20-second visualizations of each scene. Each visualization was followed by a 30-second period during which ratings were given and by a 20-second pause before the next presentation of the same scene. After the ratings were given on the final visualization of a scene, the subject was given 2 minutes to describe what he or she imagined on that (the final) visualization.

Results Obtained from Content Analysis of Narrative Reports. Three general questions were asked with regard to the data obtained from the content analysis: (1) Do the imagery inductions result in reports varying in the amounts of stimulus and response detail they contain? (2) Do the amounts of

Table 4. Scene Descriptions

Stimulus proposition condition

---

1. You are in your room preparing a speech to give the following day.
2. You are sitting on the stage before being introduced to give your speech.
3. You're at the podium looking out over the large audience.
4. You're beginning to present your speech.

Stimulus + response condition

---

1. You are in your room preparing a speech to give the following day. You're feeling tense and nervous and are having a hard time concentrating.
2. You are sitting on the stage before being introduced to give your speech. You have to go to the bathroom, and your stomach feels nervous.
3. You're at the podium looking out over the large audience. Your heart is beating hard, and your hands are sweaty.
4. You're beginning to present your speech. Your voice is shaky, and you're sweating profusely.

---

each kind of detail change over the course of scenes and repetitions? (3) How do the content analysis measures covary with ratings of the scenes and with physiological responsiveness to scenes?

The initial analyses were conducted on measures representing the sum of the frequencies of the coding categories grouped under the stimulus and the response proposition headings. The 2 (Imagery Script) × 4 (Same) × 2 (Repetition: first and last) repeated-measures analyses of variance yielded significant effects on each measure for Scene only. Stimulus propositions decreased over scenes, $F(3,102) = 13.42, p < .01$, and response propositions increased over scenes, $F(3,102) = 4.15, p < .01$. No results emerged for the Imagery Script or Repetition factors. Correlations between these measures and the other dependent measures were also nonsignificant. Reasoning that measures based on the sums of all the categories under each heading might be too gross to reflect the processes of interest, I decided to derive more focused measures on the grounds that they might be more sensitive to those processes.

Under the stimulus proposition heading, the spatial category often had disproportionately high frequencies. This was probably the result of deciding to code each preposition separately from its object. Time and energy did not permit recoding of the transcripts under new guidelines designed to separate prepositions that conveyed clear spatial information from those that were more extraneous. Thus the category was eliminated altogether on the grounds that it might be masking any results. Other categories that were used infrequently were also eliminated. The final set of categories composing the modified stimulus proposition measure included the following: objects, properties of objects, people, properties of people, and movement of people.

These were thought to be the categories that most unambiguously reflected perceptible stimulus detail in the scene.

The eligible response proposition categories were limited to those that would capture references to emotional arousal and/or to the common somatic or cognitive accompaniments of emotional arousal. This more focused set of categories consisted of processor characteristics, body parts, emotion, visceral parts, and bodily arousal.

The analyses of variance on the modified stimulus and response proposition measures also yielded significant main effects for Scene only, with the sum of stimulus propositions decreasing over the four scenes, F $(3,102)$ = $10.8, p$ = .001, and the sum of response propositions increasing over the four scenes, $F(3,102)$ = $5.2, p$ = .002. There were no main effects or interactions for either the Imagery Script or the Repetition factor.

The first general question asked with regard to the content analysis data concerned differences in the kinds of detail reported by subjects in the two treatment groups. Several interpretations can be offered for the lack of significant differences on the response proposition measure. Perhaps the two groups actually did not differ in the amount of response information they imagined, in spite of the different inductions. This interpretation is consistent with the failure to find any significant differences in heart rate responsiveness between the two treatment groups. Alternatively, subjects may not have reported differences that in fact existed.

Unlike Lang *et al. 's* subjects (Note 2), the participants in this study did not receive a training program in imagining or in reporting. The effects of this might be more apparent in the response proposition measure than in the stimulus proposition measure because people simply may not be used to describing the response aspects of their imaginal activity. A request for a description may be more likely to elicit reports of essentially visual stimuli than reports of feelings, somatic awarenesses, and characteristics of perceptual and cognitive processing. Thus the amount of processing of response information necessary to prompt a report of even one bit of response detail may be more than the amount of processing underlying an equivalent amount of reported stimulus detail.

This speculation suggested one final post hoc analysis of the two treatment groups. A test for the difference between two proportions was performed on the proportion of reports in each treatment condition that contained at least one reference to one of the modified response proposition categories. The proportion in the stimulus treatment group was .77 and in the stimulus + response group, .94; the difference between the two was significant, z = $3.86, p$ = .001. This result provides weak confirmation of the experimental manipulation: stimulus + response instructions tended to result in more references to response elements. However, that three-fourths of the subjects in the stimulus condition made some reference to response elements, and that the two conditions did not differ in total references to response elements, suggest that researchers would be well advised to exercise caution in assuming that telling subjects to imagine particular kinds of content will result in imagery limited to those contents.

The second general question concerned changes in each kind of detail over the four scenes and over the five repetitions of each scene. The decline in the amount of stimulus detail over scenes was unexpected, but it could reflect subject fatigue, because the final report was obtained at the end of approximately one hour of repeated imagining, rating, and narrating. Alternatively, it could be related to the corresponding increase in response detail that was reported. The increase in response detail over scenes is consistent with the hierarchical order in which the scenes were presented.

These results do not shed light, however, on the theoretically more interesting question of changes in imaginal content across repetitions of a given scene. Clinicians (Beck, 1970) and researchers (Mathews, 1971) have known that repeated imagination of fearful scenes leads to reduced fear. Some of the imagery-based therapeutic approaches (desensitization, implosion) are based on this principle. The therapeutic mechanisms underlying these therapies are still substantially unknown, although several candidate processes have been suggested. We had thought that a shift in the verbal report toward more stimulus information and/or less response information over repetitions of a given scene might be informative of the cognitive processing underlying fear reduction. However, the analyses on the narrative measures yielded no significant effects for the Repetition factor. Examination of the transcripts of first and last presentations of particular scenes revealed, however, that most subjects did not imagine the *same* contents on each visualization. Although some variation in choice of words between two separate reports would be expected, the differences between reports of successive imaginings of the same scene went beyond this and involved the addition and/or exclusion of large chunks of information. An intriguing task for future research is to determine if there are systematic patterns in these differences, and if there are, what functional importance they might have.

The third question asked of the content analysis measures concerned their relationship with the subjective ratings and with heart rate responsiveness. Product–moment correlations among the dependent measures were computed, using derived scores reflecting mean changes over repetitions. The correlations between heart rate responsiveness and the stimulus and response proposition measures were, respectively, $r = +.08$ (nonsignificant) and $r = +.32$ ($p = .03$). Response propositions also correlated significantly with fear ratings, $r = +.30$ ($p < .05$). The correlational nature of the data prevents a defensible causal interpretation, but these relationships are consistent with Lang's idea that the amount of reponse information processed is causally related to both physiological reactivity and subjective fear.

Conclusion. This study illustrates how content analysis as a methodology can be used to assess imaginal activity and provides some validity data for measures derived from this particular content analysis system. Content analysis data were shown to have utility in two senses. First, they helped provide an explanation for the lack of significant differences between the treatment conditions on both the heart rate responsiveness and the ratings measures. That such a high proportion of subjects in the stimulus proposition condition made some reference to response elements suggests that the results cannot be interpreted as indicating no differential effect for simulus versus stimulus + response *images.* Although the inductions differed on this dimension, the resultant images did not. On the basis of the information gained from the content analysis data, one can direct one's future efforts toward developing a better test of the hypothesis, including, perhaps, imagery training sessions to ensure that intended treatment differences are actually implemented.

Second, the data reported here provide some tentative support for the construct validity of the particular content analysis measures used, especially for the response measure. The pattern of correlations obtained among the different variables provides support for the proposition that the response detail measure is tapping the same dimension as the other two types of measures. Also, the significant scenes effect for the response detail was consistent with the content of the imagery induction.

Finally, the specific system used here, along with its categories and its measures, is an example of a general strategy for imagery assessment. Different coding systems and measures might be appropriate for different questions and purposes. This study demonstrates the potential of the general strategy for assessing imaginal activity by content analysis of narrative reports.

ACKNOWLEDGMENTS

The research and review work for this chapter were conducted while the author was supported by the National Institute of Alcohol, Drug Abuse, and Mental Health Administration's National Research Service Award No. 1-F32-MH07473-01 from the National Institute of Mental Health. Thanks to Michael J. Mahoney for his sponsorship of the fellowship and to Thomas D. Borkovec for the use of his research facilities.

Reference Notes

1. Lang, P. J. *A bio-informational theory of emotional imagery.* Presidential address to the annual meeting of the Society for Psychophysiological Research, Madison, Wisconsin, 1978.
2. Lang, P., Kozak, M., Miller, G., Levin, D., & McLean, A. *Emotional imagery: Conceptual structure and pattern of somato-visceral response.* Unpublished manuscript, 1979.

References

Anderson, J. Arguments concerning representations for mental imagery. *Psychological Review,* 1978, *85,* 249–278.

Anderson, M. P. Imaging as a self-control response to enhance voluntary tolerance of an aversive stimulus (Doctoral dissertation, University of Texas at Austin, 1975). *Dissertation Abstracts International,* 1975, 36 (2-B), 899–900.

Anderson, M. P. Imaginal processes: Therapeutic applications and theoretical models. In M. J. Mahoney (Ed.), *Psychotherapy process: Current issues and future directions.* New York: Plenum Press, 1980.

Anderson, M. P., & Borkovec, T. D. Imagery processing and physiological responsiveness during repeated exposure to two types of phobic imagery. *Behaviour Research and Therapy,* 1980, *18,* 537–540.

Antrobus, J., Fein, G., Jordan, L., Ellman, S., & Arkin, A. Measurement and design in research on sleep reports. In A. Arkin, J. Antrobus, & S. Ellman (Eds.), *The mind in sleep.* Hillsdale, N.J.: Erlbaum, 1978.

Antrobus, J., Schnee, R., Lynne, A., Silverman, S., Offer, V., & Boback, P. *Psycholinguistic coding manual for reports of sleep and stimulus independent waking state experience.* Princeton, N.J.: Educational Testing Service Test Collection, 1977.

Arkin, A., Antrobus, J., & Ellman, S. *The mind in sleep: Psychology and psychophysiology.* Hillsdale, N.J.: Erlbaum, 1978.

Barber, T., & Hahn, K. Experimental studies in "hypnotic" behavior: Physiological and subjective effects of imagined pain. *Journal of Nervous and Mental Disease,* 1964, *139,* 416–425.

Beck, A. Role of fantasies in psychotherapy and psychopathology. *Journal of Nervous and Mental Disease,* 1970, *150,* 3–17.

Bennett, G., Seashore, H., & Wesman, P. *Differential aptitude tests.* New York: The Psychological Corporation, 1959.

Berelson, B. *Content analysis in communications research.* Glencoe, Ill.: The Free Press, 1952.

Betts, G. *The distribution and function of mental imagery* (Contributions to Education Series, No. 26). New York: Columbia University Teachers College, 1909.

Borkovec, T., & Sides, J. The contribution of relaxation and expectancy to fear reduction via graded, imaginal exposure to feared stimuli. *Behaviour Research and Therapy,* 1979, *17,* 529–540.

Cautela, J., & McCullough, L. Covert condition: A learning-theory perspective on imagery. In J. Singer & K. Pope (Eds.), *The power of human imagination.* New York: Plenum Press, 1978.

Crowne, D. P., & Marlowe, D. *The approval-motive: Studies in evaluative dependence.* New York: Wiley, 1964.

Danaher, B., & Thoresen, C. Imagery assessment by self-report and behavior measures. *Behaviour Research and Therapy,* 1972, *10,* 131–138.

Davidson, R., & Schwartz, G. Brain mechanisms subserving self-generated imagery: Electrophysiological specificity and patterning. *Psychophysiology,* 1977, *14,* 598–602.

DiVesta, F., Ingersoll, G., & Sunshine, R. A factor analysis of imagery tests. *Journal of Verbal Learning and Verbal Behavior,* 1971, *10,* 471–479.

Dyckman, J., & Cowan, P. Imaging vividness and the outcome of *in vivo* and imagined scene desensitization. *Journal of Consulting and Clinical Psychology,* 1978, *46,* 1155–1156.

Ernest, C. Imagery ability and cognition: A critical review. *Journal of Mental Imagery,* 1977, *1,* 181–216.

Ernest, C., & Paivio, A. Imagery and verbal associative latencies as a function of imagery ability. *Canadian Journal of Psychology,* 1971, *25,* 83–90.

Foulkes, D., & Rechtschaffen, A. Presleep determinants of dream content: Effects of two films. *Perceptual and Motor Skills,* 1964, *9,* 983–1005.

Fusella, V.J. *Blocking of an external signal through self-projected imagery: The role of inner-acceptant personality style and categories of imagery* (Doctoral dissertation, University of Utah, 1973). *Dissertation Abstracts International,* 1973, *33,* 5489B-5490B. (University Microfilms No. 73-11, 352)

Gordon, R. An investigation into some of the factors that favour the formation of stereotyped images. *British Journal of Psychology,* 1949, *39,* 156-167.

Gottschalk, L., & Gleser, G. *The measurement of psychological states through the content analysis of verbal behavior.* Berkeley: University of California Press, 1969.

Grossberg, J., & Wilson, H. Physiological concomitants accompanying the visualization of fearful and neutral situations. *Journal of Personality and Social Psychology,* 1968, *10,* 124-133.

Haber, R., & Haber, R. Eidetic imagery I: Frequency. *Perceptual and Motor Skills,* 1964, *19,* 131-138.

Hall, C. S., & Van de Castle, R. *The content analysis of dreams.* New York: Appelton-Century-Crofts, 1966.

Hiscock, M. Imagery assessment through self-report: What do imagery questionnaires really measure? *Journal of Consulting and Clinical Psychology,* 1978, *46,* 223-231.

Holsti, O. *Content analysis for the social sciences and humanities.* Reading, Mass.: Addison-Wesley, 1969.

Holt, R. On the nature and generality of mental imagery. In P. Sheehan (Ed.), *The function and nature of imagery.* New York: Academic Press, 1972.

Hurley, A. D. Covert reinforcement: The contribution of the reinforcing stimulus to treatment outcome. *Behavior Therapy,* 1976, *7,* 374-378.

Jacobson, E. Electrical measurements of neuromuscular states during mental activities. (III) Visual imagination and recollection. *American Journal of Physiology,* 1930, *95,* 694-702.

Jacobson, E. Electrical measurements of neuromuscular states during mental activities. (IV) Evidence of contraction of specific muscles during imagination. (V) Variation of specific muscles contracting during imagination. *American Journal of Physiology,* 1931, *96,* 115-121.

Kazdin, A. The effect of model identity and fear-relevant similarity on covert modeling. *Behavior Therapy,* 1974, *5,* 624-635.

Kazdin, A. Covert modeling, imagery assessment, and assertive behavior. *Journal of Consulting and Clinical Psychology,* 1975, *43,* 716-724.

Kazdin, A. Assessment of imagery during covert modeling treatment of assertive behavior. *Journal of Behavior Therapy and Experimental Psychiatry,* 1976, *7,* 213-219.

Kazdin, A. Imagery elaboration and self-efficacy in the covert modeling treatment of unassertive behavior. *Journal of Consulting and Clinical Psychology,* 1979, *47,* 725-733.

Kieras, D. Beyond pictures and words: Alternative information-processing models for imagery effects in verbal memory. *Psychological Bulletin,* 1978, *85,* 532-554.

Klinger, E. *The structure and functions of fantasy.* New York: Wiley-Interscience, 1971.

Klinger, E. Dimensions of thought and imagery in normal waking states. *Journal of Altered States of Consciousness,* 1978, *4,* 97-113. *(a)*

Klinger, E. Modes of conscious flow. In K. Pope & J. Singer (Eds.), *The stream of consciousness: Scientific investigations into the flow of human experience.* New York: Plenum Press, 1978. *(b)*

Kosslyn, S., & Pomerantz, J. Imagery, propositions, and the form of internal representations. *Cognitive Psychology,* 1977, *9,* 52-76.

Lang, P. Imagery in therapy: An information processing analysis of fear. *Behavior Therapy,* 1977, *8,* 862-886.

Likert, R., & Quasha, W. *Revised Minnesota paper form board test* (Series AA). New York: The Psychological Corporation, 1941.

McGuigan, F. J. Electrical measurement of covert processes as an explication of "higher mental events." In F. J. McGuigan & R. A. Schoonover (Eds.), *The psychophysiology of thinking.* New York: Academic Press, 1972.

McGuigan, F. J., & Schoonover, R. A. *The psychophysiology of thinking*. New York: Academic Press, 1972.

McKellar, P. Imagery from the standpoint of introspection. In P. Sheehan (Ed.), *The function and nature of imagery*. New York: Academic Press, 1972.

McLemore, C. W. Imagery in desensitization. *Behaviour Research and Therapy*, 1972, *10*, 51–57.

McLemore, C. Factorial validity of imagery measures. *Behaviour Research and Therapy*, 1976, *14*, 399–408.

Marks, D. Individual differences in the vividness of visual imagery and their effect on function. In P. Sheehan (Ed.), *The nature and function of imagery*. New York: Academic Press, 1972.

Marsden, J. Content-analysis studies of psychotherapy. 1954–1968. In A. Bergin & S. Garfield (Eds.), *Handbook of psychotherapy and behavior change*. New York: Wiley, 1971.

Marzillier, J., Carroll, D., & Newland, J. Self-report and physiological changes accompanying repeated imagining of a phobic scene. *Behaviour Research and Therapy*, 1979, *17*, 71–77.

Mathews, A. Psychophysiological approaches to the investigation of desensitization and related procedures. *Psychological Bulletin*, 1971, *76*, 73–91.

Miller, G. A. The magical number seven, plus or minus two: Some limits on our capacity to process information. *Psychological Review*, 1956, *63*, 81–97.

Neisser, U. *Cognitive psychology*. New York: Appleton-Century-Crofts, 1967.

Neisser, U. Changing conceptions of imagery. In P. Sheehan (Ed.), *The function and nature of imagery*. New York: Academic Press, 1972.

Neisser, U. *Cognitions and reality: Principles and implications of cognitive psychology*. San Francisco: W. H. Freeman, 1976.

Paivio, A. *Imagery and verbal processes*. New York: Holt, Rinehart & Winston, 1971.

Phillips, L. Training of sensory and imaginal reponses in behavior therapy. In R. Rubin, H. Fensterheim, A. Lazarus, & C. Franks (Eds.), *Advances in behavior therapy*. New York: Academic Press, 1973.

Pylyshyn, Z. What the mind's eye tells the mind's brain: A critique of mental imagery. *Psychological Bulletin*, 1973, *80*, 1–22.

Rawlings, E., & Rawlings, I. Rotary pursuit tracking following mental rehearsal as a function of voluntary control of visual imagery. *Perceptual and Motor Skills*, 1974, *38*, 302.

Rechtschaffen, A. Dream reports and dream experiences. *Experimental Neurology*, 1967, Supplement 4, 4–15.

Rehm, L. Relationships among measures of visual imagery. *Behaviour Research and Therapy*, 1973, *11*, 265–270.

Richardson, A. *Mental imagery*. New York: Springer, 1969.

Richardson, A. Voluntary control of the memory image. In P. Sheehan (Ed.), *The function and nature of imagery*. New York: Academic Press, 1972.

Richardson, A. The meaning and measurement of memory imagery. *British Journal of Psychology*, 1977, *68*, 29–43.

Rimm, D., & Bottrell, J. Four measures of visual imagination. *Behaviour Research and Therapy*, 1969, *7*, 63–69.

Sarbin, T. Imagining as muted role-taking: A historical–linguistic analysis. In P. Sheehan (Ed.), *The function and nature of imagery*. New York: Academic Press, 1972.

Schwartz, G. Psychobiological foundations of psychotherapy and behavior change. In S. Garfield & A. Bergin (Eds.), *Handbook of psychotherapy and behavior change: An empirical analysis*. New York: Wiley, 1978.

Sheehan, P. Functional similarity of imagery to perceiving: Individual differences in vividness of imagery. *Perceptual and Motor Skills*, 1966, *23*, 1011–1033.

Sheehan, P. A shortened form of Betts's Questionnaire upon Mental Imagery. *Journal of Clinical Psychology*, 1967, *23*, 386–389.

Singer, J. *Imagery and daydream methods in psychotherapy and behavior modification*. New York: Academic Press, 1974.

Singer, J., & Antrobus, J. Daydreaming, imaginal processes, and personality: A normative study. In P. Sheehan (Ed.), *The function and nature of imagery.* New York: Academic Press, 1972.

Singer, J., & Pope, K. (Eds.). *The power of human imagination: New methods in psychotherapy.* New York: Plenum Press, 1978.

Starker, S. Effects of hypnotic induction upon visual imagery. *Journal of Nervous and Mental Disease,* 1974, *159,* 433–437. *(a)*

Starker, S. Two modes of visual imagery. *Perceptual and Motor Skills,* 1974, *38,* 649–650. *(b)*

Stoyva, J., & Kamiya, J. Electrophysiological studies of dreaming as the prototype of a new strategy in the study of consciousness. *Psychological Review,* 1968, *75,* 192–205.

Thurstone, L., & Jeffrey, T. *Flags: A test of space thinking.* Chicago: Industrial Relations Center, 1956.

White, J., Sheehan, P., & Ashton, R. Imagery assessment: A survey of self-report measures. *Journal of Mental Imagery,* 1977, *1,* 145–170.

Wilson, S., & Barber, T. *The Creative Imagination Scale as a measure of hypnotic responsiveness: Applications to experimental and clinical hypnosis.* Medfield, Mass.: Medfield Foundation, 1976.

Wolpe, J. *The practice of behavior therapy* (2nd ed.). New York: Pergamon Press, 1973.

7

Personal Construct Perspectives on Cognitive Assessment

Greg J. Neimeyer and Robert A. Neimeyer

There are two ways in which one can look at psychological measurement and clinical diagnosis. On the one hand, he can seek to fix the position of the subject with respect to certain dimensions or coordinates—such as intelligence, extraversion, and so on—or to classify him as a clinical type—such as schizoid, neurotic and the like. On the other hand, he can concern himself with the subject's freedom of movement, his potentialities, the resources which can be mobilized, and what is to become of him. From the point of view of the psychology of personal constructs, in which the emphasis is upon process rather than upon fixed position, the latter represents the more enlightened approach. Let us say, then, that the primary purpose of psychological measurement . . . is to survey the pathways along which the subject is free to move, and the primary purpose of clinical diagnosis is the plotting of the most feasible course of movement.

Kelly (1955, p. 203)

Introduction

As modern cognitively oriented students of personality and behavior trace the theoretical roots of their discipline, they are increasingly acknowledging the contribution of George A. Kelly's psychology of personal constructs to their intellectual heritage. Michael Mahoney and Diane Arnkoff (1978), for example, in reviewing the history of the cognitive–behavioral interface, refer to Kelly, along with Rotter and Beck, as "three examples of early cognitive-learning cultivators whose influence is very important in contemporary work. Through their research, theories and the impact they had on students,

Greg J. Neimeyer • Counseling Center, University of California, Irvine, California.
Robert A. Neimeyer • Department of Psychology, University of Nebraska, Lincoln, Nebraska.

these three may have been the founding fathers of our current trend" (p. 691). In a similar vein, Walter Mischel, a student of Kelly, draws attention to the farsightedness of the latter theorist. In a recent paper, "George Kelly's Anticipation of Psychology: A Personal Tribute," Mischel (1980) remarks as follows:

> That George Kelly was a very deep, original, refreshing voice was always evident to all who knew him well. What has surprised me was not the brilliance with which he first spoke but the accuracy with which he anticipated the directions into which psychology would move two decades later.

> Virtually every point of George Kelly's theorizing in the 1950's . . . has proved to be a prophetic preface for the psychology of the 1970's—and, it seems safe now to predict—for many years to come. (pp. 85-86)

Ironically, however, much current cognitive psychology has developed without explicitly drawing upon Kelly's unique perspective. In retrospect this is not surprising, given that construct theory has been eclipsed until recently by theoretical systems posited on very different sets of assumptions. Surely Kelly's *The Psychology of Personal Constructs* (1955), which granted preeminence to the process by which persons creatively interpret their physical and interpersonal worlds, was an unlikely competitor in a field dominated by the theoretical perspectives that stressed overt behavior on the one hand and unconscious motivation on the other. A renaissance of interest in personal construct theory (PCT) had to await the widespread kindling of concern with what traditionally has been referred to as the "cognitive" aspect of our psychological economy.

This chapter is written in the belief that PCT can contribute scope and depth to current discussions of cognitive assessment. It will be our central aim, therefore, to suggest the diversity of methodological tools generated by this perspective. In so doing, we will be able to give only cursory attention to the broad outlines of PCT. The reader interested in developing a richer appreciation of the theory in which these techniques are grounded is encouraged to consult the primary sources listed at the end of the chapter.

Inquiry and the Quest for Meaning

Contemporary philosophers of science (e.g., Harre, 1972; Kuhn, 1970; Rychlak, 1968) have drawn attention to the fact that all scientific theorizing, whether it bears upon the natural or the social domain, rests on a fundament of philosophical assumptions about the nature of its subject matter. The discipline of psychology is, of course, no exception. If PCT can be differentiated from other psychological theories in this regard, it is only because of the clarity with which Kelly makes his philosophical commitments known to his readers. Essentially, PCT is predicated upon the assumption of "inquiring man" (Bannister & Fransella, 1971). Antithetical to both the image of the "empty organism" implied by more extreme behaviorist formulations and the need-dominated systems espoused by some students of motivation, this posture of inquiry suggests the central project of our species: to participate in the flux of events in which we are immersed and to render them meaningful in human terms.

To discern order in the physical and interpersonal realities they confront, individuals abstract recurrent themes in their experience that have some measure of generality across situations. In the course of her encounters with men, for example, an enterprising woman might become aware of the elements of condescension and mild flirtation displayed toward her. As she takes note of the recurrence of such behavior across time and perhaps across persons, she may come to "construe" certain of the men as "those who treat women stereotypically" and may discriminate them from "those who respect me for my abilities." This discrimination, or "construct," exemplifies characteristics of constructs in general; it provides a means of representing the way in which some things are alike in certain respects (e.g., "These men treat me stereotypically") and simultaneously different from others (e.g., "These men respect me for my abilities").

It is a tenet of PCT that all constructs are "bipolar," that they imply some sort of contrast, the nature of which may be more or less idiosyncratic to the individual construer. It is the implied contrast that gives constructs their personal character. Consider the difference in the meaning of the notion "studious" when embedded in the context of "studious versus shallow" as opposed to "studious versus fun to be around." Though individuals may draw upon communal discriminations in formulating their conceptual templates, they typically evolve construct systems that are in some measure unique, embodying richer personal significance than do simple dictionary antonyms.

If the world stood still for the construing individual, then life might amount to little more than the task of developing a classificatory system according to which the world's static entities might be coded. But fortunately or unfortunately, such is not the case; the universe changes along a dimension of time. Thus constructions that may have seemed reasonable at some point in the past may be invalidated by current turns of events. A profound remark by a student who I once construed as "having nothing interesting to say" may prompt me to reconstrue him, perhaps in terms of his being "quiet but intellectually intense."

According to PCT, it is the *cycle* of framing personal interpretations of the world and reassessing them in light of ensuing events that constitutes experience rather than the merely passive encoding of the stimuli that one encounters. Kelly (1970) elaborates on this point:

> Keeping in mind that events do not actually repeat themselves and that the replication we talk about is a replication of ascribed aspects only, it begins to be clear that the succession we call experience is based on the constructions we place on

what goes on. If those constructions are never altered, all that happens during a man's years is a sequence of parallel events having no psychological impact on his life. But if he invests himself—the most intimate event of all—in the enterprise, the outcome, to the extent that it differs from his expectation or enlarges upon it, dislodges the man's construction of himself. In recognizing the inconsistency be~ween his anticipation and the outcome, he concedes a discrepancy between what he was and what he is. A succession of such investments and dislodgements constitutes the human experience. (p. 18)

Constructs, in this view, are more than intellectual labels for replicative themes in life; they are significant guideposts for the business of living. Thus, if I anticipate that I will act in a "moral," as opposed to an "unscrupulous," fashion, this will have profound implications for the way I behave toward others. It is the types of constructs that persons formulate, the way in which they change over the course of time, the manner in which individual dimensions are organized into complex personal construct systems, and the implications that such constructions have for human emotionality and our life among others that constitute the subject matter of PCT. What follows is a brief exposition of the techniques that construct theorists have developed to gain access to the interpretive frameworks that individuals employ. First, however, we must digress momentarily to consider the sense in which these methods are and are not assessments of "cognitions."

Constructs and Cognition

Although it may be altogether appropriate to regard the psychology of personal constructs as contributing to the development of cognitive theorizing, PCT does chart a unique course through the mainstream of these cognitive approaches. Kelly strongly resisted having his theory identified with the cognitive approach. Reflecting on the curiously incompatible potpourri of conceptual frameworks with which psychologists had classified his position, Kelly (1969a) noted:

> I have been so puzzled over the early labeling of personal construct theory as "cognitive" that several years ago I set out to write another short book to make it clear that I wanted no part of cognitive theory. The manuscript was about a third completed when I gave a lecture at Harvard University with the title "Personal Construct Theory as a Line of Inference." Following the lecture, Professor Gordon Allport explained to the students that my theory was not a "cognitive" theory but an "emotional" theory. Later the same afternoon, Dr. Henry Murray called me aside and said, "You know, don't you, that you are really an existentialist."

> I have, of course, been called a Zen Buddhist, and last fall one of our former students, now a distinguished psychologist, who was invited back to give a lecture, spent an hour and a half in a seminar corrupting my students with the idea that I was really a behaviorist. (pp. 216–217)

In part, Kelly's rejection of the rubrics "cognitive," "emotional," "behavioral," and so on was a rejection of each as a preemptive designation of the content of his theory. In point of fact, aspects of each of these areas are represented in PCT, just as they are in the lives of those individuals to whom the theory is to apply.

More important, however, Kelly sought to disaffiliate himself from such part approaches to psychology because they suggested lines of discrimination that he sought to transcend in the formulation of his theory and the development of its fundamental notion, the construct. In explicating the latter term, Kelly (1969*b*) remarks:

> What I am describing is not *conceptualization,* as psychologists and logicians commonly understand that notion. It may not even be very good *logic.* But it is descriptive of the way man starts to make sense out of his buzzing blooming confusion. Instead of trying to classify this particular process loosely as one of "conception" or "cognition" let us abandon these formalistic notions altogether and designate it as the psychological process of *construing,* or one of forming *personal constructs.* And I must insist that the elemental *construct* I am postulating bears little resemblance to a *concept* and that *construing* is a far cry from *cognition.*
>
> It would be quite understandable, linguistic traditions being what they are, if you were to visualize construing as a verbalized or conscious act. But that need not be so. Constructs can be *preverbally* symbolized and . . . a person can have a hard time representing constructs to himself except as raw experience. There is not necessarily anything either cognitive or affective about this kind of construing. (pp. 197–198, original emphasis)

Here it is apparent that Kelly is blazing new trails in his development of the "construct" and not following the better worn paths of classical distinction. Rather, what he attempts to do is to posit as the defining feature of human functioning an activity, construing, which is superordinate to the hoary psychological distinctions between "emotion" and "cognition," between "thought" and "behavior." Still, he is aware that others following him may naturally, albeit mistakenly, take the more familiar trails. Those of us for whom such dichotomies have become "obvious" labels for certain categories of human phenomena may find construing an elusive concept.

> The difficulty in understanding personal construct theory arises out of the assumption that all discrimination . . . is essentially cognitive. But human discrimination may take place also at levels which have been called "physiological" or "emotional." Nor is discrimination necessarily a verbalized process. Man discriminates at a very primitive and behavioral level. For example, for him to be afraid on two different occasions suggests that he has somehow or other linked or identified them as constructively the same object of danger. (Kelly, 1969*a*, p. 219)

Clearly, then, constructs are not solely cognitions. Nonetheless, it is easy to confuse the two, particularly given that construct assessment strategies traditionally have relied so heavily upon verbal formulations. These linguistic signposts have served well the needs of most clinical and experimental investigations but, with time, have tended to become confused with the underlying bases of discrimination (i.e., constructs) from which they emerged. Misconceived as its verbal designation, the construct was ripe for classification as "cognition."

Despite the tendency of researchers to operationalize constructs in linguistic terms, PCT would contend that construing is as implicit in overt behavior as it is in one's "cognitive" verbalizations.[1] In all cases, it suggests the operation of certain lived discriminations, which differ only in the degree to which the individual is personally invested in them. Thus, for example, construing one's companion as "tall" might represent simply a "cognitive" recognition for one person, whereas for another who construes himself as "very short," it might carry a significant, if subtle, "emotional" resonance. Similarly, revising the "merely intellectual" understanding that the shortest distance between two points is a straight line may arouse considerable anxiety in the sophomore mathematics major who must grapple with the very different set of axioms characteristic of a non-Euclidean geometry. Our more central constructions of ourselves and our world are more clearly impassioned. Construing myself as basically "worthless" or the interpersonal world as "totally incomprehensible" obviously has profound implications for so-called affective facets of my life; they are not simply "cognitive" interpretations.

This being said, it remains true that the interests of construct theorists do converge with those of modern cognitive psychologists. Both camps are interested in illuminating the assumptive structures by means of which people impute meaning to their experience. Moreover, both have a practical and humanitarian disposition toward helping individuals revise those constructions that are too restrictive or too chaotic in order to allow them paths of movement toward a satisfying future. Let us now consider some of the techniques construct theorists employ to elucidate the construing activity of the persons whose outlooks they seek to understand.

Illustrative Assessment Techniques

Kelly's unique contribution to the field of psychological assessment was the Role Construct Repertory Test, or Reptest for short (1955, pp. 219–318). The Reptest and its popular variant, the repertory grid, are techniques that allow individuals to articulate the important dimensions or constructs

---

[1]The tendency to conceptualize constructs as verbal labels has not been universal, however. Radley (1977) offers a sophisticated theoretical treatment of the nonverbal realm, and recent approaches to the assessment of nonverbal construing will be reviewed subsequently in the chapter.

according to which they orient themselves in some aspect of their lives. Originally proposed as instruments for clinical practice and psychological research, these techniques have proven so attractive to social scientists that they have been applied in areas as diverse as urban planning (Stringer, 1974) and the anthropological investigation of folk beliefs of primitive tribes (Orley, 1976).

It is clearly beyond the scope of this chapter to detail the dozens of adaptations of repertory techniques in current use, much less recount the hundreds of published studies in which they have been employed. We will, however, survey some of the major grid and nongrid techniques generated within PCT and illustrate their use by discussing representative research efforts incorporating each. Moreover, because the type of analysis performed on data generated from the repertory grid is at least partially independent of the exact assessment technique being used, we will suggest some of the methods of scoring commonly applied to such data, referring the reader to other sources for detailed instructions wherever possible. Finally, we will conclude by discussing briefly some of the problems and prospects of such techniques, so that readers who choose to explore them further might do so in an informed and critical fashion.

Grid Techniques

As construct theorists (e.g., Bannister & Fransella, 1971; Bannister & Mair, 1968; Fransella & Bannister, 1977) repeatedly have emphasized, the name "Reptest" is something of a misnomer. Actually this name designates not a single test or questionnaire with fixed content, but a broad variety of techniques sharing certain methodological features as well as a conceptual congruence with the fundamental tenets of personal construct psychology.

In general outline, the Reptest is a form of structured interview or a self-administered instrument that provides the respondent with a number of "elements" (usually from 10 to 30) that serve as the basis for his or her constructions. Often, these elements represent various "role titles" of significant others who play a part in the person's life (e.g., mother, brother, employer, someone who appears to dislike you). However, a great variety of things have been utilized as elements, including parts of one's own body (Feldman, 1975), countries (Lemon, 1975), social issues (Epting, 1972), occupations (Shubsachs, 1975), and situations involving death and dying (Krieger, Epting, & Leitner, 1974).

The individual is asked to concentrate on preselected groupings of two or three elements and to construe them in terms of their similarities and/or contrasts along important dimensions. In so doing, the Reptest "elicits" the personal templates by means of which the individual interprets that domain of her or his experience. Most grid forms of the Reptest further require the respondent to allocate the remaining elements to one or the other of the "poles" of the elicited constructs, as will be detailed subsequently. This has the advantage of allowing not only for the analysis of an individual's construct content but also for the investigation of structural interrelationships between the dimensions. By turning our attention to a few of the techniques that have evolved in the past 25 years, we can illustrate with greater clarity the possibilities for grid administration, scoring, and interpretation that currently exist.

Ratings Grid. Many of the grids that enjoy wide use in the United States and Canada are forms of ratings grids, so called because they require the respondent to rate elements on Likert-type scales anchored by his or her constructs. The procedure for the administration of such an instrument can be illusrated by reference to an actual clinical example.

Janet R. (all names have been fictionalized to protect the client's identity) was referred to one of us (R.N.) for psychotherapy immediately after she had been diagnosed as having undergone an acute schizophrenic episode. In the initial "crisis" interview, she appeared quite confused and emotionally labile, alternating between almost dreamlike attention to minutiae in the environment and organized, although bizarre, interaction with those persons present. The unpredictability of her behavior in these interactive phases was particularly noteworthy. At these times she fluctuated rapidly among three very distinct "personalities," one highly accusatory and domineering, another very aloof and condescending, and the third almost childlike and fearful. With each shift in personality, her posture, tone of voice, and coverbal gestural repertoire changed dramatically, giving the impression of highly compartmentalized and virtually nonoverlapping interactive styles. The phenomenal reality of such compartmentalization for her was indicated by her modes of self-reference during each episode: she was not "Janet" when one of these "personalities" was "in control," but "Angela," "Cynthia," and "Cyn," respectively.

A rating form of the repertory grid was administered in the third session to help provide a diagnostic base upon which a relevant therapeutic approach could be planned. Although her dreamlike withdrawal from interaction had been attenuated by the prescription of antipsychotic medication, Janet continued to experience herself as one of the alien personalities much of the time. Because these sudden shifts remained disconcerting for her, the grid was tailored to focus upon the degree of conceptual disorganization inherent in her perception of herself and of other significant persons.

The grid began as a structured interview, during which Janet was asked to supply the first names of a list of people who occupied certain roles in her life (herself, her spouse, etc.) The role titles and fictionalized versions of the names she provided appear in Table 1. The figures chosen by the therapist to serve as elements for her grid included salient persons from her past and pres-

Table 1. Role Titles Used as Elements in Grid for Janet R.

1. Yourself (Janet)
2. Your husband (Jerry)
3. Your present therapist (Bob)
4. Someone you respect (Cory)
5. Someone who appears to dislike you (Joe)
6. Aspect of self (Angela)
7. Aspect of self (Cynthia)
8. Aspect of self (Cyn)
9. Your mother (Imogene)
10. Your father (Tom)

Note. Fictionalized versions of the names provided by the respondent appear in parentheses.

ent as well as those relatively autonomous character structures that had become elaborated as identifiable "subpersonalities" during her psychotic episode.

Following this role specification phase, the interviewer proceeded to elicit several of the major constructs Janet used to dimensionalize her intrapersonal and interpersonal world. This was accomplished by selecting two figures, as indicated in Table 2 (e.g., "Angela" and "Imogene" in Sort 1), and by instructing her as follows:

> All right, Janet, now I want you to think about _____ [first role figure] and
> _____ [second role figure]. Do you see them as mainly alike or as mainly opposite in some important respect? The similarity or difference can be anything at all. It might have to do with the kind of people they are or the way they feel, act, look, or think . . . any way at all in which they seem like one another or in contrast to one another, as long as this seems important to you.

In this first sort, Janet responded that she saw the two figures as very much the same; both were "angry and did not like men." The interviewer recorded this response and then asked her, "And what would the opposite of that be? What idea would be the opposite of _____ [being 'angry and not liking men']?" In this case, Janet replied that "being passive" connoted the opposite of her first response. This answer also was noted by the interviewer. Taken together, "angry, does not like men" versus "passive" represented the two "poles" of a construct by which she organized her perceptions of people.

This cycle of questioning was repeated for each of the remaining sorts of elements, except that when the two figures initially were perceived as opposite, the further question "And what would the opposite of that be?" was not asked. Thus, for example, when Janet contrasted Cory's being a "patriarch" with Joe's being a "matriarch," additional questioning was obviated, be-

Table 2. Element Sorts Provided to
Janet from Her Role Title List

Sort	Elements
1	6,9
2	1,8
3	2,10
4	3,8
5	4,5
6	3,7
7	4,10
8	1,6
9	5,9
10	2,7

cause both contrast poles of the construct were implied in this single answer. The constructs elicited by all ten sorts appear in column A of Table 3.

In preparation for the rating phase of the administration procedure, the interviewer recorded Janet's earlier answers on the rating response sheet depicted in Figure 1. A set of ten rating-scale overlay sheets was attached in the center of the form, so that the ten 13-point Likert scales on each sheet were flanked by the poles of one of the ten elicited constructs. At the top of each of these overlays was recorded one of the ten role figures that had served as elements. The entire packet was handed to Janet, and she was instructed aloud as follows:

> Now I want you to think about *Janet* [role figure at top of the sheet]. Where would you place Janet on this scale, which goes from "angry, does not like men" [first construct pole] on one extreme to "passive" [second construct pole] on the other extreme? For example, if you saw her as very clearly angry and not liking men, then circle a 5 or even a 6 in this direction. On the other hand, if she seems to be somewhat passive, then circle a 3 or a 4 in the other direction. Circle the 0 point if she seems to be equally angry and disliking men and passive or if the scale doesn't really seem to apply to her.

Figure 1 also depicts Janet's circled placements of Element 1, herself, on each of the construct scales. These scales were completed at her own rate for each of the remaining elements once it had been ascertained that she had understood the instructions. After all ratings had been performed, the interviewer requested that Janet "value code" each of the construct poles as positive, negative, or neutral, depending on how she regarded the possession of each of the qualities she had described. These responses appear in parentheses immediately following the construct poles in Table 3.

The analysis of data generated by such a grid can take many forms. Kelly

Table 3. Constructs Elicited from Janet R., Testings A and B

	A		B
Sort	Construct	Sort	Construct
1	Angry, does not like men (+) vs. passive (−)	1	Hate men (−) vs. compassion for men (+)
2	Assertive, in control (+) vs. aggressive (−)	2	Need to be taken care of (−) vs. independent (+)
3	Hating women (−) vs. indifferent (−)	3	Grandiosity (+) vs. "Chester Milktoast" (−)
4	Suffered from one's parents (+) vs. rejecting parents (−)	4	Sensitive (+) vs. harsh (−)
5	Powerful (+) vs. intimidated (−)	5	Control (+) vs. compassion (−)
6	Sensitive (+) vs. scared (+)	6	Strong (+) vs. helpless (−)
7	Patriarch (+) vs. matriarch (+)	7	Alcoholic (N) vs. temperate (+)
8	Accepts anger (+) vs. controlled by anger (−)	8	Anger (−) vs. jubilant (+)
9	Manipulative (+) vs. subdued (−)	9	Manipulative (−) vs. honest (+)
10	Superior (−) vs. inferior (−)	10	Afraid (−) vs. courageous (+)

Note. Symbols in parentheses denote positively (+), negatively (−), and neutrally (N) valued qualities within Janet's conceptual system.

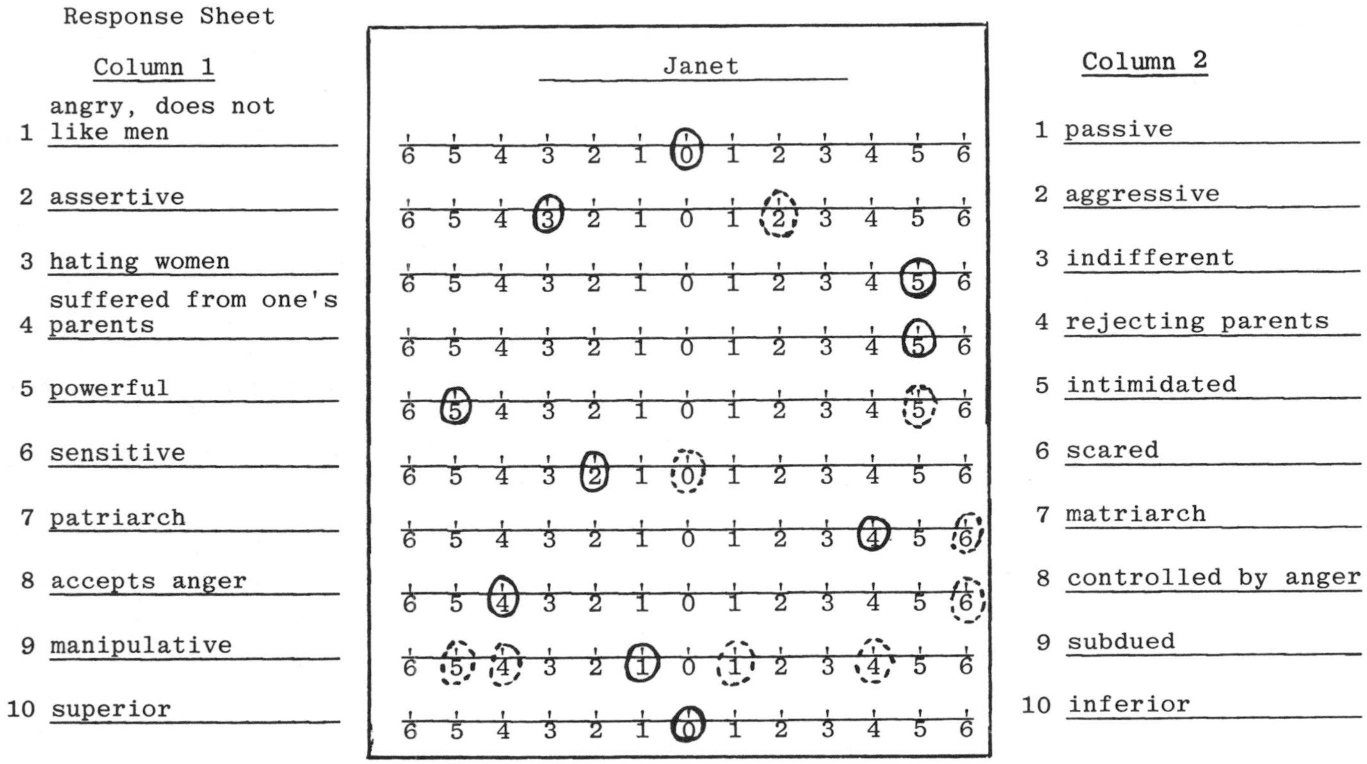

Response Sheet

Column 1

1 angry, does not like men

2 assertive

3 hating women

4 suffered from one's parents

5 powerful

6 sensitive

7 patriarch

8 accepts anger

9 manipulative

10 superior

Janet

Column 2

1 passive

2 aggressive

3 indifferent

4 rejecting parents

5 intimidated

6 scared

7 matriarch

8 controlled by anger

9 subdued

10 inferior

Figure 1. Overlay rating response sheet as completed by Janet R. prior to therapy. (Dashed circles indicate erasures, that is, instances in which Janet rated herself at one point of the scale and then changed her rating. Completed circles indicate her final self-rating.)

199

(1955, pp. 219–266) discusses the *clinical analysis* of the Reptest, concentrating upon the content of the constructs elicited and their application to specific figures. An examination of Janet's constructs (column A, Table 3) suggests that she frequently dimensionalizes her interpersonal world in terms of dimensions that may have limited commonality with constructs typically used by other people (e.g., Construct 7). The idiosyncratic nature of her discriminations may make it difficult for others to play meaningful social roles in relation to her, in Kelly's sense, because roles are defined as interactions based upon an appreciation of the individual's outlook (Kelly, 1955, p. 97). Thus we might be alert to possible expressions of estrangement from others on Janet's part in the course of therapy, perhaps coupled with her impression that others are too simple or too conventional to understand her.

A further approach to the interpretation of Janet's constructs would consider the *behavioral alternatives* implicit in her construction system. It must be remembered that constructs represent psychological pathways along which the individual is free to move; they are not merely intellectual labels for objects and occurrences. Consider the case of the man in therapy who construes human relations mainly as a matter of being "kind" versus being "hostile." If events force him to change his customarily "kind" behavior toward others, then "hostility," as he sees it, is his most palpable alternative (Kelly, 1955, p. 938). By implication, several of Janet's constructs present her with behavioral dilemmas; she can choose to be either "powerful" or "intimidated," "manipulative" or "subdued." Similarly, she is bound by her own constructions to "hate women" or be "indifferent" toward them, to "suffer from her parents" or to totally "reject" them. Within such a system, it is hardly surprising that anger, suffering, manipulation, and so on represent positively valued alternatives to her (see her value codings in Table 3), if not wholly satisfactory ones. Moreover, when such constructs are understood as structures that psychologically channel the person's processes, as the fundamental postulate of PCT suggests (Kelly, 1955, p. 46), her bizarre shifts in interactive style become more comprehensible.

From a PCT viewpoint, Janet's disjunct "personalities" can be understood as fragmented subsystems of core role structures, that is, as inferentially incompatible constructions of her own identity (cf. Kelly, 1955, pp. 83ff, 502ff). Some of the chief axes along which her self-construction fluctuates are suggested in her Reptest. Thus, "Angela," representing her predominant subsystem, is characterized in her ratings as extremely "angry" and "aggressive," as "hating women" and "rejecting her parents." "Cyn," in many respects, represents the contrast figure; she is very "passive," "intimidated," "scared," and "subdued," "suffering from her parents" rather than rejecting them. "Cynthia" seems to offer the prospect of less emotionally devastating interactions with others, although she remains an aloof and underdimensioned figure, being construed only as highly "assertive," "indifferent," and "superior," obtaining zero ratings on all other scales.

In the face of such intrapsychic contradiction, it is hardly surprising that, as Figure 1 indicates, Janet produced a confused and ambivalent pattern of ratings when instructed to place herself, as a *single* figure, within her repertory of constructs. This shifting of the element "herself" from one pole to the other of her dimensions is clinically significant, given the complete absence of such ambivalence for other figures in her grid. Such an instability in self-understanding is consonant with the conceptualization of "loose construing" that Kelly (1955, p. 856) regards as the distinguishing feature of thought-disordered schizophrenics.

More formal analysis of such grid data also can be informative in clinical diagnoses. Landfield (1971) has developed a reliable "content postcoding dictionary" for interpersonal constructions, allowing individual construct poles to be multiply coded under an appropriate subset of the 32 categories that compose his system. Applying this content-coding scheme to Janet's Reptest reponses (column A, Table 3), we discover that fully 60% of her construct poles connote "high forcefulness," suggesting that she regards this as a salient feature of her interpersonal world. Moreover, although nearly a third (30%) of her constructs would be considered indicative of "emotional arousal," none of these could be classified as "high tenderness," implying a dearth of positive emotional experiences in Janet's affectively charged perceptual universe. Finally, it is noteworthy that the 20% of her constructs that point to her being "closed to alternatives" are counterbalanced by another 20% that draw attention to her capacity for "self-sufficiency."

These observations clearly carry implications for the psychotherapeutic goals appropriate to Janet's case. For example, therapy might aim at helping her explore less forceful, invasive relationships with others, thus providing a context for the experience of positive as well as negative emotions. Furthermore, one might seek to enlist her sense of autonomy in the service of therapeutic reconstruction, a reconstruction that would be facilitated by the attenuation of those structures that bar her from seeing alternatives to her present system of understanding.

Numerous possibilities also exist for the *structural scoring* of Janet's rating grid, as opposed to an analysis of its content. Broadly speaking, structural analyses examine formal properties of the individual's grid responses (e.g., the intercorrelation of element ratings performed on two construct scales) rather than the semantic meaning of the dimensions per se. An example of such an approach is the calculation of the "functionally independent construction" (FIC) score for a sample of constructs (Landfield, 1971, 1977).

In brief, the FIC indexes the number of functionally independent construct clusters employed by the individual, with the "independence" of the dimensions being gauged by the degree of dissimilarity of element ratings in the pairs of construct dimensions under consideration. In the limiting case, an individual's construct system might be so differentiated that no two constructs seem related to one another; construing a certain role figure with a given pole of one construct carries no implications for where he or she might fall on any other construct. Such a style of construing would yield a high FIC score, indicating a degree of "cognitive complexity" that may verge on conceptual fragmentation. On the other hand, a person's construction system can be so monolithic that every construct yields essentially the same perceptual discriminations as every other. In this case, the FIC score of 1 (e.g., all constructs form one dependent cluster) points to the functional equivalence of the constructs sampled, despite their different word labels. Landfield, Page, and Lavelle (Note 1) recently have developed a computer program that calculates FIC scores for ratings grids of the type administered to Janet, as well as "ordination" and "rating extremity" scores (discussed subsequently) for the same data. The flexibility of the program makes it suitable for a wide range of applications, because it can accommodate grids containing as few as 5 constructs and 5 elements or as many as 45 of each.

The FIC score was computed for the ratings of the ten elements on the ten constructs of Janet's grid (Figure 1). Only three constructs displayed functional dependence upon one another (1, 5, and 9), suggesting that, for Janet, "angry" people tend to be perceived as "powerful" and "manipulative," whereas "passive" characters may be construed as "intimidated" and "subdued." No other constructs were significantly correlated. The resulting FIC score of 8 (i.e., one cluster of constructs plus seven independent dimensions) suggests considerable differentiation in her construct repertoire. Such differentiation, in the absence of a capacity to integrate one's disparate perceptions, has been associated with the breakdown of one's interpretive system and the emergence of various "pathological" behaviors, including suicide (Landfield, 1976).

In order to assess Janet's conceptual capacity to encompass the complexity implicit in her perceptual system, the "ordination for constructs" score (Leitner, Landfield, & Barr, cited in Adams-Webber, 1979, p. 60ff) was computed for the same grid data. Essentially, the score reflects the degree of flexibility with which a construct is used to rate a set of elements. For an individual to display such flexibility of construing, it is reasoned that he or she must have access to integrative, "superordinate" constructions. Janet's ordination score of 7.6 is unusually low, reinforcing the concern about her highly differentiated system leading to bewilderment for her. Thus the unintegrated complexity in her constructions of herself and others is implied by her grid and is consonant with impressions gleaned from the clinical observation of her behavior.

Finally, a rating extremity score can be computed by the same program, indicating the extent to which the respondent produces extreme and clear-cut ratings of the elements on the construct scales rather than more equivocal center-scale responses. Bonarius (1971, 1977) has adduced considerable experimental evidence to support the interpretation of such rating extremity as an indication of the "meaningfulness" of the constructs and elements involved. The relatively high total extremity score of 397 for Janet's protocol suggests that she generally dimensionalizes her interpersonal world in clear-cut, if fragmented, fashion. Still, it is noteworthy that particular figures (e.g., herself and her present therapist, with extremity scores of 29 and 27, respectively) appear much less meaningful than most other figures on her grid.

Assessment techniques based on construct theory are particularly well suited to longitudinal investigations, arising as they do from Kelly's basic philosophy that "the person is a form of motion" whose psychological processes only make sense when considered along a dimension of time (Kelly, 1955, p. 48). A clinical example of such longitudinal study is afforded by an analysis of a second grid testing of Janet R., administered after 6 months of personal-construct-oriented psychotherapy (cf. Epting, 1980; Kelly, 1955; Landfield & Leitner, 1980) with one of us (R.N.). The same element sorts were administered in this second testing, which allowed Janet latitude in expressing different constructs than those obtained on the first testing. Ratings of all elements on the newly elicited construct scales were performed as before.

An inspection of the content of Janet's dimensions on the second grid (see column B, Table 3) suggests that substantial reconstruction of her system had taken place during therapy. Constructs 1, 5, 8, and 9 in particular had been revised, resulting in a far-reaching change in her outlook. Her new-found capacity for joy, honesty, and compassion as behavioral alternatives to anger, manipulation, and hatred was evidenced in her interactions with significant others as well as on the grid itself. "Angela," "Cyn," and "Cynthia," her "subpersonalities," remained meaningful characters for her but had come to be regarded metaphorically, as labels for aspects of herself. Moreover, she came to construe them all as motivated by "fear," in contrast to her emergent sense of a holistic self ("Janet") who displayed great "courage" (Construct 10).

Categorizing these new constructions using Landfield's (1971) postcoding scheme lends further credence to these clinical impressions. The high forcefulness constructs that had dominated her earlier grid had shrunk in number, from 60% to 35%, implying her greater freedom to enact nonabrasive social roles toward others. Furthermore, although 30% of her responses continued to suggest emotional arousal, one third of these could now be classed as high tenderness, opening vistas for positive emotional experience that were closed to her at the time of the first testing. In a similar vein, those construct poles representing her being closed to alternatives had dwindled to only 10% of her total repertoire, whereas those pertaining to self-sufficiency had doubled to 40%. These shifts were very much in keeping with the autonomous, "experimental" approach to living that she had evolved over the course of therapy.

Changes in the structural indexes of Janet's grid were no less dramatic.

Constructs 2 and 5, 9 and 10, 3, 7, and 8 had cohered into three identifiable clusters, whereas Constructs 1, 4, and 6 remained functionally independent. The resulting FIC score of 6 represented a "tightening" from the previously more differentiated system having eight unrelated clusters. Concomitantly, her behavior, her perceptions of others, and especially her experience of herself became more consistent and organized. Her ordination score doubled, from 7.6 at the first testing to 14.9 at the second, reflecting her recently acquired access to superordinate constructions, which allowed her to integrate the unmanageable complexity of her earlier experience. Finally, as one would expect of a "treatment" in which the therapeutic relationship figured so importantly, the meaningfulness of the therapist figure increased substantially, from 27 to 44 points on the extremity score. More important, Janet's understanding of herself showed a similar increment in meaningfulness over the course of therapy (from 29 to 43), and the marked ambivalence in self-ratings that characterized her earlier responses was nonexistent at the second testing.

A clinical follow-up 6 months after the administration of the second grid confirmed that she had consolidated the life changes she had initiated during psychotherapy and had successfully developed her career and personal relationships along lines commensurate with her reconstruction of herself. Repertory grid technique proved sensitive in monitoring the process of therapy, capturing the uniqueness of Janet's case without sacrificing the possibility of rigorous evaluation of therapy outcome.

Rank Order Grid. The rank order grid was first described by Bannister (1963). As with other grid forms, the rank order grid technique is applicable to a wide variety of problem areas. In each case, however, the subjects' task is the same—to rank order a series of elements from those most easily subsumed under the pole of a construct to those least easily subsumed under that pole (e.g., ranking one's acquaintances from "most outgoing" to "least outgoing"). Because this grid method is used extensively in Europe and enjoys a wide range of scoring procedures, the administration, grid compilation, and scoring possibilities will be discussed in greater detail within the context of a clinical sample.

In the course of clinical work with chronic alcoholics, one of us (G.N.) obtained a 9 × 12 rank order grid from a 34-year-old male. In addition to alcoholism, particularly critical clinical issues included the individual's excessive preoccupation with maintaining control of situations and his inability to cope with minor frustrations and anxieties. The rank order grid was administered to help this patient better understand the relationships among these problem areas in his life. For this reason, nine situational constructs were chosen for use in the grid. Each construct defined a particular situation or context along which the patient could rank order a variety of elements (Table 4). Similarly, the 12 elements chosen for use in the grid were specific contexts in which the client would be likely to experience clinically relevant feelings or behavior (Table 5).

Table 4. Situations Used as Constructs in Rank Order Grid

C_1	Situation in which you feel in control of things
C_2	Situation in which you would be most likely to drink alcohol
C_3	Situation in which you would feel the most companionship
C_4	Situation that you would enjoy the most
C_5	Situation in which you would feel anxious or uneasy
C_6	Situation in which you want to make a good impression
C_7	Situation in which people are likely to be critical of you
C_8	Situation in which you are likely to laugh and be friendly
C_9	Situation that is likely to become frustrating

Given these nine constructs and 12 elements, the administration of the rank order grid proceeded as follows: Each of the constructs (C_1 through C_9) and elements (E_1 through E_{12}) was printed on a separate 3 × 5 inch index card. All element cards were then spread in front of the patient. He was presented with the first construct card (C_1) and asked, "In which of these situations (referring to the 12 element cards) would you feel most in control of things?" In this instance his response was, "When having dinner with my wife" (E_5). The numeral "1" was then recorded in the grid form at the intersection of $C_1 E_5$, as indicated in the completed grid form shown in Table 6. Discarding E_5, the therapist then repeated the question, "In which of the remaining situations would you feel most in control of things?" The response was E_7, and, accordingly, the numeral "2" was recorded at the intersection of $C_1 E_7$, as indicated in Table 6. This procedure was repeated until all 12 elements had been ordered along C_1.

Moving to C_2, the therapist again spread all 12 element cards in front of the patient and asked, "In which of these situations would you be most likely to drink alcohol?" The client's response, E_3, was then recorded by registering the number "1" in the matrix at the intersection of $C_2 E_3$. This procedure

Table 5. Contexts Used as Elements in Rank Order Grid

E_1	Spending an evening at home with your family
E_2	Spending time wrapped up in yourself
E_3	Spending an evening alone
E_4	Spending a day with your kids
E_5	Going out to dinner with your wife
E_6	Attending group therapy
E_7	Attending an Alcoholics Anonymous meeting
E_8	Spending a night in the halfway house
E_9	Going to church on Sunday
E_{10}	Walking into a favorite bar
E_{11}	Sitting at the table with a friend who's drinking a beer
E_{12}	Arguing with your wife

Table 6. Completed Rank Order Grid Matrix

Elements	Constructs								
	1	2	3	4	5	6	7	8	9
1. Family	8	10	4	4	5	5	7	8	6
2. Wrapped-Up	11	2	11	8	7	11	4	11	2
3. Alone	12	1	12	12	1	12	5	12	4
4. Kids	4	7	3	3	6	6	6	6	7
5. Dinner	1	3	5	1	12	9	12	1	3
6. Therapy	3	12	2	9	9	1	1	4	8
7. Alcoholics Anonymous	2	9	1	2	11	10	11	2	12
8. Halfway house	5	11	6	5	10	4	9	5	10
9. Church	6	8	7	10	8	8	10	3	9
10. Bar	7	6	10	7	3	3	3	7	5
11. Beer	9	4	8	6	2	2	2	9	1
12. Argument	10	5	9	11	4	7	8	10	11

Note. Numbers in the body of the grid matrix represent rankings.

continued until all 12 elements were rank ordered along all nine constructs and the grid matrix was completed. The completed matrix was then amenable to a variety of scoring procedures.

One useful approach to initiating the grid analysis is simply to calculate rank-order correlation coefficients between all possible different combinations of constructs. For example, calculate the correlations of C_1 with C_2, C_3, C_4, ... C_9; C_2 with C_3, C_4, ... C_9; and so forth. If each of these ρ's is then squared and multiplied by 100, it yields a series of relationship scores. The sum of the 36 relationship scores provides what is termed the "intensity score." Like the FIC measure for the ratings grid, the intensity score provides a useful index of the overall degree of cognitive structure in the construct sample (Bannister, 1960). The intensity score reflects the system's degree of tightness or looseness. A "tight" construct system is one that leads to unvarying predictions, whereas a "loose" system leads to varying predictions. This is so because a system marked by a high intensity score is one in which the constructs are powerfully related to one another. Hence, knowledge about the placement of an element along one construct provides a substantial predictive base for inferring the element's placement along other constructs in the system. A system marked by a low intensity score, however, does not afford such predictive potential—that is, knowledge concerning the placement of an element along any construct does not enable a tenable prediction as to its placement along other constructs in the system.

An intensity score was calculated for this particular patient and results yielded a score of 978. Although standardized norms for intensity are not yet available, clinical evidence suggests that such a score represents a fairly tight ordering of the individual's perceptual system. This finding may have prognostic significance because it reflects the client's ability to predict accurately his emotions and behaviors within an interpersonal context.

In addition to the intensity score, a measure of an individual's consistency of construing can be assessed if the same repertory grid is readministered. Such a score can be useful in monitoring the stability of an individual's construing over time. In order to calculate the consistency score, simply rank order the sums of each construct's relationship scores for both administrations and correlate these rank orderings. Because this illustrative grid was not administered a second time, however, a consistency score cannot be calculated.

One particularly useful method of analyzing the rank order data is a simple form of cluster analysis (Bannister, 1965), which is designed to provide a visual display of construct relationships. The analysis begins with the calculation of all possible correlations between constructs and the conversion of these correlations to relationship scores ($\rho^2 \times 100$). Second, the absolute value of these relationship scores is summed for each construct. For the sample grid, this procedure results in seven summed relationship scores, each score representing the amount of variance accounted for by one particular construct. The basic strategy is then to extract the two constructs accounting for the most variance to form the main axes of the visual display. In this instance the construct "feel in control of things" (C_1) accounts for the majority of the variance and, accordingly, is designated as the primary axis. The secondary axis is that dimension accounting for most of the common variance after the first dimension has been extracted but that is statistically independent ($p < .01$) of the primary axis. In this instance, C_2, "most likely to drink alcohol," constitutes the secondary axis. All other constructs can then be plotted along these two axes using the relationship scores as coordinates.

Figure 2 displays the final plotted product. It is interesting to note that this hand-calculated cluster analysis yields results virtually identical to those of sophisticated principal components analysis (Fransella & Bannister, 1977), though the latter is clearly more expeditious.

This graphic display of construct relationships provided several useful clinical insights. On the most general level, it is noteworthy that *all* constructs are plotted in quadrants I and IV. From this plotting, it was inferred that, roughly speaking, feeling "in control of things" is something of a safeguard against drinking alcohol, whereas an experienced loss of control over things may constitute a threat to the patient's sobriety. More specific observations are illuminating too. Situations in which the client enjoys the "most companionship," for instance, are also situations in which he feels very much "in control of things" as well as "least likely to drink." Situations in which he finds himself "anxious" and uneasy, conversely, are highly negatively polarized along the control dimension and moderately negatively polarized along the drinking alcohol dimension. Anxiety-producing situations, then, may in-

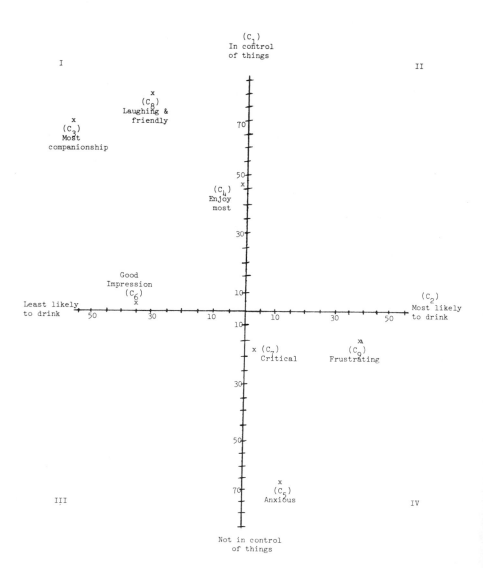

Figure 2. Constructs plotted in relation to two primary construct axes, using relationship scores.

dicate an experienced loss of control and a corresponding likelihood of drinking alcohol. Similarly, "frustrating" situations pose something of a threat to this individual's control over things and critically threaten his sobriety.

Used in this way, the rank order grid was an aid to this alcoholic in helping him discern the relationship of various interpersonal situations to his need to be in control of things as well as to his drinking behavior. In addition to providing him with some insight into the relationships among several germane clinical issues, it enabled staff to assist him in tailoring treatment plans to those problem areas most critically jeopardizing his sobriety.

The rank order grid has enjoyed application to a broad spectrum of research areas. The technique has been used most extensively in the work of Bannister (1960, 1963, 1965) and others on schizophrenic thought disorder, a line of research traced later in this chapter. Other uses of the rank order technique include such diverse applications as the study of interpersonal perceptions in marital couples (Wijesinghe & Wood, 1976), voting behavior (Fransella & Bannister, 1967), arson (Fransella & Adams, 1966), and stuttering (Fransella, 1972).

Implications Grid. In assessing an individual's construct system, it is important to discover the ways in which the axes are related to one another. Kelly's original formulation stressed the hierarchical nature of the constructs within the system. A few overarching, superordinate dimensions subsume numerous subordinate dimensions. For example, many of our finer order evaluative discriminations can be subsumed under the superordinate construct "good versus bad." Advancements in Reptest technique have sought to test this hierarchical characteristic of construing and to assess the differential impact of altering higher and lower order constructs within an individual's system.

In a major methodological innovation in PCT, Hinkle (Note 2) proposed what he termed the "implications grid" as a method for investigating construct hierarchy. He argued that more superordinate dimensions would be those carrying the greatest number of implications for the entire construct system. He first elicited a number of subordinate constructs in the standard fashion and then elicited an equal number of superordinate dimensions through the "laddering" technique. This technique elicits superordinate constructs by first asking subjects to indicate the preferred pole of each of their subordinate constructs.

Say, for example, the preferred pole of my construct "athletic versus not athletic" is "athletic." The investigator than asks, "Why?" "Athletic people get on better socially," I explain. "And why is it valuable to get on better socially?" queries the investigator. "Because people like you better," I reply. In this way, an individual can be asked to trace the superordinate implications of his or her subordinate dimensions to any prearranged level. In this case, we climbed only two rungs of the "ladder," leaving the construct "liked by people versus disliked by people" as a dimension superordinate to "athletic versus not athletic."

The next step in the implications grid is to assess the number of implications each dimension has for the entire construct system. This is accomplished by asking individuals to indicate along which other constructs they would view themselves differently, given a change in one particular construct. Suppose, for example, an individual construes herself as "very ambitious" within the context of "ambitious versus lazy." Further, suppose she were to awake one morning to find herself on the opposite side of things, say, "very lazy," and that this change reflects an enduring disposition, not a momentary lethargy. Given that she is now "very lazy," along what other constructs might she view herself differently? In essence, she would be asked to tally up the number of implied changes that resulted from that single change. This procedure would be repeated for each construct in the grid until each was paired with every other construct twice (i.e., 1 with 2, 2 with 1, etc.) and a matrix of implications is obtained.

Although a variety of statistical tests can be performed on the data (see Hinkle, Note 2), a simple perusal of the protocol is highly informative. If the grid contains comparatively few tally marks (indicating few implied changes), the likelihood is that the individual's personal template for systematizing experience is of a fairly concrete, subordinate nature. This may imply that the person is experiencing difficulty in keeping the construct system together, because the matrix manifests so few implications among constructs. Conversely, a grid teeming with tally marks may reflect a system dominated by only a few superordinate dimensions. Of course, in addition to such a general scanning, the researcher may take note of particular constructs in the system, too.

If, for example, a change in self-construction from "ambitious" to "lazy" implies changes in 15 of an individual's remaining 19 dimensions, this construct may be regarded as a relatively "core," or superordinate dimension. Conversely, the change from "blonde hair" to "brunette" may imply fewer changes and hence can be regarded as a relatively peripheral, or subordinate, dimension. In this fashion, constructs may be rank ordered according to the number of implications that each carries for the system, resulting in a ranking of relative ordination among constructs. Hinkle (Note 2) demonstrated, according to prediction, that more superordinate dimensions did, in fact, implicate more of the other dimensions in the system than did subordinate dimensions.

The implications grid has been used in a variety of other areas, including the exploration of personal identity (Bender, 1969), the study of weight change (Fransella & Crisp, 1970), and the investigation of stuttering (Fransella, 1972).

Resistance-to-Change Grid. Hinkle (Note 2) developed the "resistance-to-change grid" partly to test his hypothesis that superordinate dimensions, as defined by the implications grid, are more resistant to change than subordinate dimensions having fewer implications. In this grid, each construct is paired with every other construct once. In each pairing the subject is asked on which dimension he or she would most like to stay the same; that is, "If you *had* to change along one of these dimensions, on which one would you most like to stay the same?" A matrix of tally marks in recorded, as in the implications grid, and the results indicate the various constructs' differential resistance to change. Hinkle's findings in this regard again supported the prediction that those dimensions with the greatest number of implications also evidenced greater resistance to change.

The resistance-to-change grid has been applied in such diverse areas of study as architectural and environmental design (Honikman, 1976) and interpersonal relationship formation (Bender, 1969).

Reptest Interaction Technique. One particularly intriguing methodological innovation in interpersonal construing is the "Reptest interaction technique" (RIT; Bonarius, 1977). The RIT is a dyadic interaction technique that is played as a game. The simplest explanation of the RIT is the "administration of a Reptest by two people to each other" (Bonarius, 1977, p. 330). Participants take turns in eliciting constructs from one another (using sorts of the role figure elements provided) and then in applying those constructs to each of several role figures. This process enables each interactant to gain access to a sample of his or her partner's construct system and insight into the ways in which the system is employed in an interpersonal context.

Two recent studies have used the RIT as a structured method for facilitating interpersonal interaction in the investigation of self-disclosure. Eland, Epting, and Bonarius (1979) studied 42 dyads varying in their level of acquaintanceship. Results indicated the impact of prior relationships on the level of perceived and experienced self-disclosure in the relatively structured experimental situation. Neimeyer and Banikiotes (1980) also have used the RIT to structure the acquaintance process and have noted the usefulness of adjoining Landfield's (1971) "predictive accuracy" measure in order to assess the interactants' evolving understandings of one another over time. In addition to the use of RIT in experimental contexts, areas of potential application include communication training and marital and couples counseling.

Self-Rep Inventory. In a recent innovation of repertory grid technique, Page (Note 3) has developed what he terms the "self-rep inventory," an index of constructions of the self. Norms are being established for the instrument, and it has, to date, been administered to more than 300 individuals.

Administration is initiated by asking a person to indicate at least five positive personal characteristics (assets), five negative personal characteristics (faults), and five aspects of desired improvement (ideals). Contrasts are also elicited for each of these 15 constructs. Second, the individual selects 15 *roles* (e.g., self as "father," "brother," "student") that he or she finds personally meaningful. Third, the 15 self-roles are rated along all 15 constructs, using 13-point, Likert-type rating scales.

Using these scalar ratings, the measure permits the assessment of the interrelationship among various aspects of the self as well as the positivity and negativity of each self-role. Additionally, structural measures of integration (ordination) and differentiation (FIC) can be calculated. Of particular interest is the instrument's potential clinical utility. Because each self-role can be viewed in terms of its degree of positivity/negativity, it may be useful in assisting the clinician in differentiating particular aspects of role difficulty (e.g., problems associated with being a "father," "husband," or "student"). Similarly, the instrument may assist the therapist in determining the degree of structural fragmentation of the individual's roles. Further, the self-rep shows longitudinal potential in monitoring the change in self-constructions over time.

Threat Index. The Threat Index originally was developed as a structured interview designed to tap the respondent's orientation toward his or her own death (Krieger, Epting, & Leitner, 1974). PCT conceptualizes "threat" as the "awareness of imminent, comprehensive change in one's core structures" (Kelly, 1955, p. 489), that is, the awareness that upcoming events are likely to challenge the very roots of one's identity. Death threat, then, exists for a person to the extent that his or her construct system is not structured to anticipate the occurrence of one's own death. Operationally, this may be evaluated by the person's inability to construe his or her current life and eventual death using the same poles of a sample of important constructs. Thus construing life as "meaningful" and death as "empty" along the construct "meaningful versus empty" would be considered indicative of such a threat.

Although it provided a clinically rich perspective on the meaning of death for the individual, the original interview format of the Threat Index proved cumbersome for research use. Therefore, comparable self-administered forms of the instrument using provided dimensions (i.e., the death-relevant constructs elicited in early studies) were developed (Krieger, Epting, & Hays, 1979; Neimeyer, Dingemans, & Epting, 1977). Studies have examined the death threat characteristic of numerous populations and have reported lower death threat (relative to controls) for college students enrolled in death and dying courses and for persons who have arranged for the disposal of their bodies after death (Rainey & Epting, 1977) and higher death threat for suicide intervention workers (Neimeyer & Dingemans, 1980–1981), professionals (Krieger, 1977) and persons who remain distant from their life goals (Neimeyer & Chapman, 1980–1981). Rigdon, Epting, Neimeyer, and Krieger (1979) review the substantial literature on the psychometric properties of the Threat Index and delineate the forms of administration and scoring appropriate for its several modifications.

Nongrid Techniques

Despite the proliferation of grid techniques, it would be erroneous to identify PCT assessment strategies exclusively with the Reptest and its psychometric offspring. Especially in recent years, personal construct psychologists have shown considerable ingenuity in devising alternative assessment strategies, which, although different in format from the popular repertory grids, nonetheless are compatible with the chief principles of the theory itself. Again, only a few of these can be reviewed here, but these examples should serve to suggest the diversity of nongrid procedures now being explored.

Self-Characterization. Kelly's contribution to psychological assessment was not limited to grid methodology. In developing the "self-characterization" technique, he also pioneered the exploration of systematic, though less easily quantifiable, alternative methods. In essence, self-characterization invites the respondent (often a client in psychotherapy) to reveal those dimensions used to construe the self by couching them in a "character sketch," which imposes a modicum of structure upon the task. The instructions, as given to a hypothetical respondent, are as follows:

> I want you to write a character sketch of Harry Brown, just as if he were the principal character in a play. Write it as it might be written by a friend who knew him very *intimately* and very *sympathetically,* perhaps better than anyone ever really could know him. Be sure to write it in the third person. For example, start out by saying, "Harry Brown is. . . ." (Kelly, 1955, p. 323, original emphasis)

By requesting that the respondent describe himself from the perspective of an "intimate" and "sympathetic" imaginary friend, Kelly encourages him to write a holistic description of who he is without resorting exclusively to threatening self-incrimination. The relative lack of prescriptiveness in the instructions is also significant. Rather than specifying topical areas to be covered in the sketch (e.g., family background, interpersonal relations), they allow the individual to elaborate upon those areas containing "enough uncertainty to make exploration interesting and enough structure to make it meaningful" (Kelly, 1955, p. 334). Thus the self-characterization frequently elicits what might be regarded as the "growing edge" of the respondent's self-construction, suggesting where the client may be ripe for experimentation with new approaches to life's problems and for reconstruction of his or her outlook.

Kelly's guidelines for the analysis of such a sketch or protocol help the psychologist go beyond a merely impressionistic evaluation of the written response. He instructs the clinician to attend to the topical sequence and transition in the protocol, its organizational properties, and the clusters of related terms contained within it, which may signal the operation of an important preverbal construction. Moreover, he encourages the interpreter to take a variety of perspectives on the sketch by examining each sentence against the background of the entire protocol and by restating the client's point in other words. He directs the psychologist to the analysis of contextual areas and themes implicit in the characterization, which may indicate the grounds upon which the client is trying to extend his or her construct system and the regularities governing such elaboration. Most important, the clinician attempts to understand the principal construct dimensions invoked by the individual, taking special note of their personal meaning and the way the client shifts his or her identification within this network. Finally, the psychologist attempts to subsume or interpret the client's characterization in terms of the professional constructs represented by PCT or an alternative theoretical system.

Unfortunately, the self-characterization, although highly informative, has been employed in few formal research efforts. It has, however, been applied in the context of personal-construct-oriented psychotherapy (Bonarius, 1970; Fransella, 1972; Skene, 1973), where it often serves as the initial ground upon which reconstructive role enactment techniques can be based (cf. Kelly, 1955, pp. 360–451).

A Conversational Model for Psychological Enquiry. In an insightful elaboration of nongrid assessment techniques, Mair (1970) proposed what he terms the "conversational model for psychological enquiry." The method aims at charting the direction and nature of interpersonal understandings within the context of ongoing interactions. It consists of essentially four stages. During the first stage, interactants are invited to write two character sketches of one another—one "public" (to share with the other) and one "private" (not to share). Although interactants are encouraged to be as honest as they can be at any one time, the model recognizes that the appropriateness of disclosure is highly contextually and interpersonally dependent and that an investigation of differences between and changes within these two sketches over time can be highly informative.

The second stage of the model begins with the partners' sharing of public sketches. Interactants systematically question one another concerning clarification and elaboration of the themes in the sketches in an effort to flesh out the skeletal structure of the sketch and, in so doing, gain a better understanding of how each views the other.

Third, interactants take turns questioning one another in detail about the basis for, or evidence behind, their statements concerning the other. That is, they seek an understanding of the inferential base from which understandings were erected. Further, they examine these premises, together with their inferences, with an eye toward what they reveal about the *object* of the statements and what they reveal about the *author* of the statements. Insights from this bidirectional inquiry are noted and clearly contribute to the evolution of intrapersonal and interpersonal understandings.

Finally, the interaction ends with each member's withdrawing to consider the issues until the next prearranged interaction. In this way the longitudinal nature of this conversational method enables interactants to monitor the process and content of interpersonal development over time.

Cognitive Anxiety. In a recent elaboration of emotional construing, Mc-Coy (1977) has sought to lay the groundwork for the systematic study of affective states. From a personal construct perspective, emotional behavior may be regarded as an indicator of the state of one's construct system. Accordingly, positive emotions may be viewed as those that follow from construct validation, whereas negative emotions may be seen as resulting from construct invalidation (McCoy, Note 4). Consistent with this conceptualization is the recent theoretical and methodological work pertaining to cognitive anxiety.

Cognitive anxiety results from an individual's awareness that an insufficient basis of information or comprehension impairs judgment, organization, and planning (Viney & Westbrook, 1976). As such, it represents the recognition of the inadequacy of one's construct system for systematizing events (Kelly, 1955). Viney and Westbrook (1976) have detailed the following five different forms that such recognition can take:

1. Extremely novel stimuli not before experienced and therefore not covered by the construct system.
2. Extra constructs needed but not available.
3. Incongruous stimuli leading to conflict within the construct system.
4. Unavailable responses, generating uncertainty.
5. Cognitive processing overload or interference (e.g., too high a rate of stimulus presentation).

Using such a scheme, researchers can score written or transcribed verbal protocols for cognitive anxiety similar to the way in which "cognitive thought listings" (cf. Caccioppo & Petty, Chapter 10, this volume) are postcoded. The scoring system counts statements that fit into these various categories, providing different weights to references expressing cognitive anxiety (1) experienced by the self, (2) experienced by others, and (3) expressed but denied. Interestingly, because this nongrid construct assessment of cognitive anxiety provides five qualitatively distinct postcoding categories, it may permit not only an overall quantitative index of anxiety but also a potentially useful qualitative assessment.

Interview Techniques for Children. In the course of his intriguing work with children, Ravenette (1975, 1977) has developed a creative repertoire of nongrid techniques for eliciting constructs in preadolescent populations. His most recent elaboration (Ravenette, 1980) details several such techniques, which aptly illustrate the broader outlines of his assessment approach.

In one technique, entitled "troubles with school," the child is invited to choose three out of eight drawings pertaining to situations in school. Each drawing is in black ink on white paper and is loosely detailed but well-structured thematically. Each situation chosen serves as the focus of a detailed inquiry, during which the following six questions are posed (Ravenette, 1980, p. 46):

1. What do you think is happening?
2. Who do you think is troubled or upset and why?
3. How do you think this came about?
4. If that child were you, what would you think/feel/do? What difference would that make to anyone? As a result of all this, would you feel good or bad and why?
5. If the child were not you, what sort of boy/girl would you say he/she was?

During the course of this inquiry, the investigator discovers the way in which the child makes sense of troubled situations (e.g., his or her constructs concerning the area; Questions 1 through 3) and the child's degree of awareness concerning his or her own thoughts, feelings, and actions and, most centrally, their perceived degree of impact upon others (Question 4). The latter is crucial because it intimately involves the child's sense of self-potency in the world. The investigator also learns the child's reaction(s) to possible alternative identities and hence to the possibility of change (Question 5). Additionally, this permits insight into the kind of person that the child believes he or she is not, lending balance to an understanding of the child's self-perceptions.

A second technique, entitled "portrait gallery," aims at the self-exploration of feelings. Two faces are drawn, one to stand for a "sad" child and one for a "happy" child. The child is asked to distinguish the two and to say three things about each of them. Further, the child is presented with blank faces and is asked to fill in each of them to represent other feeling states and to say three things about each of them. Despite the technique's simplicity, it provides particularly rich interpersonal insight. It enables the investigator to determine many implicative relationships within the child's affective world. For example, what does being "sad," "mad," and "nervous" mean to the child? What implications does each state carry for his or her thoughts, feelings, and behavior? What are the underlying assumptions of the various affective states (e.g., Is it "cowardly" to cry, "bad" to get angry?).

A third technique is called "the good and the bad of it." This method assumes as its premise that every good thing can be viewed as bad in some respect, and vice versa. This is essentially a concretized version of PCT's fundamental assumption, "constructive alternativism" (i.e., that an object or event is always open to alternate constructions). This technique focuses on an aspect of the child that he or she regards as "bad" for himself or herself at the moment. The investigator asks how the child would prefer things to be. This yields two contrasting states, about each of which the child is asked to find something "good" and something "bad." Say, for example, a boy were to regard himself as "bad" for "cutting up so much" in class, whereas he would prefer to be "more serious." "Cutting up" is seen as "bad" because "it gets me in trouble" and as "good" because "other kids laugh and like me." Alternately, being "more serious" is seen as "bad" because "none of the kids would like me anymore" and as "good" because "I'd make better marks."

This procedure accomplishes two things. First, it clearly urges the child to move into constructive alternativism. The implicit message suggests that nothing is absolute, that there are good and bad things about everything. In itself, this may be enlightening and liberating for the child who feels bound by his or her constructions. Second, this technique allows the child to trace the superordinate implications of his or her construct system. For example, it may constitute an important realization that "cutting up in class" implies "being liked by others," whereas "being serious" implies "interpersonal isolation." In this way the child becomes better able to understand the relationships among the various things he thinks, feels, and does.

In sum, Ravenette has creatively engineered a variety of nongrid assessment procedures that imaginatively tap children's construing. Although the focus of convenience for these particular techniques is clearly the preadolescent age group, similar measures could be fruitfully adapted for use with other age groups.

Illustrative Lines of Investigation

Schizophrenic Thought Disorder

It is not surprising that, as a clinically based personality theory, PCT has given extensive attention to several clinical issues. Perhaps foremost among these has been the systematic investigation of schizophrenic thought disorder.

In his pioneering work in the area, Bannister (1963) proposed what he termed the "serial invalidation hypothesis." This explanatory notion holds that thought disorder results from repeatedly unsuccessful construing. As an individual's predictions of an event along a number of constructs are repeatedly invalidated, that individual is forced to change his or her evaluations along these dimensions, gradually weakening the interrelationships among constructs. This eventuates in "loosened construing." As mentioned previously, a loose construct system is one that leads to varying predictions, whereas a tight system is one that leads to unvarying predictions. In the loose system, knowledge about an event's placement along one dimension provides little predictive value regarding its placement along other dimensions in the system. Consequently, the end product of serial invalidation is the experience of an unpredictable, chaotic world, or in short, thought disorder. Numerous research investigations have addressed the efficacy of this serial invalidation model.

For example, a series of four experimental studies published by Bannister (1963, 1965) supported this model by demonstrating that over a 20-day period repeated experimental validation resulted in a general tightening of the construct relationships, whereas repeated invalidation resulted in a loosening of these construct relationships. Subsequent research sought to differentiate various psychiatric and nonpsychiatric populations on this dimension of "tightness to looseness." Bannister and Fransella (1965), for example, constructed a rank order grid in which subjects ordered a series of photographs along six "psychological" constructs (mean, honest, sincere, kind, stupid, and selfish). The test differentiated a group of thought-disordered schizophrenics from non-thought-disordered schizophrenics, depressives, neurotics, organics, and normals in terms of construct system intensity and consistency. As predicted, the thought-disordered sample evidenced significantly lower construct system intensity (i.e., loosened construing) and consistency (stability).

In an attempt to further define the relationship of thought disorder to construct system loosening, Bannister and Salmon (1966) argued that thought disorder should be differentially manifest in various subsystems of the construct system. Deriving from the work of Bateson, Jackson, Haley, and Weakland (1956), they reasoned that thought disorder appeared to have a specific interpersonal focus. Accordingly, a number of studies were designed (McPherson, Armstrong, & Heather, 1975; McPherson, Blackburn, Draffan, & McFayden, 1973; McPherson, Buckley, & Draffan, 1971) to test the degree of structure (intensity) and stability (consistency) of normal and thought-disordered subjects' systems in relation to "psychological" and "physical" construing.

In general, two types of rank order grids were administered. The first required subjects to rank order photographs of unknown people along psychological constructs pertaining to personality characteristics (e.g., kind, mean, honest), whereas the second required subjects to rank order the same photographs along physical constructs relating to somatic attributes (e.g., well-built, elderly, energetic). Results consistently demonstrated three things. First, all subjects demonstrated greater intensity and consistency in using physical constructs than in using psychological ones. Second, thought-disordered individuals evidenced some impairment of physical construing relative to that of their normal counterparts. Third, the thought-disordered group evidenced massive impairment in the intensity and consistency of their construing along psychological channels relative to that of normals. Taken collectively, these results have been interpreted as evidence for the differential focus of thought disorder as well as for the serial invalidation model.

Recent investigations have challenged Bannister's original conceptualization of loosened construing, however. For example, Haynes and Phillips (1973) noted that Kelly's (1955) conceptualization of a loose construct is somewhat different from Bannister's. Kelly holds that constructs themselves are "loose" when used in an inconsistent fashion. This would give rise to lower consistency (stability), but not necessarily to lower intensity (intrasystem correlation), in the system of an individual marked by loose constructs. Alternately, Bannister argues that construing can become loose by a repeated weakening of the relationships among constructs. This would give rise to lower consistency *and* intensity in the construct sample. Reasoning in this fashion, Haynes and Phillips (1973) hypothesized that, if thought disorder is related to both intensity and consistency, then intensity alone (with consistency removed statistically) should still differentiate samples of thought-disordered and non-thought-disordered individuals. Such was not the case, however. They concluded that their data show "no evidence that thought disorder is characterized by 'loosened construing' in Bannister's sense of weak relationships between constructs," although "they are perfectly consistent with, indeed strongly support the proposition that it is characterized by 'loose constructs' in Kelly's sense of inconsistently used constructs" (Haynes & Phillips, 1973, p. 215).

Although the precise relationship of thought disorder to construct system impairment remains uncertain, this evolving literature suggests the fruitfulness of further investigation. Additionally, it illustrates the fecundity of an approach that displays an interpenetration of theory and method.

The Acquaintance Process

In a series of systematic investigations of friendship formation, Duck (1973) corroborated his "filter theory" of friendship development. As the basic premise of this early work, Duck adhered to a similarity–attraction hypothesis. He argued that individuals sharing similar constructs would find communication and validation of mutual constructions easier and hence find one another more attractive than a dissimilar person. Most important, however, Duck suggested that different types of similarity (e.g., attitude agreement, personality similarity, construct similarity) should be differentially attractive at various *stages* of friendship development. Accordingly, individuals who fail to meet the necessary criterion for similarity during any particular stage would be "filtered" out of the pool of prospective friendships.

Several studies have supported this conceptualization by demonstrating the differential attractiveness of various types of similarity at different levels of acquaintance (Duck, 1973; Duck & Craig, 1978; Duck & Spencer, 1972; McCarthy & Duck, 1976). Construct similarity, in particular, has been related systematically to friendship choice (Duck, 1973) as well as to continued friendship development (Duck, 1975). Further, the *type* of construing has been shown to undergo a characteristic shift over the acquaintance process (Duck, 1973; Neimeyer & Merluzzi, Note 5). Typically, upon first encounter, interactants characterize one another in relatively concrete physical terms (e.g., tall, cute, blonde). Gradually, as acquaintance continues, however, these dimensions are eschewed for progressively higher order, more abstract bases of discrimination (e.g., sensitive, ambitious, playful). The application (Neimeyer & Neimeyer, 1977), similarity (Duck, 1975), and meaningfulness (Neimeyer, Banikiotes, & Ianni, 1979) of these psychological constructs have been especially useful in differentiating friendships from more casual acquaintances (Lea, 1979) and in predicting friendship maintenance and collapse (Duck & Allison, 1978). Although very recent, the study of friendship collapse (Duck, 1977, Note 6) is already documenting the functional relationship of construct dissimilarity to relationship deterioration. For example, it appears as though construct dissimilarity at relatively core psychological levels is highly predictive of relationship collapse (Duck &

Allison, 1978). In this way, the continued investigation of interpersonal development and deterioration holds intriguing implications for integrating aspects of social psychology, personality theory, and clinical practice.

In an independent line of work, Landfield (1977, 1979) has investigated structural changes associated with increased sociality. As the major vehicle for his investigations, he developed the "interpersonal transaction group." Designed to facilitate the acquaintance process, the group combines aspects of large group and dyadic interactions. Group size can vary somewhat (usually between 6 and 12 members) but must remain a multiple of two. The number of interpersonal transaction sessions is prearranged and usually varies between 8 and 20. Each session is composed of three phases.

During the first phase, group members convene collectively to discuss the session's upcoming activities, and the importance of nonjudgmental sharing is emphasized. The first topic for dyadic discussion in the second phase is also announced. The second phase constitutes the most important aspect of the procedure and consists of the "serial rotation" of dyadic interactions, a sequence that continues until each member has interacted with every other member for a brief period (from 4 to 8 minutes) during which interactants discuss a given topic or issue. Upon completion of the first serial rotation procedure, another topic is announced and the rotation sequence is repeated. Following this interaction phase is the third phase, in which participants again convene collectively and issues and insights are shared with the entire group. At appropriate intervals (e.g., after sessions 1, 10, and 20 in a 20-session group) a ratings Reptest (using fellow group members as elements) is administered to each person, and measures of "predictive accuracy," "positivity," and "meaningfulness" are obtained from members' scalar ratings of one another. Structural measures of integration (ordination) and differentiation (FIC) (cf. the ratings grid discussed previously) are also derived. Using such grid analyses as indexes of change, Landfield (1979) has documented the significantly greater meaningfulness, positiveness, and predictive accuracy (empathy) of group members' perceptions of one another over time as compared to a comparable control group. Independent observations in applied settings (R. Neimeyer, G. Fairbairn, cited in Landfield, 1979) corroborate the value of interpersonal transaction groups for interpersonal facilitation.

Nonverbal Construing

Although PCT does not regard constructs as explicit cognitive or verbal affairs, it is true that the great majority of research studies have operationalized constructs as linguistic discriminations. Some pioneering work, however, has sought to overcome this traditional bias by exploring constructions conveyed by nonverbal symbols.

Riedel (1970), for example, devised a matrix within which individuals could depict schematically the nature of the role constructs governing their interactions with significant others. His results imply that younger children and psychotics, in contrast to adolescents and nonpsychiatric medical patients, have a more variable sense of self in various role relations. Van Harten (reported in Bonarius, 1971) had respondents using contrasting inkblot cards to represent the poles of their constructs. As he had predicted, ratings of elements performed on scales anchored by these nonverbal symbols were more extreme if the respondent regarded the dimensions as personally relevant. This finding provided additional validation for Bonarius's "meaningfulness" interpretation of rating scale extremity. G. Neimeyer (Note 7) extended this work into the area of interpersonal construing. By asking participants to flank rating scales with "verbal" and "nonverbal" constructs (the latter symbolized by photographs), he discovered that placements of role figures were equally extreme on both sets of dimensions. He concluded that respondents perceived the language and nonlanguage constructs to be equally meaningful.

R. Neimeyer has attempted to delineate structural properties of what he terms "tacit construing," defined as "all those constructions which are not verbally articulated, regardless of their point of emergence in the individual's lifespan. They may or may not be symbolized in a nonlanguage modality" (R. Neimeyer, 1980*b*, p. 105). In order to gain access to these elusive areas within a person's construct system, he has developed the tacit construing technique, which provides a variety of visual, plastic, and textural materials that can be used to symbolize tacit dimensions in a ratings grid format. Data obtained on adult respondents suggest that these unspoken discriminations occupy central, superordinate positions within the overall system and that they may be more intensely meaningful than their verbal counterparts when applied to certain aspects of experience. Moreover, provocative sex differences have been evidenced in the use of tacit construing. Although the females studied have equaled males in the complexity of their verbal networks of constructs, they appear to be more differentiated than the latter in their use of nonverbal, perhaps more "intuitive" discriminations. Such results contribute to a clearer understanding of this largely ignored domain and illustrate what may be discovered when exclusive reliance on the verbal Reptest is abandoned.

Psychotherapy Process and Outcome

Given the sensitivity of repertory techniques to intraindividual variation over time, it is not surprising that construct theorists have employed them to monitor the process of psychotherapeutic change. Fransella (1972), for example, conducted a longitudinal investigation of a treatment of stuttering. She argued, from a PCT perspective, that persons stutter because in that way they can interpret interpersonal events most effectively, thereby rendering them meaningful and to some degree predictable. Theoretically, as children, stutterers were never in a position to elaborate constructions of themselves as fluent speakers and hence became unable to achieve anticipatory security regarding the reactions of others to them were they to abandon their familiar disfluent roles. To trace therapeutic change in the construct systems of these clients, Fransella periodically administered to each a "bipolar" variant of the implications grid (Fransella, 1972; Fransella & Bannister, 1977) throughout treatment. Therapy was technically eclectic but theoretically consistent, as is generally true of personal construct psychotherapy (cf. Epting, 1980; Landfield & Leitner, 1980). One important aim of treatment was to encourage "social role taking" (e.g., understanding the outlook of the other person who the stutterer engaged in interaction). This was facilitated by in-session discussions as well as extratherapy behavioral experiments with fluency.

As had been predicted, grid testing indicated that the clients saw significantly fewer implications for themselves as nonstutterers than as stutterers at the beginning of treatment, a picture that reversed by termination. Concomitantly, two measures of speech disfluency registered significant decreases during therapy, with 81% of the stutterers improving at least 50%. Most important, Fransella found evidence in support of her primary hypothesis that reductions in speech disfluency were related to an increase in the number of implications associated with being a nonstutterer. Conversely, those individuals evidencing the least improvement were shown to have the greatest number of implications for self-as-stutterer. Finding themselves highly "implicatively bound" to viewing themselves as stutterers, these individuals were highly resistant to change.

Carr (1970, 1980) has approached the study of therapy outcome from a somewhat different methodological and theoretical perspective. Recognizing that a modicum of "cognitive compatibility" between interactants is necessary to ensure communication, he hypothesized that client–therapist pairs manifesting similar levels of construct "differentiation" would show greater therapeutic gain than would more discrepant pairs. Differentiation was assessed by means of the Interpersonal Discrimination Task (IDT), which measures the number of discriminations made among a set of stimulus persons along each respondent's personal construct dimensions (Carr, 1965).

Results supported his predictions. Clients whose pretherapy differentiation scores more nearly matched those of their psychiatric resident therapists showed significantly more improvement in terms of both reported symptom reduction and their own ratings of outcome than did those clients less conceptually congruent with their therapists. Furthermore, posttherapy assessment using the IDT indicated that dyads whose scores were initially discrepant tended to converge in differentiation over the 12 weeks of therapy. Carr interpreted this as an attempt on the part of both therapist and client to approximate the conceptual style of one another, in order to provide a more adequate basis for further interaction. These findings were replicated in a subsequent investigation (cited in Carr & Posthuma, 1975), which further suggested that differentiation compatibility need not be consciously apprehended by the members of the dyad in order to have an impact on therapy outcome.

Landfield (1971) has analyzed still other facets of the interplay between client and therapist construction systems over the course of psychotherapy. He administered repertory grids to a heterogeneous sample of clients and their therapists, the latter differing in their theoretical persuasions, throughout the therapeutic sequence. Landfield then pooled the dimensions for each therapy dyad and asked each individual to rate his or her (1) "actual" self, (2) "ideal" self, and (3) partner on scales anchored by all of their constructs.

As he had hypothesized, premature termination of treatment was found to be more likely in those dyads in which clinician and client perceived one another as less meaningful figures (as indexed by the extremity of their ratings of one another) and in those cases when the two interactants showed less construct similarity (as determined by Landfield's content postcoding system, discussed previously). Moreover, results implied that, although *gross* organizational discrepancy in client–therapist construct systems (as gauged by difference in FIC scores) could result in premature termination, *moderate* levels of discrepancy were associated with client improvement, as judged by independent evaluators. Perhaps even more interesting was the finding that improvement was associated with a shift in the client's "actual-self" rating toward the "ideal" of the therapist, but only when the shift was plotted within the personal construct system of the client. How many studies of psychotherapy outcome have failed to yield significant findings only because improvement has been indexed exclusively along "objective" provided scales rather than measured along the personal channels of the clients' network of understandings?

In sum, construct theorists have begun to illuminate the workings of psychotherapy and the determinants of its outcome. It seems safe to conclude that PCT offers the clinical researcher not only a rich fund of hypotheses concerning individual and interactional processes occurring in therapy but also a sophisticated methodology by means of which the tenability of such hypotheses can be assessed.

Developmental Psychology

It is only recently that PCT has begun to elaborate a developmental psychology, one that explicitly deals with the construing processes of children as well as of adults. The recency of this concern is largely attributable to Kelly's reluctance to posit "separate" assumptions for persons of different ages and to his belief that a comprehensive theory needs to encompass psychological change irrespective of the age at which it occurs. Nonetheless, it is inarguable that understanding the processes of the child presents a unique challenge to the adult (O'Reilly, 1977). Construct psychologists who have taken up these challenges have attempted a "downward extension" of their efforts with regard to theory and methodology as well as research.

A PCT approach to the study of children begins with the recognition that development, even in the earliest years of life, is a deeply interpersonal process. Thus, although the infant seems to possess certain rudimentary bipolar discriminations (e.g., "hunger vs. no hunger") at least from birth (Tyler, Note 8), this inchoate construing begins to assume characteristically human form only under the tutelage of a caring adult (Shotter, 1970). Because the parents' construct systems represent the "enabling structure" within which the child will begin to know the world and himself or herself, it becomes crucial to study the interplay of both parental and child constructions (O'Reilly, 1977). For example, the mother's perception that she and her child share similar constructs would be expected to facilitate their forming an empathic role relationship, one that would conduce to the child's evolving a progressively more organized construct system with increasing maturity (Salmon, 1970).

Although general support for a PCT interpretation of parent and child behavior is provided by current cognitive developmental research (Mancuso, 1977), a number of grid techniques have been developed that permit the testing of hypotheses unique to construct theory (e.g., Ravenette, 1975, 1977, 1980; Salmon, 1976). Barratt (1977), for example, devised a picture-sorting grid to assess the interpersonal constructions of children aged 8 to 14 years. As he had hypothesized, the percentage of constructs whose content concerned superficial roles occupied by the construed figures decreased with age, whereas those relating to the behavior and personality of the figures increased concomitantly. Moreover, the constructs employed by older children tended to be more "other-oriented" and more discriminating than those employed by younger respondents, a finding that corroborated Applebee's (1976) observation that children tend to recognize more "shades of grey" within a construct dimension as they grow older. Barratt also noted that more mature children were less sex-stereotypic in their perception of peers and that they were better able to generate hypotheses about why a particular construction seemed to fit a particular figure. Females appeared generally precocious on all of these trends.

Bannister and Agnew (1977) investigated somewhat similar themes in the child's construing of self. They found that, with increasing age, children were better able to recognize their earlier self-descriptions as distinct from those of others. Furthermore, in doing so, they seemed to rely less on simple memory, instead emphasizing such features of the descriptions as the general psychological appropriateness of the statement to them. The investigators reasoned that such findings evidenced the maturing child's greater number of self-constructions, as well as an increase in the strength and variety of their implications.

Honess (1980), noting the theoretical compatibility of Kelly's (1955) and

Werner's (1957) theories, used assessment techniques derived from the former to test hypotheses derived from the latter. According to Werner, development entails increasing "system differentiation" and "hierarchic integration" of the child's psychological structures. Operationally, Honess argued, increasing differentiation should be reflected by a decrease in the number of construct implications in grids completed by mature children, whereas emerging integration should be signaled by the evolution of more abstract, psychologically relevant constructions as the children aged. Analysis of the grid responses of more than 200 children aged 8 to 16 years evidenced both these trends, thereby supporting both the validity of Werner's theory and the viability of grid technique in assessing such development.

Other construct theory investigators have focused less on elucidating general developmental trends and more on describing problems endemic to certain populations of children. Hayden, Nasby, and Davids (1977), for example, studied the interpersonal conceptual structures of emotionally disturbed boys, using an innovative grid method that tested the child's capacity to both construe and predict the sequence of a photographed boy's behavior. As they had predicted, those boys possessing more differentiated interpersonal construct systems were found to engage in more adaptive behaviors toward others than did their less conceptually differentiated peers. Moreover, those children showing greater predictive accuracy in ordering the behavioral sequence represented in the photographs were also rated as more appropriate in their interpersonal demeanor. The latter finding is congruent with the stress PCT places upon an empathic sociality in the development of adequate constructions to channel the child's behavior toward others.

Although most research to date has concentrated on the child's own constructions of self and others, some attention also has been given to the interactive context within which the child's construing develops. Epting, Zempel, and Rubio (1980), for instance, have examined maternal construct systems and their relationship to parent–child interactions. In line with Salmon's (1970) theorizing, they found that mothers who construed themselves and their children in similar terms displayed more warmth and noncommanding verbalization with their children in an experimental situation. The impact that parents can have upon the child's construing is illustrated by the work of Lifshitz (1976). She theorized that the differentiation of the child's social perception is initiated in the context of the child–mother–father triad. Such differentiation, she felt, would be impaired if the triad were incomplete, as in the case of the father's death. To examine this hypothesis, she tested children whose fathers had been killed in war and found, as predicted, that those who were orphaned earlier than 7 years of age were less conceptually complex than children with living fathers or those who were orphaned later. Furthermore, she discovered that the less differentiated the child's system, the more restless his or her classroom behavior, a finding that parallels the observations of Hayden *et al.* (1977).

In conclusion, the studies reviewed here are only pioneering explorations of the domain represented by developmental psychology. They do, however, suggest the fecundity of utilizing PCT resources, both theoretical and methodological, in investigating the evolution of construct systems in childhood as well as in adult life.

Conclusion

Having dealt with a variety of grid and nongrid techniques generated by personal construct theory, and with their representative areas of application, it may be useful to conclude with a few words concerning the strengths and weaknesses of such assessment procedures. An initial focus for such a discussion is provided by Sarason's (1979) thoughtful analysis of cognitive theorizing generally and cognitive therapy especially. Essentially, he points to three major lacunae characteristic of these contemporary approaches: investigations of cognitive histories, recognition of the multiple levels of cognitive accessibility, and attention to interactions among cognitions. He argues cogently that cognitive psychology would be strengthened were these factors taken into account in psychotherapy and, presumably, in cognitive assessment as well.

For the cognitive research psychologist as well as the clinician, construct assessment procedures offer possibilities for addressing these traditional shortcomings. Kelly's theory, for example, recognizes the importance of historical continuity in the construing process. Both in his discussion of the "experience corollary" (1955, 1970) and in his actual therapy (R. Neimeyer, 1980), he attends to the temporal dimensions of construing and the impact that previously formulated constructions have upon the individual's present conceptual system. Empirically, this emphasis is reflected in longitudinal research efforts and in recent attempts to assess child development using a number of innovative grid and interview approaches.

Second, Sarason (1979) stresses the dearth of theorizing concerning the differential accessibility of cognitions, some of which exist at relatively conscious levels and others of which "go underground" but nonetheless remain operative in the person's psychological economy. Personal construct theory recognizes a similar distinction between peripheral dimensions and those more superordinate reference axes that represent the core of one's system. Moreover, it is acknowledged that, although one's constructions often may be amenable to verbal articulation, many important constructs lack adequate linguistic labels and thus may operate at a lower level of awareness (Kelly, 1955, p. 466). Construct theorists, however, go beyond an abstract recognition of the multiple levels of construing; they also have provided methodologies with which such levels can be explored. Landfield's (1976) ordination measure, Hinkle's laddering procedure (cited in Bannister & Mair, 1968), and Duck's (1973) content postcoding scheme all provide means by which the level of a given construct can be inferred. Moreover, other investigators (e.g., R. Neimeyer, 1980; Riedel, 1970) have devised instruments permitting the elicitation of constructs that may be altogether unverbalizable. In combination with the several indexes of construct system structure, such measures tap what Arnkoff (1980) has referred to as the "deep structural rules" that form the fundament of the individual's model of the world.

Third, as Sarason (1979) asserts, the psychologist must be alert to interactions among cognitions, because they usually exist in complex networks rather than as specific, isolable units. Grid techniques can be particularly helpful to the clinician or researcher who shares this concern, because the diversity of structural analyses appropriate to them are designed to elucidate just such interactions. Slater's (1964) principal components analyses of grid data, Bannister's (1960) intensity score, Hinkle's implications grid (Note 2) and its bipolar adaptation by Fransella (Fransella & Bannister, 1977), and Landfield's (1977) functionally independent construction score represent only a few of the approaches developed to examine interrelationships among the constructs that compose the individual's system.

Construct assessment strategies have other important advantages as well. Because they comprise techniques and approaches to analysis rather than tests with fixed content, they can be tailored by the imaginative psychologist to address virtually any topic or problem area. Additionally, as Salmon (1976) notes, such techniques share with projective techniques a focus upon the individual's subjective world, whereas with questionnaires and rating scales they share the possibility of quantitative as well as qualitative analysis. Moreover, because PCT assessments are not closely tethered to the verbal abilities of the respondent, they are not limited to use with intelligent adults, yielding meaningful results for children as young as 4 years (e.g., Allison, Note 9). Other work has suggested the suitability of construct techniques for the study of complex interpersonal as well as intrapersonal processes (e.g., Carr, 1980; Duck, 1973, 1977; Landfield, 1971). Perhaps the greatest advantage to such assessment procedures, however, is their articulation within the coherent theoretical system that Kelly and his successors have propounded. This cross-fertilization of theory and method gives PCT-derived grids and structured interviews an advantage enjoyed by few other cognitive assessment strategies.

The clear strengths of PCT techniques, however, should not blind investigators to their equally real limitations. As Bavelas, Chan, and Guthrie (1976) have demonstrated empirically, grids are poorly suited to the evaluation of "traits," which are conceived of as unchanging features of an individual's personality structure. In a similar vein, PCT assessment procedures are limited in their appropriateness for purely normative investigation, because few rigorous norms exist for the various structural and content scores derivable from them. More seriously, however, traditional grids depict only a slice of psychological life. If readministered in a longitudinal investigation, they may suggest changes in the construct system over time; they do not, however, assess the process of construing itself, a step that may require theoretical as well as methodological refinements (Radley, 1977).

Paradoxically, the very attractiveness of PCT assessment strategies may be their greatest weakness, insofar as this may encourage their indiscriminate use by persons who may not take the time to explore the theory that alone renders them intelligible. Contemporary psychologists have a disconcerting propensity to seek safety in numbers, and the plethora of quantitative indexes derivable from the average grid is dangerous for just this reason. Several authors (e.g., Bannister & Mair, 1968; Fransella & Bannister, 1977) have noted that construct assessment techniques are vitiated by a literalistic concentration on isolated grid scores to the neglect of a more subtle appreciation of their meaning in the total interpersonal and theoretical context within which they are embedded. Only if psychologists are able to ground their disciplined investigations in an empathic and discriminating understanding can they hope to devise and employ methodologies that respect the point of view of their subject matter—the person being assessed.

Reference Notes

1. Landfield, A. W., Page, M., & Lavelle, D. *The Landfield trichotomous ratio program: Revised version.* Unpublished manuscript, University of Nebraska, 1979.
2. Hinkle, D. *The change of personal constructs from the viewpoint of a theory of construct implications.* Unpublished doctoral thesis, Ohio State University, 1965.
3. Page, M. Unpublished data on the self-rep inventory. University of Nebraska, 1979.
4. McCoy, M. M. *Positive and negative emotion: A personal construct theory interpretation.* Paper presented to the Third International Congress on Personal Construct Psychology, Breukelen, The Netherlands, July 1979.
5. Neimeyer, G. J., & Merluzzi, T. V. *Group structure and group process: Explorations in therapeutic sociality.* Paper presented to the Third International Congress on Personal Construct Psychology, Breukelen, The Netherlands, July 1979.
6. Duck, S. W. *Personal constructs in the development and collapse of personal relationships.* Paper presented to the Third International Congress on Personal Construct Psychology, Breukelen, The Netherlands, July 1979.
7. Neimeyer, G. J. *Exploring nonverbal constructs.* Unpublished data, University of Florida, 1977.
8. Tyler, M. *Kelly's "road to freedom?"* Paper presented at the Third International Congress for Personal Construct Psychology, Breukelen, The Netherlands, July 1979.
9. Allison, B. *The development of personal construct systems.* Unpublished manuscript, Memorial University, St. John's, Newfoundland, Canada, 1972.

References[2]

*Adams-Webber, J. *Personal construct theory: Concepts and applications.* New York: Wiley, 1979.
Applebee, A. N. The development of children's response to repertory grids. *British Journal of Social and Clinical Psychology,* 1976, *15,* 101–102.

[2]Symbols preceding references represent the following: *suggested readings in research; †suggested readings in theory; ‡suggested readings in technique; §suggested readings in psychotherapy.

Arnkoff, D. Psychotherapy from the perspective of cognitive theory. In M. J. Mahoney (Ed.), *Psychotherapy process.* New York: Plenum Press, 1980.

Bannister, D. Conceptual structure in thought disordered schizophrenics. *Journal of Mental Science,* 1960, *106,* 1230-1249.

Bannister, D. The genesis of schizophrenic thought disorder: A serial invalidation hypothesis. *British Journal of Psychiatry,* 1963, *109,* 680-686.

Bannister, D. The genesis of schizophrenic thought disorder: Re-test of the serial invalidation hypothesis. *British Journal of Psychiatry,* 1965, *111,* 377-382.

Bannister, D., & Agnes, J. The child's construeing of self. In A. W. Landfield (Ed.), *Nebraska symposium on motivation, 1976* (Vol. 24). Lincoln: University of Nebraska Press, 1977.

Bannister, D., & Fransella, F. A repertory grid test of schizophrenic thought disorder. *British Journal of Social and Clinical Psychology,* 1965, *2,* 95-102.

†Bannister, D., & Fransella, F. *Inquiring man.* New York: Penguin, 1971.

*‡Bannister, D., & Mair, J. M. M. *The evaluation of personal constructs.* London and New York: Academic Press, 1968.

Bannister, D., & Salmon, P. Schizophrenic thought disorder: Specific or diffuse? *British Journal of Medical Psychology,* 1966, *39,* 215-219.

Barratt, B. B. The development of peer perception systems in childhood and early adolescence. *Social Behavior and Personality,* 1977, *5,* 2, 351-360.

Bateson, G., Jackson, D., Haley, J., & Weakland, J. Towards a theory of schizophrenia. *Behavioural Science,* 1956, *4,* 251.

Bavelas, J. B., Chan, A. S., & Guthrie, J. A. Reliability and validity of traits measured by Kelly's repertory grid. *Canadian Journal of Behavioural Science,* 1976, *8,* 1, 23-38.

Bender, M. P. To smile at or avert the eyes from: The formation of relationships among students. *Research in Education,* 1969, *2,* 32-51.

Bonarius, H. Fixed role therapy: A double paradox. *British Journal of Medical Psychology,* 1970, *43,* 213-219.

*‡Bonarius, H. An interaction model of extreme response style. In A. W. Landfield (Ed.), *Nebraska symposium on motivation, 1976* (Vol. 24). Lincoln: University of Nebraska Press, 1977.

Bonarius, J. C. J. *Personal construct psychology and extreme response style.* Amsterdam: Swets & Zeitlinger, 1971.

Carr, J. E. The role of conceptual organization in interpersonal discrimination. *Journal of Psychology,* 1965, *59,* 159-176.

Carr, J. E. Differentiation similarity of patient and therapist and the outcome of psychotherapy. *Journal of Abnormal Psychology,* 1970, *76,* 3, 361-369.

Carr, J. E. Personal construct theory and psychotherapy research. In A. W. Landfield & L. Leitner (Eds.), *Personal construct psychology: Psychotherapy and personality.* New York: Wiley, 1980.

Carr, J. E., & Posthuma, A. The role of cognitive process in social interaction. *International Journal of Social Psychiatry,* 1975, *21,* 157-165.

*Duck, S. W. *Personal relationships and personal constructs.* London: Wiley, 1973.

Duck, S. W. Personality similarity and friendship choices by adolescents. *European Journal of Social Psychology,* 1975, *5,* 351-365.

Duck, S. W. Inquiry, hypothesis and the quest for validation: Personal construct systems in the development of acquaintance. In S. W. Duck (Ed.), *Theories of interpersonal attraction.* London: Academic Press, 1977.

Duck, S. W., & Allison, D. I liked you but I can't live with you: A study of lapsed friendships. *Social Behavior and Personality,* 1978, *8*(1), 43-47.

Duck, S. W., & Craig, G. Personality similarity and the development of friendship: A longitudinal study. *British Journal of Social and Clinical Psychology,* 1978, *17,* 237-242.

Duck, S. W., & Spencer, C. Personal constructs and friendship formation. *Journal of Personality and Social Psychology,* 1972, *23,* 40-45.

Eland, F. A., Epting, F. R., & Bonarius, H. Self-disclosure and the Rep-test interaction technique. In P. Stringer & D. Bannister (Eds.), *Constructs of sociality and individuality*. London: Academic Press, 1979.

Epting, F. R. The stability of cognitive complexity in construing social issues. *British Journal of Social and Clinical Psychology*, 1972, *11*, 122–125.

§Epting, F. R. *Personal construct theory psychotherapy*. London and New York: Wiley, 1980.

Epting, F. R., Zempel, C. E., & Rubio, C. T. Construct similarity and maternal warmth. *Social Behavior and Personality*, 1980.

Feldman, M. M. The body image and object relations: Exploration of a method utilizing repertory grid technique. *British Journal of Medical Psychology*, 1975, *48*, 317.

*§Fransella, F. *Personal change and reconstruction*. New York: Academic Press, 1972.

Fransella, F., & Adams, B. An illustration of the use of repertory grid technique in a clinical setting. *British Journal of Social and Clinical Psychology*, 1966, *5*, 51–62.

Fransella, F., & Bannister, D. A validation of repertory grid technique as a measure of political construing. *Acta Psychologica*, 1967, *26*, 97–106.

‡Fransella, F., & Bannister, D. *A manual for repertory grid technique*. New York: Academic Press, 1977.

Fransella, F., & Crisp, A. H. Conceptual organization and weight change. *Psychotherapy and Psychosomatics*, 1970, *18*, 176–185.

Harre, R. *The philosophies of science*. London: Oxford Press, 1972.

Hayden, B., Nasby, W., & Davids, A. Interpersonal conceptual structures, predictive accuracy, and social adjustment of emotionally disturbed boys. *Journal of Abnormal Psychology*, 1977, *86*(3), 315–320.

Haynes, E. T., & Phillips, J. P. N. Inconsistency, loose construing and schizophrenic thought disorder. *British Journal of Psychiatry*, 1973, *123*, 209–217.

Honess, T. Children's implicit theories of their peers: A developmental analysis. *British Journal of Psychology*, 1980.

Honikman, B. Construct theory as an approach to the architectural and environmental design. In P. Slater (Ed.), *Explorations of interpersonal space* (Vol. 1). London: Wiley, 1976.

†‡§Kelly, G. A. *The psychology of personal constructs* (Vols. 1 & 2). New York: Norton, 1955.

§Kelly, G. A. The psychotherapeutic relationship. In B. Maher (Ed.), *Clinical psychology and personality*. New York: Wiley, 1969. *(a)*

Kelly, G. A. In whom confide: On whom depend for what? In B. Maher (Ed.), *Clinical psychology and personality*. New York: Wiley, 1969. *(b)*

†Kelly, G. A. A brief introduction to personal construct theory. In D. Bannister (Ed.), *Perspectives in personal construct theory*. New York: Academic Press, 1970.

Krieger, S. R. Death orientation and the specialty choice and training of physicians (Doctoral dissertation, University of Florida). *Dissertation Abstracts International*, 1977, *37*, 3616B.

Krieger, S. R., Epting, F. R., & Hays, C. H. Validity and reliability of provided constructs in assessing death threat. *Omega*, 1979, *10*, 87–95.

Krieger, S. R., Epting, F. R., & Leitner, L. Personal constructs and attitudes toward death. *Omega*, 1974, *5*, 299.

Kuhn, T. S. *The structure of scientific revolutions*. Chicago: University of Chicago Press, 1970.

*§Landfield, A. W. *Personal construct systems in psychotherapy*. Chicago: Rand-McNally, 1971.

Landfield, A. A personal construct approach to suicidal behavior. In P. Slater (Ed.), *Explorations of intrapersonal space* (Vol. 1). New York: Wiley, 1976.

Landfield, A. W. Interpretive man. In A. W. Landfield (Ed.), *Nebraska symposium on motivation, 1976* (Vol. 24). Lincoln: University of Nebraska Press, 1977.

Landfield, A. W. Exploring socialization through the interpersonal transaction group. In P. Stringer & D. Bannister (Eds.), *Constructs of sociality and individuality*. New York: Academic Press, 1979.

*†‡§Landfield, A. W., & Leitner, L. (Eds.). *Personal construct psychology: Psychotherapy and personality*. New York: Wiley, 1980.

Lea, M. Personality similarity in unreciprocated friendships. *British Journal of Social and Clinical Psychology,* 1979, *18,* 393-394.

Lemon, N. Linguistic developments and conceptualization. *Journal of Cross-Cultural Psychology,* 1975, *6,* 173-182.

Lifshitz, M. Long range effects of father's loss: The cognitive complexity of bereaved children and their school adjustment. *British Journal of Medical Psychology,* 1976, *49,* 187-197.

Mahoney, M. J., & Arnkoff, D. Cognitive and self-control therapies. In S. L. Garfield & A. E. Bergin (Eds.), *Handbook of psychotherapy and behavior change* (2nd ed.). New York: Wiley, 1978.

Mair, J. M. M. Psychologists are human too. In D. Bannister (Ed.), *Perspectives in personal construct theory.* New York: Academic Press, 1970.

Mancuso, J. C. Current motivational models in the elaboration of personal construct theory. In A. W. Landfield (Ed.), *Nebraska symposium on motivation, 1976* (Vol. 24). Lincoln: University of Nebraska Press, 1977.

McCarthy, B., & Duck, S. W. Friendship duration and responses to attitudinal agreement-disagreement. *British Journal of Social and Clinical Psychology,* 1976, *15,* 377-386.

†McCoy, M. M. A reconstruction of emotion. In D. Bannister (Ed.), *New perspectives in personal construct theory.* New York: Academic Press, 1977.

McPherson, F. M., Armstrong, J., & Heather, B. B. Psychological construing, "difficulty" and thought disorder. *British Journal of Medical Psychology,* 1975, *48,* 303-315.

McPherson, F. M., Blackburn, I. M., Draffan, J. W., & McFayden, M. A further study of the grid test of thought disorder. *British Journal of Social and Clinical Psychology,* 1973, *12,* 420-427.

McPherson, F. M., Buckley, I., & Draffan, J. W. "Psychological" constructs thought process disorder and flattening of affect. *British Journal of Social and Clinical Psychology,* 1971, *10,* 267-270.

Mischel, W. George Kelly's anticipation of psychology: A personal tribute. In M. J. Mahoney (Ed.), *Psychotherapy process.* New York: Plenum Press, 1980.

Neimeyer, G. J., & Banikiotes, P. G. Self-disclosure flexibility, empathy, and perceptions of adjustment and attraction. *Journal of Counseling Psychology,* 1980.

Neimeyer, G. J., Banikiotes, P. G., & Ianni, L. E. Self-disclosure and psychological construing: A personal construct approach to interpersonal perception. *Social Behavior and Personality,* 1979, *7,* 161-165.

Neimeyer, R. A. Addendum note on tacit construing. In A. W. Landfield (Ed.), *Nebraska symposium on motivation, 1976* (Vol. 24). Lincoln: University Nebraska Press, 1977.

Neimeyer, R. A. George Kelly as therapist: A review of his tapes. In A. W. Landfield & L. Leitner (Eds.), *Personal construct psychology: Psychotherapy and personality.* New York: Wiley, 1980. *(a)*

Neimeyer, R. A. The structure and meaningfulness of tacit construing. In H. Bonarius, R. Holland, & S. Rosenberg (Eds.), *Personal construct theory: Recent advances in theory and practice.* London: Macmillian, 1980.

Neimeyer, R. A., & Chapman, K. M. Self-ideal discrepancy and fear of death: The test of an existential hypothesis. *Omega,* 1980-1981, *11,* 233-240.

Neimeyer, R. A., & Dingemans, P. Death orientation in the suicide intervention worker. *Omega,* 1980-1981, *11,* 15-23.

Neimeyer, R. A., Dingemans, P., & Epting, F. R. Convergent validity, situational stability and meaningfulness of the Threat Index. *Omega,* 1977, *8*(3), 251-265.

Neimeyer, R. A., & Neimeyer, G. J. A personal construct approach to the perception of disclosure targets. *Perceptual and Motor Skills,* 1977, *44,* 791-794.

O'Reilly, J. The interplay between mothers and their children. In D. Bannister (Ed.), *New perspectives in personal construct theory.* New York: Academic Press, 1977.

Orley, J. The use of grid technique in social anthropology. In P. Slater (Ed.), *Explorations of interpersonal space* (Vol. 1). London: Wiley, 1976.

Radley, A. Living on the horizon. In D. Bannister (Ed.), *New perspectives in personal construct theory.* New York: Academic Press, 1977.

Rainey, L. C., & Epting, F. R. Death threat constructions in the student and the prudent. *Omega,* 1977, *8,* 19–28.

Ravenette, A. T. Grid techniques for children. *Journal of Child Psychology and Psychiatry,* 1975, *16,* 79–83.

††Ravenette, A. T. Personal construct theory: An approach to the psychological investigation of children and young people. In D. Bannister (Ed.), *New perspectives in personal construct theory.* New York: Academic Press, 1977.

Ravenette, A. T. The exploration of consciousness: Personal construct intervention with children. In A. W. Landfield & L. Leitner (Eds.), *Personal construct psychology: Psychotherapy and personality.* New York: Wiley, 1980.

Riedel, W. An investigation of personal constructs through nonverbal tasks. *Journal of Abnormal Psychology,* 1970, *76*(2), 173–179.

Rigdon, M. A., Epting, F. R., Neimeyer, R. A., & Krieger, S. R. The Threat Index: A research report. *Death Education,* 1979, *3,* 245–270.

Rychlak, J. *A philosophy of science for personality theory.* Boston: Houghton Mifflin,1968.

Salmon, P. A psychology of personal growth. In D. Bannister (Ed.), *Perspectives in personal construct theory.* New York: Academic Press, 1970.

Salmon, P. Grid measures with child subjects. In P. Slater (Ed.), *Explorations of intrapersonal space* (Vol. 1). New York: Wiley, 1976.

Sarason, I. G. Three lacunae of cognitive therapy. *Cognitive Therapy and Research,* 1979, *3,* 223–235.

Shotter, J. Men, the man-makers. In D. Bannister (Ed.), *Perspectives in personal construct theory.* New York: Academic Press, 1970.

Shubsachs, A. P. W. To repeat or not to repeat? Are frequently used constructs more important to the subject? *British Journal of Medical Psychology,* 1975, *48,* 31–37.

Skene, R. A. Construct shift in the treatment of a case of homosexuality. *British Journal of Medical Psychology,* 1973, *46,* 287–292.

‡Slater, P. *The principal components of a repertory grid.* London: Vincent Andrew, 1964.

Stringer, P. A use of repertory grid measures for evaluating map formats. *British Journal of Psychology,* 1974, *65,* 23–24.

Viney, L. L., & Westbrook, T. Cognitive anxiety: A method of content analysis for verbal samples. *Journal of Personality Assessment,* 1976, *40,* 140–150.

Werner, H. *The comparative psychology of mental development.* New York: International Universities Press, 1957.

Wijesinghe, O. B. A., & Wood, R. R. A repertory grid study of interpersonal perception within a married couple. *British Journal of Medical Psychology,* 1976, *49,* 287–293.

8

Think-Aloud Approaches to Cognitive Assessment

Myles Genest and Dennis C. Turk

All things considered then, we may reasonably question whether we can at present throw over introspection altogether, unless we are prepared to content ourselves with the two ends of a series of events of which the intercalary links are frequently most complex and significant. These links are now often accessible to us only in mental terms.

Angell (1913, p. 266)

Introduction

Although there has been renewed interest in the cognitive mediation of behavior, we should not forget that, with the exception of a few aberrational periods in certain areas, cognition has held a primary position in the field of psychology since the discipline first branched out from philosophy. Indeed, in 1913 the question hotly debated was is *behavior* a legitimate category of study for psychology (e.g., Angell, 1913; Watson, 1913)? It was generally maintained that "psychology is a study of the science of consciousness," whereas "the world of physical objects . . . is looked upon merely as means to an end" (Watson, 1913, p. 158). Led by Watson, a new focus on overt behavior gained predominance in the field for some time, although not without reluctance.

When she abandons the stronghold of consciousness as her peculiar institution,

Myles Genest • Department of Psychology, University of Saskatchewan, Saskatoon, Saskatchewan, Canada.
Dennis C. Turk • Department of Psychology, Yale University, New Haven, Connecticut.

psychology is moderately certain to find that as an autonomous government she has ceased to exist and has become a mere dependency of biology or some other overlord. (Angell, 1913, p. 268)

The more recent interest in cognitive factors among behaviorally oriented psychologists (Mahoney, 1974, 1980; Mahoney & Arnkoff, 1978) has resulted in increasing concern for systematic, reliable, and valid procedures by which to assess covert processes. Four basic focuses have been evident in the research strategies in this area: (1) selection of subjects on the basis of dispositional variables, (2) direct manipulation of subjects' interpretations of stimuli or events, (3) indirect manipulations of subjects' interpretations of stimuli or events, and (4) utilization of self-report data (Lazarus, Averill, & Opton, 1970). This chapter has as its focus one group of self-report data collection methods, which we have clustered under the generic term "think-aloud." In this grouping we will include continuous monologues, event recording, thought sampling, and reconstructive techniques.

Before turning to this set of methods, we will briefly describe the other strategies in order to place our topic in context. Another primary concern of the chapter is to identify and discuss the major objections to using self-reports of cognitions that must be addressed by cognitive researchers before data obtained from think-aloud procedures are deemed legitimate. Some objections will be shown to be groundless, whereas others will point to the real limitations and constraints on both think-aloud and other self-report methods.

A Perspective on Self-Report Strategies

Four Approaches to Studying Covert Processes

The first approach to studying covert processes entails the selection of subjects on the basis of personality- or species-based predispositions to behave in particular ways. For example, subjects who vary along some personality dimension (e.g., repression–sensitization) are presented with a particular stimulus. Differential responses to the stimulus are attributed to characteristics composing the personality dimension. In this manner, subjects' responses are attributed to cognitive processes that are *thought* to underlie the particular disposition. In the example of repression–sensitization, the subjects' responses are thought to be mediated by the characteristics of either repression (tendency to deny threatening information) or sensitization (tendency to employ intellectualizing modes of defence) (e.g., Lazarus & Alfert, 1964).

The second approach involves direct intervention to alter the manner in which stimuli are interpreted. That is, different orientations toward or sets of the stimuli are provided by the investigator. Differential responding to the stimuli may thus be manipulated by the way in which the stimuli are presented. The delay of gratification paradigm employed by Mischel and others (e.g., Mischel, 1973; Mischel & Baker, 1975; Mischel, Ebbesen, & Zeiss, 1972; Mischel & Patterson, 1976; Moore, 1977) characterizes this approach. Subjects, usually young children, are offered one of two rewards—a less desirable one that the subject may have immediately or a more desirable one that is available only after some period. Different cognitive strategies are provided to help the subject delay. For example, if the less desirable reward is a pretzel and the more desirable reward is a marshmallow, subjects may be told to imagine the pretzel as a brown log and the marshmallow as a fluffy cloud to help them delay (Mischel & Moore, Note 1).

Similar approaches are employed in pain tolerance studies in which subjects are told to engage in some distracting mental activity to enable them to endure the aversive sensations for a longer period (e.g., to imagine that they are on the beach in Hawaii, reciting poetry to themselves). Following the presentation of such cognitive strategies, differential tolerance times are attributed to the use of such cognitive coping techniques (e.g., Barber & Cooper, 1972; Kanfer & Goldfoot, 1966).

The third approach is designed to manipulate the environmental parameters of which cognitive interpretations or appraisals are a function. Seligman's (1975) "learned helplessness" approach is an example. In this paradigm, subjects are led to believe either that they can or that they cannot control the outcome of some task as a function of their own behavior. That is, the apparent response contingency of the outcome is manipulated. Decrements in response initiation for the "no control" group are then attributed to the cognitive process characterized by "learned helplessness": some subjects show decrements in performance because they believe that their efforts are futile.

In all three of these approaches, inferences about cognitive factors and cognitive mediation are based on the individuals' behaviors or products, with little information available about the cognitive processes that were present between the presentation of the stimuli and the subsequent response.

> What happens between the time a stimulus affects a peripheral organ and the later time at which some reaction is made, we can often only judge with approximate accuracy provided the individual concerned tells us what has passed in his mind during the interim. . . . In other words, we have not at present any techn˙ que for ascertaining the train of neural units intermediate between a specific sen sorial stimulation and a specific delayed response. This gap we must bridge with information gleaned from essentially introspective sources or else leave it open. (Angell, 1913, p. 266)

Angell's point is no less pertinent today than it was in 1913.

The fourth approach to studying covert processes, then, is based on self-report data provided by subjects. Such data enable the investigator to make inferences about the causes of subjects' responses and provide information about the processes that may have mediated the responses.

Self-Reports

In clinical practice, the recent emphasis on cognitive processes in the production and maintenance of maladaptive behavior has, by necessity, placed increased reliance on self-reports (Kanfer & Goldstein, 1980; Meichenbaum, 1977; Thoresen & Mahoney, 1974). The development of cognitive-behavior modification approaches is heavily dependent on internal cognitive processes in both assessment and therapy. Cognitive approaches have emphasized the production and maintenance of maladaptive behaviors by irrational beliefs (Ellis, 1962), distorted thinking styles (Beck, 1976), or dysfunctional internal dialogues (Meichenbaum, 1976, 1977). According to the proponents of cognitive-behavior modification, maladaptive cognitions play an important role in contributing to maladaptive behavior and emotional disturbance, and thus therapy focuses on the modification of dysfunctional cognitions (cf. Mahoney & Arnkoff, 1978; Shaw & Dobson, Chapter 12, this volume).

Self-reports of cognitions may be obtained by a variety of different procedures. Many of these procedures and their specific applications are reviewed in this volume. In the major portion of this chapter, we will examine one set of such self-report procedures that we believe is of particular potential utility in facilitating the understanding of not just the products, but also the processes, of cognition. Our review of think-aloud procedures will include such methods as thought sampling by means of interruption, event recording and self-monitoring, continuous monologues, and videotape reconstruction.

We are casting a wide net to encompass procedures that, sometimes appearing different, share the common characteristic of providing samples of cognitive events or processes. Rather than limiting our discussion to a very narrowly defined set of procedures, we are running the risk of overlapping with other (arbitrarily designated) categories in our own (also arbitrary) categorization. Each of the procedures requires subjects to provide reports of the ongoing thoughts, images, and feelings they are experiencing or have just experienced. That is, the subjects are asked to provide reports, either behaviorally (by pushing a button to indicate a category of specific thoughts at a specific time or when thoughts shift from one category to another; see Pope, 1978) or verbally, as these thoughts occur. Think-aloud techniques may be distinguished both from assessments obtained from subjects subsequent to the performance of the task (retrospectively) and from less direct methods that are based on rating scales, responses to stimuli, and other indirect indexes of thought content (e.g., see Chapter 6, this volume, by Anderson; Chapter 13, by Glass & Merluzzi; Chapter 5, by Sobel; and Chapter 10, by Cacioppo & Petty).

Think-aloud procedures have been employed to study the process and organization of thought and the influence of ongoing thought in a variety of areas, from problem solving (e.g., Gagne & Smith, 1962; Ericsson, Note 2) and creativity (e.g., Meichenbaum, Henshaw, & Himel, 1980) to the clinical impact of dysfunctional (defensive) thoughts (e.g., in free association). Nevertheless, the approach is often avoided or criticized because it is confused with introspection as employed by Titchener and Kulpe (Boring, 1953; Dodge, 1912; Titchener, 1909, 1912). Recently, the use of self-report cognitive data has been broadly attacked (Nisbett & Wilson, 1977; Wilson & Nisbett, 1978) as not useful and often misleading. We feel that this controversy has muddied the waters, stirring together both legitimate constraints and limitations to the use of procedures such as think-aloud methods and some ostensibly serious, but actually irrelevant, objections. It is therefore necessary to address some of these conceptual issues before examining the think-aloud methodology in detail.

Access to Cognitive Antecedents of Behavior

Think-aloud protocols and other methods of collecting self-report data concerning cognitive processes have both recently been attacked (Nisbett & Bellows, 1977; Nisbett & Wilson, 1977) and long been neglected (see Ericsson & Simon, Note 3). Since Watson's skeptical conclusion that a verbal report could seldom have any value in an account of behavior, "direct" methods of studying cognitions (i.e., reports by the subjects of their own cognitions as opposed to inferences based on outcome behaviors) fell into disuse among behavioral investigators—that is, until relatively recently. Watson's point is clear in this illustration:

> The behaviorist . . . in studying skating, would take up the whole system of responses of the skater from and including the moment of fastening on the skates until they were removed. . . . After he had made a complete and searching analysis, what would be lacking? The individual's own account, of course. For the sake of completeness we will take it down. Our claim is that, in the great majority of cases, a report by the subject throws very little light upon the act he is engaged in. Let us ask him the question, however, "What were you thinking about while you were skating?" . . . the reply one usually gets to such a question . . . "What was I thinking about? I was wondering whether that 'queen' over there in the red sweater was watching me!" (Watson, 1920, pp. 99–100)

Watson, then, contended that the information provided by an open-ended verbal report of thought is generally irrelevant and useless.

Nisbett and Wilson (1977) went further, contending that accounts of causality that are based on cognitive self-reports are often wrong. With this, too, Watson was in agreement. Watson's example of the inaccurate report of a golfer's and a tennis player's analysis of their own actions served to discredit the veracity of self-report-based accounts of behavior. Furthermore, Nisbett and Wilson argued, when these causal reports are correct, they are only correct because either (1) the subject made the same observations as an outside observer would have or (2) it was the subject's predictive model or causal theory that allowed an accurate probabilistic prediction, irrespective of the particular data available in the specific case. Thus Nisbett and Wilson's argument can be viewed as consistent with Watson's evaluation of the uselessness of cognitive self-report data.

The Usefulness/Uselessness of Verbal Reports of Thinking

Let us take up Watson's initial point first: that verbal accounts provide no useful information. First, it is important to note that Watson did not challenge the accuracy of a verbal report of thought. Indeed, his 1920 paper stands as a defense of the transparent validity of thinking aloud. Watson (1920) contended that "thinking is . . . largely a verbal process" (p. 104), and "thinking aloud" he considered to be essentially representative of thinking covertly. His point, however, was that this information was useless. The skater's account of his distraction by the "queen in the red sweater" was, for Watson, irrelevant.

Watson's rejection of thinking aloud on this basis is quite understandable *for Watson's purposes*. The observations made, the data collected, and, ultimately, the conclusions drawn, however, are a function of the biases, theories, and beliefs the investigator brings to an investigation (Bowers, 1973; Kuhn, 1962; Polanyi, 1964). In this hypothetical case, Watson was concerned with constructing descriptive behavioral accounts of the figures cut by a skater. He found he could, in principle, do that quite adequately by making use of physical, observable events, such as the following:

> Arm and leg movements, the way the ankles function, the compensatory movements of the trunk, with the effort put forth by the skater as shown by the ease and grace of the movements, with the fact as to whether he was perspiring or whether he showed only signs of exhilaration or other emotional changes, etc. (Watson, 1920, p. 99)

The skater's preoccupation with an attractive spectator was not necessary for a complete account in these terms.

The situation would have been different, however, had Watson been interested in other sorts of phenomena and other sorts of accounts. Had he, for example, been attempting to explain why the single axel jump just made was not the same as the one completed two minutes previously, an account based only on the mechanics of the skater's movements would not have seemed terribly enlightening. A lean of two more degrees to the left, an increased angle on the inside edge, and so forth, might describe the kinetics involved, but they do not strike us as the sorts of "explanations" in which psychologists are generally interested when asking such questions. Why were the figures today better or worse than the ones the day before?

If one is asking these sorts of questions, then the skater's accounts become potentially useful. Knowing that the skater was particularly concerned with impressing the "queen in the red sweater" today, for instance, can be valuable in understanding the quality of his skating. Presumably, an expert skater does not have to think in detail about every movement. The "mental gymnastics" are no longer necessary when skills become overlearned and control progresses to a higher level of organization than conscious, thoughtful direction of every detail (Smith & Miller, 1978). In fact, once this overlearning has occurred, conscious thought about an overlearned behavior can interfere with its execution (e.g., Kendler, Kendler, & Carrick, 1966). This would likely be the case in Watson's example, which is why he found the skater's account irrelevant to an understanding of the execution of the maneuver. This does not mean, though, that the mental activity does not have some effect on the figure. Indeed, several investigators have suggested that the mental activity of athletes can have a clear effect on their performances (e.g., Mahoney & Avener, 1977; Mahoney & Epstein, Chapter 14, this volume).

If, then, Watson had been interested in accounting for differences between today's and yesterday's performance, or between the performance of this and that skater or this and that particular figure, the data that he found useless might well have been quite valuable. The verbal data were not necessary for his purposes. This does not imply that they are never useful. This volume provides ample evidence for the potential value of verbal reports.

The Accuracy of Verbal Reports of Thinking

Nisbett and Wilson's (1977) primary point, which Watson (1920) also expressed, was that causal accounts based on self-reports are generally incorrect and that, when they are correct, it is for the wrong reasons. These contentions have sparked several articulate replies, to which the reader is referred for extended discussion (Bowers, 1979; Smith & Miller, 1978; Ericsson & Simon, Note 3, Chapter 2, this volume; Adair & Spinner, Note 4; Hurlburt, Note 5). We will limit ourselves to two points, which are the most pertinent for this discussion.

Appropriate Situations for Use of Self-Report. The first point is that Nisbett and Wilson do not distinguish between the situations in which it does and does not make sense to use subjective cognitive accounts as data. In the same way in which Watson found the skater's account irrelevant for his purposes, one can imagine innumerable other instances in which cognitive information would *not* be helpful. One could, nevertheless, as Nisbett and Wilson have done, proceed to ask people for cognitive accounts in such situations;

because they are asked, they will probably provide them. Their willingness to do so does not in itself mean that their accounts are relevant or likely to be correct, however. In fact, as Nisbett and Wilson contend, in such instances people are likely to fall back on their implicit theories about "how people work" in order to come up with some plausible cognitive explanation. Their accuracy will then be no more and no less than a function of how good their theory is. It will not be a function of their actual cognitions. Thus, arguing the null hypothesis, one can generate unlimited examples of the uselessness and inaccuracy of cognitive accounts, examples that are themselves as totally gratuitous as providing bushels and bushels of red apples as evidence that all apples are red.

A further point is that Nisbett and Wilson's evidence is based on relatively trivial sorts of judgments. It is questionable whether their data would be similar if their subjects were responding in more personally relevant or important situations or if their assessments were more complete.

Distinction between Data and Causality. The second point is the distinction between data and causality. Nisbett and Wilson's claim is that people cannot construct accurate causal accounts of their behavior based on introspective access. It is important to be clear here about the difference between the introspective access and the causal account (Bowers, 1979).

It is clear that people do not have access to causal connections. Causal connections are *inferences*, whether they are made by Watson, Nisbett and Wilson, or David Hume (1739–1740/1888), whose forceful argument of this point has yet to be successfully challenged. Causality does not exist as a property of data. It is a concept, inferred by the observer upon making repeated observations of an invariant relationship. The most that anyone can reasonably do is to infer a connection between two events when the one repeatedly and invariantly follows the other. It is through such observations of invariant relationships and systematic elimination of reasonable alternative explanations that all causal connections are "made."

So it cannot be that Nisbett and Wilson are arguing that the subject does not have introspective access to accurate causality, for of course he or she does not. Nor does the observer have access to objective, accurate causality. It must be, then, that their quarrel is over the particular data used by the subject when giving an introspectively-based account. But this presents some difficulty. It seems to us that one must assume that subjects have unique access to some data, data from private cognitive experiences to which the observer is not privy. Given this, the only point that can be raised concerns the heuristic value of such data. Are they relevant in inferring causality in a given instance? If they are, then surely the subject must have an advantage over the observer. If they are not relevant—well, then, they simply are not useful, which is the point we dealt with previously.

This reasoning, however, still does not imply that such data are never useful. They may not be in the instances cited by Nisbett and Wilson and by

Watson. It is an empirical question whether such data are useful in any other particular situations. Smith and Miller (1978) noted that Nisbett and Wilson seemed to have chosen instances in which introspective information was singularly useless, but that in other situations, such information could be considerably more helpful.

In summary, the neglect of verbal reports of thinking occasioned by the early behaviorist critique (Watson, 1920) and the distrust evidenced in Nisbett and Wilson's (1977) paper do not challenge the validity of such reports but do question their relevance. The question of relevance is a perfectly legitimate one, deserving of empirical attention. The answer, however, will be different in different areas of investigation rather than being necessarily negative.

The Usefulness/Uselessness of Verbal Reports of Thinking Revisited

Our own proclivities lead us to advocate the collection of "cognitive data" in order to help understand much of human behavior. We believe that such data are indeed relevant to explanations of many phenomena that are currently of interest to psychologists. Going one step further, we can note that, in the clinical context, the diagnostic process and all forms of psychotherapy rely to a greater or lesser extent on the clients' self-reports as primary sources of data.

The most frequent initial statement made by diagnosticians or therapists is likely to be "Tell me about your problem," "What brings you here?," or some such variant. These initial queries are usually followed by others that require clients to report on antecedent events, consequents of various behavior, thoughts, preoccupations, fantasies, reactions of other people, causal connections they have made, and so on. The clients' responses to these probes often form the basis for additional diagnostic procedures, and the diagnosis itself and may dictate the nature of the treatment provided.

Reported fear of heights might lead to the use of a fear survey schedule (e.g., Lang & Lazovik, 1963) or *in vivo* observations and to subsequent systematic desensitization, in which the clients' verbal reports of cognitions are taken quite seriously. Reports of social anxiety might suggest a role-playing, analogue assessment and perhaps assertion-skills training. Patients' reported feelings of worthlessness and suicidal ideation might precipitate the use of cognitive therapy or, if severe enough, electroconvulsive shock therapy. Descriptions of auditory hallucinations might instigate a regimen of antipsychotic medication. The treatment selected will, of course, also depend upon the therapeutic orientation of the therapists and upon the credence given to the clients' self-reports. The important point, however, is that self-reports of the clients' own thoughts and feelings are used in some respect in this process of diagnosis and treatment.

Rogerian and other humanistically oriented therapists consider clients' self-reports as veridical. They make the tacit assumption that clients can and will provide reliable and valid responses. Psychodynamically oriented therapists, on the other hand, tend to mistrust clients' self-reports because of the emphasis on unconscious distortions and defensive maneuvers. However, dynamic therapists consider retrospective accounts, free associations, and responses to projective tests as reliable bits of data that may be interpreted by the analyst (see Sobel, Chapter 5, this volume). Behaviorally oriented therapists tend to agree with the dynamic view in that they also view self-reports as somehow untrustworthy, misrepresenting the determinants of behavior, but not necessarily useless.

Cognitive self-reports may be the only techniques, or the best ones available, to establish certain facts that are inaccessible to other forms of measurement (e.g., maladaptive beliefs about competence). Many authors have acknowledged that clients appraise their environments and behaviors, ascribing subjective meaning to their problems (Bandura, 1978; Lazarus, 1980; Mischel, 1973). Self-reports can clarify the clients' idiosyncratic perceptions. The use of self-reports may also bring to light facts that might otherwise be overlooked and may stimulate the diagnostician, therapist, or investigator to ask new questions.

To illustrate the latter point, consider a patient with symptoms of Raynaud's disease (a problem of constriction and reduction of peripheral blood flow that includes such symptoms as sensations of "cold" in the affected area, which may be quite painful) described by Schwartz (1973). The patient, a practicing psychoanalyst, was being treated with biofeedback to increase peripheral blood flow. The patient interpreted the purpose of the reinforcement slides that were used as an opportunity to free associate. One time, the slide projector jammed, and the screen showed only a bright white light. The patient viewed this as a cue to free associate about sunny, warm beaches. He used these "hot thoughts" to control the temperature of his feet outside the laboratory. Only the patient's self-reports led to the identification of the utility of cognitive mediation in the development of his self-control of bodily processes. Knowledge of the use of this strategy became apparent only from the patient's self-report of his internal processes during the biofeedback training.

Increasing numbers of behavior therapists have begun to explore, study, and utilize treatment methods that include covert processes in the target domain (Goldfried & Goldfried, 1980; Mahoney, 1974). Cognitive–behavioral approaches utilize self-reports for both assessment and change of such covert behaviors as thinking, planning, problem solving, decision making, and fantasizing. The theoretical basis of the various cognitive-behavior modification approaches rests on the assumption that cognitions do, indeed, mediate behavior. For example, Ellis (1962) suggested the following:

> If . . . people essentially become emotionally disturbed because they unthinkingly accept certain illogical premises or irrational ideas, then there is good

reason to believe that they can be somehow persuaded or taught to think more logically and rationally and thereby undermine their disturbances. (p. 94)

Beck (1976) has gone so far as to postulate that patterns of maladaptive cognitions are common to each neurotic disorder. Meichenbaum has suggested that cognitive information is relevant to understanding inadequate performance across a variety of task and skill domains. He summarized the point this way:

> I would like to suggest, in the same spirit in which Pasteur offered a germ theory of disease (saying: "If you encounter a disease, especially one that spreads quickly, look for a microorganism"), the following axiom of cognitive ethology: "If you encounter inadequate performance at a task, especially if such inadequate performance is evident across tasks and settings, look for negative self-referent ideation. (Meichenbaum, 1980)

Limitations. Despite the growing use of cognitive data, we must remain cognizant of the limitations of such information. For example, self-reports may be incomplete, reactive to environmental influence (i.e., demand characteristics, social desirability, and evaluation apprehension), inconsistent with observations of behavior, idiosyncratic, and confounded by investigator bias in the interpretation from the actual data. In short, self-observation, information storage, recall, and reporting are all subject to distortions.

Although this must be acknowledged, none of the alternative assessment procedures has proven to be completely satisfactory or unproblematic. For example, the validity of projective techniques has been seriously challenged (e.g., Mischel, 1968; Sobel, Chapter 5, this volume). The ecological validity of analogue role-playing tests has been questioned (Bellack, Hersen, & Turner, 1978). Methodological problems in behavioral observations have been acknowledged (e.g., Wildman & Erickson, 1977). And even physiological measurements have been reported to be less accurate than self-reports (Hilgard, 1969).

Some of the critiques of cognitive investigations in the past can be instructive in helping to avoid pitfalls in what Hurlburt has called "the second experimental introspection of thinking" (Note 5, p. 1). The first introspectionists required analytic judgment by the subjects, who were viewed as "ideal observers," and much training. (In Wundt's laboratory, subjects were required to practice 10,000 introspections before they were considered ready to participate in a genuine experiment.) Such subjects were considered to be unaffected by knowledge of the purpose of the experiment (Boring, 1953; Ericsson & Simon, Chapter 3, this volume; Lieberman, 1979). It is today understandable that such assumptions eventually led to concern with the extent to which introspectionist accounts were reliable, as well as with the objectivity of such reports (e.g., Watson, 1913). Moreover, the subjects in these studies were mostly professors and graduate students who were not naive to the experimental hypotheses under study, thus raising the additional concern of subjective bias. All of these are concerns that still need to be kept in mind, although they are generally less blatantly violated nowadays.

Thinking aloud, however, has been judged guilty by association. Yet thinking aloud has little in common with classical introspectionism beyond the reliance on ongoing verbal self-report. In studies that employ think-aloud procedures, naive subjects are asked to provide continuous or episodic (when cued) verbal monologues, behavioral indications of cognitions of which they are aware, or signals whenever specific predetermined thoughts occur. The investigator or clinician employing such approaches is seeking the subject's direct expression of thought while minimizing the analytic steps and the self-reflection involved in classical introspection. When Freud asked his clients to free associate, or "think aloud," they were expected to report whatever thoughts passed through their conscious awareness. In the same manner, when Jung asked his clients to engage in a word association test, the instruction was to provide the first word that came to mind following the presentation of the stimulus word. In both of these situations, interpretation of the self-report data was left to the clinician, not to the client.

Cognitive Reports as Data. One lesson from earlier introspectionist attempts is that we should treat cognitive reports merely as data and not as somehow more superior explanations of behavior. That is, when we ask subjects for verbal accounts of their actions, simply because they report something, such as "I did this and that because I thought about X," does not mean that we should take at face value the causality of X in leading to "this and that." We should not take these reports as causal explanations. Rather, we should collect the verbalizations *qua* verbalizations, in the same manner as we would collect bits of observational data. In fact, conceiving of verbalizations as bits of observational data, that is, *our* observation that "when presented with stimulus Y the subject said such and such," helps to keep our relationship to these reports clear. We accept them as data—nothing more, nothing less—and can use them to help us find answers to questions in the same way in which we use any other types of data. We can categorize our observations of verbal behavior, quantify them, analyze them, and so on. If they are functional in predicting behavior, then they have some value. If not, we are presumably on the wrong track.

For example, in an experiment concerning problem solving, the investigator might ask the subject to provide a continuous monologue of all thoughts that occurred while the subject attempted to solve the various tasks (e.g., Genest & Mann, Note 6). In the experimental situation as well as the clinical one, the investigator is interested not only in the content of the subjects' verbal reports but also in the cognitive processes that are in evidence. Genest and Mann (Note 6) reported an investigation of the effects of alcohol on attentional tasks, such as the digit symbol task. The subjects' think-aloud protocols provided not only information relevant to how they carried out the tasks but also much self-evaluative data. Some subjects, for example, attended a great deal to the perceptual alterations that the alcohol (or placebo) had on their ability to carry out the task, and this sometimes resulted in a negative (or for some subjects, a positive) evaluation of their capacity to complete it adequately.

An additional example will illustrate what is meant by cognitive processes and how thinking aloud can help uncover them. Imagine that you are at a party and are talking with a friend who notices a woman enter the room. He recognizes her but cannot recall her name. You ask your friend to try to report aloud all the thoughts he engages in as he attempts to recall the name. He might provide something like the following account:

> Red hair . . . where have I seen that red hair? . . . with a green dress, like the color of the wallpaper in my dentist's office . . . who was she with? . . . a tall man with a beard . . . that's it, at the Smith's house . . . she was introduced to me . . . Mary? Millie? Marlene? I'm not getting it. Alice? No, Betty? No, Carol? Doris? No, but something like that . . . Lois . . . no . . . I think it does start with a "d." Yeah, Dorothy. Her name is Dorothy. Dorothy Green.[1]

In this example, it appears as if the subject first tried to place the woman in the context in which he had first met her: whom she was with, her dress, something about color. He engaged in what appeared to be some irrelevant associations; he monitored his progress in resolving the problem, using one strategy; and he decided to adopt a different approach, that of going through the alphabet to arrive at her name. At one point he tried to rhyme Doris and Lois but identified that the salient feature was the first letter rather than the rhyme. Finally, he connected the name beginning with a "d" with the color from his prior strategy. Regardless of the strategy for retrieving the name, however, it is the details of the cognitive processes that may provide the most interesting information. If we did not ask for the flow of ideation, we would only be aware of the product, that is, whether or not the individual was able to retrieve the name. This success or failure is only the end product of performance. As such, it does not disclose the *how* of success or the *why* of failure.

We should take note here that we are sidestepping—quite legitimately—the nefarious issues associated with accepting verbal data as "causal accounts" in and of themselves. We need not concern ourselves with the issue of internal versus external causes, apparent versus "real" causes, underlying unconscious versus superficial conscious determinants, and so on (see, e.g., Moore, 1979). We examine our cognitive data to test hypotheses. The sources of these data do not reflect on the legitimacy of such an undertaking.

Rather, it is incumbent upon investigators and clinicians who believe

---

[1]We are indebted to Don Meichenbaum for the suggestion that led to this example.

cognitions are important to demonstrate that accurate predictions of behavior can be made on the basis of clients' self-reports of their covert processes. Klinger (1978) noted that "the validity process [for self-reports] resides in ruling out artifacts, in replications, and ultimately in the usefulness of data or theory for making other forms of prediction and perhaps control" (p. 227). Can self-reports of cognitions actually predict behavior in criterion situations?

A preliminary affirmative answer to this question has been provided by Bandura, Adams, and Beyer (1977). Bandura *et al.* were able to demonstrate that clients' self-reports of efficacy expectations (their beliefs in their ability to perform in a specific manner) were powerful predictors of nonavoidant behavior in fear-provoking situations. Related to this answer is Bellack and Hersen's (1977) suggestion that subjective *quantitative* judgments are likely to be unreliable, although *nonquantitative* judgments may be quite reliable (e.g., "I have suicidal thoughts"), as may be judgments of very low- or zero-frequency responses (e.g., "I have never had sex").

Investigators who have adopted the cognitive-behavior perspective have provided substantial data that consistently demonstrate marked individual differences in the reporting of cognitions by clients and that these differences appear to have important relationships with overt behavior (e.g., Glasgow & Arkowitz, 1975; Glass, Gottman, & Shmurak, 1976; Goldfried & D'Zurilla, 1969; Goldfried & Sobocinski, 1975; Nelson, 1977; Schwartz & Gottman, 1976; Genest, Meichenbaum, & Turk, Note 7; Larsen, Note 8; Levine, Note 9). Lieberman (1979) recently drew the same general conclusion concerning this literature:

> In a number of different settings . . . subjects' reports of their hypotheses and strategies have proved to be highly correlated with their subsequent behavior and, indeed, have often proved to be by far the most accurate predictors available. It would be foolish, of course, to claim that introspective reports would always be this reliable—the history of classical introspection has clearly shown that they are not. That same history, however, makes it equally clear that certain kinds of reports *are* useful. (p. 328, original emphasis)

If mental events do influence behavior, as such empirical studies and anecdotal reports suggest, then it is important to develop methods that will enable the measurement of these internal events accurately. Because most indexes of such covert processes can be obtained only by self-report techniques, it is most important that these techniques be developed and refined. They may be usefully employed in such clinically relevant tasks as studying the influence of maladaptive cognitions on specific emotional disorders (as suggested by Beck, 1976) and determining whether the modification of dysfunctional cognitions is the mechanism by which behavior change is accomplished (Kendall & Korgeski, 1979).

We now turn to an examination of the think-aloud methodology.

Think-Aloud Methods

Ericsson and Simon (Note 3) noted that thinking aloud continues to be criticized on at least three bases. First, the verbalizations that occur concurrently with the specific thoughts are reactive and may alter the cognitive processes under study. Second, the subject may report only a portion of the thoughts that pass through his or her short-term memory. Thus the self-reports may be incomplete and fragmentary. Third, because many thoughts may be occurring simultaneously, the subject may report thoughts that are irrelevant to the actual mechanisms of thinking related to the thought processes of interest.

These criticisms underscore the point that thinking aloud may be limited in its utility. Nevertheless, acknowledgment of methodological limitations does not require complete elimination of such reports from the class of acceptable sources of data, as we have discussed. Even overt behaviors and physiological responses can be falsified or can provide inaccurate data (e.g., Bandura, 1978; Laws & Holmen, 1978). The goal should be to reduce circumstances that encourage dishonesty or other reactive biases (Bowers, 1967) and to employ several converging operations in order to enhance our knowledge and increase our ability to understand, predict, and control behavior. Lieberman (1979) suggested that we should be interested not just in the question of whether self-report data obtained through think-aloud procedures are accurate or misleading but also in recognizing those situations in which such data are accurate and reliable.

Mischel (1973) noted that clinicians guided by concepts about underlying genotypic dispositions have not been able to predict behavior better than have the clients' or subjects' own self-reports. Bandura (1977) underscored the utility of subjects' self-ratings by demonstrating that self-ratings of subjects' feelings of self-efficacy were better predictors of future performance than even past behavior was. We will examine think-aloud methods in detail by considering several dimensions in turn.

Timing

At first blush, the issue of the timing of think-aloud reports may seem trivial or superfluous. Surely thinking aloud involves reporting thoughts as they occur. It is likely, however, that any requests for subjects to "think aloud" will result in at least some delay between the thought and its verbalization or between the process of thinking and the attempt to put it into words. This is especially the case with more complex cognitive events. Even the task of pressing a button to signal the occurrence of a given thought is often likely to result in the button pressing's *following* the thought, rather than being exactly simultaneous with it, without the subject's awareness of this.

In a sense, then, almost all cognitive reports are retrospective, because a cognitive process must occur before it can be reported. Furthermore, within the general category that we are considering, considerable variation is possible in the details of the timing of reports.

Continuous Monologues

> And how he kissed me under the Moorish wall and I thought well as well him as another and then I asked him with my eyes to ask again yes and then he asked me would I yes to say yes my mountain flower and first I put my arms around him yes and drew him down to me so he could feel my breasts all perfume yes and his heart was going like mad and yes I said yes I will Yes. (Joyce, 1914/1961, p. 783)

This quotation from Molly Bloom's closing soliloquy in *Ulysses* demonstrates not only the "unusual frankness" (for 1914) that resulted in a U.S. ban on the book but also the "serious experiment" on which the Honorable John M. Woolsey commented in handing down his dismissal of the libel charges:

> Joyce has attempted—it seems to me, with astonishing success—to show how the screen of consciousness with its ever-shifting kaleidoscopic impressions carries, as it were on a plastic palimpsest, not only what is in the focus of each man's observation of the actual things about him, but also in a penumbral zone residua of past impressions, some recent and some drawn up by association from the domain of the subconscious. He shows how each of these impressions affects the life and behavior of the character which he is describing. (Woolsey, 1933, in Joyce, 1913/1961, p. ix)

Although it may not always meet with the "astonishing success" of Joyce's efforts, the continuous monologue approach shares some of the same ends. The procedure is aimed at having people engage in ordinary activities (e.g., chess playing, problem solving) and verbalize all of their conscious thoughts as they occur. (Joyce went beyond this in an attempt to cover much material that was semiconscious or unconscious as well.) That is, subjects are asked to verbalize ongoing thoughts simultaneously with the conduct of some task provided by the experimenter. Following Joyce's pioneering, this approach, in literary circles, has been referred to as "stream of consciousness." In certain business settings a variant of this approach is known as "brainstorming." During brainstorming sessions, individuals are asked to report all the thoughts they have regarding a specific subject without censoring these thoughts in any way. Among psychoanalytically oriented psychotherapists, the technique of free association is analogous.

Private Speech. One form of a continuous monologue is private speech, which is usually studied in children. Indeed, it is probably the type of report with the least delay and the fewest intervening steps between thought processes and reports. Speech that is aloud but not intended for anyone other than the speaker is likely to reflect the thought processes that are occurring at that time fairly closely (Flavell, Beach, & Chinsky, 1966; Meichenbaum &

Goodman, 1979; Piaget, 1923/1955). Vygotsky (1934/1962) suggested that private speech "is speech for oneself intimately and usefully connected with the child's thinking" (p. 113). Recording and analyzing such speech provides an opportunity for sampling the flow of cognition without influencing its natural progression. Meichenbaum and Goodman (1979) have considered the methodological problems in studying private speech, and Zivin's (1979) volume provides some examples of studies that have tapped this dimension of behavior.

One obvious problem with private speech methods is the lack of control over the speech that is produced. One cannot assume that the child will talk about what the experimenter is interested in, and the absence of speech is generally uninterpretable. Some manipulations of the situation (e.g., providing a moderately challenging task, causing some failure, or using a fantasy-play setting) can assist in increasing the incidence of private speech, but the investigator wishing to collect these reports is essentially limited to studying a given range of situations and types of verbalizations.

Occasionally, unpredicted occurrences of private speech can provide clinical leads and sources of data. Weisman and Sobel (1979), for example, recounted the occurrence of spontaneous self-instructional language during a 67-year-old cancer patient's block design subtest of the WAIS:

> There we are . . . now that's better . . . a white one here . . . yes, then that one . . . it'll have to go like that . . . first this one, then another red . . . now this is a real humdinger . . . two reds go here . . . good. (p. 5)

Weisman and Sobel found, upon inquiry, that the patient often used such positive, self-guiding speech in other situations. It seemed to serve several very adaptive functions for her and contributed to what the authors called her "superb coping strategies."

Free Associations. A close relative to private speech is the method of free association. In theory, the verbalizations produced by the patient during psychoanalysis ought to be faithful reproductions of thought content. The patient is to do the following:

> Tell everything that passes through his mind, and, as nearly as this is humanly possible, to tell it in the order and in the form in which it comes to him. Thus, he is asked to think aloud in the presence of the psychoanalyst with that simple and naive form of undirected musing which everyone uses in the solitude of his own chambers. (Kubie, 1950, p. 45)

Indeed, the orthodox claim is that "free associations . . . approximate a random sample of our psychological processes" (Kubie, 1950, p. 46). The instructions used by analysts are closely paralleled by some current laboratory investigations of cognitive processes. Klinger (1974), for example, instructed subjects to think out loud while engaging in several different activities. He introduced this to subjects as "a process of verbalizing continuously rather than retrospectively reporting segments of content" (p. 44). Such instructions ought to encourage minimal delay and maximum correspondence between the cognitive events of interest and their reporting.

We should note, however, that the patient who is free associating in the presence of the analyst and the subject who is thinking aloud while performing a task are both operating under a specific set of instructions and setting-related constraints. It would be naive to assume that their reports were uninfluenced by these instructions. (For example, see Haley's 1963 analysis of the powerful effects of such subtle demand characteristics in the psychoanalytic setting.)

Another variation of the continuous monologue approach is to have subjects engage in some task (e.g., observing films with different emotional content) and then to ask them to spend time after the task verbalizing all of their thoughts. (This will be reported in more detail in the section on reconstructive procedures.) This method enables investigators to examine the determinants of the content of thought—for example, physical surroundings, immediately previous activities, or everyday events in the subjects' lives (e.g., Horowitz, 1975; Klinger, 1971; Pope, 1977).

Advantages and Disadvantages of Continuous Monologues. The advantages of the continuous monologue approach over other cognitive assessment approaches include nonreliance on retrospective memory and distortions, facilitation of the detailed investigation of moment-to-moment *sequences* of conscious thought, and minimization of subjects' causal inferences.

Some of the disadvantages include the fact that providing a continuous monologue, and thus "putting thoughts into words," is a particularly demanding task. This transformation may slow the subject down, distort cognitive events, and necessitate omission of some content either because of time constraints or because the subjects cannot find the right words to describe their thoughts. Recall trying to report a dream to someone. Often, finding the appropriate terms is difficult, and you may have found yourself having to add information to make the experience comprehensible for someone else. Or, imagine you were trying to tell someone how you recognized someone's face. Often such an attempt will distort the process or fail to capture it accurately, especially a process that occurs quite rapidly.

When it is possible to provide a report, the amount of cognitive information produced in a short time interval may be overwhelming, as is evident in the often-cited description of the early introspectionists' methods: "A ten-second period of thinking sometimes required as many minutes to recount and make clear to E" (Woodworth, 1938, p. 783).

Furthermore, as discussed previously, providing continuous monologues may be a particular problem in reporting overlearned or automatized activities, such as certain motor behaviors (e.g., driving a standard transmission car) or certain well-rehearsed cognitive and perceptual activities (e.g., reading, ordering food at a restaurant; see Abelson, Note 10). We have subtle sets of well-established programs and well-ordered hierarchies of expectations. These permit certain material to be processed extremely rapidly and without moment-to-moment conscious awareness. The processes underlying such automatized behavior may be relatively inaccessible, although conscious sequences of thoughts may have been identifiable when the behavior was first developing.

This discussion relates to yet another difficulty. Indivduals brought into a laboratory or recruited for a study are likely to become self-conscious. This self-consciousness may be thought provoking and habit inhibiting (Langer, Blank, & Chanowitz, 1978). Moreover, just as placing a mirror in front of subjects can alter their attributional processes (Buss & Scheier, 1976; Duval & Wicklund, 1973), so may placing a microphone (and, either concretely or by implication, a tape recorder and someone else's ear) in front of them affect the way in which they approach, perform, and evaluate a task. One likely effect is an increase in self-awareness, or the directing of attention inwardly (Duval & Wicklund, 1972; Wicklund & Duval, 1971). In this way, the verbalizations produced by the subjects may be distorted by the very method required — spontaneous self-verbalizations. Thus we may be left with the situation in which we are studying the response of thinking subjects, when, in fact, people most often would not be consciously "thinking" as much about what they are doing. Some evidence also suggests that continuous monologues lead subjects to spend more time engaging in certain thoughts (e.g., Pope, 1977) than they would otherwise.

Of course, such reactivity problems can be present in any study, but they are a particular concern when reliance is placed on subjects' self-reports. (See Duval & Wicklund, 1972, for a detailed discussion of the influence of subjective self-awareness.)

Audiotape Recording. The least obtrusive and reactive method of collecting oral reports is, of course, by tape recording private speech without subjects' awareness (e.g., Goodman, Note 11). Ethical considerations and the limited usefulness of private speech samples (discussed previously) often preclude this possibility.

Other uses of audiotapes, however, are often possible. They can be used to record responses to interviews (Genest & Turk, 1979; Spanos, Radtke-Bodorik, Ferguson, & Jones, 1979; Genest & Mann, Note 6) or verbalizations that subjects produce during a task (Meichenbaum, Henshaw, & Himel, 1980).

Tape recordings allow for more completeness and spontaneity than is possible by other means. At the same time, they can provide an overwhelming amount of data for analysis. To maximize the validity and reliability of the analyses, it is generally advisable to transcribe reports verbatim. Transcription will inevitably introduce some error variance, because clear, totally comprehensible recordings are difficult to obtain, and the transcriptions themselves will likely involve some errors.

Quantification and Analysis. Once reports have been transcribed, one faces the problem of how to use the raw data. The narrations obtained may be idiosyncratic, making comparisons across individuals difficult. Reports may also use terms that are ambiguous and hard to quantify. How, then, can qualitative, idiosyncratic reports be quantified?

There are three possibilities: (1) derive overall indexes based on global ratings of the transcripts by judges (these can also be derived from the audiotapes themselves); (2) unitize, or "chunk," the transcripts into time segments and then have raters score each segment on the dimensions of interest; or (3) unitize into some naturally occurring units, such as sentence structure, pauses, and so on.

Although global ratings may be useful in some circumstances, we should note the potential pitfalls of such ratings. The sources of error in making judgments under conditions of uncertainty have received much attention (e.g., Chapman & Chapman, 1967, 1969; Ross, 1977; Tversky & Kahneman, 1973, 1974). Results from a study by Kent, O'Leary, Diament, and Dietz (1974), for example, have underlined the potential consequences of such errors. These investigators found that global evaluations were more subject to distorting effects, such as expectation bias, than were evaluations made on the basis of more specific, smaller units of observations. On the other hand, in other studies (e.g., Jones, Ried, & Patterson, 1974; Mash & McElwee, 1974) the use of smaller units, and therefore more discriminations by the observers, has resulted in a decrease in reliability.

In reality, these results were not contradictory, because the errors in each of the studies can be understood not just in terms of the size of the unit being rated but also in terms of the multiple influences on the reliability of scoring. Such influences include the complexity of the behavior being observed, the complexity of the scoring system and the judgments it requires, the frequency of the classes being observed, the degree of certainty versus uncertainty with which classification can be made, and so on. (See Johnson & Bolstad, 1973; Kent & Foster, 1977; and O'Leary & Kent, 1973, for a detailed discussion of these issues.) Such issues are, of course, relevant to both global and smaller unit ratings. They are particularly worthy of notice at this point, however, because some of the critical comments concerning verbal reports have concerned themselves primarily with rather ill-defined, global judgments (e.g., Nisbett & Wilson, 1977; Tversky & Kahneman, 1974).

Global judgments need not be of this sort, however. Attention to the characteristics of the ratings made (such as noted previously) can increase the reliability and validity of scoring systems. One method of enhancing the reliability of global judgments that has been used with verbal transcripts is to have judges score tapes or transcripts for the simple presence or absence of particular characteristics or categories of content. Brown and Chaves (Note 12), for example, had judges read transcriptions of tape-recorded interviews with dental patients and score the open-ended cognitive self-reports for the presence or absence of several classes of cognitive coping strategies.

Chunking transcripts by time introduces the additional minor technical problem of producing time signals on the tape recording. More important, it involves a designation of units that is irrespective of content. Nevertheless, the method is straightforward in determining units for analysis (requiring no subjective judgments), which in itself may make it attractive for some purposes (Goor & Sommerfeld, 1975).

Using naturally occurring characteristics of the protocols for unitizing is more complex. Henshaw (1978), for example, derived separate units from transcripts obtained during think-aloud problem solving by using the following cues: (1) sentence structure, (2) naturalistic phrasing, (3) changes in content, and (4) pauses in the subject's ideational flow. Goodman (1978, Note 11) and Martin and Murray (Note 13) have used similar criteria. Following is an example of a protocol segment that has been unitized by Henshaw's criteria (units are separated by obliques — subjects had been asked to think of unusual uses for bricks):

> You could use bricks as a candle holder/(pause) stick a candle in the hole in the middle/you could even use the big bricks as a lamp/put a light bulb in each of the separate hollow parts in the center/(silence)/um let's see/(pause) you could scrape things with bricks/(silence)/I'm trying to think of what else they could be used for/(pause) to heat hot water, like boil water/(pause) you heat up a brick/(pause) and drop in in a pot of water/(pause) and the water will boil/. (Meichenbaum *et al.*, 1980)

It is evident in this segment that unitizing was not accomplished on the basis of content alone. Paralinguistic cues, such as pauses and shifts in tone, speed, and inflection, are necessary. It is therefore ideal to have the unitizing done while raters follow transcripts and review the audiotapes or videotapes. Goodman (Note 11) reported that her judges agreed on 97% of the units that they arrived at using videotapes and transcriptions in scoring the verbalizations of preschool children.

Once protocols are unitized, further steps in the analysis will depend upon the particular dimensions of interest to the investigator. Each unit can be scored for the presence or absence of particular content, affect, and so on.

Categorization can also be accomplished on the basis of function. For example, Craighead, Kimball, and Rehak (1979) were interested in certain types of self-statements that were present during social rejection imagery. The authors hypothesized that subjects for whom social approval was very important would emit more negative and fewer positive task-relevant self-statements when they visualized social rejection scenes. The authors employed the continuous monitoring technique and scored the data according to four categories: positive and negative self-statements and positive and negative task-relevant ideation. The authors' hypothesis was confirmed: Groups differed significantly in the frequency of negative self-statements, with those indicating higher needs for social approval having a greater number of negative self-statements.

Scoring can be based on other variables. Kohlberg, Yaeger, and Hjertholm (1968), for example, have classified children's private speech into developmental levels. Records can be scored for the levels of the speech produced. Another possibility is to examine the flow of cognitions, sequences of categories, or relationship of specific categories or patterns to other aspects of the person's experience. Henshaw (1978) found, for example, that low-creative subjects were more likely than high-creative subjects to follow up certain kinds of verbalizations (e.g., "reviewing information given") with "inhibitive mediation," or statements reflecting a negative attitude or evaluation of themselves or the situation. It is not only the particular content that may be of interest, then, but also the *sequences* of cognitions and their interrelationships with other variables. Goodman (1978), for example, related the sequence of ideation to the sequence of behavior of preschoolers who were solving jigsaw puzzles. She found that specific classes of private speech preceded specific classes of motoric acts.

The particular types of classifications used and the analyses undertaken can range as much in the study of self-reports as they can in the study of any other aspects of behavior (see Notarius, Chapter 11, this volume).

Random Sampling of Thoughts

An alternative to asking subjects to verbalize continuously is to ask them to report thoughts that have occurred during a given segment of time. Generally, this method involves having subjects interrupted at random intervals by an experimenter (e.g., Antrobus, Singer, & Greenberg, 1965; Foulkes & Fleisher, 1975) or having them carry a portable electronic quasi-random interval generator, which emits a beep occasionally, signaling them to make a record of cognitions by whatever method has been agreed upon (e.g., Hurlburt, 1979; Hurlburt & Sipprelle, 1978; Klinger, Barta, & Glas, Note 14).

Klinger, for example, has signaled subjects at intervals and asked them to narrate "their last thoughts" (Klinger *et al.*, Note 14, p. 4). Similarly, Hurlburt (1979) requested subjects to report "the thought which was occurring at the instant the signal began" (p. 105). Such "samples" of thought content are more clearly retrospective than are productions of private speech or speech following free-association-type instructions, although there still may be a minimal delay between thought and its report. The size of the "chunk" reported and the delay in reporting are variable dimensions with this method.

The thought-sampling approach is based on time-sampling approaches employed in industrial settings to study patterns of work (Tippett, 1935) and in behavioral observations (e.g., Kazdin, 1975; O'Leary & O'Leary, 1972). In both of these instances, a sample of behavior is obtained, and generalizations are made to other samples of time.

One of the earliest uses of thought sampling was the research conducted by Aserinsky and Kleitman (1953) on dreams and sleep. These investigators would wake subjects from either REM or non-REM sleep and ask them to report what they had been thinking.

In a recent study employing thought sampling, Zachary (1977) exposed subjects to emotionally arousing or nonarousing, ambiguous or nonambiguous films. After they viewed the films, subjects were left alone for 20 to 30 minutes and were interrupted at 20 predetermined intervals and asked to report what they had been thinking. Subjects' verbal reports were rated according to whether they were (1) film-related, (2) future-oriented, (3) present-oriented, (4) past-oriented, or (5) current concerns. Using this technique, Zachary was able to demonstrate that the content of films did influence the nature of subsequent thoughts. Horowitz (1975) has used a similar procedure to study the impact of films in causing intrusive thinking.

The thought-sampling approach has been employed innovatively by Hurlburt (1979) to circumvent two of the problems associated with many laboratory studies, namely, artificiality and restricted time span. Hurlburt (1979) employed a shirt-pocket-sized, portable quasi-random interval generator, which subjects carried from the time they awoke until the time they went to bed for at least 3 consecutive days. Signals occurred between a few seconds and 60 minutes apart, with a mean intersignal interval of 30 minutes. Subjects were instructed to respond to each signal by recording (1) the thoughts that were occurring at the time of the signal, (2) the activity they were engaged in, and (3) what time of day it was. Hurlburt employed six scales to quantify aspects of thinking: tense (past, present, and future), affective tone, sex, aggression, human interaction, and relatedness. Using this approach, Hurlburt was able to identify the frequency and consistency of certain categories of thought over extended periods in naturalistic settings.

Csikszentmihalyi and his colleagues have used a similar method to sample thoughts, activities, and moods (Csikszentmihalyi, 1978; Csikszentmihalyi, Larson, & Prescott, 1977). These investigators have examined the relationship between focus of attention and other aspects of experience using electronic paging devices to signal subjects for reports during their daily activities. In a study with adolescents, Csikszentmihalyi *et al.* (1977) found that subjects experienced their highest levels of concentration and enjoyment during games and sports activities, whereas their lowest levels occurred while they were watching television (which occupied three times as much of their time). In an investigation of workers in their work and home environments, Csikszentmihalyi (1978) found the highest mood ratings to be associated with voluntary, as opposed to forced, activities and even more clearly with activities during which subjects' attention was focused on what they were doing rather than elsewhere. This congruence of activity and attention was stronger than the voluntary–forced dimension in its relation to feelings of creativity, freedom, alertness, and satisfaction.

Advantages and Disadvantages of Random Sampling. Some of the particular advantages of thought sampling over the continuous monologue approach include the following: (1) thought sampling causes less frequent intrusions into the ongoing flow of ideation and behavior; (2) it is more flexible and can be employed to collect data in more naturalistic settings and over extended periods; and (3) subjects may be somewhat less self-conscious of the task because they are not restricted to a laboratory setting. Hurlburt (1979) has also found that recordings made on the spot provide different estimates of at least some cognitive events than do post hoc records. From a sample of 778 reported thoughts provided by five female and five male undergraduates, Hurlburt (1979) noted the following:

> One result seems clear: people are not good estimators of the relative frequencies of their thought classes, even if they themselves intuitively define the classes. There must be some other factor or factors besides frequency which can cause such distortions in cognitive estimates. (p. 109)

Hurlburt's comment points to both the advantages and disadvantages of this method. It can provide reliable, random samples of thoughts, but at the same time it may not be simply random samples of thoughts that are of interest. Infrequent events may be important, particularly to the clinician, but the random sampling method may completely miss or greatly underrepresent rare events that may be critical. Even this "limitation," however, may be clinically useful. At times the clinician attempts to have clients demonstrate for themselves that they are distorting or overreacting to events or that they have "irrational" or mistaken beliefs about the world. Frequently, the clinician will have clients collect data that bear on the beliefs that are targeted, in order to challenge their basis. Random sampling of the clients' cognitions can provide one means of doing this.

Thought sampling also shares many of the limitations noted for the continuous monologue approach: problems in quantification and idiosyncratic responding and in the inaccessibility of some information. In addition, thought sampling generally depends to a greater degree on memory and may be more subject to distortion than continuous monologues. The thought-sampling approach does not permit study of the moment-by-moment sequence of cognitive events, but is more static. As an analogy, we might think of the continuous monologue approach as providing a motion picutre of conscious events. Whereas thought sampling provides repeated snapshots.

Event Recording

The event-recording procedure requires subjects to indicate whenever a certain kind of previously defined event occurs in consciousness. This approach requires that subjects attend closely to the occurrence of specified conscious events. Individuals may be asked simply to acknowledge the presence of certain thoughts or to describe them in detail when they occur. Alternatively, records may be made at a standard time each day, for example, each evening or following each meal.

In essence, this constitutes a form of self-monitoring, which has received attention in the behavioral literature (e.g., Ewart, 1978; Lipinski, Black, Nelson, & Ciminero, 1975; Lipinski & Nelson, 1974; Mahoney, 1977; Nelson, 1977; Sieck & McFall, 1976; Snyder, 1974). Subjects or clients wishing to change some behavior (e.g., smoking or overeating) are often asked to keep records of behaviors related to target complaints. They may record antecedent and consequent events surrounding the maladaptive behaviors, as well as the frequency of occurrence. As clinicians have become more concerned about the influence of cognitions on maladaptive behavior, event recording of thought processes has become important.

For example, Beck, Rush, and Kovacs (Note 15) were interested in the circumstances surrounding the production of automatic thoughts by depressed patients, as well as the frequency of such thoughts. Beck *et al.* assigned their patients the task of spending a half hour per day thinking about and writing down their maladaptive automatic thoughts. They were also to record thoughts accompanying increased negative affect and precipitating environmental events. Such self-monitoring provides baseline information regarding the presence and frequency of maladaptive thoughts, as well as situational determinants. The data also lead to therapy designed to make clients aware of self-defeating thoughts and of the environmental contingencies that maintain them.

Recently, Marlatt and Gordon (1979) asked clients who previously had given up drinking and had then relapsed to record the following information immediately following a drink: time of day, presence or absence of others, brief description of the situation, and a rating of subsequent mood or feeling state. Typical patterns identified from this event recording are used to prevent future relapses.

In a more traditional, laboratory study, Pope (1977) focused on structural characteristics of ongoing thought sequences. Pope used both continuous monologues and event recording to examine shifts in thought between the external environment and internally generated ideation. Raters identified significantly fewer shifts and less remote thought content with continuous monologues than with event recording. This suggests that translating thoughts into words may slow down reports and cause each segment to occupy more time than it does when it is unspoken. These data further underscore some of the disadvantages of the continuous monologue approach.

Advantages and Disadvantages of Event Recording. Event recording relies on subjects' understanding of categories of thoughts and behaviors of interest to the experimenter or clinician. This understanding, coupled with those circumstances of extended, extralaboratory monitoring, results in a particular problem. Self-monitoring may be extremely reactive, with attention to specific behaviors resulting in alteration of their frequency as well as in changes in other characteristics of the thoughts or behaviors (Nelson, 1977). Particularly weak areas are potential falsification of records, selective reporting, and other sources of inaccuracies. (See Ciminero, Nelson, & Lipinski, 1977, for a detailed discussion of these issues.) As was discussed with the thought-sampling approach, some of the sequential nature of moment-to-moment thoughts and behaviors is sacrificed by specifying the categories of thoughts to be recorded.

What is maintained, however, by the event-recording procedure, is the potential of gaining rich information concerning perhaps infrequent, but important, occurrences. Furthermore, the heightened reactivity of the method may have clinical utility (e.g., in reducing marital discord somewhat simply by monitoring it). Also, because the occurrence of intense affect or of a particular targeted event can be used by subjects or clients to signal the appropriate time at which to make a record, cognitive events can be observed and reported with minimal delay rather than depending upon recall at a later date, such as a therapy session several days later. Cognitive therapists have emphasized the collection of cognitive samples as soon as possible after the period of interest if they are to reflect the cognitive processes during that period (e.g., Beck, Rush, Shaw, & Emery, 1979).

Rating Scales

As noted previously, subjects who provide continuous monologues or thought samples are likely to provide idiosyncratic and often ambiguous narratives that may be hard to quantify. An additional problem with relatively unstructured approaches like thought sampling and continuous monologues is that subjects may not attend to specific aspects of cognitive events that are of particular interest to the investigator. To circumvent these problems, some investigators have employed specific rating scales in conjuction with thought sampling.

With this variation, subjects are typically asked to rate their conscious events on some specified dimensions. This task, of course, requires that the subjects be trained in advance with regard to the specific variables they will be reporting. Simplicity and comprehensiveness of the descriptions of the variables are critical. Antrobus *et al.* (1966) requested that subjects simply indicate the presence or absence of thoughts about the immediate situation or about things other than the immediate situation. Because of the need for simplicity, however, data obtained with some rating scales may be somewhat sterile.

Nevertheless, these scales may be able to make good use of people's access to their own private experiences. Relying on subjects to rate their cognitions can encourage some thoughtfulness in responding, taking time, making a search for relevant information, considering alternatives, and so on. Although the result of a process such as this is more complex than the immediate report of a "raw" train of thought, it may be no less valid as a source of data. An excellent example of such written reports is the Concern Dimensions Questionnaires (CDQs) developed by Klinger and his colleagues (Klinger, Barta, & Maxeiner, 1980, Note 16). These instruments are important pioneering efforts in this area and deserve particular attention.

The CDQ Scales. In the course of an extensive research program concerned with the motivation of human behavior, Klinger has developed several ways of assessing cognitive experiences. His investigations have centered on a concept that he identifies as "current concern;" which refers to "the state of the organism between commitment to a goal and either attainment of the goal or disengagement from it" (Klinger, 1977, p. 37). Klinger (1977) elaborates on the concept as follows:

> By this definition, people are normally in the grip of several or even numerous current concerns at a time. For instance, a student may be committed to pursuing a degree, completing certain courses, maintaining or improving a relationship with a close friend, finding a part-time job, eating dinner, skiing at year's end, and so on. Each of the ends to which he or she is committed constitutes an incentive (because he or she is attracted to it) and a goal (because he or she is committed to striving for it), and about each he or she has a different current concern (the construct that represents his or her state of being committed to that goal). (p. 37)

Of interest is the connection between people's current concerns and their ongoing cognitions. Klinger (1975, 1977) suggested that current concerns would influence cognitive experiences, with environmental stimuli that are associated with current concerns being more attended to than those that are irrelevant to the current concerns. To aid in the investigation of the differential effects of different kinds of current concerns, Klinger and his colleagues developed several versions of the Concern Dimensions Questionnaire (Klinger *et al.,* 1980, Note 16). These questionnaires first ask subjects to list a certain number of things they have thought about most "today and yesterday," as well as a number of important things in their lives that they have thought about little or not at all. Subjects then rank order all of these things according to how much time they have spent thinking about them and characterize each of them on a number of scales, such as degree of commitment, positivity, negativity, probability of success, and nearness (Klinger *et al.*, Note 16, p. 9).

There are several conclusions of interest here that derive from work with the CDQs (Klinger *et al.*, Note 16). Questionnaire indexes were compared with cognitive reports collected by means of quasi-random sampling. Subjects who had completed the CDQ carried electronic beepers, which emitted a soft signal tone at unpredictable intervals, averaging one every 40 minutes. When they heard the tone, subjects wrote down and characterized the thoughts that had immediately preceded the signal, as well as the environmental setting and their activity at that time. Comparisons were then carried out of the data collected by this random sampling procedure with the measures obtained from the CDQs. These analyses indicated that the CDQs provided valid indexes predictive of thought content as sampled randomly during the 24-hour period following CDQ administration. In particular, the CDQ variables of value and imminence of current concerns were highly significant predictors of thought content frequency, and affective items were the most effective value variables.

Such findings are encouraging for the further development of similar instruments. The findings of Klinger *et al.* suggest that carefully constructed scales can indeed lead to valid and reliable data based on subjects' reflective, introspective reports of their ongoing stream of cognitions. A major disadvantage of the procedure is the time it takes to complete the questionnaire. For particular clinical uses, this might not be a serious drawback, however. Furthermore, Klinger's ground-breaking efforts with his instruments ought to lead to further development of these methods for other particular applications, and, with refinement, scales can become focused enough to permit abbreviation. The essential aspect of the method is that subjects are induced reflectively to produce a written record of some selection of their stream of cognitive events and to rate that selection on various dimensions. Klinger and his associates have also been making use of lengthier, orally administered forms of cognitive measures (Klinger *et al.*, 1980).

Reconstructive Procedures

Instead of sampling or concurrently collecting cognitive data, one may attempt to have subjects reconstruct a train of cognitions and report on them during the reconstruction (e.g., Meichenbaum, 1977; Sheehan, McConkey, & Cross, 1978; Smye, 1978; Genest & Mann, Note 6; Genest *et al.*, Note 7). Investigators employing this approach usually videotape subjects engaging in some task and then allow the subjects to view the tapes. The subjects may be asked to provide continuous monologues (Genest & Mann, Note 6; Genest *et al.*, Note 7) to report reactions while observing themselves (Sheehan *et al.*, 1978), or to record the occurrence of specific cognitive events. Hollandsworth, Glazeski, Kirkland, Jones, and Van Norman (1979), for example, gave subject 40 minutes to work on a test and then requested their ongoing verbal reports of thoughts as they watched a videotape of the entire testing session. This procedure has the advantage of reducing the interference of the data gathering with the task in which the subject is engaged. No interruptions are necessary until the task is completed, and in some circumstances this may be critically important.

In the Genest *et al.* (Note 7) study, subjects were videotaped while their arms were immersed in a tank of ice water maintained at 2°C (to induce nonharmful pain). Subjects provided reports of pain intensity during the stress exposure. Following the removal of the arm from the water, subjects viewed videotapes with the experimenter. The pain ratings and behavioral indicators of distress (e.g., grimaces) were cues to help the subject recall "the thoughts and feelings in as much detail as you can." Subjects' reports were then categorized into ten categories of thought.

We should note that this procedure attempts to have subjects "relive" the same time period and essentially think aloud as they are reliving it rather than having to try to reconstruct the sequence of thoughts, images, and so on without any internal or external cues. This type of procedure can be viewed as an attempt to have subjects reexperience the same sequence of cognitive events and report on them *concurrently* rather than retrospectively. Whether such attempts to reexperience are successful or whether subjects are simply remembering in the usual sense a sequence of thoughts, is an important issue and is worthy of investigation, for it is the difference between retrieval from short-term versus long-term memory, the latter of which adds irrelevant sources of variance to the data (Ericsson & Simon, Note 3). Furthermore, it is as yet unclear how much the "prompts," such as videotapes, add to the cognitive reports. They may, in fact, be unnecessary, with adequate reports being available from subjects without any aids.

Nevertheless, experimenters and clinicians frequently attempt to have subjects and patients reexperience the thoughts and emotions from a prior period (e.g., using role play, imagery, and the therapist–patient interaction) and report on them as they are happening. The issue that needs to be addressed in individual instances as well as in general is whether such a procedure is resulting merely in subjects' or clients' post hoc rationalizations or interpretations of their cognitions, based on other aspects of the situation (e.g., perceived demands, behavioral performance). (For further discussion see Meichenbaum on cognitive–behavioral assessment, 1977, pp. 248–259, and McFall's chapter on behavioral analogue assessments, 1977.)

A Note on Structure

The structuring of the techniques that have been described ranges from the free association of the analyst's couch to the endorsement ratings of a standard self-statement list in the Assertive Self-Statement Test (Schwartz & Gottman, 1976). Clearly, such structural differences will have an impact on the data. The trend in data collection has been away from unstructured procedures and toward more structure, particularly with developments in behavioral assessment (e.g., see volumes by Ciminero, Calhoun, & Adams, 1977; Cone & Hawkins, 1977; Hersen & Bellack, 1976). In attempting to collect more situation-specific information, behavioral researchers and therapists have developed a multitude of questionnaires, tests, interview schedules, and inventories, with more numerous, more specific stimuli than the earlier, psychodynamically based assessment procedures, such as projective tests. The advantages of greater structure are obvious—a greater potential for consistency across assessors and subjects, which aids in establishing validity and reliability.

The most serious drawback to great structure is its rigidity. Because a preestablished structure defines the range of information that will be requested, it does not permit new, unanticipated data to emerge. Procedures involving less structure are more flexible. Interesting leads can be followed up by the assessor, or new hypotheses that emerge can be tested within the course of an interview. Relationships among variables in the newly developing area of cognitive–behavioral research and therapy are not all charted by any means. Relatively flexible assessment procedures, therefore, offer the valuable potential for the perception of unexpected relationships.

It is a recurrent theme of this chapter that several concurrent approaches to cognitive data collection should be employed, and the point is relevant here also. Particularly in the early development of hypotheses, the use of less structured methods is appropriate. As specific, testable hypotheses are formulated, more structured data collection methods may facilitate investigations. Premature employment of such structures, however, may preclude the possibility that unanticipated, yet relevant, data may come to light. General discussions of clinical assessment have made a similar case (e.g., Linehan, 1977; Mischel, 1968; Sundberg, 1977).

An experiment conducted by Spanos *et al.* (1979) illustrates the problem. In a study of the effects of hypnotic susceptibility, suggestions for analgesia, and cognitive strategies on pain, the experimenters had subjects immerse their hands and forearms in ice water (the cold-pressor task). Subjects were interviewed in an open-ended manner concerning their cognitions, with such questions as "Try as fully as possible to tell me what was going through your mind during the time that your hand was in the water." The interview protocols for the subjects were then scored by raters for the presence of various coping strategies (such as distraction, relaxation, dissociative thoughts) and noncoping cognitions (such as negative self-statements, "catastrophizing" images). The design included a pretest cold-pressor trial, treatment (involving hypnosis and suggestions), and a posttest cold-pressor trial.

Following the posttest cold-pressor trial, 52 of the 96 subjects' protocols (i.e., 54%) were rated as including a cognitive "strategy" for coping with the pain. Thus a relatively unstructured, open-ended inquiry suggested that about half of the subjects were intentionally doing something to cognitively cope with the experimental pain. Spanos *et al.* also directly asked subjects whether they did anything to cope with the pain. Of the 52 subjects, 29 (56%) stated that they did not.

> For example, one subject was classified as using distraction because he testified that "I was counting in my head, sort of counting off seconds. It was just a way of sort of changing the subject, taking your mind off it. . . . " Nevertheless, this subject answered no when asked if he had done anything to help him feel less pain. (Spanos *et al.*, 1979, p. 286)

In other words, the structured inquiry led to quite a different finding than did the more open-ended procedure.

This finding harks back to our comments concerning access to antecedent cognitive causality. It seems that Spanos *et al.*'s subjects were unable to use appropriately the cognitive information available to them to answer the specific question accurately. They nevertheless did have access to the appropriate information, because they had already provided it when asked to.

The problem was in the search made or in the inferences drawn, or in both—that is, in the problem-solving heuristics—and not in the availability of data.

Thus, when a structured probe incorporates a request for causal inferences to be made, for data to be summarized, or for some transformations to be accomplished between the raw cognitive data and the report, the report may not accurately reflect what is intended.

Conclusion

In describing the variations of thinking aloud, we have emphasized the advantages and limitations of each approach. As the last example illustrates, none of the approaches, by itself, is problem-free. The choice of procedures to be used will, as always, depend upon the questions being addressed and the situation under investigation. Both researchers and clinicians who wish to employ the techniques we have described must be aware of the problems inherent in them and must weigh these against the potential utility of the information that can be obtained.

Reference Notes

1. Mischel, W., & Moore, B. *Cognitive transformations of the stimulus in delay of gratification.* Unpublished manuscript, Stanford University, 1973.
2. Ericsson, K. A. *Instruction to verbalize as a means to study problem solving processes with with the 8-puzzle: A preliminary study* (Report No. 458 from the Department of Psychology). Stockholm University, Stockholm, Sweden, 1975.
3. Ericsson, K. A., & Simon, H. A. *Retrospective verbal reports as data* (C.I.P. Working Paper). Unpublished manuscript, Carnegie–Mellon University, August 1978.
4. Adair, J. G., & Spinner, B. *Subjects' access to cognitive processes: Demand characteristics and verbal report.* Unpublished manuscript, University of Manitoba, 1979.
5. Hurlburt, R. T. *Random sampling of cognition: Submethods and an historical perspective.* Paper presented at the annual meeting of the American Psychological Association, Toronto, August 1978.
6. Genest, M., & Mann, R. *Assessing cognitions during the experience of pain and during impairment by alcohol.* Paper presented at the 12th annual convention of the Association for the Advancement of Behavior Therapy, Chicago, November 1978.
7. Genest, M., Meichenbaum, D. H., & Turk, D. C. *A cognitive–behavioral approach to the management of pain.* Paper presented at the 11th annual convention of the Association for the Advancement of Behavior Therapy, Atlanta, December 1977.
8. Larsen, K. *The effects of social anxiety and performance feedback on cognitions and self-evaluations.* Unpublished master's thesis, Notre Dame University, 1978.
9. Levine, H. M. *Report on a stress management course with patients from a family medical center setting.* Paper presented at the NATO Advanced Study Institute, "Environmental Stress, Life Crisis, and Social Adaptation," Cambridge, England, August 1978.
10. Abelson, R. *Scripts.* Invited address to the Midwestern Psychological Association meeting, Chicago, May 1978.

11. Goodman, S. H. *Children's private speech and their disposition to use cognitive mediational processes.* Unpublished master's thesis, University of Waterloo, 1975.
12. Brown, J. M., & Chaves, J. F. *Guide for scoring strategies.* Unpublished scoring manual, School of Dental Medicine, Southern Illinois University at Edwardsville, undated.
13. Martin, R., & Murray, J. *Manual for scoring private speech.* Unpublished manuscript, University of Rochester, 1975.
14. Klinger, E., Barta, S. G., & Glas, R. A. *Thought content and gap time in basketball.* Paper presented at Sport Psychology Symposium, University of Minnesota, Duluth, 1979.
15. Beck, A. T., Rush, A. J., & Kovacs, M. *Individual treatment manual for cognitive/behavioral psychotherapy for depression.* Unpublished manuscript, University of Pennsylvania, 1978.
16. Klinger, E., Barta, S. G., & Maxeiner, M. E. *Motivational correlates of thought content frequency and commitment.* Unpublished manuscript, University of Minnesota, 1979.

References

Angell, J. R. Behavior as a category of psychology. *The Psychological Review,* 1913, *20,* 255–270.
Antrobus, J. S., Singer, J. L., & Greenberg, S. Studies in the stream of consciousness: Experimental enhancement and suppression of spontaneous cognitive processes. *Perceptual and Motor Skills,* 1966, *23,* 399–417.
Aserinsky, E., & Kleitman, N. Regularly occurring periods of eye mobility and concomitant phenomena during sleep. *Science,* 1953, *118,* 273–374.
Bandura, A. Self-efficacy: Toward a unifying theory of behavioral change. *Psychological Review,* 1977, *84,* 191–215.
Bandura, A. On paradigms and recycled ideologies. *Cognitive Therapy and Research,* 1978, *2,* 79–103.
Bandura, A., Adams, N. E., & Beyer, J. Cognitive processes mediating behavioral change. *Journal of Personality and Social Psychology,* 1977, *35,* 125–139.
Barber, T. X., & Cooper, B. J. Effects on pain of experimentally induced and spontaneous distractions. *Psychological Reports,* 1972, *31,* 647–651.
Beck, A. T. *Cognitive therapy and the emotional disorders.* New York: International Universities Press, 1976.
Beck, A. T., Rush, A. J., Shaw, B. F., & Emery, G. *Cognitive therapy of depression.* New York: Guilford Press, 1979.
Bellack, A. S., & Hersen, M. Self-report inventories in behavioral assessment. In J. D. Cone & R. P. Hawkins (Eds.), *Behavioral assessment: New directions in clinical psychology.* New York: Brunner/Mazel, 1977.
Bellack, A. S., Hersen, M., & Turner, S.M. Role-play tests for assessing social skills: Are they valid? *Behavior Therapy,* 1978, *9,* 448–461.
Boring, E. G. A history of introspection. *Psychological Bulletin,* 1953, *50,* 169–189.
Bowers, K. S. The effect of demands for honesty on reports of visual and auditory hallucinations. *International Journal of Clinical and Experimental Hypnosis,* 1967, *15,* 31–36.
Bowers, K. S. Situationism in psychology: An analysis and a critique. *Psychological Review,* 1973, *80,* 307–336.
Bowers, K. S. Time distortion and hypnotic ability: Underestimating the duration of hypnosis. *Journal of Abnormal Psychology,* 1979, *88,* 435–439.
Buss, D. M., & Scheier, M. F. Self-consciousness, self-awareness, and self-attribution. *Journal of Research in Personality,* 1976, *10,* 463–468.
Chapman, L., & Chapman, J. The genesis of popular but erroneous psychodiagnostic observations. *Journal of Abnormal Psychology,* 1967, *72,* 193–204.

Chapman, L., & Chapman, J. Illusory correlations as an obstacle to the use of valid psycho-diagnostic signs. *Journal of Abnormal Psychology*, 1969, *74*, 271–280.

Ciminero, A. R., Calhoun, K. S., & Adams, H. E. (Eds.). *Handbook of behavioral assessment*. New York: Wiley, 1977.

Ciminero, A. R., Nelson, R. O., & Lipinski, D. P. Self-monitoring procedures. In A. R. Ciminero, K. S. Calhoun, & H. E. Adams (Eds.), *Handbook of behavioral assessment*. New York: Wiley, 1977.

Cone, J. D., & Hawkins, R. P. (Eds.) *Behavioral assessment: New directions in clinical psychology*. New York: Brunner/Mazel, 1977.

Craighead, W. E., Kimball, W. H., & Rehak, P. J. Mood changes, physiological responses and self-statements during social rejection imagery. *Journal of Consulting and Clinical Psychology*, 1979, *47*, 385–396.

Csikszentmihalyi, M. Attention and the holistic approach to behavior. In K. S. Pope & J. L. Singer (Eds.), *The stream of consciousness: Scientific investigations into the flow of human experience*. New York: Plenum Press, 1978.

Csikszentmihalyi, M., Larson, R., & Prescott, S. The ecology of adolescent activities and experiences. *Journal of Youth and Adolescence*, 1977, *6*, 281–294.

Dodge, R. The theory and limitations of introspection. *American Journal of Psychology*, 1912, *23*, 214–229.

Duval, S., & Wicklund, R. A. *A theory of objective self-awareness*. New York: Academic Press, 1972.

Duval, S., & Wicklund, R. A. Effects of objective self-awareness on attribution of causality. *Journal of Experimental Social Psychology*, 1973, *9*, 17–31.

Ellis, A. *Reason and emotion in psychotherapy*. New York: Lyle Stuart Press, 1962.

Ewart, C. K. Self-observation in natural environments: Reactive effects of behavior desirability and goal-setting. *Cognitive Therapy and Research*, 1978, *2*, 39–56.

Flavell, J., Beach, D., & Chinsky, J. Spontaneous verbal rehearsal in a memory task as a function of age. *Child Development*, 1966, *37*, 283–299.

Foulkes, D., & Fleisher, S. Mental activity in relaxed wakefulness. *Journal of Abnormal Psychology*, 1975, *84*, 66–75.

Gagne, R. H., & Smith, E. C. A study of the effects of verbalization on problem solving. *Journal of Experimental Psychology*, 1962, *63*, 12–18.

Genest, M., & Turk, D. C. A proposed model for behavioral group therapy with pain patients. In D. Upper & S. M. Ross (Eds.), *Behavioral group therapy. An annual review*. Champaign, Ill.: Research Press, 1979.

Glasgow, R., & Arkowitz, H. The behavioral assessment of male and female social competence in dyadic heterosexual interactions. *Behavior Therapy*, 1975, *6*, 488–498.

Glass, C. R., Gottman, J. M., & Shmurak, S. H. Response-acquisition and cognitive self-statement modification approaches to dating-skills training. *Journal of Counseling Psychology*, 1976, *23*, 520–526.

Goldfried, M. R., & D'Zurilla, T. J. A behavior-analytic model for assessing competence. In C. D. Spielberger (Ed.), *Current topics in clinical and community psychology* (Vol. 1). New York: Academic Press, 1969.

Goldfried, M. R., & Goldfried, A. P. Cognitive change methods. In F. H. Kanfer & A. P. Goldstein (Eds.), *Helping people change: A textbook of methods* (2nd ed.). New York: Pergamon Press, 1980.

Goldfried, M. R., & Sobocinski, D. The effect of irrational beliefs on emotional arousal. *Journal of Consulting and Clinical Psychology*, 1975, *43*, 504–510.

Goodman, S. H. *The integration of verbal and motor behavior in preschool children*. Unpublished doctoral dissertation, University of Waterloo, 1978.

Goor, A., & Sommerfeld, R. A comparison of problem-solving processes of creative students and non-creative students. *Journal of Educational Psychology*, 1975, *67*, 495–505.

Haley, J. *Strategies of psychotherapy*. New York: Grune & Stratton, 1963.

Henshaw, D. *A cognitive analysis of creative problem-solving.* Unpublished doctoral dissertation, University of Waterloo, 1978.

Hersen, M., & Bellack, A. S. (Eds.). *Behavioral assessment: A practical handbook.* New York: Pergamon Press, 1976.

Hilgard, E. R. Pain as a puzzle for psychology and physiology. *American Psychologist,* 1969, *24,* 103–113.

Hollandsworth, J.G., Jr., Glazeski, R. C., Kirkland, K., Jones, G. E., & Van Norman, L. R. An analysis of the nature and effects of test anxiety: Cognitive, behavioral, and physiological components. *Cognitive Therapy and Research,* 1979, *3,* 165–180.

Horowitz, M. J. Intrusive and repetitive thoughts after experimental stress. *Archives of General Psychiatry,* 1975, *32,* 1457–1463.

Hume, D. *A treatise of human nature* (L. Selby-Bigge, Ed.). London: Oxford University Press, 1888. (Originally published, 1739–1740.)

Hurlburt, R. T. Random sampling of cognitions and behavior. *Journal of Research in Personality,* 1979, *13,* 103–111.

Hurlburt, R. T., & Sipprelle, C. N. Random sampling of cognitions in alleviating anxiety attacks. *Cognitive Therapy and Research,* 1978, *2,* 165–169.

Johnson, S. M., & Bolstad, O. D. Methodological issues in naturalistic observation: Some problems and solutions for field research. In L. A. Hamerlynck, L. C. Handy, & E. J. Mash (Eds.), *Behavior change: Methodology, concepts, and practice.* Champaign, Ill.: Research Press, 1973.

Jones, R. R., Ried, J. B., & Patterson, G. R. Naturalistic observation in clinical assessment. In P. McReynolds (Ed.), *Advances in psychological assessment* (Vol. 3). San Francisco: Jossey-Bass, 1974.

Joyce, J. *Ulysses.* New York: The Modern Library, 1961. (Originally published, 1914.)

Kanfer, F. H., & Goldfoot, D. A. Self-control and tolerance of noxious stimulation. *Psychological Reports,* 1966, *18,* 79–85.

Kanfer, F. H., & Goldstein, A. P. (Eds.). *Helping people change: A textbook of methods.* New York: Pergamon Press, 1980.

Kazdin, A. E. *Behavior modification in applied settings.* Homewood, Ill.: Dorsey, 1975.

Kendall, P. C., & Korgeski, G. P. Assessment and cognitive–behavioral interventions. *Cognitive Therapy and Research,* 1979, *3,* 1–21.

Kendler, T., Kendler, H., & Carrick, M. Verbal labels and inferential problem solution of children. *Child Development,* 1966, *37,* 749–736.

Kent, R. N., & Foster, S. L. Direct observational procedures: Methodological issues in naturalistic settings. In A. R. Ciminero, K. S. Calhoun, & H. E. Adams (Eds.), *Handbook of behavioral assessment.* New York: Wiley, 1977.

Kent, R. N., O'Leary, K. D., Diament, C., & Dietz, A. Expectation biases in observational evaluation of therapeutic change. *Journal of Consulting and Clinical Psychology,* 1974, *42,* 774–780.

Klinger, E. *Structure and functions of fantasy.* New York: Wiley, 1971.

Klinger, E. Utterances to evaluate steps and control attention distinguish operant from respondent thought while thinking out loud. *Bulletin of the Psychonomic Society,* 1974, *4,* 44–46.

Klinger, E. Consequences of commitment to and disengagement from incentives. *Psychological review,* 1975, *82,* 1–25.

Klinger, E. *Meaning and void.* Minneapolis: University of Minnesota, 1977.

Klinger, E. Dimensions of thought and imagery in normal waking states. *Journal of Altered States of Consciousness,* 1978, *4,* 97–113.

Klinger, E., Barta, S. G., & Maxeiner, M. A. Current concerns: Assessing therapeutically relevant motivation. In P. C. Kendall & S. D. Hollon (Eds.), *Cognitive–behavioral interventions: Assessment.* New York: Academic Press, 1980.

Kohlberg, L., Yaeger, J., & Hjertholm, E. The development of private speech: Four studies and a review of theories. *Child Development*, 1968, *39*, 691–736.

Kubie, L. S. *Practical and theoretical aspects of psychoanalysis*. New York: International Universities Press, 1950.

Kuhn, T. S. *The structure of scientific revolutions*. Chicago: University of Chicago Press, 1962.

Lang, P., & Lazovik, A. Experimental desensitization of a phobia. *Journal of Abnormal Psychology*, 1963, *66*, 519–525.

Langer, E. J., Blank, A., & Chanowitz, B. The mindlessness of ostensibly thoughtful action: The role of "placebic" information in interpersonal interaction. *Journal of Personality and Social Psychology*, 1978, *36*, 635–642.

Laws, D. R., & Holmen, M. L. Sexual response faking by pedophiles. *Criminal Justice and Behavior*, 1978, *5*, 343–356.

Lazarus, R. S. Cognitive behavior therapy as psychodynamics revisited. In M. J. Mahoney (Ed.), *Psychotherapy process: Current issues and future directions*. New York: Plenum Press, 1980.

Lazarus, R., & Alfert, E. Short-circuiting of threat by experimentally altering cognitive appraisal. *Journal of Abnormal and Social Psychology*, 1964, *69*, 195–205.

Lazarus, R., Averill, J. R., & Opton, E. M., Jr. Towards a cognitive theory of emotion. In M. Arnold (Ed.), *Third international symposium on feelings and emotions*. New York: Academic Press, 1970.

Lieberman, D. A. Behaviorism and the mind: A (limited) call for a return to introspection. *American Psychologist*, 1979, *34*, 319–333.

Linehan, M. M. Issues in behavioral interviewing. In J. D. Cone & R. P. Hawkins (Eds.), *Behavioral assessment: New directions in clinical psychology*. New York: Brunner/Mazel, 1977.

Lipinski, D. P., Black, J. L., Nelson, R. O., & Ciminero, A. R. Influence of motivational variables on the reactivity and reliability of self-recording. *Journal of Consulting and Clinical Psychology*, 1975, *43*, 637–646.

Lipinski, D. P., & Nelson, R. O. The reactivity and unreliability of self-recording. *Journal of Consulting and Clinical Psychology*, 1974, *42*, 110–123.

Mahoney, M. J. *Cognition and behavior modification*. Cambridge, Mass.: Ballinger, 1974.

Mahoney, M. J. Some applied issues in self-monitoring. In J. D. Cone & R. P. Hawkins (Eds.), *Behavioral assessment: New directions in clinical psychology*. New York: Brunner/Mazel, 1977.

Mahoney, M. J. (Ed.). *Psychotherapy process. Current issues and future directions*. New York: Plenum Press: 1980.

Mahoney, M. J., & Arnkoff, D. Cognitive and self-control therapies. In S. Garfield & A. Bergin (Eds.), *Handbook of psychotherapy and behavior change: An empirical analysis*. New York: Wiley, 1978.

Mahoney, M. J., & Avener, M. Psychology of the elite athlete: An exploratory study. *Cognitive Therapy and Research*, 1977, *1*, 135–141.

Marlatt, G. A., & Gordon, J. R. Determinants of relapse: Implications for the maintenance of behavior change. In P. O. Davidson (Ed.), *Behavioral medicine: Changing health lifestyles*. New York: Brunner/Mazel, 1979.

Mash, E. J., & McElwee, J. D. Situational effects on observer accuracy: Behavior predictability, prior experience, and complexity of coding categories. *Child Development*, 1974, *45*, 367–377.

McFall, R. M. Analogue methods in behavioral assessment: Issues and prospects. In J. D. Cone & R. P. Hawkins (Eds.), *Behavioral assessment: New directions in clinical psychology*. New York: Brunner/Mazel, 1977.

Meichenbaum, D. A cognitive-behavior modification approach to assessment. In M. Hersen

& A. Bellack (Eds.), *Behavioral assessment: A practical handbook*. New York: Pergamon Press, 1975.

Meichenbaum, D. Toward a cognitive theory of self-control. In G. Schwartz & D. Shapiro (Eds.), *Consciousness and self-regulation: Advances in research* (Vol. 1). New York: Plenum Press, 1976.

Meichenbaum, D. *Cognitive–behavior modification: An integrative approach*. New York: Plenum Press, 1977.

Meichenbaum, D. A cognitive–behavioral perspective on intelligence. *Intelligence: A Multidisiplinary Journal*, 1980.

Meichenbaum, D., & Goodman, S. H. Clinical use of private speech and critical questions about its study in naturalistic settings. In G. Ziven (Ed.), *The development of self-regulation through private speech*. New York: Wiley, 1979.

Meichenbaum, D., Henshaw, D., & Himel, N. Coping with stress as a problem-solving process. In W. Krohne & L. Laux (Eds.), *Achievement stress and anxiety*. Washington, D.C.: Hemisphere Publishing, 1980.

Mischel, W. *Personality and assessment*. New York: Wiley, 1968.

Mischel, W. Toward a cognitive social learning reconceptualization of personality. *Psychological Review*, 1973, *80*, 252–283.

Mischel, W., & Baker, N. Cognitive transformations of reward objects through instructions. *Journal of Personality and Social Psychology*, 1975, *31*, 254–261.

Mischel, W., Ebbesen, E., & Zeiss, A. Cognitive and attentional mechanisms in delay of gratification. *Journal of Personality and Social Psychology*, 1972, *21*, 204–218.

Mischel, W., & Patterson, C. J. Substantive and structural elements of effective plans for self-control. *Journal of Personality and Social Psychology*, 1976, *34*, 942–950.

Moore, B. S. Cognitive representation of rewards in delay of gratification. *Cognitive Therapy and Research*, 1977, *1*, 73–83.

Moore, M. S. Responsibility for unconsciously motivated action. *International Journal of Law and Psychiatry*, 1979, *2*, 323–347.

Nelson, R. O. Methodological issues in assessment via self-monitoring. In J.D. Cone & R. P. Hawkins (Eds.), *Behavioral assessment: New directions in clinical psychology*. New York: Brunner/Mazel, 1977.

Nisbett, R. E., & Bellows, N. Verbal reports about causal influences on social judgments: Private access versus public theories. *Journal of Personality and Social Psychology*, 1977, *35*, 613–624.

Nisbett, R. E., & Wilson, T. D. Telling more than we can know: Verbal reports on mental processes. *Psychological Review*, 1977, *84*, 231–259.

O'Leary, K. D., & Kent, R. Behavior modification for social action: Research tactics and problems. In L. A. Hamerlynck, L. C. Handy, & E. J. Mash (Eds.), *Behavior change: Methodology, concepts, and practice*. Champaign, Ill.: Research Press, 1973.

O'Leary, K. D., & O'Leary, S. G. (Eds.). *Classroom management: The successful use of behavior modification*. New York: Pergamon Press, 1972.

Piaget, J. [*The language and thought of the child*] (M. Gabain, trans.). New York: Meridian, 1955. (Originally published, 1923.)

Polanyi, M. *Personal knowledge: Towards a post-critical philosophy*. New York: Harper, 1964.

Pope, K. S. *The flow of consciousness*. Unpublished doctoral dissertation, Yale University, 1977.

Pope, K. S. How gender, solitude, and posture influence the stream of consciousness. In K. S. Pope & J. L. Singer (Eds.), *The stream of consciousness*. New York: Plenum Press, 1978.

Ross, L. The intuitive psychologist and his shortcomings: Distortions in the attribution process. *Advances in Experimental Social Psychology*, 1977, *10*, 173–220.

Schwartz, G. E. Biofeedback as therapy: Some theoretical and practical issues. *American Psychologist*, 1973, *28*, 666–673.

Schwartz, R., & Gottman, J. Toward a task analysis of assertive behavior. *Journal of Consulting and Clinical Psychology*, 1976, *44*, 910–920.

Seligman, M. E. P. *Helplessness: On depression, development and death.* San Francisco: W. H. Freeman, 1975.

Sheehan, P. W., McConkey, K. M., & Cross, D. Experimental analysis of hypnosis: Some new observations on hypnotic phenomena. *Journal of Abnormal Psychology*, 1978, *87*, 570–573.

Sieck, W. A., & McFall, R. M. Some determinants of self-monitoring effects. *Journal of Consulting and Clinical Psychology*, 1976, *44*, 958–965.

Smith, E. R., & Miller, F. D. Limits on perception of cognitive processes: A reply to Nisbett and Wilson. *Psychological Review*, 1978, *85*, 355–362.

Smye, M. D. Behavioral and cognitive assessment through role-playing. *Psychology*, 1978, *15*, 35–48.

Snyder, M. Self-monitoring of expressive behavior. *Journal of Personality and Social Psychology*, 1974, *30*, 526–537.

Spanos, N. P., Radtke-Bodorik, H. L., Ferguson, J. D., & Jones, B. The effects of hypnotic susceptibility, suggestions for analgesia, and the utilization of cognitive strategies on the reduction of pain. *Journal of Abnormal Psychology*, 1979, *88*, 282–292.

Sundberg, N. D. *Assessment of persons.* Englewood Cliffs, N.J.: Prentice-Hall, 1977.

Thoresen, C. E., & Mahoney, M. J. *Behavioral self-control.* New York: Holt, Rinehart & Winston, 1974.

Tippett, C. H. C. A snap reading method of making time studies of machines and operatives in factory surveys. *Journal of the British Tactile Institute Transactions*, 1935, *26*, 51–55.

Titchener, E. B. *Experimental psychology of the thought processes.* New York: Macmillan, 1909.

Titchener, E. B. Prologomena to a study of introspection. *American Journal of Psychology*, 1912, *23*, 427–448.

Tversky, A., & Kahneman, D. Availability: A heuristic for judging frequency and probability. *Cognitive Psychology*, 1973, *5*, 207–232.

Tversky, A., & Kahneman, D. Judgment under uncertainty: Heuristics and biases. *Science*, 1974, *185*, 1124–1131.

Vygotsky, L. [*Thought and language*] (E. Hanfmann & G. Vakar, Eds. and trans.). Cambridge, Mass.: Massachusetts Institute of Technology Press, 1962. (Originally published, 1934.)

Watson, J.B. Psychology as the behaviorist views it. *Psychological Review*, 1913, *20*, 158–177.

Watson, J. B. Is thinking merely the action of language mechanisms? *British Journal of Psychology*, 1920, *11*, 87–104.

Weisman, A., & Sobel, H. J. Coping with cancer through self-instruction: A hypothesis. *Journal of Human Stress*, 1979, *5*, 3–8.

Wicklund, R. A., & Duval, S. Opinion change and performance facilitation as a result of objective self-awareness. *Journal of Experimental Social Psychology*, 1971, *7*, 319–342.

Wildman, B. G., & Erickson, M. T. Methodological problems in behavioral observation. In J. D. Cone & R. P. Hawkins (Eds.), *Behavioral assessment: New directions in clinical psychology.* New York: Brunner/Mazel, 1977.

Wilson, T. D., & Nisbett, R. E. The accuracy of verbal reports about the effects of stimuli on evaluations and behavior. *Social Psychology*, 1978, *41*, 118–131.

Woodworth, R. S. *Experimental psychology.* New York: Holt, Rinehart & Winston, 1938.

Zachary, R. *Cognitive and affective determinants of ongoing thought.* Unpublished doctoral dissertation, Yale University, 1978.

Zivin, G. (Ed.). *The development of self-regulation through private speech.* New York: Wiley, 1979.

9

Issues in Electrophysiology and Cognition

F. J. McGuigan

Sources of Electrophysiological Signals

The question of the nature of cognition is, I believe, to be solved by directly measuring mental processes through psychophysiological techniques. In considering the question of how and where in the body cognitive acts occur, an objective scientist would eschew any predisposing biases, considering it possible that any or all bodily systems might serve some cognitive function. In fact, research has indicated that most bodily systems are active in cognitive activities.

Accounts of brain functioning during thought may be found in Delafresnaye (1954), Eccles (1966), and Young (1970). The eye apparently performs important activities during all types of cognitive acts—Hebb (1968), for instance, held that peripheral events, especially eye movement, are essential during the formation of images. Chase (1973) detailed visual system functioning during various mental acts. Visceral phenomena have been theoretically and empirically implicated in cognitive processes in a variety of ways. Theoretically, Watson (1930) defined "emotion" as visceral responding, and, empirically, the esophagus (e.g., Jacobson, 1925), intestinal activity (e.g., Davis, Garafolo, & Gault, 1957), electrodermal responding (e.g., Grings, 1973a, 1973b), and the autonomic system in general (e.g., Lacey, 1950; Lacey & Lacey, 1974) have been intensively studied.

Finally, there is extensive historical and contemporary implication that the skeletal musculature is covertly active during thought processes (e.g., Langfeld, 1933; Smith, 1969). The importance of cognitive motor responding has been particularly emphasized in Russia and in the United States since

F. J. McGuigan • Performance Research Laboratory, University of Louisville, Louisville, Kentucky.

the latter part of the 19th century (McGuigan & Szegal, 1980). Sechenov (1935/1863), the father of cognitive psychophysiological theorizing and empirical research in Russia, emphasized the importance of reflexes and responses, as in his doctrine that "all the endless diversity of the external manifestations of the activity of the brain can be finally regarded as one phenomenon—that of muscular movement" (1965, p. 309). The work of Bechterev (1923), Galperin (1969), Leontiev (1959), Pavlov (cf. 1941), and Vigotsky (1962) continued Sechenov's work into contemporary Soviet psychology.

In the United States, Titchener (1909) emphasized the role of the skeletal musculature for the development of meaning in his context theory of meaning, though the early behaviorists were primarily responsible for inclining psychology toward contemporary concentration on the skeletal musculature. Among those workers in the behavioristic tradition who theorized about the role of skeletal muscles in the higher mental processes were Dunlap (1912), Holt (1937), Hunter (1924), Langfeld (1931), and Watson (1914). In the early 1930s, Jacobson (1932) further advanced the concept of neuromuscular functioning as an explication of cognitive activities.

Electropsychology: Covert Behavior Electrophysiologically Measured

The goal of psychology is to understand behavior, though our science has developed with primary emphasis on overt behavior. Psychologists have accomplished much by studying relationships between overt response patterns and external environmental events. In the early part of the century, we theorized about covert behavior, but the technology for studying small-scale responses was simply not available. With the recent development of sensitive psychophysiological measurement techniques, impressive progress in the understanding of covert behavior has been achieved. The past successes from relating overt behavior to stimuli in the external environment can be equaled or surpassed by understanding the "internal world" of covert processes to which psychology has recently turned with vigor.

The distinction between overt and covert behavior is not sharp. Overt events (waving the hand, speaking aloud) are clearly overt; just as clearly, some events are hidden from ordinary observation (a slight thumb twitch, the brief contraction of a small muscle in the tongue, an increase in cardiac rate). However, there is a "twilight zone" between these extremes in which some events are difficult to classify as overt or covert—a slight whisper, a partial blink of the eyes, or an arrested nod of the head, for example. It is theoretically irrelevant, however, whether events are overt, covert, or in the twilight zone. Just because a specialized apparatus is required for the observation of small-scale behavior does not mean that overt and covert behavior differ in kind or in quality. Nor is it theoretically relevant that events in the twilight zone may be studied more effectively by the methods of observing covert behavior than by the classical methods of observing overt behavior. The important point is that the task of psychology is to understand behavior, *all* behavior. To accomplish this task, psychologists must concentrate some of their energies on that subrealm of behavior that is covert.

The problem with studying overt responses is not one of observation, but of recording and measurement. Covert events, on the other hand, can be observed only through the use of equipment that extends the scope of our senses. Just because magnification is required to observe covert phenomena, however, does not render those phenomena mystical. Numerous kinds of apparatuses have been developed to detect events that could not otherwise be studied. The microscope and the telescope are obvious examples and serve to emphasize that covert processes are like any (physicalistic) event but that they must be amplified for study.

The frequent reference in the psychological literature to "covert behavior," "implicit response," "subvocalization," "silent speech," and "inner speech" attests to the historical and contemporary importance of covert concepts. Our primary purpose is to study such covert processes psychophysiologically, and our long-term goal is to develop concepts and principles that will constitute a mature science of covert processes. The consequence will be a more complete science of psychology than one built merely on the study of overt behavior.

In this chapter, I will focus on methods by which covert processes are sensed, amplified, recorded, and quantified. Because the electrical components of these covert processes are the most prominently sensed, the term "electrophysiology" is frequently used to denote this area of study. However, because we are interested in psychological processes, perhaps the term "electropsychology," employed by Hefferline, Keenan, Harford, and Birch (1960), is more appropriate. As defined by these authors, "electropsychology" refers to the study of those small-scale bodily events during cognition that are electrically measured.

The Evolution of Electrophysiology

The various activities of the body involve chemical, mechanical, and electrical processes. Measures of chemical reactions are best left to the biochemist and physiologist. In psychophysiological research, numerous measures of mechanical reactions have been used. The mechanical measurement of covert behavior started in the early 1900s, when experimenters enthusiastically and creatively sought objective evidence of "implicit language habits," a critical concept in behavioristic theories of thinking. Techniques to record covert speech during thought involved such devices as inflated ballons and flattened wine glasses placed on or about the tongue; such "sensors" then had mechanical connections to recording systems of tambours and kymographs. The extreme of mechanical measurement was Thorson's

(1925) device, which magnified tongue movements by a factor of about 4.5 (Figure 1). It is obvious that during the first quarter of this century adequate technology was simply lacking, and the few reported successful measurements of small-scale, covert processes invite skepticism.

The technological breakthrough came in the 1920s with Jacobson's (1927) pioneering electrical quantification of covert behavioral events and with Berger's (1929) electrical recording of brain events. In developing progressive relaxation, begun in 1908, Jacobson needed a sensitive measure of muscular tension as a criterion for the degree of improvement of his patients. His first index of tension was a kymographic measure of the amplitude of the knee-jerk response, a reflex that does not occur in the well-relaxed person. Later Jacobson employed a string galvanometer, a primitive electromyograph with which one inserts electrodes into muscles; the voltage generated by active muscles produces vibration of a wire whose shadow can be recorded. However, the string galvanometer lacked sufficient sensitivity to measure amplitudes of a microvolt (one millionth of a volt). With Bell Telephone Laboratories, Jacobson developed an integrating neurovoltmeter, which he used successfully in both his scientific and his clinical work. Jacobson was then able to show that muscle tonus could be reduced to a level of zero microvolts by the use of progressive relaxation technics (cf. Jacobson, 1929). His use of the neurovoltmeter in scientific investigations in the 1930s

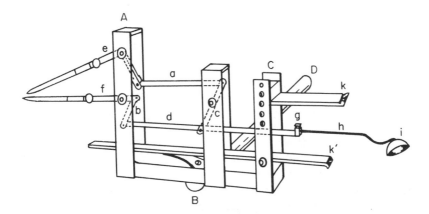

Figure 1. Thorson's experimental apparatus (× 4.5). Rigid frame (ABC) supported in adjustable clamp by a rod (BD). Metal suction cup (i) for attachment to tongue. Aluminum bar (a) attached to suction cup by aluminum wire (h), adjustable by the set screw (g), and transmitting movements through the links and bell cranks (b, c, d, and e) to the writing points. The writing points are adjustable horizontally by thumb screws acting against light bronze springs. (From ''The Relation of Tongue Movements to Internal Speech,'' by A. M. Thorson, *Journal of Experimental Psychology,* 1925, *8,* 1–32.)

allowed him to conclude that muscle responses were present during all mental acts.

However, in these early days scientists were not sure what their electrical measurements indicated. Consequently, Jacobson (1932) carefully established differences between covert electromyographic movement and the galvanic skin response, including differences in voltage, latency, frequency, wave form, direction of potential, and tissue of origin. Jacobson's pioneering work has led to great advances in electromyography, as has Berger's (1929) well-known research in electroencephalography. Berger published the first tracings of electrical activity from over the human skull, though he had difficulty in finding acceptance for his conclusions among the scientific community. As Lindsley (1969) pointed out, neurophysiologists of the day were reluctant to think that any events other than the well-known spike potentials occurred in the nervous systems.

Acceptance of the slow alpha potentials occurred only when confirmed by Adrian and Matthews (1934), no doubt enhanced by the prestige that Lord Adrian added to the cause. Even then, those who did believe that the signals were generated by the brain regarded them as rather dull because the alpha frequencies were so constant and thus could not be indicative of momentary thoughts. (See Lindsley, 1969, pp. 2–15, for some of these important historical developments in electroencephalography.) Today the controversy as to the source of alpha waves continues. We have, for instance, the startling conclusion of Lippold (1970a, 1970b, 1970c; Lippold & Novotny, 1970) that alpha waves are generated by the eyes and resonate from the back of the skull.

These two pioneering efforts by Jacobson and Berger thus launched quantitative electromyography and electroencephalography, respectively. The vacuum tube was then applied with increasing frequency for the solution of cognitive problems through psychophysiological techniques. Other prominent research included the classical study of linguistic muscle responses in the deaf during problem solving, dreaming, and so forth, by Max (1935, 1937) and an extensive series of experiments by R. C. Davis (e.g., 1939).

As versatile as the vacuum tube proved to be, the development of solid-state electronics, especially the operational amplifier constructed of transistors that replaced the vacuum tube, has led to a new, more highly advanced stage of psychophysiological measurement. We have truly witnessed an exponentially increasing amount of research in the psychophysiologists' laboratories, especially on cognitive problems.

The Nature of Bioelectrical Phenomena

Thus electrical techniques have come to provide the most sensitive measures of response events. Because responses are psychophysiologically measured, let us briefly consider how electrical signals are generated within bodily tissues.

All cells in nerve, muscle, and glandular tissues (as well as in many plants) are enveloped by membranes. In a resting cell there is a difference in electrical potential between the inside and the outside of the cell's membrane, such that the inside is electrically negative relative to the outside. When a stimulus is applied to the resting cell, an electrical event called an "action potential" is generated. The action potential occurs because the stimulus produces a localized depolarization that is propagated along the cell.

The propagated depolarization (due to selective ionic movement through the cell's semipermeable membrane) may be electrically sensed in single cells or in groups of cells. The resulting action potentials may be detected by electrodes placed in or on the body, and it is such electrically sensed events that produce signals that are transmitted to amplifiers for further processing. Such processed signals constitute the response measure to be studied. Let us now consider some of these response measures that are prominent in psychology, after which I will specify the stages by which they are studied.

The Taxonomy of Covert Processes

Table 1 presents a number of the more commonly measured events studied in cognitive psychophysiology, starting with a primary division between "response events" and "neurophysiological processes." The general term "covert processes" (or "covert events") thus includes both behavioral (response) and nervous system (neural) phenomena. After this basic division of covert processes into responses (muscular and glandular events) on the one hand and central nervous system (CNS) reactions on the other, the table shows that muscle responses and brain events are most effectively studied through their electrical manifestations (electromyography and electroencephalography, respectively). This separation of responses and CNS reactions indicates that the two classes of events are intrinsically different phenomena, though both are components of neuromuscular circuits that function during internal information processing. No doubt responses obey different laws than do neural events, so that it is most efficient to classify responses and CNS reactions separately and then to study their interactions within neuromuscular circuits. How brain and muscle interact is a major, important, and difficult problem for the psychophysiologist.

In Table 1 there is a further separation of responses in the oral regions of the body (IA) from the nonoral bodily areas (IB). If a covert oral response produces internal speech, it is a covert *linguistic* oral response. There is considerable empirical justification for the conclusion that certain classes of covert oral behavior function linguistically (McGuigan, 1978). During silent linguistic processing, the tongue yields the most sensitive data, the lips are the next most sensitive region, and the jaw, chin, and laryngeal regions are relatively insensitive. Pneumograms (IA2) are important measures of covert

Table 1. A Summary Classification of Psychophysiologically Measured
Covert Processes

The two major classes of covert processes are:
 I. Covert responses, which consist of, and only of, muscular and glandular events
II. Neurophysiological processes, principally measured in the normal human through electrical
    techniques

 I. Covert responses
    A. Covert oral responses
       1. Skeletal muscle electromyographic measures from the larynx, lips, chin, tongue, jaw,
          and so forth
       2. Pneumograms
       3. Audio measures of subvocalization (involuntary "whispering")
    B. Covert nonoral responses
       1. Skeletal muscle electromyographic measures from fingers, arms, legs, and so forth
       2. Visceral muscle activity (electrogastrogram)
       3. Eye responses (electrooculogram, electroretinogram, pupillogram)
       4. Cardiovascular measures (heart rate, electrocardiogram, finger pulse volume, blood
          pressure)
       5. Electrodermal measures (galvanic skin response, skin conductance, etc.)
II. Neurophysiological measures
    In the normal human, electrical activity is studied and recorded with a variety of techni-
    ques—for example, electroencephalograms, evoked potentials, and contingent negative
    variation (the "expectancy" wave)

oral responses, and breathing rate generally increases during linguistic tasks.
Breathing amplitude has been found to increase during auditory hallucinations. Audio measures of subvocalization (IA3) allow us to monitor both the
internal linguistic processes of children during silent reading and the verbal
content of schizophrenics who are engaged in auditory hallucinations.

Measures of nonoral responses (IB1) during linguistic processing allow
us to monitor covert finger activity in deaf individuals during their cognitive
activities or covert eye behavior (IB3) during dreams and waking mentation.
Visceral muscular, cardiovascular (IB4), and electrodermal (IB5) recordings
are valuable in studies of emotion and arousal.

Neurophysiological measures (II) should eventually lead to a better
understanding of the brain during thought, but this exceedingly complex
organ will undoubtedly require more advanced techniques of study than we
can yet imagine.

With this overview of covert processes, let us now consider the psychophysiological characteristics of some of the more important processes in
greater detail. Research indicates that skeletal speech muscle responding
and eye activity are the most indicative of cognitive functioning, though we
are advancing with our understanding of neurophysiological processes,
too.

Selected Covert Responses

Skeletal Muscle Responses. Electromyography allows us to record the covert muscle responses that are especially prominent during cognitive functioning. The recording of muscle action potentials through electromyography provides the electromyogram, which is a record of the electrical properties of muscular activity.

An efferent neural impulse, which arrives at the central region of a muscle fiber, produces a rapid contraction of the entire fiber. Accompanying localized depolarizations of the muscle fibers within a muscle are then transmitted along the semipermeable membrane that surrounds the muscle fiber. During contraction, membrane polarity is reversed, yielding the major electrical signal that may be electromyographically recorded.

To record the action potential given off by contracting muscle fibers, the voltage difference between two electrodes is recorded. The action potential may be detected either by surface electrodes attached to the skin or by inserted electrodes (needle electrodes or hair-fine wires) localized subcutaneously in the region of the muscle fiber or fibers of interest. Inserted electrodes have an advantage over surface electrodes when the researcher seeks to study localized, subcutaneous events. An example of such use comes from Faaborg-Anderson and Edfeldt (1958), who studied contrasting muscle action potentials in neighboring muscles in the throat during silent reading.

Because surface electrodes are exposed to signals from many fibers, and to a greater length of each fiber, high-amplitude electrical signals may still be detected at the surface. Consequently, the surface electrode potential is a summation over both space and time. With surface electrodes being capable of detecting signals less than 1 μV (one microvolt) in amplitude (given other suitable laboratory conditions) from a wide bodily region, they are likely to enhance the investigator's chances of detecting critical response events.

The phenomena sensed with muscular electrodes are quite varied and often extremely difficult to detect, as in the instance of very rapid or low-amplitude spikes. The covert arm and eye responses detected by McGuigan and Pavek (1972) that differentiated a person's "yes" versus "no" thoughts, for instance, could not have been possible without sensitive computer analysis.

Visceral Muscle Activity. Visceral activity is of considerable cognitive importance, probably functioning to add "emotional tone" to semantic interpretation. Among the relatively small amount of psychophysiological research involving visceral muscle activity, there have been some interesting findings, and it is likely that much important linguistic processing research will be conducted in the foreseeable future. A variety of techniques has been used for the study of these visceral events (swallowing a balloon or magnet, fluoroscopy, etc.), but electrical recording techniques are preferable because they reduce the likelihood of artifacts and appear generally more sensitive.

Electrical records of smooth muscle activity in the abdomen are referred to as "electrogastrograms" (EGGs).

Eye Responses. The electrical method of registering eye movements is the prominent one. Most commonly, electrodes are placed just posterior to the external canthi of both eyes. Hence, eye movements in the horizontal plane produce a transorbital potential that may be led into amplifiers and recorded. Vertical as well as horizontal signals may be obtained by locating an additional pair of electrodes above and below one eye.

Measures of covert eye responses have been extremely valuable in identifying important components of covert response patterns during a variety of thought processes. At the current level of analysis, it has been important to implicate any signal from the eye region as a component of mental activity, regardless of the technical source (electrooculograms—EOGs; electroencephalograms—EEGs; electromyograms—EMGs; etc.). Electrical signals thus result not only from the EOG standing potential between the cornea and the retina but also from numerous small saccadic movements and grosser movements that can be directly observed. Lindsay and Norman (1972) classified these complex eye movements into four categories: (1) very small and fast responses that occur from 30 to 70 times each second; (2) large oscillatory movements; (3) slow drifts of a few visual minutes one way or the other; and (4) rapid jerks with amplitudes about 5 minutes apart, often correcting for the slow drifts. Refined analysis can isolate the precise source of composite signals from the eye region, if and when desired.

Neurophysiological Processes

Our major source of information about neurophysiological activity in the normal human derives from electrical reactions recorded from the surface of the skull. As was noted, Berger (1929) had difficulty in finding acceptance for his conclusions among the scientific community, and even today there is no consensus as to the principles by which some 10 billion cerebral neurons generate the various brain waves. Although we appear to be making good progress, we must recognize that brain events constitute, in all probability, the most complex phenomena in nature and probably will be the last to yield to an adequate understanding.

Brain waves have been classified primarily by their frequency range, possibly because the amplitude values are so much more variable among people. Approximate defining frequency ranges for various brain wave classes are presented in Table 2.

Efforts to develop lawful relationships involving the ever-changing patterns of electrical gradients generated by the brain have resulted in a wide variety of methods of analysis. Classification of brain waves through complex frequency analyses and the plotting of gradients are illustrative techniques.

Table 2. Classes of Electroencephalographically Recorded Brain Waves Defined by Their Frequency Ranges

Brain wave class	Frequency
Sub-delta	0–.5 Hz
Delta	.5–4 Hz
Theta	4–8 Hz
Alpha	8–13 Hz
Sigma	13–15 Hz
Beta	15–30 Hz
Gamma	30–50 Hz

One popular method for studying the electrical activity of the brain is that of averaging evoked potentials from the human scalp, yielding an event that is not apparent in the spontaneous EEG. Signal averaging was developed by Dawson in 1947; he superimposed a number of synchronized EEG traces (evoked by a common stimulus) on a cathode-ray oscilloscope (CRO) and recorded the traces on a single photographic record. In this way a consistent, time-locked relationship appears as a consequence of the commonality of the individual traces in the group traces, revealing the evoked potential. The importance of Dawson's work was that it led to improved methods for recording evoked potentials, namely, signal averaging with the use of small commercial computers that calculated average transients. A veritable flood of research on the evoked potential has followed.

Another major advance in electrical measurement of brain activity was the recording of the contingent negative variation (CNV), which also is not readily observable in the raw trace. Typically, the signal-to-noise ratio must be increased, which is possible through the computer averaging technique. The CNV is a slow negative shift in the EEG baseline that is readily recordable when there is a contingency between two successive stimuli. The first stimulus is followed after a constant time interval by the second stimulus, to which the subject must make a response. For instance, the CNV can be seen in the EEG trace if a light flash (S_1) is followed by a continuous tone (S_2). The slow negative potential (CNV) can be observed within the S_1-S_2 interval, and a subject's overt pressing response would then terminate the tone and also the negativity of the CNV.

The widespread interest in electrical brain potentials may be witnessed in such disparate fields as psychiatry, neurology, electroencephalography, psychology, ophthalmology, audiology, computer science, and engineering. The early promise of advancing our understanding of brain functioning through these electrical techniques has been realized to some extent, but we should recognize that the field is still in its infancy.

This completes the survey of some of the principal covert processes that are psychophysiologically measured during cognitive functions. It is particularly within the past two decades that extremely versatile electronic systems have been developed to allow sensitive electrical recording of signals generated by the body, and it is the electrical measurement of covert processes that has yielded the most valuable findings. As a consequence, the psychophysiological study of covert processes has been progressing exponentially. I shall now turn to the electrophysiological laboratory system required for electropsychology.

Electrophysiological Methods for Studying Cognitive Processes

There are four essential features of an electropsychology laboratory for the study of covert processes: (1) sensors, which detect the signals of interest; (2) amplifiers, which modify the signals sensed; (3) readout devices, which display and record the signals; and (4) quantification systems, which render the analog signals into numerical values.

An Inexpensive Laboratory

The researcher who is just starting in this field is probably poorly financed and often must start with what is readily available. Though one constructing his or her own laboratory cannot expect to start with a sophisticated one (it might even be a disadvantage to do so), one *can* profitably start somewhere. Where one starts and how far one advances depend principally upon one's ingenuity, motivation, and, to a lesser extent, research funding. The dedicated researcher will almost always find a way.

For sensors, one could employ quite inexpensive electrodes (such as some offered by Grass Instruments Company) and could also find inexpensive amplifiers. Excellent, if dated, stock vacuum-tube amplifiers (such as Tektronics 122's) are available at low cost. Those who know solid-state electronics can develop effective operational amplifiers for a few dollars. Inexpensive oscilloscopes can be obtained for monitoring, though these are not absolutely essential.

The major problem comes with a recording device. Inexpensive recording systems might be purchased from suppliers that deal in used equipment or might be obtained free from companies such as Western Electric or from "government surplus." One could even eliminate a recording system if there is access to an institutional computer. In this case a program for integrating signals per unit time (or otherwise quantifying signals) could allow the signals to be conducted directly into a university's computer from the amplifiers. This would provide an ideal and probably inexpensive printout system. If one does record signals as on a strip chart, the time-proven quantification system of hand measurement, as discussed later, is always available.

A variety of other problems, discussed later, can be effectively handled by the beginning researcher, such as the problem of external (interfering) signals. Ideally, an electronically "quiet" area (e.g., a basement) could be found in which to locate the laboratory. The experimenter could then start off with inexpensive copper screening, checking signals on an oscilloscope to determine the relative effectiveness inside and outside the shielding. A more effective shielding is especially treated magnetic sheets of metal available from manufacturers. Some signals may not need shielding out at all, such as perhaps those sensed in brain wave recording. With the effective use of filters and of differential amplifiers with a high common mode rejection ratio, shielding may generally be eliminated.

The Laboratory Units

Figure 2 shows the four major components of a relatively advanced psychophysiological laboratory. To the left, one can note that the sensors are contained in a specially shielded subject room and that they enter the amplifiers, located in a second room. The amplified signals are recorded on a direct recorder and also on a data tape recorder; the signals are simultaneously monitored by CROs and can be displayed for detailed study on a storage oscilloscope. Finally, the signals enter a quantification system, which may be on-line or may be employed at a later time, receiving data stored on magnetic tape on a tape recorder.

Sensors. The sensor is a device that detects the signal of interest. If the event of interest has prominent electrical characteristics, then a pair of electrodes may be fixed on or in the appropriate location of the body, and a difference in electrical potential between the two electrodes may be detected. Examples of bodily events that yield electrical signals are the activities of muscles and of cerebral neurons. These two classes of events may be directly studied through electronic means, yielding EMGs and EEGs, respectively.

Most covert processes of interest here have electrical components and can be sensed directly by means of electrodes. (In addition to EMG, ECG, and EEG, there is an almost endless series of abbreviations beginning with "E" for "electro," as in "electrooculograms," "electrogastrograms," and "electroretinograms.")

A variety of acceptable electrodes is commercially available from suppliers. Gold electrodes are quite satisfactory (inexpensive and sturdy gold electrodes are available from Grass Instruments Company), and, because of their great stability (gold does not tarnish when exposed to atmospheric contaminants as silver does), are even preferable to others. Silver–silver chloride electrodes are also electrochemically quite stable.

More than one pair of electrodes should be attached to the subject so that measurements may be made simultaneously from a number of bodily locations. The value of data from concomitant measures was emphasized in

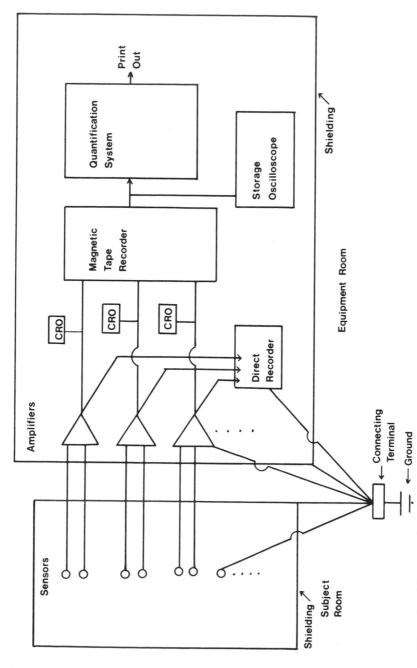

Figure 2. A laboratory for studying covert processes, with emphasis on its four major features. The shielded rooms, the shielded equipment, and the subject are all connected to a common ground.

McGuigan (1978)—one important advantage is that the procedure avoids the problem of suggestion. If only one set of electrodes is attached, the suggestion is obvious to the subject that something special should occur at that bodily location. Accordingly, electrodes attached only at the eyes might result in heightened frequency of blinking, and so on. If the experimenter has only one recording channel in the laboratory, then dummy (nonfunctional) electrodes should be attached at other locations of the body.

Transducers. A transducer is a device that changes one kind of energy into another. Most frequently in psychophysiology, a transducer is used to change some physical quantity, force, or property of the body into electrical energy. If the bodily process of interest does not have prominent electrical aspects, a transducer can be used to convert its energy into an electrical signal. In measuring respiration, for example, the primary mechanical signal (a change in chest size) is commonly sensed with a bellows-type pneumograph about the chest. As one breathes, the changing chest size produces changes in the air pressure in the bellows. A rubber tube conducts the pressure changes into a pressure transducer, which emits an electrical signal proportional to the degree of change in chest size.

Transducing bodily events to electrical signals allows us to process and display the events electronically, thereby maximizing the amount of information obtained. One can appreciate the value placed on transducing signals by noting the great number and variety of transducers that have been developed.

Signal Modification: Amplifiers. Once an electrical signal is sensed (either directly or by means of a transducer), it is led from a subject to a signal modifying unit—the second of the four essential laboratory components. Because the signals of covert processes are of such small amplitude, the signal modification unit is an amplifier.

Because amplifiers vary in an extremely large number of ways, considerable care should be exercised in selecting the one most appropriate for the particular covert process being studied. Amplifier requirements are determined primarily by the amplitude and frequency ranges of the signal being studied. The frequency of EMG is in the range of 20 to perhaps several thousand Hz (considering overtones of the basic signal, too). Consequently, for EMG recording, one would select an amplifier capable of processing signals in the range between several Hz and at least 1000 Hz. For covert processes of low amplitude (as in electromyographic signals of less than a microvolt), specialized amplifiers with low noise are required. In fact, it is of utmost importance that the total laboratory system be designed to minimize noise and to maximize the signal of interest in order to optimize the signal-to-noise ratio. Amplifiers are critical components of that system, and, if they are of low quality, they can contribute sizably to the total system noise.

Readout Systems. The third feature of the laboratory system is the readout device, a unit by which the signal is observed. Readout devices may provide only a momentary signal for study, as in the case of the CRO, or they may consist of recording systems that provide a permanent record of the phenomenon. A laboratory typically includes both kinds, the CRO for monitoring purposes, and the permanent recording system for the later study of the phenomenon.

The most frequently used recording system is some type of ink-writing polygraph, such as the "electroencephalograph." (The quotation marks are used because "electroencephalograph" is a term often loosely used for polygraphs that record a variety of psychophysiological measures besides brain waves.) Although psychophysiology has made great progress with the use of the ink-writing polygraph, this type of system is not recommended for such covert processes as EMGs, because EMGs range into the higher frequencies. The disadvantage of ink-writing polygraphs for recording such processes is that even the improved versions provide a linear (i.e., faithful) response recording only up to about 200 Hz; hence EMG frequencies are often too high for a mechanical recording system to follow. Another disadvantage is the inertia of the system; it does not provide a true tracing because of lag and overshoot. For EMGs that have a frequency range extending well above 200 Hz, a high-frequency recorder is much preferred. High-frequency recorders typically use an optical system. For instance, the input signal from the amplifier drives a miniature mirror that reflects ultraviolet light onto photosensitive paper; the signal, recorded on the paper, can then be preserved through chemical fixing processes. Such an optical system can provide a linear response recording as high as 10,000 Hz.

When direct tracings are recorded, as with ink-writing or high-frequency recorders, the experimenter's ability to quantify the data is restricted because the phenomena can only be quantified from the paper records. For this reason, an excellent addition to a laboratory is a multichannel data tape recorder, which will record the signals from the amplifiers on magnetic tape; frequency-modulated tape recorders are preferable to direct-recording tape recorders because of less distortion of amplitude and wave form and high repeatability from one playback to the next. The magnetic tape may then be played into a readout device (an ink-writing polygraph, a high-frequency recorder, or a CRO); for instance, the signals from the magnetic tape may be "frozen" for study on a storage CRO or photographed with a CRO camera. The data stored on tape in the original form may also be used for other methods of analysis (such as feeding them into a computer). This added flexibility is quite important, because with it the experimenter can try a variety of techniques of data analysis, some of which may be suggested only after observing the original tracings. This mention of different techniques of data analysis brings us to the fourth feature of the laboratory—the quantification system. Before concluding here, however, it is important to mention that the recording system should have several channels (tracks) to allow the simultaneous recording of several different covert processes.

Quantification Systems. Investigations conducted in the area of covert processes may be divided into two general classes: (1) those of brief, momentary phenomena and (2) those of sustained, long-term events. The investigator studying a momentary event may be most interested in an amplitude measure, although other parameters, such as duration and latency, may also be important. The amplitude of the measured event should be compared to some control or baseline value in order to ascertain whether or not the event actually occurred. For example, if one were trying to condition an EMG response, continuous EMG recordings would be made. The experimenter would then expect heightened EMG values following the presentation of the conditional stimulus, relative to a baseline measure.

In the study of longer term records, signals may be quantified by either amplitude or frequency measures, depending on their characteristics. If the signal is a cyclical, repetitive one, frequency measures are typically used (though amplitude measures are not thereby precluded). For example, the pneumogram, electrocardiogram, or peripheral pulse are usually quantified by counting the number of cycles per unit of time and converting to a rate, such as number of respirations, heart beats, or pulses per minute. Of course, rate is also a primary technique for classifying brain waves (see Table 2).

Where the signal is not cyclical and values are required for relatively long intervals of time, amplitude measures may be obtained in several different ways. Perhaps the simplest technique is to measure the height of the tracing with a ruler; one would thus compute peak-to-peak amplitude by measuring from the highest point of an event (such as an EMG spike) to the lowest.

In measuring signals over long intervals of time, data may be sampled by preselecting temporal intervals during which the measure will be taken. More typically, the total tracing may be subdivided into smaller time intervals; in this case the maximum amplitude of a spike that occurs during each smaller interval (e.g., each 10-second period of a 30-minute record) is measured, and the mean of these maximum amplitude values is computed. The EMG is a good example of a record for which this procedure is used, so that changes in maximum amplitude are studied as a function of time and experimental condition.

Hand-measuring techniques are quite simple, though typically time consuming, and thus they are often replaced by various automated procedures. An integration device (which sums the amplitude of the signal from the subject as a function of time) is perhaps the most popular procedure for quantifying sustained records by amplitude measures (integrators are typically included in standard ink-writing polygraphs). Again, the EMG is a good example of a measure for which the use of an amplitude integrator is helpful.

In addition to recording or integrating data on line (directly from the subject without storage) by means of either low- or high-frequency recorders, the advisability of including a multichannel magnetic tape recorder in the laboratory has been mentioned. The tape recorder and the direct recorder could be in parallel in the system so that the signals from the amplifier would be directly recorded and also stored on magnetic tape for other kinds of analysis. Because the stored signals are in analog form, the magnetic tape would be entered into some type of analog-to-digital conversion system, so that the data might be printed out in quantified digital form. For instance, the continuous analog psychophysiological signal stored on the magnetic tape may be digitized automatically by an analog-to-digital converter such that the quantity of integrated voltage per unit of time may be typed out in microvolt units. The particular analysis depends on the nature of the experimenter's problem, but a wide variety of analog-to-digital quantification systems is available. Computers that contain analog-to-digital converters are appropriate for this purpose, or more limited systems may be put together from standard units sold by electronic manufacturers. With the use of such systems, the experimenter can arrange for printing or plotting an integrated value per unit of time, the frequency of the signal, an average of the signals, and so forth. Such analysis can also be programmed for on-line computation, providing, of course, that the experimenter knows sufficiently well in advance how the data are to be analyzed.

Other Guidelines

Although complex laboratory equipment is necessary for the study of covert processes, the laboratory system should still be kept as simple as possible. A primary conclusion is that one should have as few apparatuses as is reasonably possible and should never develop equipment that is more complicated than necessary to get the job done. Researchers must be wary of the pitfalls that they can encounter if they become so enamored of apparatus construction, computer programming, statistical analysis, and the like that they needlessly complicate their task and perhaps even lose sight of their original research goal. In short, everything else being equal, the simpler the laboratory system, the more efficiently the research can be conducted.

Another general principle that should guide the psychophysiologist is that ultimately the psychophysiologist has to make his or her own decisions about how best to accomplish individual purposes in his or her own laboratory. Although it is advisable to study the many valuable references on psychophysiological and electronic techniques, and although experts can offer much general advice, such information does not necessarily apply in the unique situation of any individual psychophysiological laboratory. This is reminiscent of Einstein's comment about mathematicians to the effect that a mathematician can tell you an awful lot of things, but seldom what you want to know at the moment. To solve the problem of the moment, the psychophysiologist might try out a number of different types of supplies and equipment (manufacturers often furnish apparatuses on trial) and keep records of performance under a variety of conditions, eventually selecting those that provide relatively good recording under the existing laboratory conditions. For example, one should try several different kinds of electrodes, jellies, and pastes and evaluate several different methods of application of these (styrofoam pads, tape, etc.). Such experiences establish a sound basis for future standard laboratory procedures. One may find that the more expensive items are not necessarily the best.

Often, relatively simple and inexpensive items are equal or superior to more complex and expensive ones. For example, over the years I have tried out a large number of different kinds of electrodes and have concluded that the relatively inexpensive ones manufactured by Grass Instruments Company are completely satisfactory. They provide excellent recordings and remain usable for years, compared to some that must be discarded after several months.

Finally, I conclude this discussion with a general point applicable to all laboratory components: it is important to have confidence in the manufacturer so that the stated specifications may be believed.

Theoretical Integration of Electrically Measured Cognitive Processes

In the introduction, I specified as our goal the understanding of behavior, both overt and covert. The traditional psychological approach to achieve this goal has been to develop stimulus–response laws, including the hypothesizing of a variety of logical constructs. The psychologist, working strictly at the level of observable external stimuli (S) and overt responses (R), has thus been hampered by an inability to do more than indirectly infer the nature of the processes intervening between the S and the R. More recently, with the knowledge explosion in psychophysiology, we are making progress in filling those gaps between S and R through the direct measurement of covert processes. An illustrative methodology for directly studying such hypothesized events is given in the work of McGuigan and Boness (1975). Figure 3 gives a sample of their psychophysiologically recorded events, and Figure 4, a plot of the temporal relationships among those events.

However, the psychophysiologist's approach also has had shortcomings but for a different reason, namely, because of the lack of a guiding theoretical framework for the empirical measurement of psychophysiological phenomena. What we have learned through psychophysiological measurement has been initiated primarily by basic, low-level, limited empirical hypotheses rather than by more general, higher level theoretical constructs. By wedding the behavioristic and psychophysiological approaches, efforts within both domains should be enhanced through mutually facilitating techniques, approaches, and findings. The purpose in this section, therefore, is to attempt to interweave behaviorism and psychophysiology.

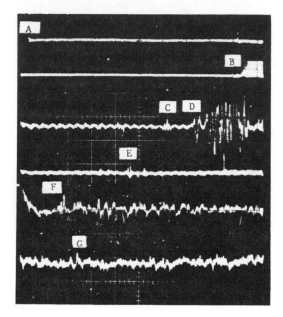

Figure 3. Sample tracings of the major physiologically recorded events. Blank (A) indicates stimulus presentation; B, overt response; C, isolated covert reaction in the active limb; D, onset of the covert response in the active limb that builds up to the overt response that produces B; E, isolated covert response in the passive limb; F, covert response in the tongue; G, covert response in the eye. Amplitude is 50 μV per division, except for tongue, which is 100 μV per division. Each horizontal centimeter is 50 msec.

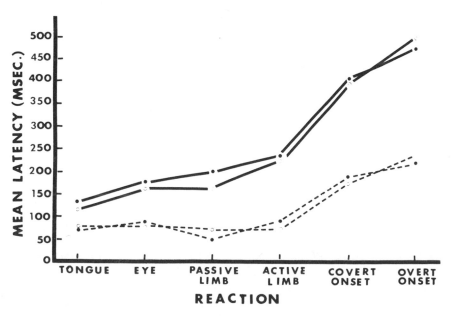

Figure 4. Mean latency of the earliest identified reaction for each bodily region. The top two traces are for choice reaction time, whereas the bottom two traces are for simple reaction time. Filled circles are for linguistic stimuli, unfilled circles, for nonlinguistic stimuli.

Developing a Model

We assume that an adequate understanding of any behavioral unit cannot be achieved when it is isolated from the rest of the body. Rather, a model of complex interactions of the various bodily systems is required in order to understand behavior and neural reactions, both of which are required for an understanding of cognitive functioning. Steps in developing a formal theory of covert processes require three hypothetical constructs and their interrelationships, as shown in Figure 5. These three constructs—the covert oral response (r_O), the covert nonoral response $(r_{\bar{O}})$, and the covert neurophysiological reaction (ρ_N)—may be evoked by external linguistic stimuli (S_L). The enormously complex interactions among these three classes of events are summarized by single arrows, indicating that each class of reaction sets off instances of every other class as responses and neural reactions relate within neuromuscular circuits. The ongoing interactions of these three classes of events result in an overt response (R_L) that is the termination of this neurobehavioral unit.

At a theoretical level, the covert response has traditionally been considered a hypothetical construct (X) defined according to classical procedures such as those employed by Hull (1943) or Tolman (1932). Hypothetical con-

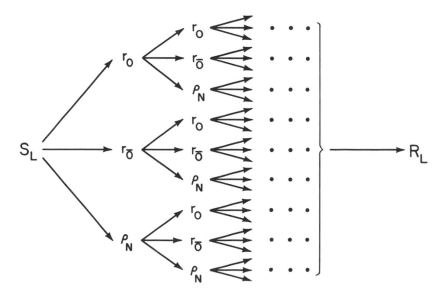

Figure 5. Representation of three classes of hypothetical constructs: covert oral responses (r_O), covert nonoral responses $(r_{\bar{O}})$, and covert neurophysiological processes (ρ_N). Complex interactions are represented here with arrows, though the representation of them as neuromuscular circuit components in Figure 7 is more realistic.

structs are defined by means of functional relationships between external stimuli (*S*) that anchor them on the antecedent side and overt responses (*R*) that anchor them on the consequent side (hence the paradigm *S*-(*X*)-*R*). For example, Hull's covert fractional anticipatory goal response (r_G) was defined by externally observable stimuli and responses according to the functional relationships specified by the paradigm S-r_G-s_G-R. Essentially the same approach to theoretical covert reactions has been used by many others (as listed in McGuigan, 1978).

Although behavioristic paradigms for anchoring constructs of covert processes have been quite successfully employed—the outstanding success of Osgood and his colleagues (e.g., Osgood & Hoosain, 1974) in measuring meaning (r_M) through such techniques as the semantic differential is an excellent example—psychophysiologists seek to compliment this classical approach by means of psychophysiological techniques. In this regard, hypothetical constructs are considered to have "reality status" and thus are potentially observable (as distinguished from intervening variables; cf. MacCorquodale & Meehl, 1948). The three major classes of covert processes (covert oral responses, covert nonoral responses, and covert neurophysiological processes) can thus also be empirically anchored directly through the psychophysiological methods specified in Table 1.

Figure 6 graphically illustrates this approach in which the hypothetical constructs are operationally defined in terms of the techniques of electromyography, electroencephalography, electrooculography, and so forth (Table 1). Note that the three hypothetical constructs (ρ_N, r_O, and $r_{\bar{O}}$) in-

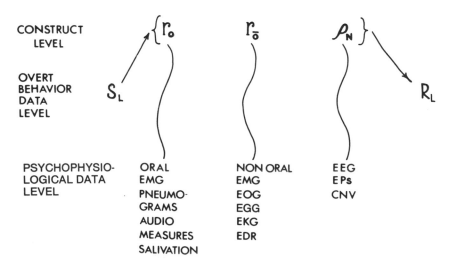

Figure 6. Three hypothetical constructs directly measured through psychophysiological methods.

tervening between the external linguistic stimulus (S_L) and the overt linguistic response (R_L) are directly tied to their psychophysiological data bases as well as to their indirect data bases (S_L and R_L). Reichenbach (1932) referred to this relationship between the formal constructs and the data level as that of a coordinating definition; Northrop (1948) identified the relation as an epistemic correlation.

Neuromuscular Circuits. In considering how the various bodily systems represented by the constructs of covert oral behavior, covert nonoral behavior, and neurophysiological reactions interact, we can consider the neuromuscular information-processing model represented in Figure 7. The basic notion is that the various cognitive phenomena with which psychology has dealt over the years occur when there is selective activation of the composite circuits represented in Figure 7. Perceptions, thoughts, ideas, images, hallucinations, dreams, or whatever, by this model, are common-sense terms denoting cognitive events produced during internal information processing when various of these circuits are activated.

Elsewhere we have detailed some of the abundant anatomical and physiological evidence about these specific circuits (loops) between a wide variety of peripheral mechanisms and the brain (McGuigan, 1978). The first class of circuit (designated Ia in Figure 7) occurs when stimuli excite receptors, whereupon afferent neural impulses evoke brain events that result in efferent impulses back to the receptor. Such loops must reverberate for some time following stimulus reception. There is also the probability of extra-CNS loops between receptors and other peripheral mechanisms, such as the receptor–speech muscle–brain circuits designated by the symbols Ib and Ib'.

The second general class of circuit (which would function for sensory integration) would consist of intracerebral loops (II). These may include circuits between the cortex and subcortical regions (cf. Penfield, 1969) as well as complex transcortical loops, such as Hebb's (1949) cell assemblies. The third class of circuit involves cerebral–speech muscle activity (IIIa) and cerebral–somatic muscle activity (IIIb).

Hence, when external linguistic stimuli impinge on the organism, the first class of circuit (Ib and Ib') is activated, following which sensory integration (for separate input from the two eyes, the two ears, etc.) occurs when circuit class II reverberates. Simultaneously, there is skeletal speech muscle and nonspeech muscle activity through the circuit classes IIIa and IIIb. These latter circuits are important for the generation of linguistic codes, which are then transmitted to and from the linguistic regions of the brain for lexical-semantic processing. It is during this latter stage (circuit class IV) that meaningful perception (interpretation) of the external stimuli occurs.

A rather detailed consideration of how this internal information-processing model may be used to explicate the "higher mental processes" may be found in McGuigan (1978, pp. 329–439). This neuromuscular circuit model is mentioned here merely for heuristic value in guiding our psychophysiologi-

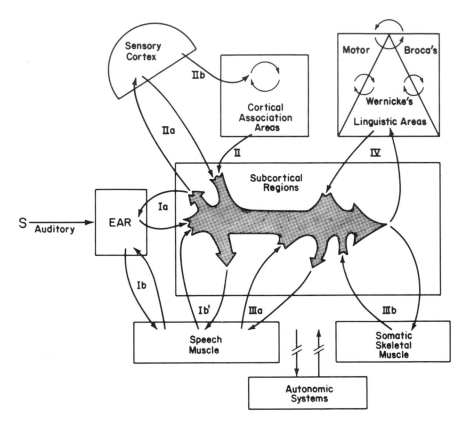

Figure 7. A neuromuscular circuit model for internal information processing.

cal laboratory research. The task for the cognitive psychophysiologist is to measure components of these neuromuscular circuits and to temporally relate those measured events to trace out the circuits that are critical during cognitive functioning, as shown in Figure 8.

In discussing this figure, McGuigan and Pavek (1972) stated the following:

> Complex feedback loops might function to integrate the speech musculature (lips, tongue, etc.) with the speech regions of the brain, and with the eye, related perhaps to a covert nod or shake of the head (indicated by the response in the neck region). Differential linguistic patterns should be identifiable at this instant, as in the case of duration of eye response. . . . Concomitant with this intraperipheral and interperipheral and central integration in which a YES–NO decision is reached, and part of the almost simultaneous running off of these feedback loops, a "command" is issued to the passive arm that is inhibitory in nature—it may be that the active arm can only overtly respond once the passive

arm is commanded to "not respond" (hence, a more rapid response in the passive arm relative to that in the active arm . . . such an inhibitory response, involving as it does the skeletal musculature, might be the behavioral counterpart of inhibitory neural activity, as reported by Hernández-Péon, Scherrer, and Jouvet (1956). Finally, continuing this line of speculation, after the complex decision (YES or NO) was made, the dominant motor cortex was uniquely activated, "commanding" the overt response to be made in the active arm. (p. 244)

These considerations clearly illustrate the necessity of taking simultaneous records from a number of bodily systems. By employing all of the psychophysiological variables specified in Table 1, and new ones, too, we should make progress toward the direct measurement of the various cognitive events that are of primary concern to the psychologist and to other interested scientists.

A summary of the various kinds of circuits and their functioning is presented in Figure 9. Note that complex interactions between the speech muscle and central nervous system occur in the generation of the type of

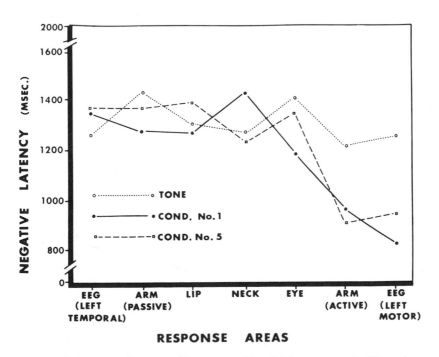

Figure 8. Relative mean latencies of responses identified in various bodily regions. (The higher the data point on the vertical scale, the earlier the response followed stimulus termination.)

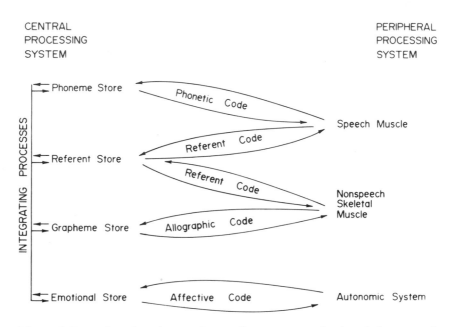

CENTRAL
PROCESSING
SYSTEM

PERIPHERAL
PROCESSING
SYSTEM

INTEGRATING PROCESSES

Phoneme Store

Referent Store

Grapheme Store

Emotional Store

Phonetic Code

Referent Code

Referent Code

Allographic Code

Affective Code

Speech Muscle

Nonspeech
Skeletal
Muscle

Autonomic System

Figure 9. In conjunction, these various volleys are transmitted to their appropriate regions of the brain (the verbal coding to the linguistic regions for lexical–semantic processing, the nonverbal coding to other regions of the brain for nonlinguistic processing).

linguistic code referred to as a "phonetic code" and in those nonoral skeletal muscle components that function in the generation of the type of linguistic code referred to as an "allographic code" (as detailed in McGuigan, 1978). Note also the neuromuscular circuits that function during nonverbal thought by generating a "referent-level code". Finally, there are circuits involving the autonomic system for adding emotional tone to our mental activity. In conjunction, these various volleys are transmitted to and from their appropriate regions of the brain (the verbal coding to and from the linguistic regions for lexical–semantic processing, the nonverbal coding perhaps to selected regions of the minor hemisphere for nonlinguistic processing, and the autonomic systems with the subcortical regions of the brain for emotional processing).

Understanding Cognitive Functions

"Cognitive activities" in all of their diversity (dreams, thoughts, images, hallucinations, ideas, etc.) are thus to be considered as labels in the vernacular that served to start our science. If they exist, and overwhelming data indicate that they do, they can be measured through the tools of science. Classical psychology has indirectly measured them by means of their consequences for overt behavior, and psychophysiology directly measures them principally through electrical techniques. As such scientific explication progresses, we can increasingly replace common-sense terms with precise well-defined, scientific terms, as Binet did with "intelligence."

It is an amazing thought that the human mind consists of operations performed by the selective activation of neuromuscular circuits. Yet, no other interpretation is reasonable. Centuries of philosophical speculation and of empirical specifications of "blind alleys" and "true pathways" have been necessary to arrive at this insight. We have arrived at the threshold of understanding cognitive functions, and, peering into the future, I can envision highly sophisticated research in which internal information processes are precisely sensed, recorded, quantified, and lawfully related. I strongly suspect that information received from the external environment, as well as that generated internally, is processed through the complex interactions of several kinds of linguistic and nonlinguistic codes. Yet, codes themselves are meaningless and have value only when interpreted. The great problem of psychology that lies before us is to specify how internally transmitted and generated codes are interpreted. Specification of the mechanism by which codes are interpreted and by which codes are generated for controlling behavior through self-programming operations should constitute a sufficient explication of what we refer to as "the human mind."

Current Research in Cognitive Psychophysiology

These considerations for the development of the neuromuscular circuit model of cognitive activity will, I hope, provide guidance for the increasing amount of research relevant to the field. This empirical research has been fairly thoroughly summarized through about 1977 (McGuigan, 1979), but the additional data since then are somewhat scattered. A brief mention of more recent research into various facets of psychophysiology may be helpful in illustrating how very much alive these developing notions are.

Especially impressive is the systematic work by Cacioppo and his colleagues. They have conducted a variety of studies on patterns of covert somatic responses that interface the brain to the external environment. (See, especially, the summary by Cacioppo & Petty, in press, Note 1.) This work effectively extends the area of psychophysiology to cognitive, clinical, and social subfields.

Another line of development that is similarly encouraging has been the work by Schwartz and his colleagues. In particular, in a series of studies, Schwartz (1975), Schwartz, Fair, Mandel, Salt, Mieske, and Klerman (1978), and Schwartz, Fair, Salt, Mandel, and Klerman (1976a, 1976b) have successfully electromyographically measured affective imagery in terms of facial muscle pattern. Other aspects of these works are elaborated by Cacioppo and Petty in Chapter 10, this volume.

Consequences of a Science of Covert Behavior for Clinical Practice

Tension Control: An Overview

A science of covert behavior has numerous technological consequences for society (McGuigan, 1978). I will deal here with some of the clinical disorders resulting from chronic muscular states produced by the stresses of the modern world. These stresses literally reek havoc on the systems of the body by producing states of overtension. The omnipresence of tension disorders in our society attests to the fact that few successfully cope with the tension's of everyday living. Indeed, tension disorders are more common than the common cold, and they constitute unique problems for many professional fields. Overtension is evidenced by bruxism (nocturnal tooth grinding), headaches, hypertension, coronary heart disease, colitis, anxiety, excessive fatigue, constipation, diarrhea, phobias, and so forth.

An initial problem often encountered in the scientific study of relaxation is the diversity of definitions for the terms "relaxation" and "tension"; "relaxation" can mean anything from a Florida vacation to smoking a good cigar. The accepted classical scientific definitions of the terms "tension" and "relaxation" have to do with states of the skeletal musculature. Tension is the contraction (shortening) of skeletal muscle fibers, and relaxation is the lengthening of muscle fibers. The consequences of these simple, straightforward, scientific definitions are enormous, as Jacobson (1929), the pioneer in the field of relaxation has shown in his voluminous work.

The task of learning to use one's muscles efficiently is not an easy one. There are some 1030 separate striated muscles in the human body (which compose almost half of our body weight), and a lifetime of injudicious use of these muscles indirectly leads to chronic malfunction of various bodily systems. The accumulated data clearly indicate a strong functional relationship between state of the skeletal musculature and level of autonomic activity, as illustrated in Figure 10. In particular, consistent, chronic tension of the skeletal musculature increases activity of the cardiovascular system, the gastrointestinal system, and so forth. Overtenseness can be a critical factor leading to such problems as coronary heart disease or stomach or intestinal ulcers. Conversely, when we produce a tranquil state of the skeletal musculature, autonomic activity decreases, whereupon we often witness a lowering of blood pressure and a loosening of the smooth musculature of the intestines, which relieves a spastic colon. Precisely how the skeletal muscles control these autonomic systems is poorly understood at present. It seems apparent that there are complex central nervous system and hormonal

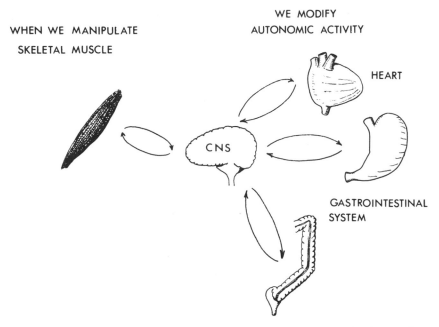

WHEN WE MANIPULATE
SKELETAL MUSCLE

WE MODIFY
AUTONOMIC ACTIVITY

HEART

CNS

GASTROINTESTINAL
SYSTEM

Figure 10. A model of the functional relationship between the skeletal musculature and other bodily functions. As tension increases, central nervous system and autonomic functions are heightened. Relaxation of the skeletal musculature produces a tranquil state throughout the body.

mediating processes; one suggestion is that muscular relaxation reduces proprioceptive input to the hypothalamus, which in turn reduces hypothalamic cortical discharges (Gellhorn & Kiely, 1972).

Numerous techniques have been proposed to achieve relaxation, ranging from natural, general bodily control (as in progressive relaxation), to treating localized symptoms with auxiliary equipment (as in biofeedback), to meditative techniques imported from the "wisdom of the Eastern religions." Recently there has been a heightened interest in the scientific validity of these techniques. Progressive relaxation has a long and venerable history of clinical and experimental validation; muscle biofeedback is also in the scientific mainstream, though it less successfully satisfies such scientific criteria of evaluation as specified by Borkovec (1977).

Progressive Relaxation

In progressive relaxation, one learns to "observe" the internal sensory world as well as one observes the external environment. In acquiring heightened internal sensory observation, one employs two simple, straight-forward, physiological principles: (1) learning to recognize ("observe") a state of tension and (2) contrasting that tension state with the elimination of tension (relaxation). The learner emphasizes that he or she was the one who successfully eliminated the tension that was recognized in a given part of the body. Each of the major muscle groups is systematically tensed so that the learner can identify the unique tension or control signal produced by that muscle group. This sensation is called the "control signal" because it literally is a control for neuromuscular circuits, as diagrammed in Figure 11. Just as one learns to drive an automobile or a jet airplane by means of an accelerator, one can control the human body by means of the skeletal muscles.

Volleys of afferent neural impulses, generated by the various possible receptors imbedded in the muscles, constitute the control signal. These af-ferent neural impulses are directed to (and from) the brain within neuromus-cular circuits. By learning internal sensory observation, one can observe the control signals that are signs of tension wherever they may occur throughout the skeletal musculature. The goal of progressive relaxation is to achieve a state in which the body automatically monitors all of the control signals in-stantaneously and relieves those tensions that are not desired. To eliminate any unnecessary tension, one must first learn to recognize it. An efficiently run organism automatically relaxes all of the muscles that are not required for the act being performed, having learned to unconsciously recognize con-trol signals for unnecessarily contracted muscles and to relax those tensions away. In short, one can learn to relax selectively (differentially) those muscles not required for the act being performed. "Differential relaxation" thus is defined as the process of contracting only those muscles necessary for carry-ing out the purpose at hand, while relaxing all others in the body.

"Self-operations control" is a synonym for "progressive relaxation" and emphasizes the importance of the active programming of one's own body to accomplish the purposes that one sets for oneself. Self-operations control (progressive relaxation) has two general phases: (1) the self-programming phase, in which one decides life goals and strategies for accomplishing those goals, and (2) the phase in which one learns techniques for carrying out these purposes. One needs to learn not only how and when to expend energies but also how to estimate the optimal amount of energy required for a given pur-pose. Often a person may decide in the self-programming phase that some act is or is not worthwhile. Many ongoing conversations simply are not worth one's effort, particularly if they are emotionally wasteful. A progressive relaxation student will not argue heatedly or castigate another driver, because such activities are obviously only wasteful of energy, accomplishing nothing. Cost estimation is important, and one can become skillful in automatically estimating one's moment-to-moment energy expenditure. Life is difficult enough as it is, and it is important for one with high purposes to keep his or her eye on the doughnut and not on the hole.

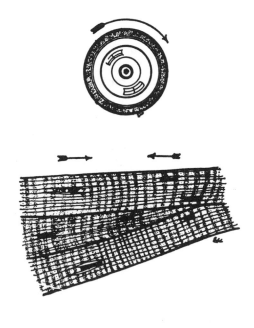

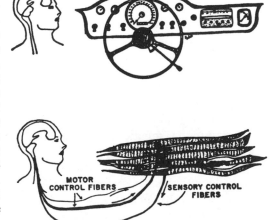

Figure 11. "You run your car by manipulating the controls on and near the dashboard, whereby you make the wheels move at the rate and in the direction you desire. Likewise, you can run yourself by going on and off with the power in the controls which lie in your muscles, whereupon your muscles contract and relax in the patterns which suit your effort-purposes." (From *Self-operations control*, by E. Jacobson. Chicago: National Foundation for Progressive Relaxation, 1964, p. 2.)

In summary, with progressive relaxation, one seeks to relax differential-ly 24 hours a day as one moves through life. This means that for both waking and sleeping life one specifies for oneself the goal at hand and tenses precisely those muscles necessary to accomplish that goal, whether it be cleaning the teeth, reading a book, or going to sleep. All other tensions detected during the act at hand should be relaxed away.

Controlling Mental Processes. The act of going to sleep provides us with the opportunity for understanding how we control thoughts and ideas. When one sets for oneself the purpose of lying down in bed at night to sleep, one should differentially relax almost all of the skeletal musculature. Minimal ex-ertion is required to maintain the vegetative processes, as in breathing, cir-culation, and digestion. An instance of misprogramming is trying to fall asleep while engaging in active thought processes. Insomnia, rather than sleep, is often the result. If one wishes to review the day's activities or to plan for the morrow, one might do that most efficiently by sitting up or taking a walk. However, if sleep is the goal, then one should lie down and relax the en-tire body, including the neuromuscular circuits responsible for thought.

Thoughts are physical acts of the body that occur when selected neuromuscular circuits are activated, as depicted in Figure 7. The scientific and clinical evidence supporting this model of thought is substantial (McGuigan, 1978). According to this view, mental processes are internal information-processing events that occur when selected muscles tense (especially those in the oral and visual regions) to activate afferent circuits to and then from the brain. Any interruption of these circuits will eliminate the processing of information and thus eliminate thoughts. The simplest and most normal way to cause the circuits to be tranquil is by relaxing the tensed muscles. If one relaxes the tongue, the lips, the jaws, the cheeks, and the muscles of the neck, a large proportion of one's thought content is eliminated, especially that having to do with linguistic (verbal) mental ac-tivity.

The model of the mind represented in Figure 7 has considerable techno-logical as well as scientific significance. The conclusion that muscles are in-timately involved in thought allows for the practical application of differen-tial relaxation to eliminate undesired thoughts (as in phobias, worries) and is an additional personal energy conservation procedure. We thus control our external and internal activities through the skeletal muscles, orchestrating central and autonomic activities, as we seek to guide our thoughts and emo-tions systematically and efficiently. A wise person rationally determines when and when not to be emotional. An advocate of tension control does not suggest the elimination of one's emotional life. Emotions can be good or bad, depending on what they are and on when they are allowed to flow.

Bruxism. As dentists are quite aware, the habit of grinding one's teeth, especially during sleep, is a very common one. Often the result is a wearing away of the teeth, which, in turn, may produce other bodily malfunctions. In the application of progressive relaxation, special attention is paid to the relaxation of the masseter (jaw), and as a result, bruxism is one of the earliest tension problems to be eliminated.

Coronary Heart Disease and Essential Hypertension. The epidemic proportions of some one million cardiovascular disease fatalities and of 700,000 deaths due to heart attacks per year are well recognized internationally. The problem is because the disease is progressing to earlier age levels, commanding an increasing amount of our research attention. As Hillman (1976) has summarized, progressive relaxation has been shown to be effective in controlling high blood pressure. When one meets the stresses of everyday living, the activities of the skeletal musculature increase, causing, in turn, increased cardiovascular activity (Figure 10). If the stresses that caused the increased cardiovascular activity continue, the initially intermittent smooth muscle overexertion of the arterioles can become chronic, resulting in consistent high blood pressure. If an individual seeks proper treatment prior to organic damage, blood pressure can be lowered, as with clinical progressive relaxation. For example, Figure 12 shows a consistent decrease in blood pressure in selected patients treated with progressive relaxation. Follow-up data indicate that the decrease is lasting.

Gastrointestinal Disorders, Headaches, Phobias, and Other Applications of Progressive Relaxation. As noted in discussing Figure 10, chronic constriction of the skeletal musculature, slight though it might be, can produce disastrous effects on the gastrointestinal tract. Such small tensions, consistently applied over the years, working away 24 hours a day, may not be considered important. However, just as a consistent dripping of water can work its way through a large boulder, the continuous state of overtenseness that many people experience can overdrive many systems of the body. Common gastrointestinal results are a spastic colon and ulcers, with attendant constipation and diarrhea. Almost uniformly, the overtense individual will also report chronic fatigue, which is especially apparent at the end of the day.

Through the years, Jacobson has reported on a number of successful applications of progressive relaxation for treating such problems. The approach is to treat the entire skeletal musculature, but with the process of treatment the clinician especially concentrates on the afflicted portions of the body. Thus, in the case of a malformed colon, relaxation of the abdominal muscles is especially practiced. Jacobson (Note 2) has estimated that perhaps 90% of the cases of constipation and diarrhea result from the overtenseness that is concentrated in the abdominal region and that chronic constriction of the upper gastrointestinal tract in the esophagus produces maladaptive fear (as evidenced by phobias).

In the application of clinical progressive relaxation for the treatment of a phobia, the patient imagines fearful acts of increasing intensity, after each

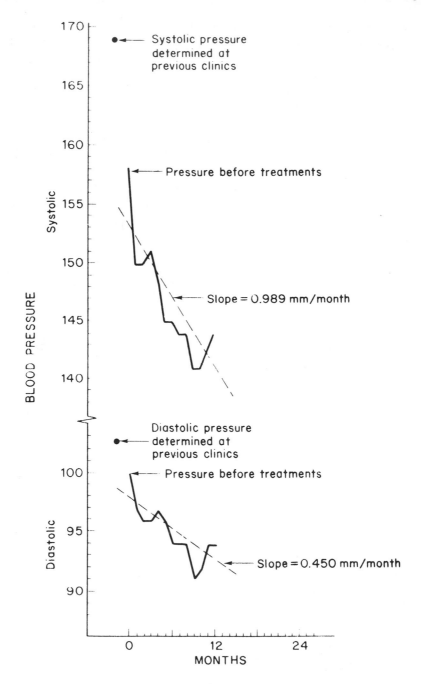

Figure 12. Mean decrease of blood pressure in selected patients treated with clinical progressive relaxation. Follow-up data indicate that the decrease is lasting.

component of which the musculature is relaxed. In a classic case (Jacobson, 1934), a patient who feared heights started by imagining a feather dropping and gradually worked up to imagining hanging down from tall heights. Eventually, the patient rented an office high up in a skyscraper.

In treating a phobia, the clinician also employs techniques for relaxing the body—especially the esophagus—and for controlling one's thoughts—especially visual ones, which engage the muscles of the eyes. The learner eventually experiences relatively tranquil states throughout the body, particularly in the visual region and also in the esophagus. As a consequence, when the muscular components of the neuromuscular circuits (Figure 7) are unactivated, thoughts that are components of the phobia disappear. Again, in the treatment of headaches, one relaxes the entire skeletal musculature, with concentration on the eye muscles (those of the neck, the eyes proper, and the brow).

Conclusion. The successful student of self-operations control becomes self-reliant in order to carry out the purposes that he or she sets for himself or herself. One does not become dependent on the teacher. For the greatest benefit of society, Jacobson (1973) advocated the teaching of progressive relaxation to children, who, incidentally, acquire the skills more efficiently and more rapidly than do adults. If the technique is acquired early, children are then equipped to employ it automatically and habitually throughout their lives. Great advances in preventative medicine and clinical psychology could be achieved by thus educating our young. Such progress comes slowly, but just as we eventually learned to brush our teeth and to bathe our bodies frequently, perhaps we will eventually learn to relax differentially.

Behavior Therapy

The resemblance between clinical progressive relaxation and what has more recently come to be know as behavior therapy or behavior modification is readily apparent. Behavior modification was derived partly from principles of conditioning, as in the work of Wolpe (1975) and Cautela (1973). Cautela employed methods referred to as "covert conditioning" in clinical situations where the assumption was that empirical generalizations of overt operant conditioning apply to the manipulation of covert processes as well. In the application of such conditioning procedures as covert sensitization, covert positive reinforcement, covert negative reinforcement, and covert extinction, small-scale muscular behavior presumably is systematically manipulated to eliminate the pathological condition.

The entire field of behavior modification and associated enterprises is so enormous that I will only pay lip service to it here. The consequences for society are indeed great, and these technological approaches deserve our continued observation and study within the context of a science of covert processes.

Biofeedback

Recently, biofeedback has been widely advocated as a tension control procedure. Like many other scientific procedures, biofeedback has potential values and drawbacks. It is clearly a valuable and interesting laboratory phenomenon, and we have learned much about the operation of the human body by employing it. The pitfall is that people have seized on the phenomenon often as an instant cure-all for whatever problems they may have.

In biofeedback, internal bodily signals are transduced so that one may directly observe them on an oscilloscope or by listening to sounds. In electrocardiography, for instance, one can directly observe the electrical activity of one's heart. We can thus see, hear, or otherwise monitor such internal events as brain waves, cardiovascular activity, galvanic skin responses, skin temperature, and activities of the smooth and striated muscles. Any bodily organ that generates signals can be transduced so that the activity is externally observable and thus "fed back" into the body's biological receptors. No doubt basic scientific findings with biofeedback will have great significance for the further development of science. Although psychology has traditionally been concerned with the relationship of one's behavior to the external world, it is increasingly turning to the exploration of relationships between overt behavior and internal events, as evidenced by the flood of scientific interest in biofeedback.

Clinically, biofeedback was first used about 1950 by Jacobson (cf. 1957). Electromyographic signals were transduced so that his patients could visually monitor their tensions on the CRO. The technique was eventually abandoned for clinical use because the student became dependent upon the feedback signal, relaxing only selected muscle groups and only in the presence of that signal. The preferable technique is progressive relaxation, wherein the individual monitors *all* tension signals from *all* muscles under *all* life circumstances, without the necessity of auxiliary equipment. We have long known that learning to relax one muscle group (by whatever technique) has only a localized effect on that particular region of the body—relaxing the tongue, for instance, does not result in relaxation of muscles well removed from that bodily region (e.g., McGuigan, 1971; Gatchel, Korman, Weiss, Smith, & Clark, 1978). The skeletal musculature simply does not act as a unified system, so that if, through biofeedback, one does learn to relax the forehead muscle, this localized relaxation is independent of tension states in the remainder of the skeletal muscles, each group of which must be relaxed in turn. In a sense, one might say that after successful tension reduction of one muscle through biofeedback, there are only about 1029 yet to go. Other difficulties in this area have been summarized by Tarler-Benlolo (1978).

A second major problem with muscle biofeedback concerns generalization and permanence of the effect. The behavioral modification might not transfer to everyday life situations, and the modification might not be permanent (McGuigan, 1971).

Muscle biofeedback may eventually find useful and even powerful application in the public domain as a clinical technique, but to date there is little scientific validation for the procedure. However, we are witness to numerous biofeedback clinics that are actively engaged in therapy throughout the country. Although patients report relief of symptoms through various biofeedback procedures, these reports are not sufficient to justify the technological application of such procedures. Biofeedback, like any relaxation technique, should be well validated. As Wolpe (1975) pointed out, a valid therapy should produce a success rate in excess of the 50–60% one can expect from any therapy simply as a result of the "placebo effect."

Reference Notes

1. Cacioppo, J. T., & Petty, R. E. Electromyographic specificity as a function of depth and type of processing. In *Psychophysiological research: 101 years of exploring covert functions.* Symposium presented at the 87th annual convention of the American Psychological Association, New York, September 1979.
2. Jacobson, E. Personal communication.

References

Adrian, E. D., & Matthews, B. H. C. The Berger rhythm: Potential changes from the occipital lobes of man. *Brain*, 1934, *57*, 355–385.

Bechterev, V. M. *Foundations of general reflexology of man.* Moscow: Gosizdat, 1923.

Berger, H. Uber das elektrekephalogramm des Menschen. *Archiv fuer Psychiatrie und Nervenkrankheiten*, 1929, *87*, 527–570.

Borkovec, T. D. Therapy outcome research: Group design and methodology. In F. J. McGuigan (Ed.), *Tension control: Proceedings of the third meeting of the American Association for the Advancement of Tension Control.* Louisville: AAATC, 1977.

Cacioppo, J. T., & Petty, R. E. Electromyograms as measures of extent and affectivity of information processing. *American Psychologist,* in press.

Cautela, J. R. Covert processes and behavior modification. *Journal of Nervous and Mental Disease*, 1973, *157*, 27.

Chase, W. G. (Ed.). *Visual information processing.* New York: Academic Press, 1973.

Davis, R. C. Patterns of muscular activity during "mental work" and their constancy. *Journal of Experimental Psychology*, 1939, *24*, 451–465.

Davis, R. C. Garafolo, L. & Gault, F. P. An exploration of abdominal potentials. *Journal of Comparative and Physiological Psychology*, 1957, *50*, 519–523.

Dawson, G. D. Cerebral responses to electrical stimulation of peripheral nerves in man. *Journal of Neurology and Neurosurgical Psychiatry*, 1947, *10*, 134–140.

Delafresnaye, J. F. *Brain mechanisms and consciousness.* Oxford: Blackwell Scientific Publications, Ltd., 1954.

Dunlap, K. *A system of psychology*. New York: Scribner's, 1912.

Eccles, J. C. *Brain and conscious experience*. New York: Springer-Verlag, 1966.

Faaborg-Anderson, K., & Edfeldt, A. W. Electromyography of intrinsic and extrinsic laryngeal muscles during silent speech: Correlation with reading activity. *Acta Oto-Laryngologica*, 1958, *49*, 478–482.

Galperin, P. Y. Stages in the development of mental acts. In M. Cole & I. Maltzman (Eds.), *A handbook of contemporary Soviet psychology*. New York: Basic Books, 1969.

Gatchel, R. J., Korman, M., Weiss, C. B., Smith, D., & Clark, L. A multiple-response evaluation of EMG biofeedback performance during training and stress-induction conditions. *Psychophysiology*, 1978, *15*, 253–258.

Gellhorn, E., & Kiely, W. F. Mystical states of consciousness: Neurophysical and clinical aspects. *Journal of Nervous and Mental Disease*, 1972, *154*, 399–405.

Grings, W. W. The role of consciousness and cognition in autonomic behavior change. In F. J. McGuigan & R. A. Schoonover (Eds.), *The psychophysiology of thinking*. New York: Academic Press, 1973. (*a*)

Grings, W. W. Cognitive factors in electrodermal conditioning. *Psychological Bulletin*, 1973, *79*, 200–210. (*b*)

Hebb, D. O. *The organization of behavior*. New York: Wiley, 1949.

Hebb, D. O. Concerning imagery. *Psychological Review,* 1968, *75*, 466–477.

Hefferline, R. F., Keenan, B., Harford, R. A., & Birch, J. Electronics in psychology. *Columbia Engineering Quarterly*, 1960, *13*, 10–15.

Hernández-Peón, R., Scherrer, H., & Jouvet, M. Modification of electric activity in cochlear nucleus during "attention" in unanesthetized cats. *Science*, 1956, *123*, 331–332.

Hillman, E. C., Jr. The effect of tension control on blood pressure. In F. J. McGuigan (Ed.), *Tension control: Proceedings of the second meeting of the American Association for the Advancement of Tension Control*. Chicago: University Publications, 1976.

Holt, E. B. Materialism and the criterion of the psychic. *Psychological Review*, 1937, *44*, 33–53.

Hull, C. L. *Principles of behavior*. New York: Appleton-Century-Crofts, 1943.

Hunter, W. S. The problem of consciousness. *Psychological Review*, 1924, *31*, 1–37.

Jacobson, E. Voluntary relaxation of the esophagus. *American Journal of Physiology*, 1925, *72*, 387–394.

Jacobson, E. Action currents from muscular contractions during conscious processes. *Science*, 1927, *66*, 403.

Jacobson, E. *Progressive relaxation*. Chicago: University of Chicago Press, 1929.

Jacobson, E. Electrophysiology of mental activities. *American Journal of Psychology*, 1932, *44*, 677–694.

Jacobson, E. *You must relax: Practical methods for reducing the tensions of modern living*. New York: McGraw-Hill, 1934.

Jacobson, E. *You must relax* (4th ed.). New York: McGraw-Hill, 1957.

Jacobson, E. *Self-operations control*. Chicago: National Foundation for Progressive Relaxation, 1964.

Jacobson, E. *Teaching and learning: New methods for old arts*. Chicago: National Foundation for Progressive Relaxation, 1973.

Lacey, J. I. Individual differences in somatic response patterns. *Journal of Comparative and Physiological Psychology*, 1950, *43*, 338–350.

Lacey, B. C., & Lacey, J. I. Studies of heart rate and other bodily processes in sensorimotor behavior. In P. A. Obrist, A. H. Black, J. Brener, & L. V. DiCara (Eds.), *Cardiovascular psychophysiology: Current issues in response mechanisms, biofeedback, and methodology*. Chicago: Aldine-Atherton, 1974.

Langfeld, H. S. A response interpretation of consciousness. *Psychological Review*, 1931, *38*, 87–108.

Langfeld, H. S. The historical development of response psychology. *Science*, 1933, *77*, 243–250.

Leontiev, A. N. *Problems of psychic development*. Moscow: APN RSFSR Press, 1959.

Lindsay, P. H., & Norman, D. A. *Human information processing. An introduction to psychology*. New York: Academic Press, 1972.

Lindsley, D. B. Average evoked potentials—achievements, failures and prospects. In E. Donchin & D. B. Lindsley (Eds.), *Average evoked potentials*. Washington, D.C.: NASA SP-191, 1969.

Lippold, O. Origin of the alpha rhythm. *Nature*, 1970, 226, 616–618. (*a*)

Lippold, O. Bilateral separation in alpha rhythm recording. *Nature*, 1970, 226, 459–460. (*b*)

Lippold, O. Are alpha waves artifactual? *New Scientist,* March 12, 1970, 506–507. *(c)*

Lippold, O. C. J., & Novotny, G. E. K. Is alpha rhythm an artifact? *Lancet*, 1970, 1, 976–979.

MacCorquodale, K., & Meehl, P. E. On a distinction between hypothetical constructs and intervening variables. *Psychological Review*, 1948, 55, 95–107.

Max L. W. An experimental study of the motor theory of consciousness: III. Action-current responses in deaf mutes during sleep, sensory stimulation and dreams. *Journal of Comparative Psychology*, 1935, 19, 469–486.

Max, L. W. An experimental study of the motor theory of consciousness: IV. Action-current responses in the deaf during awakening, kinaesthetic imagery and abstract thinking. *Journal of Comparative Psychology*, 1937, 24, 301–344.

McGuigan, F. J. External auditory feedback from covert oral behavior during silent reading. *Psychonomic Science*, 1971, 25, 212–214.

McGuigan, F. J. *Cognitive psychophysiology: Principles of covert behavior*. Englewood Cliffs, N.J.: Prentice-Hall, 1978.

McGuigan, F. J. *Psychophysiological measurement of covert behavior: A guide for the laboratory*. Hillsdale, N.J.: Erlbaum, 1979.

McGuigan, F. J. & Boness, D. J. What happens between an external stimulus and an overt response? A study of covert responses. *Pavlovian Journal of Biological Science*, 1975, 10, 112–119.

McGuigan, F. J., & Pavek, G. V. On the psychophysiological identification of covert nonoral language processes. *Journal of Experimental Psychology*, 1972, 92, 237–245.

McGuigan, F. J., & Szegal, B. Covert behavior and mental processes in Russian psychology. *Pavlovian Journal of Biological Science,* 1980, 15, 35–41.

Northrop, F. S. C. *The logic of the sciences and the humanities*. New York: Macmillan, 1948.

Osgood, C. E., & Hoosain, R. Salience of the word as a unit in the perception of language. *Perception and Psychophysics*, 1974, 15, 168–192.

Pavlov, I. P. *Lectures on conditioned reflexes* (Vol. II): *Conditioned reflexes and psychiatry*. New York: International Publishers, 1941.

Penfield, W. Consciousness, memory, and man's conditioned reflexes. In Karl H. Pribram (Ed.), *On the biology of learning*. New York: Harcourt Brace Jovanovich, 1969.

Reichenbach, H. *Atom and cosmos*. London: Allen & Unwin, 1931.

Schwartz, G. E. Biofeedback, self-regulation, and the patterning of physiological processes. *American Scientist*, 1975, 63, 314–324.

Schwartz, G. E., Fair, P. L., Mandel, M. R., Salt, P., Mieske, M., & Klerman, G. L. Facial electromyography in the assessment of improvement in depression. *Psychosomatic Medicine*, 1978, 40, 355–360.

Schwartz, G. E. Fair, P. L., Salt, P., Mandel, M. R., & Klerman, G. L. Facial muscle patterning to affective imagery in depressed and nondepressed subjects. *Science,* 1976, 192, 489–491. *(a)*

Schwartz, G. E., Fair, P. L., Salt, P., Mandel, M. R., & Klerman, G. L. Facial expression and imagery in depression: An electromyographic study. *Psychosomatic Medicine*, 1976, 38, 337–347. (*b*)

Sechenov, I. M. Reflexes of the brain. In I. M. Sechenov, *Selected works*. Moscow and Leningrad: State Publishing House for Biological and Medical Literature, 1935. (Originally published in St. Petersburg, 1863.)

Smith, M. O. History of the motor theories of attention. *Journal of General Psychology*, 1969, *80*, 243–257.

Tarler-Benlolo, L. The role of relaxation in biofeedback training: A critical review of the literature. *Psychological Bulletin*, 1978, *85*, 727–755.

Thorson, A. M. The relation of tongue movements to internal speech. *Journal of Experimental Psychology*, 1925, *8*, 1–32.

Titchener, E. B. *Lectures on the experimental psychology of the thought-processes.* New York: Macmillan, 1909.

Tolman, E. C. *Purposive behavior in animals and men.* New York: Appleton-Century-Crofts, 1932.

Vigotsky, L. S. *Thought and language.* New York: Wiley, 1962.

Watson, J. B. *Behavior: An introduction to comparative psychology.* New York: Holt, 1914.

Watson, J. B. *Behaviorism* (Rev. ed.). Chicago: University of Chicago Press, 1930. (Reissued New York, W. W. Norton & Co., 1970.)

Wolpe, J. Relaxation as an instrument for breaking adverse emotional habit. In F. J. McGuigan (Ed.), *Tension control: Proceedings of the first meeting of the American Association for the Advancement of Tension Control.* Blacksburg, Va.: University Publications, 1975.

Young, R. M. *Mind, brain and adaptation in the nineteenth century.* New York: Oxford University Press, 1970.

10

Social Psychological Procedures for Cognitive Response Assessment: The Thought-Listing Technique

John T. Cacioppo and Richard E. Petty

The various cognitive-behavior therapies share the notion that a person's idiosyncratic cognitions and ways of thinking are at the root of many emotional and behavioral disorders (Ellis, 1977; Meichenbaum, 1977). The goal of treatment, therefore, is often the modification of a client's self-statements. However, before a person's self-statements can be modified, one must determine what constitutes the internal dialogue.

As social psychologists, we have been interested in what people say to themselves when they are exposed to persuasive communications designed to change their attitudes on personally important issues. Previous investigators, beginning with Carl Hovland and his colleagues in the 1950s, believed that the primary determinant of whether or not attitude change would occur and endure was the extent to which the audience was able to comprehend and retain the arguments contained in the persuasive message (Hovland, Janis, & Kelley, 1953; Hovland, Lumsdaine, & Sheffield, 1949). This view of the persuasion process is analagous to therapies that emphasize the client's ability to understand and follow direct instructions from his or her therapist (cf. Shaffer & Galinsky, 1974, pp. 223–225).

More recently, it has been shown that the ability to learn the information (e.g., message arguments) espoused by the source is not as important in attitude change processes as how individuals cognitively respond to or elaborate upon that information (Cacioppo & Petty, 1980b; Greenwald,

John T. Cacioppo • Department of Psychology, The University of Iowa, Iowa City, Iowa.
Richard E. Petty • Department of Psychology, University of Missouri, Columbia, Missouri.

1968; Petty, Ostrom, & Brock, 1981). This cognitive response approach to persuasion emphasizes how people personally evaluate the information provided. Ultimately, it is the person's own self-statements that produce change or resistance. If the audience generates favorable thoughts about a message, persuasion results; if counterarguments are produced, resistance results. This emphasis on the importance of a person's self-statements (cognitive responses) in determining attitudes and behavior is analogous to the emphasis on self-talk and internal dialogues in the various cognitive-behavior modification therapies. The dilemma for both persuasion researchers and cognitive-behavior modifiers, then, is to assess what it is that a person says to himself or herself when various stimuli are presented (cf. Kendall & Korgeski, 1979).

Measures of Cognitive Responses: An Overview

The purpose of this chapter is to survey some of the procedures found in social psychology for assessing cognitive responses. By "cognitive responses," we mean those thoughts that pass through a person's mind as he or she anticipates, receives, or reflects upon a message designed to change beliefs, attitudes, or behaviors. Although we focus on procedures designed to measure thoughts elicited by persuasive messages, the techniques outlined would also be applicable for use in monitoring a person's thoughts when confronted with any personally significant stimulus or situation. We begin this survey of cognitive response assessment with a brief section on mechanical procedures. An overview of nonmechanical measurement procedures is then followed by a detailed discussion of a self-report technique that we have employed in our own research to tap what persons say to themselves.

Mechanical Assessment Procedures

In Hovland's pioneering work on attitudes, subjects were instructed to press buttons indicating their agreement or disagreement with an advocative message. (Hovland et al., 1949). A similar procedure, called the "signal stopping technique," has been used recently to measure the evaluative nature of a person's stream of thoughts (Carter, Ruggels, Jackson, & Heffner, 1973). Messages were delivered in print form by a computer to subjects at a console. Subjects were instructed (and encouraged) that, at any time they wanted to stop the incoming information, they were to press a slash (/) symbol on their console. In some experiments, subjects were also instructed to record in the margin their reason for stopping. In other studies, subjects used the following "stop" symbols: /A—stop to agree; /D—stop to disagree; /T—stop to think; and /?—stop to question.

Employing the latter procedure for monitoring cognitive responses, Carter and Simpson (1970, cited in Carter et al., 1973) presented messages containing either proattitudinal, neutral, or counterattitudinal information to subjects. They found that subjects stopped more to agree than to disagree with the message when the information contained in the message was proattitudinal and that the opposite was true when the information contained in the message was counterattitudinal. The average number of stops to agree and disagree did not differ when the information was neutral. These results suggest that the signal stopping technique may prove useful in future research on cognitive response, particularly if a computer (or sophisticated hardware) is used to provide minute-by-minute (or second-by-second, etc.) changes in responding to a stimulus.

Unfortunately, this technique has several disadvantages. Assessment must be done individually or at individual terminals, and the sensitivity of this assessment technique is unknown. Some individuals may enjoy playing with the computer, whereas others may be angered or intimidated by the impersonal interaction; these idiosyncratic responses to the contextual cues may obliterate subtle differences in cognitive response.

In marketing research, a person's cognitive responses to stimuli are sometimes tapped with a dial-turning technique (cf. Peterman, 1940). Subjects listen to the advocative message and turn a dial to designate their agreement with what is being said as it is being said. The turning of the dial denotes intensity as well as direction of agreement/disagreement. This and the preceding techniques could easily be adapted to suit the measurement needs of a researcher or practitioner. For instance, a dial could be turned to the right to indicate a positive self-statement and so on. Moreover, this latter procedure has the unique advantage of providing measures of intensity as well as of direction.

Electrophysiological Techniques. Nevertheless, a concern with procedures that require subjects to "do something" before, during, or after the presentation of a stimulus is that the request itself may elicit or alter the cognitive responses measured. That is, the measurement procedure may be reactive. Love (1972) attempted to avoid this problem by videotaping the shoulders and faces of subjects as they listened to an advocative message. Raters then scored the nonverbal cues (facial expressions) of subjects as denoting positive or negative affect. Following the early outlines of Darwin (1872/1904), Love sought to quantify distinctive facial expressions that characterized cognitive responses. Unfortunately, this videotape measure proved to be insensitive for detecting the fast and subtle changes of expression emitted by subjects (Haggard & Issacs, 1966). New hope for this theoretical approach, however, has been created by the work of Schwartz and his colleagues (Schwartz, 1975; Schwartz, Fair, Salt, Mandel, & Klerman, 1976). They found that facial electromyographic patterns reflect favorable and unfavorable imagery, even though neither judges nor subjects could visually distinguish the facial expressions.

We have found that this technique reflects the affective nature of one's thoughts as well (Cacioppo & Petty, 1979a). In our first experiment, subjects expected to hear discrepant communications (messages that take a position counter to that of the subject) and were requested to "collect their thoughts" following each forewarning. As discrepancy increased, anticipatory counterargumentation increased, whereas production of favorable thoughts and agreement decreased. In addition, following forewarnings, oral, muscle, cardiac, and respiratory activity increased, whereas nonoral muscle activity remained constant and quiescent.

In a second experiment, subjects anticipated and heard either a proattitudinal, counterattitudinal, or neutral communication. They evaluated more positively and generated more favorable thoughts and fewer counterarguments to the proattitudinal than to the counterattitudinal advocative message but rated similarly the neutral and proattitudinal messages. As in the first study, incipient oral muscle activity increased following the forewarning of an involving counterattitudinal message, and it increased for all messages during their presentation. Moreover, patterns of subtle facial muscle changes reflected the affective nature of the cognitive responding when subjects anticipated and heard the communication.

These results provide evidence that electrophysiological assessments offer objective, concurrent, and independent measures of cognitive response in persuasion and suggest that people actively elaborate upon personally important stimuli. The major disadvantages of electrophysiological techniques are that (1) to employ them requires expensive equipment and specialized knowledge, (2) persons have to be tested individually, and (3) the information obtained is often sparse, if not ambiguous. These techniques seem most valuable, at this point, in providing convergent validation for simpler, more practical techniques (cf. Cacioppo & Sandman, 1980; McGuigan, Chapter 9, this volume).

Reaction-Time Procedures. Reaction-time procedures, employed commonly by experimental psychologists in the study of verbal learning and verbal behavior, have also been used in the study of cognitive responses in impression formation (Lingle, Geva, Ostrom, Leippe, & Baumgardner, 1979; Lingle & Ostrom, 1979, 1981) and in relation to the self (Cantor & Mischel, 1977; Markus, 1977; Rogers, Kuiper, & Kirker, 1977), with longer reaction times indicating more extensive (deeper) processing.[1] For example, more

---

[1]Mean reaction time and mean speed (its reciprocal) have been used in studies of cognition as if the choice between these dependent measures mattered little. Surprisingly, however, these measures do not necessarily yield similar results; Wainer (1977) discussed an instance in which the conclusions to be drawn from the analyses of each of these measures were exactly opposite. Wainer (1977) suggests three solutions: (1) choose the measure for which a clear theoretical rationale exists; (2) employ an alternative measure of central tendency (e.g., the median) instead of the mean and then proceed with the appropriate order statistics; or (3) employ a trimmed mean in which a specified percentage of the distribution of data is eliminated from each end of the distribution (the justification for trimming comes from a heterogeneity-of-variance problem in the data). In any case, both the mean reaction time and the mean speed should be examined; if results are contradictory, one of the three suggestions of Wainer should be employed to remove the ambiguity of the results.

elaborate analyses of a word are involved when determining whether it describes oneself than when determining whether the letters are printed in upper-case letters. The former task takes longer to perform, produces a more lasting memory for the word that is analyzed, and is accompanied by greater increases in localized muscle activity over the speech muscles than the latter task (Cacioppo & Petty, 1979c, in press-*a*).

Variations of the reaction-time procedure may provide information about the type of cognitive responses elicited. One such technique involves measuring reaction times to the Stroop test. The Stroop test consists of rectangles (or X's) and words (typically, names of colors) printed in a variety of colors. Generally, the colors of rectangles are identified more quickly than are colors in which names of other colors are printed (Stroop, 1938). This difference presumably is due to a semantic interference effect. The subject viewing *X*'s printed in some color has very little distracting information in the way of accessing the color name. The subject viewing a *word* printed in a color, however, has the tendency to allocate at least some of his or her attention to determining the meaning of the word, which hinders accessing the color name. The interference effect is especially noticeable when the printed word is highly accessible in memory, which occurs when the printed word represents the name of a different color or is associated with some word presented previously (Schiebe, Shaver, & Carrier, 1967; Warren, 1972, 1974).

For example, suppose that we want to determine whether a person relates the word "dog" more closely to "cat" (a normal response) or "man" (an abnormal response). We could do this by using reaction-time measures in the following manner: The person would be instructed that, each time a word was presented visually, he or she should quickly identify the name of the color in which the word was printed. A number of words (e.g., cat, man) would then be presented visually to the person, each printed in one of a variety of colors, and each preceded by a spoken work (e.g., "dog"). After a number of pairings of these words (and their synonyms), we should be able to secure a fairly stable estimate of the size of the interference effect that exists between dog–cat and between dog–man. The longer the average time it takes a person to identify the name of the color in which "cat" or "man" was printed (assuming the presentation of each was preceded by the word "dog"), the greater the interference effect. Because the interference effect is directly related to the strength of the association between words, we would judge the person as possessing an abnormal view of dogs and men only if the color-naming latencies for the dog–man pairings were significantly longer than those observed for the dog–cat pairings.

Geller and Shaver (1976) used this effect to identify whether or not people were generating self-relevant or self-evaluative thoughts. Some subjects were placed in a state of "objective self-awareness," which theoretically activates self-examination; this was accomplished by placing subjects in front of a mirror and camera. Other subjects served in a control group (no mirror or camera). As predicted by objective self-awareness theory, subjects who had been placed in front of a mirror and camera responded more slowly to self-relevant words (but not other types of words) than subjects in the control condition.

A Limitation of Mechanical Techniques. It is apparent from this brief survey of mechanical techniques that there are several ingenious methods for assessing what a person is thinking. An important limitation of these techniques, however, is that individuals have more (and more types of) thoughts than can be placed in a scale or test; consequently, the dimensions (or types of words) composing the test may not be the most important ones to study. McGuire and Padawer-Singer (1976) echo this concern in their comments on the existing research on self-concepts:

> This low yield (with respect to research on self-concepts) we attribute primarily to researchers having measured the self-concept almost exclusively by information-losing "reactive" methods, that is, by studying subjects' reactions to a dimension chosen a priori by the researcher. (p. 743)

To date, the profile of *spontaneous* cognitive responses has been ascertainable most easily by listing, reporting, and recalling procedures. These nonmechanical means of assessing cognitive responses are addressed next.

Spoken and Written Assessment Procedures

One of the most common means of obtaining cognitive responses in research has been to instruct subjects to either list (write) or report aloud their thoughts. Each of these techniques has its unique merits (cf. Meichenbaum, 1977; Wright, 1974a). Verbal measures are advantageous because they can be obtained quickly (it is easier to speak than to write), which minimizes the forgetting of one's actual responses to a stimulus. The written listing procedure, though slower, can be administered easily in group settings, is relatively private and nonthreatening, and requires only pencil and paper. Both have the advantage that they can be administered in a manner that does not restrict the dimensions obtained.

Some have suggested that persons be taught to monitor and record their thoughts and feelings in their daily lives, for instance, following an unexpected bleep (Hurlburt & Sipprelle, 1978). We have found a related diary technique unsuitable for hypothesis testing in a study on migraine headaches (Quinatar, Cacioppo, Monyak, Alvarez, & Snyder, 1980). We found vast differences in our subjects's willingness and ability to record consistently and accurately their cognitive and emotional responses at the onset of a migraine headache. The vast differences in the situations and the people encountered also proved problematic. We found that the greatest potential of the technique was in its power to generate testable hypotheses by helping us to identify important dimensions of a person's reportable subjective reactions. The measure most helpful to us in *testing* hypotheses regarding cognitive response has been the thought-listing technique.

The Thought-Listing Technique

A self-report device called the "thought-listing procedure" was developed by Brock and Greenwald at Ohio State University in the late 1960s (Brock, 1967; Greenwald, 1968). This procedure is suitable for obtaining either spoken (Cacioppo, 1979) or written (Petty, Wells, & Brock, 1976) listings, though the latter are more typical. In this section, we discuss the rationale for this procedure and the substantial data that now exist. We conclude the chapter with a discussion of the procedure's reliability, validity, and sensitivity.

Thought-Listing Instructions

Three different types of instructions have been used to obtain thought listings. Subjects have been asked to list (1) thoughts elicited by the stimulus (e.g., Roberts & Maccoby, 1973), (2) general thoughts on the topic about the communication or problem (e.g., Greenwald, 1968; Peterman, 1940), and (3) all thoughts that occurred to them while they anticipated and/or attended to a stimulus (e.g., Cacioppo & Petty, 1979b; Goor & Sommerfeld, 1975; Petty & Cacioppo, 1977).

The request to list the thoughts elicited by the stimulus assumes that subjects are able to distinguish the thoughts that are elicited by the stimulus from those that are not. Thus it is assumed that subjects are able to determine the cognitive effects of the stimulus, an assumption that is quite dubious (Nisbett & Bellows, 1977; Nisbett & Wilson, 1977; Reese, 1971). In the second and third instructional procedures, subjects are not asked to identify the cognitive effects of the stimulus, and thus there is no assumption about the subject's ability to identify the stimulus that elicited the cognitive responses. The instruction to list all thoughts that occurred to the individuals during the preceding moments is, of course, the least restrictive of the instructions.

The instructions given to subjects for listing thoughts *are* consequential. We have found that instructing them to report thoughts on a particular problem or issue versus instructing them to report all of the thoughts that occurred during a certain period produced different listings. In some of the conditions of a previous experiment, subjects anticipated a counterattitudinal communication on a highly involving topic (Petty & Cacioppo, 1977). Of these subjects, half were asked to list all of the thoughts that they were thinking prior to the discrepant message, and half were asked to write only those thoughts that were pertinent to the topic of the message.

We found that, when subjects were instructed to "try to record only those ideas that you were thinking during the last few minutes," the demand to produce a particular type of cognitive response was minimal; the thoughts listed were predominantly unfavorable or unrelated to the counterattitudinal issue. When subjects were asked to list their thoughts on a particular topic or issue, however, significantly more favorable and fewer neutral/irrelevant thoughts were reported. That is, the "topic instruction" produced an experimental demand for subjects to report responses relevant to the topic and apparently compelled them to show their "open-mindedness" and "intelligence" by generating thoughts on both sides of the issue. Because each of these profiles of thoughts may be of interest to an investigator, the instructions that provide the most useful results depend upon the aims of the particular research.

Thought-Listing Interval

Another factor that influences the profile of cognitive responses obtained is the amount of time given to subjects to report their responses (Miller & Baron, 1973; Osterhouse & Brock, 1970; Wright, 1974a). In the first part of this section, we report the rationale for, and the results of, imposing time limits for thought listings. In the second part, a distinction is made between the cognitive responses that are reported during the presentation of a communication and those that are reported following a communication.

Time Limits for Thought Listing. In general, investigators want to assess the cognitive responses elicited by a stimulus in order to study their role in the mediation of affective or behavioral change. The purpose of imposing a time limit to listing thoughts is to increase the likelihood that we measure only those responses that are elicited by the stimulus and those few responses that are readily accessible and could easily be elicited by the stimulus.

The time provided for listing cognitive responses has ranged from 45 seconds (Miller & Baron, 1973) to 10 minutes or longer (Cacioppo, Sandman, & Walker, 1978; Greenwald, 1968), but the time interval used most commonly has been 2 to 3 minutes (Brock, 1967; Cacioppo & Petty, 1979b; Petty & Cacioppo, 1979a, 1979b; Petty et al., 1976; Wright, 1973). Of course, the optimal interval depends on the purpose of the particular experiment and the nature of the experimental materials (e.g., the length of the message, situation, or interaction). As a rule of thumb, if only the most salient thoughts are desired, then a brief interval would be better than a long one. If the interval is too long, a subject would have time to reflect on, generate additions to , select among, and delete portions of his or her cognitive responses.

Time of Measurement. Another concern is whether the profile of cognitive responses differs as a function of when they are obtained. There is a paucity of evidence concerning this question, and the evidence that exists is conflicting: some research indicates that the responses measured during and after a stimulus presentation or situation are very similar (Greenwald, 1968), and other research suggests that the responses reported afterward are more unfavorable than responses reported during the presentation (Roberts & Maccoby, 1973). This entire question can be resolved by determining whether the responses reported *during* or *after* the situation or stimulus presentation more accurately reflect the cognitive responses elicited normally (i.e., when no measurements are taken). When looked at in this way, measuring cognitive responses immediately after a stimulus seems best.

Obtaining cognitive responses after the stimulus (e.g., a communication) can be accomplished without the subject's foreknowledge and does not require interruption of or distraction from the stimulus presentation. Obtaining responses during the stimulus presentation, however, requires that the subject know during the presentation that his or her cognitive reactions are being monitored; moreover, subjects must either interrupt the presentation or distract themselves from it to report their cognitive reactions to it. The primary disadvantage of measuring thoughts during the stimulus, then, is that the assessment may seriously distort the responses elicited naturally by the stimulus. On the other hand, the unexpected, immediate poststimulus measure of cognitive response suffers from loss of retention of cognitions, though this loss is minor (Wright, 1974a).

The usefulness of a cognitive response measure taken *after* the stimulus presentation would be enhanced greatly if it did not affect the reported emotion or behavior under investigation (i.e., if it were nonreactive) because separate groups of subjects would not be needed to measure the cognitive responses and the outcome variable. Evidence relevant to this issue is provided by several experiments in which subjects were asked to list their thoughts either before or after they rated their attitudes (Calder, Insko, & Yandell, 1974; Insko, Turnbull, & Yandell, 1974), by an experiment in which subjects were either asked or not asked to list thoughts while all subjects reported their attitudes (Petty & Cacioppo, 1977), and by an experiment in which electrophysiological procedures were used to trace cognitive responses (Cacioppo & Petty 1979a). In each experiment, the written thought-listing procedure was used to obtain cognitive responses. If the thought-listing method of obtaining cognitive responses is reactive, the first two variations would alter the reported attitude; in the case of the electrophysiological study, the cognitive and physiological responses would be unrelated to one another. These studies indicated that attitude (the outcome variable) was *not* affected by obtaining cognitive responses; further, a concordance between cognitive and physiological responses was evident. These results suggest that the thought-listing procedure is not reactive.

A note of caution is perhaps in order here. We found high correlations between cognitive response and attitudes when the stimulus (an advocative message) was personally relevant but much lower correlations between these variables when the stimulus was *not* personally relevant (Petty & Cacioppo, 1979a, 1979b). This latter instance suggests that the stimulus was of such low importance or personal relevance that it did not elicit much thought on the part of the individual. Under these conditions, an instruction to list cognitive responses about the issue before measurement of the outcome variable (e.g., attitude) may "force" cognitive consideration of the issue and alter the outcome observed. Instructions to list everything about which subjects thought,

318   *John T. Cacioppo and Richard E. Petty*

or measurement of cognitive responses after the outcome variable should avoid this possible problem. *(retention can be a problem; should we show stimuli again?)*

Scoring Thought Listings

To classify the cognitive responses, they must first be "unitized" (Meichenbaum, Henshaw, & Himel, 1980), which means that the protocols must be broken down into individual units of cognitive response. Three methods of unitizing cognitive response protocols seem most prevalent. In the first method, subjects are instructed prior to listing their thoughts to list one thought or idea per box. The exact instructions from Petty and Cacioppo (1977) are as follows:

> We are now interested in what you were thinking about during the presentation of the message on the tape. You might have had ideas all favorable to the recommendation on the tape, all opposed, all irrelevant to the recommendation on the tape, or a mixture of the three. Any case is fine; simply list what it was that you were thinking during the tape-presentation. The next page contains the form we have prepared for you to use to record your thoughts and ideas. Simply write down the first idea you had in the first box, the second idea in the second box, etc. Pleas put only one idea or thought in a box. You should try to record only those ideas that you were thinking *during* the message. Please state your thoughts and ideas as concisely as possible . . . a phrase is sufficient. IGNORE SPELLING, GRAMMAR, AND PUNCTUATION. You will have 2½ minutes to write your thoughts. We have deliberately provided more space than we think most people will need to insure that everyone would have plenty of room to write the ideas they had during the message. So don't worry if you don't fill every space. Just write down whatever your thoughts were during the message. Please be completely honest and list all of the thoughts that you had. (p. 648)

Twelve 8-inch (20.32 cm) horizontal lines, each about 1 inch (2.54 cm) from the one above it, created the boxes in which subjects were to write their thoughts. This method is effective if cognitive responses are obtained using the thought-listing procedure but requires slight modification if spoken procedures are used (e.g., subjects must denote individual thoughts with a key word or pause—cf. Cacioppo, 1979).

The second method is similar to the first, except that judges, rather than subjects, determine what constitutes an idea or thought. Predetermined criteria are used by the judges. One common criterion is that a stated idea, whether grammatically correct or not, constitutes a unit. Other criteria might rely upon the use of semicolons, compound sentences, and so forth.

In the third method of unitizing cognitive responses, no search for a cogent idea is made. Rather, an arbitrary number of words (Miller & Baron, 1973) or unit of time (Goor & Sommerfeld, 1975; Meichenbaum *et al.*, 1980) serves as the unit of cognitive response. Of course, a person's thoughts and ideas seldom, if ever, are generated in intervals of short duration and/or of equivalent length. Hence a highly contrived unitization of the protocol results; this makes it very difficult later to rate these unitized cognitive responses reliably along various dimensions.

Once the responses are unitized, their content can be analyzed, which involves classifying them along various dimensions. It is to that topic that we turn next.

Dimensions of Cognitive Response

Three dimensions that have characterized the classification of responses in research on attitude change (cf. Cacioppo, Harkins, & Petty, 1981) are: (1) "polarity"—the degree to which the response is in favor of or opposed to the referent; (2) "origin"—the primary source of the information contained in the person's response; and (3) "target"—at what the response is directed. These three orthogonal categories can serve generally as dimensions for systematically classifying the cognitive responses to any designated referent. In research and theory on persuasion, the referent has been the advocative message; in theory and research on behavior deficits and on personality, the referent may be the person, or "self." Of course, the referent need not be restricted to these alternatives, and dimensions need not be restricted to the three that have been listed. For instance, a fourth dimension, the irrationality of the responses, has been called for in the literature and also is discussed briefly in this section.

Polarity Dimension. The most consistent finding in cognitive-response research has been that there is a relationship between the favorableness of the responses elicited by the referent and the evaluation of the referent, whether it be a communication (e.g., Brock, 1967; Greenwald, 1968; Wright, 1974b) or the self (Cacioppo, Glass, & Merluzzi, 1979; Glass, Gottman, & Schmurak, 1976; Lazarus, 1966; Mirels & McPeek, 1977; Gergen & Gibbs, Note 1). The polarity dimension comprises (1) "favorable thoughts"—statements that are positive toward or supportive of a referent (e.g., the self or message); (2) "neutral/irrelevant thoughts"—statements that neither favor nor oppose the referent; and (3) "unfavorable thoughts"—statements that are negative toward or in opposition to the referent.

Scoring the reported thoughts along the polarity dimension is done as follows:

1. Statements involving the referent (e.g., self, advocated position) that mention specific undersirable attributes or negative associations, challenges to the validity of the situation or stimulus, and statements of negative affect about the referent are counted as unfavorable thoughts. Examples of unfavorable thoughts about the self or experimental setting generated by men waiting to interact with an un-

familiar woman (cf. Cacioppo, Glass, & Merluzzi, 1979) included
"I'm a little nervous" and "I hope this experiment ends soon."[2]

2. Statements in favor of the referent that mention specific desirable attributes or positive associations, statements that support the validity
or value of the situation or stimulus, and the statements of positive affect about the referent are scored as favorable thoughts. Examples of
favorable thoughts included "I hope we start soon" and "This
should be fun."

3. All remaining statements should express no affect with regards to the
referent and are scored as neutral/irrelevant thoughts. Examples of
neutral/irrelevant thoughts included "I hope my math test won't be
too hard" and "I wonder what she looks like."

Each statement is scored as one and only one of the preceding. Data
reduction then involves simply summing the number of statements in each
category. The three sums (e.g., three unfavorable, one favorable, and two
neutral thoughts) serve as measures of polarity response.

As should be evident from these examples, the categorization of a
cognitive response requires an interpretation of the responses. This can best
be accomplished by reading all of the thoughts listed by a subject prior to
scoring any of the listed thoughts. It is imperative, therefore, that the scorer
be blind to the experimental conditions and, preferably, to the experimental
hypothesis. (We have noticed, too, that trained, but psychologically unso-
phisticated, judges are sometimes better at scoring cognitive responses than
psychology graduate students and faculty, who tend to see "subconscious
motives" in many of the comments. The simpler, more naive perspective may
be preferable.)

Origin Dimension. Classifying cognitive responses according to their
origin was first proposed by Greenwald (1968). Three classifications of
origin, which are modifications of those proposed by Greenwald (1968), are
as follows: (1) "externally originated thoughts"—statements or paraphrases
of information provided in the stimulus; (2) "modified externally originated
thoughts"—statements that are reactions to the information provided in the
stimulus; and (3) "internally originated thoughts"—statements not traceable
directly to the materials constituting the stimulus.

Scoring the reported thoughts along the origin dimension has been done
as follows:

1. Statements that are direct quotes, paraphrases, or restatements of the
information given to subjects (e.g., instructions, message arguments)

---

[2]Subjects in this study were instructed to list everything they were thinking about during
the preceding several minutes. It is possible that instructions to list only their thoughts about
themselves would provide more specific (i.e., fewer irrelevant) responses and hence might increase even more the sensitivity of this measure.

are counted as externally originated thoughts. Thus any statement that repeats an instruction or response made by an experimenter or confederate (e.g., recall) is scored as externally originated. Examples of externally originated thoughts are "I am to wait here until the experimenter returns" and "I am going to talk to some girl."

2. Statements that are elaborations, qualifications, or examples of materials constituting the stimulus (e.g., specific replies to instructions, message arguments) are counted as modified externally originated thoughts. Examples of such thoughts are "I hope I will like the girl" and "I wonder what questions she will ask me."

3. All remaining statements should be expressions not traceable directly to something heard or seen (e.g., responses pertinent to the stimulus or issue but not to a specific instance in the situation; responses irrelevant to the stimulus or issue) and are counted as internally originated thoughts. Examples of these statements include "I am always nervous when meeting a new girl" and "I didn't bring an umbrella and it looks like rain."

Each statement is scored along this dimension once and only once; data reduction requires summing separately the number of statements classified as externally originated, modified externally originated, and internally originated thoughts. The sums serve as measures of origin response.

Research employing basically this origin classification system has revealed that, in some cases, internally originated thoughts weighted by polarity are most highly related to affect (Greenwald, 1968; Roberts & Maccoby, 1973) and that, in other cases, externally originated thoughts weighted by polarity are related most highly to affect (Calder *et al.*, 1974; Insko *et al.*, 1974). Although various reasons may account for this discrepancy, one possibility is that the subjects' prior knowledge of, and ability to generate responses to, the stimulus may affect whether internally, modified externally, or externally originated thoughts are most important in changing affective states and behavior. For instance, subjects may find it easy and adaptive to generate responses (i.e., internally and modified externally originated thoughts) to a situation about which they have some prior information (e.g., eliminating editorial comments in the news media—Roberts & Maccoby, 1973). In support of this analysis are the results of numerous experiments on role playing, which demonstrate that, so long as subjects have some prior familiarity with a topic, more attitude change results when arguments are actively self-generated than when arguments are received passively (e.g., Janis & King, 1954).

When subjects have little prior knowledge on an issue, as when judging a defendant's guilt in a hypothetical case (Calder *et al.*, 1974), they probably have to rely on the information contained in the situation rather than upon their preexisting cognitions about the case because no thoughts about the stimulus exist prior to exposure. For example, during jury selections, judges attempt to select jurors who are characterized by just such a cognitive state. Experimental evidence for this notion is provided by McGuire's (e.g., McGuire & Papageorgis, 1962) experiments on inoculation theory, which demonstrate that, when subjects have little familiarity with defending their positions on an issue, such as cultural truisms, externally originated defenses (passive) are initially superior to self-generated defenses (active) in producing resistance to persuasion. Thus the discrepancy that exists concerning the relative importance of internally, modified externally, and externally originated thoughts may be attributable to differences in the amount of preexisting information that subjects have about the situation.

The clinical implications of this model are straightforward. Therapeutic techniques that require active involvement on the part of the client should be most effective when the problem is entrenched deeply in past experience and when the client views the advocated change as discrepant. On the other hand, therapeutic techniques that require relatively passive participation on the part of the client should be most effective when the client's problem is due, in part, to a lack of experience or knowledge.

Target Dimension. The target of the cognitive response provides information about the effect of the stimulus on the recipient's focus of attention. In the past, targets have been classified into the following categories: (1) "stimulus thoughts"—statements pertaining to the situation or issue, and (2) "source thoughts"—statements pertaining to the source of the stimuli. Lasswell's (1948) and Abelson's (1968) analyses of the persuasion process suggest additional targets that might be fruitful to study: (3) "recipient (or audience) thoughts"—statements pertaining to the recipient(s) of the stimulus, including the self, and (4) "channel thoughts"—statements pertaining to the medium through which the stimulus is transmitted.

Scoring the reported thoughts along the target dimension could be done as follows:

1. Statements whose object is the stimulus, or one or more informational items, stated or implied, concerning the stimulus, are counted as stimulus thoughts. Examples of stimulus thoughts would include "I wonder what the discussion will be like" and "What is this experiment really about?"
2. Statements whose object is the source of the stimuli are counted as source thoughts, examples of which include "I wonder what the experimenter wants me to do next" and "Why would he tell me that?"
3. Statements whose object is the expected, actual, or potential recipient(s) of the stimulus are counted as recipient thoughts. "I'm very nervous" and "If she's as nervous as I am, I'm going to laugh" are examples of recipient thoughts.
4. Statements that have as their object the medium or modality through which the stimulus is presented are counted as channel thoughts. "I

prefer talking face-to-face with a new girl" and "Are we going to have to talk into microphones?" are instances of channel thoughts.

5. Responses whose object is anything irrelevant to the targets designated are scored as irrelevant thoughts. Examples of irrelevant comments are "I was thinking about the upcoming Chicago Bears football game" and "I am going to be late for music practice if I don't hurry."

Each statement is scored as one and only one of the preceding; data reduction is accomplished by summing the number of statements in each category. The total number of each category of thought (stimulus, source, recipient, channel, and irrelevant thought) serves as the dependent measure.

Reality Dimension. There are, no doubt, a variety of other dimensions that might be important, including saliency (i.e., how often the response is emitted—Smith, Bruner, & White, 1956), emotionality (i.e., the degree to which a response is affect-laden, regardless of polarity—Janis & Mann, 1977; Miller & Baron, 1973), and reality (i.e., the extent to which the response is based on and reflects the acceptance of objective reality—Ellis, 1962, 1977; Maultsby, 1970, 1977). For instance, concerning the latter, cognitive responses could be classified as follows: (1) "objective-reality thoughts"— statements that exemplify a reasoned and objective commerce with the environment; (2) "distorted thoughts"—statements that are based upon unrealistic desires or fears rather than upon actual states of being and affairs; and (3) "unclassifiable thoughts"—statements that are either too brief or too obtuse to categorize as either of the preceding thoughts.

Scoring the reported thoughts along the reality dimension might be done as follows:

1. Statements, assertions, or conclusions that are accepted as valid by objective observers, and statements that adhere to the rules of logic are scored as objective reality thoughts. Examples are "I will soon be discussing campus issues with some girl" and "The experimenter has been gone several minutes now" (when, in fact, the experimenter had been gone several minutes).

2. Statements that involve overgeneralization; statements that exaggerate the significance of an event; statements, assertions, or conclusions that would not be validated by objective observers; and statements based upon an inaccurate or illogical premise are counted as distorted thoughts. Examples of distorted thoughts include "I feel I should get the girl every time" and "I should have gotten a better grade on that test" (when, in fact, the test was graded fairly).

3. Statements that defy classification under one of the preceding categories are counted as unclassifiable thoughts. Examples include "Nothing" and "That woman."

Again, each statement is scored as only one of the preceding; data reduction involves summing the number of statements scored for each category.

McGuire (1969, 1980) has conducted research employing a classification scheme similar to the one that is suggested here. He found that simply asking individuals to think about (attitudinal) conclusions of syllogisms led to increased logical consistency in the syllogisms. He also found evidence of added wishful (distorted) thinking by these instructions. Specifically, cognitive responses in McGuire's research were assessed by asking individuals to supply probability estimates for various statements of belief. He found that subjects assigned higher probabilities to desirable outcomes and lower probabilities to undesirable outcomes than would be demanded by a strict probabilistic (logical) analysis. McGuire concluded that affective change over time is the result of both logical and wishful (distorted) thought processes.

Note that the method suggested here for scoring objective-reality and distorted thoughts is quite compatible with Maultsby's (1970) and Ellis's (1977) discussions of rational and irrational thoughts. The reader is also referred to the literature reviews of Di Giuseppe and Miller (1977) and Ellis (1977) for evidence of the utility of distinguishing between these types of cognitive responses.

Other Dimensions. A major disadvantage of employing predetermined dimensions for the classification of cognitive responses is that researchers may overlook important and recurrent themes present in a person's responses. The dimensions described in this chapter have been discussed in the social psychological literature, but much can be gained in the hypothesis-generation phase of research by approaching the thought listings with no predetermined ideas about which dimensions are "relevant" (McGuire & Padawer-Singer, 1976).

Judging and Combining Thought Listings

Once cognitive responses have been obtained and classification schemes have been selected, there is the need to judge the responses (i.e., assign each response to a particular category along each dimension) and to combine the responses along each dimension to obtain an index of each individual's responses. Quantitative analyses can then be performed.

With respect to the task of categorizing the responses, three methods have been employed:

1. "Judge rating." Individuals that are familiar with the scoring categories, but not with the experimental hypotheses, assign each response to a particular category (within each dimension) on the basis of their understanding of the meaning of the response (Brock, 1967; Cook, 1969; Insko *et al.*, 1974; Roberts & Maccoby, 1973).
2. "Subject rating." After completing the dependent variable, subjects

are instructed how to categorize their responses (e.g., "Place a plus next to the thoughts that are favorable to yourself, a minus next to the thoughts that are unfavorable to yourself, and a zero next to the thoughts that are neutral or irrelevant to yourself"—Cacioppo, Glass, & Merluzzi, 1979; Calder *et al.*, 1974; Cialdini, Levin, Herman, Kozlowski, & Petty, 1976; Greenwald, 1968).

3. "Judge and subject ratings." Both subjects and judges rate the responses. If there is disagreement between the independent judges' ratings, there are various reasonable means of resolution, including employing the subject's rating if it breaks the tie (e.g., Petty & Cacioppo, 1977; Petty *et al.*, 1976), averaging the judges' ratings (e.g., Petty, Cacioppo, & Heesacker, 1981), obtaining a third judge's opinion to break the tie (e.g., Cacioppo & Petty, 1980*a*), or resolving any discrepancies in discussions between the judges (e.g., Cacioppo, Petty, & Snyder, 1979).

Independent judges have demonstrated a high degree of agreement in their classification of responses along the polarity dimension (e.g., Insko *et al.*, 1974) but not along the origin dimension (e.g., Greenwald, 1968). Though ratings by subjects and judges are correlated highly (Petty *et al.*, 1976), subjects rating their own responses circumvents both the problem of low interrater reliability and the problem of judges' misinterpreting the meaning of responses. Subjects, of course, are not always willing and/or able to comply with the request to classify their thoughts (cf. Cacioppo, Petty, & Snyder, 1979), a problem that is exacerbated by the selection of several dimensions along which subjects must classify their thoughts. The procedure of using both judges' ratings and subjects' ratings represents a compromise method.

Some of the listed cognitive responses are more extreme than others (e.g., more favorable or unfavorable, more assuredly distorted or objective-reality thoughts). What are the effects of weighting the responses in accordance with their extremity? What happens if, instead of just counting the number of favorable thoughts generated, the thoughts were weighted such that "1" indicated slightly favorable, "2" indicated moderately favorable, and "3" indicated very favorable? The research results indicate that weighting the responses along the polarity dimension neither alters nor strengthens the effects found by using the simpler frequency counts. This null effect has been obtained when using subjects' ratings (Calder *et al.*, 1974; Cullen, 1968; Greenwald, 1968) and when using judges' ratings (Roberts & Maccoby, 1973).

Alternatively, weighting inferential beliefs (responses) on the basis of the subjects' certainty that the responses were applicable and on the basis of their extremity appears to be an effective method of increasing the predictability of the attitude toward a person in an impression formation task (Jaccard & Fishbein, 1975). Similarly, Petty (1977) determined that subject weightings of the "certainty" of belief in cognitive responses scored along the polarity dimension strenghtened their covariation with attitude change. This latter procedure may prove especially useful in future research of cognitive responses, emotions, and behavior.

Finally, neither simple counts nor weightings of the responses by their extremity and certainty reduces individual differences in the total number of thoughts reported. One method of controlling for these differences in total thought production is to calculate a ratio score, with the difference score serving as the numerator and the total number of responses from the two categories as the denominator—for example, (favorable − unfavorable thoughts)/(favorable + unfavorable thoughts) (Cullen, 1968; Petty & Brock, 1979).

The Stream of Cognitive Responses

Development of techniques for assessing the sequence in which cognitive responses are generated has begun only recently (see Notarius, Chapter 11, this volume). Meichenbaum et al. (1980) investigated the probabilistic and temporal sequence of cognitive responses during the performance of creativity tests; the think-aloud procedure was employed to obtain the cognitive responses, which were unitized differently for each of the sequential analyses performed. For the probabilistic analysis, unitization of the verbal protocols was accomplished by having judges determine what constituted a cognitive response on the basis of content and paralinguistic cues (e.g., pauses). Comments by Meichenbaum et al. (1980) are informative regarding the use of stream analysis:

> The results thus far have indicated that high versus low creative subjects differed significantly in the frequencies with which they emitted various categories of verbal behavior. These results, however, leave open the question of how high and low creative subjects might differ in their patterns of verbal behavior. One way of addressing this question is to compare high versus low creative subjects on the frequencies of the various categories of response which follow each specific category. This provides an opportunity to examine the patterning of thoughts over time.

Meichenbaum et al. (1980) compared the effects of the grouping variable (i.e., high- versus low-creative individuals) on the various conditional probabilities. The potential of this procedure manifested in identifying differing sequences of cognitive response attributable to the grouping variable. For instance, Meichenbaum et al. reported that low-creative individuals were more likely than high-creative individuals to follow an unfavorable thought with another unfavorable thought. High-creative individuals tended to generate task-relevant or favorable thoughts after they expressed an unfavorable thought. The exact method by which these comparisons are conducted depends upon whether the grouping variable(s) affected the frequency and types of thoughts produced. Gottman and Notarius (1978) provide a cogent presentation of the statistical procedures for conducting these probabilistic analyses; the interested reader may wish to consult their work.

Meichenbaum *et al.* (1980) also conducted an analysis of the temporal sequence of cognitive response. Unitization of the verbal protocols for the temporal analysis was achieved by dividing each protocol at every 5-second interval; one 5-second interval constituted a unit of cognitive response. The number of cognitive responses within each category generated within various (equal-length) time intervals (e.g., the first half versus the last half of the protocol) was analyzed to obtain the temporal sequence of cognitive response. This temporal analysis has the following potential merits: (1) the cognitive responses elicited by components of the stimulus presentation (e.g., particular informational items) can be identified, (2) differences in the general sequence of cognitive response are discernible (e.g., by counterbalancing the ordering of the informational items composing a stimulus presentation), and (3) the effects of grouping variables on either of the preceding can be determined. For instance, Beaber (1975) used a similar procedure and found that individuals initially responded emotionally, but that in time responded rationally, to the contents of a discrepant message.

We recently have studied the sequence of cognitive and affective responses to repeated, rather than single, exposures to a stimulus (Cacioppo & Petty, 1979*b*, 1980*a*). Individuals heard a personally relevant, counterattitudinal communication either one, three, or five times. They then rated their agreement with the message, and listed their thoughts (unitizing them as they did so by placing one idea or thought in a box). Classification of the cognitive responses was done both by subjects and by judges, and analyses were performed using the frequency counts of each type of response along the polarity dimension. We found that only topic-relevant thoughts were related to attitude change. More important, the production of unfavorable thoughts decreased and then increased, whereas agreement and favorable-thought production increased and then decreased as the subjects heard the communicative stimulus again and again.

This example underscores the major benefit of this type of sequence analysis: The pattern of cognitive response can be examined as the information in (or motor response to) a stimulus becomes overlearned, more familiar, or the object of more thought. It is theoretically possible to employ a probabilistic or a temporal analysis in combination with a repeated-exposure analysis (e.g., by examining changes in conditional probabilities as a function of exposure frequency) to provide yet more specific temporal information about the person's stream of thought. The selection of the method of assessing cognitive-response sequence depends, of course, upon the purpose of the research.

In sum, cognitive responses can be assessed using mechanical, observational, or instructional techniques. Instructional techniques, used most frequently, involve either the spoken or written report of thoughts and feelings. The classification of the cognitive responses can be done by judges, subjects, or both. Frequency counts of the items within each category of cognitive response provide a satisfactory measure of the relative prominence or profile of the different cognitive response categories. Recent research suggests that the associations between cognitive responses and the outcome variable are strengthened by including ratings of certainty (saliency) and extremity for cognitive responses.

Assessing the Structural Bases of Cognitive Responses

Cognitive organizations or schemas provide the means by which persons organize objects and events in their environment. Obviously, then, cognitive organization affects the way people respond to their environment. One of the first social psychologists to measure cognitive structure was Zajonc (1960). He had subjects describe a stimulus person "by freely listing the qualities and attributes that characterized" a person about whom they had read a letter (Zajonc, 1960, p. 160). In other words, Zajonc obtained the cognitive responses (one per index card) elicited by a description of a fictitious person. He then calculated four measures of cognitive structure:

1. "Differentiation" is a measure of the extent to which a person is capable of identifying the discriminating objects and events. The simple total of characteristics listed is the measure of differentiation. For example, if one were interested in studying the structure of cognitive responses to a stimulus, the total number of stimulus-relevant thoughts listed could serve as the measure.
2. The extent to which different categories are used determines "complexity." The cognitive responses that subjects list can come from a single category or multiple categories. Complexity is measured by asking the subjects to arrange the reported cognitive responses into their categories and subcategories and by counting the number of categories utilized.
3. "Unity" is a measure of the interdependence of the cognitive responses. It is assessed by having the subjects indicate which cognitive responses would change if one were changed or untrue. The greater the number of changes resulting from a change in each of the cognitive responses, the greater the unity.
4. "Organization" is the degree to which one cognitive response or a set of cognitive responses is central or dominates the relationship among all the cognitive responses. To the extent that changes in one cognitive response result in changes in other related cognitive responses, the initial cognitive response would be central.

Zajonc (1960) provides procedures for calculating each of these aspects of cognitive structure.

An alternate structural analysis has been suggested recently in research on personality. Some have argued that past experience and categorizations form structures (schemata) that affect perceptions and recollections of events and that function to process information efficiently (with a concomitant loss of actual detail; e.g., Abelson, 1976; Bartlett, 1932; Neisser, 1976). Markus (1977) provided evidence that self-schemata facilitate the processing of information about the self and that they contain behavioral examples and self-predictions. Cantor and Mischel (1977) demonstrated the prototypical character of schemata, which they found biased recognition of self-related, but unpresented, items.

Recently, we have explored the question of how self-schemata influence attitudinal processing (Cacioppo, Petty, & Sidera, Note 2). Sixty introductory psychology students were shown 30 slides of trait adjectives, 15 of which were prerated as indicating a "religious" person, and 15 of which were prerated as indicating a "legal" person. Classification of subjects to group (religious or legal) was done using their "me" (self-descriptive) and "not-me" (not-self-descriptive) decisions and response times to the 30 words (cf. Markus, 1977). One week later, subjects heard one of four counterattitudinal messages, which had been developed in pilot tests to represent either a legal or a religious perspective on the topics of capital punishment or abortion. These messages were equated across perspectives for persuasiveness and familiarity. After hearing one of the four messages, subjects rated its persuasiveness, listed their thoughts in the manner described, and completed a surprise recognition test.

We found that a persuasive message that was in accord with the subject's self-schema was rated as more persuasive than one that was not. In addition, a schema-consistent message elicited more total thoughts, more externally originated thoughts (e.g., quotes), and more thoughts with the message as target. These results suggest that a developed self-schema facilitates total thought production and, more specifically, increases topic-relevant thinking. In other words, the person's cognitive structure affected the attitudinal processing of a related issue. The study of the influence on affect and behavior of self-schemata seems to portend a fuller understanding of why individuals respond cognitively as they do.

Cognitive Response Stereotypy

Finally, neuropsychological studies of human information processing suggest the utility of one additional measure of cognitive response: the degree to which one particular type of cognitive response (e.g., favorable or unfavorable thoughts) dominates the entire profile of cognitive responses (cf. Cacioppo, Petty, & Quinatar, Note 3). Specifically, research on functional cerebral asymmetry indicates that the right (minor) compared to the left (major) hemisphere processes information in a prosodic, thematic manner (Cacioppo & Petty, in press-*b*; Tucker, 1981). This suggests that the thoughts, associations, and elaborations that are produced when, for instance, listening to a communication, are especially likely to adhere to a common theme when the right hemisphere is relatively utilized. Conversely, relative utilization of the left, rather than the right, hemisphere should be associated with more divergent (piecemeal) analyses of the communication and hence less stereotypy in the cognitive responses.

To test this notion, we conducted several experiments in which subjects anticipated and heard either a proattitudinal or counterattitudinal message (Cacioppo & Petty, Note 4). Immediately following the message presentation, subjects listed everything they had been thinking about and, afterward, went back through their listed thoughts and scored them along the polarity dimension. Throughout the session, we monitored the electroencephalographic activity over the right and left associative (parietal) areas of the brain. Afterward, we calculated electroencephalographic ratio scores to determine which side of the brain of each subject was being relatively utilized; at the conclusion of the study, we conducted a median split between subjects, using these ratios to determine who displayed relative left versus right hemispheric involvement while anticipating and listening to the persuasive communication.

The next task was to derive the measure of cognitive response stereotypy. To do this, we used a nomothetic criterion to identify the predominant and the nonpredominant cognitive responses. In pilot testing, we had found that most people responded to our proattitudinal message by listing favorable thoughts, whereas most responded to our counterattitudinal message by listing unfavorable thoughts. Hence, by our nomothetic criterion, "favorable thoughts" was the predominant cognitive response, and "unfavorable thoughts" the nonpredominant cognitive response when the message was proattitudinal; the opposite was the case when the message was counterattitudinal. We calculated the degree of cognitive response stereotypy by subtracting the number of nonpredominant cognitive responses generated by each individual from the number of predominant cognitive responses produced by each. Thus we obtained a measure of cognitive response stereotypy for each subject in the study. We analyzed this measure in the same manner in which we analyzed the other measures obtained (e.g., attitudes).

As expected, we found that subjects who displayed relative right hemispheric involvement while anticipating and listening to the persuasive communication generated a more stereotyped profile of cognitive responses. Interestingly, median splits on the electroencephalographic ratios obtained during a prewarning basal interval did not portend this effect, which is consistent with the notion that there are predictable relationships between relative cerebral hemispheric involvement and the means by which attitudes are developed and changed. More important here, perhaps, is the utility of the measure of cognitive response stereotypy that is illustrated in this research.[3]

In sum, the research concerning the measurement of cognitive responses has focused on a variety of empirical means of obtaining and analyzing cognitive reactions to a stimulus. Most of this work has been conducted on the level of analyzing and classifying single responses. The work on the stream of cognitive response and and on analyses of cognitive organization offers a potentially rich area of research in which the reciprocal organismic–environmental interactions can be studied.

Some Final Considerations

How useful is the thought-listing procedure for tapping a person's self-statements? Can the procedure be employed successfully in an attempt to monitor the covert verbalizations or images that are produced as some task is anticipated or performed? Is the thought-listing procedure useful in psychological research and treatment?

Several important issues must be addressed in answering these questions, namely:

1. Is the measure reliable?
2. Is the measure sensitive to environmental interventions and individual differences?
3. Are the thoughts that are measured determinants or post hoc rationalizations of the observed outcome variable?
4. Can the thought-listing procedure serve as both an independent and a dependent variable?[4]

Reliability

A perfectly reliable measure is internally consistent (split-half reliability) and yields the same result on repeated testings (test–retest reliability). In

---

[3] Rather than using the nomothetic procedure for identifying predominant and nonpredominant cognitive responses that we have outlined, an idiographic criterion could be used. In this alternative method, the predominant cognitive response is considered to be whatever type of cognitive response is most abundant within each individual's thought listing. This can be calculated simply by taking the absolute value of the difference between the number of favorable and unfavorable thoughts generated by each subject. When we calculated this index in the study described here, we obtained essentially the same results. This idiographic criterion is especially useful, however, when the goal of the study is to examine a particular individual's thought processes and when thought listings by this individual in response to a variety of stimuli are available. The reader might recognize the parallels between our notions of nomothetic and idiographic stereotypy in cognitive response and psychophysiologists' notions of stimulus and individual response stereotypy in bodily reactions (cf. Engel, 1972).

[4] Other important issues concern the reactivity and the validity of the thought-listing measure. Because we addressed these issues previously in this chapter, we have excluded discussion of them in this section.

1968, Cullen compared the reliability of the thought-listing procedure with that of several respected attitude asessments (the Likert and Thurstone scales). Subjects responded to messages on two topics (birth control and segregation) by completing attitude and thought-listing measures (the order of assessment was counterbalanced across subjects). Cullen found that both split-half and test–retest reliabilities were acceptably high for these measures and that order of measurement made no difference. Specifically, she found that the average split-half reliability was $+.78$ for thought-listings, $+.83$ for Likert scales, and $+.55$ for Thurstone scales. The average test–retest reliability was $+.64$ for thought listings, $+.83$ for Likert scales, and $+.53$ for Thurstone scales. These data suggest that the thought-listing procedure obtains reliable information from a subject.

Sensitivity

Is the thought-listing measure sensitive to interventions? To test this, we conducted some studies in which we attempted to disrupt the subjects' thought processes (e.g., Cacioppo *et al.*, 1978; Petty *et al.*, 1976) and other studies in which we attempted to facilitate thinking (e.g., Cacioppo & Petty, 1979*b*; Petty & Cacioppo, 1979*b*).

Disrupting Cognitive Elaboration. We constructed two communications for a study in which thought processes were disrupted (Petty *et al.*, 1976). One contained rather weak arguments, and we expected that subjects would primarily counterargue this low-quality message while hearing it. We reasoned that, if we could impair cognitive elaboration while leaving comprehension relatively intact, then we could disrupt primarily counterarguments and make the person more susceptible to the speaker's appeal. The second message contained very strong arguments on the same topic. For this high-quality message, we expected subjects to be generating favorable thoughts to themselves regarding the advocacy as they listened to it. If we impaired cognitive elaboration in this instance, then we would expect to disrupt primarily favorable thoughts about the advocacy, thereby leading to less attitude change than if no disruption of thoughts occurred.

To test these hypotheses, Petty *et al.* presented a discrepant message (increasing tuition) to the subjects. Half heard the low-quality communication (weak arguments) for increasing tuition, whereas half heard the high-quality communication (strong arguments). In addition, half of the subjects engaged in a distracting task during the message, whereas half did not. The results confirmed the hypotheses: Distraction decreased counterargumentation and increased attitude change for the low-quality communication, but it decreased favorable thoughts and attitude change for the high-quality communication. This study has been replicated recently using different topics and distractors but yielding, in essence, the same effect (Lammars & Becker, 1980).

Enhancing Cognitive Elaboration. In other studies, we exposed subjects repeatedly to a persuasive communication. We reasoned that repeated presentations would provide subjects with additional opportunities to think about and elaborate upon the arguments given for adopting a discrepant position. Hence facilitated thought should increase attitude change if the arguments are strong (at least until repetition becomes tedious) and decrease attitude change if the arguments are weak. In our first studies, we tested and found support for the first notion, that it, that a moderate number of presentations of a high-quality communication increased attitude change (Cacioppo & Petty, 1979*b*, 1980*a*).

We recently completed a study in which subjects heard a high- or low-quality communication for instituting senior comprehensive exams (a discrepant message). Some subjects heard the message once, whereas others heard it three times. As expected, moderate repetition reduced counterarguing and increased attitude change when the arguements were strong, but it increased counterarguing and decreased attitude change when the arguements were weak. Together, these studies indicate that the thought-listing measure is sensitive to manipulations of information processing and illustrate the importance of self-statements in mediating affective responses to communications.

Reflecting Motivational Changes. Cognitive response processes operate at the service of two general factors: the *motivation* and the *ability* to think about and elaborate upon some stimulus or event. (Freud, for instance referred to repression in order to indicate motivated forgetting or nonthinking about some traumatic event.) The issue of the sensitivity of the thought-listing procedure can be extended to these two factors as well. Simply stated, does the thought-listing procedure reflect changes in cognitive response when a person's motivation or ability to think about some stimulus has been manipulated? Again, the answer seems to be a firm "yes."

One of the best known findings in social psychology is that the real or imagined presence of other people inhibits individuals from helping in emergencies (Latané & Darley, 1970). This social laziness is not limited to emergency (e.g., Ingham, Levinger, Graves, & Peckham, 1974; Petty, Williams, Harkins, & Latané, 1977) or even to physical tasks (Petty, Harkins, & Williams, 1980; Petty, Harkins, Williams, & Latané, 1977). The "social loafing" elicited by the presence of others who could also perform or assist in a task appears to be motivational in origin, as the effect is evident even when care is taken to ensure that participants are equally able to perform the task when alone and when with others.

Petty, Harkins, and Williams (1980) have shown that the implied or real presence of others working on the same cognitive task lessens the cognitive work an individual devotes to the task. More important here, this motivational effect was evident in thought listings. For instance, when evaluating a high-quality communication, individual evaluators generated more favorable thoughts and evaluated the stimulus more positively than group evaluators; when evaluating a low-quality communication, however, individual evaluators generated more unfavorable thoughts and evaluated the stimulus more negatively than group evaluators.

We have also found the thought listing to reflect enhancements of a person's motivation to think about a stimulus (Petty & Cacioppo, 1979b). Again, we used two forms of communication advocating the same position, one constituted by weak message arguments (low-quality communication), and one by strong arguments (high-quality communication). This time, however, subjects were told that the advocacy (instituting senior comprehensive exams) would occur at some distant school (low personal involvement, low motivation) or at their university (high involvement, high motivation). Increasing involvement enhanced persuasion for the high-quality communication but reduced persuasion for the low-quality communication. Moreover, thought listings revealed that the production of favorable thoughts was enhanced by involvement for the high-quality communication, whereas unfavorable thought production was enhanced by the more involving low-quality communication.

Collectively, these studies suggest that the thought-listing procedure can be used to detect differences in cognitive response caused by environmental influences on a person's motivation to think about a stimulus or event.

Reflecting Alterations of Ability. The thought listing has in several studies also proven quite sensitive to environmental influences on a person's ability to think about a stimulus or event. The distraction studies we reviewed above (e.g., Petty *et al.*, 1976) are based upon the logic that the person's ability to elaborate upon the stimulus was impaired. The level of distraction in these studies was finely determined so that reception of the message arguments was left intact while disabling subjects from elaborating as completely as normal upon these arguments. As we noted, these conditions had a dampening effect on any cognitive and attitudinal changes normally caused by these stimuli—and these effects were evident in the thought listings.

Enhancing a person's ability to process has been illustrated in the thought-listing technique by Cacioppo (1979). We found that under certain conditions an accelerated heart rate enhanced the performance on intellective tasks of people wearing pacemakers. In a second study, subjects wearing implanted cardiac pacemakers read counterattitudinal communications when their heart rate was either accelerated or not accelerated. These subjects were more resistant to these communications (which consisted of weak arguments) when their heart rate was accelerated than when it was not. This change in their ability to elaborate cognitively was evident on the thought-listing measures as well (cf. Cacioppo & Petty, in press-c).

Reflecting Individual Differences. It is often more important in clinical matters to assess dispositional, rather than situational, differences in thought processes. How does the thought-listing procedure fare in assessing individual differences? The data are sparse but encouraging.

In one study, we pretested a large number of male undergraduates and selected for further examination (i.e., a second session) those who scored either high or low on Watson and Friend's (1969) scale of social anxiety (Cacioppo, Glass, & Merluzzi, 1979). During the second session, subjects (who were tested individually) were told that they would be discussing campus issues with a female undergraduate. Each subjects was asked to wait quietly for a few minutes while the experimenter retrieved a "prediscussion questionnaire." When the experimenter returned 3 minutes later, the subject was asked to complete thought-listing and self-evaluation measures.

We found that anticipating a discussion with an unfamiliar woman led to the spontaneous generation of more negative self-statements and more negative self-evaluations by high, as opposed to low, socially anxious men. Moreover, the self-statements listed by high and low socially anxious men were clearly distinguishable and were highly related to self-evaluations.

The Role of Cognitive Responses

This finding brings us to an important theoretical as well as methodological question: Are the responses that are measured with the thought-listing technique determinants or post hoc rationalizations of the observed emotional responses? The logic of the distraction studies discussed previously argues that they are determinants. Similarly, studies in which thought has been facilitated suggest that they are determinants (cf. Petty & Cacioppo, 1981). For instance, slightly speeding up the heart beat of pacemaker patients improved their performance in intellective tasks—and increased their counterargumentation, total thought production, and resistance to discrepant communications (Cacioppo, 1979).

Besides these experimental means, we have employed path analytic procedures in an attempt to determine the most likely causal sequence of the cognitive and affective responses we observed. For example, if a manipulation influences cognitive *and* affective responses, then one of the following causal models is likely:

1. Manipulation———▶Cognitive responses———▶Affective responses
2. Manipulation———▶Affective response———▶Cognitive responses
3. Manipulation⟨ Cognitive responses / Affective responses

Path analytic techniques provide a means of selecting from among these various models. The logic behind path analysis is fairly straightforward. If the effects on some "criterion" measure (e.g., affective response) are mediated by the effects of the manipulation on some other ("predictor") variable (e.g., cognitive responses), then stastically eliminating the predictor variable should eliminate the effects that the manipulation seemed to have on the criterion variable. Typically, path analyses have revealed that the person's cognitive responses to persuasive communication mediated the affective response (Cacioppo *et al.*, 1981; Insko, *et al.*, 1974; Osterhouse & Brock, 1970).

Finally, we discussed previously how personal involvement increases the cognitive elaboration of a communication as it is presented. If the thought-listing procedure taps post hoc rationalizations, then the correlation between these thoughts and affective responses should be about the same, regardless of issue involvement. On the other hand, if thought listings are tapping the actual (and accessible) cognitive responses to the communication, then the correlation between cognitive and affective responses should be higher when there is high, rather than low, issue involvement because the former elicits greater relevant cognitive elaboration. As mentioned previously, high-in-volvment issues produce stronger correlations among cognitive and affective responses than do low-involvement issues (Petty & Cacioppo, 1979*a*, 1979*b*).

Thought Listing as an Independent Variable

The thought-listing procedure has proven useful as a reliable and sensitive dependent variable; it has been employed successfully as an independent variable as well. One example of this is in research on the determinants of enduring attitude changes.

Most attitude changes that are produced in the laboratory are relatively short lived; there is little or no maintenance of the new attitude. Hovland (1959) and his colleagues originally believed that attitude change would persist if subjects could subsequently recall the arguments contained in the communication. Of course, from the cognitive response point of view, attitude change is not produced or maintained by argument learning but by the elicitation and retention of favorable thoughts about the advocacy. That is, attitude change may persist to the extent that subjects at some later time are able to recall the favorable cognitions that were elicited initially by the communication.

To test this, we asked subjects to read five arguments on an involving topic and to list five of their own thoughts on the topic (Petty, 1977). Subjects then memorized either their own five thoughts or the five message arguments. Attitudes on the topic were measured both immediately and one week later. The results supported the cognitive response view. Immediate attitude change was related more highly to the cognitive responses than to message learning. In addition, attitude change persisted more among those who memorized their own thoughts than among those who memorized message arguments.

The use of thought listing as an independent variable is important for other areas of psychology for at least two reasons. First, there is the obvious advantage for theory testing that we capitalized upon in the study described.

For instance, recall that we found that highly socially anxious men were more likely to generate negative self-statements when awaiting their interaction with a woman than were less anxious men (Cacioppo, Glass, & Merluzzi, 1979). This study did not indicate whether or not these self-statements were instrumental in eliciting or heightening the anxiety and self-evaluations; the use of thought listing as an independent variable provides a means by which to test the causal role of a person's self-statements in bringing about the subsequently observed affective and self-evaluative responses.

Second, thought listing as an independent variable is important for its application in therapy. As a component of a treatment intervention, a therapist might want to select a subset of thoughts and have the client memorize these (e.g., the favorable self-statements in a phobic situation) to facilitate the client's affective and behavioral change.

In sum, the thought-listing procedure has provided a reliable and valid measure of cognitive responses. The procedure does not appear to be reactive, because it does not affect the responses to the task under investigation. Thought listings appear to be sensitive to environmental manipulations and to individual differences. The measure appears to tap thoughts that mediate affective responses rather than post hoc rationalizations for these responses. Finally, it has proven useful as an independent variable in assessing cognitions in research. Perhaps one of the most promising and exciting prospects for the thought-listing technique is its application as an independent variable to assessing and treating the underlying problems in an individual's thought processes.

ACKNOWLEDGMENTS

We would like to thank Donald Meichenbaum, Michael Mahoney, and the editors of this book for their helpful comments on an earlier draft of this chapter. Preparation of this chapter was supported by a University Faculty Scholar Award and by National Science Foundation Grant No. BNS80-23589.

Reference Notes

1. Gergen, K. J., & Gibbs, M. *Role playing and modifying the self-concept.* Paper presented at the meeting of the Eastern Psychological Association, Atlantic City, N.J., April 1965.
2. Cacioppo, J. T., Petty, R. E., & Sidera, J. *Self-schema and the processing of attitudinal information.* Manuscript under review, 1981.
3. Cacioppo, J. T., Petty, R. E., & Quinatar, L. R. *Individual differences in relative hemispheric alpha abundance and cognitive responses to a persuasive communication.* Manuscript under review, 1981.
4. Cacioppo, J. T., & Petty, R. E. The association between hemispheric dominance and cognitive responses to persuasive communications. In S. Cook (Chair), *Social psychophysiology I: The brain, the body, and social psychology.* Symposium presented at the meeting of the American Psychological Association, Montreal, Canada, September 1980.

References

Abelson, R. P. Computer, polls, and public opinion—Some puzzles and paradoxes. *Transaction*, 1968, *5*, 20–27.

Abelson, R. P. Script processing in attitude formation and decision making. In J. S. Carroll & J. W. Payne (Eds.), *Cognition and social behavior*. Hillsdale, N.J.: Erlbaum, 1976.

Bartlett, F. C. *Remembering: A study in experimental and social psychology*. New York: Macmillan, 1932.

Beaber, R. J. *The general characteristics of covert resistance mechanisms and their relationship to attitude change and speaker perception*. Unpublished doctoral dissertation, The University of Southern California, 1975.

Brock, T. C. Communication discrepancy and intent to persuade as determinants of counterargument production. *Journal of Experimental Social Psychology*, 1967, *3*, 269–309.

Cacioppo, J. T. The effects of exogenous changes in heart rate on facilitation of thought and resistance to persuasion. *Journal of Personality and Social Psychology*, 1979, *37*, 487–496.

Cacioppo, J. T., Glass, C. R., & Merluzzi, T. V. Self-statements and self-evaluations: A cognitive response analysis of heterosocial anxiety. *Cognitive Therapy and Research*, 1979, *3*, 249–262.

Cacioppo, J. T., Harkins, S. G., & Petty, R. E. The nature of cognitive responses to persuasive appeals. In R. E. Petty, T. M. Ostrom, & T. C. Brock (Eds.), *Cognitive responses in persuasion*. Hillsdale, N.J.: Erlbaum, 1981.

Cacioppo, J. T., & Petty, R. E. Attitudes and cognitive response: An electrophysiological approach. *Journal of Personality and Social Psychology*, 1979, *37*, 2181–2199. (*a*)

Cacioppo, J. T., & Petty, R. E. The effects of message repetition and position on cognitive response, recall, and persuasion. *Journal of Personality and Social Psychology*, 1979, *37*, 97–109. (*b*)

Cacioppo, J. T., & Petty, R. E. Lip and nonpreferred forearm EMG activity as a function of orienting task. *Journal of Biological Psychology*, 1979, *9*, 103–113. (*c*)

Cacioppo, J. T., & Petty, R. E. Persuasiveness of communications is affected by exposure frequency and message quality: A theoretical and empirical analysis of persisting attitude change. In J. H. Leigh & C. R. Martin, Jr. (Eds.), *Current issues and research in advertising*. Ann Arbor, Mich.: University of Michigan, 1980. (*a*)

Cacioppo, J. T., & Petty, R. E. Sex differences in influenceability: Toward specifying the underlying processes. *Personality and Social Psychology Bulletin*, 1980, *6*, 651–656. (*b*)

Cacioppo, J. T., & Petty, R. E. Electromyographic specificity during covert information processing. *Psychophysiology*, in press. (*a*)

Cacioppo, J. T., & Petty, R. E. Lateral asymmetry in the expression of cognition and emotion. *Journal of Experimental Psychology: Human Perception and Performance*, in press. (*b*)

Cacioppo, J. T., & Petty, R. E. (Eds.). *Focus on cardiovascular psychophysiology*. New York: Guilford Press, in press. (*c*)

Cacioppo, J. T., Petty, R. E., & Snyder, C. W. Cognitive and affective response as a function of relative hemispheric involvement. *The International Journal of Neuroscience*, 1979, *9*, 81–89.

Cacioppo, J. T., & Sandman, C. A. Psychophysiological functioning, cognitive responding, and attitudes. In R. E. Petty, T. M. Ostrom, & T. C. Brock (Eds.), *Cognitive responses in persuasive communications*. Hillsdale, N.J.: Erlbaum, 1981.

Cacioppo, J. T., Sandman, C. A., & Walker, B. B. The effects of operant heart rate conditioning on cognitive elaboration and attitude change. *Psychophysiology*, 1978, *15*, 330–338.

Calder, B. J., Insko, C. A., & Yandell, B. The relation of cognitive and memorial processes to persuasion in a simulated jury trial. *Journal of Applied Social Psychology*, 1974, *4*, 62–93.

Cantor, N., & Mischel, W. Traits as prototypes: Effects on recognition memory. *Journal of Personality and Social Psychology*, 1977, *35*, 38–48.

Carter, R. F., Ruggels, W. L., Jackson, K. M., & Heffner, M. Application of signaled stopping technique to communication research. In P. Clarke (Ed.), *New models for mass communication research*. Beverly Hills, Calif.: Sage Publications, 1973.

Cialdini, R. B., Levin, A., Herman, C. P., Kozlowski, L. T., & Petty, R. E. Elastic shifts of opinion: Determinants of direction and durability. *Journal of Personality and Social Psychology*, 1976, *34*, 663–672.

Cook, T. D. Competence, counterarguing, and attitude change. *Journal of Personality*, 1969, *37*, 342–358.

Cullen, D. M. *Attitude measurement by cognitive sampling*. Unpublished doctoral dissertation, The Ohio State University, 1968.

Darwin, C. *The expression of the emotions in man and animals*. London: John Murray, 1904. (First ed., 1872.)

Di Giuseppe, R. A., & Miller, N. J. A review of outcome studies on rational–emotive therapy. In A. Ellis & R. Grieger (Eds.), *Handbook of rational–emotive therapy*. New York: Springer, 1977.

Duval, S., & Wicklund, R. A. *A theory of objective self-awareness*. New York: Academic Press, 1972.

Ellis, A. *Reason and emotion in psychotherapy*. New York: Lyle Stuart, 1962.

Ellis, A. Research data supporting the clinical and personality hypotheses of RET and other cognitive-behavior therapies. In A. Ellis & R. Grieger (Eds.), *Handbook of rational–emotive therapy*. New York: Springer, 1977.

Engel, B. T. Response specificity. In N. S. Greenfield & R. A. Sternbach (Eds.), *Handbook of psychophysiology*. New York: Holt, Rinehart & Winston, 1972.

Geller, V., & Shaver, P. Cognitive consequences of self-awareness. *Journal of Experimental Social Psychology*, 1976, *12*, 99–108.

Glass, C. R., Gottman, J. M., & Shmurak, S. M. Response-acquisition and cognitive self-statement modification approaches to dating-skills training. *Journal of Counseling Psychology*, 1976, *23*, 520–526.

Goor, A., & Sommerfeld, R. A comparison of problem-solving processes of creative students and noncreative students. *Journal of Educational Psychology*, 1975, *67*, 495–505.

Gottman, J. M., & Notarius, C. Sequential analysis of observational data using Markov chains. In T. R. Kratochwill (Ed.), *Single subject research*. New York: Academic Press, 1978.

Greenwald, A. G. Cognitive learning, cognitive response to persuasion, and attitude change. In A. G. Greenwald, T. C. Brock, & T. M. Ostrom (Eds.), *Psychological foundations of attitudes*. New York: Academic Press, 1968.

Haggard, E. A., & Issacs, F. S. Micromomentary facial expressions as indicators of ego mechanisms in psychotherapy. In L. A. Gottschalk & A. H. Averback (Eds.), *Methods of research in psychotherapy*. New York: Appleton-Century-Crofts, 1966.

Hovland, C. Reconciling conflicting results derived from experimental and survey studies of attitude change. *American Psychologist*, 1959, *14*, 8–17.

Hovland, C. I., Janis, I. L., & Kelley, H. H. *Communication and persuasion*. New Haven: Yale University Press, 1953.

Hovland, C. I., Lumsdaine, A. A., & Sheffield, F. D. *Experiments on mass communication*. Princeton: Princeton University Press, 1949.

Hurlburt, R. T., & Sipprelle, C. N. Random sampling of cognitions in alleviating anxiety attacks. *Cognitive Therapy and Research*, 1978, *2*, 165–169.

Ingham, A. G., Levinger, G., Graves, J., & Peckham, V. The Ringelmann effect: Studies of group size and group performance. *Journal of Experimental Social Psychology*, 1974, *10*, 371–384.

Insko, C. A., Turnbull, W., & Yandell, B. Facilitative and inhibiting effects of distraction on attitude change. *Sociometry*, 1974, *37*, 509–528.

Jaccard, J. J., & Fishbein, M. Inferential beliefs and order effects in personality impression formation. *Journal of Personality and Social Psychology*, 1975, *31*, 1031–1040.

Janis, I. L., & King, B. T. The influence of role playing on opinion change. *Journal of Abnormal and Social Psychology*, 1954, *49*, 211–218.

Janis, I. L., & Mann, L. *Decision making: A psychological analysis of conflict, choice, and commitment.* New York: The Free Press, 1977.

Kendall, P. C., & Korgeski, G. P. Assessment and cognitive–behavioral interventions. *Cognitive Therapy and Research*, 1979, *3*, 1-21.

Lammars, B., & Becker, L. A. Distraction effects on the perceived extremity of a communication and on cognitive responses. *Personality and Social Psychology Bulletin*, 1980, *6*, 261-266.

Lasswell, H. D. The structure and function of communication in society. In L. Bryson (Ed.), *Communication of ideas.* New York: Harper, 1948.

Latané, B., & Darley, J. M. *The unresponsive bystander: Why doesn't he help?* New York: Appleton-Century-Crofts, 1970.

Lazarus, R. S. *Psychological stress and coping process.* New York: McGraw-Hill, 1966.

Lingle, J. H., Geva, H., Ostrom, T. M., Leippe, M. R., & Baumgardner, M. H. Thematic effects of person judgments on impression organization. *Journal of Personality and Social Psychology,* 1979, *37,* 674-687.

Lingle, J. H., & Ostrom, T. M. Retrieval selectivity in memory-based impression judgments. *Journal of Personality and Social Psychology*, 1979, *37*, 180-194.

Lingle, J. H., & Ostrom, T. M. Principles of memory and cognition in attitude formation. In R. E. Petty, T. M. Ostrom, & T. C. Brock (Eds.), *Cognitive responses in persuasive communications.* Hillsdale, N.J.: Erlbaum, 1981.

Love, R. *A videotape technique for the measurement of cognitive response to persuasion.* Unpublished doctoral dissertation, The Ohio State University, 1972.

Markus, H. Self-schemata and processing information about the self. *Journal of Personality and Social Psychology*, 1977, *35*, 63-78.

Maultsby, M. C., Jr. Routine tape recorder use in RET. *Rational Living*, 1970, *5*, 8-23.

Maultsby, M. C., Jr. Rational–emotive imagery. In A. Ellis & R. Grieger (Eds.), *Handbook of rational-emotive therapy.* New York: Springer, 1977.

McGuigan, F. J. *Cognitive psychophysiology: Principles of covert behavior.* Englewood Cliffs, N.J.: Prentice-Hall, 1978.

McGuire, W. J. The nature of attitudes and attitude change. In G. Lindzey & E. Aronson (Eds.), *The handbook of social psychology* (Vol. 3, 2nd ed.). Reading Mass.: Addison-Wesley, 1969.

McGuire, W. J. The probabilogical model of cognitive structure and attitude change. In R. E. Petty, T. M. Ostrom, & T. C. Brock (Eds.), *Cognitive responses in persuasion.* Hillsdale, N.J.: Erlbaum, 1980.

McGuire, W. J., & Padawer-Singer, A. Trait salience in the spontaneous self-concept. *Journal of Personality and Social Psychology*, 1976, *33*, 743-754.

McGuire, W. J., & Papageorgis, D. Effectiveness of forewarning in developing resistance to persuasion. *Public Opinion Quarterly*, 1962, *26*, 24-34.

Meichenbaum, D. *Cognitive-behavior modification: An integrative approach.* New York: Plenum Press, 1977.

Meichenbaum, D., Henshaw, D., & Himel, N. Coping with stress as a problem-solving process. In W. Krohne & L. Laux (Eds.), *Achievement stress and anxiety.* Washington, D.C.: Hemisphere, 1980.

Miller, N., & Baron, R. S. On measuring counterarguing. *Journal for the Theory of Social Behavior*, 1973, *3*, 101-118.

Mirels, H. L., & McPeek, R. W. Self-advocacy and self-esteem. *Journal of Consulting and Clinical Psychology*, 1977, *45*, 1132-1138.

Neisser, U. *Cognition and reality.* San Francisco: W. H. Freeman, 1976.

Nisbett, R. E., & Bellows, N. Verbal reports about causal influences on social judgments: Private access versus public theories. *Journal of Personality and Social Psychology*, 1977, *35*, 613-624.

Nisbett, R. E., & Wilson, T. D. Telling more than we can know: Verbal reports on mental processes. *Psychological Review*, 1977, *84*, 231–259.

Osterhouse, R. A., & Brock, T. C. Distraction increases yielding to propaganda by inhibiting counterarguing. *Journal of Personality and Social Psychology*, 1970, *15*, 344–358.

Peterman, J. N., III. Program research. The Program Analyzer—A new technique in studying liked and disliked items in radio programs. *Journal of Applied Psychology*, 1940, *23*, 725–741.

Petty, R. E. *A cognitive response and analysis of the temporal persistence of attitude changes induced by persuasive communications*. Unpublished doctoral dissertation, The Ohio State University, 1977.

Petty, R. E., & Brock, T. C. The effects of Barnum assessment on cognitive behavior. *Journal of Consulting and Clinical Psychology*, 1979, *47*, 201–203.

Petty, R. E., & Cacioppo, J. T. Forewarning, cognitive responding, and resistance to persuasion. *Journal of Personality and Social Psychology*, 1977, *35*, 645–655.

Petty, R. E., & Cacioppo, J. T. Effects of forewarning of persuasive intent and involvement on cognitive responses and persuasion. *Personality and Social Psychology Bulletin*, 1979, *5*, 173–176. (*a*)

Petty, R. E., & Cacioppo, J. T. Issue involvement can increase or decrease persuasion by enhancing message relevant cognitions. *Journal of Personality and Social Psychology*, 1979, *37*, 1915–1926. (*b*)

Petty, R. E., & Cacioppo, J. T. *Attitudes and persuasion: Classic and contemporary approaches*. Dubuque, Ia.: Wm. C. Brown, 1981.

Petty, R. E., Cacioppo, J. T., & Heesacker, M. The use of rhetorical questions in persuasion: A cognitive response analysis. *Journal of Personality and Social Psychology*, 1981, *40*, 432–440.

Petty, R. E., Harkins, S. G., & Williams, K. D. The effects of group diffusion of cognitive effort on attitudes: An information processing view. *Journal of Personality and Social Psychology*, 1980, *38*, 81–92.

Petty, R. E., Harkins, S. G., Williams, K.D., & Latané, B. Social inhibition of helping yourself: Effort and evaluation. *Personality and Social Psychology Bulletin*, 1977, *3*, 579–582.

Petty, R. E., Ostrom, T. M., & Brock, T. C. (Eds.). *Cognitive responses in persuasion*. Hillsdale, N.J.: Erlbaum, 1981.

Petty, R. E., Wells, G. L., & Brock, T. C. Distraction can enhance or reduce yielding to propaganda: Thought disruption versus effort justification. *Journal of Personality and Social Psychology*, 1976, *34*, 874–884.

Petty, R. E., Williams, K. D., Harkins, S. G., & Latané, B. Social inhibition of helping yourself: Bystander response to a cheeseburger. *Personality and Social Psychology Bulletin*, 1977, *3*, 575–578.

Quinatar, L. R., Cacioppo, J. T., Monyak, N., Alvarez, L., & Snyder, C. W. The effects of cranial vasoconstriction and paced respiration on migraine. *Psychophysiology*, 1980, *17*, 284. (Abstract)

Reese, H. W. The study of covert verbal and nonverbal mediation. In A. Jacobs & L. Sachs (Eds.), *The psychology of private events: Perspectives on covert response systems*. New York: Academic Press, 1971.

Roberts, D. F., & Maccoby, N. Information processing and persuasion: Counterarguing behavior. In P. Clarke (Ed.), *New models for mass communication*. Beverly Hills, Calif.: Sage Publications, 1973.

Rogers, T. B., Kuiper, N. A., & Kirker, W. S. Self-reference and the encoding of personal information. *Journal of Personality and Social Psychology*, 1977, *35*, 677–688.

Schiebe, K. E., Shaver, P. R., & Carrier, S. C. Color association values and response interference on variants of the Stroop test. *Acta Psychologica*, 1967, *26*, 286–295.

Schwartz, G. E. Biofeedback, self-regulation, and the patterning of physiological processes. *American Scientist*, 1975, *63*, 314–324.

Schwartz, G. E., Fair, P. L., Salt, P., Mandel, M. R., & Klerman, G. L. Facial expression and imagery in depression: An electromyographic study. *Psychosomatic Medicine*, 1976, *38*, 337–347.

Shaffer, J. B., & Galinsky, M. D. *Models of group therapy and sensitivity training.* Englewood Cliffs, N.J.: Prentice-Hall, 1974.

Smith, M. B., Bruner, J. S., & White, R. W. *Opinions and personality.* New York: 1956.

Stroop, J. R. Factors affecting speed in serial verbal reactions. *Psychological Monographs*, 1938, *50*, 38–48.

Tucker, D. M. Lateral brain function, emotion, and conceptualization. *Psychological Bulletin*, 1981, *89*, 19–46.

Wainer, H. Speed vs. reaction time as a measure of cognitive performance. *Memory and Cognition*, 1977, *5*, 278–280.

Warren, R. E. Stimulus encoding and memory. *Journal of Experimental Psychology*, 1972, *94*, 90–100.

Warren, R. E. Association, directionality, and stimulus encoding. *Journal of Experimental Psychology*, 1974, *102*, 151–158.

Watson, D., & Friend, R. Measurement of social-evaluative anxiety. *Journal of Consulting and Clinical Psychology*, 1969, *33*, 448–457.

Wright, P. L. The cognitive processes mediating acceptance of advertising. *Journal of Marketing Research*, 1973, *10*, 53–62.

Wright, P. L. On the direct monitoring of cognitive response to advertising. In G. D. Hughes & M. L. Ray (Eds.), *Buyer/consumer information processing.* Chapel Hill: The University of North Carolina Press, 1974. (*a*)

Wright, P. L. Analyzing media effects on advertising responses. *Public Opinion Quarterly*, 1974, *38*, 192–205. (*b*)

Zajonc, R. B. The process of cognitive tuning in communication. *Journal of Abnormal and Social Psychology*, 1960, *61*, 159–167.

11

Assessing Sequential Dependency in Cognitive Performance Data

Clifford I. Notarius

There is an increasing interest in the behavioral sciences in capturing the importance of time and sequence inherent in the phenomenon of study. The usual focus on response rates of various behavioral categories ignores the sequential patterning of behavior. Response rates give us information about the frequency of occurrence of behavior, whereas sequence analysis yields information about the patterns and interdependency of behavior. For example, the tendency for aggressive behavior to follow an insult among children who are playing is a question that sequential analysis can answer; frequency data would tell us only how often aggressive behavior occurred.

Recently, several sources have presented overviews of the different strategies available for assessing streams of behavior (Bakeman, 1978; Castellan, 1979; Gottman & Notarius, 1978; Raush, 1972). This chapter illustrates application of these strategies in cognitive assessment situations. The utility of these methods in this specific domain will remain to be determined by the applications that I hope will be stimulated by this chapter.

Types of Data

Cognitive assessment entails both methodological and conceptual issues. Kendall and Korgeski (1979) have suggested seven approaches to assessing cognitions: *in vivo* thought sampling and the assessment of im-

---

Clifford I. Notarius • Department of Psychology, The Catholic University of America, Washington, D.C.

agery, cognitive style, beliefs, attributions, self-efficacy expectations, and self-statements. Because sequential analysis is aimed at describing the patterning of behavior, it is useful only when the dimensions of time and/or sequence are important and when the behavior of interest is variable over time. Thus *in vivo* thought sampling and self-statements or thought-listing assessments are most likely to suggest sequential analyses, whereas cognitive style assessments are not.

In general, Bakeman, Cairns, and Applebaum (1979) have distinguished five types of sequential data. The first two types represent continuous series arising from the measurement of a continuous variable at successive time periods. Time-series data consist of a series of scores, with each score representing a measurement at each time period. Multiple time-series data are similar, except that more than one variable is measured at each interval.

In contrast to the continuous series data, there are three types of discrete sequential data that are more applicable to cognitive assessment. The discrete sequential data, described by Bakeman *et al.* (1979), include event sequence, timed-event sequence, and multiple timed-event sequence data. For event sequence data, a stream of behavior is broken down into a sequence of events that are usually defined as mutually exclusive and exhaustive. Valence scores assigned to consecutive thoughts generated by a thought-listing procedure illustrate this type of data. For time-event sequence data, the duration and the sequence of events or behavior are recorded. For example, a coder watching a person and coding one of four behaviors every 6 seconds would yield a timed-event sequential record. For multiple timed-event sequence data, the researcher considers combinations of behaviors that occur in specified timed intervals.

These five types of data are not meant to constitute an exhaustive catalog of sequential data types nor are they immutable. For example, timed-event sequence data can be collapsed across time periods to produce event sequence data in which each observation (unit of analysis) represents the transition to a new behavior without respect to the duration of each behavior.

At this point, it will be useful to consider a cognitive assessment situation that might be appropriate for sequential analysis methods. One such situation concerns the change in cognitions expected to follow a cognitively oriented therapy. To demonstrate that cognitive change is responsible for treatment outcome, it should be possible to monitor the *process* of cognitive performance change in individuals receiving an intervention program conceptualized as altering dysfunctional cognitions. To accomplish this, the researcher/therapist must monitor cognitive performance before treatment, during treatment, and after treatment. Because it is unlikely that cognitive change will occur on an all-or-none basis, we expect that there will be a gradual transition to more functional cognitive performance. Thus, at the beginning of treatment, we might expect negative self-statements to lead to other negative statements in a manner characteristic of a positive feedback loop. With an effective intervention, we would expect a gradual interruption of this cycle with the introduction of positive coping statements. To the extent that we able to tap this process, sequential analysis methods can enable us to map out this transition process from negative to positive self-statements.

The power of sequential analysis derives from its ability to go beyond the sheer frequency of occurrence of behaviors. In the therapy situation just described, it may be inadequate simply to tally the relative proportion of positive to negative thought. Rather, it is more likely that the treatment effect is demonstrated by a disruption in the negative thought cycle rather than by a complete block of all negative thoughts. The process can easily be mapped out over an intervention period with sequential analyses methods.

In the general case, sequential analysis allows the researcher/therapist to go beyond the simple frequency of occurrence of cognitive performance by examining the more informative process of cognitive performance over time. The *in vivo* thought-sampling techniques and the thought-listing procedure lend themselves to this type of analysis. Other methods depend on the creativity of the investigator in tapping the flow of internal events as they occur. For example, a response box might be constructed, with a series of buttons defining any dimension of interest to the investigator (e.g., threat, valence of thoughts, potency). The subject would be instructed to press the appropriate button at specified intervals or whenever a situationally defined event occurs. These subjective ratings, along with observed situational events and behaviors, can be processed to identify the patterning and interrelationships among situational, cognitive, and behavioral events happening in a behavioral stream. A similar procedure was used to assess the phenomenological intent and impact of marital interaction (Gottman, Notarius, Markman, Bank, Yoppi, & Rubin, 1976).

In the remaining portion of this chapter, specific techniques of sequential analysis will be illustrated, and methodological considerations in applying these methods will be presented.

Describing Sequences

A clear method of presenting sequential analysis is by way of example. Cacioppo, Glass, and Merluzzi (1979) studied the cognitive responses of two groups of male subjects differing in levels of heterosocial anxiety as they anticipated interacting with a woman. In their experiment, subjects were told that they would discuss college life with a female student for approximately 5 minutes. Prior to the meeting, the experimenter left the subject for 3 minutes to fetch a questionnaire from his office. The subject was asked to sit quietly until the experimenter returned. After 3 minutes, the experimenter returned with the "prediscussion questionnaire" and asked the subject to list all thoughts that he had had during the preceding 3 minutes. The thought-listing procedure (see Cacioppo & Petty, Chapter 10, this volume) generated a series of thoughts as they occurred to a subject at the time at which the request was made to write them down. Cacioppo *et al.* then had judges score the thoughts for either positive $(+)$, negative $(-)$, or neutral/irrelevant (0) self-statements. These coding data were reduced and submitted to an analysis of variance by summing the number of statements falling into each category for each subject.

The analysis of variance results indicated that the high heterosocially anxious males had more negative and less positive self-statements than the low heterosocially anxious males. These frequency data provide an index of differences between the two groups in production levels of types of cognitive responses. We might also consider the influence of time and sequence by posing the question "Does the order in which cognitive self-statements are reported contribute to our understanding of group differences between high and low heterosocially anxious males?" Or we might wonder, "Do the two groups each generate an equal number of positive statements to point *p*, after which time the high anxious drift toward increasing negative thoughts, while the low anxious maintain a preponderance of positive thoughts?"

Let us "walk through" a hypothetical data set to understand how we can answer the first question. Each subject's record will consist of a series of $+$, $-$, and 0 codes assigned, in temporal order, to each thought listed—for example, one subject might have listed two positive thoughts followed by neutral and then three negative thoughts, or "$+ + 0 - - -$." For the moment, we will want to pool subjects into two groups, the low anxious and the high anxious. As an initial data reduction procedure, we can produce a conditional frequency table with entries indicating the frequency with which each code follows every other code. Sample data from ten subjects are listed in Table 1; the frequency with which each code follows an immediate consequent thought in all subjects is shown in the top half of Table 2. By dividing each row cell by the respective row marginal, we obtain the conditional probability of a consequent thought following a specific antecedent thought; these probabilities are shown in the bottom half of Table 2.

Table 1. Hypothetical Coded Data from Thought-Listing Procedure Used with Ten Subjects

Low heterosocially anxious males		High heterosocially anxious males	
Subject	Data	Subject	Data
1	$00 + - + - + + +$	31	$+ + - - - 0 - + +$
2	$+ + 0 + - + - + +$	32	$+ 000 + - - - + +$
3	$- 00 + - + - 0 -$	33	$- - - + 00 + + 00 +$
4	$+ - + - + - + - -$	34	$+ 00 + + + - - - 0$
5	$- - 000 - 0 + 0 + 0$	35	$- - 0 - 0 + 0 +$

Table 2. *Frequency and Conditional Probabilities of Hypothetical Data Generated by Thought-Listing Procedure*

Low heterosocially anxious males	High heterosocially anxious males

Frequency matrices

		Consequent							Consequent			
		0	+	−					0	+	−	
Antecedent	0	31	40	16	87		Antecedent	0	35	48	17	100
	+	24	33	80	137			+	41	55	28	124
	−	32	64	15	111			−	24	21	66	111
					335							335

Conditional probability matrices

		Consequent					Consequent		
		0	+	−			0	+	−
Antecedent	0	.36	.46	.18		Antecedent 0	.35	.48	.17
	+	.18	.24	.58		+	.33	.44	.23
	−	.29	.57	.14		−	.22	.19	.59

Examination of these conditional probabilities, or the first-order transition matrices, reveals several important differences between the high- and low-anxious subjects. Let us focus on the occurrence of a negative thought. We note that in the low-anxious subjects, the most likely consequent thought, given that a negative thought had just occurred, was a positive thought. This relationship is conveniently given as $p(+/-) = .57$. Compare this .57 conditional probability to $p(+/-) = .19$ in high-anxious subjects. In the high-anxious group the most likely consequent to a negative thought is another negative thought; $p(-/-) = .59$. These relationships suggest that high-anxious subjects are caught in a "negative thought cycle," whereas low-anxious subjects tend to react to a negative thought with a positive thought. (Remember, these data are fictitious.) Note that, if only the number of negative thoughts were compared, the researcher would have concluded that there were *no* differences between high and low heterosocially anxious males because each had identical frequencies of negative thoughts ($f- = 111$) and identical relative frequencies ($p- = 111/335 = .331$).

Although we know that the high-anxious males differ from the low-anxious males in their tendencies to follow one negative thought with another, it would be useful to have some index to gauge whether or not this pattern differs from chance expectations. Bakeman (1978) has suggested using the binomial test Z score to establish whether or not observed patterns differ from chance occurrences. Our question is, "Among high heterosocially anxious males, does the tendency for a negative thought to follow another negative thought occur more often than chance would lead us to expect?"

The binomial test proceeds as follows:

$$Z = (X - NP)/(NPQ)^{1/2}$$

in which X is the observed frequency of event j (consequent negative thought) following event i (antecedent negative thought) ($X = 66$); NP is the predicted frequency, f_{ij}, of event j following event i (making the null hypothesis of no patterning, the probability of event j following event i should be equal to the probability of event j anywhere in the sequence; thus P_{ij} predicted $= P_j$ and f_{ij} predicted $= f_i P_j$; so the predicted probability of a negative thought following another negative thought is $111/335 = .331$, and the predicted frequency of a negative thought following another negative thought is $111 \times .331 = 36.78$); and NPQ is the variance of the difference between predicted and observed values (N = frequency of event i, P = probability of event i, $Q = 1 - P$; thus $NPQ = (111) \times (.331) \times (.669) = 24.54$). Substituting these values yields

$$Z = (66 - 36.78)/(111 \times .331 \times .669)^{1/2}$$

$$= 29.22/4.95$$

$$= 5.89$$

In interpreting the Z index, Bakeman (1978) writes: "Given the lack of independence between successive time intervals (or events), it seems best to treat the Z score solely as an index rather than assigning p values to it" (p. 70). In current practice, a Z index of 2.0 has been considered sufficient to establish a behavior pattern beyond chance expectations. Thus our observed Z index of 5.90 supports the occurrence of the sequence negative thought → negative thought in high heterosocially anxious males beyond chance levels.

Graphic Summaries

It is sometimes convenient to present the conditional probabilities in the form of state transition diagrams, especially when the number of categories coded is small. The state transition diagram presents the information of the first-order transition matrix in a format in which the direction of sequences is easily observed. Returning to our first example, the state transition matrix of the high heterosocially anxious males is presented in Figure 1. A state transition matrix for an individual may also be informative to the researcher, clinician, and client in assessing individual behavior patterns.

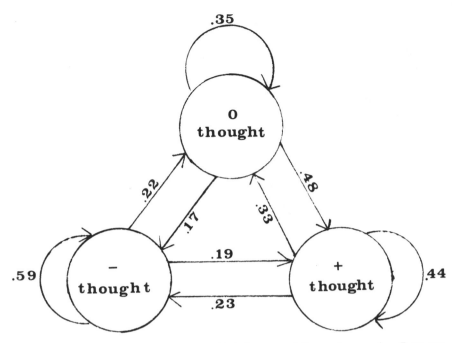

Figure 1. State transition diagram for high heterosocially anxious males. Data are hypothetical.

Looking Behind an Immediate Antecedent

The method just presented is easily extended beyond an examination of a single antecedent. A second-order model examines the probability that event *k* is significantly affected by events *i* and *j* that immediately preceded it. The analysis parallels that in the preceding example, beginning with the construction of a new matrix in which each antecedent event consists of the dyadic sequence *i, j*. Although this method for detecting patterning between lagged antecedents and a consequent behavior is straightforward, there is a better solution for uncovering sequential dependencies that extend beyond the relationship of a consequent and its immediate antecedent event. This solution is Sackett's (1977, Note 1) lag sequential analysis.

Sackett's Lag Sequential Analysis

Sackett (1977, Note 1) has proposed a powerful procedure for identifying sequencing of events that allows one to target specific patterns of interest rather than describing every possible two-event sequence. Using this analysis, a specific code (event) is selected as a criterion, and transition probabilities of all other codes are computed with respect to the selected criterion as a function of lag forward or backward from this criterion. Computer programs are available with which to perform these analyses.[1] The procedure is repeated for as many criterion codes as are of interest. The advantage of this procedure is that it allows the investigator to examine the pattern of events preceding or following a selected criterion behavior and conveniently maps out sequences that are longer than two events.

Continuing with our example, we might select a negative thought as the criterion code and seek to identify the pattern of thoughts at each of three states (lags) following the occurrence of the negative criterion thought. We would examine the probability of each code immediately following the negative thought (Lag 1), at two events following the negative thought (Lag 2), and at three events following the negative thought (Lag 3). This procedure is best illustrated graphically by looking at the probability profiles that are generated. In each case, the criterion code is a negative thought, and we examine the conditional probabilities of all other states at each lag with respect to this criterion. The graphs are presented in Figure 2.

In examining the graphs, peaks in the profile indicate sequential positions following (or preceding) the criterion at which a given state is more likely to occur, whereas troughs indicate sequential positions at which the given state is less likely to occur. If there are no sequential dependencies between a selected criterion and a given state, then its conditional probabilities at various lags should be equal to its simple, unconditional probability. The extent to which the conditional probability differs from the simple probability is measured by the Z index.

Examination of the three graphs in Figure 2 suggests the following sequence: negative thought, neutral thought, positive thought, neutral thought. This pattern is revealed by the peak at Lag 1 of a neutral thought, given a negative thought; a peak at Lag 2 of a positive thought, given a negative thought; and a peak at Lag 3 of a neutral thought, given a negative thought. To test whether this suggested pattern occurs beyond chance expectations, the following two steps are followed: (1) determine that the Z scores of each peak consequent, given a negative thought as the criterion, are greater than 2.0 and (2) determine that the Z scores of the intermediate Lag 1 connections, neutral thought to positive thought and positive thought to neutral thought, are each greater than 2.0. Step 2 is accomplished by first making the most probable event at Lag 2 to the original criterion (a neutral thought) the new criterion and assessing the most likely consequent (a positive thought) at Lag 1 to the new criterion. If this comparison reveals a Z score greater than

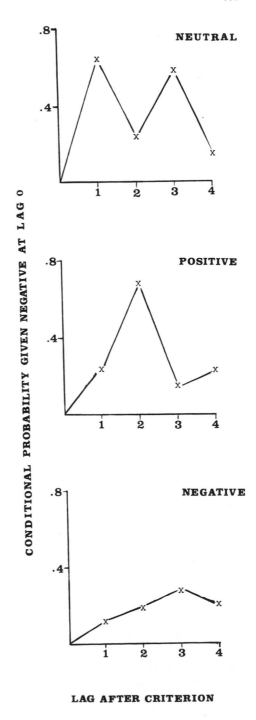

Figure 2. Lagged conditional probabilities for neutral thought, positive thought, and negative thought, given that a negative thought had occurred. Data are hypothetical.

2.0, the final dependency can be established by making positive thought the criterion and assessing the tendency for neutral thought to occur at Lag 1.

To summarize, the sequence negative thought, neutral thought, positive thought, neutral thought is *identified* and shown to occur more often than by chance by demonstrating sequential dependencies between a negative thought and neutral thought at Lag 1, a positive thought at Lag 2, and a neutral thought at Lag 3 *and* by demonstrating a sequential dependency (i.e., Lag 1 Z scores greater than 2.0) between the intermediate steps, neutral thought and positive thought, and positive thought and neutral thought. An example of lag sequential analysis (of marital interaction) is presented by Gottman, Markman, and Notarius (1977).

Stability of Event Sequences

Previously in this chapter, we asked a question concerning the stability of antecedent–consequent pairings over time. Using analyses on frequency or contingency tables, Castellan (1979) illustrates how this question may be answered. As a first step, the data must be grouped according to time blocks, or blocks of behavior pairs. Suppose that we have observed 100 antecedent events, A_i, and have recorded the following consequent state, C_j, of each occurrence. Further, suppose that there were three possible consequent states that could follow A_i. Note that in this procedure each antecedent event is analyzed separately.

The analysis proceeds by dividing up the blocks of behavior into equal divisions; let us say that we chose four sequence blocks, each with 25 $A_i \rightarrow C_j$ behavior pairs. A contingency table is then prepared, with behavior blocks on one marginal (e.g., rows) and consequents on the other marginal (e.g., columns). The table might appear as in Table 3. Note that the behavior blocks might, alternatively, represent time blocks—for example, 15-minute intervals.

To test the hypothesis that the probability of consequent C_j is constant across blocks 1 through 4, we compute the following test statistic:

$$\chi_i^2 = \sum_{b=1}^{B} \sum_j \frac{[f_{ij}(b) - f_i^A(b)\,(f_{ij}/f_i^A)]^2}{f_i^A(b)\,(f_{ij}/f_i^A)}$$

where $f_{ij}(b)$ is the frequency of occurrence of the antecedent (A_i)-consequent (C_j) pair in block b; f_i^A is the total frequency of occurrence of the antecedent (A_i) in block b; and f_{ij}/f_i^A is the estimate of the conditional probability of C_j, given that antecedent A_i has occurred overall in blocks 1 to N. This test statistic is asymptotically distributed as chi-square, with $(B-1)(J-1)$ degrees of freedom.

Table 3. Contingency Table to Examine Stability
of Event Sequences for a Hypothetical Example

Behavior block[a]	Consequent C_j		
	C_1	C_2	C_3
1	7	12	6
2	9	8	8
3	4	5	16
4	3	4	18

[a]For antecedent A_j.

Although the formula looks a bit complex, it remains a calculation of the familiar $x^2 = (O_{ij} - E_{ij})^2 / E_{ij}$. The observed frequency of occurrence in this case is the observed frequency of the specific antecedent–consequent pair in a specific behavior (or time) block, and the estimated value is an estimate of this pairing based on the conditional probability observed between the specific antecedent $\rightarrow$ consequent event overall. Thus the estimated value represents the conditional probability of a specific consequent to follow a chosen antecedent (frequency of consequent, C_j, across all behavior blocks divided by the total of all consequents to that antecedent) multiplied by the sum total of consequents occurring across a specific behavior block; the estimate is of a specific consequent in each block to the chosen antecedent.

In our example:

$$\chi_i^2 = \frac{[7 - (25)(23/100)]^2}{(25)(23/100)} + \frac{[12 - (25)(29/100)]^2}{(25)(29/100)} + \ldots$$

$$+ \frac{[18 - (25)(48/100]^2}{(25)(48/100)}$$

$$= \frac{(7 - 5.75)^2}{5.75} + \frac{(12 - 7.25)^2}{7.25} + \frac{(6 - 12)^2}{12} + \frac{(9 - 5.75)^2}{5.75}$$

$$+ \frac{(8 - 7.25)^2}{7.25} + \frac{(8 - 12)^2}{12} + \frac{(4 - 5.75)^2}{5.75}$$

$$+ \frac{(5 - 7.25)^2}{7.25} + \frac{(16 - 12)^2}{12} + \frac{(3 - 5.75)^2}{5.75}$$

$$+ \frac{(4 - 7.25)^2}{7.25} + \frac{(18 - 12)^2}{12}$$

$$= (.27) + (3.11) + (3.0) + (1.84) + (.08) + (1.33) + (.53) + (.70)$$
$$+ (1.33) + (1.32) + (1.46) + (3.0)$$
$$= 17.968 \qquad df = (4 - 1)(3 - 1) = 6$$

Had we, in fact, obtained this value, we would conclude that there is a shift in the transitions of consequents C_1, C_2, C_3 following antecedent A_i. Inspection of the matrix clearly indicates that the probability of the behavior pair $A_i \rightarrow C_3$ is more likely in behavior blocks 3 and 4 than in behavior blocks 1 and 2.

In this example, only one antecedent, A_i, was examined. If there is interest in other antecedents of those possible consequents, the preceding process is repeated with a new transition table created for each antecedent of interest. In addition, it is also possible to test the hypothesis of stable or constant transitions from all antecedents. This is accomplished by performing the preceding test for each antecedent, A_i, and summing the resultant χ_i^2. The test statistic is

$$\chi^2 = \sum_i \sum_b \sum_j \frac{[f_{ij}(b) - f_i^A(b)(f_{ij}/f_i^A)]^2}{f_i^A(b)(f_{ij}/f_i^A)}$$

which is asymptotically distributed as chi-square, with $I(J - 1)(B - 1)$ degrees of freedom.

The reader may be interested in other analyses of contingency tables, some of which provide alternatives to the methods presented throughout this chapter. Castellan (1979) provides a useful summary of these procedures, along with guidelines for appropriate use of these statistics.

Methodological Considerations

If we step back for a moment and place this chapter in the context of a research plan, it is clear that the material deals mostly with rather late-occurring activities, that is, data reduction and analysis.

As with any analytic tool, sequential analysis is only as good as the data with which it has to work. The issues of reliability and validity of observational data and cognitive performance data are of critical importance. Though not discussed, it is assumed that the user of the analysis strategies discussed in this chapter has first addressed the reliability and validity of the variables under study. Once the researcher is convinced that the measurements are meaningful, it is then appropriate to proceed with the analyses.

Determining reliability for sequential analyses deserves a special comment. In computing a reliability estimate, it makes the most sense to strive for consistency between the level of analysis and the level of inference demanded of the data. If one is interested in comparing the relative frequency of code occurrences, then it is appropriate to estimate reliability of the coding schedule on the overall distribution of coding results. However, if one is interested in determining sequential dependencies, it is necessary to compute reliability estimates with respect to the basic unit entering the analysis, a time or behavior block. Thus comparison of rates of agreement between two coders across an entire setting is not appropriate for sequential analysis. Instead, reliability must be estimated for each time or behavior block. Further discussion of strategies for estimating reliability coefficients can be found in Haynes (1978), Kent and Foster (1977), and Mitchell (1979).

As anyone who has studied interaction knows, a tremendous amount of data is generated. For this reason, it is wise for the experimenter to specify the questions of interest prior to getting swamped by a mass of "potentially" significant information. There is always room to explore interesting hypotheses in the context of understanding one's results; however, without a clear path through observational data, it is all too possible to get lost.

There are also several potential problems that researchers should be aware of when doing sequential analysis. One problem concerns the stability of contingencies under study. In most applications, an experimenter considers data from a whole period of observation and makes an implicit assumption that contingencies between variables are stable or constant over the observation period(s). If there is reason to suspect that the contingencies change after point p, then this assumption is violated. As discussed previously, if there are a sufficient number of observations, it is then possible to assess the stability of the contingencies prior to pooling the data from an entire session.

Bakeman *et al.* (1979) identify a potential problem with the unit of analysis in sequential analyses. Researchers developing coding systems have tended to observe and encode elemental behavioral units. This strategy optimizes reliability but results in a "microscopic" level of analysis. Bakeman *et al.* point out that patterns of acts (e.g., "themes") should be considered along with the small, elemental units of analysis that are typically focused on. In working only with discrete events, it is possible to ignore processes that govern larger, integrated behavioral events: "The information yielded by a contingency analysis of discrete acts may not be the same as an analysis of patterns, simply because the events that *elicit* patterns may not be the same as those that *maintain* their internal organization" (Bakeman *et al.*, 1979, p. 233).

Summary

This chapter has been concerned with methods of describing sequential dependencies in cognitive assessment situations. The techniques presented are based on the simple use of conditional probabilities to describe patterns in a behavioral stream. Although the techniques themselves are not complex, creating a situation that enables an assessment of a stream of cognitive events will present the researcher with a challenge.

In looking toward the future, the descriptive techniques offered in this chapter may provide a first step in building a *model* of cognitive performance. As we develop better tools for observing and describing behavioral and cognitive events, we will be better able to formulate and test models that can account for the phenomena identified through sequential analysis. In recognition of the speculative basis of this chapter in the area of cognitive assessment, it is fitting to note in closing that the theoretical utility of assessing sequential dependencies in cognitive assessment situations remains to be determined.

Reference Note

1. Sackett, G. P. *A nonparametric lag sequential analysis for studying dependency among responses in observational scoring systems.* Unpublished manuscript, University of Washington, 1974.

References

Bakeman, R. Untangling streams of behavior: Sequential analyses of observation data. In G. P. Sackett (Ed.), *Observing behavior* (Vol. II): *Data collection and analysis methods.* Baltimore: University Park Press, 1978.

Bakeman, R., Cairns, R. B., & Applebaum, M. Note on describing and analyzing interactional data: Some first steps and common pitfalls. In R. B. Cairns (Ed.), *The analysis of social interactions: Methods, issues, and illustrations.* Hillsdale, N.J.: Erlbaum, 1979.

Cacioppo, J. T., Glass, C. R., & Merluzzi, T. V. Self-statements and self-evaluations: A cognitive-response analysis of social anxiety. *Cognitive Therapy and Research,* 1979, *3,* 249-262.

Castellan, N. J. The analysis of behavior sequences. In R. B. Cairns (Ed.), *The analysis of social interactions: Methods, issues, and illustrations.* Hillsdale, N.J.: Erlbaum, 1979.

Gottman, J. M., Markman, H. J., & Notarius, C. I. The topography of marital conflict: A sequential analysis of verbal and nonverbal behavior. *Journal of Marriage and the Family,* 1977, *39,* 461-477.

Gottman, J. M., & Notarius, C. I. Sequential analysis of observational data using Markov chains. In T. Kratochwill (Ed.), *Strategies to evaluate change in single-subject research.* New York: Academic Press, 1978.

Gottman, J. M., Notarius, C. I., Markman, H. J., Bank, S., Yoppi, B., & Rubin, M. E. Behavior exchange theory and marital decision making. *Journal of Personality and Social Psychology,* 1976, *34,* 14-23.

Haynes, S. N. *Principles of behavioral assessment.* New York: Gardner Press, 1978.

Kendell, P. C., & Korgeski, G. P. Assessment and cognitive-behavior interventions. *Cognitive Therapy and Research,* 1979, *3,* 1-21.

Kent, R. N., & Foster, S. L. Direct observational procedures: Methodological issues in naturalistic settings. In A. R. Ciminero, K. S. Calhoun, & H. E. Adams (Eds.), *Handbook of behavioral assessment.* New York: Wiley, 1977.

Mitchell, S. K. Interobserver agreement, reliability, and generalizability of data collected in observational studies. *Psychological Bulletin,* 1979, *86,* 376-390.

Raush, H. L. Process and change—A Markov model of interaction. *Family Process,* 1972, *11,* 275–298.

Sackett, G. P. The lag sequential analysis of contingency and cyclicity in behavioral interaction research. In J. Osfsky (Ed.), *Handbook of infant development.* New York: Wiley, 1977.

Part III
Clinical Implications

12

Cognitive Assessment
of Depression

Brian F. Shaw and Keith S. Dobson

Introduction

Judging from the number of scientific publications alone, the study of cognitive factors in depression has received increasing attention in the past decade. There appears to be a "cognitive revolution" (Dember, 1974) in psychology, and some writers (e.g., Beck, 1967, 1976) have posited a primary role of cognition in the maintenance, if not the etiology, of depression. This chapter addresses the questions "How can we reliably measure depressive or depressogenic cognition?" and "What is the validity of these measurements?"

Neisser (1967, p. 4) defined "cognition" as "all the processes by which the sensory input is transformed, reduced, elaborated, stored, recovered, and used." As such, the cognitive processes include sensation, perception, imagery, attention, recall, memory, problem solving, and thinking; in short, all of the processes generally defined under the rubric of information processing (Mahoney, 1974) and problem solving (D'Zurilla & Goldfried, 1971). It is important to distinguish between cognitive content (e.g., images, assumptions, ideation, automatic thoughts) and cognitive processes (e.g., transfer of information from short-term memory to long-term memory). "Cognitive content," as used here, refers to individuals' self-reports of their thinking (i.e., their ideation). "Cognitive processes" are the set of heuristic postulates derived from cognitions.

Brian F. Shaw • Departments of Psychiatry and Psychology, University Hospital and The University of Western Ontario, London, Ontario, Canada.
Keith S. Dobson • Department of Psychiatry, The University of Western Ontario, London, Ontario, Canada.

As will be seen later, most efforts to study cognitive factors in depression have focused on descriptions of the cognitions related to depression. The processes by which stimuli are transformed, reduced, elaborated, stored, recovered, and used have understandably received less attention. Information about cognitive content can be obtained rather simply from the self-reports of subjects. Data on the cognitive processes in depression, however, must be inferred from individuals' reports or behavior and must be viewed from a theoretical perspective. The data obtained are a function of the adequacy of the experimental conditions used (e.g., see Paivio, 1975). Typically, the assessment of cognition has involved traditional psychometric methods, experimental paradigms from cognitive psychology have only recently been employed.

Before beginning our excursion toward a better understanding of the cognitive assessment of depression, we will map our plan. The chapter is written in three major sections: (1) a review of past empirically based attempts to describe cognitive variables associated with depression; (2) a review of current research strategies; and (3) a discussion of directions for future investigations. The term "depression" refers to the rather complex group of affective, cognitive, behavioral, and physiological changes that many investigators consider a syndrome (see Beck, 1967, or Feighner, Robins, Guze, Woodruff, Winokur, & Muñoz, 1972). We have excluded findings on manic–depressive patients, as these individuals may be different in their cognitive responses (Dupue & Monroe, 1978; Miller, 1975).

We will distinguish between subtypes of depressives where possible. Subtyping in depression as it relates to cognition is poorly understood. Many clinicians and researchers endorse the reactive–endogenous dichotomy, whereas others prefer different groupings (e.g., psychotic–neurotic, primary–secondary). The debate continues, but, clearly, subtypes that have predictive validity with respect to variables such as treatment outcome or suicidal risk are most desirable. Studies that concern depressed mood, as opposed to the syndrome of depression, will be identified as such. Similarly, studies using analog populations (e.g., college students) will also be identified to avoid risky overgeneralizations (see Shaw, 1979).

Contributions of Cognitive Assessment to Depression Research

The assessment of cognitive contents and processes related to depression is important for at least four reasons. First, assessment serves to describe the cognitive phenomena of depression. These descriptive studies have much to offer when relatively little is known about the psychological characteristics of the population of interest. Data of this type are necessary for describing the range of cognitive changes in depression and, perhaps more important, for differentiating cognitive phenomena that are unique to depression. Differential diagnosis is concerned with the characteristic onset, course, and prognosis of a disorder, and thus cognitions that differentiate groups hold the most promise.

Second, cognitive assessment serves to elicit the formulation of theories of depression in which the functional relationship of cognition and depression can be considered (e.g., see Blaney, 1977; Shaw & Beck, 1977). Assessment based on the theoretical models of depression may be used to predict the onset, course, and termination of the disorder. In addition, using these data, persons at risk for depression (Shaw, 1979) and the variables (e.g., personality, biochemical, behavioral) related to potentially predisposing cognitive factors may be discovered.

Third, assessment data may provide new information about cognitive processes. Our understanding about how knowledge is represented and processed (Siegler, 1976) is limited. The assessment of cognition in depression has the potential of providing data concerning information processing. For example, what are the effects of mood on memory, or what is the probability of certain stimuli eliciting specific schemas? This potential has been only minimally pursued (e.g., Bower, Montiero, & Gilligan, 1978; Kuiper & Derry, 1980), but as long as standard cognitive psychology paradigms are employed, the population of depressed subjects serves as a useful validation group.

Fourth, if cognitive variables are shown to be functionally related to depression, then cognitive–behavioral clinicians and researchers will be able to determine the changes in cognition that occur as a function of treatment. Psychotherapists, in particular, will require information about the quality and quantity of cognitive change necessary to treating a person's depression or to preventing future depressive episodes. This type of information can only be provided within the range of fidelity offered by cognitive assessment.

Characteristic Cognitions and Cognitive Processes in Depression

Within the content of cognition as defined by Neisser (1967), six different areas of assessment have developed. The areas are (1) perception, (2) imagery, (3) memory, (4) attribution, (5) problem solving, and (6) thinking styles and constructs. In this section we intend to review the major studies citing examples of assessment in these six areas.

Perception

A number of studies have revealed possible perceptual deficits associated with depression (see Miller, 1975, for a review). In general, depressed individuals, compared to a mixed group of neurotics, require more intense heat stimuli and greater muscular work before reporting pain or physically withdrawing from the stimulus (Hemphill, Hall, & Crookes, 1962). Depressed patients also show increased visual threshold changes in response to emotional words (Dixon & Lear, 1962).

Negative Self-Perception. If one views perception from a broad perspective, subsuming the individual's percepts of the self, prior experiences, and the future (using Beck's cognitive triad, 1967, 1976), then this area has easily received the most attention from researchers. The outstanding characteristic of depressive self-percepts is their negative valence. Lewinsohn and his colleagues (Lewinsohn, Mischel, Chaplin, & Barton, 1980; Lewinsohn & Muñoz, Note 1; Lewinsohn & Talkington, Note 2) have repeatedly suggested that depressed individuals have a negative perception expressed in expectancies for their performance. For example, Lewinsohn *et al.* (1980) demonstrated that depressed individuals rated themselves as less socially competent than a nondepressed control group. Interestingly, this perception was also validated by the nondepressed controls, who rated the depressives as being less socially competent. The depressives thus appeared to be "realistic." In fact, the control group subjects were found to perceive themselves more favorably than they were seen by others, suggesting what Lewinsohn *et al.* (1980) described as an "illusory glow" in normal self-perception.

In a similar type of research paradigm, but using impersonal tasks (e.g., word associations, WAIS digit symbol), Lobitz and Post (1979) found a pattern of results similar to that of Lewinsohn *et al.* (1980). In their study, depressed and nondepressed psychiatric control subjects made ratings that were components of self-reinforcement. Included in these were ratings of self-expectation and self-evaluation, two types of self-perception. For both of these measures, the depressed subjects rated themselves both as having done worse after the task was completed and as likely to do worse in the future. Additionally, the depressed subjects rated "others" as more likely to succeed and to have done well. There were, however, no objective performance differences between groups.

Perception of Experiences. In the preceding types of research, Likert rating scales were employed to gather information about how depressed individuals view themselves. In a similar manner, depressed individuals have been compared to normals with respect to their perception of their experiences. For example, in a study in which subjects completed the Social Readjustment Rating Questionnaire (Holmes & Rahe, 1967) and the Beck Depression Inventory (BDI) (Beck, Ward, Mendelson, Mock, & Erbaugh, 1961), Schless, Schwartz, Goetz, and Mendels (1974) found that subjects who were depressed rated significantly more life change than nondepressed subjects. Similarly, Hammen (1978) administered to a large group of college students the Life Events Inventory (Cochrane & Robertson, 1973), the BDI (Beck *et al.*, 1961), and a measure of cognitive distortion originally used in a study by Hammen and Krantz (1976). Depressed subjects who experienced increasing amounts of life change manifested decreasing levels of cognitive distortion.

Depressed subjects with low life stress, in particular, appeared to distort more than other subjects.

Two laboratory tasks have been used to examine depressive perceptions of subjects' experiences. The first approach involves the experimental manipulation of reinforcement given to subjects. In the earliest of these studies, Wener and Rehm (1975), using a contrived social task, demonstrated that depressed subjects underestimated the absolute number of times they had produced a correct response. These results suggest either a selective attentional factor or selective negative recall of success in depression.

Nelson and Craighead (1977) extended the findings of Wener and Rehm (1975) by providing depressed and nondepressed students with both positive and negative feedback about their performance. As was predicted, the depressed subjects systematically distorted the positive feedback in a negative direction. Interestingly, the nondepressed subjects systematically distorted the negative feedback in a positive direction (the normal positive bias). Thus, in keeping with the cognitive theory of depression (Beck, 1967), both groups appeared to have a cognitive schema about themselves that potentiated the misperception, selective attention, or remembrance of one type of feedback.

Because the studies by Wener and Rehm (1975) and Nelson and Craighead (1977) had been conducted with college students, DeMonbreun and Craighead (1977) investigated the perceptions of hospitalized depressed patients using the same experimental task as Nelson and Craighead. Their study also attempted to extend Nelson and Craighead's study by determining whether cognitive biases manifested by depressives and normal subjects were manifested with neutral feedback. They tested subjects' immediate perceptions and, later, subjects' recall of the feedback. A negative feedback condition was not employed. For high rates of positive feedback only, the depressed subjects distorted the information in a negative manner, thus replicating Nelson and Craighead's results. Under neutral feedback conditions, however, no differences between the groups were obtained. The distortions obtained were noted only at the time of delayed recall; no subject group was inaccurate in its immediate perception of the feedback given.

More recently, the status of these results has been called into question. An attempt to replicate the DeMonbreun and Craighead (1977) results by Craighead, Hickey, and DeMonbreun (1979) has been unsuccessful. Clearly, more work of this type is needed in order to show when the cognitive distortions occur (i.e., whether at the immediate perception or later).

The other major laboratory task used to evaluate depressives' perceptions of their experiences or of the world involves the ratings of others (person perception). Lunghi (1977) measured the interpersonal evaluations of depressed inpatients and normal controls. He found that depressives tend toward poorer self-ratings and more negative evaluations of their relationships. He suggested that the negative views of depressives were either accurate or a function of a generalized negative bias. Steiner (1975) found simi-

lar results in his study of depressed female college students. The depressed
subjects rated themselves as interpersonally incompetent.

In the consideration of depressives' perceptions of others, Coyne's
(1976) discussion of the interaction between the depressed person and his or
her environment is important. Coyne (1976) emphasized the "changing environment" of the depressive, in which "irritated, yet inhibited and increasingly guilt-ridden, members of the social environment continue to give verbal
assurance of support and acceptance" (p. 34). In this situation the verbal
messages are not concordant with the affective time, and the depressed person is unable to determine the true nature of the social relationships.

Meltzer (Note 3) pursued the question of a differential mood response to
others in a task involving visual and audio stimuli. She presented slides of
people whose faces reflected happiness, neutrality, or hostility, along with
audiotaped passages of positive, neutral, or negative communication, to a
group of seven depressed inpatients and seven normal controls matched on
age. The depressed group was not significantly different from the control
group on a measure of affective reactivity (i.e., changes in mood as a function
of mixed communications).

The attempt to examine the perceptions of interpersonal relationships
may lead to a better understanding of the social behavior of depressed persons. It would be useful to employ an *in vivo* procedure to test the congruence
between the depressives' ratings of their social interactions and the perceptions of others. A number of variables could be considered, including the
"mixed message" of supportive statements given by others in an angry tone
(Coyne, 1976).

Future Time Perspective. The final area of study on the perceptions of
depressed patients concerns their future time perspective. There is strongly
uniform evidence that depressives anticipate future failure. The negative expectations are manifested in the expression of hopelessness (cf. Erickson,
Post, & Paige, 1975). The assessment of hopelessness has received considerable attention. Beck, Weissman, Lester, and Trexler (1974) devised the
Hopelessness Scale to quantify the degree of negative expectancy. The Hopelessness Scale consists of 20 items and has high internal reliability and strong
concurrent validity (Beck *et al.,* 1974). The value of the scale resides in the
clinical importance of hopelessness and, in particular, in the predictive significance that hopelessness has for suicide (Minkoff, Bergman, Beck, & Beck,
1973).

A number of investigators (e.g., Melges & Bowlby, 1969; Stuart, 1962)
have found an association between depression and a restricted time perspective. Depressives tend toward a past orientation (Dilling & Rabin, 1967), conceptualize smaller intervals of time in the future (Miller, 1975), and even
given inaccurate estimates of time intervals (Mezey & Cohen, 1961). Furthermore, it appears that hopelessness is the major mediating variable between

depression and suicidal behavior (Beck, Kovacs, & Weissman, 1979; Wetzel, 1976).

The study of expectancies for future outcome as a function of skilled behavior has constituted a major research thrust in the psychology of depression. Briefly, the experimental paradigm involves engaging the subject in a problem-solving task and eliciting his or her predictions of outcome (e.g., "There's an 80% chance I'll fail"). Success or failure feedback is typically provided, and the expectancies of subjects are measured following this experimentally controlled manipulation.

The learned helplessness model of depression (Seligman, 1974) predicts that depressed persons, compared to other psychologically disordered individuals, perceive reinforcement in skills tasks as more independent of their responses. One method of testing this model has been to assess changes in expectancies using the aforementioned design. Abramson, Garber, Edwards, and Seligman (1978) found that unipolar depressed inpatients showed *smaller* changes in expectancy of future success after failure than did normal and schizophrenic control groups. This finding is consistent with the view that responding and reinforcement are perceived as independent. In contrast to these findings, Smolen (1978) assessed a group of depressed patients on a skilled task and found that their expectancy changes were essentially the same as the controls. Notably, the Abramson, Garber, Edwards, and Seligman (1978) study carefully assessed and controlled for the presence of schizophrenia, whereas Smolen (1978) combined depressed schizophrenics and depressed nonschizophrenics. The difference in diagnosis may account for the discrepant findings.

There have been other studies on expectancy during skilled problem-solving tasks, and these are discussed in the section on problem solving.

Imagery

The detection of possible imaging differences between depressives and normals is an area that has not been pursued. In fact, only one investigation was found that directly assessed the imagery styles of depressives. In this study (Jessup & Baker, Note 4) college volunteers were split into high- and low-depression groups on the basis of their BDI scores. They were then instructed either to imagine or to narrate verbally their reactions to different scenes (positive, neutral, or negative types). Eight ratings, such as vividness, depressiveness, anxiousness, and interest, were requested once the scene was imaged. The nonverbal scenes were rated as more vivid, stronger, and less able to generate a happy mood. There were no differences in the processing styles (e.g., visual versus verbal) of depressives and controls.

In another study the influence of imagery on mood was called into question (Craighead, Kimball, & Rehak, 1979). Although these authors did not define their research groups on the basis of depression, they failed to find an influence of social rejection imagery on negative affect, as might be expected if imagery mediated depression in college students. Imagery has received insufficient attention to consider what future projects need to be undertaken. Preferences for verbal versus visual imagery may be one area of study in the future.

Encoding, Recall, and Memory

Tulving (1962) demonstrated that, in the recall of putatively "unrelated" words, idiosyncratic clustering occurs. Research has shown that the recall of material in depressives is organized in such a way that negative material has a higher probability of recall than positively valenced material. Lishman (1972) presented subjects with a word list with both positively and negatively toned words and found that the depressed subjects' recall of negative words was significantly better than their recall of positive words. Lloyd and Lishman (1975) further established that the severity of depression is significantly related to the speed of recall of pleasant and unpleasant experiences. With increased levels of depression, more negative material was recalled. Interestingly, this result disappeared when the subjects were retested following remission of the depression. Thus depressed persons' recalling of negatively toned material may be specific to the time of the depressive period.

Laboratory studies investigating the recall aspects of depressive cognitions have tended to corroborate the notion that depressives recall negative material better than positive material. As noted previously, depressed subjects, compared to normals, underestimate the amount of "correct" feedback they have received following a skill task (Wener & Rehm, 1975). Other studies using a similar methodology (i.e., providing different levels of reinforcement) have revealed that depressed subjects recall more punishment and less reinforcement than nondepressed subjects (DeMonbreun & Craighead, 1977; Nelson & Craighead, 1977).

A critical question in the research on recall biases in depression is whether the biases reflect retrieval or encoding problems. This is the issue of "encoding specificity" (Tulving & Thompson, 1973). The recall of material appears to depend on two factors: (1) what is encoded or perceived, in the sense of registering in short-term memory, and (2) what is retrieved, or the effectiveness of recall cues (Klatzky, 1975). Some preliminary work by Davis (1979) has shown that, by using a depth-of-processing encoding model (Craik & Lockhart, 1972), differences between college student depressives and normals are shown in incidental recall *only* when the items asked for recall are pertinent to the self. Davis has termed this reponse "self-referent encoding." He posits that the self-referent encoding differences found in depression result from the existence of a negative self-schema. It is the negative schema that allows the encoding of words concordant with the self-image at the time. Further, he showed that the longer the depressive episode, the stronger the negative self-referential recall. This finding suggests a developmental aspect of negative schemas: longer periods of use are related to a more pervasive schema.

There is considerable uncertainty about the existence of actual memory deficits in depression. The term "memory deficit" is typically used to describe a performance decrement attributable to a deficit in any stage of a standard memory model (see Atkinson & Shiffrin, 1968; Bransford, 1979; Norman, 1969). It is, however, generally accepted that depressed patients complain of memory impairments (Kahn, Zarit, Hilbert, & Niederehe, 1975; Sternberg & Jarvik, 1976).

Some studies (Glass, Uhlenhuth, & Weinreb, 1978; Levy & Maxwell, 1968; Russell & Beckhuis, 1976) have concluded that depression is associated with objective memory deficits, whereas others (Miller & Lewis, 1977) have not found differences between depressed and control groups. One serious problem with the research on memory functioning in depression is the confounding of potentially significant variables. First, many of the studies include patients who have received antidepressant medication and/or electroconvulsive treatment. The effects of these treatments that may be associated with memory are serious confounds because these treatments are almost always used with depressed patients only. Second, the sample of subjects studied is frequently restricted to the elderly, and, again, it is impossible at present to differentiate the effects of the interaction between age and depression.

Attribution

There has been a recent articulation of the attributional reformulation of the learned helplessness model of depression (Abramson, Seligman, & Teasdale, 1978). Coincident with the reformulation of learned helplessness, there has been a plethora of studies examining various aspects of attributional processes in depression. Although the basic status of the learned helplessness model as a viable model of depression remains uncertain (Buchwald, Coyne, & Cole, 1978; Wortman & Dintzer, 1978) it is worthwhile to discuss the research findings related to attribution processes in depression.

In general, the new model (see special issue of the *Journal of Abnormal Psychology,* 1978) predicts that, following failure, depressives tend to make internal attributions (effort, skill), whereas nondepressives tend to make external attributions (luck, task difficulty). Conversely, following success, depressives tend to make external attributions. This general pattern has been reported several times with a college student sample (Fitch, 1970; Kuiper, 1978; Rizley, 1978) and appears to be fairly robust with respect to the particulars of the experimental procedure.

These findings corroborate earlier research (Miller & Ross, 1975; Sobel, 1974; Stevens & Jones, 1976) and are comprehensible within the framework of self-serving biases. That is, by adopting the aforementioned attributional style, normals can maintain their positive views about themselves even in the face of low rates of reinforcement. The attributions adopted by the depressives, however, are not understandable from the point of view of self-serving biases as it is not self-enhancing to attribute failure to oneself. As a function of a depressive cognitive schema (Beck, 1967, 1976; Beck & Shaw, 1977), it may be that the attributional style of depressives is concordant with their perceptions about themselves. One important area for future research will be to determine if the attributions made by depressives under success and failure feedback are specific to the depressive condition, or if this style is a more pervasive approach or trait.

In the area of attribution, it will be critical to determine whether differences exist between clinical depressives and analogue subjects. The relationship between various types of situations and responses and the attributions functionally related to depression also need to be assessed. For example, it will be important to understand attributions of depressives with the Abramson, Seligman, and Teasdale (1978) framework across different situations and under different conditions.

One study (Breiter, Note 5) evaluated goal setting (i.e., expectations for future success) on a social judgment test, as well as attribution ratings after the testing. One important methodological point concerned subject definition. Breiter (Note 5) studied two groups of subjects who scored as depressed on the BDI and the D30 scale (Dempsey, 1964). One group (labeled "depressed") met the additional inclusion criteria of probable depression using the Feighner *et al.* (1972) diagnostic criteria. The second group (labeled "sad") did not meet this additional criteria. Interestingly, members of the "sad" group made significantly more internal attributions for their performance than did members of the normal control and "depressed" groups. The ratio of internal and external attributions of the depressed group and the normal controls did not differ. In this study, success and failure feedback was not given as in past studies. Nevertheless, the findings do suggest that greater attention be given to the generalizability of analogue studies.

The assessment of attributional patterns of depressed persons will undoubtedly be facilitated by the attributional style scale developed by Semmel, Abramson, Seligman, and vonBaeyer (Note 6). This scale was used in the Seligman, Abramson, Semmel, and vonBaeyer (1979) study of college students. One important feature of the scale is that it assesses three attributional dimensions relevant to learned helplessness: internal–external, stable–unstable, and global–specific (see Abramson, Seligman, & Teasdale, 1978).

Problem Solving

"Problem solving" as defined by D'Zurilla and Goldfried (1971) involves the identification of the problem, the generation of possible solutions, the selection of one possible solution (decision making), and an assessment of the efficacy of the chosen solution. We are aware of only a few studies that have examined possible deficits in these stages of problem-solving ability for depressives. Depression has not generally been shown to be associated with intellectual deterioration (Miller, 1975). Similarly, there is some evidence that the actual performance of depressed individuals on problem-solving tasks is equivalent to that of controls.

Two types of problems have been employed. First, a number of studies (Loeb, Beck, & Diggory, 1971; Giles, Note 7; Shaw, Note 8) have examined depressives' abilities to complete tasks such as card sorting (a task assessing visuo-motor skills) and anagrams (Sacco & Hokanson, 1978). Second, two studies (Giles, Note 7; Gotlib & Asarnow, 1979) examined the interpersonal problem-solving abilities of depressives.

Impersonal Abilities. Loeb *et al.* (1971) employed the card-sorting method to assess depressives' perceptions. In addition, however, they computed an actual performance score (i.e., the average number of seconds taken to sort each card) and found no performance differences between the depressed and nondepressed male outpatients. Shaw (Note 8) replicated this finding in a group of depressed and normal control college students, and Giles (Note 7) replicated the Loeb *et al.* (1971) study with female inpatients in depressed, nondepressed psychiatric, and normal groups. Smolen (1978) compared depressed and nondepressed psychiatric patients on card-sorting and peg-sorting tasks and also failed to find significant performance differences.

Sacco and Hokanson (1978) studied depressed and nondepressed college students' abilities to solve anagrams, using three dependent variables: number of failures, number of trials required to learn the anagram pattern, and average response latency. There were no significant group differences in anagram performance. Gotlib and Asarnow (1979) evaluated depressed and nondepressed students and found no group differences on anagram performance. A study by Dobson and Dobson (in press) has shown that an important variable in impersonal problem-solving studies is the difficulty of the task employed. In that study, a task was employed that required analogue depressive subjects to solve problems under a variety of different semantic rules of increasing difficulty. Although the major problem-solving variable did not distinguish between the two groups, there was a significant interaction between rule difficulty and the groups. Only for the two most difficult problems were there significant group differences.

Interpersonal Problem-Solving Abilities. One interpersonal task that has been used by several investigators is the Means–End Problem-Solving (MEPS) task (Platt & Spivack, 1972). The MEPS requires subjects to produce a means for a person to achieve some goal in a social conflict situation. As such, it is a measure of interpersonal problem-solving ability. In a study comparing depressed college students to their nondepressed counterparts,

Krumm (Note 9) did not observe significant differences in the total number of means provided or in the number of coping means produced. These negative findings were replicated with independent groups of depressed and nondepressed college students (Giles, Dobson, & Shaw, Note 10).

In clinical populations, however, significant differences have been noted between depressives and nondepressed subjects. Giles (Note 7) demonstrated that depressed female inpatients provided significantly fewer relevant solutions to the MEPS problems. In addition, Gotlib and Asarnow (1979), in their study of depressed and nondepressed students, noted signficant differences between groups on the number of relevant means for the MEPS situations. Taken as a whole, these results suggest that, although depressives may not have a general problem-solving deficit, at least some manifest a deficiency in their interpersonal capabilities. Further research is needed to identify the salient characteristics of the deficient subjects.

Unfortunately, very few problem-solving studies of the type proposed by D'Zurilla and Goldfried (1971) have been completed in the area of depression. Thus, although the use of such assessment techniques as the MEPS provides a way in which to assess one stage of problem solving as defined by D'Zurilla and Goldfried (1971), namely, generation of alternatives, most of the other aspects of problem solving remain unexplored. If researchers and clinicians are to understand how problem definition and decision making occur in depression, a more rigorous examination of the component processes (such as orientation to problems, interpretation of problems, establishment of coping alternatives, decision making, solution implementation, and verification) is necessary.

Thinking Styles and Constructs

Thinking styles and personal constructs have been investigated in depressives in three major ways: through specification of thinking errors, identification of automatic thoughts or irrational belief systems, and assessment of the nature of response biases such as conservatism.

Identifying Thinking Errors. Beck (1970) proposed a typology of thinking errors found in depression. Following his general view that depressives distort reality, he identified the following errors (pp. 190–191):

1. "Arbitrary inference"—the process of drawing a conclusion in the absence of evidence to support the conclusion.
2. "Selective abstraction"—the process of focusing on a detail taken out of context and conceptualizing the entire experience on the basis of this element, thereby ignoring other, more salient features of the situation.
3. "Overgeneralization"—the process of drawing a general conclusion on the basis of a single incident.

4. "Magnification and minimization"—the process of evaluating situations in a manner that reflects a distortion of the incident or of its significance.

Krantz and Hammen (1979) developed a questionnaire to assess depressive distortion, encompassing many of the thinking errors noted by Beck (1970). The questionnaire consists of six stories, followed by items that belong in one of four categories (i.e., combinations of depressed–nondepressed and distorted–nondistorted dimensions). Three of the stories had mainly "social–interpersonal themes," and the other three had "predominantly achievement competence themes." Krantz and Hammen (1979) studied a range of populations (from college students to inpatients) and concluded that the relatively more depressed (defined as depressed mood) subjects had significantly higher depressive–distortion scores. One problem with this research, understandable in its early phase, is that the situations used were relevant to college students and had to be adapted for inpatients. On the other hand, the type of situation (interpersonal vs. achievement) did not influence the major findings, and thus the situational characteristics may not be a powerful factor.

Stake, Warren, and Rogers (Note 11) explored the relationship among coping strategies, cognitive distortions, and depression in a study of 211 college undergraduates (119 women and 92 men). They developed an objectively scored measure of maladaptive thinking, the "interpretation inventory." This inventory consists of 21 questions, each consisting of an event, a distorted cognitive response to the event, and a 5-point quantitative rating from "never" to "always." Coping strategies were measured by an adaption of Rippere's (1977) list of strategies.

Subjects who had high cognitive-distortion scores and who indicated using a limited repertoire of coping strategies had the highest depression scores. High cognitive-distortion scores combined with many coping strategies, however, resulted in depression scores in the normal range. This finding supports Rippere's (1977) idea that individual coping strategies must be considered in the theory and treatment of depression.

Weintraub, Segal, and Beck (1974) developed a "cognitive total test," a story completion test with five introductions, to assess depressive cognitive content. In a sample of male college student volunteers, they showed a significant association between negative cognitive content and depressed mood. The reliability and validity of this instrument have not been pursued.

Any of these tests may be useful in identifying the thinking errors uniquely related to depression. The Weintraub *et al.* (1974) test could be extended to examine cognitive distortion as well as content. It is important to recognize that thinking errors are not necessarily unique to depression (Krantz & Hammen, 1979); thus research examining depressed subjects versus other psychologically disordered groups is indicated.

Identifying Depressive Thoughts or Beliefs. The second way in which thinking styles have been investigated is through questionnaires tapping depressive thoughts or beliefs. In cognitive therapy (Beck, Rush, Shaw, & Emery, 1979), two main levels of intervention are utilized: interventions to alter specific automatic thoughts and interventions to modify assumptions or beliefs that are assumed to be related to depression. Instruments to assess these two levels of thinking have been developed.

Hollon and Kendall (1980) devised a 30-item questionnaire to measure the frequency of occurrence of automatic negative thoughts associated with depression. College undergraduates were used as subjects in the initial construction and cross-validation of the scale. The "automatic thoughts questionnaire" score discriminated between psychometrically depressed and nondepressed groups; thus the first stage of validation of the instrument has been accomplished.

To assess assumptions or beliefs, two scales have been employed: the "dysfunctional attitude scale" (Weissman & Beck, Note 12) and Jones's (1968) Irrational Beliefs Test. Nelson (1977) assessed the correlation between the IBT and the BDI with college students. The IBT assesses the extent to which the person adheres to ten of the beliefs that were proposed by Ellis (1962) to underlie psychological disturbance. There was a moderate correlation ($r = +.53$) between these measures.

Weissman and Beck (Note 12) have started a series of investigations on the dysfunctional attitude scale. The initial objective was to determine the relationship between attitudes and a tendency to become depressed. The scale, developed with undergraduates, consists of two parallel forms of 40 items designed to assess maladaptive beliefs. Like all of the scales assessing discrete thoughts or beliefs, this scale requires further investigation.

Beck's (1967, 1974, 1976; Beck, Rush, Shaw, & Emery, 1979) assumption of schemata that in some manner predispose an individual to depression has been central to many of the attempts to operationalize a depressogenic thinking style. Beck and Shaw (1977) have stated:

> Depression is likely to be precipitated when a depression-prone individual (i.e., an individual who has incorporated a constellation of negative schemas) is either subjected to specific stresses which activate this negative self-schema or to a series of specific events which are not highly structured individually but have an additive effect. (p. 125)

Currently, only the dysfunctional attitude scale is an attempt to assess directly an individual's susceptibility to the stresses that might eventuate in depression. Later in the chapter we will introduce other methods of approaching this issue.

Assessing the Nature of Response Biases. The third area relevant to thinking style is the notion of "conservatism," that is, the measurable "bias" characterized by the individual who responds only when he or she is certain of the "correct" answer. Conservatism is particularly problematic for the assessment of cognitive functioning (e.g., memory assessment), but the bias may also produce problems in the person's daily living. For example, the depressed individual may avoid situations in which there is uncertainty because of a general sense of perceived incompetence (Golin, Terrell, Wetiz, & Drost, 1979.)

One example of the potential confounding introduced by a conservative response style is illustrated by Miller and Lewis's (1977) study. They found that the depressives' nonverbal recognition memory was similar to that of the normals. The depressed patients, however, adopted a more conservative response strategy, which was significantly different from a group of demented patients and normal controls (matched for age and sex). There were a number of problems that restrict generalization of the results, such as the use of the recognition memory task with no control for intellectual functioning and the restricted age range (the actual range was not presented, but all subjects were over 65, and the mean was 77 years). Nevertheless, the signal detection methodology used by Miller and Lewis (1977) was valuable in distinguishing subjects who performed badly because of poor memory from those who performed badly because of altered decision processes.

Conservatism in depression has also been demonstrated in depressed college students (defined by BDI scores). Using a task in which a card-selection strategy leads to the solution of a problem, Dobson and Dobson (in press) demonstrated that depressed college students used more cards than nondepressed controls to solve the problems, thus implicating a more conservative strategy. By continuing to choose cards that offered them only redundant information, they demonstrated a desire to be certain of their response before offering it to the experimenter. Interestingly, these differences betwteen depressives and controls became more acute as the difficulty of the problem increased.

Current Strategies in the Cognitive Assessment of Depression

This section is a biased presentation of current cognitive research in depression—biased, because we will focus primarily on the work from our laboratories. The main purpose is to provide information about new approaches, methodologies, and problematic areas. The studies in this section move from descriptive to theoretical investigations and include such content areas as expectancy and depression, the role of situations in depression, thinking errors, and methods for assessing the depressive cognitive schema.

The Relationship of Depression to Other Aspects of Psychotherapy

One problem we have identified in the cognitive assessment of depression is the relationship of depression to other aspects of psychopathology. This problem is perhaps best illustrated by the cognitive theory of depression

(Beck & Shaw, 1977; Shaw, 1979), which posits a negative view of the self as a primary factor in depression. If one considers the negative view of the self (or negative self-concept or negative self-theory), it quickly becomes apparent that this construct is a broad one and that it is associated with other psychological disorders as well as depression. Epstein (1973) provides an excellent review of the self-concept. There is considerable clinical and research evidence to suggest that a negative self-concept has a significant relationship to conditions such as anxiety (Epstein, Note 13) and schizophrenia (Epstein, 1973). Thus it appears that we are left with a long road to follow in developing predictive, cognitive instruments of depression versus anxiety or schizophrenia.

We have started investigations in the attempt to disengage anxiety from depression. Dobson (1980) constructed a scale to assess tendencies toward depression using an interactional model (cf. Endler & Magnussen's work on anxiety, 1976). Within the interactional approach to anxiety, it is recognized that the interaction between situations and persons (including cognitions) accounts for at least as much variance as either aspect alone. In a similar vein, it may be that depressive cognitions are required for depression, but a depressogenic situation is also required; interaction between certain cognitions and certain situations may be necessary to precipitate a clinical depression. For example, Hammen (1978) found an interactional pattern of results in that a person's level of life stress interacted with the degree of cognitive distortion employed. Other work is needed to articulate more fully the relationship between certain thought processes and environmental stressors.

Dobson (1980) has constructed an interactional inventory to identify individuals prone to depression. As part of this construction, college student subjects rated a series of 69 situations as to their potential for invoking anxiety and depression. Results of factor analyses of these data, coupled with an analysis of the different anxiety and depression response patterns of males and females, have led to the construction of the "differential anxiety and depression inventory" (DADI). The situation scales for depression, in order of decreasing magnitude based upon the factor analyses, are presented in Table 1. Some of the preliminary results as to the properties of the depression scales are also presented, including test–retest reliabilities over 16-day intervals and standardized Cronbach alpha coefficients, the latter being an index of internal scale homogeneity.

As can be seen in Table 1, the types of situations that can engender depression appear to be relatively consistent between males and females—three of the four situations are the same. More interesting, perhaps, was the finding that the order of relative importance of the common situations is not the same for both sexes. At present, the DADI is undergoing further validation procedures. Preliminary studies aimed at employing the DADI to predict individuals' responses to different situations have also been started. These findings support the belief that the DADI will be useful in identifying in-

Table 1. Properties of the Differential Anxiety and Depression Inventory

Situation type	Mean[a]	SD	Coefficient α[b]	Test–retest reliability[c]
		Male form		
1. Anticipating situations	23.202	5.268	.683	.548
2. Assertiveness/persistence	23.874	5.943	.845	.454
3. Social exits	28.319	6.643	.856	.668
4. Physically dangerous	24.714	6.097	.850	.585
		Female form		
1. Social exits	27.293	8.326	.820	.678
2. Anticipating situations	22.955	6.824	.795	.806
3. Assertiveness/persistence	21.108	6.492	.848	.505
4. Artificial evaluation situations	19.955	5.878	.811	.558

Note. From Dobson (1980).
[a]For males, $n = 119$; for females, $n = 157$.
[b]For both males and females, $n = 40$.
[c]For males, $n = 45$; for females, $n = 46$.

dividual differences in the susceptibility of people to depressive situations.

Giles (Note 7) evaluated Beck's (1967) cognitive triad in depression. She compared depressed, nondepressed, and normal control female inpatients on two types of tasks, interpersonal and intrapersonal. One important finding was that the depressed subjects could be discriminated from the others on measures of expectancy of success, level of aspiration, and evaluation of their actual performance. Giles (1980) concluded that this set of cognitions reflected a decidedly negative bias in information processing.

Shaw (Note 8) analyzed similar rating data in an attempt to predict psychotherapy responders from nonresponders. He assessed two groups of depressed college students who were receiving some type of psychological therapy (cognitive therapy, behavioral social skills therapy, or nondirective therapy). These subjects were divided into two groups on the basis of the success of treatment, defined as a BDI score of less than 10. The probability-of-success estimate (the subject's rating of the chances of reaching a certain goal) was found to discriminate responders from nonresponders. This measure has been referred to by some investigators as a measure of one's self-concept (Loeb *et al.*, 1971).

Giles (Note 7) proposed that the negative cognitions in her study might be accounted for by the negative belief about the self. The data on expectancy rating appear to be important, because they reflect the individual's beliefs about his or her skilled behavior. The type of task is not a significant factor. This cognitive information can easily be correlated with behavioral measures such as the coping strategy used to obtain a range of subject responsiveness. Knowledge of cognitive and behavioral responses to specific skilled tasks may be predictive of treatment success—that is, if neither cognitions nor skilled behavior change, then the probability of relapse is higher. Giles and Shaw are currently following the patients from the Giles (Note 7) study in order to determine the predictive validity of the measures. It is important to determine the central cognitions in depression, and this type of assessment appears to be consistently related to depression.

Two safeguards to unwarranted conclusions are needed in future research. First, replication of studies is always important, particularly when a field is rapidly expanding. Second, constructs such as cognitive distortion need to be assessed and validated by a number of methods. Shaw, Croker, and Burns (Note 14) have undertaken a study to assess thinking errors in depression. They obtained groups of depressed inpatients (females) and normal control subjects and determined responses to a range of situations. These situations sampled areas such as failure to achieve a goal and interpersonal conflict. The subjects' responses were rated for the type and degree of distortion (following Beck's 1976 nosology). No differences were found between groups on the measure of cognitive distortion. However, the groups were differentiated on their self-reported use of a number of coping strategies. The correlation between the measure of cognitive distortions and the BDI was $+.60$ ($n = 26$, $p < .001$.) On the cognitive distortion measure, a wide variance of response was noted in the depressed group, indicating that some other variables (e.g., severity of depression, number of coping strategies) may be mediating the relationship between depression and cognitive distortion. This hypothesis is currently being pursued.

In future studies we will need to determine patterns of thinking that are *unique* to depression. Otherwise, the notion of cognitive distortion may simply reflect a general stress response. A simple confirmation of the degree of distress (and not necessarily the degree of psychopathology) would not be interesting from a theoretical perspective.

The Negative Self-Schema in Depression

A second construct frequently related to depression is the negative cognitive schema. We discussed one approach to the individual's view of the self, namely, the assessment of expectancies for success. Another way to assess the type of negative self-schema in depression is illustrated by the work of Kuiper and Derry (1980). These investigators employed the Craik and Lockhart

(1972) depth-of-processing paradigm to investigate the self-schema of depressed patients.

Recall that this is the same paradigm employed by Davis (1979). Kuiper and Derry (1980) proposed that depressed patients may not demonstrate the typical recall of self-referent material. (The authors used descriptive words from Jackson's Personality Research Form, 1974.) They suggested an encoding process in depression that required both positive *and* negative stimuli and not just the typical psychopathological adjectives usually used in this paradigm. Furthermore, they suggested covariation between depression and the degree of depressive content in the self-schema. They proposed that there is a point at which the individual's self-schema is in transition. When a person is mildly depressed, the schematic organization is disorganized, but it becomes more clearly negative with increasing depressive symptoms. This model appears to be similar to proposals of a disorganization in the self-schema that may or may not be associated with other types of psychopathology (e.g., schizophrenia).

Shaw (Note 15) and his colleagues designed a study to test the hypothesis that depression results in memory impairment. Standard instruments to measure intelligence and general memory functioning were employed. In addition, subjects were given two recognition memory tasks that allow a signal detection analysis of the data. Thus information about the individual's response style with the actual memory functioning was obtained in order to test the hypothesis that depressed patients are conservative (i.e., that they do not guess) in their responding to questions about their memory.

To date, only preliminary results on 15 unipolar depressed patients and 15 normals matched for sex and similar in age (mean ages of 47.6 and 43.4 years, respectively) can be reported. Our previous criticism of research without a psychiatric control group applies here. One finding deserves comment at this point. The groups differed significantly on the memory strength (d') measure from the verbal recognition memory test. This finding may reflect a true (i.e., unbiased by response style) memory deficit for verbal material. We are in the process of collecting more data, but the preliminary result underlines the need for cautious interpretation of theoretical notions such as cognitive schema that require verbal memory.

Future Studies

We are at a point where careful consideration must be given to the types of paradigms and methodologies employed in our assessment research. We should take note of the historical referent in the research of schizophrenia. For many years, researchers in schizophrenia have seemingly tracked down every identified cognitive deficit in patient populations. An almost infinite number of deficits can be alluded to today (Wynne, Cromwell, & Matthyse,

1978), although the final clinical import of these deficits remains at issue. Depression researchers would be well advised to attempt to tie their research to theory whenever possible.

One potentially advantageous paradigm is the information-processing model in which the assessment of cognitions is directly facilitated. As well, "led by a new paradigm, scientists adopt new instruments and look in new places" (Kuhn, 1970, p. 111). Because the information-processing paradigm is one that has been developed for the explicit purpose of assessing cognitive processes, depression researches who adopt this approach will be aided in their development of new methodologies. Broga and Neufeld (1980) present an excellent review of the information-processing model as used in schizophrenia.

There are other models and areas of investigation that can lead to new discoveries in depression. For example, the previously cited work on self-referential encoding (Davis, 1979; Kuiper, 1978) utilizes a relatively tight methodology to develop a theoretical system related to the self and to the manner in which a negative self-schema may be developed. This type of research is an explicit example of a theoretically derived investigation. Methodologically, these studies must determine whether deficits are a function of encoding biases or of retrieval processes. Nevertheless, the findings are tied to a predictive as well as descriptive model.

Another general area that requires extensive investigation is that of memory. As several writers have noted (Beck, 1967, 1976; Hammen, 1978; Shaw, 1979), if depression is to develop, then a strong component of the process must be a memory trace or structure priming depressives to remember their negative past and to distort their memories in a negative direction. (This has been termed the "loser ideal" by Beck & Shaw, 1977.)

Yet another manner in which memory and the negative self-schema may be assessed through cognitive psychology paradigms can be seen in the research in recall. Recent work in this area suggests that some prior retrieval or recall facilitates later recall of that same material (Darley & Murdock, 1971; Hogan & Kintsch, 1971; Thompson, Wenger, & Bartling, 1978). From examination of the research methods used in these experiments and from the theoretical background provided by the negative self-schema notion, it may be possible to devise effects of depressed mood on the accessibility of past pleasant or unpleasant real-life experiences. Teasdale and Fogarty (1979) conducted a study that addressed this issue. Sixteen students were made happy or depressed by a mood-induction procedure. It took depressed subjects longer to retrieve pleasant memories than it took them to retrieve unpleasant memories. The study is important because it suggests that mood has an effect on the retrieval of long-term memories.

A fourth methodology to address theoretically important issues in depression is signal detection theory analysis. This method has already been discussed in the research on memory. Another potential use is in examining depressives' response biases. Thus the propensity that a depressed individual has to identify certain types of affectively laden words may be found to be related to the ease with which these words are identified with the self. This easy access or response bias may help to perpetuate a negative self-image and a depressogenic self-schema.

Studies examining cognitive problems and/or deficits in depression have typically employed the comparative methodology (i.e., depressed vs. control group). This method of inquiry is instructive because it provides a description of the group differences in depression. It falls short in that predictions of recovery, duration of depression, and likelihood of relapse cannot be made. These predictions require longitudinal studies with the depressed groups.

Similarly, the descriptive methodology utilized in the majority of the depression literature is unable to increase our knowledge of the process of depression. Thus, although "one-shot" research designs provide information about certain cognitive characteristics, it is uncertain whether these characteristics remain over time. In addition, there may be significant moderator variables between depression and cognitive distortion. A case in point is the study by Hammen (1978). She found that depressed individuals who had experienced a high level of life stressors exhibited little cognitive distortion, whereas other individuals who were equally depressed but who had experienced a lower level of life stressors manifested substantial cognitive distortion.

The issue at hand is which cognitions change over time. It is a well-established fact in cognitive psychology that recall of an incident or memory facilitates more recall (Lachman & Laughery, 1968; Thompson *et al.*, 1978; Tulving, 1962). In depression it may be possible to demonstrate that negative schemas are easier to recall through subsequent processing of material related to them. In fact, this suggestion has been made by Davis (1979). Again, longitudinal studies on depression-prone individuals that track several cognitive variables are indicated.

Methodologically, the future of cognitive assessment may lie in neomentalistic (Paivio, 1975) studies. "Neomentalism" has been defined as the objective study of the structure, functions, and development of mental representations. Instead of utilizing introspective methods, the methodology is behavioral in focus. Three general classes of operations are employed: the attributes of the stimulus material, various experimental manipulations, and individual differences variables. Some of the best examples of this paradigm in the cognitive psychology literature are discussed by Paivio (1975). The emphasis is on the control processes (i.e., the components that operate on stored information). For example, the instruction to imagine onself cutting up a cube into equal parts illustrates one control process. By studying control processes, we will move further in our understanding of what depressed individuals *do* cognitively as well as what they *have* and *are* (Mischel, 1973).

Therapy has been relatively unaffected by the extensive literature on cognitive functioning. Even cognitive therapy (Beck, Rush, Shaw, & Emery, 1979) takes as its data base a different type of cognitive information than that gained in most research studies. There are, of course, increasing attempts to narrow the gap between therapeutic procedures and research. Kendall and Korgeski (1979) make a similar point. Without valid methods to assess the cognitions that are associated with depression, we will not be able to determine whether the target processes in cognitive therapy (or any therapy) are changed by the treatment.

The research done in any area is only as good as the methodologies and assessment techniques used. In depression a wide range of assessment tools has been developed, and a number still need to be developed. This chapter is a call to researchers to direct their attention to the methods they employ in their work. Where possible, the methods should yield results that can be clearly linked to theory, and the implications for theory should be clearly defined. We need to define the cognitions that we are assessing and to conduct the assessment with maximum reliability and validity. Only in this manner will the area be advanced.

Reference Notes

1. Lewinsohn, P. M., & Muñoz, R. *Measurements of expectations and cognitions in depressed patients.* Paper presented at the annual meeting of the Association for the Advancement of Behavior Therapy, Chicago, December 1978.
2. Lewinsohn, P. M., & Talkington, J. *Studies on the measurement of unpleasant events and the relations with depression.* Unpublished manuscript, University of Oregon, 1978.
3. Meltzer, S. S. *The effect of depression on the interpretation of communication.* Unpublished B.A. thesis, The University of Western Ontario, 1979.
4. Jessup, B. A., & Baker, L. *Psychophyiology of verbal and visual imagery: Implications for therapy.* Paper presented at the annual meeting of the Association for the Advancement of Behavior Therapy, Chicago, December 1978.
5. Breiter, H. *Goal setting and depression.* Unpublished master's thesis, The University of Western Ontario, 1978.
6. Semmel, A., Abramson, L., Seligman, M. E. P., & vonBaeyer, C. *A scale for measuring attributing style.* Unpublished manuscript, University of Pennsylvania, 1979.
7. Giles, D. E. *Cognitive-perceptual abnormalities in depression.* Unpublished manuscript, The University of Western Ontario, 1980.
8. Shaw, B. F. *Predictive value of probability of success estimates for skilled tasks in depression.* Unpublished manuscript, The University of Western Ontario, 1979.
9. Krumm, H. *A comparison of the attributions and interpersonal problem solving skills of mildly depressed and nondepressed subjects.* Unpublished B.A. thesis, The University of Western Ontario, 1978.
10. Giles, D., Dobson, K. S., & Shaw, B. F. *Interpersonal goal-setting and problem-solving in analog and clinically depressed groups.* Unpublished manuscript, The University of Western Ontario, 1980.
11. Stake, J. E., Warren, N. J., & Rogers, H. E. *Coping strategies as mediators in the relationship between cognitive distortions and depression.* Unpublished manuscript, The University of Missouri—St. Louis, 1979.

12. Weissman, A. N., & Beck, A. T. *Development and validation of the dysfunctional attitude scale: A preliminary investigation.* Paper presented at the meeting of the American Educational Research Association, Toronto, 1978.
13. Epstein, S. *Natural healing processes of the mind: Acute schizophrenic disorganization.* Unpublished manuscript, 1976.
14. Shaw, B. F., Croker, W., & Burns, D. *Thinking styles and coping strategies in depression: An empirical investigation.* Unpublished manuscript, The University of Western Ontario, 1978.
15. Shaw, B. F. *Depression and memory functioning: A signal detection analysis.* Manuscript in progress, The University of Western Ontario, 1980.

References

Abramson, L. Y., Garber, J., Edwards, N. B., & Seligman, M. E. P. Expectancy changes in depression and schizophrenia. *Journal of Abnormal Psychology,* 1978, *87*(1), 102–109.

Abramson, L. Y., Seligman, M. E. P., & Teasdale, J. D. Learned helplessness in humans: Critique and reformulation. *Journal of Abnormal Psychology,* 1978, *87*(1), 49–74.

Atkinson, R. C., & Shiffrin, R. M. Human memory: A proposed system and its control processes. In K. W. Spence & J. T. Spence (Eds.), *The psychology of learning and motivation: Advances in research and theory* (Vol. 2). New York: Academic Press, 1968.

Beck, A. T. *Depression: Clinical, experimental, and therapeutic aspects.* New York: Harper & Row, 1967.

Beck, A. T. Cognitive therapy: Nature and relation to behavior therapy. *Behavior Therapy,* 1970, *1*, 184–200.

Beck, A. T. The development of depression: A cognitive model. In R. J. Friedman & M. M. Katz (Eds.), *The psychology of depression: Contemporary theory and research.* New York: Wiley, 1974.

Beck, A. T. *Cognitive therapy and the emotional disorders.* New York: International Universities Press, 1976.

Beck, A. T., Kovacs, M., & Weissman, A. Assessment of suicidal intent: The scale of suicide ideation. *Journal of Consulting and Clinical Psychology,* 1979, *47*(2), 343–352.

Beck, A. T., Rush, A. J., Shaw, B. F., & Emery, G. *Cognitive therapy of depression.* New York: Guilford Press, 1979.

Beck, A. T., & Shaw, B. F. Cognitive approaches to depression. In A. Ellis & R. Grieger (Eds.), *Handbook of rational-emotive therapy.* New York: Springer, 1977.

Beck, A. T., Ward, C., Mendelson, M., Mock, J., & Erbaugh, J. An inventory for measuring depression. *Archives of General Psychiatry,* 1961, *4*, 561–571.

Beck, A. T., Weissman, A., Lester, D., & Trexler, L. The measurement of pessimism: The hopelessness scale. *Journal of Consulting and Clinical Psychology,* 1974, *42*(6), 861–865.

Blaney, P. H. Contemporary theories of depression: Critique and comparison. *Journal of Abnormal Psychology,* 1977, *86*(3), 203–223.

Bower, G. H., Montiero, K. P., & Gilligan, S. G. Emotional mood as a context for learning and recall. *Journal of Verbal Learning and Verbal Behavior,* 1978, *17*, 573–385.

Bransford, J. D. *Human cognition: Learning, understanding and remembering.* Belmont, Calif.: Wadsworth Publishing Co., 1978.

Broga, M. I., & Neufeld, R. W. J. Schizophrenic deficits in the light of information processing accounts of cognition. *Psychological Bulletin,* in press.

Buchwald, A. M., Coyne, I. C., & Cole, C. S. A critical evaluation of the learned helplessness model of depression. *Journal of Abnormal Psychology,* 1978, *87*, 180–193.

Cochrane, R., & Robertson, A. The Life Events Inventory: A measure of the relative severity of psycho-social stressors. *Journal of Psychosomatic Research,* 1973, *17*, 135–139.

Coyne, J. C. Toward an interactional description of depression. *Psychiatry,* 1976, *39*, 28–40.

Craighead, W. E., Hickey, K. S., & DeMonbreun, B. G. Distortion of perception and recall of neutral feedback in depression. *Cognitive Therapy and Research,* 1979, *3*(3), 291–298.

Craighead, W. E., Kimball, W. H., & Rehak, P. J. Mood changes, physiological response, and self-statements during social rejection imagery. *Journal of Consulting and Clinical Psychology,* 1979, *47*(2), 385–396.

Craik, F. I. M., & Lockhart, R. S. Levels of processing: A framework for memory research. *Journal of Verbal Learning and Verbal Behavior,* 1972, *11,* 671–684.

Darley, C. F., & Murdock, B. B. Effects of prior recall testing on final recall and recognition. *Journal of Experimental Psychology,* 1971, *91,* 66–73.

Davis, H. Self-reference and the encoding of personal information in depression. *Cognitive Therapy and Research,* 1979, *3,* 97–110.

Dember, W. N. Motivation and the cognitive revolution. *American Psychologist,* 1974, *29,* 161–168.

DeMonbreun, B. G., & Craighead, W. E. Distortion of perception and recall of positive and neutral feedback in depression. *Cognitive Therapy and Research,* 1977, *1*(4), 311–329.

Dempsey, P. A unidimensional depression scale for the MMPI. *Journal of Consulting Psychology,* 1964, *28,* 364–370.

Dilling, C. A., & Rabin, A. I. Temporal experience in depressive states and schizophrenia. *Journal of Consulting Psychology,* 1967, *31*(6), 604–408.

Dixon, N. F., & Lear, T. E. Perceptual regulations and mental disorder. *Journal of Mental Science,* 1962, *108,* 356–361.

Dobson, K. S. *Assessing the interface between anxiety and depression.* Unpublished doctoral dissertation, The University of Western Ontario, 1980.

Dobson, D. J. G., & Dobson, K. S. Problem solving efficiency in depressed and nondepressed college students. *Cognitive Therapy and Research,* in press.

Dupue, R. A., & Monroe, S. M. The unipolar–bipolar distinction in the depressive disorders. *Psychological Bulletin,* 1978, *85,* 1001–1029.

D'Zurilla, T. J., & Goldfried, M. R. Problem-solving and behavior modification. *Journal of Abnormal Psychology,* 1971, *78*(1), 107–126.

Ellis, A. *Reason and emotion in psychotherapy.* New York: Lyle Stuart, 1962.

Endler, N. S., & Magnussen, D. Toward an interactional psychology of personality. *Psychological Bulletin,* 1976, *83,* 956–974.

Epstein, S. The self concept revisited. *American Psychologist,* 1973, *28,* 404–416.

Erickson, R. C., Post, R. D., & Paige, A. B. Hope as a psychiatric variable. *Journal of Clinical Psychology,* 1975, *31,* 324–330.

Feighner, J. P., Robins, E., Guze, S. B., Woodruff, R. A., Winokur, G., & Muñoz, R. Diagnostic criteria for use in psychiatric research. *Archives of General Psychiatry,* 1972, *26,* 57–63.

Fitch, G. Effects of self-esteem, perceived performance, and choice on causal attributions. *Journal of Personality and Social Psychology,* 1970, *16,* 311–315.

Glass, R. M., Uhlenhuth, E. H., & Weinreb, H. Imipramine reversible cognitive deficit in outpatient depressives. *Psychopharmacology Bulletin,* 1978, *14,* 10–13.

Golin, S., Terrell, F., Weitz, J., & Drost, P. L. The illusion of controls among depressed patients. *Journal of Abnormal Psychology,* 1979, *88,* 454–457.

Gotlib, I. H., & Asarnow, R. F. Interpersonal and impersonal problem-solving skills in mildly and clinically depressed university students. *Journal of Consulting and Clinical Psychology,* 1979, *47*(1), 86–95.

Hammen, C. Depression, distortion, and life stress in college students. *Cognitive Therapy and Research,* 1978, *2,* 189–192.

Hammen, C. L., & Krantz, S. Effects of success and failure on depression cognitions. *Journal of Abnormal Psychology,* 1975, *85*(6), 577–586.

Hemphill, R. E., Hall, K. R. L., & Crookes, T. E. A preliminary report on fatigue and pain tolerance in depressive and psychoneurotic patients. *Journal of Mental Science,* 1952, *98,* 433–440.

Hogan, R. M., & Kintsch, W. Differential effects of study and test trials on long-term recognition and recall. *Journal of Verbal Learning and Verbal Behavior,* 1971, *10,* 562–567.

Hollon, S. D., & Kendall, P. C. Cognitive self-statements in depression: Development of an Automatic Thoughts Questionnaire. *Cognitive Therapy and Research,* 1980, *4,* 383–395.

Holmes, T. H., & Rahe, R. H. The social readjustment rating scale. *Journal of Psychometric Research,* 1967, *11,* 213–218.

Jackson, D. N. *Personality research form manual.* Goshen, N.Y.: Research Psychologists Press, 1974.

Jones, R. *A factored measure of Ellis's irrational belief systems with personality and maladjustment correlated.* Unpublished doctoral dissertation, Texas Technological College, 1968.

Journal of Abnormal Psychology, 1978, *87*(1).

Kahn, R., Zarit, S., Hilbert, N., & Niederehe, G. Memory complaint and impairment in the aged. *Archives of General Psychiatry,* 1975, *32,* 1569–173.

Kendall, P. C., & Korgeski, G. P. Assessment and cognitive–behavioral interventions. *Cognitive Therapy and Research,* 1979, *3*(1), 1–21.

Klatzky, R. L. *Human memory: Structures and processes.* San Francisco: W. H. Freeman, 1975.

Krantz, S., & Hammen, C. L. Assessment of cognitive bias in depression. *Journal of Abnormal Psychology,* 1979, *88*(6), 611–619.

Kuhn, T. S. *The structure of scientific revolutions.* Chicago: University of Chicago Press, 1970.

Kuiper, N. A. Depression and causal attributions for success and failure. *Journal of Personality and Social Psychology,* 1978, *36*(3), 236–246.

Kuiper, N. A., & Derry, P. A. The self as a cognitive prototype: An application to person perception and depression. In N. Cantor & J. Kihlstrom (Eds.), *Cognition, social interaction, and personality.* Hillsdale, N.J.: Erlbaum, 1980.

Lachman, R., & Laughery, K. R. Is a test trial a training trial in free recall learning? *Journal of Experimental Psychology,* 1968, *76,* 40–50.

Levy, R., & Maxwell, A. E. The effect of verbal context on the recall of schizophrenia and other psychiatric patients. *British Journal of Psychiatry,* 1968, *114,* 311–316.

Lewinsohn, P. M., Mischel, W., Chaplin, W., & Barton, R. Social competence and depression: The role of illusory self-perception. *Journal of Abnormal Psychology,* 1980, *89,* 203–212.

Lishman, W. A. Selective factors in memory. Part 2: Affective disorders. *Psychological Medicine,* 1972, *2,* 248–253.

Lloyd, G. G., & Lishman, W. A. Effect of depression on the speed of recall of pleasant and unpleasant experiences. *Psychological Medicine,* 1975, *5,* 173–180.

Lobitz, W. C., & Post, R. D. Parameters of self-reinforcement and depression. *Journal of Abnormal Psychology,* 1979, *88*(1), 33–41.

Loeb, A., Beck, A. T., & Diggory, J. Differential effects of success and failure on depressive and nondepressed patients. *Journal of Nervous and Mental Disease,* 1971, *152*(2), 106–114.

Lunghi, E. The stability of mood and social perception measures in a sample of depressive inpatients. *British Journal of Psychiatry,* 1977, *130,* 598–604.

Mahoney, M. J. *Cognition and behavior modification.* Cambridge, Mass.: Ballinger, 1974.

Melges, F. T., & Bowlby, J. Types of hopelessness in psychopathological process. *Archives of General Psychiatry,* 1969, *20,* 690–699.

Mezey, A. G., & Cohen, S. I. The effect of depressive illness on time judgment and time experience. *Journal of Neurology, Neurosurgery, and Psychiatry,* 1961, *24,* 269–276.

Miller, D. T., & Ross, M. Self-serving biases in the attribution of causality: Fact or fiction. *Psychological Bulletin,* 1975, *82,* 213–225.

Miller, E., & Lewis, P. Recognition memory in elderly patients with depression and dementia: A signal detection analysis. *Journal of Abnormal Psychology,* 1977, 86, *1,* 84–86.

Miller, W. R. Psychological deficit in depression. *Psychological Bulletin,* 1975, *82*(2), 238–260.

Minkoff, K., Bergman, E., Beck, A. T., & Beck, R. Hopelessness, depression, and attempted suicide. *American Journal of Psychiatry,* 1973, *130,* 455–459.

Mischel, W. Toward a cognitive social learning reconceptualization of personality. *Psychological Review,* 1973, *80,* 252–283.

Neisser, U. *Cognitive psychology.* New York: Appleton-Century-Crofts, 1967.

Nelson, R. Irrational beliefs in depression. *Journal of Consulting and Clinical Psychology,* 1977, *45,* 1190–1197.

Nelson, R. E., & Craighead, W. E. Selective recall of positive and negative feedback, self-controlled behaviors, and depression. *Journal of Abnormal Psychology,* 1977, *86,* 379–388.

Norman, D. A. *Memory and attention.* New York: Wiley, 1969.

Paivio, A. Neomentalism. *Canadian Journal of Psychology,* 1975, *29,* 263–291.

Platt, J., & Spivack, G. Problem-solving thinking of psychiatric patients. *Journal of Consulting and Clinical Psychology,* 1972, *39,* 148–151.

Rippere, V. Commonsense beliefs about depression and antidepressive behavior: A study of social consensus. *Behaviour Research and Therapy,* 1977, *15,* 465–473.

Rizley, R. Depression and distortion in the attribution of causality. *Journal of Abnormal Psychology,* 1978, *87,* 32–49.

Russell, P., & Beckhuis, M. Organization in memory: A comparison of psychotics and normals. *Journal of Abnormal Psychology,* 1976, *85,* 527–534.

Sacco, W. P., & Hokanson, J. E. Expectations of success and anagram performance of depressives in a public and private setting. *Journal of Abnormal Psychology,* 1978, *87*(1), 122–130.

Schless, A. P., Schwartz, L., Goetz, C., & Mendels, J. How depressives view the significance of life events. *British Journal of Psychiatry,* 1974, *125,* 406–410.

Seligman, M. E. P. Depression and learned helplessness. In R. J. Friedman & M. M. Katz (Eds.), *The psychology of depression: Contemporary theory and research.* Washington, D.C.: Hemisphere, 1974.

Seligman, M. E. P., Abramson, L., Semmel, A., & vonBaeyer, C. Depressive attributional style. *Journal of Abnormal Psychology,* 1979, *88,* 242–247.

Shaw, B. F. The theoretical and empirical foundations of a cognitive model of depression. In P. Pliner, I. Spigel, & K. Blankstein (Eds.), *Perception of emotion in self and others.* New York: Plenum Press, 1979.

Shaw, B. F., & Beck, A. T. The treatment of depression with cognitive therapy. In A. Ellis & R. Grieger (Eds.), *Handbook of rational-emotive theory and practice.* New York: Springer, 1977.

Siegler, R. S. Where is the logic? *Contemporary Psychology,* 1976, *21,* 462–464.

Smolen, R. C. Expectancies, mood and performance of depressed and nondepressed psychiatric inpatients on chance and skill tests. *Journal of Abnormal Psychology,* 1978, *87*(1), 91–101.

Sobel, R. S. The effects of success, failure, and locus of control on post-performance attributions of causality. *Journal of General Psychology,* 1974, *91,* 29–34.

Steiner, R. E. A cognitive developmental analysis of depression: Interpersonal problem-solving and event interpretation among depressed and nondepressed women. *Dissertation Abstracts International,* 1975, *35*(800B), 4197.

Sternberg, D. E., & Jarvik, M. E. Memory functions in depression. *Archives of General Psychiatry,* 1976, *33,* 219–224.

Stevens, L., & Jones, E. E. Defensive attribution and the Kelly cube. *Journal of Personality of Social Psychology,* 1976, *34,* 809–920.

Stuart, J. L. *Intercorrelations of depressive tendencies, time perspective, and cognitive style variables.* Unpublished doctoral dissertation, Vanderbilt University, 1962.

Teasdale, J. D., & Fogarty, S. J. Differential effects of induced mood on retrieval of pleasant and unpleasant events from episodic memory. *Journal of Abnormal Psychology,* 1979, *88*(3), 248–257.

Thompson, C. P., Wenger, S., & Bartling, C. A. How recall facilitates subsequent recall: A reappraisal. *Journal of Experimental Psychology: Human Learning and Memory,* 1978, *4*(3), 210–221.

Tulving, E. Subjective organization in free recall of "unrelated" words. *Psychological Review,* 1962, *69,* 344–354.

Tulving, E., & Thompson, D. M. Encoding specificity and retrieval processes in episodic memory. *Psychological Review,* 1973, *80,* 352–373.

Weintraub, M., Segal, R., & Beck, A. T. An investigation of cognition and affect in the depressive experience of normal men. *Journal of Consulting and Clinical Psychology,* 1974, *42,* 911.

Wener, A. E., & Rehm, L. P. Depressive affect: A test of behavioral hypotheses. *Journal of Abnormal Psychology,* 1975, *84,* 221–227.

Wetzel, R. D. Hopelessness, depression and suicide intent. *Archives of General Psychiatry,* 1976, *33,* 1069–1073.

Wortman, C. B., & Dintzer, L. Is an attributional analysis of the learned helplessness phenomenon viable? A critique of the Abramson–Seligman–Teasdale reformulation. *Journal of Abnormal Psychology,* 1978, *87*(1), 75–90.

Wynne, L. C., Cromwell, R. L., & Matthyse, S. *The nature of schizophrenia: New approaches to research and treatment.* New York: Wiley, 1978.

13

Cognitive Assessment of Social-Evaluative Anxiety

Carol R. Glass and Thomas V. Merluzzi

This chapter will review recent advances in the development and application of cognitive assessment techniques for the study of test anxiety, speech anxiety, nonassertiveness, and heterosocial competence. Because of this broad emphasis, we will use the term "social-evaluative anxiety" as a more concise description of these four problem areas. The reader should realize that heterosocial difficulties and nonassertiveness encompass much more than a high level of social anxiety, and we do not mean simply to equate these terms.

We begin with the background for a cognitive conceptualization of social-evaluative concerns. A brief review of recent cognitive therapy outcome studies for social-evaluative anxiety further serves to highlight both the need for cognitive assessment and the questions that remain unanswered. The major thrust of the chapter is to review the methods employed to assess the irrational beliefs, self-statements, expectations, problem-solving and coping strategies, and self-evaluations of individuals who display social, test, or speech anxiety. We conclude with some speculations on the use of cognitive assessment in outcome and process research and with suggestions for future research.

A Cognitive Model of Social-Evaluative Concerns

Researchers in the field of test and speech anxiety and social competence have typically chosen one of three models to explain the etiology of these dif-

Carol R. Glass • Department of Psychology, The Catholic University of America, Washington, D.C. *Thomas V. Merluzzi* • Department of Psychology, University of Notre Dame, Notre Dame, Indiana.

ficulties (Curran, 1977). The first conceptualization focuses on the role of conditioned anxiety and maintains that test or social anxiety has been acquired through a learning process whereby a previously neutral stimulus situation has become fear inducing. The second model considers that difficulties in social-evaluative situations arise from skill deficits or an inadequate behavioral repertoire. Thus nonassertive persons lack appropriate assertive responses, shy men and women have a deficiency of good interpersonal skills for conversation and relationship formation, and test-anxious individuals may be anxious because they are aware they failed to acquire good study and test-taking skills.

A cognitive conceptualization of an individual's difficulties in evaluative and social situations stresses the role of negative or maladaptive self-statements, unrealistic expectations, irrational beliefs, negative self-evaluations, and faulty cognitive appraisal. This third model is the most relevant for our presentation and discussion of cognitive assessment. The way in which a person appraises or construes an actual or anticipated outcome in a given situation can be seen as an important determinant of stress (Lazarus, 1966, 1980). Ellis (1962), Beck (1976), and Meichenbaum (1977) similarly have recognized the role of cognition—irrational beliefs, faulty thinking styles, negative self-statements—in maintaining maladaptive emotional reactions. The following sections will briefly explicate current theory and research pertaining to the cognitive conceptualization of test and speech anxiety, nonassertiveness, and heterosocial competence.

Test and Speech Anxiety

Wine (1971, 1980) and Sarason (1972) have conceptualized test anxiety as a form of task-irrelevant self-preoccupation characterized by self-awareness, self-doubt, self-depreciation, and ruminative self-critical worry in evaluative situations. This attentional focus away from the task to be solved thus influences overt behavior and psychological reactivity. Sarason (1978) maintains that test-anxious individuals (1) see the situation as difficult and threatening, (2) see themselves as ineffective in handling the tasks, (3) focus on the undesirable consequences of personal inadequacy, (4) show a strong self-deprecatory preoccupation that interferes with task-relevant cognitive activity, and (5) anticipate failure and loss of regard by others. High-test-anxious individuals are thus prone to self-centered interfering responses in evaluative situations.

Test anxiety has also been conceptualized as consisting of both a worry and an emotionality component (Liebert & Morris, 1967). The worry, or cognitive, component refers to an attentional focus on concerns about performance, consequences of failure, negative self-evaluation and evaluation of one's ability relative to others (Deffenbacher, 1980). Both Liebert and Morris's (1967) Worry–Emotionality Inventory and Osterhouse's (1972) Inventory of Test Anxiety contain a measure of the worry component. Because these inventories were designed to assess the more general construct of state test anxiety, they will not be considered in our discussion of cognitive assessment. Nonetheless, this area of research may be of interest to those concerned with cognitive factors in test anxiety; those readers are referred to Deffenbacher (1978, 1980) for a thorough review.

Although the role of cognition in speech anxiety has not been theoretically developed to the same extent as in test anxiety, we may speculate that a similar cognitive conceptualization may hold. Appropriate interventions for both test anxiety and speech anxiety thus might include self-instructions to facilitate focusing on the task in order to inhibit negative self-relevant thinking. In addition, the identification of irrational beliefs that contribute to evaluation anxiety, and the replacement of negative self-statements with positive coping ones, are relevant adjuncts to redirecting attention.

Previous research has identified a number of situational factors that also must be considered in order to develop a comprehensive account of test anxiety. Sarason (1975) has shown that test performance is affected by (1) the nature of the task instructions, (2) task difficulty, (3) time pressure, and (4) manipulated expectations. The cognitive model of test anxiety would predict that these four variables affect an individual's self-focused attention and negative evaluations of ability, thus contributing to poorer performance. The development of cognitive assessment will greatly increase our ability to test such predictions.

Assertiveness and Heterosocial Competence

As Galassi and Galassi (1979) note, equating heterosocial problems with skill deficits has biased research efforts, because heterosocial difficulty may not uniformly arise from a lack of skills. Similarly, the term "social anxiety" implies that the problem is equated with a particular explanatory model. In fact, Galassi and Galassi (1979) conclude that there is "more evidence that heterosocial problems are characterized (not necessarily caused) by deficits in cognitive rather than behavior skills" (p. 176). Recent research has attempted to clarify the nature of the cognitive deficit that may be present in individuals with difficulties in assertiveness and heterosocial interaction. Bellack (1979) has urged that extensive effort be devoted to such a task.

Arkowitz (1977) has suggested that anxiety and avoidance are due to the presence of (1) overly negative self-evaluations of social performance (Clark & Arkowitz, 1975; Glasgow & Arkowitz, 1975), (2) an internal dialogue consisting of many negative self-statements (Cacioppo, Glass, & Merluzzi, 1979; Glass, Gottman, & Shmurak, 1976), (3) excessively high standards for performance (Bandura, 1969), (4) selective attention and memory for positive versus negative information about oneself and social performance (O'Banion & Arkowitz, 1977), and (5) pathological patterns of attribution for social success and social failure (Miller & Arkowitz, 1977). A similar role of cognition in assertiveness has been described by Lange and Jakubowski (1976) and Schwartz and Gottman (1976), who stress the presence of irrational beliefs and negative self-statements in nonassertive individuals. Although research on social anxiety has developed independently from the area of text anxiety, we would speculate that Wine's (1980) attentional theory of test anxiety might be quite relevant to problems of shyness and interpersonal anxiety as well.

In sum, test, speech, assertiveness, and social competence problems have recently been conceptualized in ways that emphasize the cognitive component of the problem. Before beginning our discussion of cognitive assessment, we will give a brief overview of approaches to cognitive therapy that have arisen from the cognitive conceptualization. Social, test, and speech anxiety have been among the most popular targets for cognitive therapy interventions. Yet, it is strikingly apparent that cognitive therapy approaches consistently lack a deliberate attempt to assess cognitive change.

Cognitive Therapy Approaches for Social-Evaluative Anxiety

Controlled research on the efficacy of cognitive therapy for the problems of test and speech anxiety, nonassertiveness, and heterosocial anxiety has appeared only within the past 10 years. Such research has firmly established that cognitive interventions significantly contribute to affective and behavior change. We will argue, however, that strong confirmation of changes in the actual cognitive appraisal process has not been consistently demonstrated.

Further difficulties arise from a general lack of consistency in the names used to refer to cognitive therapy approaches. In a review of 49 therapy outcome studies employing cognitive interventions for test and speech anxiety, nonassertiveness, and interpersonal–heterosocial problems, we discovered no fewer than 24 different names used to describe the treatment approaches. These include, for example, "cognitive-behavior modification," "cognitive modification," "self-statement modification," "cognitive therapy," "cognitive restructuring," and "rational restructuring." Because the focus of this chapter is on assessment and not on therapy, we will include applications of cognitive assessment across a broad range of cognitive therapy approaches. Although cognitive assessment also may be useful for outcome studies of noncognitive therapies, only one more behavioral approach to test anxiety (Hutchings, Denney, Basgal, & Houston, in press) has attempted to assess cognitive change (coping strategies).

Table 1 summarizes some relevant information concerning cognitive therapy outcome research in this area. It can be seen that only about one quarter of all cognitive intervention studies for social-evaluative anxiety employed any kind of cognitive assessment. Of the 13 studies that did assess

Table 1. Summary of Cognitive Therapy Outcome Studies

Author	Cognitive intervention	Cognitive assessment
	Test anxiety	
Arnkoff (1980*b*)	Belief therapy, self-statement therapy	Irrational beliefs, self-statements
Bruch (1978)	Cognitive modeling	Self-statements, problem-solving rules, coping instructions
Collins, Dansereau, Holley, Garland, and McDonald (in press)	Self-coaching	
Deffenbacher and Hahnloser (in press)	Cognitive modification	
Finger and Galassi (1977)	Attentional treatment	
Goldfried, Linehan, and Smith (1978)	Systematic rational restructuring	
Holroyd (1976)	Cognitive therapy	
Hussian and Lawrence (1978)	Stress inoculation	
Hussian and Lawrence (Note 1)	Stress inoculation	
Kirkland and Hollandsworth (1980)	Attentional control, adaptive self-instructional statements	Self-statements, attentional focus
Little and Jackson (1974)	Attentional training	
May (1976)	Cognitive modification, insight therapy, coping behavior rehearsal	
McCordick, Kaplan, Finn, and Smith (1979)	Cognitive-behavior modification	
Meichenbaum (1972)	Cognitive modification	
Montgomery (1971)	Rational–emotive therapy	

Table 1. (continued)

Author	Cognitive intervention	Cognitive assessment
	Test anxiety	
Osarchuk (1976)	Rational restructuring, self-control desensitization	
Sarason (1973)	Cognitive modeling	
	Speech anxiety	
Casas (1976)	Systematic rational re-structuring, self-control desensitization	Irrational beliefs
Fremouw and Zitter (1978)	Cognitive restructuring-relaxation	
Glogower, Fremouw, and McCroskey (1978)	Cognitive restructuring	
Jaremko and Walker (Note 2)	Stress inoculation	Self-efficacy
Karst and Trexler (1970)	Rational–emotive therapy	
Meichenbaum, Gilmore, and Fedoravicius (1971)	"Insight" treatment	
Norman (1975)	Self-instructional training	
Thorpe, Amatu, Blakey, and Burns (1976)	"Insight" treatment	
Trexler and Karst (1972)	Rational–emotive therapy	Irrational beliefs
Weissberg (1977)	Cognitive modification, desensitization with coping imagery	
	Assertiveness	
Carmody (1978)	Rational–emotive therapy, self-instruction	
Craighead (1979)	Self-instructional training	Irrational beliefs
Derry and Stone (1979)	Cognitive self-statement therapy	Irrational beliefs, self-statements

(continued)

Table 1. (continued)

Author	Cognitive intervention	Cognitive assessment
Assertiveness		
Kazdin (1974)	Covert modeling	
Kazdin (1976)	Covert modeling	
Linehan, Goldfried, and Goldfried (1979)	Systematic rational restructuring	
Nietzel, Martorano, and Melnick (1977)	Covert modeling	
Rakos (1979)	Part of "assertiveness training"	Irrational and coping cognitions
Safran, Alden, and Davidson (1980)	Cognitive restructuring	
Thorpe (1974)	Self-instructional training	
Tiegerman and Kassinove (1977)	Cognitive–rational therapy	
Twentyman, Pharr, and Connor (1980)	Covert rehearsal, self-statement modification, problem solving	
Wolfe and Fodor (1977)	Rational behavior therapy	
Interpersonal/heterosocial		
DiLoreto (1971)	Rational–emotive therapy	
Elder, Edelstein, and Fremouw (in press)	Cognitive restructuring	
Glass, Gottman, and Shmurak (1976)	Cognitive self-statement modification	
Gormally, Varvil-Weld, Raphael, and Sipps (in press)	Rational reevaluation	Irrational beliefs, subjective utility
Kanter and Goldfried (1979)	Systematic rational restructuring, self-control desensitization	Irrational beliefs

Table 1. (continued)

Author	Cognitive intervention	Cognitive assessment
	Interpersonal/heterosocial	
Kramer (1975)	Practice dating + cognitive restructuring	Irrational beliefs
Malkiewich and Merluzzi (1980)	Cognitive restructuring	Self-statements
Rehm and Marston (1968)	Self-reinforcement	
West, Goethe, and Kallman (1980)	Behavioral–cognitive approach	

cognitive variables, all but 5 relied on only *one* cognitive measure. Eight employed Jones's (1969) Irrational Beliefs Test (IBT), even though the therapy itself may not have been conceptualized as attempting to change such beliefs.

Most outcome research in this area has been of the "Grand Prix" variety (Glass & Smith, Note 3), in which investigators pit some form of cognitive therapy against a behavioral approach such as relaxation training, systematic desensitization, or skills training. A few of the more interesting studies have performed component analyses of cognitive restructuring or have looked at the role of different types of coping statements while examining the active ingredients that contribute to psychotherapeutic change. In order to illustrate the unanswered questions that remain in outcome research as a result of the lack of cognitive assessment, we will review one study that is typical of the "cognitive versus behavior therapy" variety and three studies that have attempted some form of component analysis. The reader is urged to consult Goldfried (1979) for a more complete review of cognitive therapy for social-evaluative anxiety.

Glass *et al.* (1976) compared the relative effectiveness of cognitive self-statement modification, social skills training, and combination treatment groups with a waiting-list control group for college men who reported heterosocial shyness and anxiety. Treatments and assessment were empirically derived using a behavioral–analytic model (Goldfried & D'Zurilla, 1969). All three treatment groups were judged to be significantly more skillful than the controls in taped role-playing situations in which they had received training. Subjects who received the cognitive component, however, performed significantly better on untrained situations than those who did not have a cognitive component. The cognitive self-statement group made significantly more telephone calls and made a better impression on the women they called as part of an *in vivo* assessment, suggesting greater generalization for the cognitive approach than for response acquisition.

The results of this study demonstrated that self-statement modification affected *behavior*. Was the cognitive approach actually successful in changing the nature of subjects' *self-statements*? We would at least need to show that subjects showed change on cognitive measures before concluding that such cognitive elements accounted for the success of the treatment. It is possible that subjects who learned new social skills also altered their internal dialogues in situations involving the opposite sex. Looking for answers to these questions will enable us to gain a more thorough understanding of the processes involved in change.

The failure to assess cognitive change is not limited to research that compares behavioral and cognitive interventions but is also evident in component analyses of cognitive therapy. Studies by Carmody (1978) and by Glogower, Fremouw, and McCroskey (1978) addressed the issue of the relative importance of examining and challenging negative self-statements versus learning and practicing new positive self-statements.

Carmody (1978) found few differences between behavioral assertion training, a "rational–emotive" treatment in which subjects examined and challenged maladaptive self-statements (and practiced positive self-statements and behavior), and a "self-instructional" therapy that focused solely on producing positive self-instructions. However, all treatment groups were superior to a waiting-list control group. Treatment groups did not differ on self-report inventories of assertiveness and social-evaluative anxiety or on behavioral ratings of videotaped role-playing situations, yet the rational–emotive group was superior to the waiting-list and self-instructional groups in refusing demands made by an unknown confederate in a waiting-room situation. Carmody (1978) speculated that "some form of cognitive restructuring occurs as a result of strictly behavioral intervention" (p. 251). The lack of cognitive assessment has prevented us from knowing whether, in fact, this was the case. It would be interesting to see whether subjects actually did use a different series of coping self-statements as a result of Carmody's interventions, not only in the behavioral group but also in the cognitive treatments.

Glogower *et al.*'s (1978) component analysis of cognitive restructuring for speech anxiety found knowledge and rehearsal of positive statements to be more important than awareness of negative self-statements. However, it was a combination of the two that was consistently most effective in changing actual speech and self-report of communication apprehension relative to a waiting-list control group and a group that merely discussed situations and labeled feelings. Even some subjects in the discussion group and the negative self-statement awareness group indicated on a posttreatment questionnaire that they made positive self-statements in anxiety-provoking situations. However, we would need a more direct assessment of the nature of subjects' internal dialogue in evaluative situations in order to understand (1) the way in which speech-anxious and nonanxious individuals naturally attempt to cope with stress and anxiety and (2) how different interventions change this coping process.

A final illustrative study, which examined cognitive interventions for speech anxiety (Thorpe, Amatu, Blakey, & Burns, 1976), addressed two treatment issues: (1) specific insight into irrational beliefs and self-statements relevant to speech anxiety versus a general focus on irrational thinking styles and (2) the addition of overt self-instruction rehearsal to insight treatments. Results indicated that subjects who did not rehearse productive ideas or self-instructions improved more on self-report measures of speech anxiety and social anxiety than subjects who did rehearse. There were no group differences on several other measures of speech anxiety and fear of negative evaluations, although general focus groups reported less social anxiety than specific insight groups. The lack of control groups and of knowledge of whether treatments were equated for therapist and client expectations for effectiveness limits the generalizability of the results. We are again unable to further our understanding of the process through which cognitive therapy produces change and do not know whether subjects in the different conditions actually *did* change their irrational beliefs and self-instructions as the treatments intended.

These four studies serve as examples of good outcome research on cognitive therapy components and effectiveness. Many interesting questions concerning the nature of cognitive change and the relationship among cognitions, affect, and behavior could not be answered, however, suggesting the need for including assessment in the cognitive domain. Studies that find cognitive approaches to be effective in reducing heterosocial avoidance or test anxiety do *not* provide conclusive evidence for a cognitive model of social competence or evaluation anxiety. It is circular to infer etiology from treatment effectiveness (Davison, 1968). We must be able to evaluate more directly whether cognitions (irrational beliefs, negative self-statements, efficacy expectations, etc.) play a role in arousing and maintaining social-evaluative anxiety. Two important issues, which we will discuss at the conclusion of this chapter, concern (1) the relationship among cognition, affect, behavior, and psychophysiological response and (2) the personal subjective meanings that cognitions may have for the individual.

The major purpose of this chapter, then, is to describe the development and use of cognitive assessment methods that can increase our knowledge of social-evaluative anxiety. Although we have mentioned that many studies have lacked such assessment, several excellent examples exist of the use of cognitive assessment in outcome research. These studies (Arnkoff, 1980*b*;

L. Craighead, 1979; Derry & Stone, 1979; Gormally, Varvil-Weld, Raphael, & Sipps, in press) will be reviewed later in the chapter. The feasibility and importance of cognitive assessment in this area and the need for additional research will be stressed.

Cognitive Assessment of Social-Evaluative Anxiety

A few years ago, Mahoney (1977) described the development of more reliable methods for assessing cognitive phenomena as one of the major tasks facing the cognitive-learning perspecitve in psychotherapy. One of the reasons behavior therapy has progressed and developed is the time and effort that has been spent in developing adequate behavioral assessment. In fact, Kendall and Korgeski (1979) claim that "advances in therapeutic intervention are directly related to prior advances in the accuracy of assessment" (p. 1). After reviewing cognitive–behavioral interventions for anxiety reduction, Goldfried (1979) concludes that, "if we ever hope to develop the field of cognitive-behavior therapy, it is crucial that we have more complete understanding of the interrelationship of cognition and experience" (p. 141). Meichenbaum (1977; Meichenbaum & Butler, 1979) has stressed similar concerns.

The remainder of this chapter will illustrate the development and application of cognitive assessment techniques for research on the nature and treatment of social-evaluative anxiety. Specifically, we will discuss the assessment of cognitive content in five areas: (1) irrational beliefs, (2) self-statements, (3) expectations and self-efficacy, (4) problem-solving and coping strategies, and (5) self-evaluations of performance and perception of feedback.

Assessment of Irrational Beliefs

Irrational Beliefs Test. Jones's (1969) Irrational Beliefs Test was one of the earliest and most frequently used cognitive assessment measures (see Table 2). The IBT is a 100-item self-report inventory that asks individuals to respond on a 5-point scale to the extent to which they hold certain beliefs. Using factor analysis, Jones (1969) identified a number of belief statements that made up ten factors representing Ellis's (1962) irrational beliefs. According to Jones, the resulting instrument, the IBT, showed satisfactory concurrent validity and internal consistency of subscales. Responses to items such as "I hate to fail at anything," "I want everyone to like me," and "I can't stand to take chances" are summed to yield a total score and ten subscale scores that correspond to each irrational belief. These beliefs include "demand for approval" and "high self-expectations."

In one of the first studies to use the IBT, Goldfried and Sobocinski (1975) examined the relationship between irrational beliefs and emotional arousal. Significant correlations were found between irrational beliefs and

Table 2. Summary of Studies on Assessment of Irrational Beliefs

Author	Problem and nature of study	Cognitive assessment
Arnkoff (1980b)[a]	Test anxiety; outcome	Irrational Beliefs Test (IBT)
Casas (1976)	Speech anxiety; outcome	IBT
Craighead (1979)[a]	Assertiveness; outcome	IBT, irrational beliefs about assertion
Craighead, Kimball, and Rehak (1979)[a]	Replication of Goldfried and Sobocinski	IBT
Curran, Wallander, and Fischetti (1980)[a]	Heterosocial; contrasted groups	IBT
Derry and Stone (1979)[a]	Assertiveness; outcome	IBT
Glass, Merluzzi, Biever, and Larsen (in press)	Social anxiety; contrasted groups	IBT
Goldfried and Sobocinski (1975)	Social-evaluative anxiety; correlational and contrasted IBT groups	IBT
Gormally, Sipps, Raphael, Varvil-Weld, and Edwin (in press)[a]	Heterosocial; contrasted groups	IBT
Gormally, Varvil-Weld, Raphael, and Sipps (in press)[a]	Heterosocial; outcome	IBT
Jones (1969)	Development and validation	IBT
Kanter and Goldfried (1979)	Interpersonal anxiety; outcome	IBT
Kramer (1975)	Heterosocial; outcome	IBT
Lohr and Bonge (in press)	Validational	IBT
Sutton-Simon and Goldfried (1979)	Social anxiety and acrophobia; correlational	IBT
Trexler and Karst (1972)	Speech anxiety; outcome	IBT
Alden and Cappe (1981)[a]	Assertiveness; contrasted groups	Irrational Beliefs Inventory (IBI)

(continued)

Table 2. (continued)

Author	Problem and nature of study	Cognitive assessment
Alden and Safran (1978)	Assertiveness; contrasted groups	IBI
Alden, Safran, and Weideman (1978)	Assertiveness; outcome	IBI
Lohr and Bonge (Note 4)	Development and validation	Situational Irrational Cognitions Inventory (SICI)
Lohr, Brandt, and Bonge (Note 5)	Development and validation	SICI
Fodor (Note 6)	Heterosocial assertiveness	Projective
Morelli and Friedman (1978)	Included social anxiety; correlational	Modified S-R Inventory of General Trait Anxiousness
Rakos (1979)	Assertiveness; outcome	Subjective behavior rating scale (8 of 17 items)

[a]Reference includes additional forms of cognitive assessment (see other tables).

paper-and-pencil measures of social, test, and speech anxiety. In a second experiment, women who either did or did not strongly endorse a belief in the extreme importance of social approval imagined themselves in social situations in which social rejection occurred. Subjects who strongly held this belief reacted with greater anxiety and hostility, as measured by an adjective checklist, than did subjects for whom this belief was less important. Craighead, Kimball, and Rehak (1979), however, were not able to replicate these results. Although anxiety, hostility, and depression were higher after social rejection imagery, there were no significant differences between subjects who strongly or weakly endorsed the irrational social approval belief.

Because the IBT was their only cognitive measure, Goldfried and Sobocinski did not assess the relationship between irrational beliefs and the nature of the subject's internal dialogue in response to the social situations. Studies by Sutton-Simon and Goldfried (1979) and Craighead *et al.* (1979) have addressed this issue and will be reviewed in the self-statement section of this chapter because they also illustrate the use of expressive or concurrent assessment of internal dialogue.

The IBT has been used primarily in cognitive therapy outcome research.

A fairly consistent trend indicates that subjects receiving cognitive interventions show significantly lower IBT total and subscale scores relative to waiting-list controls. These results have been reported in studies of test anxiety (Arnkoff, 1980*b*), speech anxiety (Trexler & Karst, 1972), and interpersonal anxiety (Kanter & Goldfried, 1979). Kramer (1975) found that a program of practice dating and cognitive restructuring for infrequent daters produced significant treatment decreases on IBT subscales of demand for approval and emotional irresponsibility and a trend toward significance on reaction to frustration. Similarly, Craighead (1979) found that subjects who received self-instructional assertiveness training improved, relative to expectancy and waiting-list controls, on subscales of demand for approval and high self-expectations. Derry and Stone (1979), however, found no posttreatment IBT differences between treatment groups, and Casas (1976) failed to find treatment-versus control-group differences in studies of assertiveness and speech anxiety.

There are several possible reasons for this discrepancy. The four treatment groups (no controls) employed by Derry and Stone received only 70 minutes of training, perhaps too short a period for irrational beliefs to change. Casas found treatment effects on only one of several behavioral, physiological, and self-report measures of speech and evaluation anxiety. The studies that found significant differences on the IBT employed between four and seven therapy sessions and yielded similar significant differences between treatment and control subjects on a large number of anxiety inventories and behavioral measures.

Finally, we need to consider the possibility that the problem may be with the instrument and not with the studies. The IBT is certainly in need of further validation, even though Lohr and Bonge (in press) recently have submitted the IBT to an independent factorial validation using a larger sample size than Jones ($n = 897$) and a randomly ordered questionnaire format. Except for one subscale (frustration reactive), patterns of component loadings were similar to those found by Jones (1969). The first ten components accounted for about 37% of the total scale variance. Lohr and Bonge also developed a factor-derived scoring procedure that led to an improvement in IBT factor purity. Although further research is needed in order to determine the range of usefulness of the IBT, it remains the most frequently used measure of irrational beliefs. However, just because a measure is used a great deal does not mean that it is valid, and the popularity of the IBT may be due mainly to a lack of competitors. It would seem that a measure with factors that account for only 37% of the total variance should be used with caution in both research and clinical settings.

Other Measures of Irrational Beliefs. Although they have been developed primarily for research purposes and have not received independent validation, a number of measures of irrational beliefs have appeared recently in the literature. The Irrational Beliefs Inventory (IBI) is a briefer, 11-item scale developed by Alden and colleagues, who examined the role of irrational beliefs in nonassertive behavior. Subjects are asked to respond on 9-point scales to items such as "I believe I should be competent at everything I attempt." Each item corresponds to one of Ellis's irrational beliefs.

In their research, Alden and Safran (1978) compared nonassertive subjects who scored highest and lowest on the IBI. Individuals who endorsed irrational beliefs most strongly also described themselves, on the Gambrill–Richey Assertion Inventory, as more uncomfortable and less assertive. Although there were no differences in subjects' knowledge of assertive responses, judges rated high scorers as less assertive in role-playing situations, and high scorers rated their own anxiety as greater than did subjects who endorsed irrational beliefs less strongly. Similarly, Alden and Cappe (1981) found that subjects who described themselves as "quite assertive" showed less endorsement of irrational beliefs on the IBI than "quite unassertive" subjects. Finally, in a therapy outcome study (Alden, Safran, & Weideman, 1978), cognitive-behavior modification and skills training groups showed lower posttreatment scores on the IBI compared to waiting-list controls. These studies nicely illustrate how cognitive measures can be used in both assessment- and outcome-oriented research.

In another study, Morelli and Friedman (1978) added to the S-R Inventory of General Trait Anxiousness five statements to measure irrational responses (e.g., "It is awful"; "Not the end of the world"). They found a highly significant correlation between anxiety and irrationality scores for all four general situations on this inventory, including a social interaction scene. Rakos (1979) devised an original subjective behavior rating scale, which assessed irrational and coping cognitions in addition to assertiveness and discomfort (e.g., "I can control my own anxiety"; "Being rejected by another person is awful and lowers my worth as a person"). The eight statements were rated on an 11-point scale. Subjects who received cognitive and behavioral self-administered assertiveness training reported significantly more rational cognitions than subjects who received self-administered relaxation training. Although these studies offer some interesting results, they do not provide data on the psychometric properties of these measures of irrational beliefs.

Measures of irrational beliefs appear to have utility for client screening and for research on the role of cognition in social-evaluative anxiety in addition to contributing to multimodal assessment of therapy change. A more fruitful direction than the development of general measures of irrational beliefs, however, may be the development of situation- or problem-specific methods. Rather than to assume that irrationality is a general "trait," it may be important to concern ourselves with specific types of irrationality.

In her well-designed outcome study with nonassertive subjects,

Craighead (1979) employed a measure of irrational beliefs about assertion in addition to the IBT. Craighead's scale consisted of 24 general-belief statements about the value and consequences of assertive responding. Two different self-instructional training groups showed significant improvement compared to a discussion placebo group, which, in turn, showed significant improvement relative to a waiting-list control group. This measure allowed for a direct manipulation check to confirm that cognitive therapy successfully accomplished the objective of modifying unproductive beliefs. That there was a significant difference between the discussion and waiting-list groups on the Craighead scale but not on the IBT suggests that general irrationality may be more difficult to change than irrational beliefs specific to the target of intervention.

A program of research by Lohr (Lohr & Bonge, Note 4; Lohr *et al.,* Note 5) has focused on the development and validation of a new measure, the "Situational Irrational Cognitions Inventory" (SICI). Subjects are asked (1) to examine irrational "syllogistic" interpretations that follow a number of social vignettes and (2) to rate the degree to which they agree with each interpretation and how anxious they would feel in a similar situation. The SICI consists of 50 items, so that each of Ellis's irrational beliefs is represented by five vignettes. Following is an example:

> Your class is discussing a subject upon which there are mixed feelings and opinions. You state one of your opinions about the subject, and immediately several people begin to strongly argue against your opinion. You know you shouldn't have said anything in class, and now they're going to think you're dumb. (Lohr *et al.,* Note 5, p. 36)

Subjects categorized on the IBT as highly irrational were more likely to agree with irrational interpretations of problematic social situations and estimated a greater degree of emotional upset in these situations than did persons who scored low on the IBT. However, there were no differences in ratings when social situations on the SICI did not lead to personal involvement for the main character.

In contrast to these questionnaires and inventories, which require ratings or responses to listed irrational ideas or beliefs, Fodor (Note 6) has developed an interesting projective measure of irrational thinking in heterosocial assertiveness behavior. Subjects' responses to a TAT-like picture of a woman and a man interacting are rated on a variety of dimensions, including feeling tone, degree of assertiveness, resolution of conflict, and self-statements accompanying assertive responses. Certain self-statements are related to one of seven irrational beliefs. For example, comments such as "What's the use?" are scored under the belief that "I have little ability to change or control the world." Other beliefs include "It would be awful if I hurt the other person" and "Other people should be condemned for treating me this way.'' Fodor's method illustrates a nonquestionnaire technique for assessing irrational beliefs and raises important issues concerning the relationship between self-statements and irrational beliefs.

Although irrational beliefs appear to be important targets for study, recent studies have not devoted much time and effort to the validation of inventories of such beliefs. The majority of studies have uncritically used the IBT, probably because it is more frequently found in the previous literature. To parallel a statement by Goldfried and Linehan (1977), controlled outcome research on cognitive therapy is only as good as our measures of cognitive (and behavioral and affective) change. We must pay considerably more attention to the psychometric properties of cognitive assessment instruments or risk proliferating the use of individually developed and unvalidated measures.

Assessment of Self-Statements

The assessment of self-statements has been a major area of study for researchers interested in the nature and treatment of social-evaluative anxiety. Studies have examined (1) the role of cognition in competent versus incompetent performance, (2) the relationship between cognition and affective and psychophysiological response, (3) the change in clients' internal dialogue as a function of cognitive therapy, and (4) the effect of different instructions on the level of task-interfering cognitions prior to a test or social interaction.

In addition, a number of different methods have been employed to assess "self-talk." We have organized these into six basic areas, based on the nature of the task that the subject is asked to complete. These methods include (1) recognition, (2) recall, (3) prompted recall, (4) projective, (5) expressive, and (6) naturalistic approaches. Studies dealing with assessment of self-statements in these areas are summarized in Table 3.

Recognition Methods. Structured questionnaires have frequently been used to assess self-statements. Subjects generally complete such a measure after a particular task (e.g., role-playing assertiveness situations). They are asked to indicate how frequently each of a predetermined list of thoughts occurred while they were working on the task. Most structured questionnaires attempt to measure the frequency of specific thoughts that are postulated to make it either more or less difficult to cope with a situation. Although such questionnaires have been developed for the study of depression (Hollon & Kendall, 1980), creativity (Henshaw, 1979), and coping with illness and stress (Kendall, Williams, Pechacek, Graham, Shisslak, & Herzof, 1979), we will focus exclusively on the use of such measures for the assessment of cognitive factors in assertiveness and social and evaluation anxiety.

The most frequently used measure, the Assertion Self-Statement Test (ASST), was developed by Schwartz and Gottman (1976) as part of their task analysis of assertive behavior. After completing a number of taped role-

Table 3. Summary of Studies on Assessment of Self-Statements

Author	Problem and nature of study	Cognitive assessment
	Recognition methods	
Bruch (in press-*b*)[a]	Assertiveness; contrasted groups	Assertion Self-Statement Test (ASST)
Craighead (1979)[a]	Assertiveness; outcome	ASST
Derry and Stone (1979)[a]	Assertiveness; outcome	ASST
Pitcher and Meikle (1980)	Assertiveness; contrasted groups	ASST
Rhyne and Hanson (Note 7)	Assertiveness; contrasted groups	ASST
Schwartz and Gottman (1976)	Assertiveness; contrasted groups	ASST
Taskey and Rich (Note 8)	Assertiveness; outcome	ASST
Glass, Merluzzi, Biever, and Larsen (in press)[a]	Development and validation	Social Interaction Self-Statement Test, thought listing
Hollandsworth, Glazeski, Kirkland, Jones, and VanNorman (1979)[a]	Test anxiety; contrasted groups	Cognitive Interference Questionnaire (CIQ), videotape thought reconstruction (VTR)
Kirkland and Hollandsworth (1980)	Test anxiety; outcome	CIQ, attentional interference scale
Sarason (1978)	Test anxiety; development	CIQ
Sarason and Stoops (1978)	Test anxiety; contrasted groups	CIQ
Galassi, Frierson, and Sharer (in press)	Test anxiety; contrasted groups	Checklist of positive and negative thoughts
Keane and Lisman (1980)	Heterosocial; contrasted groups	Irrational Statements Inventory
LaPointe and Harrell (1978)	Interpersonal conflict; correlational	Thoughts–feelings ratings

(continued)

Table 3. (continued)

Author	Problem and nature of study	Cognitive assessment
Recall methods		
Arnkoff (1980*b*)[a]	Test anxiety; outcome	Thought listing
Bruch (1978)[a]	Test anxiety; analogue outcome	Thought listing
Cacioppo, Glass, and Merluzzi (1979)[a]	Social anxiety; contrasted groups	Thought listing
Glass, Merluzzi, and Cacioppo (Note 9)	Social anxiety; contrasted groups	Thought listing
Malklewich and Merluzzi (1980)	Social anxiety; outcome	Thought listing
Merluzzi, Cacioppo, and Glass (Note 10)	Social anxiety; contrasted groups	Thought listing
Prompted recall		
Smye and Wine (1980)	Social competence; contrasted groups	Behavioral Social Interaction Test: VTR
Steffen and Lucas (Note 11)	Social competence; contrasted groups	VTR
Projective methods		
Breznitz (1971)	Social anxiety; correlational	Projective
Weston and Glass (Note 12)	Social competence; contrasted groups	Projective
Expressive (concurrent) methods		
Crager (1959)	Test anxiety; contrasted groups	Thinking aloud
Craighead, Kimball, and Rehak (1979)	Social rejection; contrasted groups	Taped current thoughts

Table 3. (continued)

Author	Problem and nature of study	Cognitive assessment
	Expressive (concurrent) methods	
Hurlburt and Sipprelle (1978)	Anxiety; case study	Random thought sampling
Sutton-Simon and Gold-fried (1979)[a]	Social anxiety and acro-phobia; correlational	Sentence completion

[a]Reference includes additional forms of cognitive assessment (see other tables).

playing situations, undergraduate students were asked to respond to 17 positive and 17 negative self-statements on a 5-point scale from "hardly ever had the thought" to "very often had the thought." "I was worried what the other person would think about me if I refused" is an example of a negative, inhibitive thought, which would make it harder to refuse the request. "I was thinking that there didn't seem to be any reason not to state my position" is a positive, facilitative self-statement, which might make refusal easier. Subjects then indicated the sequence of strategies they used (e.g., negative and then positive; always positive). Although nonassertive undergraduates did not differ from assertive undergraduates in their knowledge of assertive responses or in their ability to demonstrate an assertive response to a friend, they performed significantly poorer in their role-played responses to actual requests, reported more anxiety, and demonstrated different cognitive responses on the ASST. Specifically, assertive students made more positive and fewer negative self-statements than nonassertive students (and reported significantly more positive than negative self-statements). On the basis of their results, Schwartz and Gottman (1976) concluded that "the most likely source of non-assertiveness in low assertive subjects could be related to the nature of their cognitive positive and negative self-statements" (p. 918).

The ASST has been used in four additional task analyses of assertive behavior and in at least two outcome studies. Bruch (in press-*b*) and Pitcher and Meikle (1980) extended the task analysis to the study of positive (commendatory) as well as negative (refusal) assertiveness. Pitcher and Meikle revised the ASST into two forms, which measured self-statements in negative or positive assertion situations. Each scale consisted of five assertion-facilitating and five assertion-inhibiting self-statements. The appropriate form was administered immediately after role-playing situations involving positive or negative assertion. Although there were no cognitive differences between high- and low-assertive subjects in positive assertion situations, high-assertive subjects reported significantly more facilitating than inhibiting self-statements in negative situations. There was a nonsignificant trend for low-assertive subjects to report more inhibiting than facilitating thoughts. Finally, high-assertive subjects had more facilitating and fewer inhibiting self-statements than low-assertive subjects, replicating Schwartz and Gottman's findings for assertive refusal situations.

Bruch (in press-*b*) directly replicated Schwartz and Gottman but added written and role-playing tests of positive assertion (tenderness expression) and three additional cognitive measures: MEPS, cognitive complexity, and the Subjective Probability of Consequences Scale. The ASST results almost exactly paralleled the original study, with high-assertive subjects emitting significantly more positive and fewer negative self-statements than low-assertive subjects in assertive refusal situations. High-assertive subjects also endorsed significantly more positive than negative self-statements. Bruch's study is exemplary in its use of a variety of cognitive measures. Results from the subjective probability instrument will be discussed in a subsequent section of this chapter.

Rhyne and Hanson (Note 7) have extended the task analysis of assertion to psychiatric inpatients. Although they found significant differences between high- and low-assertive patients on all three behavioral-response formats (knowledge, hypothetical response, role-play), results on the ASST again replicated those of Schwartz and Gottman. Such results suggest that nonassertiveness among psychiatric patients is due not only to the presence of maladaptive and inhibiting self-statements but to an inadequate behavioral repertoire as well. High-assertive subjects, compared to low-assertive subjects reported a significantly greater number of positive self-statements and fewer negative self-statements and, unlike low assertives, indicated significantly more positive than negative self-statements. Heimberg, Chiauzzi, Becker, and Madrazo-Peterson (Note 13) have recently completed a similar investigation using a clinical population.

Finally, two outcome studies cited in the previous section employed the ASST in addition to the IBT as a measure of cognitive change. Derry and Stone (1979) found no posttest differences in positive self-statements on the ASST, but found that subjects in the behavioral-rehearsal plus cognitive self-statement condition endorsed fewer negative self-statements than either subjects in behavior rehearsal plus attribution training or behavior rehearsal alone. The latter contrast was also significant at follow-up. Craighead (1979) reported that self-instructional training resulted in a significant increase in the frequency of positive self-statements relative to no-treatment controls and in a significant decrease in negative self-statements relative to no-treatment and expectancy controls. Recall that similar differences were found on the IBT and on Craighead's assertion-specific measure of irrational beliefs.

The consistency of findings in these studies helps to establish the utility of the ASST as a measure of cognitive self-statements in assertion-related situations. Glass and Merluzzi (Glass *et al.,* in press; Glass & Merluzzi, Note 14) have developed a similar scale for use in heterosocial situations. In developing the "Social Interaction Self-Statement Test" (SISST), we thought it crucial to obtain self-statements firsthand from a large group of subjects. It is important to attend to such content validity concerns rather than to allow self-statement questionnaires to be based on items from previous questionnaires or on what appears to be valid to the authors.

Pilot subjects were given descriptions of ten heterosocial situations and asked to list their thoughts as they imagined they were personally involved in each interaction. Two trained judges read all self-statements and classified them as negative, positive, or neutral in valence. Sixty-five self-statements that were unanimously classified as positive or negative and reported by at least two pilot subjects were given to eight raters who evaluated each statement on an 11-point scale from negative to positive. We selected the 15 negative and 15 positive self-statements with the most extreme mean ratings and lowest standard deviations to compose the SISST. These items were presented in the same format as that of the previously described ASST (Schwartz & Gottman, 1976). Examples of SISST items include "She probably won't be interested in me" (negative) and "This will be a good opportunity" (positive).

Our research (Glass *et al.,* in press) has shown a significant relationship between positive and negative self-statement scores on the SISST and various measures of social anxiety (Social Avoidance and Distress Scale, Watson & Friend, 1969) and social skill (Survey of Heterosocial Interaction, Twentyman & McFall, 1975; Survey of Heterosocial Interaction for Females, Williams & Ciminero, 1979). Socially competent (high-skill, low-anxiety) subjects demonstrated more positive and fewer negative self-statements than low-competent (low-skill, high-anxiety) subjects. In addition, low-competent subjects had significantly more negative than positive self-statements; the opposite was true for the socially competent group.

It is important to note that self-statements were also related to situational self-evaluations. Subjects who frequently emitted negative self-talk also tended to rate their tension level as higher and their skill level as lower on 7-point self-ratings immediately after role-playing situations or a face-to-face interaction. Frequent positive self-statements, on the other hand, were related to higher skill self-ratings and lower perceived tension. It is perhaps even more notable that SISST-negative (but not SISST-positive) scores correlated significantly with confederates' and judges' ratings of subject skill and anxiety. Thus the other person involved in the interaction tended to rate subjects with higher levels of negative internal dialogue as less skillful and more tense.

A similar questionnaire for use with test-anxious subjects was developed by Sarason (1978). The Cognitive Interference Questionnaire (CIQ) is a measure of negative self-statements and attention during evaluative (test) situations. The CIQ consists of 11 5-point scales on which subjects respond to "how often each thought occurred while working on the task" and a 7-point scale concerning the "degree to which you felt your mind wandered." Sarason and Stoops (1978) gave high-, moderate-, and low-test-anxious subjects either achievement-orienting or neutral instructions to solve a series of anagrams after a 4-minute wait. The CIQ was administered after the task, and the authors found a significantly higher level of task-interfering cognitions in high- as compared to moderate- or low-test-anxious subjects. For the high-anxious group alone, achievement-orienting instructions also led to a significantly higher level of interfering thoughts than did neutral instructions. Thus high-test-anxious subjects were particularly preoccupied with how poorly they were doing, how others were faring, and what the examiner would think of them. This study provides direct support for Wine's (1971, 1980) model of a task-irrelevant process in high-test-anxious individuals. It would also be important to know what subjects were thinking about during the waiting period, after the instructions but before the task.

Hollandsworth, Glazeski, Kirkland, Jones, and VanNorman (1979) used Sarason's CIQ in an interesting study of the cognitive, behavioral, and physiological components of test anxiety. Six subjects with either high or low levels of test anxiety, yet a moderate level of general anxiety, performed an evaluative task. Measures of heart rate, skin resistance, and respiration were recorded during the task. In addition to the CIQ and two standard self-report measures of anxiety, Hollandsworth *et al.* (1979) used a videotape thought-reconstruction measure (see discussion of prompted recall methods). On the average, low-test-anxious subjects reported fewer interfering thoughts than high-anxious subjects and did not think about how poorly they were doing or about getting confused. Interestingly, low-test-anxious subjects also showed a greater degree of cardiac and respiratory arousal before the test and after testing began.

Most recently, the CIQ has been used as a measure in outcome research on test anxiety (Kirkland & Hollandsworth, 1980). Subjects who were trained in test-taking attentional skills (including adaptive self-instructional statements) thought less frequently about the level of their ability during posttreatment evaluative tasks than did subjects in cue-controlled relaxation, meditation, or practice control conditions. Both skills and relaxation groups thought less frequently than the practice control group about how much time was left, and attentional-skills subjects also had lower overall CIQ scores than did the controls. Hollandsworth's own attentional interference scale (Glazeski, Hollandsworth, & Jones, Note 15) yielded similar results. Skills-training subjects reported that they thought less frequently about how poorly they were doing and were able to concentrate more than controls.

Not all recognition measures of self-statements rely on posttask inventories and frequency ratings of cognitions. Galassi *et al.* (in press) used a self-statement checklist of positive and negative thoughts to assess students' internal dialogue at one of three different times during a course examination: (1) after reading the test for the first time, (2) about halfway through the test, and (3) approximately 10 minutes before completing the test. The checklist contained 18 positive and 19 negative thoughts likely to affect concentration and performance. Results showed that high-test-anxious students had significantly fewer positive, task-relevant cognitions than both low- and moderate-test-anxious students. Low-, moderate-, and high-test-anxious groups differed significantly from each other in the number of negative, task-irrelevant thoughts. Students assessed toward the end of the test reported significantly more negative thoughts than the other two groups. This result emphasizes the importance of assessing cognitive responses over time.

A similar measure of the content of internal dialogue, which did not attempt to address issues of thought frequency or order, was developed by Keane and Lisman (1980) as part of a study that assessed the effects of alcohol on men's heterosocial anxiety and performance. The Irrational Statements Inventory is a 20-item true-false checklist of negative self-statements and beliefs adapted from Watson and Friend's (1969) Fear of Negative Evaluation Scale. Three items represent general irrational beliefs (e.g., "Evaluations which other people make of me cause me little concern"), and 17 are specific worries, fears, and feelings relevant to subjects' conversation with a woman (e.g., "I was worried that I would say the wrong things"). High socially anxious men who were given alcohol prior to an interaction with a female confederate reported more negative self-statements during the interaction than high-anxious men who were given a placebo. Keane and Lisman suggest that the poorer behavioral performance of these heterosocially anxious men may have been mediated by negative self-statements that were disinhibited by the presence of alcohol.

Structured questionnaires appear to show high potential as a measure of self-statements. Already we have increased our knowledge of the contributions of cognitive appraisal to problems of shyness, test anxiety, and nonassertiveness. The questionnaires are extremely easy to administer and score and do not require extensive rating systems. However, performance on structured questionnaires may reflect post hoc reappraisals of what subjects feel they *could* have been thinking. In other words, the recognition nature of the task may add to the possibility that such retrospective accounts are distorted. This format, however, could also allow for more accurate responding because of increased accessibility of thoughts, although the questionnaire may not contain representative thoughts for all individuals. The frequency of specific self-statements may not be the most important aspect of internal dialogue to study, because the salience or meaning of a thought to the individual may be more relevant. This issue will be discussed in a subsequent section of the chapter.

Recall Methods. Allowing subjects to list or describe what they were thinking during an immediately preceding period helps to reduce the post hoc reappraisal problem and does not limit subjects to a predetermined number of self-statements. The recall method most frequently employed is the thought-listing technique, previously discussed in detail by Cacioppo and Petty (Chapter 10, this volume). The reader is referred to their chapter for instructions and scoring criteria. We will focus here on the use of thought listings in clinically relevant situations with socially anxious and test-anxious individuals.

Cacioppo *et al.* (1979) used thought listings in their study of social anxiety. After a short period, during which male subjects waited to interact with an unfamiliar woman, subjects were asked to list all the thoughts that had gone through their minds. High socially anxious men listed more negative and fewer positive self-statements than low socially anxious subjects. In related studies, Glass *et al.* (Note 9) found that men who expected to interact with a woman reported higher levels of state anxiety and listed a greater number of negative self-statements than men who expected to interact with another man. Merluzzi *et al.* (Note 10) found that high socially anxious men's thoughts were focused more on themselves whereas low socially anxious men's thoughts were focused more on an impending interaction or on the other person involved. These findings suggest a difference not only in the valence of cognitive responses (positive, negative, or neutral/irrelevant) but also in the target or locus of attention.

In addition, thought listings have been used as dependent variables in three therapy outcome studies. Arnkoff (1980*b*) used a thought-listing procedure to explore the posttherapy internal dialogue of text-anxious subjects. In addition to physiological and anxiety measures, subjects completed a thought listing after a period in which they thought about their upcoming final exam (one hour away). Arnkoff scored the results on the valence dimension and calculated the proportion of positive, negative, and neutral thoughts compared to total listed thoughts. This approach offers an alternative to categorical frequency analysis. Although subjects who learned to challenge their maladaptive beliefs regarding achievement showed significantly fewer negative self-statements than waiting-list controls, subjects who learned to use self-statements regarding worry, attention, and relaxation during a test showed not only significantly fewer negative self-statements but also significantly more positive self-statements than waiting-list controls. Recall from the previous section that both cognitive therapy groups had significantly deceased scores on the IBT relative to control subjects.

A study by Bruch (1978) employed cognitive modeling of problem-solving rules or coping self-instructions with test-anxious female subjects. The women were stopped at three different times during an anagram test and were asked to list things they did or thought about while solving the anagrams. These protocols were scored for the number of negative self-statements as well as for the use of imitative or idiosyncratic problem-solving rules and coping instructions. Negative self-statements were positively correlated with time to complete the test (poorer performance) and inversely related to the use of problem-solving rules. A comparison group of low-test-anxious women reported very few negative self-statements.

Finally, in a therapy outcome study with socially anxious men (Malkiewich & Merluzzi, 1980), subjects engaged in a pretreatment and a post-treatment 8-minute conversation with two other group members. Immediately after the conversation, subjects were asked to list the thoughts that they had had during the conversation. Although no differences were found for positive or neutral thoughts, rational restructuring and systematic desensitization significantly reduced negative self-statements relative to waiting-list controls.

Prompted Recall Methods. A third method of self-statement assessment is prompted recall. Subjects are again asked to recall previous thoughts but are given some structure in the form of a visual, spoken, and/or written prompt. Videotape-aided thought reconstruction is perhaps the best example of this method. Like thought listing, such procedures require well-developed scoring systems.

Videotape thought reconstruction involves videotaping a subject's behavior in an actual or role-playing situation (often a problematic one), playing back the videotape for the individual, and asking him or her to recall the thoughts (and/or feelings) experienced while in the original situation. We have alternatively used the term "thought dubbing" to describe this procedure (Glass & Merluzzi, Note 14), which in some ways is similar to the process in which actors and actresses dub in a sound track after a movie scene is filmed. This approach is also similar to Kagan's interpersonal process recall (Kagan & Krathwohl, 1967), where therapists under supervision are videotaped during a therapy session and trained to recall their feelings and thoughts while viewing the videotape. The effect of training on results obtained from videotape-aided thought reconstruction remains an interesing question.

Smye and Wine (1980) have used this technique as part of their Behavioral Social Interaction Test. In their study, male and female high school students responded to 26 videotaped vignettes of problematic social situations. In addition to obtaining ratings of overt behavior, Smye and Wine played back the videotape and asked subjects to recall what they were thinking during the social interaction test, especially right before and right after their spoken responses. Thoughts were coded into 26 categories, such as "positive description of feelings" and "evaluation of test." Results showed that women, compared to men, evaluated others more negatively, denied their impact on others, had fewer cognitions to avoid or escape the situation, and tended less to deny the impact of others on themselves. Thus, although men were more overtly aggressive, the addition of cognitive assessment demonstrated that women were more covertly negative toward others. A cluster analysis also revealed fewer and smaller categories of cognitions for men than for women.

Steffen and Lucas (Note 11) used a similar methodology, in which high

and low socially competent men were shown a videotape of role-play interaction they had had with a female confederate. Subjects were told to stop the
tape and report their thoughts if there were any points at which they could
recall what they had been thinking at the time. In addition, the experimenters
asked subjects 29 questions concerning the "mental processes you employ
when interacting with someone for the first time" (Steffen & Lucas, Note 11,
p. 7). Results indicated that high socially competent men, as compared to low
socially competent men, described more original strategies of action, were
able to generate more strategies to initiate conversations, and were more
aware of their thoughts about the interaction and about the appearance of,
and their feelings toward, their partner in the interaction. They also made
more favorable statements, including those in which they referred to
themselves. Note that Steffen and Lucas assessed problem-solving strategies
as well as self-statements using videotape-aided thought recall.

Videotape reconstruction has also been used to identify cognitive aspects
of test anxiety. The Hollandsworth *et al.* (1979) study was discussed previously in the section on recognition methods. In addition to finding that low-test-
anxious subjects reported fewer interfering thoughts on the CIQ, the authors
asked high- and low-test-anxious subjects to view a videotape of their task
performance and to relate what they were thinking and feeling as they worked
on the test. The tape was stopped at several predesignated points or if certain
behaviors occurred. After breaking the internal dialogue into discrete
statements, judges categorized these self-statements as task-facilitative (on
task, positive) or task-debilitative (off task, negative). On the average, low-
test-anxious subjects reported a substantially greater percentage of
facilitative statements.

Videotape methods appear to be a broad and creative way to measure
subjects' thoughts. As with other retrospective techniques, there is a possibility that results reflect a post hoc rationalization rather than an actual narrative of thoughts during the original situation. It is therefore important to
compare videotape methods with less reactive measures. Our faith in such
assessment will increase as data are gathered on its reliability and validity and
as cognitive assessment is shown to aid our ability to *predict* and *explain* complex events.

Projective Methods. Sobel (Chapter 5, this volume) has described in
detail the use of projective methods to assess cognitive coping strategies.
Previously in this chapter, we described Fodor's (Note 6) projective measure
of irrational beliefs in a heterosocial assertiveness situation. Projective
measures have also been used to assess self-statements. These methods differ
from those already described in that subjects do not indicate the nature of
their own internal dialogue, but rather what the central character in a picture
or vignette is thinking. For example, Weston and Glass (Note 12) used hand-
puppet characters to assess self-statements and problem solving in popular
and unpopular children. The children put on a puppet's "thinking cap" and

related what the puppet was thinking when faced with various situations involving social conflict.

Breznitz (1971), in his study of worrying, used a slightly different task. Subjects projected their own thoughts and feelings onto a social intelligence test after the following scene was described: "A person is waiting for another person to come. The person who is late is very dear to the one who is waiting" (p. 275). Undergraduate subjects responded to a checklist of 14 thoughts and feelings most "appropriate" for the person who was waiting. These thoughts ranged in intensity and focus and constituted scales of rejection, aggression, possible accident, and diminishing optimism. Thoughts of rejection (e.g., "He forgot to come") were followed more often by aggression-scale thoughts (e.g., "This is making me angry") than by any other category.

Although projective methods have not often been used in self-statement assessment, they offer interesting possibilities. Because it is possible to question the extent to which projective measures yield data relevant to an individual's actual cognitions, validation is crucial. Like recall methods, many projective methods require the development of detailed and reliable scoring systems.

Expressive Methods. The fifth category of self-statement assessment, expressive or concurrent methods, includes techniques that assess ongoing thoughts accompanying a situation. Subjects can be asked either (1) to imagine they are in a particular situation and to express what they are thinking or (2) to record thoughts during an actual task or life event. Such methods may attempt to capture an expression of the individual's "stream of thoughts" over a period of time, although assessment during actual task performance comes much closer to meeting this goal. We will discuss two studies that use an imagery-based setting and two that obtained a protocol of thoughts during a laboratory task and daily experiences.

Sutton-Simon and Goldfried (1979) related IBT scores to subjects' actual positive and negative self-statements and to measures of social anxiety and fear of heights. Using a sentence completion technique, subjects were shown descriptions of social, height-involving, and neutral situations and were asked to complete sentence stems describing how they felt and what they thought—for example, "In this situation, I'm feeling _____"; I'm feeling this way because I'm thinking _____" (p. 197). Although the tendency to hold irrational beliefs was significantly associated with level of social anxiety and acrophobia and tended to correlate with negative self-statements emitted in social situations, there was little correlation with negative self-statements in height-related situations. This suggests that irrational beliefs may reflect a situation-specific, and not a general, tendency to emit negative self-statements and raises important questions for future research.

In a replication and extension of Goldfried and Sobocinski's (1975) study, Craighead *et al.* (1979) used tape recordings to assess subjects' reactions following imagined scenes of social rejection. Taped answers to the question "What thoughts are racing through your head?" (p. 387) were scored for the presence of positive and negative self-statements and task-referent statements. The number of negative self-referent statements was significantly correlated with mood scale increases in feelings of anxiety, hostility, and depression; positive self-referent statements were correlated with a decrease in depression during social rejection imagery. Female subjects who scored high on the IBT social approval scale emitted significantly more negative self-referent statements compared to those who scored lowest on this scale.

A more *in vivo* approach to the assessment of ongoing self-statements asks subjects to think aloud while performing a task. Cognitive psychologists Newell and Simon (1972), in their work on computer models of human problem solving, elicited such protocols from subjects solving cryptarithmetic problems. In what may be one of the first applications of think-aloud assessment in clinical psychology, Crager (1959) sought to demonstrate the existence of interfering "personal negative statements" while undergraduates performed an achievement-oriented task. High- and low-test-anxious subjects were asked to "talk out loud" and to describe what they were doing, how they were trying to solve the anagram, and anything else that came to mind. Crager videotaped all protocols and scored them for personal negative statements as well as eight other variables, such as number of words and personal pronouns used, total time taken, and number of cues needed. High-test-anxious women emitted significantly more personal negative statements than low-test-anxious women and needed significantly more time and cues in order to reach the correct solutions. No such distinctions were found between high- and low-test-anxious men.

A sampling procedure has been used by Klinger (1978) and Hurlburt (1979) to record subjects' thoughts at random times during the day. At present, no data are available that directly relate to the assessment of social or evaluation anxiety. In a related study, Hurlburt and Sipprelle (1978) reported the case of a 48-year-old man who was undergoing therapy for anxiety attacks. A signal generator presented a tone to the client's earphone at random intervals, at which time the man recorded his current thought and level of anxiety. The authors reported that, although the number of negative cognitions remained the same, the client reported less anxiety associated with such thoughts after therapy. This result suggests that we must be careful to attend not only to the frequency or content of self-statements but also to the subjective meaning they hold for the individual.

These results underscore the importance of developing a methodology for the reliable assessment of self-verbalizations *during* the situation, as well as retrospective reports using recall and recognition methods. However, it is unclear what effect the process of thinking out loud will have on performance and the internal dialogue itself. This may become more of a problem, and thinking aloud may become a more inappropriate methodology, as the situation or task becomes increasingly social in nature. Although a subject could be asked to think aloud while anticipating an interaction, it would be exceptionally difficult to continue once the interaction had begun! (See Genest & Turk, Chapter 8, this volume, for a more detailed discussion of the advantages and disadvantages of think-aloud and random-thought-sampling methods.)

A final consideration must focus on the ecological validity of most expressive methods. There may be large differences between what test-anxious individuals say to themselves in artificial test situations and their internal dialogue during an actual classroom exam. As far as we know, think-aloud recording methods have not been employed in such real-life settings with test-anxious or socially anxious subjects.

Naturalistic Methods. The final method for assessing self-statements involves the naturalistic recording of spontaneous verbalizations. This procedure has been especially valuable in studies with children, but we were unable to find research in topic areas relevant to this chapter. The reader can refer to Genest and Turk (Chapter 8, this volume) for a presentation of the methodology of this approach.

Self-statement assessment generally involves retrospective or ongoing methods. We shall now turn our attention to the assessment of future possibilities: the assessment of predicted consequences and experiences.

Assessment of Expectations and Self-Efficacy

Bandura's theory of self-efficacy (Bandura, 1977) has received a good deal of attention in recent years. Curiously, only one study has described a measure of self-efficacy in the context of assertion or social-evaluative anxiety (see Table 4). Jaremko and Walker (Note 2) asked speech-anxious subjects to rate the extent to which they felt able to perform ten specific behaviors involved in preparing and giving a speech. At follow-up, subjects who received a stress-inoculation program showed a significant increase in self-efficacy expectations from pretreatment levels. Immediately after treatment, only the stress-inoculation group, which focused on reversal of affect, showed a significant change. The stress-inoculation group that rehearsed general self-statements did not demonstrate self-efficacy change.

Another theoretical approach that has influenced recent cognitive assessment is decision theory (Edwards, 1954), which postulates that behavior is a function of both evaluations and expectations of particular consequences of a given behavior. "Subjective expected utility" (SEU) is calculated as the sum of a subject's ratings of the utilities or benefits of a series of positive and negative consequences, weighted by the probability that he or she thinks each consequence will occur. It is thus a measure of the response cost or subjective risk of certain behaviors.

Fiedler and Beach (1978) used SEU values to examine the conditions

Table 4. Summary of Studies on Assessment of Expectations and Self-Efficacy

Author	Problem and nature of study	Cognitive assessment
Bruch (in press-b)[a]	Assertiveness; contrasted groups	Subjective Probability of Consequences Scale
Eisler, Frederiksen, and Peterson (1978)	Assertiveness; contrasted groups	Generalized Expectations of Others Questionnaire
Fiedler and Beach (1978)	Assertiveness; contrasted groups	Subjective expected utility
Gormally, Sipps, Raphael, Varvil-Weld, and Edwin (in press)[a]	Heterosocial; contrasted groups	Situational expectancies inventory
Gormally, Varvil-Weld, Raphael, and Sipps (in press)[a]	Heterosocial; outcome	Situational expectancies inventory
Jaremko and Walker (Note 2)	Speech anxiety; outcome	Self-efficacy

[a]Reference includes additional forms of cognitive assessment (see other tables).

under which a person chooses to act assertively. High-, medium-, and low-assertive subjects first rated each of ten negative and ten positive consequences for their utility or desirability. These consequences were presented again following each of nine scenes, and subjects were asked to rate the probability of each consequence, first assuming that they complied with the request, second, assuming that they refused. The authors also asked subjects to state if they actually would have complied or refused (behavioral intent).

Although assertiveness and anxiety level were not related to behavioral intent or SEU in the Fiedler and Beach study, the latter two values were highly related. Individuals with high levels of behavioral intent expected that positive consequences would accompany assertive refusal and that nonrefusal would lead to negative consequences. Subjects also had a higher SEU for refusal in situations involving authorities versus peers and in situations with males more than females.

Previously in this chapter, we described Bruch's (in press-b) task analysis of positive and negative assertive behavior. In addition to Schwartz and Gottman's (1976) ASST and behavioral measures of assertion, Bruch administered the Subjective Probability of Consequences Scale, a paragraph completion measure of cognitive complexity, and the Means–End Problem-Solving (MEPS) procedure (Spivack, Platt, & Shure, 1976), which will be described in a later section. The Subjective Probability of Consequences Scale asks subjects to rate the probability of various consequences of refusal and compliance, based on three situations from the Conflict Resolution Inventory (McFall & Lillesand, 1971). Following a decision to comply, high-assertive subjects expected fewer positive consequences. They also expected a lower probability of negative consequences following a decision to refuse a request. In addition, expectations of negative consequences of compliance and of positive consequences of refusal were significantly correlated with ASST-positive scores; ASST-negative scores were correlated with expected positive consequences of compliance and negative consequences of refusal.

Not all applications of SEU measures have focused on assertiveness. Gormally, Sipps, Raphael, Varvil-Weld, and Edwin (in press) developed a situational expectancies inventory for heterosocially anxious college men. Subjects were asked to imagine themselves in each of four situations describing an initiation of a social overture to a female stranger. For each situation, they then rated how they would feel if the woman rejected the overture (negative affect) and how they would feel if she responded positively (positive affect). These feelings were described by checking a point on a scale ranging from − 100 ("horrible") through 0 ("neutral") to + l00 ("ecstatic"). Subjects also described the perceived probability of being rejected in each situation by use of a 5-point scale ranging from 0% (rejection not at all likely) to 100% (rejection is certain).

The clinical sample of high heterosocially anxious men was significantly different from competent daters on three of the four situations. Socially anxious men expected to feel worse if their overtures were rejected, and more euphoric if accepted, and estimated a higher probability of rejection than did the socially competent men. Gormally, Sipps, Raphael, Varvil-Weld, and Edwin (in press) suggest that low-frequency daters may thus be "catastrophizing" as well as "ecstatisizing" their interactions with women. Consistent with this hypothesis, the clinical sample estimated the same amount of risk in starting a casual conversation as the competent daters assigned to asking for a date. Because Gormally *et al.* used multiple measures of cognitive response, they were able to test the relationship between situational expectancies and irrational beliefs (IBT). Correlations ranged from absolute values of .20 to .61. Greater irrationality was associated with higher estimates of being rejected, feeling more positive after acceptance, and feeling more negative after the rejection of a social initiation.

Eisler *et al.* (1978) used a measure of expectations not formally derived from decision theory, the Generalized Expectations of Others Questionnaire, in a study with assertive and unassertive psychiatric patients. Results showed that high-assertive men generally expected that others would respond to them in a more positive manner in social situations. The authors conclude that "how a person performs is related to cognitive constructions of how he perceives the situation, the ability to select responses from a range of alternatives, and the expected consequences of alternatives'' (Eisler *et al.,* 1978, p. 42).

Expectations and perceptions of self-efficacy appear to be easily assessed, important components of successful or competent performance. Such findings raise important questions of whether treatment should deal with changing performance or with changing such expectations and perceptions more directly. Because previous research has tended to focus on social competence, further applications to test and speech anxiety are needed. We would urge researchers to develop measures using empirically derived positive and negative behavioral consequences of refusal or compliance, as Kuperminc and Heimberg (Note 16) have done.

Assessment of Problem-Solving and Coping Strategies

Most research on the role of problem-solving or coping strategies in social competence has been with children. Because Krasnor and Rubin (Chapter 15, this volume) discuss this topic in detail, this chapter will deal primarily with applications of cognitive assessment with adults (see Table 5). We begin with a description of recent work by Richard Lazarus and his colleagues.

Lazarus (1980) has recognized that stress and conflict may result not only in impaired performance but also sometimes in constant or even improved performance. Thus emotions (or stress) are seen as products of cognition, resulting from the way we *appraise* or construe our environment, but also as affecting cognitive appraisal in turn. Coping includes both problem-solving instrumental action and palliative management of the somatic and subjective components of stress. Coyne and Lazarus (1979) stress the importance of assessing cognitive appraisal as people engage in ongoing transactions with the environment. They add, however, that self-reports of cognitive activity should be seen as just one subset of the data, which would also focus on characteristics of the person and his or her environment, observed patterning of emotions, physiological responses, coping, and the fit or congruence of all of these factors.

The assessment of coping can be approached in a number of different ways (Lazarus, 1980). Coping can be viewed as a pattern or constellation of many acts and thoughts over time. Alternatively, coping can be studied through people's awareness of current tactics and thoughts, as assessed by checklists and clinical interviews. Finally, coping effectiveness could be evaluated in terms of what works for different individuals in various situations. Folkman and Lazarus (1980), in a study of naturalistic stress, coping, and daily life in middle-aged individuals, developed several measures of coping processes. A coping interview asked subjects to describe stressful events during the previous month and elicited a detailed account of thoughts,

Table 5. Summary of Studies on Assessment of Problem-Solving
and Coping Strategies

Author	Problem and nature of study	Cognitive assessment
Bruch (1978)[a]	Test anxiety; correlational analogue outcome	Problem-solving rules and coping instructions
Bruch (in press-*a*)	Test anxiety; contrasted groups	Questionnaire of How You Take Tests
Bruch (in press-*b*)[a]	Assertiveness; contrasted groups	Means–End Problem Solving
Folkman and Lazarus (1980)	Naturalistic stress and coping	Coping interview, checklist, and questionnaire
Getter and Nowinski (in press)	Social competence; development and validation	Interpersonal Problem-Solving Assessment Technique
Hutchings, Denney, Basgal, and Houston (in press)	Test anxiety; outcome (behavioral approach)	Cognitive coping question-naire (coping strategies)
Steffen and Lucas (Note 11)[a]	Social competence; contrasted groups	Videotape-aided reconstruction

[a]Reference includes additional forms of cognitive assessment (see other tables).

emotions, and actions in each coping episode. Subjects also completed a monthly coping questionnaire, where they described the most stressful event of the month. Finally, a ways-of-coping checklist assessed behavioral and cognitive coping strategies employed in specific situations. These strategies included information seeking, direct action, and problem solving as well as defensive coping mechanisms such as avoidance and intellectualization.

Other investigators have focused more exclusively upon the assessment of problem-solving forms of coping, stressing the generation of alternatives, means–ends thinking, performance strategies, and styles of managing interpersonal conflict. Bruch (in press-*b*) included a Means–End Problem-Solving procedure (Spivack *et al.,* 1976) in his task analysis of assertive behavior. After being presented with nine stories in which a need was aroused in the main character at the beginning and was satisfied by the story's end, subjects made up a story to fill in the details of what the character did. Thus the MEPS represents a more projective assessment of problem solving. The descriptions were scored to reveal the number and percentage of relevant means employed, added details, obstacles and their enumeration, and total time. High-, moderate-, and low-assertive subjects did not differ on the MEPS. However, group differences were found on different cognitive measures such as the ASST and the Subjective Probability of Consequences Scale. This illustrates the importance of viewing cognitive variables as independent and perhaps functionally distinct.

Bruch (in press-*a*) has also studied problem-solving strategies in a task analysis of competence in evaluative situations. His Questionnaire of How You Take Tests asks subjects to recall their strategies while responding to different formats of questions, a form of post hoc "cognitive role play." The number of relevant test-taking strategies (e.g., check work, deduce answer, clarify meaning, recall material) and the effectiveness or quality of each strategy were computed for high-, medium-, and low-math-anxious and high-, medium-, and low-test-anxious undergraduates. Although the questionnaire was unrelated to American College Test (ACT) scores, low-test-anxious subjects scored significantly higher than high-test-anxious subjects on total strategy score and strategies on essay and matching questions. A similar pattern was found for high- and low-math-anxious subjects on math problem strategies. This research suggests the importance of studying the knowledge of test-taking strategies (tactics, rules, or procedures that increase the probability of correct question interpretation and solution) in addition to self-instructions that help one to cope with anxiety-arousing thoughts and direct attention.

A final example of the assessment of interpersonal problem-solving and thinking styles can be found in the work of Getter and Nowinski (in press), who have developed a promising scale for assessing components of interpersonal effectiveness across six types of social situations. After reading descriptions of situations involving interpersonal conflict, subjects were asked to list as many alternative solutions as they could before indicating which one they would actually choose in the situation. The major scoring categories of the Interpersonal Problem-Solving Assessment Technique (IPSAT)—effectiveness, avoidance, appropriateness, dependency, and solution productivity—were derived from Rotter's social learning theory, giving this inventory a strong theoretical grounding.

The authors provide a detailed scoring manual (Nowinski & Getter, Note 17) and preliminary evidence of good interscorer reliability and of both convergent and discriminant validity. Clinical and nonclinical samples of college students produced IPSAT scores that were significantly different in clinically meaningful ways. As predicted, the number of effective and avoidant solutions on the IPSAT was significantly related to undergraduates' scores on a measure of assertiveness. Avoidant and inappropriate solutions were also related to the need for heterosexuality (social activity level) on the Edwards Personal Preference Schedule. The IPSAT provides an interesting alternative for the cognitive assessment of problem solving and of styles of coping in interpersonal situations.

Assessment of Self-Evaluations and Attributions

In addition to expectations of future positive and negative consequences, research has focused on differential evaluations of past performance (see Table 6). The initial research in this area was done by Arkowitz and his colleagues. After completing a 10-minute interaction with another subject of the opposite sex, subjects were asked to complete a social interac-

Table 6. Summary of Studies on Assessment of Self-Evaluations and Attributions

Author	Problem and nature of study	Cognitive assessment
Alden and Cappe (1981)[a]	Assertiveness; contrasted groups	Self-evaluations of assertiveness, effectiveness, and anxiety
Cacioppo, Glass, and Merluzzi (1979)[a]	Heterosocial; contrasted groups	Self-evaluations (semantic differential)
Clark and Arkowitz (1975)	Heterosocial; contrasted groups	Self-evaluations of social skill and anxiety
Curran, Wallander, and Fischetti (1980)[a]	Heterosocial; contrasted groups	Self-evaluations of social skill
Glasgow and Arkowitz (1975)	Heterosocial; contrasted groups	Self-evaluations of social skill and anxiety
Glass, Merluzzi, Biever, and Larsen (in press)[a]	Social/heterosocial anxiety; contrasted groups	Self-evaluations of social skill and anxiety
Holroyd, Westbrook, Wolf, and Badhorn (1978)	Test anxiety; contrasted groups	Self-evaluation of performance, attributions
Miller and Arkowitz (1977)	Heterosocial; contrasted groups	Attributions
O'Banion and Arkowitz (1977)	Heterosocial; contrasted groups	Memory for feedback
Smith and Sarason (1975)	Social anxiety; contrasted groups	Perception of negative feedback

[a]Reference includes additional forms of cognitive assessment (see other tables).

tion questionnaire, which involved rating themselves and their partners on social skill, anxiety, and attractiveness (Glasgow & Arkowitz, 1975). Although both men and women who dated often rated *themselves* as significantly more skillful and less anxious than did low-frequency daters, *partners* did not rate high- and low-dating men differently. Few behavioral variables significantly distinguished the two criterion groups.

Clark and Arkowitz (1975) found similar results for high and low socially anxious men. Although judges did not differentiate between criterion groups in their ratings of subject skill in two brief, live heterosocial interactions, high socially anxious men rated themselves as significantly less skillful than did low socially anxious men, thus underestimating their level of skill relative to judges' ratings. Social inhibition in men could thus be explained better by overly critical self-evaluations than by a hypothesized skills deficit.

Curran *et al.* (1980) divided male undergraduates into three criterion groups based on combined assessment of levels of both social skill and anxiety. After viewing a videotape of their performance in a role-playing dating interaction, high-anxious/low-skilled men accurately rated their skill level (accuracy being determined by similarity to judges' ratings); high-anxious/high-skilled men underestimated their level of social skill. Although these subjects rated themselves as slightly below average, judges actually rated them as slightly above average in skill. The degree of discrepancy was unrelated to the presence of irrational beliefs on the IBT, however. This study illustrates the necessity of assessing both behavioral and cognitive factors in research and therapy with socially anxious or shy clients.

Self-evaluations have also been studied in the area of assertiveness (Alden & Cappe, 1981). Subjects who described themselves as quite assertive or quite unassertive were asked to rate a videotape of their own performance on four role-playing assertion situations. Although there were no differences in observers' ratings of performance, and although low-assertive subjects did not differ in ratings of models' role-plays, they rated *themselves* as less assertive, less effective, and more anxious than did high-assertive subjects. Low-assertive subjects were also more likely to endorse irrational beliefs on the IBT.

Several other cognitive variables have been studied that also involve postperformance assessment and that may be associated with negative self-evaluations. Miller and Arkowitz (1977) looked at factors of anxiety and perceived causation after male undergraduates encountered either an accepting or a rejecting female confederate. They found no support for an attribution–social anxiety relationship, although attributions were related to expectancy–experience discrepancies. O'Banion and Arkowitz (1977) found that high socially anxious female undergraduates, following a brief interaction with a male confederate, selectively remembered negative feedback about themselves better than positive feedback and reactions. Similarly, Smith and Sarason (1975) found that high socially anxious subjects perceived negatively toned interpersonal feedback as more negative than did low socially anxious individuals. Feedback evoked more negative affect and greater expectancy for receiving negative evaluations in the future. The perception and distortion of feedback is also a major research issue in depression (see Shaw and Dobson, Chapter 12, this volume).

Holroyd, Westbrook, Wolf, and Badhorn (1978) conducted an interesting study that examined the role of evaluative self-awareness in the cognitive, attentional, and physiological processes of high- and low-test-anxious women. Subjects completed two performance tasks under evaluative, nonevaluative, or self-awareness-inducing conditions. Later, high-test-anxious women indicated that they spent more time worrying while working on the anagram task and evaluated their relative performance more negatively than did low-test-anxious women. There were no differences in causal attributions made for the difficulty encountered with the anagrams. However, the self-evaluations of high- (but not low-) test-anxious subjects were *unrelated* to their actual anagram solution times. When actual performance was controlled, high-test-anxious subjects were still more negative in their self-evaluations. The authors suggest that high-test-anxious women were negatively biased in their performance evaluations, which were not influenced by actual performance.

It would be interesting to relate these findings on self-evaluations, self-efficacy, and reactions to negative feedback to other current research on the relationships between negative self-statements and social-evaluative anxiety. In what way are self-statements and self-evaluations related? Could these measures be tapping the same processes? Preliminary evidence suggests that self-evaluations are related to endorsement of irrational beliefs (Alden & Cappe, 1981). Cacioppo *et al.* (1979) also found that self-evaluations on a semantic differential measure were significantly related to the number of negative self-statements indicated on the thought-listing measure.

Conclusion: Crucial Issues in Cognitive Assessment

This chapter has reviewed the methods used to assess irrational beliefs, self-statements, expectations, problem-solving and coping strategies, and self-evaluations in social-evaluative anxiety. In just a few years, there has been an increase in our knowledge regarding test anxiety, nonassertiveness, and shyness, which is attributable to the identification of cognitive factors associated with such behavior. In this final section, we will address several issues that are in need of further analysis: (1) the role of cognitive assessment in therapy outcome and process research, (2) the need for validation, (3) the relationship between cognition and emotion, (4) the importance of situational variables, (5) the idiosyncratic nature and subjective meaning of self-statements, and (6) the search for a unifying theory to guide cognitive assessment in this area.

Therapy Outcome and Process Research

When working with nonassertive or shy clients, it is all too common to assume the existence of a behavioral deficit and to focus research and treatment on social skills training. The introduction of cognitive assessment makes it possible to identify both cognitive and behavioral skill deficits, allowing for the matching of client to treatment program. Approaches to therapy must be individually tailored to the needs of each client. On the other hand, new evidence on the role of cognition in social anxiety should not automatically lead us to select cognitive therapy or restructuring as the treatment of choice. In fact, Bandura (1977) hypotheses that behavioral performance may be the best means to effecting cognitive (self-efficacy) change.

A second issue concerns the contribution of cognitive assessment to exploring the nature of change in cognitive therapy. As Galassi and Galassi (1979) state, cognitive treatment studies must produce changes on the SISST or other cognitive measures as a prerequisite for concluding that therapy was effective because of a cognitive mechanism. However, it is conceivable that cognitive therapy is effective for reasons other than those immediately apparent from an examination of therapy procedures. Although a treatment program may focus on changing a shy client's negative self-statements and may indeed demonstrate cognitive self-statement *and* behavioral change, the reason for change may be at a different level than the mere substitution of positive thoughts for negative ones.

Arnkoff (1980*a*) argues for the existence of "deep structural rules," which underlie fearful and defensive behavior and which are modified or altered through the process of psychotherapy. It is important to study not only the *outcome,* or effectiveness, of cognitive therapy but also the *process* and nature of change. Do positive coping self-statements actually replace negative cognitions? If so, how do these negative statements "disappear," and how is the client's new internal dialogue integrated into his or her belief system? Can you change the belief system without changing self-statements? Perhaps we are not eliminating negative self-statements but changing the way people react to them. An increasing interest in the process of change in cognitive therapy is demonstrated by the contributions to Mahoney's (1980) recent book on the psychotherapy process.

Validation

As may be apparent from the material reviewed in this chapter, the field of cognitive assessment is coming dangerously close to repeating the mistakes of the behavioral assessment movement. Specifically, there is a dearth of actual validity studies as researchers rush to develop new, creative methods to measure cognitive content and processes in their specific areas of interest.

Many of these measures are developed for potential use in a particular psychotherapy outcome study. Others are developed to become part of a battery of instruments used in contrasted group studies to assess differences between individuals who are high- and low-test-anxious, assertive, depressed, and so forth. Still other researchers, who have begun to realize the importance of cognitive factors in various disorders, choose to use existing measures (such as the IBT) because they want to assess cognition in addition to behavior and it "looks" valid as a measure of irrational beliefs. Thus some measures get used repeatedly because they have been used before, eventhough sufficient attention has not been paid to questions of validity and to whether they assess what the researcher is interested in assessing.

Cone (Note 18) has proposed a multicontent–multimethod–multibehavior system that offers some interesting possibilities for cognitive assessment. The system's content includes cognitive, motoric, and physiological areas; methods refer to interviews, self-reports, ratings by others, self-monitoring, and direct observation by others in controlled (analogue) and natural environments (Cone & Hawkins, 1977). He distinguishes "cognitive" as a system or referent of assessment instead of using the term to refer to self-report (as opposed to observational) methods of assessment.

This multifactor approach conceivably could be extended to include specific methods employed in cognitive assessment (recall, recognition, projective, expressive, etc.) as well as different targets for assessment, such as beliefs, self-statements, or expectations. It is important to determine whether correlations between assessments have more to do with the methods used than with the underlying processes being measured.

As Klinger (1978) has stated, the "validating process resides in ruling out artifacts, in replications, and, ultimately, in the usefulness of data or theory for making possible other forms of prediction and perhaps control" (p. 227). Perhaps we need to declare a state of "nonproliferation" in measure development and instead lend our empirical expertise to validation of measures and our theoretical strengths to the development of a solid conceptual framework to underlie our assessment efforts. Ideally, there might not be separate fields of "cognitive assessment," "behavioral assessment," and "physiological assessment," but rather a comprehensive assessment of the individual as a whole.

Cognition, Emotion, and Arousal

Researchers interested in social-evaluative anxiety should also be careful not to assume a simple causal connection between cognition and affect. It is important that emotion or anxiety not be seen only as a product of the cognitive appraisal process.

Richard Lazarus (1980; Lazarus, Kanner, & Folkman, 1979) has stressed that cognitive appraisal is also influenced by emotion and motivation and views these three factors as interdependent processes. Meichenbaum and Butler (1979) similarly view cognition and emotion as interactive, ongoing streams of experience. They suggest, for example, that emotion may interfere with the adoption and maintenance of a problem-solving set. It is too simplistic, therefore, to assess the role of cognition in social anxiety using a structured questionnaire and then to conclude only that the anxiety experienced has been caused by the presence of negative self-statements in the client's internal dialogue. What impact does anxiety, in turn, have on cognitive processes?

Lazarus *et al.* (1979) also make the thought-provoking point that faulty, irrational premises and beliefs do not necessarily lead to psychopathology or emotional difficulty. It is possible, they argue, that false assumptions, irrational beliefs, and the cognitive appraisals they foster may also lead to positively toned emotions. In some cases, normally functioning people do and think things that maintain illusions and inaccurate perceptions in order to feel good. We would urge researchers, in addition to studying test-anxious and nonassertive people, to pay equal attention to socially competent individuals and to those who demonstrate outstanding test and speech performance. When faced with difficult or anxiety-provoking situations, what coping mechanisms do they employ? Recent developments in cognitive assessment may also allow us to test Lazarus's speculations on the role of "irrational" cognition in positive emotional states.

Situational Variables

Cognitive assessment of social-evaluative anxiety has also paid little attention to the role of the situational context, although it would seem logical that different situations might necessitate different negative self-statements and expectations. Important variables could be the familiarity of the situation (or the other person), its complexity, possible consequences, and the importance of the situation to the individual. For example, what is it about a situation that would lead one to consider it threatening?

Lazarus (1980) has used the term "transaction" to describe the dynamic interchange between a person and the environment that gives rise to particular thoughts and feelings. Stress, he claims, arises from demands that tax or exceed available resources as appraised by the person, who can view a stressful encounter as a threat or a challenge. In addition to normative, between-subjects comparisons, we need research into intraindividual (ipsative) performance across time and situations (Lazarus, 1980). The person × situation interaction remains an important issue for cognitive assessment, especially as it relates to assertiveness and heterosocial competence.

The decision/expectancy model employed by Fiedler and Beach (1978) in their research on the decision to be assertive focuses on some interesting possibilities. Recall that Fiedler and Beach found that this decision was deter-mined partly by subjects' perceptions of the probability of potential conse-quences in assertive situations. Merluzzi and Rudy (Note 19), using multidi-mensional scaling, found that the relative salience or weighing attached to various dimensions of assertive situations varied as a function of level of assertiveness. Thus subjects' perceptions of the meaning or importance of situations may be significant targets for future research.

Subjective Meaning of Self-Statements

In addition to the meaning attached to the situation, self-statements themselves have associated meanings to the individual. Meichenbaum and Butler (1979) have referred to "personal meanings," and Goldfried (1979), to "connotative meaning structures," "latent meaning," and "symbolic significance." Current measures, such as the ASST and thought listings, assess the relative frequency of positive and negative self-statements. Fre-quency may not be as important as *when* a thought occurs (or what it means). Although two subjects both may have the thought "She's probably not in-terested in me," this may mean "I'm a real loser" to one of the subjects but "I'll have to turn on the charm, then" to another. Thus one thought is seen as a challenge and implies a belief in one's social skills, and the other reflects a belief in one's inferiority. It is clear from this example that the subjective meaning of one's thoughts can play a key role in influencing action. Clinical experience has shown us that men who date frequently may actually ex-perience a greater amount of rejection than shy men, because they simply keep trying more often and more persistently.

A thought-listing measure can potentially be used to obtain subjects' ratings of their own thoughts, although the nature of the instructions and/or training given to subjects and judges before rating these listed thoughts may be extremely influential. In addition to ratings on dimensions of valence (positive–negative–neutral), it may be possible to assess subjects' evaluations of the importance or influence of various self-statements. Sequential analysis of thought-listing or think-aloud data (see Notarius, Chapter 11, this volume) represents another promising direction for the assessment of mean-ing.

A Theoretical Framework for Cognitive Assessment

Thus far the cognitive assessment of social-evaluative anxiety remains a collection of diverse techniques. We lack an integrative framework or model to guide our efforts at assessing the cognitive processes that may be fun-damental to social and test anxiety. This chapter has emphasized various methods by which researchers have assessed irrational beliefs, self-statements, expectations, problem-solving and coping styles, and self-evaluations. This research, however, has treated these variables as isolated entities, without moving toward a conception of the cognitive structures or schemata underlying these converging operations.

Arnkoff's (1980a) cognitive theory of psychotherapy would suggest that self-statements may represent a surface representation of a deeper cognitive schema. Where should irrational beliefs fall in this analysis? It is possible that certain belief systems would engender various self-statements in appropriate situations. In addition to cognitive content, we need to look at cognitive processes evoked in social and evaluative situations: problem solving, consequence appraisal, misperception, forgetting and encoding of information, standard setting, and self-evaluations. Kelly's (1955) personal construct theory (see Neimeyer & Neimeyer, Chapter 7, this volume) may also offer a useful model.

Cognitive and developmental psychology offer a wealth of ideas that may be useful for theory development in clinical cognitive assessment. Mahoney (1977) has emphasized the need to look to cognitive psychology for methods of perceptual and conceptual assessment. The concept of breadth and depth of processing (Craik & Tulving, 1975) has implications for the organization of the self-schema and the differential accessibility of cognitive events. For example, Davis (1979) has demonstrated that depressed individuals show deficits in processing self-referential information. Also, Schwartz (1975) suggests that high arousal leads to the diminished ability to organize responses into categories and to encode a broad range of features. One might wonder whether it is possible to speak of internal dialogues at different levels of processing. Merluzzi, Rudy, and Glass (Chapter 4, this volume) provide a more detailed review of the depth-of-processing literature.

An exciting area of research concerns the process of metamemory and metacognition (Belmont & Butterfield, 1977; Borkowski & Cavanaugh, 1978), which refer to the awareness of one's own cognitive processes and knowledge of helpful strategies to aid memory and information retrieval. Meichenbaum and Asarnow (1979) have written about the implications of metacognitive theory and cognitive-behavior modification for classroom teaching. Similarly, metacognition may play a role in an individual's knowledge of his or her available coping strategies and abilities to self-monitor, self-evaluate, and self-reinforce coping attempts (elements of Kanfer & Karoly's 1972 model of self-control).

An important paper by Flavell (Note 20) sets out a model of monitoring social-cognitive enterprises, referring to metacognitive knowledge that can be translated into conscious metacognitive experiences activated by various retrieval uses inherent in certain situations. These metacognitive experiences include thoughts about your own beliefs, thoughts, abilities, and feelings. Metacognitive experiences in social situations can affect goal setting, action toward goals, and additions to, revisions in, and deletions from the store of metacognitive knowledge. Mischel (1979) similarly refers to the study of what children know about "plans" and about strategies for forming and implementing them, of the awareness of our own information-processing and self-control strategies, and of how our own thoughts influence coping (see also Mischel, Chapter 16, this volume). In a potentially stressful situation, knowledge of one's own coping resources is an important part of the cognitive appraisal process.

The future of theory in this area will depend largely on the integration of diverse areas of cognitive science. For example, current research in experimental cognitive psychology, social cognition, cognitive development, and social learning theory has much to contribute to more adequate assessment and to theories of psychopathology. Atheoretical approaches to research in psychopathology with isolated assessment methods will likely lead to fragmented models or approaches. Thus, although this chapter is offered as a review of approaches with a proposed taxonomy of techniques, it is our hope that such methods for cognitive assessment will lead to more definitive theory and research in cognitive clinical science.

ACKNOWLEDGMENTS

The authors would like to thank Diane Arnkoff and Jim Gormally for their excellent comments on an earlier draft of this chapter.

Reference Notes

1. Hussian, R. A., & Lawrence, P. S. *Modification of test anxiety by self-administered stress inoculation training.* Unpublished manuscript, University of North Carolina—Greensboro, 1979.
2. Jaremko, M. E., & Walker, G. R. *The content of coping statements in the cognitive restructuring component of stress inoculation.* Unpublished manuscript, University of Richmond, 1978.
3. Glass, G. V., & Smith, M. L. *Meta-analysis of psychotherapy outcome studies.* Paper presented at the meeting of the Society for Psychotherapy Research, San Diego, June 1976.
4. Lohr, J. M., & Bonge, D. *Situational Irrational Cognitions Inventory: A second report.* Paper presented at the meeting of the Association for the Advancement of Behavior Therapy, San Francisco, December 1979.
5. Lohr, J. M., Brandt, J. A., & Bonge, D. *The Situational Irrational Cognitions Inventory: A preliminary report.* Paper presented at the meeting of the Association for the Advancement of Behavior Therapy, New York, December 1977.
6. Fodor, I. *A projective measure of assertiveness.* Unpublished manuscript, New York University, 1972.
7. Rhyne, L. D., & Hanson, T. R. *An analysis of the response deficit in nonassertive inpatients.* Manuscript submitted for publication, 1979.
8. Taskey, K. J., & Rich, A. R. *Effects of demand characteristics and format variations in role-playing assessment.* Paper presented at the meeting of the American Psychological Association, New York, August 1979.
9. Glass, C. R., Merluzzi, T. V., & Cacioppo, J. T. *The effects of social anxiety and sex of part-*

ner on spontaneous self-statements and state anxiety. Paper presented at the meeting of the Association for the Advancement of Behavior Therapy, Chicago, November 1978.
10. Merluzzi, T. V., Cacioppo, J. T., & Glass, C. R. *Cognitive responses and attentional factors in high and low socially anxious males.* Unpublished manuscript, University of Notre Dame, 1979.
11. Steffen, J. J., & Lucas, J. *Social strategies and expectations as components of social competence.* Manuscript submitted for publication, 1980.
12. Weston, J., & Glass, C. R. *A cognitive-behavioral analysis of social skills in peer interactions of middle childhood.* Unpublished manuscript, Catholic University, 1980.
13. Heimberg, R. G., Chiauzzi, E., Becker, R. E., & Madrazo-Peterson, R. *Task analysis of assertive behavior: Differences in the behavior of college students and psychiatric patients.* Unpublished manuscript, State University of New York at Albany, 1980.
14. Glass, C. R., & Merluzzi, T. V. *Approaches to the cognitive assessment of social anxiety.* Symposium paper presented at the meeting of the Association for the Advancement of Behavior Therapy, Chicago, November 1978.
15. Glazeski, R. C., Hollandsworth, J. G., & Jones, G. E. *An investigation of the role of physiological arousal in test anxiety.* Paper presented at the meeting of the Association for the Advancement for Behavior Therapy, San Francisco, December 1979.
16. Kuperminc, M., & Heimberg, R. G. *Cognitive factors in the decision to behave assertively: A further investigation of the effects of perceived future consequences on present behavior.* Unpublished manuscript, State University of New York at Albany, 1980.
17. Nowinski, J. K., & Getter, H. *Interpersonal Problem Solving Assessment Technique scoring manual.* Unpublished manuscript, University of Connecticut, 1977.
18. Cone, J. D. *The behavioral assessment grid (BAG): A taxonomy for behavioral assessment.* Paper presented at the meeting of the Association for the Advancement of Behavior Therapy, New York, December 1976.
19. Merluzzi, T. V., & Rudy, T. *Towards an information processing decision making analysis of behavior.* Symposium paper presented at the meeting of the American Psychological Association, Montreal, September 1980.
20. Flavell, J. H. *Monitoring social-cognitive enterprises: Something else that may develop in the area of social cognition.* Paper presented at the Social Science Research Council Committee on Social and Affective Development during Childhood, January 1979.

References

Alden, L., & Cappe, R. Nonassertiveness: Skill deficit or selective self-evaluation? *Behavior Therapy,* 1981, *12,* 107–114.
Alden, L. E., & Safran, J. Irrational beliefs and nonassertive behavior. *Cognitive Therapy and Research,* 1978, *2,* 357–364.
Alden, L., Safran, J., & Weidman, R. A comparison of cognitive and skills training strategies in the treatment of unassertive clients. *Behavior Therapy,* 1978, *9,* 843–846.
Arkowitz, H. Measurement and modification of minimal dating behavior. In M. Hersen (Ed.), *Progress in behavior modification* (Vol. 5). New York: Academic Press, 1977.
Arnkoff, D. B. Psychotherapy from the perspective of cognitive theory. In M. Mahoney (Ed.), *Psychotherapy process: Current issues and future directions.* New York: Plenum Press, 1980. (a)
Arnkoff, D. B. Self-statement therapy and belief therapy in the treatment of test anxiety (Doctoral dissertation, Pennsylvania State University, 1979). *Dissertation Abstracts International,* 1980, *40,* 4469B. (University Microfilms No. 80-05970) (b)
Bandura, A. *Principles of behavior modification.* New York: Holt, Rinehart & Winston, 1969.
Bandura, A. Self-efficacy: Toward a unifying theory of behavioral change. *Psychological Review,* 1977, *84,* 191–215.

Beck, A. T. *Cognitive therapy and the emotional disorders.* New York: International Universities Press, 1976.

Bellack, A. S. A critical appraisal of strategies for assessing social skill. *Behavioral Assessment,* 1979, *1,* 157–176.

Belmont, J., & Butterfield, E. The instructional approach to developmental cognitive research. In R. Kail & J. Hagen (Eds.), *Perspectives in the development of memory and cognition.* Hillsdale, N.J.: Erlbaum, 1977.

Borkowski, J., & Cavanaugh, J. Maintenance and generalization of skills and strategies by the retarded. In N. Ellis (Ed.), *Handbook of mental deficiency: Psychological theory and research.* Hillsdale, N.J.: Erlbaum, 1978.

Breznitz, S. A study of worrying. *British Journal of Social and Clinical Psychology,* 1971, *10,* 271–279.

Bruch, M. A. Type of cognitive modeling, imitation of modeled tactics, and modification of test anxiety. *Cognitive Therapy and Research,* 1978, *2,* 147–164.

Bruch, M. A. Relationship of test-taking strategies to test anxiety and performance: Task analysis of competence in evaluative situations. *Cognitive Therapy and Research,* in press. (*a*)

Bruch, M. A. A task analysis of assertive behavior revisited: Replication and extension. *Behavior Therapy,* in press. (*b*)

Cacioppo, J. T., Glass, C. R., & Merluzzi, T. V. Self-statements and self-evaluations: A cognitive response analysis of heterosexual social anxiety. *Cognitive Therapy and Research,* 1979, *3,* 249–262.

Carmody, T. P. Rational–emotive, self-instructional, and behavioral assertion training: Facilitating maintenance. *Cognitive Therapy and Research,* 1978, *2,* 241–253.

Casas, J. M. A comparison of two mediational self-control techniques for the treatment of speech anxiety (Doctoral dissertation, Stanford University, 1975). *Dissertation Abstracts International,* 1976, *36,* 4681B. (University Microfilms No. 76-5701)

Clark, J. V., & Arkowitz, H. Social anxiety and self-evaluation of interpersonal performance. *Psychological Reports,* 1975, *36,* 211–221.

Collins, K. W., Dansereau, D. F., Holley, C. D., Garland, J. C., & McDonald, B. A. Control of affective responses during academic tasks. *Journal of Educational Psychology,* in press.

Cone, J. D., & Hawkins, R. P. Current status and future directions in behavioral assessment. In J. D. Cone & R. P. Hawkins (Eds.), *Behavioral assessment: New directions in clinical psychology.* New York: Brunner/Mazel, 1977.

Coyne, J. C., & Lazarus, R. S. Cognition, stress and coping: A transactional perspective. In I. L. Kutash & L. B. Schlesinger (Eds.), *Pressure point: Perspectives on stress and anxiety.* San Francisco: Jossey-Bass, 1979.

Crager, R. L. The relation of anxiety, sex and instructions to performance and verbal behavior during anagram solution (Doctoral dissertation, University of Washington, 1959). *Dissertation Abstracts,* 1959, *20,* 2900. (University Microfilms No. 59-5457)

Craighead, L. W. Self-instructional training for assertive-refusal behavior. *Behavior Therapy,* 1979, *10,* 529–542.

Craighead, W. E., Kimball, W. H., & Rehak, P. J. Mood changes, physiological responses, and self-statements during social rejection imagery. *Journal of Consulting and Clinical Psychology,* 1979, *47,* 385–396.

Craik, F. I. M., & Tulving, E. Depth of processing and the retention of words in episodic memory. *Journal of Experimental Psychology—General,* 1975, *104,* 268–294.

Curran, J. P. Skills training as an approach to the treatment of heterosexual social anxiety: A review. *Psychological Bulletin,* 1977, *84,* 140–157.

Curran, J. P., Wallander, J. L., & Fischetti, M. The importance of behavioral and cognitive factors in heterosexual-social anxiety. *Journal of Personality,* 1980, *48,* 285–292.

Davis, H. Self-reference and the encoding of personal information in depression. *Cognitive Therapy and Research,* 1979, *3,* 97–110.

Davison, G. C. Systematic desensitization as a counter-conditioning process. *Journal of Abnormal Psychology,* 1968, *73,* 91–99.

Deffenbacher, J. L. Worry, emotionality and task-generated interference in test anxiety: An empirical test of attentional theory. *Journal of Educational Psychology,* 1978, *70,* 248–254.

Deffenbacher, J. L. Worry and emotionality in test anxiety. In I. G. Sarason (Ed.), *Test anxiety: Theory, research and applications.* Hillsdale, N.J.: Erlbaum, 1980.

Deffenbacher, J. L., & Hahnloser, R. M. Cognitive and relaxation coping skills in stress inoculation. *Cognitive Therapy and Research,* in press.

Derry, P. A., & Stone, G. L. Effects of cognitive adjunct treatments on assertiveness. *Cognitive Therapy and Research,* 1979, *3,* 213–221.

DiLoreto, A. O. *Comparative psychotherapy: An experimental analysis.* Chicago: Aldine-Atherton, 1971.

Edwards, W. The theory of decision making. *Psychological Bulletin,* 1954, *51,* 380–417.

Eisler, R. M., Frederiksen, L. W., & Peterson, G. L. The relationship of cognitive variables to the expression of assertiveness. *Behavior Therapy,* 1978, *9,* 419–427.

Elder, J. P., Edelstein, B. A., & Fremouw, W. J. A comparison of response acquisition and cognitive restructuring in the enhancement of social competence of college freshmen. *Cognitive Therapy and Research,* in press.

Ellis, A. *Reason and emotion in psychotherapy.* New York: Lyle Stuart, 1962.

Fiedler, D., & Beach, L. R. On the decision to be assertive. *Journal of Consulting and Clinical Psychology,* 1978, *46,* 537–546.

Finger, R., & Galassi, J. P. Effects of modifying cognitive versus emotionality responses in the treatment of test anxiety. *Journal of Consulting and Clinical Psychology,* 1977, *45,* 280–287.

Folkman, S., & Lazarus, R. S. An analysis of coping in a middle-aged community sample. *Journal of Health and Social Behavior,* 1980, *21,* 219–239.

Fremouw, W. J., & Zitter, R. A comparison of skills training and cognitive restructuring–relaxation for the treatment of speech anxiety. *Behavior Therapy,* 1978, *9,* 248–259.

Galassi, J. P., Frierson, H. T., & Sharer, R. The cognitions of high, moderate and low test anxious students during an actual test situation. *Journal of Consulting and Clinical Psychology,* in press.

Galassi, J. P., & Galassi, M. D. Modification of heterosocial skills deficits. In M. Hersen & A. S. Bellack (Eds.), *Research and practice in social skills training.* New York: Plenum Press, 1979.

Getter, H., & Nowinski, J. K. A free response test of interpersonal effectiveness. *Journal of Personality Assessment,* in press.

Glasgow, R. E., & Arkowitz, H. The behavioral assessment of male and female social competence in dyadic heterosocial interactions. *Behavior Therapy,* 1975, *6,* 488–498.

Glass, C. R., Gottman, J. M., & Shmurak, S. H. Response acquisition and cognitive self-statement modification approaches to dating skill training. *Journal of Counseling Psychology,* 1976, *23,* 520–526.

Glass, C. R., Merluzzi, T. V., Biever, J. L., & Larsen, K. H. Cognitive assessment of social anxiety: Development and validation of a self-statement questionnaire. *Cognitive Therapy and Research,* in press.

Glogower, F. D., Fremouw, W. J., & McCroskey, J. C. A component analysis of cognitive restructuring. *Cognitive Therapy and Research,* 1978, *2,* 209–223.

Goldfried, M. R. Anxiety reduction through cognitive–behavioral intervention. In P. Kendall & S. Hollon (Eds.), *Cognitive–behavioral interventions: Theory, research and procedures.* New York: Academic Press, 1979.

Goldfried, M. R., & D'Zurilla, T. J. A behavioral–analytic model for assessing competence. In C. D. Spielberger (Ed.), *Current topics in clinical and community psychology.* New York: Academic Press, 1969.

Goldfried, M. R., & Linehan, M. M. Basic issues in behavioral assessment. In A. R. Ciminero, K. S. Calhoun, & H. E. Adams (Eds.), *Handbook of behavioral assessment.* New York: Wiley, 1977.

Goldfried, M. R., Linehan, M. M., & Smith, J. L. The reduction of test anxiety through rational restructuring. *Journal of Consulting and Clinical Psychology, 1978, 46,* 32–39.

Goldfried, M. R., & Sobocinski, D. Effect of irrational beliefs on emotional arousal. *Journal of Consulting and Clinical Psychology, 1975, 43,* 504–510.

Gormally, J., Sipps, Raphael, R., Varvil-Weld, D., & Edwin, D. Cognitive analysis of social anxiety according to Beck and Ellis. *Journal of Consulting and Clinical Psychology,* in press.

Gormally, J., Varvil-Weld, D., Raphael, R., & Sipps, G. Treatment of socially anxious college men using cognitive counseling and skills training. *Journal of Counseling Psychology,* in press.

Henshaw, D. A cognitive analysis of creative problem-solving (Doctoral dissertation, University of Waterloo, 1978). *Dissertation Abstracts International, 1979, 39,* 4580B.

Hollandsworth, J. G., Jr., Glazeski, R. C., Kirkland, K., Jones, G. E., & VanNorman, L. R. An analysis of the nature and effects of test anxiety: Cognitive, behavioral and physiological components. *Cognitive Therapy and Research, 1979, 3,* 165–180.

Hollon, S. D., & Kendall, P. C. Cognitive self-statements in depression: Development of an automatic thoughts questionnaire. *Cognitive Therapy and Research, 1980, 4,* 383–395.

Holroyd, K. A. Cognition and desensitization in the group treatment of test anxiety. *Journal of Consulting and Clinical Psychology, 1976, 44,* 991–1001.

Holroyd, K. A., Westbrook, T., Wolf, M., & Badhorn, E. Performance, cognition, and physiological responding in test anxiety. *Journal of Abnormal Psychology, 1978, 87,* 442–451.

Hurlburt, R. T. Random sampling of cognitions and behavior. *Journal of Research in Personality, 1979, 13,* 103–111.

Hurlburt, R. T., & Sipprelle, C. N. Random sampling of cognitions in alleviating anxiety attacks. *Cognitive Therapy and Research, 1978, 2,* 165–169.

Hussian, R. A., & Lawrence, P. S. The reduction of test, state and trait anxiety by test-specific and generalized stress-inoculation training. *Cognitive Therapy and Research, 1978, 2,* 25–37.

Hutchings, D. F., Denney, D. R., Basgal, J., & Houston, B. K. Anxiety management and applied relaxation in reducing general anxiety. *Behaviour Research and Therapy,* in press.

Jones, R. G. A factored measure of Ellis' Irrational Belief System (Doctoral dissertation, Texas Technological College, 1968). *Dissertation Abstracts, 1969, 29,* 4379B–4380B. (University Microfilms No. 69-6443)

Kagan, N., & Krathwohl, D. R. *Studies in human interaction: Interpersonal Process Recall stimulated by videotape.* East Lansing, Mich.: Michigan State University, 1967.

Kanfer, F. H., & Karoly, P. Self-control: A behavioristic journey into the lion's den. *Behavior Therapy, 1972, 3,* 398–416.

Kanter, N. J., & Goldfried, M. R. Relative effectiveness of rational restructuring and self-control desensitization in the reduction of interpersonal anxiety. *Behavior Therapy, 1979, 10,* 472–490.

Karst, T. O., & Trexler, L. D. Initial study using fixed-role and rational–emotive therapy in treating public speaking anxiety. *Journal of Consulting and Clinical Psychology, 1970, 34,* 360–366.

Kazdin, A. E. Effects of covert modeling and model reinforcement on assertive behavior. *Journal of Abnormal Psychology, 1974, 83,* 240–252.

Kazdin, A. E. Effects of covert modeling, multiple models and model reinforcement on assertive behavior. *Behavior Therapy, 1976, 7,* 211–222.

Keane, T. M., & Lisman, S. A. Alcohol and social anxiety in males: Behavioral, cognitive, and physiological effects. *Journal of Abnormal Psychology, 1980, 89,* 213–223.

Kelly, G. A. *The psychology of personal constructs.* New York: Norton, 1955.

Kendall, P. C., & Korgeski, G. P. Assessment and cognitive–behavioral interventions. *Cognitive Therapy and Research, 1979, 3,* 1–22.

Kendall, P. C., Williams, L., Pechacek, T. F., Graham, L. E., Shisslak, C., & Herzof, N. Cog-

Carol R. Glass and Thomas V. Merluzzi

nitive-behavioral and patient education interventions in cardiac catheterization procedures: The Palo Alto Medical Psychology Project. *Journal of Consulting and Clinical
Psychology,* 1979, *47,* 48-59.

Kirkland, K., & Hollandsworth, J. G., Jr. Effective test-taking: Skills-acquisition versus anxie-
ty-reduction techniques. *Journal of Consulting and Clinical Psychology,* 1980, *48,* 431-
439.

Klinger, E. Modes of normal conscious flow. In K. S. Pope & J. L. Singer (Eds.), *The stream of
consciousness.* New York: Plenum Press, 1978.

Kramer, S. R. Effectiveness of behavior rehearsal and practive dating to increase heterosexual
social interaction (Doctoral dissertation, University of Texas, 1975). *Dissertation Abstracts
International,* 1975, *36,* 913B. (University Microfilms No. 75-16693)

Lange, A., & Jakubowski, P. *Responsible assertive behavior.* Champaign, Ill.: Research Press,
1976.

LaPointe, K. A., & Harrell, T. H. Thoughts and feelings: Correlational relationships and cross-
situational consistency. *Cognitive Therapy and Research,* 1978, *2,* 311-322.

Lazarus, R. S. *Psychological stress and the coping process.* New York: McGraw-Hill, 1966.

Lazarus, R. S. The stress and coping paradigm. In C. Eisdorfer, D. Cohen, A. Kleinman, & P.
Maxim (Eds.), *Theoretical bases for psychopathology.* New York: Spectrum, 1980.

Lazarus, R. S., Kanner, A. D., & Folkman, S. Emotions: A cognitive-phenomenological analysis. In R. Plutchik & H. Kellerman (Eds.), *Emotion: Theory, research and experience* (Vol.
1): *Theories of emotion.* New York: Academic Press, 1979.

Liebert, R. M., & Morris, L. W. Cognitive and emotional components of test anxiety: A distinction and some initial data. *Psychological Reports,* 1967, *20,* 975-978.

Linehan, M. M., Goldfried, M. R., & Goldfried, A. P. Assertion therapy: Skill training or cognitive restructuring. *Behavior Therapy,* 1979, *10,* 372-388.

Little, S., & Jackson, B. The treatment of test anxiety through attentional and relaxation training. *Psychotherapy: Theory, Research and Practice,* 1974, *11,* 175-178.

Lohr, J. M., & Bonge, D. The factorial validity of the Irrational Beliefs Test: A psychometric investigation. *Cognitive Therapy and Research,* in press.

Mahoney, M. J. Reflections on the cognitive-learning trend in psychotherapy. *American Psychologist,* 1977, *32,* 5-13.

Mahoney, M. J. (Ed.). *Psychotherapy process: Current issues and future directions.* New York:
Plenum Press, 1980.

Malkiewich, L. E., & Merluzzi, T. V. Rational restructuring vs. desensitization with clients of
diverse conceptual level: A test of a client-treatment matching model. *Journal of Counseling Psychology,* 1980, *27,* 453-461.

May, R. L. The treatment of test anxiety by cognitive modification: An examination of treatment components (Doctoral dissertation, University of Kansas, 1975). *Dissertation Abstracts International,* 1976, *37,* 468B. (University Microfilms No. 76-16752)

McCordick, S. M., Kaplan, R. M., Finn, M. E., & Smith, S. H. Cognitive behavior modification
and modeling for test anxiety. *Journal of Consulting and Clinical Psychology,* 1979, *47,*
419-420.

McFall, R. M., & Lillesand, D. B. Behavior rehearsal with modeling and coaching in assertion
training. *Journal of Abnormal Psychology,* 1971, *77,* 313-323.

Meichenbaum, D. H. Cognitive modification of test anxious college students. *Journal of Consulting and Clinical Psychology,* 1972, *39,* 370-380.

Meichenbaum, D. H. *Cognitive-behavior modification.* New York: Plenum Press, 1977.

Meichenbaum, D. H., & Asarnow, J. Cognitive-behavior modification and metacognitive
development: Implications for the classroom. In P. Kendall & S. Hollon (Eds.), *Cognitive-
behavioral interventions: Theory, research, and procedures.* New York: Academic Press,
1979.

Meichenbaum, D., & Butler, L. Cognitive ethology: Assessing the streams of cognition and emotion. In K. Blankstein, P. Pliner, & J. Polivy (Eds.), *Advances in the study of communication and affect: Assessment and modification of emotional behavior* (Vol. 6). New York: Plenum Press, 1979.

Meichenbaum, D. H., Gilmore, J. B., & Fedoravicius, A. Group instruction vs. group desensitization in treating speech anxiety. *Journal of Consulting and Clinical Psychology,* 1971, *36,* 410–421.

Miller, W. R., & Arkowitz, H. Anxiety and perceived causation in social success and failure experiences: Disconfirmation of an attribution hypothesis in two experiments. *Journal of Abnormal Psychology,* 1977, *86,* 665–668.

Mischel, W. On the interface of cognition and personality: Beyond the person–situation debate. *American Psychologist,* 1979, *34,* 740–754.

Montgomery, A. G. Comparison of the effectiveness of systematic desensitization, rational emotive therapy, implosive therapy and no treatment in reducing test anxiety in college students (Doctoral dissertation, Washington University, 1971). *Dissertation Abstracts International,* 1971, *32,* 1861A. (University Microfilms No. 71-27337)

Morelli, G., & Friedman, B. Cognitive correlates of multidimensional trait anxiety. *Psychological Reports,* 1978, *42,* 611–614.

Newell, A., & Simon, H. A. *Human problem solving.* Englewood Cliffs, N.J.: Prentice-Hall, 1972.

Nietzel, M. T., Martorano, R. P., & Melnick, J. The effects of covert modeling with and without reply training on the development and generalization of assertive responses. *Behavior Therapy,* 1977, *8,* 183–192.

Norman, W. H. The efficacy of self-instructional training in the treatment of speech anxiety (Doctoral dissertation, Pennsylvania State University, 1975). *Dissertation Abstracts International,* 1975, *36,* 1663B. (University Microfilms No. 75-22704)

O'Banion, K., & Arkowitz, H. Social anxiety and selective memory for affective information about the self. *Social Behavior and Personality,* 1977, *5,* 321–328.

Osarchuk, M. A comparison of a cognitive, a behavior therapy and a cognitive + behavior therapy treatment of test anxious college students (Doctoral dissertation, Adelphi University, 1974). *Dissertation Abstracts International,* 1976, *36,* 3619B. (University Microfilms No. 76-01425)

Osterhouse, R. A. Desensitization and study-skills training as treatment for two types of test-anxious students. *Journal of Counseling Psychology,* 1972, *19,* 301–307.

Pitcher, S. W., & Meikle, S. The topography of assertive behavior in positive and negative situations. *Behavior Therapy,* 1980, *11,* 532–547.

Rakos, R. F. The empirical assessment of a self-administered assertiveness training program (Doctoral dissertation, Kent State University, 1978). *Dissertation Abstracts International,* 1979, *39,* 5580B. (University Microfilms No. 79-9972)

Rehm, L. P., & Marston, A. R. Reduction of social anxiety through modification of self-reinforcement: An instigation therapy technique. *Journal of Consulting and Clinical Psychology,* 1968, *32,* 565–574.

Safran, J. D., Alden, L. E., & Davidson, P. O. Client anxiety level as a moderator variable in assertion training. *Cognitive Therapy and Research,* 1980, *4,* 189–200.

Sarason, I. G. Experimental approaches to test anxiety: Attention and the uses of information. In C. D. Spielberger (Ed.), *Anxiety: Current trends in theory and research* (Vol. 2). New York: Academic Press, 1972.

Sarason, I. G. Test anxiety and cognitive modeling. *Journal of Personality and Social Psychology,* 1973, *28,* 58–61.

Sarason, I. G. Test anxiety, attention and the general problem of anxiety. In C. D. Spielberger & I. G. Sarason (Eds.), *Stress and anxiety* (Vol. 1). Washington, D.C.: Hemisphere, 1975.

Sarason, I. G. The test anxiety scale: Concept and research. In C. D. Spielberger & I. G. Sarason (Eds.), *Stress and anxiety* (Vol. 5). Washington, D.C.: Hemisphere, 1978.

Sarason, I. G., & Stoops, R. Test anxiety and the passage of time. *Journal of Consulting and Clinical Psychology,* 1978, *46,* 102–109.

Schwartz, R. M., & Gottman, J. M. Toward a task analysis of assertive behavior. *Journal of Consulting and Clinical Psychology,* 1976, *44,* 910–920.

Schwartz, S. Individual differences in cognition: Some relationships between personality and memory. *Journal of Research in Personality,* 1975, *9,* 217–222.

Smith, R. E., & Sarason, I. G. Social anxiety and the evaluation of negative interpersonal feedback. *Journal of Consulting and Clinical Psychology,* 1975, *43,* 429.

Smye, M. D., & Wine, J. D. A comparison of female and male adolescents' social behavior and cognitions. *Sex Roles,* 1980, *6,* 213–230.

Spivack, G., Platt, J., & Shure, M. *The problem solving approach to adjustment.* San Francisco: Jossey-Bass, 1976.

Sutton-Simon, K., & Goldfried, M. R. Faulty thinking patterns in two types of anxiety. *Cognitive Therapy and Research,* 1979, *3,* 193–203.

Thorpe, G. L. Short-term effectiveness of systematic desensitization, modeling and behavioral rehearsal, and self-instructional training in facilitating assertive refusal behavior (Doctoral dissertation, Rutgers: The State University, 1973). *Dissertation Abstracts International,* 1974, *34,* 5213B. (University Microfilms No. 74-8828)

Thorpe, G. L., Amatu, H. I., Blakey, R. S., & Burns, L. E. Contributions of overt instructional rehearsal and "specific insight" to the effectiveness of self-instructional training: A preliminary study. *Behavior Therapy,* 1976, *7,* 504–511.

Tiegerman, S., & Kassinove, H. Effects of assertive training and cognitive components of rational therapy on assertive behaviors and interpersonal anxiety. *Psychological Reports,* 1977, *40,* 535–542.

Trexler, L. D., & Karst, T. O. Rational–emotive therapy, placebo and no-treatment effects on public-speaking anxiety. *Journal of Abnormal Psychology,* 1972, *79,* 60–67.

Twentyman, C. T., & McFall, R. M. Behavioral training of social skills in shy males. *Journal of Consulting and Clinical Psychology,* 1975, *43,* 384–395.

Twentyman, C. T., Pharr, D. R., & Connor, J. M. A comparison of three covert assertion therapy training procedures. *Journal of Clinical Psychology,* 1980, *36,* 520–525.

Watson, D., & Friend, R. Measurement of social-evaluative anxiety. *Journal of Consulting and Clinical Psychology,* 1969, *33,* 448–457.

Weissberg, M. A comparison of direct and vicarious treatments of speech anxiety: Desensitization, desensitization with coping imagery, and cognitive modification. *Behavior Therapy,* 1977, *8,* 606–620.

West, B. L., Goethe, K. E., & Kallman, W. M. Heterosocial skills training: A behavioral–cognitive approach. In D. Upper & S. Ross (Eds.), *Behavioral group therapy, 1980: An annual review.* Champaign, Ill: Research Press, 1980.

Williams, C. L., & Ciminero, A. R. Development and validation of a heterosocial skills inventory: The Survey of Heterosexual Interactions for Females. *Journal of Consulting and Clinical Psychology,* 1978, *46,* 1547–1548.

Wine, J. Test anxiety and direction of attention. *Psychological Bulletin,* 1971, *76,* 92–104.

Wine, J. Cognitive-attentional theory of test anxiety. In I. Sarason (Ed.), *Test anxiety: Theory, research and application.* Hillsdale, N.J.: Erlbaum, 1980.

Wolfe, J. L., & Fodor, I. G. Modifying assertive behavior in women: A comparison of three approaches. *Behavior Therapy,* 1977, *8,* 567–574.

14

The Assessment of Cognition in Athletes

Michael J. Mahoney and Martha L. Epstein

Introduction

Although the psychologist's task has always been one of tracing the etiology of consistent patterns in human experience, new areas in which to direct this effort are continually opening up. The realm of sport is one that recently has caught the attention of many psychologists. Sport psychology in America can be traced back to several important pioneers, the most notable of whom is Coleman Roberts Griffith. As a result of his work at the University of Illinois, he has come to be described by some as the father of sport psychology (Kroll & Lewis, 1970).

Griffith was an unusual professional hybrid when, in 1918, he began attending to performance-related factors in basketball and football. He applied his skills in experimental psychology to a wide range of interests, including athletic reaction time, flexibility, muscular steadiness, and a number of psychomotor skills. Exploring the topic of competitive motivation, he corresponded with Knute Rockne and found that, contrary to still-popular lore, Rockne's pregame talks were not intended to heighten the players' arousal so much as to "make our boys take the game less seriously."

Most relevant to sport personology, perhaps, were Griffith's efforts to understand the psychological parameters of athletic excellence. Griffith was the first sport psychologist to note the phenomenon of unconscious, auto-

Michael J. Mahoney and Martha L. Epstein • Department of Psychology, The Pennsylvania State University, University Park, Pennsylvania.

matic psychomotor skills as they relate to athletic performance. The experience of performing well in stressful competition without later recall of the presence of conscious thoughts, images, or self-instructions during the performance is widely cited in contemporary interviews with athletes. Griffith referred to this experience as an "automatic skill response" and illustrated it through an interview with the famous Harold "Red" Grange after the 1924 Michigan–Illinois football game. Grange had scored four touchdowns in the first 12 minutes of the game, and yet, when interviewed by Griffith, he could not remember a single detail of any of his runs.

The trait versus nontrait controversy that currently plagues many areas of psychology was not raging during Griffith's tenure as America's foremost sport psychologist. However, the seeds of the conflict were planted even before Griffith turned his attention to the psychology of sport. Historically, the most popular candidates for "causing" or explaining individual differences have been personality traits. Indeed, until the advent of behaviorism, the psychology of personality was dominated by trait theories. Early behavioristic writers began to vigorously attack the adequacy of trait approaches and argued, instead, for a nonmediational analysis of human experience in terms of environmental inputs and behavioral outputs (Skinner, 1953; Watson, 1913). The rejection of mediation was a costly move, however, in that it left the behaviorist theoretically bankrupt. Although behaviorism offered clear improvements in the descriptive realm, it seemed to offer little progress in the area of explanation.

That humans and infrahumans alike exhibit salient consistencies in performance would not have been problematic for behaviorists if such consistencies had been perfectly correlated with situational consistencies. The correlation was far from perfect, however, and the need for further explanation became apparent. Constructs such as stimulus generalization and response generalization were called upon to explain stability across ostensibly different situations. For the nonmediational theorists, these behavioral consistencies were accounted for by positing an enduring *internal* organismic change. Infinite chains of miniature stimuli and responses were invoked to legitimate the behavioristic return to constructs inside the organism. Furthermore, some behaviors were said to be "rule-governed" (Skinner, 1974), whereas others were simply relegated to the versatile concept of "reinforcement history." These mediational constructs were appropriately camouflaged in terms that made them sound observable and therefore allegedly scientific.

This state of affairs was modified substantially when some behaviorally oriented theorists began to explicitly endorse the legitimacy of inference and mediation in the analysis of human behavior (e.g., Bandura, 1969; Mahoney, 1974). Although its welcome was hardly universal, cognitive-behavior modification was soon commanding more and more attention from both behavioral and nonbehavioral quarters. Interestingly, the liberality that reenfranchised the concept of cognition did not extend to the concept of traits, which continued to be viewed as unpromising mediational constructs (e.g., Mischel, 1968). Following the example of their predecessors who had also recognized stability in behavior, cognitive-behavior modifiers simply relabeled their mediational consistencies as "beliefs," "cognitive skills," and "cognitive consistencies." Currently, cognitive–behavioral psychologists seem comfortable with the concept of cross-situational cognitive consistencies so long as they are not called "traits." Debates about person variables, situation variables, and person–situation interactions, however, continue to stimulate lively exchange (e.g., Bandura, 1978; Bowers, 1973; Endler & Magnusson, 1976; Epstein, 1979; Mischel, 1973).

Whether called "cognitive consistencies" or "traits," these cross-situational behavioral consistencies have sparked a heated controversy among sport psychologists. Some sport researchers interested in athletic personality—most notably Ogilvie and Tutko (1966) and, to a lesser extent, Vanek and Cratty (1970)—endorse a trait-based research approach. On the other hand, a growing number of sport psychologists are becoming vigorously opposed to the trait approach (e.g., Fisher, 1977; Martens, 1975; Rushall, 1970; Singer, Harris, Kroll, Martens, & Sechrest, 1977). The primary argument between the two camps has focused on the predictive validity of trait versus alternative approaches (Mischel, 1968) to understanding and anticipating athletic performance. For sport psychologists, the alternative to a trait approach has been primarily a skills analysis of athletic behavior. Our review will therefore involve separate analyses of the trait and skills approaches to the study of athletes.

Sport Personology: The Search for Athletic Traits

As psychological testing began to flourish (particularly after World War II), there were sporadic attempts to identify the "athletic personality." None of these was as captivating or enduring, however, as that of Bruce Ogilvie and Thomas Tutko of San Jose State College. In 1966 they published the volume *Problem Athletes and How to Handle Them*. They also developed the first personality inventory specifically aimed at the athlete—the Athletic Motivation Inventory. Many viewed this as a significant improvement over the growing tendency to use pathology-based tests (e.g., the MMPI) to distinguish athletes from nonathletes and/or elite athletes from average performers.

Although sport personology has been researched for many years, the purpose of this research was not closely examined until recently, when it came under attack. Was the goal to select athletes on the basis of their psychological makeup or to measure the effects of athletic competition on psychological functioning? With rare exception, the primary goal seemed to be the former.

For example, it is clear that, although researchers such as Ogilvie (1968) have explored the potential impact of sports competition on the athlete's personality, the effect of the latter on the former has been of primary concern.

> We can state with some certitude that those [athletes] who retain their motivation for competition will have most of the following personality traits: ambition, organization, deference, dominance, endurance and aggression. There will be fewer introverted types in adult-level competition. (p. 78)

The apparent inclination is to identify athletic personality profiles and to select and train athletes who already have these personality prerequisites. This inclination is noted by Martens (1975) in his commentary on Ogilvie and Tutko's claim that they can identify elite athletes on the basis of their personality profiles:

> Based on their assertion they offer for a fee to assess athletes' personalities and from this information they will predict success as well as suggest to the coach ways to "handle" an athlete in order that the athlete may maximize his potential. This dubious enterprise is unsubstantiated by any reported data by Ogilvie and Tutko. (p. 16)

It has been suggested by other critics of the personology approach that the hostility and/or apprehensiveness of some athletes and coaches toward sport psychologists stem primarily from such allegedly exaggerated assertions. The recent decision by the Professional Football Players Association to prohibit psychological testing of players may be a case in point. A less extreme evaluation of sport personology is offered by Kane (1978) and Morgan (1978). They emphasize the potential promise of a combined trait–state analysis of athletic performance. We shall return to this recommendation in the final section of this chapter.

At present, the controversy over the trait versus the nontrait paradigm is perhaps the most hotly debated issue among sport psychologists. Some contend that the search for an "athletic personality," whether generic or sport-specific, is doomed to failure because of its endorsement of an unviable trait approach to personality. This is, however, only one of many criticisms leveled against sport personologists. It seems appropriate at this point to enumerate and evaluate the other popular criticisms of sport personology. These have included the following:

1. Many of the assessment instruments used in sport personality research were designed for abnormal populations. Their validity when used on normal groups is therefore questionable.
2. Research on the personality profiles of athletes will always lag behind the level of precision and consensual knowledge in personality psychology in general, which is, at this point, embarrassingly low.
3. Extant research on the athletic personality—although voluminous—has been disorganized and methodologically inadequate.

4. Most sport personality research has lacked an inadequate theoretical framework.
5. The personality traits allegedly related to athletic performance have seldom withstood replication across athletes, sports, or even different teams.
6. It is not clear from the evidence available that the so-called athletic personality is distinguishable from the personality of any other person who is highly motivated to excel in a given area.

The viability and accuracy of these various criticisms are, of course, denied by many sport personologists and substantially qualified by others such as Kane (1978) and Morgan (1978). One of the most telling bits of evidence here, however, is offered in Martens's (1975) review of 202 manuscripts on sport personology prepared between 1950 and 1973. Only 10% of the reported data were derived from an experimental manipulation. The remaining 90% comprised scattered interviews, theoretical papers, and correlational studies, which often ended with unwarranted claims for causality and generalizability. Our own evaluation of the state of affairs in sport personality research is well stated by Martens (1975):

> What reliable knowledge has been obtained from the millions of dollars spent, the thousands of hours devoted, and the thousands of subjects tested in the study of sport personality? The answer is very disappointing. It is nearly impossible to find any consistent results in the literature. Few investigations report reliable evidence and those that do are of questionable validity. Unfortunately, after years of study we know very little about personality as related to sport. (p. 14)

As will be reiterated in our conclusion, we also concur with Martens's contention—which is echoed by Morgan (1978)—that neither the trait nor the state approach is adequate. An interactional approach appears to offer a new and interesting direction for future research, yet, like the trait and state approaches, it, too, is not appropriate for every line of inquiry.

Skillpower: The Search for Athletic Psychological Skills

The difference between a trait and a skill is perhaps a naively simple question to pose, but its unequivocal answer is probably as instructive as it is elusive. What is the difference, for example, between Mischel's (1973) cross-situational "cognitive consistencies" and the personality traits of which he has been so critical? A number of possible differentiating factors come to mind—malleability, inheritance, interrelationship, and mode of assessment (e.g., behavioral performance vs. self-report). The primary goal of this chapter is not to resolve this question, however, and we shall resist the temptation to pursue it. Suffice it to say that the long-held dichotomy between traits and skills may be more semantic than we have realized and that at least some of our intellectual battles in this arena may have been fought out of mis-communication rather than disagreement.

Research on psychological factors other than traits also has an extensive history in sport science. As early as 1940, for example, Shaw published a review of the many extant studies relating imaginal weight lifting to electrical changes in muscle activity. Shaw's contemporaries working in the areas of motor learning and human performance also studied the roles of attention and memory in the acquisition and refinement of sports skills. The infiltration of behavior modification into sport psychology added further impetus to the trend toward a skills approach to athletic training (Rushall & Siedentop, 1972). Likewise, several more cognitively oriented researchers reinforced the notion that the current psychological experiences of the athlete could dramatically affect his or her performance (e.g., Epstein & Fenz, 1962; Fenz, 1975; Mahoney, 1979). Competitive athletes must learn to cope with anxiety, frustration, personal injuries, failures, and a wide range of experiences that may influence their performance and satisfaction. There is increasing interest in the possibility that more successful athletes may have developed certain psychological skills that serve to optimize performance. The Olympic athlete, for example, may be more adept at focused task concentration or at directing anxiety in constructive, rather than destructive, directions.

Attempts to identify sports-relevant psychological skills have ranged from unstructured interviews to formal psychometric instruments. Mahoney and Avener (1977), for example, employed a specially constructed questionnaire to evaluate various psychological processes in Olympic gymnasts. The 13 finalists for the 1976 U.S. men's Olympic team completed a 25-item questionnaire dealing with coping skills, competitive anxiety, self-confidence, mental imagery, self-talk, dream content, performance standards, and attributions of success and failure. Responses to the questionnaire were correlated with final competitive standing—qualifying versus not qualifying for the Olympic team.

Better competitors reported thinking more about gymnastics in everyday life as well as dreaming more about their sport. Moreover, better gymnasts tended to have dreams in which their performance was moderately successful. Olympic team qualifiers also reported greater self-confidence and a greater frequency of self-talk during practice and competitive situations. Although all the gymnasts reported using imaginal rehearsal, there was an interesting tendency for better athletes to employ a first-person imaginal perspective (internal imagery) and for less skilled gymnasts to rely more on imagery characterized by a third-person perspective (external imagery). Qualifiers for the U.S. team also differed from nonqualifiers in their pattern of self-reported anxiety over the week preceding their performance as well as during the actual competition. The generalizability of these findings is not known, and Mahoney and Avener stressed the need for future research in this area of sport psychology.

A modified correlational–experimental design was used by Shelton and Mahoney (1978) to assess the impact of weight lifters' "psyching up" strategies on subsequent physical performance. Before the first two attempts at compressing a dynamometer, all subjects were instructed to count backward out loud from a four-digit number for 30 seconds. Control subjects repeated this procedure before their third and last attempt to compress the dynamometer, whereas experimental subjects were requested to employ their usual psyching up strategy before the last trial. Results showed that weight lifters in the experimental group improved significantly between the second and third trials and that athletes who used their psyching up techniques significantly outperformed those who did not. Reports of the cognitive strategies were divided into the following four categories: (1) attentional focus, (2) self-efficacy and ability statements, (3) purposeful arousal, and (4) imagery. Attentional focus was used most frequently, followed by cognitions involving self-efficacy.

The studies by Mahoney and Avener (1977) and Shelton and Mahoney (1978) are examples of the new skills approach to sport psychology research. Overall, however, this facet of sports research remains undeveloped, suffering from a paucity of psychometrically validated assessment instruments. The existing instruments and new directions toward skills assessment are briefly noted here.

The Modified TAT

Fenz and Epstein (1962) modified the Thematic Apperception Test to meet the needs of their research on cognitive and physiological patterns in sky divers. They asked their subjects to construct a story around pictures that were of variable relevance to parachuting. This was an ingenious modification of a standard instrument, and one may well wonder why cognitive–behavioral researchers have not followed suit in other areas such as speech anxiety and obesity.

In the Fenz and Epstein research, denial of fear was reported as a popular defense mechanism among novice parachutists and is illustrated by TAT stories depicting a calm and relaxed hero:

> He is not afraid at all, just looks that way, because of the wind that is blowing in his face. He will have a wonderful jump. It will be great, just great! (Fenz, 1975, p. 313).

Of particular interest is the fact that many of these same inexperienced jumpers were also very explicit in admitting their fear. As Fenz (1975) puts it, "when not denying fear, they acknowledge it with great intensity" (p. 332).

A perennial problem with projective instruments is, of course, their interpretation. The inferential leap from the experiences attributed to a protagonist in a TAT story to the current psychological processes in the subject is a controversial point that is well beyond the scope of this chapter. It will only be noted that unconscious processes are undeniably operative in humans and that one need not subscribe to psychoanalytic theory to accept this contention. The occurrence of self-deception, for example, is a phenomenon that appears to be receiving increasing experimental attention (cf. Nisbett & Wilson, 1977; Russell, 1978; Sackeim & Gur, 1978). In this context, we may be well advised to guard against ignoring phenomena simply because they have emanated from a competing or personally disfavored perspective.

Another heuristic finding in the Fenz and Epstein research was the apparent shift in attentional focus as a subject became more experienced and competent.

> It seems clear that the experienced jumper becomes increasingly more externally task oriented, whereas the novice jumper ruminates on his own fears or expends much of his energy defending against them. (Fenz, 1975, p. 331)

This shift, which is consistent with several extant views on coping, was clearly reflected in TAT stores that depicted either a task-oriented protagonist or one preoccupied with performance dangers. The cognitive researcher who would enlist this finding as corroboration for a particular model of coping, however, must be ready to defend his or her selective confidence in projective instruments that offer only corroborative (vs. disconfirmatory) evidence.

From this seminal work in the area, it would appear that modified projective tasks could offer valuable information about cognitive processes in the athlete. Scoring formats and correlations with other measures of cognition would offer some empirical anchors for excursions into this realm. Indeed, in light of contemporary models of human cognition, a more extensive assessment of the potential promise of projective instruments is probably long overdue.

The Sport Competition Anxiety Test

In 1977 Rainer Martens published the *Sport Competition Anxiety Test* (SCAT), a "sport-specific trait anxiety inventory" (p. iv) that is described as being superior to other trait anxiety instruments in predicting the state anxiety of athletes. The SCAT, which has both adult and child forms, consists of 15 self-descriptive statements, 10 of which are relevant to anxiety. "Before I compete I feel relaxed" and "Before I compete I feel uneasy" are two examples of the anxiety-relevant items. Subjects rate the 15 self-statements on a 3-point scale (hardly ever, sometimes, often), depending on how they usually feel when in competitive situations.

Prior to publication, the SCAT was extensively researched on thousands of subjects. Data on item discrimination, reliability, content validity, and construct validity are presented in the Martens's monograph, along with commentaries by Janet T. Spence and Charles D. Spielberger. The test is enjoying increasing use among sport scientists as a measure of competitive anxiety. It is unclear at this point, however, to what extent it addresses some of the cognitive processes that may or may not covary with the more somatic aspects of anxiety.

The Test of Attentional and Interpersonal Skills

Robert M. Nideffer (1976*a*, 1976*b*) has developed the Test of Attentional and Interpersonal Skills (TAIS). Although its relevance is not intentionally restricted to sports, Nideffer is primarily concerned with its promise in identifying athletes whose "attentional styles" may conflict with the demands of their sport.

His test divides human attention into two primary dimensions—direction (internal or external) and width (broad or narrow). Using this classification system, Nideffer constructed a questionnaire with the following six subscales: (1) broad-external (BET), (2) external overload (OET), (3) broad-internal (BIT), (4) internal overload (OIT), (5) narrow effective focus (NSR), and (6) errors of underinclusion (RED). A person who scores high on the broad-external dimension, for example, is construed as one who deals effectively with a considerable amount of environmental stimuli, whereas a person who is high on the external overload scale is seen as being easily distracted by external events. Nideffer argues that the magnitude of individual scale scores is of interest but that the "profile configuration" of scores is more important to interpreting the TAIS. He suggests that individuals who score higher on the BET, BIT, and NSR scales than on the OET, OIT, and RED scales have generally good attentional styles, whereas specific profiles are more likely to be compatible with and reinforced by certain sports. This assertion, however, must await empirical evaluation. Preliminary data on reliability, construct validity, and predictive validity are available.

Measures of Imagery

Although imaginal activities have long been regarded as important in the athlete (Corbin, 1972; Richardson, 1967*a*, 1967*b*), very few imagery assessment instruments are available to the sports researcher other than those borrowed from the learning laboratory (Richardson, 1977). These instruments range widely in their psychometric merits, and none specifically addresses the various demands of athletic competition.

In a recent study dealing with the role of different kinds of imagery in skill acquisition (Epstein, Note 1), it appeared that the task of assessing imaginal activities may be complicated by temporal and task-dependent shifts in imagery content. A questionnaire that required imagining four separate scenes and answering 12 questions about each image was used to assess natural imaginal style. Questionnaire items concerned the vividness of tactile, auditory, kinesthetic, and olfactory imaginal sensations; the degree of difficulty in concentrating on and controlling images; and the "external" versus "internal" nature of images. As noted briefly in the discussion of Mahoney and Avener's 1977 study, external images are characterized by a third-person perspective. Such images are primarily visual and resemble viewing oneself on a videotape or movie. Internal images, on the other hand, are experienced from the imager's own perspective and often incorporate kinesthetic sensations.

In addition to answering the structured imagery questionnaire, subjects verbally described their images, and these descriptions were then analyzed. Of particular interest is the fact that individuals frequently switched between the external and the internal modes both within and across images, and the place where these perspective shifts occurred was quite consistent across subjects. Furthermore, a few subjects reported images that were simultaneously external and internal. It appears that the researchers who are interested in imaginal processes in athletes are left in the unenviable position of facing a potentially important phenomenon that may be elusively dynamic and for which there is no psychometrically adequate assessment.

Some have suggested using a "clock test" to assess the aforementioned internal–external dimension of imagery. With the athlete's eyes closed, a clock is traced on his or her forehead, and the hands are "set" to read 3 o'clock. The athlete is then asked to tell the time on this clock. It is believed that internal imagers will report 9 o'clock and that external imagers will report 3 o'clock (Mahoney, 1979). At this stage, most of this belief is purely speculative. However, in an exploratory study (Epstein, 1979), a slight relationship was found between the clock test and other measures of internal–external imagery for males, although females showed no such relationship.

Thought Sampling

Klinger and his associates appear to be the first researchers to apply the method of thought sampling to athletes (Klinger, Barta, & Glas, Note 2). They asked members of a college basketball team to participate in a thought-sampling project. Athletes' thoughts were tape recorded whenever they (1) left the game for a substitute player or (2) were tapped on the shoulder while sitting on the bench. Content analyses revealed some interesting shifts in cognitive processes—from task focus to self-evaluation—covarying with the momentary state of the game. When the player's team was doing well, cognitive focus tended to be planful and task-relevant. When the opposing team was doing well, however, thought content tended to change toward self-consciousness and self-evaluation.

This exploratory study suggests that thought sampling may be a viable and valuable method for assessing athletes' thoughts *in vivo*. Although there are obvious limitations to the technique, its further evaluation would appear to be warranted.

Summary and Implications

As mentioned at the beginning of this chapter, the ongoing debate between sport personologists and skills researchers is one that hardly needs additional fuel. We have organized our brief review into these two sections because this division seemed to reflect the most salient point of contention among contemporary workers. As to the trait–situation controversy that plagues sport personologists and other personality researchers, it seems increasingly clear that neither extreme position is likely to be adequate. Indeed, there has been cogent argument that the contention between these two is itself ill-conceived:

> The trait position, the situationist position, and the interactionist position are often presented as different approaches to the issue of stability in behavior, with the implication that only one of them can be right. Actually, all of them can be right, because they identify not three different solutions to the same problem, but three different problems. The interactionist wishes to study the behavior of people with certain attributes in situations with certain attributes. The trait theorist wishes to study consistent behavioral tendencies in individuals over a sample of situations. The situationist is concerned with the general effects of situations over a sample of individuals. (Epstein, 1979, p. 1104)

If it is true that the trait paradigm, the situational paradigm, and the interactional paradigm in fact focus on three separate issues, then it is clear that the solution that sport scientists are seeking may come not from finding the one correct approach to personality research, but from raising and investigating specific and well-defined questions (something that has been sorely lacking in this area of research). The debate between traits and skills researchers may be similarly ill-conceived: they may be fighting about the correct solution to one problem when, all along, they are actually addressing two different and equally important issues.

Aside from the paradigmatic issues of a purely skills approach versus a purely trait approach, or of naive personology versus naive situationism versus naive interactionism, it should be clear that our assessment of cognitive processes in athletes remains very poorly developed. Indeed, given the crudeness of extant measures, one might expect much more instrument variance than has far been reported. That at least some cognitive patterns—albeit crudely assessed—seem to be replicable across sports (e.g., Meyers, Cooke, Cullen, & Liles, 1979) can be cautiously interpreted with optimism. We know that our current instruments involve substantial measurement error. That at least some replicable patterns seem to be emerging suggests that the signal-to-noise ratio is nonetheless surmountable (implying, of course, a strong "signal" of cognitive influence overriding the instrument noise). The warrant for this rather optimistic conjecture must await further refinements and evaluations in the study of cognition in athletes.

Reference Notes

1. Epstein, M. L. *The relationship of mental imagery and mental practice to performance of a motor task.* Unpublished master's thesis, The Pennsylvania State University, 1980.
2. Klinger, E., Barta, S. G., & Glas, R. A. *Thought content and gap time in basketball.* Paper presented to the University of Minnesota Sport Psychology Symposium, Duluth, 1979.

References

Bandura, A. *Principles of behavior modification.* New York: Holt, Rinehart & Winston, 1969.
Bandura, A. The self system in reciprocal determinism. *American Psychologist,* 1978, *33,* 344–358.
Bowers, K. S. Situationism in psychology: An analysis and a critique. *Psychological Review,* 1973, *80,* 307–336.
Corbin, C. B. Mental practice. In W. P. Morgan (Ed.), *Ergogenic aids and muscular performance.* New York: Academic Press, 1972.
Endler, N. S., & Magnusson, D. (Eds.). *Interactional psychology and personality.* New York: Wiley, 1976.
Epstein, S. The stability of behavior: I. On predicting most of the people much of the time. *Journal of Personality and Social Psychology,* 1979, *37,* 1097–1126.
Epstein, S., & Fenz, W. D. Theory and experiment on the measurement of approach–avoidance conflict. *Journal of Abnormal and Social Psychology,* 1962, *64,* 97–112.
Fenz, W. D. Strategies for coping with stress. In I. G. Sarason & C. D. Spielberger (Eds.), *Stress and anxiety* (Vol. 2). Washington, D.C.: Hemisphere, 1975.
Fenz, W. D., & Epstein, S. Measurement of approach–avoidance conflict along a stimulus dimension by a thematic apperception test. *Journal of Personality,* 1962, *30,* 613–632.
Fisher, A. C. Sport personality assessment: Adversary proceedings. In C. O. Dotson, V. L. Katch, & J. Schick (Eds.), *Research and practice in physical education.* Champaign, Ill.: Human Kinetics Publishers, 1977.
Kane, J. E. Personality research: The current controversy and implications for sports studies. In W. F. Straub (Ed.), *Sport psychology: An analysis of athlete behavior.* Ithaca, N.Y.: Mouvement Publications, 1978.
Kroll, W., & Lewis, G. America's first sport psychologist. *Quest,* 1970, *13,* 1–4.
Mahoney, M. J. *Cognition and behavior modification.* Cambridge, Mass.: Ballinger, 1974.
Mahoney, M. J. Cognitive skills and athletic performance. In P. C. Kendall & S. D. Hollon (Eds.), *Cognitive–behavioral intervention: Theory, research, and procedures.* New York: Academic Press, 1979.
Mahoney, M. J., & Avener, M. Psychology of the elite athlete: An exploratory study. *Cognitive Therapy and Research,* 1977, *1,* 135–141.
Martens, R. The paradigmatic crisis in American sport personology. *Sportwissenschaft,* 1975, *5,* 9–24.
Martens, R. *Sport competition anxiety test.* Champaign, Ill.: Human Kinetics Publishers, 1977.
Meyers, A. W., Cooke, C. J., Cullen, J., & Liles, L. Psychological aspects of athletic competitors: A replication across sports. *Cognitive Therapy and Research,* 1979, *3,* 361–366.
Mischel, W. *Personality and assessment.* New York: Wiley, 1968.
Mischel, W. Toward a cognitive social learning reconceptualization of personality. *Psychological Review,* 1973, *80,* 252–283.
Morgan, W. P. Sport personology: The credulous–skeptical argument in perspective. In W. F. Straub (Ed.), *Sport psychology: An analysis of athlete behavior.* Ithaca, N.Y.: Mouvement Publications, 1978.

Nideffer, R. M. *The inner athlete*. New York: Thomas Crowell, 1976. *(a)*

Nideffer, R. M. Test of attentional and interpersonal style. *Journal of Personality and Social Psychology,* 1976, *34,* 394–404. *(b)*

Nisbett, R. E., & Wilson, T. D. Telling more than we can know: Verbal reports on mental processes. *Psychological Review,* 1977, *84,* 231–259.

Ogilvie, B. C. Psychological consistencies within the personality of high-level competitors. *Journal of the American Medical Association,* 1968, *205,* 156–162.

Ogilvie, B. C., & Tutko, T. A. *Problem athletes and how to handle them.* London: Pelham, 1966.

Richardson, A. Mental practice: A review and discussion. Part I. *Research Quarterly,* 1967, *38,* 95–107. *(a)*

Richardson, A. Mental practice: A review and discussion. Part II. *Research Quarterly,* 1967, *38,* 263–273. *(b)*

Richardson, A. The meaning and measurement of memory imagery. *British Journal of Psychology,* 1977, *68,* 29–43.

Rushall, B. S. An evaluation of the relationship between personality and physical performance categories. In G. S. Kenyon (Ed.), *Contemporary psychology of sport.* Chicago: Athletic Institute, 1970.

Rushall, B. S., & Siedentop, D. *The development and control of behavior in sport and physical education.* Philadelphia: Lea & Febiger, 1972.

Russell, J. M. Saying, feeling, and self-deception. *Behaviorism,* 1978, *6,* 27–43.

Sackeim, H. A., & Gur, R. C. Self-deception, self-confrontation, and consciousness. In G. E. Schwartz & D. Shapiro (Eds.), *Consciousness and self-regulation: Advances in research and theory* (Vol. 2). New York: Plenum Press, 1978.

Shaw, W. A. The relation of muscular action potentials to imaginal weight lifting. *Archives of Psychology,* 1940, *247,* 1–50.

Shelton, T. O., & Mahoney, M. J. The content and effect of "psyching up" strategies in weight lifters. *Cognitive Therapy and Research,* 1978, *2,* 275–284.

Singer, R. N., Harris, D., Kroll, W., Martens, R., & Sechrest, L. Psychological testing of athletes. *Journal of Physical Education and Recreation,* 1977, *48,* 30–32.

Skinner, B. F. *Science and human behavior.* New York: Macmillan, 1953.

Skinner, B. F. *About behaviorism.* New York: Knopf, 1974.

Vanek, M., & Cratty, B. J. *Psychology and the superior athlete.* New York: Macmillan, 1970.

Watson, J. B. Psychology as the behaviorist views it. *Psychological Review,* 1913, *20,* 158–177.

15

The Assessment of Social Problem-Solving Skills in Young Children

Linda Rose Krasnor and Kenneth H. Rubin

Introduction

Assessment of the impact of early education and socialization practices has recently undergo a major shift in focus. The blossoming of novel preschool and elementary school curricula in the 1950s and 1960s was accompanied by a call for evidence to ascertain the beneficial effects of such costly interventions. At that time, attention was focused clearly on academically oriented outcomes. In a similar vein, research concerning socialization practices centered on the familial precursors of achievement motivation and the development of behaviors relevant to academic excellence.

During the 1970s, psychologists and educators alike came to realize that assessment of intellectual skills alone is inadequate and that one reasonable outcome of home and school experience is the development of social competence (Anderson & Messick, 1974; O'Malley, 1977; Webb, Oliveri, & Harnick, 1977; Zigler & Trickett, 1978). Centering on the school environment, research has been directed at discovering relationships between indexes of academic excellence and measures of interpersonal competence (Kohn, 1977; White & Watts, 1973). Given the significance of social skills for academic adjustment, curricula have been developed to improve social competencies

Linda Rose Krasnor and Kenneth H. Rubin • Department of Psychology, University of Waterloo, Waterloo, Ontario, Canada.

(e.g., Spivack & Shure, 1974). Researchers have also begun to explore the cognitive underpinnings of social skills (Flavell, Note 1).

The rapid acceleration of social competence research has, not surprisingly, been accompanied by the introduction of a wide variety of assessment instruments. These measures have reflected different dimensions of social competence (e.g., acceptability, popularity, effectiveness of behavior). As such, it appears that social competence should not be regarded as a unidimensional construct (Connolly & Doyle, Note 2).

The purpose of this chapter is to examine critically the assessment of one broad area of social competence, namely, the ability of young children to manage interpersonal problems. In our examination of the social problem-solving literature, we will attempt to provide the reader with answers to the following questions:

1. How has social problem solving generally been defined in the developmental and clinical literature, and how can this definition be expanded to include a broader range of social competencies?
2. Why is social problem solving a significant topic of study?
3. What are the current tools available for assessing social problem solving?
4. What is the psychometric strength of the extant battery of social problem-solving measures?
5. What social problem-solving skills are in the behavioral repertoires of young children?

After dealing with these questions, we will introduce a process-oriented model of social problem-solving (SPS) strategy selection. We will also suggest potential methods for testing the strength of our newly developed model.

Definition and Varying Theoretical Concerns

We assume that social behavior is goal-directed. The goals range from simply establishing social contact to eliciting complex cooperative behaviors from peers or adults. "Others" are potentially rich resources to the child—sources of materials, information, assistance, comfort, and so forth. How well a child utilizes these resources reflects how effectively he or she can communicate personal needs, as well as the responsiveness of the child's social environment to their expression. It has been suggested that the child's ability to elicit the satisfaction of his or her needs from others is in itself a major component of social competence (Ainsworth & Bell, 1974; Charlesworth, 1976; Goldberg, 1977; Humphrey, 1976; Weinstein, 1969; White & Watts, 1973). It is the *choice* of social goals and of the social behaviors that are intended as means to achieve these goals that we define as the "social problem-solving process."

Given this admittedly broad and imprecise definition, it is nevertheless the case that research concerning SPS has had a relatively varied, lengthy, and respected history. Sociobiologists, for example, have acknowledged the adaptive characteristics of SPS skills. Humphrey (1976), Kummer (1971), and Leakey and Lewin (1978) have all suggested that the requirements of resolving the complex social problems of group living spurred the emergence of increased intellectual functioning in evolutionary development. This distinctively Piagetian (Piaget, 1926) argument concerning the causal role of social interaction vis-à-vis intellectual growth has also found support in the contemporary developmental psychology literature (Damon, 1977). Resolution of social conflicts is seen by social-cognitive developmentalists as eliciting the growth of perspective-taking skills, which, in turn, aid in the growth of sophisticated SPS (Chandler, 1977; Spivack, Platt, & Shure, 1976).

Another viewpoint that may be relevant to SPS development stems from recent work by Schank and Abelson (1977), who have brought the procedures and analytic techniques of artificial intelligence and information processing to the field of social action. Research within this area, especially that concerning the characteristics of expert performance (e.g., Simon, 1976), can be expanded to include the SPS process; we shall develop this connection subsequently.

Contributions of sociobiology, psycholinguistics (Ervin-Tripp, 1977; Garvey, 1974), and developmental, social (Langer, 1978), and cognitive psychology aside, it is clear that the most visible and influential presentation of SPS work stems from the clinical literature. The most highly cited research is that of Spivack and Shure (Shure & Spivack, 1978; Spivack *et al.,* 1976; Spivack & Shure, 1974). From this research has emerged a series of training programs and assessment procedures concerning interpersonal problem-solving skills.

Borrowing from Damon (1977) and Cooney and Selman (1978), we will refer to those assessment procedures employed by Spivack and Shure, among others, as "hypothetical–reflective." The term reflects two characteristics of this approach: (1) the use of hypothetical situations and (2) the attempt to measure considered "thinking" responses.

Typically in hypothetical–reflective studies, the social goal is clearly presented. Such goals have included the acquisition of a toy that is in the possession of another child and the avoidance of adult anger (Spivack & Shure, 1974). Strategies to meet these clearly defined goals are then elicited from the child. This procedure reflects investigative concerns with classical cognitive problem-solving approaches, in which strategies can be generated and assessed in a well-defined, restricted context. Responses to the problems are judged by means of a priori criteria that remain stable throughout the paradigmatic interview. This approach assumes that motivation to achieve the goal is consistent across subjects and situations. Responses are elicited in verbal form, and an adult tester is present. A review of SPS research that has employed the hypothetical–reflective assessment procedure follows.

Assessing Social Problem Solving:
The Hypothetical–Reflective Method

As mentioned previously, the major method of assessing SPS skills in children has been to elicit verbal responses to hypothetical social dilemmas. The dual goals of this hypothetical–reflective method are (1) to gather knowledge concerning children's social cognitions and (2) to gather information that will allow useful inferences with respect to the child's social behavior. In the following discussion, we will attempt to determine the degree to which hypothetical–reflective SPS measures have successfully met these goals.

Hypothetical–Reflective Assessments

The development of hypothetical–reflective tests to assess SPS skills has been a major focus in the work of Spivack and Shure and their colleagues (Spivack *et al.,* 1976; Spivack & Shure, 1974). These authors have suggested five major components of the SPS process: (1) the ability to generate alternative solutions to social problems, (2) consideration of potential consequences to social acts and the ability to articulate consequences, (3) step-by-step means to social goals, (4) sensitivity to interpersonal problems, and (5) the understanding of the motives and behaviors of others. We will focus here on the first three components; these specific skills have been shown to be most effective in distinguishing deviant from "normal" children (Spivack *et al.,* 1976) and have attracted the most research attention.

Probably the most widely used SPS measure for young children has been the Preschool Interpersonal Problem-Solving (PIPS) test (Spivack & Shure, 1974). This test follows the general form of most of the hypothetical–reflective instruments in which a series of stories is presented verbally to the child, accompanied by either pictures or props. A social goal is clearly defined for the child, who is asked to generate verbal responses to questions concerning means, solutions, or consequences.

In the PIPS, assessment focuses on the ability to generate alternative solutions to two types of common social dilemmas: (1) a peer-oriented problem in which a child seeks to obtain a toy that is in the possession of another child and (2) an adult-oriented dilemma in which a child seeks to avoid his mother's anger after damaging property.

Within each of these two categories, the child is presented with a minimum of seven dilemmas and is asked to offer a single solution to each (e.g., "Johnny has been playing with this truck for a long time, all morning, and now Jimmy wants a chance to play with it. What can Johnny do or say so that he can play with the truck?"). The characters and objects are changed in each story in order to maintain the child's interest. Additional stories are presented if the child continues to generate new solutions. The child's score consists of the total number of different relevant solutions.

Spivack *et al.* (1976) have also developed a similar test for older children, consisting of four peer-oriented and three authority-oriented problems. Unlike the PIPS, however, the child is asked to generate as many solutions as possible for each story (e.g., "Tell me all you can think of . . . "; "What else could he do?").

Adaptations of the PIPS have been used in a number of other studies designed to explore alternative solutions. Alterations have included changes in content and presentation as well as in scoring. Asher, Renshaw, Geraci, and Dor (Note 3) used a test that centers on friendship dilemmas (getting to know children, management of conflict, maintenance of interaction). Siegal (Note 4) used a hypothetical–reflective format to study children's reliance on adult advice in problematic situations. Krasnor and Rubin (Note 5) employed three problem themes: obtaining a toy from a peer, getting an adult to do something for a child, and helping a peer in distress. Several studies have attempted to elicit multiple solutions from single stories (e.g., Krasnor & Rubin, Note 5; Elias, Larcen, Zlotlow, & Chinsky, Note 6) as opposed to a format in which only a single alternative is elicited for each story. A scoring change for the PIPS was suggested by Enright and Enright (Note 7) to adjust for spontaneity of responses. Total score consisted of the number of alternatives generated by the child divided by the number of alternatives plus the number of tester probes.

The second SPS skill, that of articulating consequences of hypothetical social acts, has been assessed by the "What Happens Next?" game (Spivack *et al.*, 1976; Spivack & Shure, 1974). The preschooler is given a social problem and the solution (e.g., character grabs a toy from another child) and is asked "What might happen next?". After each response, new characters and objects are presented in a new story. A child's score is the total number of relevant, but different, responses. A minimum of five stories is presented in each of two content areas. The adaptation of this test for older children has a different orientation. The child receives a score for the number of "pros and cons" generated in response to stories presenting a "temptation to transgress."

The third SPS skill is the ability to plan means to reach a prespecified goal. Means–end thinking has been assessed by the Means–End Problem-Solving (MEPS) test for children (Spivack *et al.*, 1976). This instrument purportedly measures the ability to specifically plan goal-directed strategies in step-by-step fashion and to consider alternative actions and potential obstacles. The test consists of six stories, each of which includes only the beginning and the end of the tale. The child is asked how the given end could have been achieved. An example of a MEPS story is as follows:

> Al (Joyce) has moved into the neighborhood. He (she) didn't know anyone and felt very lonely. The story ends with Al (Joyce) having many good friends and feeling at home in the neighborhood. What happens in between Al's (Joyce's) moving in and feeling lonely, and when he (she) ends up with many good friends? (p. 65)

A promising new instrument has been developed by Elias and his colleagues (Elias *et al.,* Note 6) to measure a variety of SPS skills simultaneously. The social problem situation analysis measure (SPSAM) consists of a series of hypothetical peer- and teacher-related problem situations (being unjustly blamed by a teacher, being excluded from a peer group, and wanting something a peer has). Each story is presented by six pictures; the pictures for each story portray the action in a step-by-step sequence. The child is asked questions that will elicit responses to the following questions: (1) What is happening in the story? (2) What are the perspectives of the actors within the story? (3) What can happen next? (4) How can the outcome be reached? (5) What would the reactions of the characters be to potential obstacles? (6) What would be the reaction to a similar situation in the future?

Psychometric Considerations

The instruments just described have been used primarily to examine the interrelationships of SPS skills and social adjustment (Spivack & Shure, 1974) and to assess the effects of interpersonal skills training programs (e.g., Spivack & Shure, 1974; Krasnor & Rubin, Note 5; Enright & Enright, Note 7). Given the widespread and growing use of these measures, we would like to note some preliminary cautions. For these tests, as well as for a number of other tests purported to assess social-cognitive skill (Rubin, 1978), psychometric considerations have not received appropriate attention. Thus reliance on these measures for program evaluation or for individual assessment may be premature.

First, normative data for hypothetical–reflective instruments are not readily available. Although Elias *et al.* (Note 6) have made an impressive start in accumulating such data (at least for the SPSAM), as yet there is relatively little age- and sex-related information concerning the quantity and quality of social strategies generated in hypothetical–reflective tests.

Second, methods of gathering information concerning SPS skills vary from study to study. Children's strategies have been elicited one at a time in response to series of related stories (e.g., PIPS) or through the generation of multiple responses to a single story (e.g., SPSAM). The latter method appears to tap flexibility and sequence of strategy use more closely. For example, Elias *et al.* (Note 6) found systematic differences between initial solutions to problems and those solutions offered following the introduction of a hypothetical obstacle to the first remedy. There were greater tendencies to suggest resolution by others, nonconfrontational actions, and the seeking of help after the introduction of obstacles to the first solutions. Given the two methods of eliciting responses, normative data gathering is hindered by the possibility of finding strategy distribution varying in accord with the manner of measurement.

Third, the variety of situations investigated in any of the available sets of hypothetical–reflective measures is narrow, especially when contrasted with the scope of potential social problems that may be encountered in the social environment. Typically, a small number of adult- or peer-oriented problems, each varying with regard to content of social problem, are presented to the children. Content and target variables are thereby confounded, and there is little opportunity to assess the range of a child's SPS skill over situations and/or targets.

The narrow range of situations also makes it difficult to assess the generalizability of SPS abilities. The internal consistency of the measures is especially difficult to compute. Although Spivack *et al.* (1976) have noted significant intercorrelations between SPS skills for different contents and targets, Butler (Note 8) and Krasnor and Rubin (Note 5) have reported uneven internal consistency patterns. Elias *et al.* (Note 6) have indicated qualitative differences in strategy use in adult-oriented versus child-oriented problems; they interpret their findings as indicative of the SPSAM's sensitivity to children's abilities to discriminate between situations.

As for the skills required for successfully solving social problems, Elias *et al.* (Note 6) found five *separate* ability factors for the SPSAM: (1) understanding situations, (2) understanding characters, (3) explicitness of means–ends linkages and specificity of actions considered, (4) personal initiative, and (5) considering alternative means to goals.

Spivack *et al.* (1976) reported that the factor patterns for their four measures of skills vary in relation to the social adjustment of the children studied. For nonadjusted preschoolers, all four tests load on a single factor. For socially adjusted children, two factors emerge: one for alternate solutions, sensitivity, and consequential thinking, and a second for causality. In summary, the relationships between children's competencies to solve different types of social problems and their abilities to employ various skills when solving such problems are relatively unknown.

Validity of Hypothetical–Reflective Measures

Ecological Validity. A further area of psychometric concern is that of ecological validity. One may question how the strategies offered by children to solve hypothetical problems relate to their strategy deployment in real-life settings. A study of strategy use in hypothetical versus behavioral settings was made by Krasnor and Rubin (Note 5). We found that the probability of predicting solutions that would be observed in the free-play setting from those offered in the traditional hypothetical format (and vice versa) was low.

Ability to Predict Results of Ratings of Social Competence from Hypothetical–Reflective Tests. A second external validity issue concerns the ability to predict from the SPS hypothetical–reflective test score the results on *rated* indexes of social competence. Spivack and his colleagues offer as evidence the strength of their SPS measures in discriminating between clinical and normal populations (Spivack *et al.*, 1976). For example, PIPS performance has

been significantly related to teachers' ratings of preschoolers' social adjustment. This relationship has been shown to hold even when the effect of IQ
and verbal fluency scores have been statistically eliminated. Similar reports
relating hypothetical–reflective SPS test performance to behavioral adjustment appear in the literature for older children as well (Spivack *et al.,* 1976;
Elias *et al.,* Note 6). In a number of recent reports using Spivack-type
measures, however, nonsignificant relationships between test scores and
behavioral adjustment ratings have been found (Krasnor & Rubin, Note 5;
Butler, Note 8; Sharp, Note 9).

Another external validity source for hypothetical–reflective measures
has been peer ratings and sociometric status. The assumption has been that
children who show high SPS skills should be more popular and should be
rated as more socially competent by their peers.

Elias *et al.* (Note 6) found that several of the SPSAM variables were
significant predictors of sociometric status. For example, status markers that
could be predicted included "the child who was chosen to go to when in need
of help" and "the child who is independent." Asher *et al.* (Note 3) found that
popular and unpopular kindergartners produced different SPS strategies.
The strategies generated by unpopular children were rated as less effective
and less "relationship enhancing" than those offered by their popular age-
mates. Similarly, Ladd and Oden (1979) found that responses to hypothetical
helping situations differed among high- and low-sociometric-status children.
On the other hand, both Sharp (Note 9) and Butler (Note 8, Note 10) reported
no significant relationships between sociometric measures and hypothetical-
reflective test scores. Where significance has been found, it appears to reside
not with total SPS score, but rather with the *types* of strategies offered by
children. Unpopular children, for example, tend to give more aggressive
strategies in response to a hypothetical conflict situation than do popular
children. In nonconflict dilemmas, unpopular children's responses tended to
be more ambiguous and showed greater tendencies to rely on adult intervention (Asher *et al.,* Note 3). Similarly, Ladd and Oden (1979) found that
uniqueness of strategies was inversely related to sociometric status.

Thus, although some support has been found for the relationship between hypothetical–reflective test scores and teacher- or peer-rated behaviors,
the results have not been entirely consistent. The explanations for these discrepancies are speculative. One explanation may stem from the degree to
which the behavioral raters have access to SPS data. For example, Spivack *et
al.* (1976) found that SPS training positively altered teacher ratings of behavioral adjustment. The significant relationship between PIPS performance
and posttreatment, teacher-rated behavioral adjustment was taken as
evidence supporting the ecological validity of the laboratory PIPS measure.
In at least some of their studies, however, it is quite clear that the teachers
who rated the children were aware of the SPS treatment (or control) groups to
which the children had been assigned (Sharp, Note 9). Thus, although one

may argue that training may have altered PIPS performance, the data concerning behavioral adjustment must be viewed with caution. In a number of studies in which observers did not have access to SPS test scores or to group assignment data, ratings of social adjustment were less likely to correlate significantly with laboratory-measured performance (e.g., Krasnor & Rubin, Note 5; Sharp, Note 9). Other potential explanations for these equivocal findings include differences in the range of deviance examined in the respective samples, differences in the rating or sociometric scales, the differential use of quantitative versus qualitative SPS scale responses, and/or differences in test procedures and test content.

Relationship of Hypothetical-Reflective Tests of Social Problem-Solving Skills to Observational Indexes. Perhaps the most exacting test of ecological validity is the degree to which performance on the hypothetical-reflective tests relates to observational, rather than rated, indexes of interpersonal problem-solving skills. The few studies that have centered on this issue have produced less than positive results. Krasnor and Rubin (Note 5) found that children who generated more alternatives to hypothetical problems on a PIPS-like measure were *not* more successful in solving interpersonal problems than low scorers during observed interactions. Similarly, Enright and Sutterfield (Note 11) found nonsignificant relationships between behavioral measures (incidence of successful resolutions, amount of derogation, and number of times a child was approached by a peer) and PIPS score, once verbal abilities were statistically eliminated. Sharp (Note 9) expected to find a negative relationship between PIPS score and undesirable classroom behaviors (e.g., grab, disturb, hit). No such relationship was found. In addition, there has been little observational support for the MEPS. Butler (Note 8, Note 10) observed fifth-graders' "appropriate" versus "inappropriate" interpersonal behaviors (cf. Rasmussen, Gonso, & Gottman, Note 12) and found little relationship between MEPS performance and the peer interaction data.

The lack of correspondence between laboratory measures of social-cognitive reasoning and proposed behavioral indexes of such reasoning has recently been subject to much discussion. Cooney and Selman (1978) have proposed three domains of social-cognitive reasoning: (1) initial interpersonal orientation (the first response to a hypothetical interpersonal dilemma), (2) reflective reasoning (thoughtful, probed response to the dilemma), and (3) reasoning in action (responses to the dilemma in the natural setting).

To Cooney and Selman, a child's reflective reasoning is most likely to demonstrate the highest social-cognitive level of development. The initial response is thought to reflect more closely the child's recognition of the "need" to use reasoning in the test situation. These researchers also hypothesized that reflective reasoning would fall at the same level as, or at a higher developmental level than, that indicated by behavior, whereas the level of initial orientation responses would fall somewhere in between reflective reasoning and reasoning in action. Cooney and Selman do acknowledge, however, that for some individuals, action reasoning may be higher than reflective reasoning.

Damon (1977) suggested that time pressures and self-interest, among other factors, may account for lower levels of "practical knowledge" than those ascertained through traditional hypothetical–reflective means. An alternative prediction can be derived from the Piagetian perspective; that is, knowledge is first constructed through action and only later emerges in hypo-thetical–reflective thought. Thus Damon (1977) and Rubin and Pepler (1980) have argued that higher levels of thought may appear in the behavioral, as op-posed to the hypothetical–reflective, domain.

Langer (1978) suggested that most social behavior is unthinking and pro-ceeds according to well-learned social scripts (Schank & Abelson, 1977). In contrast to these routines of social action are social situations that call for more reflective cognitive processing. For example, the use of "metacogni-tive" knowledge (Flavell, Note 1) is relevant in situations that are novel or in which an action will have important consequences. Assessment procedures that probe a child's understanding of social action in hypothetical dilemmas can also be listed among those situations that pull for "thinking" social behavior as opposed to the more automatic scripted social behavior found in everyday interaction. Thus differences would be expected when comparing "thinking" versus "scripted" assessment situations.

Whatever the reason for the nonsignificant relationships between labor-atory and observational indexes of SPS skills, it is nevertheless the case that test score interpretation necessitates caution. The exact role of hypothetical–reflective thought in determining social behavior is unknown. Moreover, drawing inferences from scores to child behavior remains tenuous, at best.

Limitations of Hypothetical–Reflective Approach to the Assessment of Social Problem Solving. In conclusion, the hypothetical–reflective approach is characterized by the following limitations:

1. The social goals are clearly and externally defined for the child and are not of immediate personal importance.
2. Most tests lack data concerning the sequencing of strategies.
3. Relatively narrow content areas have been sampled.
4. The verbal nature of the responses may make nonverbal strategies (e.g., frown, point) less likely to be offered.
5. Demonstration of psychometric strength for many of these measures remains weak, and reliability and normative information is rarely provided (Elias *et al.,* Note 6; Butler, Note 10).
6. Hypothetical–reflective measures have not shown a direct relation-ship to the actual behavioral strategies used by the children or to ob-servational indexes of social skill (Krasnor & Rubin, Note 5; Sharp, Note 9; Butler, Note 10; Enright & Sutterfield, Note 11).

7. The presence of an adult tester may bias responding.
8. Findings concerning the relationships between teacher ratings and sociometric measures and hypothetical–reflective test scores have not been replicated across a number of recent studies (Krasnor & Rubin, Note 5; Sharp, Note 9; Butler, Note 10).

Given these limitations, a second approach to the study of SPS skills is considered in the next section. This approach, which we will label the "observational" method, has focused on actual problems as they arise in the child's daily social interactions. In hypothetical–reflective methods, the childs SPS cognitions are assessed by scoring responses to questions that follow the presentation of hypothetical situations. Inferences concerning cognitive processes are drawn from these test responses. However, cognitive processes may also be inferred from the child's behavior outside of a given test situation. By the task analysis of complex nontest behaviors, we may infer those cognitive skills necessary to perform a given task. More specifically, we can infer the understanding of social situation and SPS skill from observations of the child's social behaviors. This work represents an indirect, yet more complex, examination of SPS. The problem-solving goal must be inferred from observation. Moreover, the rate of data acquisition is highly variable. It will become clear to the reader that we are nevertheless biased toward the use of this behaviorally oriented method. Given our expressed biases, we will now define and make explicit for the reader the nature of SPS from this perspective.

Social Problem Solving: An Observational Perspective

We define SPS attempts as "goal-directed social actions." These actions include explicit verbalizations and gestures, which we refer to as "strategies." A problem is considered to be "social" when the means or strategies employed by the child involve another individual, either in an active (e.g., helping) or passive (e.g., allowing object to be taken) sense. Further, we define "episode" as a series of strategies directed at a common goal. Each strategy within an episode is of considerable interest; it is within episodes that we can take the closest look at the sequencing and flexibility of SPS behavior.

To clarify further the observational approach to SPS, we will present a recently observed preschool episode.

(Greg reaches for the train Melanie is pushing around the track.)
MELANIE: No!
GREG: May I play with you?
MELANIE: No!
GREG: Why? *(Leans over and touches train.)* I will show you something.

MELANIE: No! No! *(Greg continues to handle the train.)*

MELANIE: No! *(Greg tries to fit tracks together.)*

MELANIE: No, I don't want to.

GREG: Put this one on. *(Holds out tracks to Melanie.)*

MELANIE: No! *(Greg turns so that his back is to Melanie, putting the train on the track and pushing it around the track, saying "Choo choo" repeatedly.)*

MELANIE: Not on the track. No! Teacher he's bothering me. *(Points to Greg and looks at teacher, who does not respond.)* Don't play with these. *(Greg reaches for another train car.)*

MELANIE: No! No! No! You play with him. *(Points at Jim, who is sitting nearby.)* *(Greg turns and takes a letter tile out of the box Jim is using.)*

GREG: Melanie, put the letter on the train track. *(Greg and Melanie laugh. Greg watches as Melanie puts letter on track.)* *(Greg laughs, smiles, takes letter from Melanie's hand.)*

GREG: Put the letter on here. *(Greg laughs as Melanie moves the letter along the track.)*

In this example, both children demonstrate persistence and flexibility in their SPS attempts. Greg begins the interaction with a physical attempt to play with the train; he next tries to engage Melanie in joint play, by employing the interrogative. Upon noncompliance, he questions Melanie's reason, touches the toy, and offers his peer a "bribe" to induce engagement. Still unsuccessful, Greg uses a different approach in which he directly tries to engage her by means of a command and an offer to exchange. At this point, Greg ignores Melanie's further verbal protests and turns away to play calmly with the train. Finally, Greg makes a playful, perhaps humorous attempt to get Melanie involved. This last strategy is effective; both children laugh and play together.

Melanie's first attempts to prevent Greg from playing tend to be stereotyped and repetitive, consisting almost entirely of verbal rejections ("No!"). When Greg ignores her protests, she turns to the teacher for assistance. This strategy failing, Melanie issues a command, which Greg again ignores. Finally,she redirects Greg to an alternative playmate. Greg responds with another joint play suggestion. Melanie yields to the last of Greg's strategies, and the main episode ends as the children play together with positive affect.

The episode can be analyzed as a unit, consisting primarily of an attempt by Greg to gain access to a particular toy. From Greg's perspective, the outcome was successful. Conversely, from Melanie's perspective, the attempt to resist object loss was somewhat a failure in that she did not maintain sole possession of the activity. The episode can also be divided into subepisodes. For example, Melanie's attempt to invoke the teacher's help can be considered as a separate episode consisting of one strategy in which the outcome was clearly failure. In fact, each separate strategy can be treated as a unit in itself.

As Wright (1967) has noted, reliably dividing a stream of behavior into distinct units is a difficult task and caution must be exercised in interpreting the results of such "externally" imposed units. Similarly, the outcome is often in question, resulting from ambiguous acts in which the goals are not clearly specified. In such cases, the coding is uncertain, and it is necessary to use affect and further attempts by the child to make tentative outcome judgments.

Content Goals

In pursuing the ethological examination of children's SPS, at least five basic content goals are of concern: (1) object transfer, (2) action, (3) attention and acknowledgment, (4) instruction and information, and (5) defense. These explicit behaviors appear to represent the majority of interactional goals for young children. In stating these goals, we have tried to avoid the "sin" of inference, which is commonly involved in making motivational judgments (e.g., dominance, nurturance), but fully acknowledge that inference is, to some degree, present in all taxonomic systems (Rosenblum, 1978).

The interpersonal goals just described are generally expressed through self-oriented acts (assertive behaviors, including both aggressive and nonaggressive acts) or acts that appear to benefit others (prosocial behaviors). In the following paragraphs, we will define more specifically the range of SPS attempts.

"Object transfers" involve soliciting goods from others. On the assertive side are such actions as grabbing and taking and such speech acts as commands, requests, and statements of need. Included on the prosocial side are attempts to give objects to others. The success or failure of these attempts is usually judged by possession of the desired object for an arbitrary period of time.

"Action" includes those goals requiring the solicitation of behaviors from others. Such behaviors may include help ("Tie my shoe") or joint play ("Play cards with me"). The judgment of a goal as action-oriented rests heavily upon the observed child's explicit verbalizations. Success or failure is determined by compliance within an arbitrarily set time frame. If the action itself is directed *toward* another (e.g., spontaneous helping), it is representative of the prosocial perspective.

"Attention and acknowledgment" goals usually require a minimal response from the target; often, a simple look or verbal acknowledgment for the target appears to suffice. This category is judged through explicit verbalizations ("See what I did") and gestures (e.g., show, point, hold up). The prosocial component of this category is relatively infrequent but includes unsolicited comments and acknowledgments concerning the work of others. Also included in this category are attempts in which the goal appears to be conversation (e.g., "I had a birthday yesterday").

Goals are judged as "instructional" or "informative" when there is explicit indication of a need for information ("Where is the truck?") or direction ("How does this go?"). When such information is offered to others, the act is considered to be prosocial ("You're holding the book upside down"). Judgments within this category also depend heavily upon the content of verbalizations, although puzzled expressions directed at others may qualify as an information-seeking strategy.

Finally, the last content area is labeled "defensive" and includes actions that appear to maintain possession or position when threatened or to avoid retribution or harmful action by another. These goal-related activities are judged to be prosocial when the goal appears to be the protection of another (e.g., rescue or restoration).

The range of SPS goal-oriented behaviors is broad and includes most of the child's socially directed actions. As a construct, SPS reflects and integrates many of the different dimensions that have been sampled in the general study of social competence. Thus SPS skills may be considered an index of mastery in which the child is viewed as an active agent in the establishment and maintenance of a positive social and material environment through his or her skill at influencing others.

Advantages of the Observational Approach to the Assessment of Social Problem Solving

We have plotted how an observational approach may be taken to study interpersonal problem solving in young children. Unlike the hypothetical-reflective approach currently in vogue in the literature, the behavioral method has the advantage of allowing the exploration of the child's *effectiveness* in problem solving. Effectiveness may be judged from the child's viewpoint (i.e., are the self-initiated goals satisfied?). In addition, the acceptance of the child's strategies by others can be observed (i.e., are the child's behavioral strategies responded to with positive affect?).

A second advantage of the observational approach is that it allows the assessment of competence in the child's real-life environment. Both the child's effectiveness and the responsivity of the environment in which he or she lives, works, and plays can be explored.

A third advantage of the observational method is that it allows the investigation of the sequential nature of any given SPS episode. Through sequential analyses, a picutre of social interaction as a cumulative and interactive phenomenon may be constructed (Gottman & Parkhurst, 1980). For example, the roles of behavioral flexibility or rigidity in strategy selection may be examined for any particular individual or situation.

Finally, once the behavioral stream of SPS skills has been examined, certain inferences may be drawn concerning underlying, causally related, cognitive properties. Such properties or subskills may include perspective taking or empathy. The assessment of such variables and their relationship to the real world or SPS is preferable to simply examining their relationships to hypothetical SPS skills (Krasnor & Rubin, Note 5).

Social Problem Solving in the Natural Setting: A Brief Review

Having described the relative advantages of the behavioral approach to assessing SPS skills, it behooves us to outline briefly those studies that have examined the social repertoires of young children. We should be forthright in admitting that few researchers have explored SPS strategy employment and outcomes per se. Nevertheless, much relevant information may be garnered from an examination of the results of observational investigations concerned with social development in general. The following represents a tentative listing of references concerned with the study of the social strategies of young children used in potentially problematic interpersonal situations.

Although there is no comprehensive verbal and/or nonverbal taxonomy for the study of social strategies, considerable information has accumulated concerning the *general* distribution of prosocial (Murphy, 1937; Yarrow & Waxler, 1976; Hansen, Goldman, & Baldwin, Note 13; Holmberg, Note 14) and assertive/agonistic (Dawe, 1934; Jones, 1972; Sluckin & Smith, 1977; Strayer & Strayer 1976; Ross & Hay, Note 15) behaviors during the early years. The effectiveness of various prosocial (Hansen *et al.,* Note 13), assertive (Camras, 1977; Patterson, 1979), and social initiation (Finklestein, Dent, Gallacher, & Raney, 1978; Putallaz & Gottman, 1980) strategies has also been subject to investigation.

There is relatively less information documenting how strategies vary with respect to specific subject and task variables. Lee (1975) noted the following potentially critical variables in social interaction: the physical characteristics and behavioral and emotional states of the children, the actor's role relationship with respect to his or her social partner, and setting variables (e.g., group configuration). Other writers have speculated that such situational factors as emotional state, prior experience with a given strategy or target, and such relationship factors as dominance status are significant determinants of social strategy (Jones, 1972; Murphy, 1937). There is evidence from observational studies that young children do vary their strategies in response to sex of partner (Jacklin & Maccoby, 1978; Note 16), relative age/status of partner (Zivin, 1977; Holmberg, Note 14; Lubin & Whiting, Note 17), friendship status (Gottman & Parkhurst, 1980; Strayer, Waring, & Rushton, Note 18), and relative popularity of partner (Putallaz & Gottman, 1980).

The observation of extended social strategy sequences has received surprisingly little research attention. Such investigations would allow examination of an individual's behavioral flexibility or rigidity following strategy failure. Initial studies have been concerned with the sequencing of assertive and prosocial behaviors (Holmberg, Note 14; Barrett, Note 19), persuasive behaviors (Lubin & Whiting, Note 17), requests (Garvey, 1974; Levin & Rubin, in press), and group entry behaviors (Putallaz & Gottman, 1980).

Hypothetical-Reflective and Behavioral Assessment Reconsidered

Having reviewed the hypothetical-reflective testing of SPS skills, and having presented a case for behavioral assessment, we now emphasize that the importance of any test or observational battery must be considered with respect to its function. In general, hypothetical-reflective tests of SPS skill have been used (1) to examine social-cognitive development, (2) to measure the effects of SPS training programs, and (3) to assess individual ability.

Hypothetical-reflective tests have discriminated among groups of children varying with regard to age, sex, socioeconomic status, and social competence. They have increased our understanding of how children think about social problems. When conclusions are drawn concerning the developmental nature of *reflection* about social problems, researchers generally stand on solid ground, given that adequate psychometric considerations have been met.

These tests have also been used to document the effectiveness of SPS training curricula (e.g., Spivack & Shure, 1974). Their appropriateness for use as outcome measures depends on (1) what the trainers are purporting to alter and (2) the adequacy of the tests in representing domains of skill broader than the test questions themselves. If the focus of training is on *behavioral* change, then we could not profitably hope to assume that test responses will provide adequate outcome measures. If however, altering hypothetical-reflective *thought* is the major goal, then changes in test scores may suffice as outcome measures. Unfortunately, most of training studies to date are based on curriculum content identical to posttest assessment. Thus the hypothetical-reflective measures have failed to meet the criterion of "representativeness" because they have been constrained by training-to-task procedures.

The third potentially significant use of the hypothetical-reflective method lies in the assessment of individual SPS skill. Such a use, if feasible, would allow identification of children "at risk" to social pathology. However, normative data are few, and the relationships between rated social competence and test response are mixed. Thus the efficient and accurate identification of target subgroups is precluded, and the meaningfulness of a given individual's SPS score remains questionable.

A promising alternative method for assessing SPS skills is the "simulated situation" procedure, which represents a combination of observational and hypothetical–reflective assessment approaches. In this approach, situations are arranged to increase the probability that certain types of problem-solving behaviors will occur (Evans & Nelson, 1977). Thus a greater amount of experimental control can be exercised over the goals and task demands of the situation. At the same time, SPS behaviors can be observed. This combination of attributes differentiates the simulated situation from the hypothetical–reflective and observational approaches. Thus, in the following discussion, we will consider it a distinct alternative assessment tool.

Damon (1977) has demonstrated the utility of the simulated technique in social-cognitive developmental studies of sharing, friendship, and obedience. Several other researchers have explored SPS skills by simulated real-life SPS situations (e.g., Larcen, Chinsky, Allen, Lochman, & Selinger, Note 20). In these investigations, however, the situations were relatively "unnatural" and required the child to verbalize, rather than to act out, alternative solutions.

The simulation technique can potentially provide an opportunity to observe relatively naturalistic SPS behaviors in situations that are more standardized than those traditionally found in observational studies and without the testing constraints inherent in the hypothetical–reflective method. Although the use of simulated situations for assessment of SPS skill is currently limited by a lack of research, it is, nevertheless, a method that deserves further attention.

A Model for Assessing Social Problem-Solving Skills in Young Children

SPS does not appear to be a unidimensional construct. Not only are there "behavior versus laboratory" differences, but even within the hypothetical–reflective testing domain, a number of independent SPS factors have been discovered (Spivack *et al.*, 1976; Elias *et al.*, Note 6). We propose a four-pronged model of SPS assessment. Our model is based on a component analysis of the SPS process, assessed primarily through observational means in which underlying cognitive skills are inferred from nontest performance. Where appropriate, we will indicate how observational measurement can be supplemented by simulated situation and hypothetical–reflective methods.

Our analysis of SPS is based on an information-processing model. Although this presentation is obviously overly simplified, we hope that it will provide a new direction for the assessment of SPS skill components. As in the information-processing approach to cognitive or nonsocial problem solving (Newell & Simon, 1972), we will assume that the child has selected a goal (e.g., to obtain an object). We further assume that the child has the motivation to act on this goal.

The SPS process can thus be described as follows: First, the "task environment'' is encoded with respect to relevant situational variables (e.g., relative status of target, familiarity, age and sex of target). Second, based on the encoded variables, a social strategy is selected. The selection process accesses long-term memory storage of specific strategies and/or more general social-cognitive knowledge. If the situation is highly familiar, then access to a strategy (given relevant situational variables and the content of the goal) may be relatively automatic. If the situation is unfamiliar or highly significant, then a ''general problem-solving'' (Newell & Simon, 1972) process is implemented in which social–cognitive knowledge is used to ''think'' through strategy choices (Langer, 1978; Flavell, Note 1). Third, the strategy is attempted. Fourth, the effects of the strategy on the environment are assessed, and behavioral adjustments are made, if appropriate.

This model presents four areas of assessment of SPS skills: (1) measurement of responsiveness to key environmental and task variables, (2) measurement of available repertoire of social strategies, (3) assessment of the skill through which the child ''matches'' the chosen strategy to the given situation, and (4) assessment of strategy sequencing.

Responsiveness to Environmental and Task Variables

A child's sensitivity to key environmental and task features should be reflected as variations in strategic behaviors across different situations. One would then predict that a child should use different strategies, for example, when interacting with strangers versus friends (e.g., Gottman & Parkhurst, 1980) or with targets of different age or sex. A child who consistently uses the same strategy over a variety of situations would show little responsiveness to critical environmental features. Conversely, a child whose strategic behavior showed predictable variation with respect to these critical features would reflect sensitivity to environmental factors. Responsiveness could be tapped by means of direct observations of a child's behavior, given enough information per child over a variety of situations.

By deliberately varying situational variables in simulated situations, an assessment of the child's strategic behavior could also be made. Similarly, critical situational factors could be varied in hypothetical–reflective measures (e.g., Elias *et al.,* Note 6) to assess the child's sensitivity to content, target, and other task variables.

Repertoire of Social Strategies

To assess repertoire range, we must focus on the quantitative measurement of the different social strategies exhibited by a child. One index of a child's repertoire is a simple count of the number of different strategies that are observed across various interpersonal situations. This index represents a conservative count of the available set of strategies, and thus caution must be used in interpretation. A child who is highly successful in SPS (i.e., frequently succeeds on the first attempt), may emit fewer strategies than a child who attempts several strategies before either giving up or eventually achieving success. Thus this index should be interpreted with respect to the child's overall SPS effectiveness.

The repertoire of social strategies may also be assessed by the simulated situation and hypothetical–reflective techniques. In both methods, social situations would be varied, and the number of strategies employed or verbalized would be counted. This form of quantitative measurement has, of course, been the major focus of hypothetical–reflective research. However, as noted previously, this technique fails to indicate the variety of strategies actually used by the child.

The Match between Strategy and Situation

The match between strategy choice and interpersonal situation may be assessed as a function of two criteria: (1) the appropriateness of strategy choice and (2) the effectiveness of the chosen behavior. Strategy appropriateness may be measured by having adults rate each problem-solving behavior given a particular situation (e.g., Mummery, 1947). Another interesting, but underutilized, source of information would be appropriateness ratings by peers of the same age. Ratings of appropriateness may be applied to all three methods of strategy assessment.

A second index of appropriateness may be garnered through observations of the overt affective reactions of others within the social milieu. Inappropriate strategy choice, for example, could be measured by the proportion of a child's strategies that is responded to negatively by others. This method has the advantage of assessing appropriateness within the relevant situational context.

The second criterion of matching strategy to situation is the effectiveness of the child's problem-solving behavior. Several observational indexes of effectiveness are available: (1) the number of attempts per episode, which constitutes a measure of "efficiency" (i.e., the fewer the number of attempts, the more efficient); (2) the total number of success experiences based on the number of episodes or on the number of strategies employed; and (3) the proportion of successes to the total number of strategies or episodes.

The effectiveness of strategies generated in hypothetical–reflective tests is more difficult to judge. Ratings of effectiveness could be used (e.g., Asher *et al.,* Note 3), or the "average" effectiveness of specific strategies could be ascertained through more general observation. In both cases, however, the effectiveness judgments are independent of the immediate situational context. Simulated situations could be engineered to yield "natural" outcomes of strategy choices by allowing participants to interact in an unconstrained manner. However, this latter approach is as unpredictable as the observational method.

Strategy Sequencing

Finally, the observation of strategy sequencing requires the judgment of episodes that are aimed at meeting the same goal. The number of single-strategy episodes that end in failure reflects the number of times a child gives up after one attempt to achieve a goal. We shall define "reattempt" as a strategy generated after noncompliance from the targeted person. The number of reattempts divided by the total number of strategies receiving noncompliant responses can provide an index of persistence in the face of failure.

In episodes consisting of more than one strategy, flexibility may be assessed. "Flexibility" has been defined as changes in strategy and/or target (Lubin & Whiting, Note 17). The number of changes in strategies/targets given noncompliance divided by the total number of strategies receiving noncompliance could serve as an index of flexibility. This index could prove particularly interesting with respect to changes in response given a negative affective response from the target.

In simulated situations, the experimenter can arrange noncompliance by the target and then observe reattempts. Several researchers (e.g., Krasnor & Rubin, Note 5; Elias *et al.*, Note 6) have assessed strategy sequence using hypothetical-reflective methods, through the introduction of obstacles after a child's initial strategy was elicited.

Summary and Conclusion

We have attempted to outline how the assessment of individual SPS components could be carried out using observational data. Parallel assessment procedures have also been suggested for simulated and hypothetical-reflective methods. An outline of our discussion is provided in Table 1.

Much seminal work needs to be conducted before many of our suggestions become useful. Information is as yet unavailable, for example, concerning average or "normal" levels of flexibility, success, and ranges of strategies employed in everyday interaction. We readily acknowledge that observational procedures are costly and time consuming.

To reiterate, however, this method offers potent advantages over the alternative methods of SPS assessment. Some of these advantages are (1) the assessment of skill within the environment in which the child functions; (2) the provision of auxiliary data resulting from the self-selected nature of the child's behavior (such data include the range of goals and targets selected by the child as well as the degree of the responsiveness of the social environment to the child's initiatives); and (3) the creation of a profile that will allow a

Table 1. Assessment of Social Problem Solving by Hypothetical–Reflective, Simulated Situation, and Observational Methods

Assessment	Methodology		
	Hypothetical–reflective	Simulated situation	Observational
Situational variables	Elicit memory or description of observed social scene with respect to number of attributes and their relevancy and accuracy; assess how memory or description changes across situations.	Elicit memory or description of simulated situation across a variety of different scenes (e.g., change target, object); obtain indirect evidence by varying situations and observing variation in child's response.	Elicit memory or description of naturally occurring social events across a variety of different scenes; obtain indirect evidence by assessing variation in child's responses over different situations.
Repertoire of strategies	Present hypothetical situation; request alternative solutions; assess quantity of solutions.	Present simulated situation; manipulate so that there is no immediate success; assess quantity of solutions.	Observe in naturally occurring social situations; assess quantity of solutions.
Linkage of strategy to situation	Judge the appropriateness and effectiveness[a] of strategy choices for a variety of hypothetically presented situations.	For a variety of simulated situations, assess child's strategies for appropriateness and effectiveness.	Observe child's strategies with respect to effectiveness and appropriateness over a variety of naturally occurring social situations.
Sequence of strategies and utilitization of feedback	Assess sequence of strategies in response to hypothetical situations in which the objective is not achieved with respect to flexibility, escalation, and so forth.	Observe reaction to noncompliance in simulated situation with respect to flexibility, escalation, and so forth.	Observe reaction to noncompliance in naturally occurring social situations with respect to flexibility, escalation, and so forth; also, assess effectiveness of sequence.

[a]For the hypothetical and simulated situations, "effectiveness" must be generalized from effectiveness in general, established by prior observation; for the ethological procedure, it can be directly observed for each situation.

detailed examination of the components of SPS skill (e.g., sequencing and reaction to failure, poor success with peers but not with adults). Through the observational method, a child's SPS weaknesses and strengths could be plotted, thereby allowing more focused and efficient remediation when deemed appropriate.

The hypothetical–reflective approach may ultimately prove most useful in the exploration of social-cognitive thinking. The simulated situation procedure may prove most efficient and useful where relatively large numbers of children are to be assessed (e.g., in training program assessment). For those children whose needs are not being successfully met in their real-life environments, however, the observational assessment procedure may prove most fruitful in planning effective remediation as well as in providing an alternative way of exploring the cognitive processes underlying social behavior.

Reference Notes

1. Flavell, J. *Monitoring social-cognitive enterprises: Something else that may develop in the area of social cognition.* Paper prepared for the Social Science Research Council, January 1979.
2. Connolly, J., & Doyle, A. *Social competence in the preschool: A multivariate view.* Paper presented at the biennial meeting of the Society for Research in Child Development, San Francisco, March 1979.
3. Asher, S., Renshaw, P., Geraci, R., & Dor, A. *Peer acceptance and social skill training: The selection of program content.* Paper presented at the biennial meeting of the Society for Research in Child Development, San Francisco, March 1979.
4. Siegal, M. *Development of children's reliance on adult advice.* Paper presented at the biennial meeting of the Society for Research in Child Development, San Francisco, March 1979.
5. Krasnor, L., & Rubin, K. *Preschoolers' verbal and behavioural solutions to social problems.* Paper presented at the annual meeting of the Canadian Psychological Association, Ottawa, June 1978.
6. Elias, M., Larcen, S., Zlotlow, S., & Chinsky, J. *An innovative measure of children's cognitions in problematic interpersonal situations.* Paper presented at the annual meeting of the American Psychological Association, Toronto, August 1978.
7. Enright, R., & Enright, N. *An educational program for promoting social cognitive development in early childhood.* Paper presented at the Ninth Annual Interdisciplinary International Conference on Piagetian Theory and the Helping Professions, February 1979.
8. Butler, L. *The relationship between interpersonal problem-solving skills and peer relations and behavior.* Paper presented at the annual meeting of the Canadian Psychological Association, Ottawa, June 1978.
9. Sharp, K. *Interpersonal problem-solving capacity and behavioral adjustment in preschool children.* Paper presented at the annual meeting of the American Psychological Association, Toronto, August 1978.
10. Butler, L. *Social and behavioral correlates of peer reputation.* Paper presented at the biennial meeting of the Society for Research in Child Development, San Francisco, March 1979.
11. Enright, R., & Sutterfield, S. *An ecological validation of social cognitive development.* Paper presented at the biennial meeting of the Society for Research in Child Development, San Francisco, March 1979.

12. Rasmussen, B., Gonso, J., & Gottman, J. *Peer interaction coding system: Observer train- ing manual.* Unpublished manuscript, 1974.
13. Hansen, R., Goldman, B., & Baldwin, M. *Towards a taxonomy of altruism: An observa- tional study of spontaneous prosocial behaviour among young children.* Paper presented at the annual meeting of the Canadian Psychological Association, Quebec City, June 1975.
14. Holmberg, M. *The development of social interchange patterns from 12–42 months: Cross- sectional and short-term longitudinal analyses.* Paper presented at the biennial meeting of the Society for Research in Child Development, New Orleans, March 1977.
15. Ross, H., & Hay, D. *Conflict and conflict resolution between 21-month-old peers.* Paper presented at the biennial meeting of the Society for Research in Child Development, New Orleans, March 1977.
16. Jacklin, C., & Maccoby, E. *Peer interaction in boys and girls.* Paper presented at the biennial meeting of the Society for Research in Child Development, San Francisco, March 1979.
17. Lubin, D., & Whiting, B. *Learning techniques of persuasion: An analysis of sequences of in- teraction.* Paper presented at the biennial meeting of the Society for Research in Child Development, New Orleans, March 1977.
18. Strayer, F. F., Waring, S., & Rushton, J. *Social constraints on naturally occurring preschool altruism.* Unpublished manuscript, York University, undated.
19. Barrett, D. *Sequential constraints in children's social interactions.* Paper presented at the biennial meeting of the Society for Research in Child Development, San Francisco, March 1977.
20. Larcen, S., Chinsky, J., Allen, G., Lochman, J., & Selinger, H. *Training children in social problem solving strategies.* Paper presented at the meeting of the Midwestern Psychological Association, Chicago, 1974. (Cited in Spivack, G., Platt, J., & Shure, M. *The problem solv- ing approach to adjustment.* San Francisco: Jossey-Bass, 1976.)

References

Ainsworth, M., & Bell, S. Mother–infant interaction and the development of competence. In K. Connolly & J. Bruner (Eds.), *The growth of competence.* New York: Academic Press, 1974.

Anderson, S., & Messick, S. Social competency in young children. *Developmental Psychology,* 1974, *10,* 282–293.

Camras, L. Facial expressions used by children in a conflict situation. *Child Development,* 1977, *48,* 1431–1435.

Chandler, M. Social cognition: A selective review of current research. In W. Overton & T. Gal- lagher (Eds.), *Advances in research and theory* (Vol. 1). New York: Plenum Press, 1977.

Charlesworth, W. Human intelligence as adaptation: An ethological approach. In L. Resnick (Ed.), *The nature of intelligence.* Hillsdale, N.J.: Erlbaum, 1976.

Cooney, E., & Selman, R. Children's use of social conceptions: Towards a dynamic model of social cognition. In W. Damon (Ed.), *Social cognition.* San Francisco: Jossey-Bass, 1978.

Damon, W. *The social world of the child.* San Francisco: Jossey-Bass, 1977.

Dawe, H. An analysis of 200 quarrels of preschool children. *Child Development,* 1934, *5,* 139–157.

Ervin-Tripp, S. Wait for me, roller skate! In S. Ervin-Tripp & C. Mitchell-Kernan (Eds.), *Child discourse.* New York: Academic Press, 1977.

Evans, I., & Nelson, R. Assessment of child behavior problems. In A. Ciminero, K. Calhoun, & H. Adams (Eds.), *Handbook of behavioral assessment.* New York: Wiley, 1977.

Finklestein, N., Dent, C., Gallacher, K., & Raney, C. Social behavior of infants and toddlers in a day-care environment. *Developmental Psychology,* 1978, *14,* 257–262.

Garvey, C. Requests and responses in children's speech. *Journal of Child Language,* 1974, *2,* 41–63.

Goldberg, S. Social competence in infancy: A model of parent–infant interaction. *Merrill-Palmer Quarterly,* 1977, *23,* 163–177.

Gottman, J., & Parkhurst, J. A developmental theory of friendship and acquaintanceship processes. In A. Collins (Ed.), *Minnesota symposia on child psychology* (Vol. 13). Hillsdale, N.J.: Erlbaum, 1980.

Humphrey, N. The social function of intellect. In P. Bateson & R. Hinde (Eds.), *Growing points in ethology.* London: Cambridge University Press, 1976.

Jacklin, C., & Maccoby, E. Social behavior at thirty-three months in same-sex and mixed-sex dyads. *Child Development,* 1978, *49,* 557–569.

Jones, N. B. Categories of child–child interaction. In N. B. Jones (Ed.), *Ethological studies of child behavior.* London: Cambridge University Press, 1972.

Kohn, M. *Social competence, symptoms and underachievement in childhood: A longitudinal perspective.* New York: Wiley, 1977.

Kummer, H. *Primate societies: Group techniques of ecological adaptation.* Chicago: Aldine Press, 1971.

Ladd, G., & Oden, S. The relationship between peer acceptance and children's ideas about helpfulness. *Child Development,* 1979, *50,* 402–408.

Langer, E. Rethinking the role of thought in social interactions. In J. Harvey, W. Ickes, & R. Kidd (Eds.), *New directions in attribution research* (Vol. 2). Hillsdale, N.J.: Erlbaum, 1978.

Leakey, R., & Lewin, R. *People of the lake.* New York: Anchor Press/Doubleday, 1978.

Lee, L. Toward a cognitive theory of interpersonal development: Importance of peers. In M. Lewis & L. Rosenblum (Eds.), *Friendship and peer relations.* New York: Wiley, 1975.

Levin, E., & Rubin, K. H. Getting others to do what you want them to do: The development of children's requestive strategies. In K. Nelson (Ed.), *Child language* (Vol. 4). New York: Gardner Press, in press.

Mummery, D. V. An analytic study of ascendant behavior of preschool children. *Child Development,* 1947, *18,* 40–81.

Murphy, L. *Social behavior and child personality.* New York: Columbia University Press, 1937.

Newell, H., & Simon, H. *Human problem solving.* Englewood Cliffs, N.J.: Prentice-Hall, 1972.

O'Malley, J. M. Research perspective on social competence. *Merrill-Palmer Quarterly,* 1977, *23,* 29–44.

Patterson, G. A performance theory for coercive family interaction. In R. Cairns (Ed.), *The analysis of social interactions: Methodological issues and illustrations.* Hillsdale, N.J.: Erlbaum, 1979.

Piaget, J. *The language and thought of the child.* London: Routledge & Kegan Paul, 1926.

Putallaz, M., & Gottman, J. Social skills and group acceptance. In S. Asher & J. Gottman (Eds.), *The development of friendship: Description and intervention.* London: Cambridge University Press, 1980.

Rosenblum, L. The creation of a behavioral taxonomy. In G. Sackett (Ed.), *Observing behavior* (Vol. 2). Baltimore: University Park Press, 1978.

Rubin, K. H. Role-taking in childhood: Some methodological considerations. *Child Development,* 1978, *49,* 428–433.

Rubin, K. H., & Pepler, D. J. The relationship of child's play to social-cognitive development. In H. Foot, T. Chapman, & J. Smith (Eds.), *Friendship and childhood relationships.* London: Wiley, 1980.

Schank, R., & Abelson, S. *Scripts, plans, goals and understanding.* Hillsdale, N.J.: Erlbaum, 1977.

Shure, M., & Spivack, G. *Problem solving techniques in child rearing.* San Francisco: Jossey-Bass, 1978.

Simon, H. Identifying basic abilities underlying intelligent performance of complex tasks. In L. Resnick (Ed.), *The nature of intelligence.* Hillsdale, N.J.: Erlbaum, 1976.

Sluckin, A., & Smith, P. Two approaches to the concept of dominance in preschool children. *Child Development,* 1977, *48,* 917–923.

Spivack, G., Platt, J., & Shure, M. *The problem solving approach to adjustment.* San Francisco: Jossey-Bass, 1976.

Spivack, G., & Shure, M. *Social adjustment of young children.* San Francisco: Jossey-Bass, 1974.

Strayer, F., & Strayer, J. An ethological analysis of social agonism and dominance relations among preschool children. *Child Development,* 1976, *47,* 980–989.

Webb, R., Oliveri, M., & Harnick, F. The socialization of intelligence: Implications for educational intervention. In R. Webb (Ed.), *Social development in childhood: Day-care programs and research.* Baltimore: Johns Hopkins University Press, 1977.

Weinstein, E. The development of interpersonal competence. In D. Goslin (Ed.), *Handbook of socialization theory and research.* Chicago: Rand McNally, 1969.

White, R., & Watts, J. *Experience and environment: Major influences in the development of the young child* (Vol. 1). Englewood Cliffs, N.J.: Prentice-Hall, 1973.

Wright, H. *Recording and analyzing child behavior.* New York: Harper & Row, 1967.

Yarrow, M., & Waxler, C. Dimensions and correlates of prosocial behavior in young children. *Child Development,* 1976, *47,* 118–125.

Zigler, E., & Trickett, P. IQ, social competence, and evaluation of early childhood intervention programs. *American Psychologist,* 1978, *33,* 789–798.

Zivin, G. On becoming subtle: Age and social rank changes in the use of a facial gesture. *Child Development,* 1977, *48,* 1314–1321.

Future Directions

16

A Cognitive–Social Learning
Approach to Assessment

Walter Mischel

This volume promises to be a valuable step toward harnessing the gains from the cognitivization of psychology for the assessment of persons. The diverse and rich contributions in the preceding pages raise problems and address challenges that are among the most enduring and important in our field. To place these contributions in perspective, I want to comment on some issues and concerns in the areas of personality and cognition, especially as they relate to the basic assessment themes of this volume.

Some Preliminary Issues

Direct Self-Reports

The most direct way to find out what a person thinks, values, knows, or believes (about himself or herself or about other people) is to ask directly. Virtually all approaches to personality ask people for self-reports. In most orientations these reports serve primarily as cues or signs from which to infer the individual's underlying personality structure and dynamics. Largely because of the assumption that people engage in extensive unconscious distortion or are otherwise deceptive, the individual's own reports generally have been used by the clinician (or the test) as a basis for generating inferences and predictions about the client rather than as a means of conveying the individual's views of themselves and their ongoing experiences and expectations. Can people be "experts" about themselves? Can they assess themselves usefully? For many years psychologists, who were heavily influenced by Freudian

---

Walter Mischel • Department of Psychology, Stanford University, Stanford, California.

theory, tended to assume automatically, both in clinical practice and in research, that what a person said about himself or herself in response to direct questions was likely to be either superficial or defensively distorted and misleading. Consequently, seemingly irrelevant behaviors (casual comments, jokes, slips of the tongue) were often taken as important clues of the individual's "underlying" dispositions, whereas the client's own reports of concerns, beliefs, interests, and personality attributes were treated with suspicion and sometimes even as defenses and resistances that had to be circumvented rather than as potentially accurate descriptions that in themselves deserved serious attention. (For an alternative that draws on projective methods constructively, while bypassing assumptions about built-in unconscious defensiveness, see Sobel, Chapter 5, this volume.)

In recent years the waning of Freudian influence diminished some of these concerns. Skepticism about self-reports, however, has resurfaced again, nourished by Nisbett and Wilson's (1977) provocative article on the limits of introspective accuracy. This influential article is easily (and often) misconstrued as a valid denunciation of the value of self-reports about cognition. Fortunately, contrary arguments are now being raised, in this volume (Genest & Turk, Chapter 8) as well as elsewhere (e.g., Cantor, Mischel, & Schwartz, 1981; Smith & Miller, 1978). These rebuttals point out the severe limits of the Nisbett and Wilson thesis. They appropriately note that demonstrating that people can make erroneous causal inferences does not imply that psychologists should neglect persons' verbal reports or other data about cognition for a large number of alternative purposes.

Empirical Status

Curiously, discomfort about self-reports has been widely shared among psychologists committed to making rational decisions about alternative data sources. This vague fear persists in spite of long-standing evidence that direct self-reports fare relatively well as predictors of behavior (Mischel, 1968, 1972, 1977). To illustrate, in one study conducted many years ago, achievement concerns, somatic concerns, religious concerns, and hostility were measured by five different methods in a sophisticated multitrait–multimethod investigation by Wallace and Sechrest (1963). Their methods for measuring these traits included self-reports (in the form of self-descriptions), reputation ratings by peers, projective techniques (incomplete sentences, Rorschach, and TAT), and behavioral indexes such as scholastic average and number of visits to health services. The researchers found that self-descriptions provided convergent and discriminant validity as good as that obtained from any other source. Self-descriptions and peer ratings consistently yielded better correlations than did any other combination of methods.

Students' self-ranking of achievement needs in another comparative study predicted their actual long-term achievements (grades) better than did experts who inferred the students' achievement motivation from the TAT

(Holmes & Tyler, 1968). In an even earlier study, the TAT stories of college students were scored for ten "signs" of aggression (Lindzey & Tejessy, 1956). These signs were correlated with diverse criteria of aggression, including diagnostic council ratings based on observation and interview, scores on a projective picture frustration test, and self-ratings of aggressiveness. The self-ratings were associated with significantly more signs of aggression than were any of the other predictors.

In another context, self-predictions were found to be as accurate as indirect measures of hypnotizability, although the accuracy of all measures was modest (Melei & Hilgard, 1964). Likewise, results from research on a Peace Corps group also favored the more direct measures used when compared to interviews and projective tests (Mischel, 1965). And research on predictions of achievement and affiliation behaviors also demonstrated that under some circumstances self-reports may have reasonable accuracy (Sherwood, 1966).

These are merely examples from a larger literature that demonstrates the relative utility of direct versus indirect measures. Taken as a whole rather than singly, the studies on the comparative utility of direct and indirect personality assessment seem quite consistent: the predictions possible from a person's own simple, direct self-ratings and self-reports generally have not been exceeded by those obtained from more indirect, costly, and sophisticated personality tests, from combined test batteries, and from expert clinical judges (Mischel, 1968, 1972). These conclusions appear to apply to such diverse content areas as college achievement, job and professional success, psychotherapy outcomes, rehospitalization for psychiatric patients, and parole violations for delinquent children.

Direct self-reports compare favorably not only with indirect tests of the projective type and with clinician's judgments but also with more complex and psychometrically sophisticated personality scales. Peterson (1965), for example, showed that two extremely simple self-ratings (one on adjustment and one on introversion–extraversion) were as stable and useful as inferences from factor scores based on sophisticated personality rating schedules. Mischel and Bentler (Note 1) assessed the ability of college students to predict their own grades. In two studies, students predicted their own course grades as well as did the best other available predictors. Self-estimates remained accurate even when the students were led to believe that their self-predictions would be seen by their instructor. The students' own predictions of grades compared favorably with predictions obtained from achievement, aptitude, and personality measures in other research. In another domain, guidance personnel have been discovering that their clients' directly expressed interests may be as valuable in vocational counseling as is the most sophisticated test— the Strong Vocational Interest Blank (Dolliver, 1969; DuBois & Watson, 1950; McArthur & Stevens, 1955). And in yet another vein, individuals' self-ratings were found to be the best predictors of peers' ratings of them (Hase & Goldberg, 1967). The self-ratings were more valid than the predictions based on *any* of several scales, including the best statistical equations based on the best scale combinations.

In other research perhaps more relevant to cognition, we assessed the degree to which people presented themselves in a positive ("repressing") rather than in a self-critical ("sensitizing") fashion on a self-report scale (Mischel, Ebbesen, & Zeiss, 1973). Those who presented themselves positively on the scale also spent more time attending to positive (.51) and less time to negative (− .61) information about themselves on a behavioral measure of selective attention to statements about their personal positive and negative qualities. This respectable link between self-report and relevant behavioral data is hardly unique. More recently, for example, self-rated self-efficacy expectations were found to predict future performance (posttreatment approach behavior to previously feared objects) even better than did relevant past behavior (Bandura, 1978). Apparently people often are capable of highly accurate self-assessments in a wide range of contexts.

Limitations and Alternatives

In sum, people can be excellent sources of information about themselves. To be sure, if we want people to tell us about themselves directly, we have to ask questions that they can answer sensibly. If we ask people to predict how they will behave on a future criterion (e.g., job success, adjustment) but do not tell them the specific criterion measure that will constitute the assessment, we cannot expect them to be accurate. As already noted, we also cannot expect people to make accurate causal inferences, especially when arbitrary sequences of events are arranged by the experimenter or the "correct" explanations are implausible or obscure (Nisbett & Wilson, 1977). Likewise, we cannot expect honest self-reports unless people are convinced that their honesty will not be used against them. We might, for example, expect job candidates to predict correctly which job they will perform best, but only when all alternatives available to them in their choice are structured as equally desirable. We cannot expect people to penalize themselves.

Of course, self-reports will always be limited by the constraints of the person's own awareness. Psychologists have too often assumed that people were unaware, when, in fact, they were simply being asked the wrong questions. In the context of verbal conditioning, for example, more careful inquiries long ago revealed that people were far more insightful than was originally assumed (e.g., Spielberger & DeNike, 1966). Although a belief in the prevalence of distortions from unconscious defenses such as repression is the foundation of the commitment to an indirect sign approach in assessment, the experimental evidence for the potency—and even the existence—of such mechanisms remains remarkably fragile (e.g., Mischel, 1981). Likewise, although people may develop impressive knowledge about the world, including basic psychological principles (e.g., Flavell, 1977; Mischel, 1979, 1981), they cannot be expected to have spontaneous awareness of processes that they cannot possibly observe, such as the physiological structures operating in their own brains.

Although direct self-reports often may yield useful information, they certainly do not obviate the need for other data, depending on the purposes and nature of the assessment. Indexes of directly relevant past performance, direct behavior sampling, nonverbal behavior, base rates and actuarial data, demographic indexes, and other data all may have value for specific assessment objectives (Mischel, 1968, 1977). To assess avoidance of phobic objects (e.g., snakes), one may, for example, want to sample actual approach behavior in relevant situations rather than to rely only on self reports. If the interest is in the client's phenomenology (e.g., the subjective experience with particular phobic objects, his or her feelings of self-confidence), however, one would certainly want to obtain the relevant self-reports.

This volume amply documents that cognitive assessments need not be restricted to asking people to introspect about their subjective states. An incomplete listing of the measurements that can be harnessed in the service of cognitive assessment encompasses the sampling of optimal performance, as in ability and intelligence testing (see Sundberg, Chapter 3, this volume); the sampling of skilled social performance, as in problem-solving skills (Krasnor & Rubin, Chapter 15); electrophysiological methods (McGuigan, Chapter 9); projective methods (Sobel, Chapter 5); testing for social knowledge and metacognition (Merluzzi, Rudy, & Glass, Chapter 4); and imagery assessments (Anderson, Chapter 6). Perhaps the prototypical assessments associated with the cognitive approach are those focusing on self-statements and internal conversations, perceptions, and experiences sampled through thought listing, verbalizations about beliefs and expectancies, selective attention and memory indicators, and a variety of other data (e.g., Shaw & Dobson, Chapter 12; Mahoney & Epstein, Chapter 14; Meichenbaum & Cameron, Chapter 1; Glass & Merluzzi, Chapter 13; Cacioppo & Petty, Chapter 10; Genest & Turk, Chapter 8). A coherent view of cognitive assessment, however, requires that we consider not only what alternative methods are available for the enterprise but also what aspects of the person need assessment within the cognitive perspective.

Person Variables in the Cognitive–Social Learning Approach

> We have no direct immediate access to the world, nor to any of its properties. . . . Whatever we know about reality has been *mediated*, not only by the organs of sense but by complex systems which interpret and reinterpret sensory information. (Neisser, 1967, p. 3)

The complex systems that "interpret and reinterpret sensory information" may be viewed both as "processes" (e.g., short-term and long-term memory) and as "products" within the individual, the residues of social experience and cognitive growth. Efforts to assess individuals for the sake of research or for clinical or other applied and educational purposes require some systematic attention to these products, which may be called "cognitive-social learning person variables." Let us consider briefly how to conceptualize these products from a cognitive–social learning perspective (Mischel, 1973).

A cognitive–social learning approach to assessment begins with the belief that the discriminativeness of behavior and the complexity of the interactions between the individual and the situation suggest that we need to focus more specifically on what the person *constructs* in particular conditions instead of attempting to infer the global traits that he or she generally *has*. Of course, what people do involves much more than motor acts; we must consider what people do cognitively and affectively, not just motorically. A cognitive–social learning approach to personality assessment focuses on the individual's cognitive activities and behavior patterns, which are investigated in relation to the specific conditions that evoke, maintain, and modify them and which they, in turn, change (Mischel, 1968, 1973, 1979). The focus in this approach shifts from trying to compare and generalize about what different individuals "are like" to assessing what they *do*—behaviorally and cognitively—in relationship to the psychological conditions in which they do it. The focus shifts from describing situation-free people with broad trait adjectives to analyzing the specific interactions between conditions and the cognitions and behaviors of interest.

In my view, cognitive–social learning person variables must include the individual's *competencies* to construct (generate) diverse behaviors under appropriate conditions. In addition, we have to consider the person's *encoding and categorization* of events and people, including the self. To understand what a person will perform in particular situations also requires attention to his or her *expectancies,* the *subjective values* of any expected outcomes, and the individual's *self-regulatory systems and plans.* The contributions in this volume address (in different degrees) all these person variables. Although the variables overlap and interact, each may offer some distinctive information about the person, and each may alert us to somewhat different aspects of individuality. Each person variable may be seen both as a product of the individual's total history and as a mediator of the impact of any future experiences.

Cognitive and Behavioral Construction Competencies

Throughout the course of life, people learn about the world and their relationship to it, thus acquiring an enormous potential to generate a vast array of knowledge and organized behavior. Although the accumulation of this potential seems an obvious product of cognitive development, just what gets learned is not so obvious. The products of such socialization and cognitive growth encompass the social knowledge and rules that guide conduct, the personal constructs one generates about the self and others, and a vast array of social and cognitive skills and competencies. The concept of "cognitive and behavioral construction competencies" refers to these diverse products and is intended to be broad enough to include the wide range of psychological acquisitions that must be encompassed.

To assess competencies, we must create conditions and incentives that will encourage optimal performance. The necessary assessment conditions for this purpose are the same as those employed in ability and achievement testing (Wallace, 1966). We can use the same strategy to assess what people "know" (their available information, comprehension, and construction skills) and what social behaviors they are capable of executing. For example, to assess what children had acquired from observing a model, attractive rewards were offered to them after the observation period. Getting the rewards was contingent upon their reproducing the model's behaviors (e.g., Bandura, 1965; Grusec & Mischel, 1966). The findings demonstrated that the children had acquired much information from observing the model and could reconstruct the modeled behavior in detail but that they did so only when offered appropriate incentives.

Assessing a person's potential cognitive constructions and behavioral enactments and measuring social, interpersonal, and cognitive skills require that we test what the individual *can* do (under appropriate conditions) rather than what he "usually" does. One of the most persistent and promising individual differences dimensions seems to involve such cognitive and behavioral (social) competencies (e.g., White, 1959; Zigler & Phillips, 1961). Such competencies may have much better temporal and cross-situational stability, and more pervasive consequences for coping and adaptation, than many of the social and motivational dispositions favored in traditional personality research that ignored cognitive characteristics (Mischel, 1968).

Construction capacities tend to be relatively stable over time, as reflected in the relatively high stability found in performances closely related to cognitive and intellectual variables (Mischel, 1968, 1969). They also may contribute significantly to the impression of consistency in personality. A person who knows how to solve certain types of interpersonal problems competently or who has good self-monitoring and assertiveness skills remains *capable* of performing skillfully in relevant situations over long periods.

Cognitive competencies (as measured by "mental age" and IQ tests) seem to be among the best predictors of later social and interpersonal adjustment (e.g., Anderson, 1960). Moreover, more competent, brighter people experience more interpersonal success and better work achievements and therefore become more benignly assessed by themselves and by others on the ubiquitous evaluative "good–bad" dimension in trait ratings (e.g., Vernon, 1964). Likewise, cognitive competencies presumably are a key component of such enduring concepts as "ego strength" and "ego development." Interestingly, the large "first factor" found regularly on tests such as the MMPI (Block, 1965), usually given labels connoting "adjustment" at the positive end and "maladaptive character structure" at the negative end, may reflect the person's level of cognitive–social competence and achievement to a considerable extent. The assessment of competence in response to specific problematic situations in the direct manner developed by Goldfried and D'Zurilla (1969) is one good example.

In this volume, Krasnor and Rubin (Chapter 15) nicely illustrate the assessment of social competence. The social problem-solving approach (e.g., Shure & Spivack, 1978) with young children on which they focus exemplifies the issues, challenges, and potentialities in the assessment of competencies. In passing, it is also worth noting that Mahoney and Epstein (Chapter 14), in discussing athletes, suggest that the distinction between traits and skills seems dubious. Although the boundary between the two constructs is far from impermeable, there is a difference. To assess skills or other competencies, we examine what the person *can* do (i.e., maximal performance). To assess social (noncognitive) traits, we assess what the person is *usually like* (i.e., typical performance) by inferring the average or central tendency of relevant acts and by inferring and abstracting the gist or disposition that characterizes the person "in general." Whereas the assessment of competencies (including skills) requires conditions that allow maximum or optimum performance, the assessment of traits depends on the sampling and inferring of typical or characteristic performance and the qualities that underlie such performance.

Encoding Strategies and Constructs

The recognition that human behavior depends on the "stimulus as coded" requires that we assess how individuals perceive, think, interpret, and experience the world. By definition, a "cognitive" orientation to the assessment of persons includes a focus on stimuli as they are encoded, on events, and on people as they are represented cognitively and are seen by the perceiver. This phenomenological stance dictates attention to the individual's own personal constructs or ways of encoding experience. In this vein, George Kelly's (1955) pioneering search for assessments that illuminate the client's personal constructs rather than the clinician's preferred hypotheses provides a most impressive conceptual and empirical milestone. The impact of Kelly's perspective is still dramatic, as seen in this volume in Neimeyer and Neimeyer, Chapter 7. Their essay documents the considerable strengths of the personal construct approach, while also recognizing its complexity and limitations.

As Kelly emphasized, the subject (like the psychologist) also groups events into categories and organizes them into meaningful units. People do not describe their experiences with operational definitions: they categorize events in terms of personal constructs that may or may not overlap with those of the assessor. The tendency to categorize things and people into categories so that nonidentical events can be treated as if they were equivalent (Rosch,

Mervis, Gray, Johnson, & Boyes-Braem, 1976) is a basic feature of cognition. We continuously simplify the flood of information impinging on us from the world, grouping objects and other people, according to their similarities into natural categories of "kinds" or "types" (of chairs, of neurotics, of psychologists). These categorization schemes permit us to structure our general knowledge about events, people, and the social world, yielding coherent expectations about characteristic patterns of behavior.

Although research on social cognition has discovered much about the consequences of categorization (as in "stereotyping"), much less is known about the structure and growth of people's natural categories about the social world. A comprehensive approach requires that we also consider such questions as what are the basic natural units for the categorization of people and psychological situations? What are the gains and losses of categorizations at different levels of abstraction? What are the rules used to judge that someone does or does not fit a particular "person type" or that "John is (or is not) a typical extravert"? Questions of this kind have guided recent explorations of natural categories in social cognition (e.g., Cantor & Mischel, 1979; Cantor *et al.*, 1981) in efforts to assess how individuals categorize types of people (extraverts, social climbers) and types of psychological situations (dates, business meetings).

In these studies of social knowledge, we were guided by a categorical-prototype approach, which begins with the realization that, although the borders of categories may be fuzzy (as Wittgenstein, 1953, first noted), the central, clearest examples of each category may be quite distinct from those in other categories. Just as recent efforts in cognitive psychology have focused on the "clear," or prototypical, examples of categories rather than on the fuzzy, borderline ones, students of social knowledge need to identify the prototypical cases and the rules used to judge prototypicality in the categorization of people and psychological situations. The search for prototypes, rather than for trait dimensions will, I hope avoid some of the central assumptions of classical trait psychology and therefore may also avoid some of its conceptual and empirical limitations (Mischel, 1968). The categorical-prototype approach may have diverse implications for assessment (e.g., Buss & Craik, 1980; Wiggins, 1979, 1980), as well as providing another route for the measurement and analysis of social knowledge (Cantor *et al.*, 1981).

More informally, clinicians have long recognized the need to assess their clients' personal constructs. When a person starts to express personal constructs, he or she usually begins in very diffuse, oversimplified, global terms. For example, a client may call himself "shrewd," or "too shy," "too sharp." He also may say he wants to "feel more real," to "adjust better," to "be happier." What can the construct assessor do with these trait verbalizations? Psychodynamically oriented clinicians rely chiefly on their intuitive inferences about the symbolic and dynamic meanings of verbal behavior. Trait-oriented psychometric assessments either investigate the accuracy of the persons' statements as indexes of their nontest behavior or treat their verbalizations as signs of their position on a personality dimension. A personal construct assessment of language, on the other hand, is quite different. The main aim of such an analysis is to decipher the content of what is being conveyed and to discover its behavioral referents and consequences; it does not aim to translate what is said into signs of underlying motives, unconscious processes, or personality dimensions.

Often it is hard to find appropriate words for deeply subjective states. Talk about private experiences, including thoughts and feelings, tends to be ambiguous. For example, statements of the kind commonly presented in clinical contexts, such as "I feel so lost," generally are not clear. Instead of inquiring into *why* the person feels "lost," personal construct assessments try to discover referents for just *what* the statement means. An adequate personal construct assessment of what people say involves the analysis of what they mean. For this purpose, the assessor's initial task is like the one faced whenever behavioral referents and operational definitions are sought for unclear theoretical constructs. Just as the researcher interested in such concepts as extraversion, identity, or anxiety must find public referents to help specify what he or she means, so must the client find public referents for his or her private concepts.

In sum, Kelly's current impact on cognitive assessment goes well beyond personal constructs as operationalized by his favorite "grid" techniques or as assessed informally by clinical interrogation. It extends to the growing contemporary interests in schemata, scripts, templates, prototypes, and other cognitive frameworks and knowledge packages hypothesized as mental structures that mediate the impact of social experience and guide information processing selectively (e.g., Cantor & Mischel, 1977, 1979; Markus, 1977; Nisbett & Ross, 1980; Rogers, Rogers, & Kuiper, 1979). It is not yet clear which routes will ultimately prove to be most useful, but there is little doubt that personal and social constructs and encoding strategies will have an enduring place in the cognitive assessment of persons.

Expectancies

When one turns from what people *can* do and from how they categorize the world to what they *actually* do, one goes from construction capacity and constructs to the selection and execution of performance in specific situations. Predicting behavior in a given situation requires attention to the person's expectancies about alternative behavioral possibilities in that situation. The person's expectancies (hypotheses) guide the selection of behaviors from among the many that could be constructed in a given context.

"Behavior-outcome expectancies" are hypotheses or contingency rules that represent the "if _____, then _____" relations between behavioral alternatives and probable outcomes anticipated for particular possible behavior in particular situations. Expectancy-value theories predict that people will generate the response patterns that they expect are most likely to lead to the most subjectively valuable outcomes (consequences) in any given situation (e.g., Mischel, 1973; Rotter, 1954). When there is no new information about the behavior-outcome expectancies in any situation, performance depends on previous behavior-outcome expectancies in similar situations; new information about behavior-outcome relations in the particular situation, however, may overcome the effects of presituational expectancies, so that specific situational expectancies soon become major determinants of performance (Mischel & Staub, 1965). When the consequences expected for performance change, so does behavior, although strongly established behavior-outcome expectancies may constrain an individual's ability to adapt to changes in contingencies. The behavior-outcome expectancy construct has been central in social learning personality theories for several decades, and diverse methods are available for its assessment (Rotter, 1954; Rotter, Chance, & Phares, 1972).

A special aspect of expectancy, "self-efficacy," defined as the person's conviction that he or she can execute the behavior required by a particular situation, has come into focus more recently (Bandura, 1978). Self-efficacy is assessed by asking the person to indicate the degree of confidence that he or she can do a particular task, which is described in detail. The perceptions of one's own efficacy may be important in guiding and directing one's behavior. The close connection between high self-efficacy expectations and effective performance is illustrated in studies of people who received various treatments to help reduce their fear of snakes. A consistently high association was found between the degree to which persons improved from treatment (becoming able to handle snakes fearlessly) and their perceived self-efficacy, assessed by asking people to predict their ability to do each given act successfully (Bandura & Adams, 1977). Results of this kind suggest strong and clear links between self-perceptions of one's competence and the ability to behave competently and demonstrate again that, when the right questions are asked, people can be excellent predictors of their own behaviors.

Although expectancies seem to be clearly central person variables, it would be a mistake to transform them into generalized traitlike dispositions by endowing them with broad cross-situational consistency or by forgetting that they depend on specific stimulus conditions and on particular contexts. Empirically, "generalized expectancies" tend to be generalized only within relatively narrow, restricted limits (e.g., Mischel & Staub, 1965; Mischel, Zeiss, & Zeiss, 1974). For example, "locus of control" may have limited generality, with distinct, unrelated expectancies found for positive and negative outcomes and with highly specific behavioral correlates for each (Mischel *et al.,* 1974). If we convert expectancies into global traitlike dispositions and remove them from their close interaction with situational conditions, they may well prove to be no more useful than their many theoretical predecessors. Construed as relatively specific (and modifiable) subjective hypotheses about behavior-outcome contingencies and personal competencies, however, expectancies may be readily assessed and may serve as useful predictors of performance.

Subjective Values and Preferences

The behaviors people choose to perform also depend on the subjective values of the outcomes that they expect. Different individuals value different outcomes and also share particular values in different degrees. Therefore it is necessary to assess still another person variable: the subjective (perceived) value for the individual of particular classes of events, that is, his or her stimulus preferences and aversions. This requires assessing the major stimuli that have acquired the power to induce positive or negative emotional states in the person and to function as incentives for or reinforcers of behavior.

Subjective values can be assessed by measuring the individual's actual choices in lifelike situations, as well as verbal preferences or ratings for different choices and activities (Bullock & Merrill, 1980; Mischel & Grusec, 1966). Verbal reports (e.g., on questionnaires) about values and interests also may supply valuable information about the individual's preferences and aversions and appear to provide some of the more temporally stable data in the domain of personality (Kelly, 1955; Strong, 1955). Alternatively, people may be asked to rank order actual rewards (Rotter, 1954), or the reinforcement value of particular stimuli may be assessed directly by observing their effects on the individual's performance (e.g., Gewirtz & Baer, 1958). Reinforcement (incentive) preferences may also be assessed by providing individuals with opportunities to select the outcomes they want from a large array of alternatives, as when patients earn tokens that they may exchange for objects or activities: the "price" they are willing to pay for particular outcomes provides an index of their subjective value (e.g., Ayllon & Azrin, 1965). Good illustrations of the clinical assessment of stimulus values come from attempts to create subjective anxiety hierarchies (e.g., Wolpe, 1961).

Self-Regulatory Systems and Plans

Still another person variable that requires assessment from a cognitive-social learning perspective consists of the individual's self-regulatory systems and plans. This person variable includes a number of components, all relevant to how complex, relatively long-term patterns of goal-directed behavior are generated and maintained even when the environment offers weak supports, barriers, and conflicts. To a considerable degree, individuals regulate their own behavior and affect the quality of their performance by self-imposed goals and standards, by self-produced consequences, and by plans and self-statements. Even in the absence of external constraints, people set performance goals for themselves, criticize or praise their own behavior (depending on how well it matches their expectations and standards), and encourage or demoralize their own efforts through their own ideation. Let us consider some of the main components in this process that may be assessed independently even if they are parts of an integral self-regulatory system.

Self-Imposed Goals and Standards. Studies of goal setting and self-reinforcement (e.g., Bandura & Perloff, 1967; Bandura & Whalen, 1966; Mischel & Liebert, 1966) have made it plain for many years that even young children will not indulge themselves with freely available, immediate gratifications but will, instead, set goals and follow rules to delay gratification; far from being simply hedonistic, they impose standards and contingencies upon their own behavior.

A key feature of self-regulatory systems is the person's adoption of goals and contingency rules that guide behavior. Such rules specify the kinds of behavior appropriate (expected) under particular conditions, the performance levels (standards, goals) that the behavior must achieve, and the consequences (positive and negative) of attaining or failing to reach those standards. Like expectancies and subjective values, self-imposed goals have had a significant place in personality theorizing and research for many years (e.g., Bandura & Walters, 1963; Kanfer, 1971; Mischel, 1966; Rotter, 1954; Rotter *et al.,* 1972). The implications for applied clinical assessment, however, have not been fully realized, and the measures that have been developed in research contexts serve more as readily available prototypes for the future than as well-established, formal instruments in their own right.

Self-Statements. After the person has selected standards (terminal goals) for conduct in a particular situation, the often long and difficult route to self-reinforcement and external reinforcement with material rewards is probably mediated extensively by covert symbolic activities, such as praise and self-instructions, as the individual reaches subgoals. When reinforcing and noxious stimuli are imagined, they appear to influence behavior in the same way as when such stimuli are externally presented (e.g., Cautela, 1971). Imagined events, self-statements, and other covert activities serve to maintain goal-directed work until the performance matches or exceeds the person's terminal standards (e.g., Bandura, 1977). Progress along the route to a goal is also mediated by self-generated distractions and cognitive operations through which the person can transform the aversive "self-control" situation into one that can be mastered effectively (e.g., Mischel, 1974; Mischel, Ebbesen, & Zeiss, 1972; Mischel & Moore, 1980). Achievement of important goals generally leads to positive self-appraisal and self-reinforcement; failure to reach significant self-imposed standards tends to lead the person to indulge in psychological self-lacerations (e.g., self-condemnation).

Whereas the anticipation of success may help to sustain performance, the anticipation of failure may lead to extensive anxiety. Anxiety interferes most with effective performance when it arouses anxious, self-preoccupying thoughts (e.g., "I'm no good at this—I'll never be able to do it") in the stressed person. These thoughts compete and interfere with task-relevant thoughts (e.g., "Now I have to recheck my answers"). The result is that performance (as well as the person) suffers (Sarason, Note 2). The interference from self-preoccupying thoughts tends to be greatest when the task to be done is complex and requires many competing responses. One cannot be full of negative thoughts about oneself and simultaneously concentrate effectively on difficult work. Likewise, as the motivation to do well increases (as when success on the task is especially important), the highly anxious person may become particularly handicapped. That happens because under such highly motivating conditions test-anxious people tend to catastrophize and become even more negatively self-preoccupied, dwelling on how poorly they are doing. In contrast, the less anxious pay attention to the task and concentrate on how to master it effectively. Obviously, high self-efficacy expectations are the foundations for successful performance, whereas intrusive self-doubts can guarantee failure.

As noted in previous chapters, when people believe that there is nothing they can do to control negative or painful outcomes, they may come to expect that they are "helpless" (Seligman, 1975). That is, they may learn to expect that aversive outcomes are uncontrollable, that there is nothing they can do. In that state, they also may become apathetic, despondent, and slow to learn that they actually *can* control the outcomes. Such states of helplessness may generalize, persist, and involve feelings of depression or sadness. The state of helplessness may have especially negative and persistent effects when the person believes that it reflects his or her own enduring, widespread internal qualities (e.g., "I'm incompetent") rather than more momentary, external, or situational considerations (Abramson, Seligman, & Teasdale, 1978). Thus people's attributions have an important part in determining how a state of helplessness affects them, and the measurement of such attributions is an important ingredient of cognitive assessment (see Shaw & Dobson, Chapter 12).

Following frustration in the form of failure on a task, some individuals "fall apart," and their performance deteriorates, but other people actually improve. What causes these two different types of responses to the frustration of failure? One important cause may be how the person interprets the reasons for the experience. Children who believed their failure was due to lack of ability (called "helpless children") were found to perform more poorly after they experienced failure than did those who saw their failure as due to lack of effort (called "mastery-oriented" children). Indeed, the mastery-oriented children often actually performed better after failure. A most encouraging finding is that training the helpless children (those who attribute their failure to lack of ability) to view outcomes as the result of their own effort results in their improved performance after a failure experience (Dweck, 1975).

When faced with failure, helpless children seem to have self-defeating thoughts that virtually guarantee further failure. This became clear when groups of helpless and mastery-oriented fifth graders were instructed "to think out loud" while solving problems. When children in the two groups began to experience failure, they soon said very different things to themselves. The helpless children made statements reflecting their lack of ability, such as "I'm getting confused" or "I never did have a good memory" or "This isn't fun anymore; I give up" (Diener & Dweck, 1978, p. 458). In contrast, the mastery-oriented children never talked about their lack of ability. Instead, they seemed to search for a remedy for their failure and gave themselves instructions to try to encourage themselves and improve their performance, such as "I should slow down and try to figure this out" or "The harder it gets the harder I need to try" or "I've almost got it now" or "I love a challenge."

In sum, people continuously judge and evaluate their own behavior congratulating and condemning themselves for their own attributes and achievements. We assess our own characteristics and actions, praise or abuse our own achievements, and self-administer social and material rewards and punishments from the enormous array freely available to us. These self-regulatory processes are not limited to the individual's self-administration of such outcomes as the tokens, "prizes," or verbal approval and disapproval that have been favored in most early studies of self-reinforcement (e.g., Bandura, 1969; Kanfer & Marston, 1963; Kanfer & Phillips, 1970; Mahoney, 1974; Masters & Mokros, 1974; Mischel, Coates, & Raskoff, 1968). An especially pervasive, but, until recently, neglected, feature of self-regulation is the person's selective exposure to different types of positive and negative information (Mischel *et al.,* 1973; Mischel, Ebbesen, & Zeiss, 1976), subsequent evaluative "self-encoding" (Mischel, 1973, 1979), and the information and ideation to which the person exposes himself or herself mentally.

Almost limitless "good" and "bad" information about the self is potentially available (for example, in the form of memories), depending on where one looks and how one searches. Individuals usually can find or construct information and thoughts to support their positive or negative attributes and their successes or failures almost boundlessly. They can focus cognitively, for example, on their past, present, and expected assets or liabilities and attend either to strengths or to weaknesses by ideating about selective aspects of their perceived personalities and behaviors. Affective self-reactions, as in the enhancement of one's own self-esteem, and, in common-sense terms, the individual's personal positive and negative feelings, presumably hinge on selective attentional processes through which the individual exposes himself or herself only to particular types of information from the enormous array potentially available. By means of such selective attention, the individuals presumably can make themselves feel either good or bad, can privately congratulate or condemn themselves, and, in the extreme, can generate emotions from euphoria or depression.

Given that every person's self-perception includes some positive and some negative qualities, what determines why more attention is paid to one or the other type of attribute? As part of our program of research, I and my colleagues have been studying the interactions between situational and dispositional variables that guide the process of selective attention of different affective value for the person (e.g., Mischel *et al.,* 1973, 1976). Studies by other investigators have extended this paradigm to demonstrate that success–failure and/or positive–negative affect influence a wide variety of responses, including generosity to self and others, self-reactions, and also delay behavior in consistent, predictable ways (e.g., Isen, Shalker, Clark, & Karp, 1978; Rosenhan, Underwood, & Moore, 1974; Schwarz & Pollack, 1977; Seeman & Schwarz, 1974; Underwood, Froming, & Moore, 1977). Taken collectively, the data strongly support the conclusion that success and positive affect lead to more benign reactions to the self as well as to others. The manifestations of this positive "glow" are diverse indeed, and they even seem to influence memory for information about the self in the same manner (Mischel *et al.,* 1976).

Given the central role of selective attention, of mastery versus helplessness ideation, and of other self-statements in determining the nature and quality of performance, it becomes most important to assess systematically the relevant cognitions, attributional styles, and information preference patterns. In this volume, several chapters review and contribute to such assessment. Examples include think-aloud methods (discussed by Genest & Turk, Chapter 8), thought listing (Cacioppo & Petty, Chapter 10), the projective approach (Sobel, Chapter 5), imagery measurement (Anderson, Chapter 6), the assessment of social-evaluative anxiety (Glass & Merluzzi, Chapter 13), and the assessment of depressive schemas (Shaw & Dobson, Chapter 12).

Plans and the Activation of Metacognitions. Although there has been increasing work on the role of self-instructions in self-control apart from specific reinforcement considerations (e.g., Bem, 1967; Luria, 1961; Meichenbaum, 1977; O'Leary, 1968), less attention has been given to the planning and organization of complex behavioral sequences essential for sustained self-regulation. In recent years, exciting developments have been occurring in the study of heuristics for such cognitive activities as reading and story comprehension (e.g., Brown, 1978). At the same time, more is becoming known about the role of plans in self-control (Meichenbaum, 1977), for example, in resistance to temptation (Mischel & Patterson, 1978) and in delay of gratification (Mischel, 1979, 1980).

I and my colleagues have been finding that even young children develop a remarkable degree of knowledge and understanding about a wide range of psychological principles, including those that are basic for effective self-control. For example, children's spontaneous delay of gratification strategies show a clear developmental progression in knowledge of effective delay rules (Yates & Mischel, 1979; Mischel & Mischel, Note 3). A few preschoolers suggest a self-distraction strategy or even rehearsal of the task contingency. Most children under the age of 5 years, however, do not seem to generate clear or viable strategies for effective delay; instead, they tend to make waiting more difficult for themselves by focusing on what they want but cannot have. Our overall results suggest that, by the age of 5 or 6 years, the children clearly know that covering the rewards in a delay-of-gratification paradigm will help them wait for them, whereas looking at them or thinking about them will make it difficult. By third grade, they spontaneously generate and reasonably justify a number of potentially viable strategies and unequivocally understand the basic principles of resistance to temptation—for example, avoid looking at the rewards because "If I'm looking at them all the time, it will make me hungry . . . and I'd want to ring the bell." Often they focus on the task and contingency, reminding themselves of the task requirement and outcomes associated with each choice ("If you wait you get _____; if you don't, you only get _____"). They also often indicate the value of distraction from the rewards or of negative ideation designed to make them less tempting ("Think about gum stuck all over them").

In sum, in the course of development, children show increasing awareness of effective delay rules and come to generate the strategies necessary for successfully reducing frustration and temptation. They progress from a systematic preference for seeing and thinking about the real blocked rewards and hence the worst delay strategy (Yates & Mischel, 1979) to a clear avoidance of attention to the rewards and particularly of "consummatory" reward ideation. Systematically they come to prefer distraction from the temptation, self-instructions about the task contingency, and more abstract, nonconsummatory ideation about the rewards themselves. These developmental shifts seem to reflect a growing recognition by the child of the principle that the more cognitively available and "hot" a temptation, the more one will want it and the more difficult it will be to resist. Armed with this insight, the child can generate a diverse array of strategies for effectively managing otherwise formidable tasks and for overcoming "stimulus control" with self-control. Hence a comprehensive cognitive assessment of persons needs to determine the availability of relevant metacognitions and to analyze how such plans and strategies for mastery become cognitively activated to facilitate goal-directed behavior.

As part of our concern with cognitive competences, we also have become interested more generally in the development of children's understanding of psychological principles underlying social behavior (Mischel & Mischel, Note 4). We therefore constructed objective multiple-choice tests that confronted children with highly specific questions requiring them to predict the probable outcome of classical experiments in psychology, which we carefully described in detail, stripped of jargon. These experiments ranged from Asch's study on conformity through Bandura's work on modeling, Pavlov's classical conditioning, and Skinner's studies of reinforcement schedules. We were surprised by the amount of psychological knowledge most children seemed to have by the time they reached about 10 years. They generally knew, for example, about the aggression-facilitating effects of watching aggressive models; they knew that live modeling with guided participation is a more effective treatment for phobias than either systematic desensitization or symbolic (film-based) modeling; they knew that Harlow's frightened monkeys would cling to the milkless terry-cloth mother more than to the wire one with milk. Although the children were systematically wrong about conformity in the Asch situation and about the effects of cognitive dissonance, and although they did not know Pavlov's discovery about classical conditioning, they did know that intermittent reinforcement makes Skinner's pigeons peck longer after the food stops (at $p \leq .002$). We also obtained correlations as high as .93 (in a small sample of sixth graders, $n = 10$) with intelligence test scores, which leads us to believe that spontaneous knowledge of psychological principles about social behavior may indeed be an important ingredient of personal and cognitive competence and of the individual's self-regulatory system and therefore worth pursuing systematically. It will be challenging to assess not just the person's psychological knowledge but also the activation and utilization of that knowledge and understanding in the process of regulating and directing behavior.

Some Cautions for Cognitive Assessors

To summarize, the cognitive person variables that require assessment include people's cognitive behavioral construction competencies, that is, their competence or ability to generate desired cognitions and response patterns. It is also important to assess how individuals encode or categorize situations, other people, and themselves. Performance in any situation depends on the person's relevant expectancies, particularly on the expected outcomes associated with alternative response patterns and on expectations about one's own ability to generate the requisite behavior. Performance also depends on the subjective values of the expected outcomes for alternative choices. Finally, assessment requires attention to the self-regulatory systems and plans that each individual brings to the situation. The assessment of this final person variable requires analyses of the plans and rules people use to guide their own behavior and their ideation and self-statements as they pursue their goals.

I hope that cognitive assessment of the sort discussed throughout this volume will also enhance our understanding of how people abstract the "gist" of each other and of themselves, forming prototypes, schemata, expectations, or other cognitive representations that may function to distill essential features from the flood of impinging stimuli that otherwise overwhelms the "unprepared mind." Ultimately, an adequate approach to the understanding of a person also may require the development of a grammar of the individual, which specifies the organization and relationships among diverse parts or components of the individual's actions and attributes. A grammar of the individual would ideally also tell us how person variables such as those discussed in this chapter are organized and interrelated to function coherently in the coping process. Such a structural approach to persons is hardly a new goal for personality theorists. The hope now, however, is that a structural approach to person variables may have a better chance to be fruitful, guided by the models and methods for the analysis of human understanding that are being developed in cognitive psychology (see Merluzzi, Rudy, & Glass, Chapter 4; Ericsson & Simon, Chapter 2).

The excitement and promise created by the cognitive assessment approach and evidenced generously throughout this volume is encouraging and refreshing. However, several cautions, all of which have often been heard before (including in this volume), need to be reiterated. First, it would be preemptive to restrict assessment to cognitive variables in the person. A comprehensive assessment also requires careful attention to the analysis of situations and of the naturally occurring behaviors observed in the interactions among people in real-life settings. The study of such *in vivo* social interactions reveals dramatically how each person selects, changes, and generates conditions just as much as he or she is influenced by them. Although I have argued that clients can be their own best experts and that their self-assessments can be highly useful, situational assessments and direct observation, as well as unobtrusive nonreactive measures, are also needed to study lives in the social interactions in which they are really lived (e.g., Patterson, 1976).

Second, imprudent inferences that generalize unjustifiably from limited observations are as imprudent when practiced by the cognitively oriented assessor as they are when offered by the trait-oriented assessor or the psychodynamicist. When measurement shifted from the cognitive to the social personality domain at the start of this century, a giant conceptual leap was taken, without adequately recognizing the length of the leap. This was the leap from sampling people's relevant specific *performance* by assessing what they could do (which was the heart of intelligence testing) to asking people to report about what they are like, in general, on such broad, situation-free dimensions as friendliness, conscientiousness, or introversion. These responses were used by trait psychologists not as *samples* of the respondents' relevant behavior (e.g., self-assessments), but as *signs* or indicators of their generalized dispositions. This leap was not carefully thought through, and we have seen its implications over the past few decades as we have begun to realize the conceptual and methodological problems that arise when one does not very carefully distinguish people's subjective judgments and statements about themselves from an objective sampling of what people actually say and do, that is, their performance under specific circumstances (Mischel, 1968). If one wants to go beyond the information given, beyond what is reported or observed directly in its own right, one must justify the resulting inferences and generalizations. Such justification requires empirically demonstrating reliability, validity, stability, cross-situational consistency, and utility, and it is the assessor's burden regardless of theoretical orientation. The deeper the inference, the wider the generalizations and the greater the responsibility to justify them with evidence.

Although not exempt from the assessment problems faced by other approaches, cognitive person variables of the sort reviewed in this chapter, and cognitive assessment generally, may have special appeal to the extent that they are rooted in psychological processes (the generation and encoding of information, the choice of performance alternatives, the self-regulation of goal-directed action). These person variables interface with basic processes of mental functioning rather than describing persons more statically by locating their positions on assessor-supplied trait dimensions. The intent in selecting such variables is to strive for an approach such as that envisioned by George Kelly in 1955, who was quoted at the outset of Chapter 7 but whose comments are worth repeating here:

> There are two ways in which one can look at psychological measurement and clinical diagnosis. On the one hand, he can seek to fix the position of the subject with respect to certain dimensions or coordinates—such as intelligence, extraversion, and so on—or to classify him as a clinical type—such as schizoid, neurotic and the like. On the other hand, he can concern himself with the subject's freedom of movement, his potentialities, the resources which can be mobilized, and what is to become of him. From the point of view of the psychology of personal constructs, in which the emphasis is upon process rather than upon fixed position, the latter represents the more enlightened approach. Let us say, then, that the primary purpose of psychological measurement . . . is to survey the pathways along which the subject is free to move, and the primary purpose of clinical diagnosis is the plotting of the most feasible course of movement. (Kelly, 1955, p. 203)

ACKNOWLEDGMENT

Preparation of this chapter was facilitated by Grant MH06830 from the National Institute of Mental Health and by Grant HD MH09814 from the National Institute of Child Health and Human Development.

Reference Notes

1. Mischel, W., & Bentler, P. *The ability of persons to predict their own behavior.* Unpublished manuscript, Stanford University, 1965.
2. Sarason, I. G. *Life stress, self-preoccupation, and social supports.* Presidential address presented at the meeting of the Western Psychological Association, 1979.
3. Mischel, W., & Mischel, H. N. *The development of children's knowledge of self-control.* Paper presented at the meeting of the Society for Research in Child Development, San Francisco, March 1979.

4. Mischel, W., & Mischel, H. N. *Children's knowledge of psychological principles.* Unpublished manuscript, Stanford University, 1979.

References

Abramson, L. Y., Seligman, M. E. P., & Teasdale, J. D. Learned helplessness in humans: Critique and reformulation. *Journal of Abnormal Psychology,* 1978, *87,* 49–74.

Anderson, J. The prediction of adjustment over time. In I. Iscoe & H. Stevenson (Eds.), *Personality development in children.* Austin: University of Texas Press, 1960.

Ayllon, T., & Azrin, N. H. The measurement and reinforcement of behavior of psychotics. *Journal of the Experimental Analysis of Behavior,* 1965, *8,* 357–383.

Bandura, A. Vicarious processes: A case of no-trial learning. In L. Berkowitz (Ed.), *Advances in experimental social psychology* (Vol. 2). New York: Academic Press, 1965.

Bandura, A. *Principles of behavior modification.* New York: Holt, Rinehart & Winston, 1969.

Bandura, A. *Social learning theory.* Englewood Cliffs, N.J.: Prentice-Hall, 1977.

Bandura, A. Reflections on self-efficacy. In S. Rachman (Ed.), *Advances in behaviour research and therapy* (Vol. 1). Oxford: Pergamon Press, 1978.

Bandura, A., & Adams, N. E. Analysis of self-efficacy theory of behavioral change. *Cognitive Therapy and Research,* 1977, *1,* 287–310.

Bandura, A., & Perloff, B. Relative efficacy of self-monitored and externally imposed reinforcement systems. *Journal of Personality and Social Psychology,* 1967, *7,* 111–116.

Bandura, A., & Walters, R. H. *Social learning and personality development.* New York: Holt, Rinehart & Winston, 1963.

Bandura, A., & Whalen, C. K. The influence of antecedent reinforcement and divergent modeling cues on patterns of self-reward. *Journal of Personality and Social Psychology,* 1966, *3,* 373–382.

Bem, D. J. Self-perception: An alternative interpretation of cognitive dissonance phenomena. *Psychological Review,* 1967, *74,* 183–200.

Block, J. *The challenge of response sets.* New York: Appleton-Century-Crofts, 1965.

Brown, A. Development, schooling and the acquisition of knowledge about knowledge. In R. Anderson, R. Spiro, & W. Montague (Eds.), *Schooling and the acquisition of knowledge.* Hillsdale, N.J.: Erlbaum, 1978.

Bullock, D., & Merrill, L. The impact of personal preference on consistency through time: The case of childhood aggression. *Child Development,* 1980, *51,* 808–814.

Buss, D. M., & Craik, K. H. The frequency concept of disposition: Dominance and prototypically dominant acts. *Journal of Personality,* 1980, *48,* 379–392.

Cantor, N., & Mischel, W. Traits as prototypes: Effects on recognition memory. *Journal of Personality and Social Psychology,* 1977, *35,* 38–48.

Cantor, N., & Mischel, W. Prototypes in person perception. In L. Berkowitz (Ed.), *Advances in experimental social psychology* (Vol. 12). New York: Academic Press, 1979.

Cantor, N., Mischel, W., & Schwartz, J. Social knowledge: Structure, content, use and abuse. In A. Hastorf & A. Isen (Eds.), *Cognitive social psychology.* New York: Elsevier North-Holland, 1981.

Cautela, J. R. Covert conditioning. In A. Jacoby & L. B. Sachs (Eds.), *The psychology of private events.* New York: Academic Press, 1971.

Diener, C. O., & Dweck, C. S. An analysis of learned helplessness: Continuous changes in performance, strategy, and achievement cognitions following failure. *Journal of Personality and Social Psychology,* 1978, *36,* 451–462.

Dolliver, S. Strong Vocational Interest Blank versus expressed vocational interest: A review. *Psychological Bulletin,* 1969, *72,* 95–107.

DuBois, P. H., & Watson, R. I. The selection of patrolmen. *Journal of Applied Psychology,* 1950, *34,* 90–95.

Dweck, C. S. The role of expectations and attributions in the alleviation of learned helplessness. *Journal of Personality and Social Psychology,* 1975, *31,* 674–685.

Flavell, J. H., & Wellman, H. M. Metamemory. In R. V. Kail & J. W. Hagen (Eds.), *Perspectives on the development of memory and cognition.* Hillsdale, N.J.: Erlbaum, 1977.

Gewirtz, J. L., & Baer, D. M. The effect of brief social deprivation on behaviors for a social reinforcer. *Journal of Abnormal Social Psychology,* 1958, *56,* 49–56.

Goldfried, M. R., & D'Zurilla, T. J. A behavioral–analytic model for assessing competence. In C. D. Spielberger (Ed.), *Current topics in clinical and community psychology* (Vol. 1). New York: Academic Press, 1969.

Grusec, J., & Mischel, W. Model's characteristics as determinants of social learning. *Journal of Personality and Social Psychology,* 1966, *4,* 211–215.

Hase, H. D., & Goldberg, L. R. Comparative validity of different strategies of constructing personality inventory scales. *Psychological Bulletin,* 1967, *67,* 231–248.

Holmes, D. S., & Tyler, J. D. Direct versus projective measurement of achievement motivation. *Journal of Consulting and Clinical Psychology,* 1968, *32,* 712–717.

Isen, A. M., Shalker, T. E., Clark, M., & Karp, L. Affect, accessibility of material in memory, and behavior: A cognitive loop? *Journal of Personality and Social Psychology,* 1978, *36,* 1–12.

Kanfer, F. H. The maintenance of behavior by self-generated stimuli and reinforcement. In A. Jacobs & L. B. Sachs (Eds.), *The psychology of private events.* New York: Academic Press, 1971.

Kanfer, F. H., & Marston, A. R. Determinants of self-reinforcement in human learning. *Journal of Experimental Psychology,* 1963, *66,* 245–254.

Kanfer, F. H., & Phillips, J. S. *Learning foundations of behavior therapy.* New York: Wiley, 1970.

Kelly, E. L. Consistency of the adult personality. *American Psychologist,* 1955, 10, 659–681.

Kelly, G. A. *The psychology of personal constructs* (Vols. 1 & 2). New York: Basic Books, 1955.

Lindzey, G., & Tejessy, C. Thematic Apperception Test: Indices of aggression in relation to measures of overt and covert behavior. *American Journal of Orthopsychiatry,* 1956, *26,* 567–576.

Luria, A. R. *The role of speech in the regulation of normal and abnormal behavior.* New York: Pergamon Press, 1961.

Mahoney, M. J. *Cognition and behavior modification.* Cambridge, Mass.: Ballinger, 1974.

Markus, H. Self-schemata and processing information about the self. *Journal of Personality and Social Psychology,* 1977, *35,* 63–78.

Masters, J. C., & Mokros, J. R. Self-reinforcement processes in children. In H. Reese (Ed.), *Advances in child development and behavior* (Vol. 9). New York: Academic Press, 1974.

McArthur, C., & Stevens, L. B. The validation of expressed interests as compared with inventoried interests: A fourteen-year follow-up. *Journal of Applied Psychology,* 1955, *39,* 184–189.

Meichenbaum, D. *Cognitive-behavior modification.* New York: Plenum Press, 1977.

Melei, J. P., & Hilgard, E. R. Attitudes toward hypnosis, self-predictions, and hypnotic susceptibility. *International Journal of Clinical and Experimental Hypnosis,* 1964, *12,* 99–108.

Mischel, W. Predicting the success of Peace Corps volunteers in Nigeria. *Journal of Personality and Social Psychology,* 1965, *1,* 510–517.

Mischel, W. Theory and research on the antecedents of self-imposed delay of reward. In B. A. Maher (Ed.), *Progress in experimental personality research* (Vol. 3). New York: Academic Press, 1966.

Mischel, W. *Personality and assessment.* New York: Wiley, 1968.

Mischel, W. Continuity and change in personality. *American Psychologist,* 1969, *24,* 1012–1018.

Mischel, W. Direct versus indirect personality assessment: Evidence and implications. *Journal of Consulting and Clinical Psychology,* 1972, *38,* 319–324.

Mischel, W. Toward a cognitive social learning reconceptualization of personality. *Psychological Review,* 1973, *80,* 252–283.

Mischel, W. Processes in delay of gratification. In L. Berkowitz (Ed.), *Advances in experimental social psychology* (Vol. 7). New York: Academic Press, 1974.

Mischel, W. On the future of personality measurement. *American Psychologist,* 1977, *32,* 246–254.

Mischel, W. On the interface of cognition and personality: Beyond the person–situation debate. *American Psychologist,* 1979, *34,* 740–754.

Mischel, W. Objective and subjective rules for delay of gratification. In W. Lens (Ed.), *Cognitions in human motivation and learning.* Hillsdale, N.J.: Erlbaum, 1981.

Mischel, W. Metacognition and rules of delay. In J. Flavell & L. Ross (Eds.), *Cognitive social development: Frontiers and possible futures.* New York: Cambridge University Press, 1981.

Mischel, W., Coates, B., & Raskoff, A. Effects of success and failure on self-gratification. *Journal of Personality and Social Psychology,* 1968, *10,* 381–390.

Mischel, W., Ebbesen, E. B., & Zeiss, A. R. Cognitive and attentional mechanisms in delay of gratification. *Journal of Personality and Social Psychology,* 1972, *21,* 204–218.

Mischel, W., Ebbesen, E. B., & Zeiss, A. R. Selective attention to the self: Situational and dispositional determinants. *Journal of Personality and Social Psychology,* 1973, *27,* 129–142.

Mischel, W., Ebbesen, E. B., & Zeiss, A. R. Determinants of selective memory about the self. *Journal of Consulting and Clinical Psychology,* 1976, *44,* 92–103.

Mischel, W., & Grusec, J. Determinants of the rehearsal and transmission of neutral and aversive behaviors. *Journal of Personality and Social Psychology,* 1966, *3,* 197–205.

Mischel, W., & Leibert, R. M. Effects of discrepancies between observed and imposed reward criteria on their acquisition and transmission. *Journal of Personality and Social Psychology,* 1966, *3,* 45–53.

Mischel, W., & Moore, B. The role of ideation in voluntary delay for symbolically presented rewards. *Cognitive Therapy and Research,* 1980, *4,* 211–221.

Mischel, W., & Patterson, C. J. Effective plans for self-control in children. In W. A. Collins (Ed.), *Minnesota symposium on child psychology* (Vol. 2). Hillsdale, N.J.: Erlbaum, 1978.

Mischel, W., & Staub, E. Effects of expectancy on working and waiting for larger rewards. *Journal of Personality and Social Psychology,* 1965, *2,* 625–633.

Mischel, W., Zeiss, R., & Zeiss, A. Internal–external control and persistence: Validation and implications of the Stanford Preschool Internal–External Scale. *Journal of Personality and Social Psychology,* 1974, *29,* 265–278.

Neisser, U. *Cognitive Psychology.* New York: Appleton-Century-Crofts, 1967.

Nisbett, R. E., & Ross, L. D. *Human inference: Strategies and shortcomings of social judgment* (Century Psychology Series). Englewood Cliffs, N.J.: Prentice-Hall, 1980.

Nisbett, R. E., & Wilson, T. D. Telling more than we can know: Verbal reports on mental processes. *Psychological Review,* 1977, *84,* 231–259.

O'Leary, K. D. The effects of self-instruction on immoral behavior. *Journal of Experimental Child Psychology,* 1968, *6,* 297–301.

Patterson, G. R. Aggressive child: Victim and architect of a coercive system. In E. J. Mash, L. A. Hamerlynck, & L. C. Handy (Eds.), *Behavior modification and families.* New York: Brunner/Mazel, 1976.

Peterson, D. R. Scope and generality of verbally defined personality factors. *Psychological Review,* 1965, *72,* 48–59.

Rogers, T. B., Rogers, P. J., & Kuiper, N. A. Evidence for the self as a cognitive prototype: The "false alarms effect." *Personality and Social Psychology Bulletin,* 1979, *5,* 53–56.

Rosch, E., Mervis, C., Gray, W., Johnson, D., & Boyes-Braem, P. Basic objects in natural categories. *Cognitive Psychology,* 1976, *8,* 382–439.

Rosenhan, D. L., Underwood, B., & Moore, B. Affect moderates self-gratification and altruism. *Journal of Personality and Social Psychology,* 1974, *30,* 546–552.

Rotter, J. B. *Social learning and clinical psychology.* Englewood Cliffs, N.J.: Prentice-Hall, 1954.

Rotter, J. B., Chance, J. E., & Phares, E. J. (Eds.). *Applications of a social learning theory of personality.* New York: Holt, Rinehart & Winston, 1972.

Schwarz, J. C., & Pollack, P. R. Affect and delay of gratification. *Journal of Research in Personality,* 1977, *11,* 147–164.

Seeman, G., & Schwarz, J. C. Affective state and preference for immediate versus delayed reward. *Journal of Research in Personality,* 1974, *7,* 384–394.

Seligman, M. E. *Helplessness—On depression, development, and death.* San Francisco: Freeman, 1975.

Sherwood, J. J. Self-report and projective measures of achievement and affiliation. *Journal of Consulting Psychology,* 1966, *30,* 329–337.

Shure, M. B., & Spivack, G. *Problem solving techniques in child rearing.* San Francisco: Jossey-Bass, 1978.

Smith, E. R., & Miller, E. R. Limits on perception of cognitive processes: A reply to Nisbett and Wilson. *Psychological Review,* 1978, *85,* 355–362.

Spielberger, C. D., & DeNike, L. D. Descriptive behaviorism versus cognitive theory in verbal operant conditioning. *Psychological Review,* 1966, *73,* 306–326.

Strong, E. K., Jr. *Vocational interests 18 years after college.* Minneapolis: University of Minnesota Press, 1955.

Underwood, B., Froming, W. J., & Moore, B. S. Mood, attention, and altruism: A search for mediating variables. *Developmental Psychology,* 1977, *13,* 541–542.

Vernon, P. E. *Personality assessment: A critical survey.* New York: Wiley, 1964.

Wallace, J. An abilities conception of personality: Some implications for personality measurement. *American Psychologist,* 1966, *21,* 132–138.

Wallace, J., & Sechrest, L. Frequency hypothesis and content analysis of projective techniques. *Journal of Consulting Psychology,* 1963, *27,* 387–393.

White, R. W. Motivation reconsidered: The concept of competence. *Psychological Review,* 1959, *66,* 297–333.

Wiggins, J. S. A psychological taxonomy of trait-descriptive terms: The interpersonal domain. *Journal of Personality and Social Psychology,* 1979, *37,* 395–413.

Wiggins, J. S. Circumplex model of interpersonal behavior in personality and social psychology. In L. Wheeler (Ed.), *Review of personality and social psychology.* Beverly Hills, Calif.: Sage Press, 1980.

Wittgenstein, L. *Philosophical investigations.* New York: Macmillan, 1953.

Wolpe, J. The systematic desensitization treatment of neuroses. *Journal of Nervous and Mental Disease,* 1961, *132,* 189–203.

Yates, B. T., & Mischel, W. Young children's preferred attentional strategies for delaying gratification. *Journal of Personality and Social Psychology,* 1979, *37,* 286–300.

Zigler, E., & Phillips, L. Social competence and outcome in psychiatric disorder. *Journal of Abnormal and Social Psychology,* 1961, *63,* 264–271.

Zigler, E., & Phillips, L. Social competence and the process-reactive distinction in psychopathology. *Journal of Abnormal and Social Psychology,* 1962, *65,* 215–222.

Author Index

Abelson, R. P., 8, 13*n.*, 90, 123*n.*, 250, 263*n.*, 322, 329, 338*n.*
Abelson, S., 454, 461, 475*n.*
Abramson, L. Y., 367, 369, 370, 382*n.*, 383*n.*, 386*n.*, 492, 499*n.*
Ach, 28
Adair, J., 5, 7, 13*n.*, 239, 263*n.*
Adams, B., 209, 230*n.*
Adams, H. E., 261, 265*n.*
Adams, N. E., 246, 264*n.*, 489, 499*n.*
Adams-Webber, J., 202, 228*n.*
Adrian, E. D., 274, 305*n.*
Agnew, 224
Ainsworth, M., 453, 474*n.*
Ajzen, I., 46, 49*n.*
Alden, L. E., 394, 399, 402, 423–425, 432*n.*, 437*n.*
Alfert, E., 234, 267*n.*
Allen, G., 468, 474*n.*
Allison, B., 227, 228*n.*
Allison, D., 219, 220, 229*n.*
Allport, G., 10, 13*n.*, 59, 191
Alvarez, L., 314, 341*n.*
Amatu, H. I., 393, 397, 438*n.*
Amundsen, R., 10
Anastasi, A., 65, 74*n.*
Anderson, J. R., 17, 20, 49*n.*, 98, 101, 102, 118*n.*, 485, 499*n.*
Anderson, M. P., viii, 149–187, 152, 159, 160, 177, 178, 184*n.*, 236, 237, 483, 494
Anderson, R. C., 102, 118*n.*
Anderson, R. L., 55, 74*n.*
Anderson, S., 452, 474*n.*
Angell, J. R., 233–235, 264*n.*
Antrobus, J. S., 152, 154, 158, 166, 171, 174, 176, 184*n.*, 187*n.*, 254, 258, 264*n.*

Applebaum, M., 344, 356*n.*
Applebee, A. N., 224, 228*n.*
Argyris, C., 72, 74*n.*
Arkin, A., 166, 171, 184*n.*
Arkowitz, H., 246, 265*n.*, 390, 423, 424, 432*n.*–434*n.*, 437*n.*, 490
Armstrong, J., 218, 231*n.*
Arnkoff, D. B., 139, 146*n.*, 188, 227, 229*n.*, 234, 236, 267*n.*, 392, 397, 399, 401, 406, 412, 426, 430, 432*n.*, 433*n.*
Asarnow, J., 89, 113, 116, 121*n.*, 139, 147*n.*, 430, 436*n.*, 437*n.*
Asarnow, R. F., 371, 372, 384*n.*
Asch, 495
Aserinsky, E., 254, 264*n.*
Asher, S., 456, 460, 470, 473*n.*
Ashton, R., 153, 187*n.*
Atkinson, R. C., 369, 383*n.*
Avener, M., 239, 267*n.*, 444, 445, 448, 450*n.*
Averill, J. R., 234, 267*n.*
Ayllon, T., 490, 499*n.*
Azrin, N. H., 490, 499*n.*

Baddeley, A. D., 36, 49*n.*, 94, 118*n.*
Badhorn, E., 423, 425, 435*n.*
Baer, D. M., 490, 500*n.*
Baggett, P., 102, 118*n.*
Bainbridge, L., 5, 13*n.*
Bakeman, R., 343, 344, 348, 350*n.*, 355, 356*n.*
Baker, L., 367, 382*n.*
Baker, N., 235, 268*n.*
Baldwin, M., 466, 474*n.*
Bandura, A., 3, 13*n.*, 89, 114, 116, 118*n.*, 242, 246, 247, 264*n.*, 390, 417, 426, 432*n.*, 440, 441, 450*n.*, 482, 485, 489, 491, 493, 495, 499*n.*
Banikiotes, P. G., 211, 219, 231*n.*

Bank, S., 345, 356*n.*
Bannister, D., 189, 194, 204, 206, 207, 209,
    217–219, 222, 224, 226–228, 229*n.*,
    230*n.*
Barber, T. X., 153, 160, 184*n.*, 187*n.*, 235,
    264*n.*
Barclay, J. R., 102, 119*n.*
Baron, R. S., 316, 318, 323, 340*n.*
Barr, 202
Barratt, B. B., 224, 229*n.*
Barrett, D., 467, 474*n.*
Barron, F. X., 64, 74*n.*
Barta, S. G., 254, 258, 264*n.*, 450, 452*n.*
Bartlett, F. C., 99, 118*n.*, 329, 338*n.*
Bartling, C. A., 380, 387*n.*
Barton, R., 97, 121*n.*, 364, 385*n.*
Basgal, J., 391, 421, 435*n.*
Bateson, G., 218, 229*n.*
Baumgardner, M. H., 312, 340*n.*
Bavelas, J. B., 227, 229*n.*
Beaber, R. J., 327, 338*n.*
Beach, D., 248, 265*n.*
Beach, L. R., 417, 418, 428, 429, 434*n.*
Beattie, O., 10, 14*n.*
Bechterev, V. M., 271, 305*n.*
Beck, A. T., 95, 118*n.*, 141, 146*n.*, 182,
    184*n.*, 188, 236, 243, 257, 258, 263,
    264*n.*, 362–367, 370–374, 376–378,
    380, 382, 383*n.*–387*n.*, 389, 433*n.*
Beck, R., 366, 386*n.*
Becker, L. A., 332, 340*n.*
Becker, R. E., 408, 432*n.*
Beckhuis, M., 369, 386*n.*
Bell, S., 453, 474*n.*
Bellack, A. S., 243, 246, 261, 264*n.*, 266*n.*,
    390, 433*n.*
Bellissimo, A., 91, 117*n.*
Bellows, N., 237, 268*n.*, 315, 340*n.*
Belmont, J., 430, 433*n.*
Bem, D. J., 494, 499*n.*
Bender, M. P., 59, 210, 211, 229*n.*
Bennett, G., 159, 184*n.*
Bentler, P., 481, 498*n.*
Berelson, B., 171, 184*n.*
Berger, H., 28, 274, 278, 305*n.*
Bergman, E., 366, 386*n.*
Bersoff, D., 130, 133, 146*n.*
Bessel, 57
Betts, G., 153, 155–157, 166, 184*n.*
Beyer, J., 246, 264*n.*
Biderman, A. D., 44, 49*n.*
Biever, J. L., 399, 405, 423, 434*n.*
Binet, A., 56, 58, 62, 295

Birch, J., 272, 306*n.*
Black, J. L., 256, 267*n.*
Blackburn, I. M., 218, 231*n.*
Blackman, S., 65, 66, 70, 74*n.*, 141, 147*n.*
Blakey, R. S., 393, 397, 398*n.*, 438*n.*
Blaney, P. H., 363, 383*n.*
Blank, A., 251, 267*n.*
Block, J., 485, 499*n.*
Boback, P., 174, 184*n.*
Boll, T. J., 66, 74*n.*
Bolstad, O. D., 252, 266*n.*
Bonarius, H., 202, 211, 214, 229*n.*, 230*n.*
Bonarius, J. C. J., 211, 221, 229*n.*
Boness, D. J., 287, 307*n.*
Bonge, D., 399–401, 403, 431*n.*, 436*n.*
Boring, E. G., 24, 49*n.*, 237, 243, 264*n.*
Borkovec, T. D., 156, 177, 178, 184*n.*,
    297, 305*n.*
Borkowski, J. G., 9, 13*n.*, 81, 82, 86, 89,
    113, 115, 116, 118*n.*, 119*n.*, 430,
    433*n.*
Bottrell, J., 159, 186*n.*
Bouchard, T. J., 64, 74*n.*
Bower, G. H., 17, 49*n.*, 78, 89, 97, 98,
    117*n.*, 119*n.*, 139, 146*n.*, 363, 383*n.*
Bowers, K. S., 5, 13*n.*, 238–240, 247, 264*n.*,
    441, 450*n.*
Bowlby, J., 366, 385*n.*
Boyes-Braem, P., 487, 501*n.*
Braff, D. L., 90, 91, 121*n.*, 122*n.*
Brandt, J. A., 400, 431*n.*
Bransford, J. D., 80, 94, 97, 98, 100, 102,
    119*n.*–121*n.*, 369, 383*n.*
Breger, L., 53, 71, 74*n.*
Breiter, H., 370, 382*n.*
Brewer, W. F., 33, 49*n.*
Breznitz, S., 406, 415, 433*n.*
Bricker, P. D., 34, 49*n.*
Brock, T. C., 310, 315, 316, 319, 324, 326,
    338*n.*, 341*n.*
Brody, N., 81, 119*n.*
Broga, M. I., 380, 383*n.*
Bronfenbrenner, U., 72, 74*n.*
Brown, A., 11, 13*n.*, 113, 115, 116, 118*n.*,
    119*n.*, 494, 499*n.*
Brown, J. M., 252, 264*n.*
Brown, W. R., 56, 74*n.*
Bruch, M. A., 392, 405–407, 412, 418, 421,
    422, 433*n.*
Bruner, J. S., 323, 342*n.*
Buchwald, A. M., 369, 383*n.*
Buckley, I., 218, 231*n.*
Budoff, J., 71, 74*n.*

Buhler, K., 99, 119*n.*
Bullock, D., 490, 499*n.*
Burland, S., 4, 13*n.*
Burns, D., 378, 383*n.*
Burns, L. E., 393, 397, 398*n.*, 438*n.*
Buros, O. K., 59, 64, 66, 74*n.*
Buss, D. M., 251, 264*n.*, 489, 501*n.*
Butcher, 61
Butler, L., 4, 5, 7, 12, 13*n.*, 14*n.*, 398, 428, 429, 436*n.*, 458–462, 462*n.*, 473*n.*
Butterfield, E. C., 77, 121*n.*, 430, 433*n.*

Cacioppo, J. T., viii, 215, 237, 295, 296, 305*n.*, 309–342, 311–320, 325, 327, 329, 330, 332–336, 337*n.*, 338*n.*, 341*n.*, 346, 390, 406, 412, 423, 425, 431*n.*–433*n.*, 483, 494
Cairns, R. B., 344, 356*n.*
Calder, B. J., 41, 49*n.*, 317, 321, 325, 338*n.*
Calhoun, K. S., 261, 265*n.*
Cameron, R., viii, 3–15, 4, 13*n.*, 485
Campbell, D. T., 7, 14*n.*, 41, 49*n.*, 60
Campione, J. C., 113, 115, 116, 118*n.*
Camras, L., 466, 474*n.*
Cannell, C. F., 43, 49*n.*
Cantor, N., 312, 329, 338*n.*, 480, 487, 488, 499*n.*
Cappe, R., 399, 402, 423–425, 432*n.*
Carlmusto, M., 94, 122*n.*
Carmody, T. P., 393, 396, 433*n.*
Carpenter, P. A., 101, 119*n.*
Carr, J. E., 222, 223, 227, 229*n.*
Carrick, M., 239, 266*n.*
Carrier, S. C., 313, 341*n.*
Carroll, D., 156, 186*n.*
Carroll, J. D., 108, 109, 118*n.*, 119*n.*
Carter, R. F., 310, 338*n.*
Casas, J. M., 393, 399, 401, 433*n.*
Castellan, N. J., 343, 352, 354, 356*n.*
Cattell, J. M., 57–59, 61, 62
Cautela, J. R., 153, 165, 184*n.*, 303, 305*n.*, 491, 499*n.*
Cavanaugh, J. C., 89, 113, 116, 119*n.*, 430, 433*n.*
Ceraso, J., 98, 123*n.*
Chan, A. S., 227, 229*n.*
Chance, J. E., 489, 502*n.*
Chandler, M., 454, 474*n.*
Chang, J. J., 108, 109, 118*n.*, 119*n.*
Chanowitz, B., 251, 267*n.*
Chapanis, A., 34, 49*n.*
Chaplin, W., 97, 121*n.*, 364, 385*n.*
Chapman, D. W., 26, 27, 49*n.*

Chapman, J., 252, 264*n.*, 265*n.*
Chapman, L., 252, 264*n.*, 265*n.*
Charlesworth, W., 453, 474*n.*
Chartier, G. M., 70, 74*n.*
Chase, W. G., 39, 49*n.*, 101, 119*n.*, 270, 305*n.*
Chatelanat, G., 55, 75*n.*
Chaves, J. F., 252, 264*n.*
Checkosky, 89
Chiauzzi, E., 408, 432*n.*
Chinsky, J., 248, 265*n.*, 456, 468, 473*n.*, 474*n.*
Chomsky, N., 85, 119*n.*
Cialdini, R. B., 325, 339*n.*
Ciminero, A. R., 256, 257, 261, 265*n.*, 267*n.*, 409, 438*n.*
Clark, H. H., 39, 49*n.*, 101, 103–105, 117*n.*, 119*n.*, 120*n.*
Clark, J. V., 390, 423, 424, 433*n.*
Clark, L. A., 304, 306*n.*
Clark, M. C., 98, 99, 119*n.*, 120*n.*, 494, 500*n.*
Coates, B., 493, 501*n.*
Cochrane, R., 364, 383*n.*
Cohen, S. I., 134, 148*n.*, 366, 385*n.*
Cole, C. S., 369, 383*n.*
Collins, K. W., 392, 433*n.*
Comstock, C., 27, 49*n.*
Cone, J. D., 130, 146*n.*, 261, 265*n.*, 427, 432*n.*, 433*n.*
Confucius, 57
Connolly, J., 453, 473*n.*
Connor, J. M., 394, 438*n.*
Cook, T. D., 324, 339*n.*
Cooke, C. J., 449, 450*n.*
Cooney, E., 454, 460, 461, 474*n.*
Cooper, B. J., 235, 264*n.*
Corbin, C. B., 447, 450*n.*
Cowan, P., 156, 184*n.*
Coyne, J. C., 366, 369, 383*n.*, 420, 433*n.*
Crager, R. L., 406, 416, 433*n.*
Craig, G., 219, 229*n.*
Craighead, L. W., 398–400, 403, 415, 433*n.*
Craighead, W. E., 95–97, 120*n.*, 122*n.*, 253, 265*n.*, 365, 367, 368, 384*n.*, 386*n.*, 393, 399, 401, 406, 408, 433*n.*
Craik, F. I. M., 93, 94, 97, 98, 120*n.*, 368, 378, 384*n.*, 430, 433*n.*
Craik, K. H., 487, 499*n.*
Cratty, B. J., 441, 451*n.*
Crisp, A. H., 210, 230*n.*
Crocker, J., 105, 106, 123*n.*
Crockett, W., 141, 146*n.*

Croker, W., 384, 383*n*.
Cromwell, R. L., 379, 387*n*.
Cronbach, L. J., 55, 60, 71, 74*n*.
Crookes, T. E., 364, 384*n*.
Cross, D., 260, 269*n*.
Crowne, D. P., 157, 184*n*.
Csikszentimihalyi, M., 10, 14*n.*, 255, 265*n*.
Cullen, D. M., 325, 326, 332, 339*n*.
Cullen, J., 449, 450*n*.
Curran, J. P., 389, 399, 423, 424, 433*n*.

Dahlstrom, L. E., 69, 74*n*.
Dahlstrom, W. G., 69, 74*n*.
Damon, W., 454, 461, 468, 474*n*.
Danaher, B., 159, 184*n*.
Dansereau, D. F., 392, 433*n*.
Darley, C. F., 380, 384*n*.
Darley, J. M., 333, 339*n*.
Darwin, C., 311, 339*n*.
Davids, A., 225, 230*n*.
Davidson, P. O., 394, 437*n*.
Davidson, R., 160, 184*n*.
Davis, H., 60, 95–97, 117*n.*, 120*n.*, 368, 369, 380, 381, 384*n.*, 430, 433*n*.
Davis, R. C., 270, 274, 305*n*.
Davison, G. C., 397, 433*n*.
Dawe, H., 466, 474*n*.
Dawson, G. D., 279, 305*n*.
Deffenbacher, J. L., 389, 390, 392, 434*n*.
Deitz, S., 128, 146*n*.
Delafresnaye, J. F., 270, 305*n*.
DeLoache, J., 11, 13*n*.
Dember, W. M., 361, 384*n*.
DeMonbreun, B. G., 95–97, 120*n.*, 365, 368, 384*n*.
Dempsey, P., 370, 384*n*.
DeNike, L. D., 482, 502*n*.
Denney, D. R., 391, 421, 435*n*.
Dent, C., 466, 474*n*.
Derry, P. A., 96, 121*n.*, 363, 378, 379, 385*n.*, 393, 398, 399, 401, 405, 408, 434*n*.
Diament, C., 252, 266*n*.
Diener, C. O., 493, 499*n*.
Dietz, A., 252, 266*n*.
Diggory, J., 371, 385*n*.
Di Giuseppe, R. A., 324, 339*n*.
Dilling, C. A., 366, 386*n*.
DiLoreto, A. O., 394, 434*n*.
Dingemans, P., 212, 231*n*.
Dintzer, L., 369, 387*n*.
DiVesta, F., 157, 158, 184*n*.
Dixon, N. F., 364, 384*n*.

Dobson, D. J. G., 370, 375–377, 384*n*.
Dobson, K. S., viii, 81, 236, 361–387, 371, 372, 375, 382*n.*, 384*n.*, 425, 483, 492, 494
Docherty, E. M., 129, 148*n*.
Dodge, R., 237, 265*n*.
Dolliver, S., 481, 499*n*.
Donders, 23–25, 28
Dor, A., 456, 473*n*.
Doyle, A., 453, 473*n*.
Draffan, J. W., 218, 231*n*.
Driver, M., 141, 148*n*.
Drost, P. L., 375, 384*n*.
DuBois, P. H., 481, 499*n*.
Duck, S. W., 219, 220, 226, 227, 229*n.*, 231*n*.
Dudek, S. Z., 67, 68, 74*n*.
Duncker, K., 30, 35–38, 49*n*.
Dunlap, K., 271, 306*n*.
Dupue, R. A., 362, 384*n*.
Duval, S., 251, 265*n.*, 269*n*.
Dweck, C. S., 492, 493, 499*n.*, 500*n*.
Dyckman, J., 156, 184*n*.
Dymond, 60
D'Zurilla, T. J., 131*n.*, 135, 147*n.*, 246, 265*n.*, 361, 370, 372, 384*n.*, 395, 434*n*.

Easterbrook, J. A., 92–94, 120*n*.
Ebbesen, E. D., 235, 268*n.*, 482, 491, 493, 501*n*.
Ebbinghaus, 57
Eccles, J. C., 270, 306*n*.
Edelstein, B. A., 394, 434*n*.
Edfeldt, A. W., 277, 306*n*.
Edwards, N. B., 367, 383*n*.
Edwards, W., 417, 434*n*.
Edwin, D., 399, 418, 421, 435*n*.
Eindhoven, J. E., 32, 49*n*.
Eisler, R. M., 418–420, 434*n*.
Ekman, P., 3, 14*n*.
Eland, F. A., 211, 229*n*.
Elder, J. P., 394, 434*n*.
Elias, M., 456–459, 461, 468, 469, 471, 473*n*.
Ellis, A., 236, 242, 265*n.*, 309, 323, 324, 339*n.*, 374, 384*n.*, 389, 398, 403, 434*n*.
Ellman, S., 166, 171, 184*n*.
Ellsworth, P., 3, 14*n*.
Emery, G., 258, 264*n.*, 374, 382, 383*n*.
Endler, N. S., 61, 376, 384*n.*, 441, 450*n*.
Engel, B. T., 331, 339*n*.

English, H. B., 23, 49n.
Enright, N., 456, 457, 473n.
Enright, R., 456, 457, 460, 461, 473n.
Epstein, M. L., viii, 239, 439–451, 483, 486
Epstein, S., 139, 145, 146n., 376, 384n., 441, 444–449, 450n.
Epting, F. R., 194, 203, 211, 212, 222, 225, 229n.–232n.
Erbaugh, J., 364, 383n.
Erickson, M. T., 243, 269n.
Erickson, R. C., 366, 384n.
Ericsson, K. A., viii, 5–7, 13n., 16–51, 18, 32–34, 36, 39, 44, 48, 48n., 49n., 81, 83, 237, 239, 243, 247, 261, 263n., 497
Eriksen, C., 12, 14n., 34, 49n.
Ernest, C., 153, 157–159, 184n.
Ervin-Tripp, S., 454, 474n.
Evans, I., 468, 474n.
Ewart, C. K., 256, 265n.
Eysenck, M. W., 60, 94, 120n.

Faaborg-Anderson, K., 277, 306n.
Fair, P. L., 295, 307n., 311, 342n.
Fairbairn, G., 220, 232n.
Fazio, R. H., 46, 49n.
Fedoravicius, A., 393, 437n.
Feffer, M., 141, 142, 146n.
Feighner, J. P., 362, 370, 384n.
Fein, G., 166, 184n.
Feldman, M. M., 194, 230n.
Fenz, W. D., 444–446, 450n.
Ferguson, J. D., 251, 269n.
Feuerstein, R., 61, 71, 74n.
Fiedler, D., 417, 418, 428, 429, 434n.
Filler, J. W., 55, 75n.
Finger, R., 392, 434n.
Finkel, C. B., 96, 97, 117n.
Finkelstein, N., 466, 474n.
Finn, M. E., 392, 436n.
Fischer, C. T., 130, 146n.
Fischetti, M., 399, 423, 433n.
Fischhoff, B., 73, 76n.
Fishbein, M., 46, 49n., 325, 339n.
Fisher, A. C., 441, 450n.
Fiske, D. W., 7, 14n., 41, 43, 49n., 60
Fiske, S. T., 46, 50n.
Fitch, G., 369, 384n.
Flavell, J. H., 11, 14n., 89, 113, 114, 141, 143, 147n., 248, 265n., 430, 432n., 453, 461, 469, 473n., 482, 500n.
Fleisher, S., 254, 265n.
Fodor, I. G., 394, 400, 403, 414, 431n., 438n.

Fogarty, S. J., 99, 117n., 123n., 380, 386n.
Folkman, S., 420, 421, 427, 434n., 436n.
Follick, M., 135, 148n.
Forgus, R., 140, 147n.
Foster, S. L., 252, 266n., 355, 356n.
Foulkes, D., 170, 184n., 254, 265n.
Frank, 59
Franks, J. J., 94, 97, 102, 119n., 121n.
Fransella, F., 189, 194, 207, 209, 210, 214, 217, 221, 227, 228, 229n., 230n.
Frederiksen, L. W., 418, 434n.
Freisen, W., 3, 14n.
Fremouw, W. J., 393, 394, 396, 434n.
Freud, S., 58, 78, 244, 333, 480
Friedman, B., 400, 402, 437n.
Friend, R., 335, 342n., 409, 411, 438n.
Frierson, H. T., 405, 434n.
Froming, W. J., 494, 502n.
Fulkerson, S., 133, 147n.
Fusella, V. J., 158, 185n.

Gagne, R. H., 237, 265n.
Galassi, J. P., 390, 392, 405, 410, 426, 434n.
Galassi, M. D., 309, 342n., 390, 426, 434n.
Gall, 57
Gallacher, K., 466, 474n.
Galperin, P. Y., 271, 306n.
Galton, 57, 62
Garafolo, L., 270, 305n.
Garber, J., 367, 383n.
Gardner, R. W., 141, 147n.
Garland, J. C., 392, 433n.
Garner, W. R., 12, 14n., 81, 120n.
Garvey, C., 454, 467, 475n.
Gatchel, R. J., 304, 306n.
Gault, F. P., 270, 305n.
Geller, V., 313, 339n.
Gellhorn, E., 297, 306n.
Genest, M., vii–ix, 4, 5, 15n., 233–269, 244, 246, 251, 260, 263n., 265n., 417, 480, 483, 494
Genshaft, J., 67, 73, 75n.
Geraci, R., 456, 473n.
Gergen, D. J., 319, 337n.
Getter, H., 421, 422, 432n., 434n.
Geva, H., 312, 340n.
Gewirtz, J. L., 490, 500n.
Gibbs, M., 319, 337n.
Gibson, E. J., 143, 147n.
Giles, D. E., 371, 372, 377, 378, 382n.
Gilligan, S. G., 97, 119n., 363, 383n.
Gilmore, J. B., 393, 437n.
Glas, R. A., 254, 264n., 448, 450n.

Glasgow, R. E., 246, 265n., 423, 424, 434n.
Glass, C. R., vii–ix, 77–124, 96, 106, 117n.,
    237, 246, 265n., 319, 320, 325, 335,
    337, 338n., 339n., 345, 356n.,
    388–438, 390, 394, 395, 399, 405, 406,
    409, 412–414, 423, 430, 431n.–434n.,
    483, 494, 497
Glass, G. V., 395, 431n.
Glass, R. M., 369, 384n.
Glazeski, R. C., 260, 266n., 405, 410, 432n.,
    435n.
Gleser, G., 60, 61, 152, 155, 162, 171, 185n.
Glogower, F. D., 393, 396, 434n.
Goethe, K. E., 395, 438n.
Goetz, C., 364, 386n.
Goldberg, L. R., 55, 74n., 481, 500n.
Goldberg, S., 453, 475n.
Golden, C. J., 66, 74n.
Goldfoot, N. A., 235, 266n.
Goldfried, A. P., 242, 265n., 394, 436n.
Goldfried, M. R., 67, 74n., 89, 90, 120n.,
    130, 131n., 135, 147n., 242, 246,
    265n., 361, 370, 372, 384n., 392, 394,
    395, 398–401, 407, 415, 429, 434n.–
    436n., 438n.
Goldman, B., 466, 474n.
Goldstein, A. P., 236, 266n.
Goldstein, K. M., 65, 66, 70, 74n., 141,
    147n.,
Golin, S., 375, 384n.,
Gonso, J., 460, 474n.
Gonzales, L. R., 64, 76n.
Goodenough, 58
Goodman, S. H., 4, 14n., 249, 251, 253,
    254, 264n., 265n., 268n.
Goodnow, J. J., 64, 75n.
Goor, A., 253, 265n., 315, 318, 339n.
Gordon, J. R., 257, 267n.
Gordon, R., 157, 185n.
Gormally, J., 394, 398, 399, 418, 419, 435n.
Gotlib, I. H., 371, 372, 384n.
Gottman, J., 108, 121n., 246, 261, 265n.,
    269n., 319, 327, 339n., 343, 345, 352,
    356n., 390, 391, 394, 404, 405, 407–
    409, 434n., 438n., 460, 465–467,
    469, 474n., 475n.
Gottschalk, L., 152, 155, 162, 171, 185n.
Gough, H., 60, 69, 75n.
Graham, L. E., 404, 435n.
Grange, H., 440
Grantham, D. W., 91, 123n.
Graves, J., 333, 339n.
Gray, W., 487, 501n.

Greenberg, S., 254, 264n.
Greene, P. A., 96, 120n.
Greenspoon, J., 33, 34, 49n.
Greenwald, A. G., 309, 315, 316, 319–321,
    325, 339n.
Griffith, C. R., 439, 440
Grossberg, J., 160, 185n.
Grusec, J., 485, 490, 500n., 501n.
Gruson, L., 4, 11, 13n., 14n., 113, 120n.
Gudeman, H., 67, 76n.
Guilford, J. P., 60, 63, 64, 75n.
Gulliksen, 60
Gur, R. C., 446, 451n.
Guthrie, J. A., 227, 229n.
Guze, S. B., 362, 384n.

Haan, N., 137, 147n.
Haber, R., 166, 185n.
Haggard, E. A., 311, 339n.
Hahn, K., 160, 184n.
Hahnloser, R. M., 392, 434n.
Hake, H., 12, 14n.
Haley, J., 218, 229n.
Hall, C. S., 152, 155, 162, 171, 185n.
Hall, K. R. L., 364, 384n.
Halstead, 59
Hamill, R., 106, 117n., 118n.
Hamilton, J. L., 71, 74n.
Hammen, C. L., 4, 14n., 364, 365, 373, 376,
    380, 381, 384n., 385n.
Hanawalt, N. G., 36, 49n.
Hansen, R., 466, 474n.
Hanson, T. R., 405, 408, 431n.
Harkins, S. G., 319, 333, 338n., 341n.
Harley, J., 250, 265n.
Harnick, F., 452, 476n.
Harre, R., 189, 230n.
Harrell, T. H., 405, 436n.
Harris, D., 441, 451n.
Harrow, M., 67, 68, 75n.
Harter, S., 143, 147n.
Hartford, R. A., 272, 306n.
Hartshorne, 58
Hase, H. D., 481, 500n.
Hathaway, 59
Haviland, S. E., 101, 103, 120n.
Hawkins, R. P., 130, 146n., 261, 265n.,
    427, 433n.
Hay, D., 466, 474n.
Hayden, B., 225, 230n.
Haynes, E. T., 218, 219, 230n.
Haynes, S. N., 355, 356n.
Hays, C. H., 212, 230n.

Haywood, H. C., 55, 71, 75n.
Heather, B. B., 218, 231n.
Hebb, D. O., 270, 291, 306n.
Heesacker, M., 325, 341n.
Hefferline, R. F., 272, 306n.
Heffner, M., 310, 338n.
Heimberg, R. G., 408, 420, 432n.
Helbock, H., 30, 50n.
Hemphill, R. E., 364, 384n.
Henehan, P., 106, 118n.
Henshaw, D., 4, 14n., 237, 251, 253, 254, 266n., 268n., 318, 340n., 404, 435n.
Herman, C. P., 325, 339n.
Hernández-Peón, R., 293, 306n.
Hersen, M., 243, 246, 261, 264n.
Herzof, N., 404, 435n.
Hickey, K. S., 365, 384n.
Hilbert, N., 369, 385n.
Hilgard, E. R., 52, 75n., 243, 266n., 481, 500n.
Hillix, W. A., 35, 26, 50n.
Hillman, E. C., Jr., 301, 306n.
Himel, N., 4, 14n., 237, 251, 268n., 318, 340n.
Hinkle, D., 209, 210, 226, 227, 228n.
Hirst, W., 91, 123n.
Hirt, M., 67, 73, 75n.
Hiscock, M., 156, 158, 185n.
Hjertholm, E., 253, 267n.
Hogan, R. M., 380, 385n.
Hokanson, J. E., 371, 386n.
Hollandsworth, J. G., Jr., 260, 266n., 392, 405, 410, 414, 432n., 437n., 436n.
Holley, C. D., 392, 433n.
Hollon, S. D., 5, 14n., 374, 395n., 404, 435n.
Holmberg, M., 466, 467, 474n.
Holmen, M. L., 247, 267n.
Holmes, D. S., 481, 500n.
Holmes, T. H., 364, 385n.
Holroyd, K. A., 392, 423, 425, 435n.
Holsti, O., 162, 171, 185n.
Holt, E. B., 271, 306n.
Holt, R. R., 68, 75n., 150, 185n.
Holtzman, W. H., 68, 75n.
Honess, T., 224, 225, 230n.
Honikman, B., 211, 230n.
Hoosain, R., 290, 307n.
Horn, J. L., 63, 64, 75n., 76n.
Hornby, P. A., 102, 120n.
Horowitz, M. J., 250, 255, 266n.
Houston, B. K., 391, 421, 435n.
Hovland, C. I., 309, 310, 339n.

Huarte, J., 57
Hull, C. L., 32, 33, 49n., 289, 306n.
Hume, D., 240, 266n.
Humphrey, G., 27, 49n.
Humphrey, N., 453, 454, 475n.
Hunt, 61
Hunter, W. S., 271, 306n.
Hurlburt, R. T., 239, 243, 254–256, 266n., 314, 339n., 407, 416, 435n.
Hurley, A. D., 165, 185n.
Hussian, R. A., 392, 435n.
Hutchings, D. F., 391, 421, 435n.

Ianni, L. E., 219, 231n.
Ingersoll, G., 157, 184n.
Ingham, A. G., 333, 339n.
Insko, C. A., 317, 321, 324, 325, 338n., 339n.
Isen, A. M., 99, 120n., 494, 500n.
Issacs, F. S., 311, 339n.
Izard, C., 3, 14n.

Jaccard, J. J., 325, 339n.
Jacklin, C., 466, 475n.
Jackson, B., 392, 436n.
Jackson, D. N., 55, 58, 73, 75n., 218, 229n.
Jackson, K. M., 310, 338n.
Jacobson, E., 160, 185n., 270, 271, 273, 274, 296, 299, 301, 303, 304, 305n., 306n.
Jakubowski, P., 391, 436n.
James, W., 21, 49n.
Janis, I. L., 309, 321, 323, 339n., 340n.
Jaremko, M. E., 393, 417, 418, 431n.
Jarvik, M. E., 369, 386n.
Jeffrey, T., 159, 187n.
Jensen, A. R., 63, 75n.
Jessup, B. A., 369, 384n.
Johnson, D., 489, 503n.
Johnson, M. K., 102, 119n., 120n.
Johnson, M. P., 41, 46, 50n.
Johnson, S. C., 106, 120n.
Johnson, S. M., 252, 266n.
Jones, B., 251, 269n.
Jones, E. E., 369, 386n.
Jones, G. E., 260, 266n., 405, 410, 432n., 435n.
Jones, N. B., 466, 475n.
Jones, R. G., 374, 385n., 395, 398, 399, 401, 435n.
Jones, R. R., 252, 266n.
Jordan, L., 166, 184n.
Jouvert, M., 293, 306n.

Joyce, J., 248, 266*n.*
Jung, C., 58, 67
Jung, J., 83, 120*n.*
Just, M. A., 101, 119*n.*

Kagan, N., 413, 435*n.*
Kahn, R. L., 43, 49*n.*, 371, 387*n.*
Kahneman, D., 91–93, 120*n.*, 252, 269*n.*
Kallman, W. M., 395, 438*n.*
Kamiya, J., 182, 187*n.*
Kane, J. E., 442, 443, 450*n.*
Kanfer, F. H., 61, 235, 236, 266*n.*, 430,
    435*n.*, 491, 493, 500*n.*
Kanner, A. D., 427, 436*n.*
Kanter, N. J., 394, 399, 401, 435*n.*
Kaplan, B., 38, 51*n.*, 134, 148*n.*
Kaplan, R. M., 392, 436*n.*
Karoly, P., 430, 435*n.*
Karp, L., 99, 120*n.*, 494, 500*n.*
Karst, T. O., 393, 399, 401, 435*n.*, 438*n.*
Kassinove, H., 394, 438*n.*
Katona, G., 35, 46, 49*n.*, 50*n.*
Kazdin, A. E., 78, 121*n.*, 152, 156, 164, 166,
    167, 185*n.*, 254, 266*n.*, 394, 435*n.*
Keane, T. M., 405, 411, 435*n.*
Keefe, J. A., 65, 75*n.*
Keenan, B., 272, 306*n.*
Keller, J. W., 56, 75*n.*
Kelley, H. H., 309, 339*n.*
Kelley, E. L., 488, 498, 500*n.*
Kelly, G. A., 60, 65, 66, 75*n.*, 105, 120*n.*,
    188–193, 197, 200, 201, 203, 209,
    212–215, 218, 219, 224, 226, 227,
    230*n.*, 430, 435*n.*, 486, 490, 500*n.*
Kendall, P. C., 5, 14*n.*, 71, 75*n.*, 144, 146,
    147*n.*, 246, 266*n.*, 310, 340*n.*, 343,
    356*n.*, 374, 382*n.*, 398, 404, 435*n.*
Kendler, H., 239, 266*n.*
Kendler, T., 239, 266*n.*
Kent, R. N., 130, 147*n.*, 252, 266*n.*, 268*n.*,
    355, 356*n.*
Kiely, W. F., 297, 306*n.*
Kieras, D., 161, 162, 185*n.*
Kiesler, D., 129, 135, 147*n.*
Kimball, W. H., 253, 265*n.*, 367, 384*n.*, 399,
    400, 406, 433*n.*
King, B. T., 321, 339*n.*
Kintsch, W., 100, 120*n.*, 380, 385*n.*
Kirker, W. S., 95, 122*n.*, 312, 341*n.*
Kirkland, K., 260, 266*n.*, 392, 405, 410,
    435*n.*, 436*n.*
Klatzky, R. L., 368, 385*n.*
Klein, K., 95, 120*n.*

Kleitman, N., 254, 264*n.*
Klerman, G. L., 295, 307*n.*, 311, 342*n.*
Klinger, E., 150–152, 154, 155, 166, 168,
    172, 185*n.*, 246, 249, 250, 254, 258–
    260, 264*n.*, 266*n.*, 416, 427, 436*n.*,
    448, 450*n.*
Knutson, J., 131, 147*n.*
Kohlberg, L., 70, 253, 267*n.*
Köhler, W., 35, 50*n.*
Kohn, M., 452, 455*n.*
Korgeski, G. P., 71, 75*n.*, 144, 146, 147*n.*,
    246, 266*n.*, 310, 340*n.*, 343, 356*n.*,
    398, 435*n.*
Korman, M., 304, 306*n.*
Kosslyn, S., 149, 185*n.*
Kovacs, M., 257, 264*n.*, 367, 383*n.*
Kozak, M., 161, 183*n.*
Kozlowski, L. T., 325, 339*n.*
Kramer, S. R., 395, 399, 401, 436*n.*
Krantz, S., 365, 373, 384*n.*, 385*n.*
Krasnor, L. R., viii, 420, 452–476, 466, 471,
    473*n.*, 483, 486
Krathwohl, D. R., 413, 435*n.*
Krieger, S. R., 194, 212, 230*n.*
Kroll, W., 439, 441, 450*n.*, 451*n.*
Krumm, H., 372, 382*n.*
Kruskal, J., 106, 118*n.*
Kubie, L. S., 249, 267*n.*
Kuhn, T. S., 77, 82, 120*n.*, 189, 230*n.*, 238,
    267*n.*, 380, 385*n.*
Kuiper, N. A., 95–97, 121*n.*, 122*n.*, 312,
    341*n.*, 363, 369, 378–380, 385*n.*,
    488, 501*n.*
Külpe, 26, 27, 237
Kummer, H., 454, 475*n.*
Kuperminc, M., 420, 432*n.*
Kutner, B., 46, 50*n.*

Labov, W., 39, 50*n.*
Lacey, B. C., 270, 306*n.*
Lacey, J. I., 270, 306*n.*
Lachman, J. L., 77, 121*n.*
Lachman, R., 77, 78, 80–84, 86, 91, 93, 100,
    101, 103, 104, 121*n.*, 122*n.*, 381,
    385*n.*
Ladd, G., 459, 475*n.*
Lakoff, R., 102, 121*n.*
Lammars, B., 332, 340*n.*
Landfield, A. W., 201–203, 211, 220, 222,
    226, 227, 230*n.*, 231*n.*
Lang, P., 151, 154, 161, 163–165, 167, 169,
    172, 175, 181, 182, 183*n.*, 185*n.*, 241,
    267*n.*

Lange, A., 391, 436n.
Langer, E., 8, 14n., 251, 267n., 454, 461, 469, 475n.
Langfeld, H. S., 270, 271, 306n.
La Piere, R. T., 45, 46, 50n.
LaPointe, K. A., 405, 436n.
LaPorte, R. E., 111, 121n.
Larcen, S., 456, 468, 473n., 474n.
Larsen, K. H., 246, 263n., 399, 405, 423, 434n.
Larson, R., 255, 265n.
Lasswell, H. D., 322, 340n.
Latané, B., 333, 340n., 341n.
Laughery, K. R., 381, 385n.
Lavelle, D., 202, 228n.
Lawrence, P. S., 392, 435n.
Laws, D. R., 247, 267n.
Lazar, B. S., 67, 68, 75n.
Lazar, Z., 73, 76n.
Lazarus, R. S., 34, 50n., 135, 145, 147n., 234, 242, 267n., 319, 340n., 389, 420, 421, 427, 428, 433n., 434n., 436n.
Lazovik, A., 241, 267n.
Lea, M., 219, 231n.
Leakey, R., 454, 475n.
Lear, T. E., 364, 384n.
Ledwidge, B., 78, 121n.
Lee, L., 466, 475n.
Leippe, M. R., 312, 340n.
Leitner, L., 194, 202, 203, 212, 222, 230n.
Lemon, N., 194, 231n.
Leontiev, A. N., 271, 307n.
Lesgold, H. M., 98, 119n.
Lester, D., 366, 383n.
Levenson, R. W., 108, 121n.
Levin, A., 323, 337n.
Levin, D., 161, 183n.
Levin, E., 467, 475n.
Levine, H. M., 246, 263n.
Levinger, G., 333, 339n.
Levy, R., 369, 385n.
Lewin, R., 454, 475n.
Lewinsohn, P. M., 97, 121n., 364, 382n., 385n.
Lewis, G., 439, 450n.
Lewis, P., 369, 375, 385n.
Lezak, M. D., 66, 75n.
Lichtenstein, S., 73, 76n.
Lieberman, D. A., 243, 246, 247, 267n.
Liebert, R. M., 389, 436n., 491, 501n.
Lief, J., 111, 118n.
Lifshitz, M., 225, 231n.
Likert, R., 159, 185n., 332

Liles, L., 449, 450n.
Lillesand, D. B., 419, 436n.
Linde, C., 39, 50n.
Lindsay, P. H., 278, 307n.
Lindsley, D. B., 274, 307n.
Lindzey, G., 481, 500n.
Linehan, M. M., 262, 267n., 392, 394, 404, 434n.–436n.
Lingle, J. H., 312, 340n.
Lipinski, D. P., 256, 267n.
Lippold, O. C. J., 274, 307n.
Lishman, W. A., 368, 385n.
Lisman, S. A., 405, 411, 435n.
Little, B., 65, 73n.
Little, S., 392, 436n.
Lloyd, G. G., 368, 385n.
Lobitz, W. C., 364, 385n.
Lochman, J., 468, 474n.
Locke, E. A., 78, 121n.
Lockhart, R. S., 93, 94, 97, 120n., 368, 378, 384n.
Loeb, A., 371, 377, 385n.
Loevinger, J., 70
Lohr, J. M., 399–401, 403, 431n., 436n.
Love, R., 311, 340n.
Lubin, B., 56, 75n.
Lubin, D., 466, 467, 471, 474n.
Lucas, J., 115, 116, 118n., 406, 413, 414, 421, 432n.
Lucy, P., 103, 120n.
Lumsdaine, A. A., 309, 339n.
Lunghi, E., 365, 385n.
Luria, A. R., 494, 500n.
Lynne, A., 174, 184n.

Maccoby, E., 466, 475n.
Maccoby, N., 315, 317, 321, 324, 325, 341n.
MacCorquodale, K., 290, 307n.
MacCrimmon, D. J., 91, 117n.
Madrazo-Peterson, R., 408, 432n.
Magaro, P. A., 65, 75n.
Magnussen, D., 376, 384n., 441, 450n.
Mahoney, M. J., viii, 3, 14n., 78, 121n., 127, 131, 139, 141, 147n., 188, 234, 236, 239, 242, 256, 267n., 269n., 361, 385n., 398, 426, 430, 436n., 439–451, 440, 444, 445, 448, 450n., 483, 486, 493, 500n.
Mair, J. M. M., 194, 214, 226, 228, 229n., 231n.
Malklewich, L. E., 395, 406, 413, 436n.
Mancuso, J. C., 224, 231n.
Mandel, M. R., 295, 307n., 311, 342n.

Mandler, G., 9, 14n.
Mann, D. C., 244, 265n.
Mann, L., 323, 340n.
Mann, R., 251, 260, 263n.
Markman, H. J., 345, 352, 356n.
Marks, D., 153, 156, 159, 160, 186n.
Markus, H., 105, 106, 121n., 312, 329,
    340n., 488, 500n.
Marlatt, G. A., 4, 14n., 257, 267n.
Marler, M., 94, 122n.
Marlowe, D., 157, 184n.
Marsden, J., 162, 171, 186n.
Marston, A. R., 395, 237n., 493, 500n.
Martens, R., 441–443, 446, 450n.
Martin, R., 253, 264n.
Martorano, R. P., 394, 437n.
Marx, M. H., 35, 36, 50n.
Marzillier, J., 156, 186n.
Mash, E. J., 130, 147n., 252, 267n.
Mason, J., 3, 14n.
Masters, J. C., 493, 500n.
Matarazzo, J. D., 55, 75n.
Mathews, A., 182, 186n.
Matthews, B. H. C., 274, 305n.
Matthyse, S., 379, 387n.
Maultsby, M. C., Jr., 323, 324, 340n.
Max, L. W., 274, 307n.
Maxreiner, M. E., 258, 264n.
Maxwell, A. E., 369, 385n.
May, R. L., 58, 392, 436n.
Mayzner, M. S., 30, 50n.
McArthur, C., 481, 500n.
McCabe, S. P., 54, 73n.
McCarrell, N. S., 102, 119n.
McCarthy, B., 219, 231n.
McCleary, R. A., 34, 50n.
McConkey, K. M., 260, 269n.
McCordick, S. M., 392, 436n.
McCoy, M. M., 214, 215, 228n., 231n.
McCroskey, J. C., 393, 396, 434n.
McCullough, L., 153, 165, 184n.
McDonald, B. A., 392, 433n.
McDougall, 57
McElwee, J. D., 252, 267n.
McFall, R. M., 256, 261, 267n., 269n., 409,
    419, 436n., 438n.
McFayden, M., 218, 231n.
McGuigan, F. J., viii, 160, 167, 185n.,
    186n., 270–308, 271, 275, 277, 283,
    287, 290, 291, 294–296, 300, 304, 305,
    307n., 312, 340n., 483
McGuire, J. M., 56, 74n.
McGuire, W. J, 314, 322, 324, 340n.

McKellar, P., 150, 186n.
McKinley, 59
McLean, A., 161, 183n.
McLemore, C. W., 156, 158, 159, 186n.
McPeek, R. W., 319, 340n.
McPherson, F. M., 218, 231n.
McReynolds, P., 55–57, 61, 75n.
Meehl, P. E., 60, 73, 75n., 290, 307n.
Meichenbaum, D., viii, 3–15, 4–6, 8, 10–12,
    13n.–15n., 71, 78, 89, 113, 116, 121n.,
    130, 135, 139, 144, 147n., 236, 237,
    243, 245n., 246n., 248, 249, 251, 253,
    260, 261, 263n., 267n., 268n., 309,
    314, 318, 326, 327, 340n., 389, 392,
    393, 398, 428–430, 436n., 437n., 483,
    494, 500n.
Meikle, S., 405, 407, 437n.
Melei, J. P., 481, 500n.
Melges, F. T., 366, 385n.
Melnick, J., 394, 437n.
Meltzer, S. S., 366, 382n.
Mendels, J., 364, 386n.
Mendelson, M., 364, 383n.
Merluzzi, T. V., vii–ix, 77–124, 89, 96, 106,
    112, 117n., 118n., 219, 228n., 235–
    237, 319, 320, 325, 338n., 345, 356n.,
    388–438, 390, 395, 399, 405, 406, 409,
    412, 413, 423, 429, 430, 431n.–434n.,
    436n., 483, 494, 497
Merrill, L., 490, 499n.
Mervis, C., 487, 501n.
Messick, S., 61, 452, 474n.
Meyers, A. W., 449, 450n.
Mezey, A. G., 366, 385n.
Mieske, M., 295, 307n.
Miller, D. T., 363, 366, 369, 371, 385n.
Miller, E., 369, 375, 385n., 480, 502n.
Miller, F. D., 5, 12, 14n., 45, 50n., 239,
    241, 269n.
Miller, G. A., 121n., 161, 168, 183n., 186n.
Miller, N., 316, 318, 323, 324, 339n., 340n.
Miller, S., 90, 121n.
Miller, W. R., 362, 385n., 390, 423, 424,
    437n.
Minkoff, K., 366, 386n.
Mirels, H. L., 319, 340n.
Mischel, H. N., 115, 118n., 494, 495, 498n.
Mischel, W., viii, 41, 43, 44, 50n., 61, 73,
    75n., 97, 114, 115, 118n., 121n.,
    128–130, 133, 145, 147n., 189, 231n.,
    235, 242, 243, 247, 262, 263n., 268n.,
    312, 329, 338n., 364, 381, 385n.,
    386n., 430, 437n., 441, 443, 450n.,

479–502, 480–485, 487–491, 493–495, 497, 498*n*.–501*n*.
Mitchell, S. K., 355, 356*n*.
Mock, J., 364, 383*n*.
Mokros, J. R., 493, 500*n*.
Monroe, S. M., 362, 384*n*.
Montgomery, A. G., 392, 437*n*.
Montiero, K. P., 363, 383*n*.
Monyak, N., 314, 341*n*.
Moore, B. S., 235, 268*n*., 263*n*., 491, 494, 501*n*., 502*n*.
Moore, M. S., 245, 268*n*.
Moos, R., 142, 147*n*.
Morelli, G., 400, 402, 437*n*.
Morgan, W. P., 442, 443, 450*n*.
Morris, C. D., 94, 97, 119*n*., 121*n*.
Morris, L. W., 389, 436*n*.
Mueller, J. H., 93–95, 98, 99, 115, 121*n*., 122*n*.
Mummery, D. V., 470, 475*n*.
Muñoz, R., 362, 364, 382*n*., 384*n*.
Murdock, B. B., 380, 384*n*.
Murphy, L., 466, 475*n*.
Murray, J., 59, 253, 264*n*.
Murstein, B., 128, 147*n*.

Nasby, W., 225, 230*n*.
Neimeyer, G. J., viii, 105, 188–232, 211, 219, 221, 228*n*., 231*n*., 430, 486
Neimeyer, R. A., viii, 105, 188–232, 212, 219–221, 226, 231*n*., 232*n*., 430, 486
Neisser, U., 91, 123*n*., 150, 151, 163, 167, 186*n*., 329, 340*n*., 361, 363, 386*n*., 483, 501*n*.
Nelson, R. E., 95, 97, 122*n*., 365, 374, 386*n*.
Nelson, R. O., 246, 256, 257, 267*n*., 268*n*., 270, 276*n*.
Neufeld, R. W. J., 380, 383*n*.
Newell, A., 17–19, 36–38, 48*n*., 50*n*., 81, 122*n*., 416, 437*n*.
Newell, H., 468, 469, 475*n*.
Newland, J., 156, 186*n*.
Nideffer, R. M., 447, 451*n*.
Niederehe, G., 369, 385*n*.
Nietzel, M. T., 394, 437*n*.
Nisbett, R. E., 5, 14*n*., 41, 44, 45, 50*n*., 237–241, 252, 268*n*., 269*n*., 315, 340*n*., 341*n*., 446, 451*n*., 480, 482, 488, 501*n*.
Noppe, L. D., 65, 75*n*.
Norman, D. A., 278, 307*n*., 369, 386*n*.
Norman, W. H., 393, 437*n*.
Northrop, F. S. C., 291, 307*n*.

Notarius, C. I., viii, 226, 227, 254, 339*n*., 343–357, 345, 352, 356*n*., 429
Novaco, R., 4, 14*n*.
Novotny, G. E. K., 274, 307*n*.
Nowinski, J. K., 421, 422, 432*n*., 434*n*.

O'Banion, K., 390, 421, 424, 437*n*.
Observer, 78, 89, 122*n*.
Oden, S., 459, 475*n*.
Offer, V., 174, 184*n*.
Ogilvie, B. C., 441, 451*n*.
O'Leary, K. D., 252, 254, 266*n*., 268*n*., 494, 501*n*.
O'Leary, S. G., 254, 268*n*.
Oliveri, M., 452, 476*n*.
Olson, D., 64, 75*n*.
Olson, S. R., 41, 50*n*.
Oltmanns, T., 91, 92, 122*n*.
O'Malley, J. M., 452, 475*n*.
Opton, E. M., Jr., 234, 267*n*.
O'Reilly, J., 224, 231*n*.
Orley, J., 194, 231*n*.
Ortony, A., 102, 118*n*.
Osarchuk, M., 393, 437*n*.
Osgood, C. E., 39, 50*n*., 60, 290, 307*n*.
Osterhouse, R. A., 316, 341*n*., 389, 437*n*.
Ostrom, T. M., 310, 312, 340*n*., 341*n*.

Pachella, R. G., 87, 89, 122*n*.
Padawer-Singer, A., 314, 324, 340*n*.
Page, M., 202, 211, 228*n*.
Paige, A. B., 366, 384*n*.
Paine, C., 56, 75*n*.
Paivio, A., 153, 158, 159, 184*n*., 186*n*., 362, 381, 386*n*.
Pankratz, L. D., 55, 75*n*.
Papageorgis, D., 322, 340*n*.
Parkhurst, J., 465, 466, 469, 475*n*.
Patterson, C. J., 235, 268*n*., 494, 501*n*.
Patterson, G., 252, 266*n*., 466, 475*n*., 497, 501*n*.
Patton, E. F., 32, 50*n*.
Paunonen, S. V., 55, 58, 73, 75*n*.
Pavek, G. V., 277, 292, 307*n*.
Pavlov, I. P., 271, 307*n*., 495
Pechacek, T. F., 404, 435*n*.
Peck, V., 115, 118*n*.
Peckham, V., 333, 339*n*.
Penfield, W., 291, 307*n*.
Pepler, D. J., 461, 474*n*.
Perloff, B., 491, 499*n*.
Peterman, J. N., III, 311, 315, 341*n*.
Peterson, D. R., 481, 501*n*.

Peterson, G. L., 418, 434*n.*
Peterson, L. R., 83, 122*n.*
Peterson, M. J., 83, 122*n.*
Petty, R. E., viii, 215, 237, 295, 296, 305*n.*,
    309–342, 310, 311, 313, 315–319,
    325–327, 329, 330, 332–335, 337*n.*,
    339*n.*, 341*n.*, 346, 412, 483, 494
Phares, E. J., 489, 502*n.*
Pharr, D. R., 394, 438*n.*
Phillips, J. P. N., 218, 219, 230*n.*
Phillips, J. S., 493, 500*n.*
Phillips, L., 165, 186*n.*, 485, 502*n.*
Piaget, J., 58, 71, 140, 142, 249, 268*n.*, 454,
    475*n.*
Picasso, P., 54
Piotrowski, C., 56, 75*n.*
Pitcher, S. W., 405, 407, 437*n.*
Platt, J., 139, 148*n.*, 371, 386*n.*, 419, 438*n.*,
    454, 476*n.*
Polanyi, M., 238, 268*n.*
Pollack, P. R., 494, 502*n.*
Pollock, J., 54
Pomerantz, J., 149, 185*n.*
Pope, K. S., 149, 187*n.*, 236, 250, 251, 257,
    268*n.*
Posner, M. I., 53, 54, 72, 76*n.*
Post, R. D., 364, 366, 384*n.*, 385*n.*
Posthuma, A., 223, 229*n.*
Prescott, S., 255, 265*n.*
Psotka, J., 98, 123*n.*
Putallaz, M., 466, 467, 475*n.*
Pylyshyn, Z., 149, 161, 162, 186*n.*
Pythagorus, 57

Quasha, W., 159, 185*n.*
Quetelet, 57
Quinatar, L. R., 314, 329, 337*n.*, 341*n.*

Rabin, A. I., 366, 386*n.*
Radley, A., 193*n.*, 227, 232*n.*
Radtke-Bodorik, H. L., 251, 269*n.*
Rahe, R. H., 364, 385*n.*
Rainey, L. C., 212, 232*n.*
Rakos, R. F., 394, 400, 402, 437*n.*
Raney, C., 468, 476*n.*
Rapaport, 60
Raphael, R., 394, 398, 399, 418, 421, 435*n.*
Raskoff, A., 493, 501*n.*
Rasmussen, B., 460, 474*n.*
Raush, H. L., 343, 357*n.*
Ravenette, A. T., 215, 224, 232*n.*
Rawlings, E., 158, 186*n.*
Rawlings, I., 158, 186*n.*

Rechtschaffen, A., 162, 170, 184*n.*, 186*n.*
Reder, L. M., 98, 118*n.*
Reese, H. W., 315, 341*n.*
Rehak, P. J., 253, 265*n.*, 367, 384*n.*, 399,
    400, 406, 433*n.*
Rehm, L. P., 95, 123*n.*, 159, 186*n.*, 365,
    368, 387*n.*, 395, 437*n.*
Reichenbach, H., 291, 307*n.*
Reitan, R. M., 66, 76*n.*
Renshaw, P., 456, 473*n.*
Resnick, L. B., 56, 62, 76*n.*
Reynolds, W. M., 56, 76*n.*
Rhyne, L. D., 405, 408, 431*n.*
Rich, A. R., 405, 431*n.*
Richardson, A., 154, 156–158, 186*n.*, 447,
    451*n.*
Ried, J. B., 252, 266*n.*
Riedel, W., 220, 226, 232*n.*
Rimm, D., 159, 186*n.*
Rippere, V., 373, 386*n.*
Rivers, 57
Rizley, R., 369, 386*n.*
Roberts, D. F., 315, 321, 317, 324, 325,
    341*n.*
Robertson, A., 364, 383*n.*
Robins, E., 362, 384*n.*
Rockne, K., 439
Rogers, C., 241
Rogers, H. E., 373, 382*n.*
Rogers, P. J., 488, 501*n.*
Rogers, T. B., 60, 95, 97, 121*n.*, 122*n.*, 312,
    341*n.*, 488, 501*n.*
Rook, R., 4, 14*n.*
Rorschach, 58, 67
Rosch, E., 486, 501*n.*
Rosenblum, L., 464, 475*n.*
Rosenhan, D. L., 494, 501*n.*
Rosenthal, T. L., 89, 90, 122*n.*
Ross, H., 466, 474*n.*
Ross, L. D., 252, 268*n.*, 488, 501*n.*
Ross, M., 41, 49*n.*, 369, 385*n.*
Rothbart, M. K., 54, 72, 76*n.*
Rotter, J. B., 70, 188, 422, 489–491, 502*n.*
Rubin, K. H., viii, 420, 452–476, 456–462,
    466, 467, 471, 473*n.*–475*n.*, 483, 486,
Rubin, M. E., 345, 356*n.*
Rubio, C. T., 225, 230*n.*
Rudy, T. E., viii, 77–124, 89, 106, 112,
    117*n.*, 118*n.*, 429, 430, 432*n.*, 483,
    497
Ruggels, W. L., 310, 338*n.*
Rumelhart, D. E., 102, 122*n.*
Rush, A. J., 257, 258, 264*n.*, 374, 382, 383*n.*

Rushall, B. S., 441, 444, 451n.
Rushton, J., 466, 474n.
Russell, J. M., 446, 451n.
Russell, P., 369, 386n.
Ryan, E. B., 89, 113, 122n.
Rychlak, J., 189, 232n.

Sacco, W. P., 371, 386n.
Saccuzzo, D. P., 90, 91, 121n., 122n.
Sackeim, H. A., 446, 451n.
Sackett, G. P., 349, 357n.
Safran, J., 394, 400, 402, 432n., 437n.
Salmon, P., 218, 224, 225, 227, 229n., 232n.
Salt, P., 295, 307n., 311, 342n.
Saltz, E., 95, 120n.
Salzberg, P. M., 98, 122n.
Sandman, C. A., 312, 316, 338n.
Santostefano, S., 141, 147n.
Sarason, I. G., 4, 14n., 78, 92, 93, 99,
    122n., 128, 131, 135, 139, 146, 147n.,
    226, 227, 232n., 389, 390, 393, 404,
    409, 410, 423, 424, 437n., 438n., 492,
    498n.
Sarbin, T., 151, 154, 186n.
Saslow, 61
Schaefer, R., 129, 147n.
Schank, R. C., 103, 122n., 454, 461, 475n.
Scheier, M. F., 251, 264n.
Scherrer, H., 293, 306n.
Schiebe, K. E., 313, 341n.
Schless, A. P., 364, 386n.
Schmurak, S. M., 319, 339n.
Schnee, R., 174, 184n.
Schneider, K. C., 129, 148n.
Schön, D. A., 72, 74n.
Schoonover, R. A., 167, 186n.
Schroder, H., 141, 142, 148n.
Schulman, B., 140, 147n.
Schuman, H., 41, 46, 50n.
Schwartz, F., 73, 76n.
Schwartz, G., 160, 184n., 186n., 242, 268n.,
    295, 307n., 311, 341n., 342n.
Schwartz, J., 480, 499n.
Schwartz, L., 364, 386n.
Schwartz, R., 246, 461, 269n., 391, 404, 405,
    407–409, 430, 438n.
Schwarz, J. C., 494, 502n.
Seashore, H., 159, 184n.
Sechenov, I. M., 271, 307n.
Sechrest, L., 441, 451n., 480, 502n.
Seeman, G., 494, 502n.
Seery, J. B., 106, 118n.
Segal, E. M., 82, 122n.

Segal, R., 373, 387n.
Seligman, M. E. P., 235, 269n., 367, 369,
    370, 382n., 383n., 386n., 492, 499n.,
    502n.
Selinger, H., 468, 474n.
Selman, R., 454, 460, 461, 474n.
Semmel, A., 370, 382n., 386n.
Sentis, K, P., 106, 117n., 118n.
Shaffer, J. B., 309, 342n.
Shaffer, M., 70, 76n.
Shalker, T. E., 99, 120n., 496, 502n.
Shannon, C. E., 80, 84, 122n., 123n.
Sharer, R., 405, 434n.
Sharp, K., 459–462, 473n.
Shaver, P., 313, 339n., 341n.
Shaw, B. F., viii, 81, 236, 258, 264n., 361–
    387, 362, 370–372, 374, 376–380, 382,
    382n., 383n., 386n., 425, 483, 492,
    494
Shaw, J. C., 37, 50n., 81, 122n.
Shaw, W. A., 444, 451n.
Sheehan, P., 153, 156, 159, 186n., 187n.,
    260, 269n.
Sheffield, F. D., 309, 339n.
Shelton, T. O., 445, 451n.
Sherwood, J. J., 481, 502n.
Shiffrin, R. M., 91, 123n., 369, 383n.
Shifman, M. A., 55, 75n.
Shisslak, C., 404, 435n.
Shmurak, S. H., 246, 265n., 390, 394, 434n.
Shotter, J., 224, 232n.
Shubsachs, A. P. W., 194, 232n.
Shure, M., 139, 148n., 419, 438n., 453–457,
    467, 476n., 486, 502n.
Sidera, J., 329, 337n.
Sides, J., 156, 184n.
Sieck, W. A., 256, 269n.
Siedentop, D., 444, 451n.
Siegal, M., 456, 473n.
Siegler, R. S., 363, 386n.
Silverman, S., 174, 184n.
Simon, H. A., viii, 5–7, 13n., 16–51, 17–19,
    26, 32–34, 36–39, 44, 48, 48n.–50n.,
    58, 81, 83, 122n., 237, 239, 243, 247,
    261, 263n., 416, 437n., 454, 468,
    469, 475n., 476n., 497
Simpson, 310
Singer, J., 149, 152, 154, 155, 158, 186n.,
    187n., 254, 264n.
Singer, R. N., 441, 451n.
Sipprelle, C. N., 254, 266n., 314, 339n., 407,
    416, 435n.
Sipps, G., 394, 398, 418, 421, 435n.

Skene, R. A., 214, 232n.
Skinner, B. F., 85, 123n., 440, 451n., 495, 496
Slater, P., 227, 232n.
Slipps, R. R., 399, 431n.
Sloves, R. E., 129, 148n.
Slovic, P., 73, 76n.
Sluckin, A., 466, 476n.
Smith, D., 304, 306n.
Smith, E. C., 237, 265n.
Smith, E. E., 87, 91, 123n.
Smith, E. R., 5, 12, 14n., 45, 50n., 239, 241, 269n., 480, 502n.
Smith, J. L., 392, 435n.
Smith, M. B., 323, 342n.
Smith, M. L., 395, 431n.
Smith, M. O., 270, 308n.
Smith, P., 466, 476n.
Smith, R. E., 423, 424, 438n.
Smith, S. H., 392, 436n.
Smolen, R. C., 367, 371, 386n.
Smye, M. D., 260, 269n., 406, 413, 438n.
Snowden, L. R., 56, 76n.
Snyder, C. W., 314, 325, 338n., 341n.
Snyder, M., 256, 269n.
Sobel, H. J., viii, 127–148, 135, 137, 138, 142, 148n., 237, 242, 243, 249, 269n., 414, 480, 483
Sobel, R. S., 369, 386n.
Sobocinski, D., 246, 265n., 398–400, 415, 435n.
Solomon, S., 102, 120n.
Sommerfeld, R., 253, 265n., 315, 318, 339n.
Spanos, N. P., 251, 262, 269n.
Spearman, 58
Spelke, E., 91, 123n.
Spence, J. T., 94, 123n., 448
Spence, K. W., 94, 123n.
Spencer, C., 219, 229n.
Sperling, G., 27, 50n.
Spielberger, C. D., 446, 482, 502n.
Spinner, B., 5, 7, 13n., 239, 263n.
Spivack, G., 139, 141, 148n., 371, 386n., 419, 421, 438n., 453–459, 467, 468, 476n., 486, 502n.
Sprafkin, J. N., 130, 147n.
Spryopoulos, T., 98, 123n.
Spurzheim, 57
Srull, T. K., 105, 124n.
Stake, J. E., 373, 382n.
Starker, S., 158, 187n.
Staub, E., 489, 501n.
Steffen, J. J., 115, 116, 118n., 406, 413, 414, 421, 432n.

Steffy, R. A., 91, 117n.
Stein, B. S., 94, 98, 119n., 123n.
Steiner, R. E., 365, 386n.
Sternberg, D. E., 369, 386n.
Sternberg, R. J., 113, 123n.
Sternberg, S., 87, 89, 123n.
Steronko, R. J., 90, 123n.
Stevens, L. B., 369, 386n., 481, 500n.
Stone, G. L., 393, 398, 399, 401, 405, 408, 434n.
Stone, P. J., 85, 123n.
Stoops, R., 92, 122n., 404, 410, 438n.
Stoyva, J., 182, 187n.
Strayer, F., 466, 476n.
Strayer, J., 466, 476n.
Streufert, S., 141, 148n.
Stricker, G., 67, 74n.
Stringer, P., 194, 232n.
Strong, E. K., Jr., 58, 490, 502n.
Stroop, J. R., 313, 342n.
Stuart, F., 130, 148n.
Stuart, J. L., 366, 386n.
Stuart, R., 130, 148n.
Suchotliff, L., 142, 146n.
Suedfeld, P., 82, 123n.
Sundberg, N. D., viii, 52–76, 54, 56, 64, 70, 72, 73, 73n., 74n., 76n., 262, 269n., 483
Sunshine, R., 157, 184n.
Sutterfield, S., 460, 461, 473n.
Sutton-Simon, K., 399, 400, 407, 415, 438n.
Szegal, B., 271, 307n.

Talkington, 364
Tarler-Benlolo, L., 302, 306n.
Taskey, K. J., 405, 431n.
Taylor, M. A., 90, 123n.
Taylor, R., 99, 117n.
Taylor, S. E., 46, 50n., 105, 106, 123n.
Teasdale, J. D., 99, 123n., 369, 370, 380, 383n., 386n., 492, 499n.
Tejessy, C., 481, 500n.
Terdal, L., 130, 147n.
Terman, 58
Terrell, F., 375, 384n.
Thomasius, 57
Thompson, C. P., 380, 381, 387n.
Thompson, D. M., 368, 387n.
Thoresen, C., 159, 184n., 236, 269n.
Thorngate, 8, 15n.
Thorpe, G. L., 393, 394, 397, 438n.
Thorson, A. M., 272, 273, 308n.
Thurstone, L., 58, 159, 187n., 332
Tiegerman, S., 394, 438n.

Tippett, C. H. C., 254, 269n.
Titchener, E. B., 22, 23, 25, 26, 28, 44, 50n., 237, 269n., 271, 308n.
Tolman, E. C., 289, 308n.
Tomkins, 61
Tresselt, M. E., 30, 50n.
Trexler, L. D., 366, 383n., 393, 399, 401, 435n., 438n.
Trickett, P., 452, 476n.
Tryk, H. E., 65, 76n.
Tucker, D. M., 330, 342n.
Tulving, E., 83, 93, 98, 101, 120n., 123n., 368, 381, 387n., 430, 433n.
Turk, D. C., viii, 4, 5, 15n., 135, 136, 148n., 233–269, 246, 251, 263n., 265n., 417, 480, 483, 494
Turner, M. B., 23, 50n.
Turner, S. M., 243, 264n.
Tutko, T. A., 441, 442, 451n.
Tversky, A., 252, 269n.
Twentyman, C. T., 394, 409, 438n.
Tyler, J. D., 481, 500n.
Tyler, L. E., 54, 56, 64, 70, 73, 76n.
Tyler, M., 224, 228n.

Uhlenhuth, E. H., 369, 384n.
Underwood, G., 91, 123n., 494, 501n., 502n.
Undheim, J. O., 63, 76n.

Van de Castle, R., 152, 155, 162, 171, 185n.
Vanek, M., 441, 451n.
Van Harten, 221
Van Norman, L. R., 260, 266n., 405, 410, 435n.
Varvil-Weld, D., 394, 398, 399, 418, 421, 435n.
Vernon, P. E., 485, 502n.
Verplanck, W. S., 32, 50n.
Vigotsky, L. S., 271, 308n.
Vinacke, W. E., 32, 49n.
Viney, L. L., 215, 232n.
vonBaeyer, C., 370, 382n., 386n.
Voss, J. F., 111, 121n.
Vygotsky, L., 249, 269n.

Wachtel, P., 78, 123n., 128, 131, 141, 146, 148n.
Wainer, H., 312n., 342n.
Walker, B. B., 316, 338n.
Walker, G. R., 393, 417, 418, 431n.
Wallace, J., 140, 148n., 480, 485, 502n.
Wallach, M. A., 64, 76n.
Wallander, J. L., 399, 423, 433n.

Wallis, R. R., 56, 75n.
Walters, R. H., 491, 499n.
Wapner, S., 134, 141, 148n.
Ward, C., 364, 383n.
Waring, S., 466, 474n.
Warren, N. J., 373, 382n.
Warren, R. E., 313, 342n.
Watson, D., 335, 342n., 409, 411, 438n.
Watson, J. B., 8, 25, 28–31, 37, 39, 50n., 51n., 233, 237–241, 243, 269n., 270, 271, 308n., 440, 451n.
Watson, R. I., 481, 499n.
Watt, 28
Watts, J., 452, 453, 476n.
Waxler, C., 466, 476n.
Weakland, J., 218, 229n.
Weaver, W., 80, 123n.
Webb, R., 452, 476n.
Wechsler, 59
Wedding, D., 67, 76n.
Weidman, R., 400, 402, 432n.
Weinberg, S. L., 111, 118n.
Weiner, I. R., 67, 74n.
Weinreb, H., 369, 384n.
Weinstein, E., 453, 476n.
Weintraub, M., 373, 387n.
Weisman, A. D., 135, 137, 138, 142, 148n.
Weiss, C. B., 304, 306n.
Weissberg, M., 393, 438n.
Weissman, A. N., 249, 269n., 366, 367, 374, 383n.
Wellman, H., 11, 14n.
Wells, G. L., 315, 341n.
Welsh, G. S., 69, 74n.
Wener, A. E., 95, 123n., 365, 368, 387n.
Wenger, S., 380, 387n.
Werner, H., 38, 51n., 134, 140, 148n., 225, 232n.
Wertheimer, M., 35, 51n.
Wesman, P., 159, 184n.
West, B. L., 395, 438n.
Westbrook T., 215, 232n., 423, 425, 437n.
Weston, J., 406, 414, 432n.
Wetiz, J., 375, 384n.
Wetzel, R. D., 367, 387n.
Whalen, C. K., 491, 499n.
White, J., 153, 157, 158, 187n.
White, P., 5, 12, 15n.
White, R. W., 323, 342n., 452, 453, 476n., 485, 502n.
Whiting, B., 466, 467, 471, 474n.
Wicker, A. W., 41, 51n., 72, 76n.
Wickland, R. A., 251, 265n., 269n.
Wiggins, J. S., 73, 76n., 487, 502n.

Wijesinghe, O. B. A., 209, 232*n*.
Wildman, B. G., 243, 269*n*.
Wilkins, C., 46, 50*n*.
Williams, C. L., 409, 438*n*.
Williams, K. D., 333, 341*n*.
Williams, L., 404, 435*n*.
Wilson, A., 38, 51*n*.
Wilson, G. T., 89, 123*n*.
Wilson, H., 160, 185*n*.
Wilson, S., 153, 187*n*.
Wilson, T. D., 5, 14*n.,* 41, 44, 45, 50*n.,*
    237–241, 252, 268*n.,* 315, 341*n.,* 446,
    451*n.,* 480, 482, 501*n*.
Wine, J. D., 4, 15*n.,* 92, 93, 123*n.,* 124*n.,*
    389, 391, 406, 410, 413, 438*n*.
Winokur, G., 362, 384*n*.
Winzenz, D., 98, 119*n*.
Witkin, H., 60, 65, 76
Wittgenstein, L., 487, 502*n*.
Wolf, M., 423, 425, 435*n*.
Wolfe, J. L., 394, 438*n*.
Wolpe, J., 78, 124*n.,* 164, 187*n.,* 303, 305,
    308*n.,* 490, 502*n*.
Wood, R. R., 209, 232*n*.
Woodruff, R. A., 362, 384*n*.
Woods, D. J., 90, 123*n*.
Woodworth, R. S., 23, 26, 28, 35–37, 51*n.,*
    58, 250,
Woody, R. H., 70, 76*n*.
Worden, J. W., 137, 138, 148*n*.
Wortman, C. B., 369, 387*n*.

Wright, H., 464, 476*n*.
Wright, P. L., 314, 316, 317, 319, 342*n*.
Wulf, 36
Wundt, W., 22–25, 28, 52, 243
Wyer, R. S., 105, 117*n.,* 124*n*.
Wynne, L. C., 379, 387*n*.

Yaeger, J., 253, 267*n*.
Yandell, B., 317, 338*n*.
Yarrow, M., 466, 476*n*.
Yarrow, P. R., 46, 50*n*.
Yates, B. T., 494, 495, 502*n*.
Yerkes, 58
Yoppi, B., 345, 356*n*.
Youkilis, H., 135, 148*n*.
Young, F. W., 106, 118*n*.
Young, R. M., 270, 308*n*.

Zachary, R., 254, 255, 269*n*.
Zajonc, R. B., 73, 76*n.,* 328, 329, 342*n*.
Zanna, M. P., 46, 49*n*.
Zarit, S., 371, 387*n*.
Zeiss, A. R., 235, 268*n.,* 482, 489, 491, 493,
    501*n*.
Zempel, C. E., 225, 230*n*.
Zigler, E., 452, 485, 476*n.,* 502*n*.
Zimmerman, B. J., 89, 90, 122*n*.
Zitter, R., 393, 434*n*.
Zivin, G., 249, 269*n.,* 466, 476*n*.
Zlotlow, S., 456, 473*n*.

Subject Index

Italicized page numbers indicate material in figures and tables.

A-B-C assessment, 128
Abstraction, selective, 372
Accommodation, cognitive, 143
Achievement
    and conformance, 69
    and independence, 69
Acrophobia, *399,* 415
Action potential, electrical, 275
Advances in Psychological Assessment (Mc-
    Reynolds), *61*
Aggression
    drives for, 68
    and frequency analysis, 343
    models of, 496
    and social learning, 481
Alcohol problems, 4, 89, 204, 207–209
Allographic code, 294, *294*
Alpha waves, 274, *279*
Ambiguity, toleration of, 70
Ambition, 210
American College Test (ACT), 422
American Psychological Association (APA),
    37, *61*
Amplifiers, *282, 283*
Analgesia, 262
Antidepressive medication, 369
Anxiety, 4, 106, *110,* 204, 207, 209, 214,
    215, 241, 296, 335, 337, 388–431, 446,
    447, 491, 492, 494
    and arousal, 427, 428
    assertiveness and heterosocial competence,
        390, 391
    and assessment of self-statements, 404–
        417, *405–407*
    and attention, 92, 93
    cognitive approaches to, 391–398, *392–395*

cognitive model on, 388–391
conclusion on, 425–431
differential, 376
and expectations/self-efficacy, 417–420,
    418
heterosocial levels of, 345–347, *346, 347,*
    391, *399*
and irrational beliefs, 398–404, *399, 400*
and learning, 69
and problem solving/coping, 420–423, *421*
and self-evaluations/attributions, 423–
    425, *423*
and self-statements, 404–417, *405–407*
social, 241, 388, 390, *406, 407,* 412
speech, 155, 156, 178–183, *179, 180,* 388–
    391, *393,* 397, *399,* 400, 401, 418
test, 94, 95, 98, 99, 388–391, *392, 393,*
    401, *405, 406,* 410, 411, *421,* 422,
    423, 429
Appraisal and environmental manipulation,
    235
Appropriateness in conversation, 104
Aptitude–treatment interaction studies, 71
A-reaction, 24, 25, 28
Army Alpha test, *58*
Army Beta test, *58*
Arousal
    and anxiety, 427, 428
    purposeful, 445
    studies of, 276
Assertion Self-Statement Test (ASST), 261,
    404, *405, 406,* 408, 409, 418, 419,
    422, 429
Assertiveness, viii, 111, 112, 164, 241, 390,
    391, *393, 394, 399, 400,* 401–403, *405,*
    407–409, *418, 421, 423,* 485

Assimilation, cognitive, 143
Associative theory of learning, 37
Athletes, 439–449
  athletic traits, 441–444, 446, 449
  and attention, 447
  performance, 440
  and personality, 442, 443
  skillpower in, 443–448
    measures of, 445–448
  summary on, 449
Athletic Motivation Inventory, 441
Attention
  and anxiety, 92, 93
  control of, *392*
  deployment model of, 92, 93
  focus on, *392,* 445, 446
  and information processing, 91–93
  limits on, 17
  selective, 87, 390, 494
  span of, 26
  style of and athletics, 447
  training for, *392*
Attribution
  and depression, 369, 370
  pathological patterns of, 390, 391
Audiotapes, 251, 253
Auditory hallucinations, 241
Auditory imagery, 156 (*see also* Imagery)
"Aufgaben," 27
Authoritarian Personality, The (Adorno *et al.*), *60*
Automatic thoughts, 57
  questionnaire on, 374
  skill response, 440
Autonomic nervous system, 270, 296, 297
Avoidance, 421

Beck Depression Inventory (BDI), 364, 374, 377, 378
Behavioral Social Interaction Test, *406*
Behaviorism, 18, 25, 28–34, 242, 303 (*see also* Cognitive modification)
  approaches of, 287
  behavior modification, 3, 78, 236, 391, 402, 444
  and cognitive approach, *395*
  critique of, 241
  data in, 30, 31
  and electrophysiology, 287, 303, 305
  and introspection, 28
  issues in, 31–34
  and memory, 29, 31
  and observations, 243

and projective methods, 129
and speech, 272, 273
and systems, 28
techniques of, *61*
tradition of, 271
Behavior modification (*see* Behaviorism)
Bellevue Intelligence Scale, *59*
Bell Telephone Laboratories, 80, 81, 273
Bender Visual–Motor Gestalt Test, *59, 62,* 66
Benton Visual Retention Test, 66
Beta waves, *279*
Betts Questionnaire on Mental Imagery (QMI), 155–158, *156, 166*
Binomial test score, 348
Bioassay procedures, 3
Bioelectrical phenomena, 274, 275 (*see also* Electrophysiology)
Biofeedback, 242, 297, 304, 305
Bioinformational theory of emotional imagery, 161
Bipolar scale ratings, *110*
Blood pressure, *276, 302*
Blushing, 30
Brain
  associative areas of, 329, 330
  asymmetry in, 329, 330
  damage to, *59,* 66, 67
  functioning of, accounts of, 270
  waves of, 278, 279, *279,* 304
    classified, 285
Brain and Intelligence (Halstead), *59*
Brainstorming, 248
B-reaction, 24, 25, 28
Bruxism, 296, 300, 301
Buffer, 81

California *F* scale, 70
California Psychological Inventory (CPI), 41, *60, 69*
Cancer Problem-Solving Projective (CPSP) Test, 137–139
Cardiovascular disease, 296
Catastrophizing, 262
Categorization process, 484
Cathode-ray oscilloscope (CRO), 279, 281, *282, 283, 284, 304*
Causality, 237, 244, 262
  and data, 240, 241, 245
  inferences of, 250
  and self-reports, 239
Censoring in verbal reports, 169
Central nervous system (CNS), 275, 297

Cerebral asymmetry, 329, 330
Change in cognitive therapy, 426
Channel capacity, 84
Checklist, coping, *421*
Chemotherapy, 138
Children
    development of, 226
    and failure, 492, 493
    interviews of, 215–217
    problem solving of, 452–473
China
    assessment in, *57*
    civil service exams in, 56
Chronometry, 53, 62
Civil service examinations, 56
"Classification of Men According to Their
    Natural Gifts" (Galton), *57*
Clinical assessment as cognitive assessment,
    73
Clinical vs. Statistical Prediction (Meehl),
    60
Cluster analysis, 207
Coding (*see* Encoding/coding)
Cognitive Interference Questionnaire (CIQ),
    405, 409, 410, 414
Cognitive modification, 391, *392, 393*
    cognitive-behavior modification, 78, 236,
        391, 402
    self-statement, *394*
Cognitive processes, general, 361
    and clinical practice, 236
    and depression, 363ff.
    and think-aloud approaches, 245, 247, 248
Cognitive–rational therapy, *394*
Cognitive response, 310 (*see also* Thought-
    listing technique)
Cognitive–social learning approach to assess-
    ment, 479–498 (*see also* Learning
    theory, social)
    cautions for, 496–498
    person variables in, 483–496
        competencies, 484–486
        encoding strategies, 486–488
        expectancies, 488–490
        self-regulatory systems/plans, 490–496
        subjective values and preferences, 490
    self-reports, direct, 479–483
Colitis, 296
College Entrance Examination Board, *59*
Colon, spastic, 296, 301
Communication
    and comprehension, 103, 104
    engineering, 84

Competency, 56
    and social learning, 484–486
Complexity of cognitive responses, 65, 202,
    328
Comprehension of information, 99–105
    and communication, 103, 104
Computability in conversation, 104
Computers, 83, 286
    and electrophysiology, 277
    and information processing, 81, 82
    and language, 85, 86
    programs, 20, 350
    simulations, *87*
Computer Simulation of Personality (Cat-
    tell), *61*
Conation, 53
Concern Dimensions Questionnaires
    (CDQs), 258, 259
Conditional probabilities for thought listing,
    346, 347, 348
Conditioning, 55 (*see also* S-R psychology)
    classical, 495, 496
    covert, 303
    and learning, 82
Conflict Resolution Inventory, 419
Conformance and achievement, 69
Conformity, 495
Confucianism, *57*
Consciousness
    direct observation of, 25
    science of, 233
    and sensation, 22, 23
    structural aspects of, 22, 23
Conservatism in depression, 374, 375
Consistency, cognitive, 207, 441, 443
    of construct system, 218
Constipation, 296, 301
Constructive alternativism, 216
Construct meaningfulness, 202
Construct perspective (*see* Personal con-
    structs)
Construing, 192
Content analysis, 162–183, *173, 174, 179*
Content postcoding, 201, 203, 223, 226
Contingency, 279
    negative variation, *276*
    stability of, 355
    tables for, 354
Contingent negative variation (CNA), 279
Continuous monologues, 234, 236, 244,
    248–258
    advantages/disadvantages of, 250, 251
Controllability of imagery, 154

Conversational model for psychological
    inquiry, 214
Coping, *392, 393,* 398, 421, *421,* 430
    and anxiety, 388
    and cognitive controls, 141, 143, *394*
    interview, *421*
    responses, 132
    strategies of, 420–423, *421*
    styles of, 429
Core role structures, 200, 212
Coronary heart disease, 296, 301
Covert processes, 234–237, 242
    conditioning, 303
    electrophysiology of, 271, 272, 275–278,
        276, 282, 291, 296–305, *297, 299*
    and modeling, 152, *394*
    and personality, 234–237
    speech, 272
C-reaction, 24, 25, 28
Creative Imagination Scale, 153
Creativity, 54, 62–66, 68–70, 153, 237, 254,
    404
Criterion referenced testing, *61,* 136
Cross-cultural studies, 64, 70
Cross-ethnic studies, 64
Crystallized intelligence, 63
Cue utilization hypothesis, 93
Current concerns, 259

Data
    and causality, 240, 241
    reduction of, 354
Daydreams, 70, 152, 155, 158, 168
Decay in forgetting, 83
Decentering, cognitive, 142
Decision making, 371, 372 (*see also* Problem
    solving)
    assistance in, 56
    industry for assistance in, 56
    and test theory, 60
Delta waves, *279*
Depolarization, electrical, 275, 277 (*see also*
    Electrophysiology)
Depression, 4, 53, 66, 68, 155, 217, 361–382,
    425, 427
    and anxiety, 416
    and attribution, 369, 370
    automatic thoughts in, 257
    cognitions in, 378
    and cognitive assessment research 362, 363
    and encoding/recall/memory, 368, 369
    endogenous, 362

future studies of, 379–382
    and imagery, 367, 368
    and levels of processing, 95–97
    and memory, 368, 369
    and perception, 363–367, 371
    and problem solving, 370–372
    and recall, 368, 369
    self-schema in, negative, 378, 379
    strategies in cognitive assessment of,
        375–379
    subtypes of, 362
    and thinking styles/constructs, 372–375
    unipolar, 367
Depth-of-processing encoding model, 368
Description and Measurement of Personality
    (Cattell), *59*
Description in psychology, 23
Desensitization, 158
    self-control, *393, 394*
    for speech anxiety, 156
    systematic, 182, 241, *395,* 413, 496
Developmental psychology, 223–226
Diagnosis
    in psychotherapy, 241
    reports, 143
Diagnostic Psychological Testing
    (Rapaport), *60*
Dial-turning technique, 311
Diarrhea, 296, 301
Differential anxiety and depression
        inventory (DADI), 376, 377, *377,* (*see
        also* Anxiety)
Differential Aptitudes Test, Space Relations
        from, 159, 160
Differentiation in discrimination, 328
Direction-of-attention hypothesis, 92
Discriminability, 31
Dissociative thoughts, 262
Distorted thoughts, 236, 323–325
Distraction, 262
    and pain, 235
Divergent thinking, 63
Double images, 27
Draw-A-Man Test, *58,* 68
D-reaction, 25, 28, 48
Dreams, 150, 152, 162, 168, 171, 276
    content analysis of, 152, 155
    research on, 254
    verbal reports of, 250
Drugs, 138
    antidepressive, 369
    and creative performance, 55

Dysfunctional attitude scale, 374

EDR, *290*
Educational Testing Service, *59*
Ego
  development of, 70
  involvement of, 107
  levels of, 70
  and projective methods, 128, 131, 134, 144
  psychology, 140
  regression in service of, 68
  strength/development of, 485
  Strength scale, 69
Elasticity, cognitive, and projective tests, 142
Electrocardiogram (ECG), *276,* 281, 285, 290
Electroconvulsive shock therapy (ECT), 241, 369
Electrodermal responding and emotion, 270
Electrodes, 273, 277, 280–283, 287
Electroencephalogram (EEG), 275, *276,* 277–279, 281, 284, 290, *290,* 330
Electrogastrogram (EGG), *276,* 278, 281
Electromyogram (EMG), 273–275, *276,* 277, 278, 281, 283, 284, 285, 290, *290,* 311
Electrooculogram (EOG), *276,* 278, 281, 290, *290*
Electrophysiology, viii, 160–162, 270–305, 311–314, 483
  and behavior therapy, 287, 303, 305
  and bioelectrical phenomena, 274, 275
  and biofeedback, 304, 305
  cognitive physiology research, 295, 296
  and covert processes/behavior, 271, 272, 275–278, *276, 282,* 291, 296–305, *297, 302*
  evolution of, 272–274, *273*
  and eyes, 278
  methods of, 280–287
  model for, 289–294, *289, 290, 292–294*
  readout systems in, 283, 284
  signals of, sources for, 270, 271
  theoretical integration in, 287, *288*
Electroretinogram, *276,* 281
Embedded Figures Test, 65
Emotion, 427, 428
  and cognition, 192
  studies of, 276
  and visceral response, 270
Empathy, 220

Encoding/coding, 368, 484, 486–488, 498
  (*see also* Content postcoding)
  for content analysis, 171–178, *173, 174, 179*
  definitions, 84
  and depression, 368, 369
Encyclopedia of Clinical Assessment (Woody), 70
Endogenous depression, 362 (*see also* Depression)
Environment and testing, 72
Epistemic correlation, 291
Esophagus and emotion, 270
Ethology, cognitive, 12, 243
Event recording, 234, 236, 256–258
Evoked potentials, *276*
Examen de Ingenios (Juan Huarte), *57*
Executive processor, 81
Expectancies
  assessment of, 417–420, *418*
  and cognitive–social learning, 488–490
  of self-efficacy, 492
  subjective values of, 484
  wave of, *276*
Explorations in Personality (Murray), *59*
Expressive methods in assessments, 415–417
Externalization, conscious, 128
Extroversion, 498
Eye movement
  and electrophysiology, 278
  and images, 270

Facial expressions, emotions, 3
Factor analyses, 376
Fantasies, 68, 128, 150, 152, 155
Fatigue, 296
Fear survey schedule, 241
Feedback, 96, 292, 293, 365, 368, 370, 424, 425
Field dependence/independence, *60,* 63, 65, 66, 140
Figure drawings, 62
Filter theory and friendship development, 219, 220
Finger pulse volume, *276*
Flexibility, *472*
  defined, 471
Fluid intelligence, 63 (*see also* Intelligence)
Forgetting, 36, 37, 83, *174* (*see also* Memory)
"Formulations of the Principles of Mental Functioning" (Freud), *58*

Free associations, 33, *58*, 237, 242, 244, 248–251 (*see also* Psychoanalysis)
Free recall, 83 (*see also* Recall)
Functional analysis, assessment as, 130
Functionally independent construction (FIC) 201, 202, 204, 206, 212, 220, 223, 227
Future time perspective, 366, 367

Galvanic skin response (GSR), 19, 34, 274, 304
Galvanometer string, 273
Gambrill–Richey Association Inventory, 402
Gamma waves, *279*
Gastrointestinal disorders, 301, 303
General ability factor *(G)*, 63, 66
Generalization, 396, 440, 498
Generalized Expectations of Others Questionnaire, *418,* 419
"George Kelly's Anticipation Psychology" (Mischel), 189
Gestalt psychology, 18, 25, 30, 34–39
   data in, 35, 36
   issues in, 36–39
   long-term, 37
   and memory, 36
   reports in, 38, 39
Global ratings and uncertainty, 252
Goals, 370
   and self-regulation, 490, 491, 495
   and social action, 462, 464, 465
Goldstein–Scheerer Tests of Abstract and Concrete Thinking, 66
Gordon Test of Visual Imagery Control (TVIC), 154, 157, 158
Grass Instruments Company, 280, 281, 287
Gratification, delay of, 235, 495
Grid techniques, 193–212, *196–199, 205, 206, 208,* 209, 210, 217, 218, 222, 227
Griggs v. Duke Power, 61
Guilford test, 65
Guilt, 155
Gustatory imagery, 156

Hallucinations, 150, 241, 276
Halstead–Reitan battery, *59,* 66
Han dynasty, *57*
Headaches, 296, 301, 303, 314
Heart disease, coronary, 296, 301
Heart rate, *276,* 334
Helplessness
   and depression, 367, 369
   learned, 235
Holland Self-Directed Search, 70

Holtzman Inkblot Technique (HIT), 68
Hopelessness feelings, 366 (*see also* Depression)
Hopelessness Scale, 366
Hostility, 155 (*see also* Aggression)
Human engineering, 83, 84
Humanistic therapy, 241, 242
Hypertension, 296, 301, 303
Hypnosis, 68
   research on, 153
   susceptibility to, 262
Hypothetical–reflective method, 454–462, 467–473, *472*
   validity of, 458–462

Id, impulse discharge, 68
Ideation, 68
   consummatory reward and, 495
Identity, 212
Idiographic/normative analysis, 133
Idiot's Act, *57*
Imagery, 148–183, 445
   content analysis, 162–183
      detail in, system for, 172–178, *173, 174*
      exploratory study of, 178–183, *179, 180*
      theory on, 162–167
      types of, 171, 172
      verbal reports, 167–178
   definition of, 150, 151
   and depression, 367, 368
   dimensions of, 153–155
      content, 154, 155
      qualitative, 154
   electrophysiological assessment, 160–162
   and eye movement, 270
   goals of, 151–153
   performance tests, 158–160
   scope of, 150
   self-reports for, 155–158
Imaginary experiences, 67, 68, 151 (*see also* Imagery)
Implications grid, 209, 210, 222, 227
Implicit response, 272
Implosion, 182
Impulsivity in children, 115
Independence and achievement, 69
Indirect assessment, 41
Individual differences
   in imagery ability, 153
   and thought listing, 334, 335
Individuality, 484
Individual differences multidimensional

scaling (INDSCAL), 108, 109, *109, 110,* 111, 112
Inferences, 240, 250, 497, 498
  arbitrary, 372
  and memory, 43–46
  natural/strategic, 102, 104
Information-processing paradigm, 17–19, 24, 25, 37, 46, 47, 62, 77–117, 361, 380
  assumptions in, *87*
  and clinical sciences, 89, 90
  conclusion on, 117
  decomposing mental processing, 86–89, *87, 88*
  described, 79–82
    information in, 80, 81
    processing in, 81, 82
  and electrophysiology, 300
  historical background on, 82–86
  internal, 275
  major tenets of, 86
  neuromuscular model of, 291, 292, *292*
  and projective methods, 133
  research lines on, 67, 90–116
    attention, 91–93
    comprehension, 99–105
    levels of processing, 93–97
    metacognition, 112–116
    retrieval processes, 97–99
    schemata of processing, 105–112, *109, 110*
  stages/levels in, 90, 91, 93–97, 100
  variables in, 54
Inhibitive mediation, 254
Inner speech, 272, 397
Inoculation theory, 322
Input, 81, 100
Insight treatment, *392, 393*
Insomnia, 300
Integrative constructions, 202
Intellectualization, 421
Intelligence, 498
  and creativity, 64
  crystallized/fluid, *61*
  deficits of, 62
  and field independence, 66
  fluid, 63
  structure of, *60,* 63
  tests of, *58, 60, 61,* 62–64, 72, 483, 496
Intensity
  of construct system, 218
  scores of, 206, 207
Interactional models of depression, 376

Interference and memory, 83, 313
Internal dialogue, 272, 397
Internal Discrimination Task (IDT), 222
Interpersonal Problem-Solving Assessment Technique (IPSAT), *421,* 422, 423
Interpersonal transaction group, 220
Interpretation of Dreams, The (Freud), *58*
Interstimulus interval (ISI), 90
Interviews, 262
  of children, 215–217
  open-ended, 6
Intestinal activity and emotion, 270
Introspection, 21, 24, 25, 237, 240, 241, 243 246, 250
  analytic/psychophysical, 25–27
  and behaviorism, 28
  classical, 26
  and inspection in physics, 23
  as investigative tool, 21, 22
  reports of, 24
Introversion, 497
  and extroversion in mental disorders, *60*
Inventories and irrational beliefs, 403
Inventory of Test Anxiety, 389
IQ (*see also* Intelligence)
  bias in, *60, 61*
  and environments, 72
  as general intelligence, 63
Irrational beliefs, 236, 389, *393–395,* 398–404, *399, 400*
Irrational Beliefs Test (IBF), 374, 395, 398, *399,* 400–404, 408, 416, 427
Irrational Statements Inventory, *405,* 411

Jackson's Personality Research Form, 379
Journal of Abnormal Psychology, 369
Judgment and Reasoning in the Child (Piaget), *58*
Judgments, psychophysical, 27, 28

Kahneman attention deployment model, 92
Kinesthetic imagery, 150, 156
Kuhnian paradigm perspective, 77, 78, 82, 86
Kymographic measures, 273
KYST, 108

Laddering technique, 209, 226
Lag sequential analysis, 349–352, *351,* 355,
Language
  and memory, 100
  personal construct assessment of, 488
Larry P. v. Riles, 61

Latencies, 23
  of cognitive processes, 25
  observed, 23, 24
  structural research on, 28
Learning Potential Assessment Device, *61*
Learning theory, social, viii, 3, *61,* 115, 127,
    422 (*see also* Cognitive–social
    learning approach to assessment)
  and aggression, 481
  association in, 37
  and cognitive therapy, 78, 79
  and competency, 484–486
  and information, 89
  potentials, 63, 71
Leary Interpersonal Checklist, 41
Libidinal drives, 68
Life histories, 54
Likert-type rating scales, 158, 211
Linear regression, 108
Linguistics, 83–85, 275, 276, *276* (*see also*
    Language)
Locus of control in projective tests, 142
Longitudinal studies, 381
Long-term memory (*see* Memory)
Loosened construing, 201, 217–219

Magnification and minimalization, 373
Maladaptive character structure, 486
Manic–depressive patients, 362 (*see also*
    Depression)
Man–machine system, 84
Marital interaction, 352
Marlowe–Crowne Social Desirability Scale,
    157
Massachusetts General Hospital, 137
Mastectomy, 138
Meaningfulness, 204, 221, 270, 271
Means–End Problem-Solving (MEPS) test,
    371, 372, 408, 418, 419, 421, *421,*
    422, 456, 460
Measurement of Meaning, The (Osgood), *60*
Mediation, cognitive, 235
Memory, 29, 31, 66, 250, 363, 375, 379,
    472, 493
  and behaviorism, 29, 31
  and deficit as term, 369
  and depression, 368, 369
  and Gestalt psychology, 36
  high-speed scanning, 89
  and inferences, 43–46
  information processing in, 83
  and interference, 313
  introspective access to, 44

  and language, 100
  long-term, 20, 26, 34, 37, 43, 261, 361,
    469, 483
  and observation, 26
  and rehearsal, 83, 84
  short-term, 17, 18*n.,* 26, 27, 33, 48, 247,
    361, 368, 483
  tests of, 159, 160
  verbal reports on, 168–171
Mental retardation, identification of, 56
Mental tests as term, *57*
Messages in information processing, 80
Metacognition, 11, 112–116, 138, 141, 430,
    461, 483, 494–496
Metamemory, 116, 430
Microscopic level of analysis, 355
Minnesota Multiphasic Personality Inventory
    (MMPI), *59, 61,* 62, 69, 72, 137,
    441, 485, 486
Minnesota Paper Form Board, 159
Mixed messages, 366
Modeling, 495, 496
  cognitive, 392, 393
  covert, 152, *394*
Modified S-R Inventory of General Trait
    Anxiousness, *400*
Monologues, continuous (*see* Continuous
    monologues)
Mood states and cognition, 99, 255, 363
Moral development, stages of, 70
Motor coordination, 66, 270, 271
Multidimensional scaling, 429
Multiple regression, *110*
Multitrait–multimethod procedures, *60*
Muscles
  and electrophysiology, 277, 296–298, *297,*
    304, 305
  neuromuscular functioning, 271, 275, 291,
    292, *292*
  and thought processes, 270, 271
  tonus of, 273

Naturalistic methods, 417
Negative thought cycle, 347, 348, 350, *351,*
    390, *405*
Neobehaviorism, 82, 86 (*see also* Be-
    haviorism)
Neomentalism, 381
Neuromuscular functioning, 271 (*see also*
    Muscles)
  circuit model of, 275, 291, 292, *292*
Neurophysiological processes, 66, 275
  and electrophysiology, 278–286

Neurosis, 218, 362, 498
Neurovoltmeter, 273
Neutral thought, 350, *351,* 352
Nonassertiveness, 388
Non-REM sleep, 175 [*see also* Rapid-eye-movement (REM) sleep]
Nonverbal construing, 220, 221
Norm-referenced testing, *61*
Nursing, 68

Objective personality inventories, 62
Objective-reality thoughts, 323-325
Objective self-awareness, 313, 314
Object relations, 70
Observation
  and memory, 26
  and reaction time, *57*
  and social problems, 462-466
Office of Strategic Services, *59*
Ohio State University, 315
Olfactory imagery, 150, 156
Ordination/integration, 220, 226
  scores, 202, 204
Organic imagery, 156
Organismic perspective on development, 134
Organization and Pathology of Thought
  (Rapaport), *60*
Organization in cognitive responses, 328
Oscilloscopes, 279-281, *282,* 283, 284, 304
Output, 81, 100
Overgeneralization, 323, 362, 372
Overlearning, 239
Overt behavior, research emphasis on, 271

Pacemakers, 334
Pain
  and cognitive reconstruction, 260
  and cognitive strategies, 262
  tolerance to, and distraction, 235
Paivio's Individual Differences Questionnaire
  (IDQ), 158
Paradigms
  identification of, 86
  of information processing, 77-117
  integration within, 146
  and projective methods, 133, 134
Paranoia, 69
Pathological bias in traditional tests, 72
Peace Corps, 481
Peer ratings, 459, 480-482
Perception and depression, 363-367
Peripheral blood flow, 242
Personal constructs, 65, 188-228, 430

assessment techniques in, 193-217
  grid techniques, 194-212, *196-199, 205,*
    206, 208
  nongrid techniques, 212-217
and cognition, 191-193
  construing process, 192, 193
conclusion on, 226-228
defined, 190, 192
hierarchy in, 209
and inquiry, 189-191
investigative lines, 217-226
meaningfulness in, 202
poles of, 196, 197, 203, 222
as psychological pathways, 200
superordinate/subordinate, 209, 210
theory on, 189, 191, 193, 194, 209, 216,
  217, 220, 221, 223-228
Personal Data Sheet, *58*
Personal equation for astronomers, *57*
Personality, 481
  and athletics, 442, 443
  and cognitive consistencies, 443
  and covert processes, 234-237
  inventories of, 69, 70
  and social learning, 480
  tests of, 42, 62
Personality (Allport), *59*
Personality and Assessment (Mischel), *61*
Personality through Perception (Witkin), *60*
Person-focused approach, 9-11
Personology and athletics, 449
Phenomenal reports, 38, 39
Phobias, 69, 296, 300, 301, 303, 483, 496
Phonetic code, 294, *294*
Pictorial tasks in projective methods, 141
Pictorial thinking, 65
Placebo effect, 305
Pneumograms, 275, 276, *276,* 285, *290*
Polygraphs, ink-writing, 284, 285
Portrait gallery, 216
Positive though cycle, 347, 348, 350, *351,*
  405
Positivity, 220
Prediction, 481, 482
  accuracy in, 211, 220
  of achievement, 481
  of affiliative behavior, 481
Preschool Interpersonal Problem-Solving
  (PIPS) test, 455-460
Preverbal nonverbal construing, 227
Primary process thinking, 67, 68
Principal components analyses, 227
Private speech, 248, 249, 251, 253, 254

Problem Athletes and How to Handle Them
    (Ogilvie & Tutko), 441
Problem solving, 35–38, 135, 237, 361, 388,
    398, 412–414, 425, 430, 452–473, 486
  and anxiety, 420, 421, *421*
  and behavioral assessment, 467, 468
  definitions/theory on, 453, 454
  and depression, 370–372
  hypothetical–reflective method, 455–462,
    467, 468
    limitations of, 461, 462
    validity of, 458–462
  and informational complexity, 142
  model for assessment of, 468–471
  in natural setting, 466, 467
  observational perspective on, 462–466
    advantages of, 465, 466
  and projective tests, 142, 143, 145
  skills in, viii, 483
  social competence, 388, 389, 391, *406,
    421,* 467
  strategies of, 420–423, *421,* 428
  style of, 132
  summary/conclusion on, 471–473, *472*
  think-aloud, 10, 253
"Processes Affecting Scores . . . "
    (Cronbach), *60*
Process-oriented assessment, 54
Product-oriented assessment, 54, 71
Professional Football Players Association,
    442
PROFIT, 108, 109
Projective methods, 55, *59,* 62, 67–69,
    127–146, 242, 243, *406,* 414, 415,
    445, 446
  background/historical context of, 128–130
  basic assumptions in, 130–135
  behavioral–analytic model of, 135–137,
    144
  cognitive variables in, 139–144
  conclusion/summary on, 144–146
  definition/redefinition of, 131–135
  design/construction of, 135–139
  paradigm basis of, 133, 134
  and problem solving, 142, 143, 145
  projective analysis, 128
  in psychoanalysis, 127, 131, 144–146
  and self-instructions, 397, 440, 495
  and social learning, 480
Project Omega, 137
Psychasthenia, 69
Psyching up of athletes, 445
Psychoanalysis, 52, 53, 67, 68, 446

  and projective methods, 127, 131, 144–146
  social awareness of, 78
Psychodiagnostics (Rorschach), *58*
Psychodynamically oriented therapy, 242
Psycholinguistics, 454
  and comprehension, 100, 101
Psychological Corporation, *58*
Psychological Differentiation (Witkin), *60*
Psychological Review, 28
Psychology of Personality Constructs, The
    (Kelly), *60, 189*
Psychometrics, history of, 71
Psychometrika, 58
Psychomotor skills, 439, 440 (*see also*
    Athletes)
Psychophysiological techniques, 270, 274,
    287 (*see also* Electrophysiology)
Psychosis
  and communication problems, 105
  depression, 362
  personality, 200
  subpersonalities in, 196
Psychosituational viewpoint, 133
Psychotherapy, 63, 195, 363
  behavioral, 242
  cognitive-learning perspective in, 398, 430
  and diagnosis, 241
  humanistic, 241, 242
  personal-construct-oriented, 201, 203, 214
  process of, vii, 221–223, 426
  psychodynamic orientation, 242
  research on, 162
Pulse, peripheral, 285
Pupillogram, *276*

Q sorts, *60*
Questionnaire of How You Take Tests, *421,*
    422
Questionnaire on Mental Imagery (QMI),
    155–158, *156,* 166
Questionnaires, 5, 44, 46, 155–158, *156,* 166,
    258–261, 373, 374, *405,* 409, 410,
    414, *418,* 419, 424, 444, 447, 448
  coping, 421, *421*
  and irrational beliefs, 403
  postexperimental, 169, 170
  posttreatment, 397
  prediscussion, 345
  self-report, 152
  social skills, 108
  structured, 404, 411

Random sampling, 259

advantages/disadvantages of, 255, 256
of thoughts, 254–256
Rank order grid, 204–209, *205, 206, 208,*
217, 218
Rapid-eye-movement (REM) sleep, 162, 170,
171, 175
Rating extremity, 202
Rating scales, 258–260
Ratings grid, *196–199*
Rational behavior therapy, *394*
Rational–emotive therapy, *392–394,* 396
Rationalization, 261
Rational reevaluation, *394*
Rational restructuring, 391, *392, 393*
Raynaud's disease, 242
Reaction time
and observation, *57*
procedures in, 312–314
Reactive depression, 362 (*see also* Depression)
Reactivity, 247, 251, 258, 331*n.*
Readout systems, 283, 284
Reality, acceptance of, 323
Recall
and depression, 368, 369
free, 83
methods of, 411, 412
Reconstructive techniques, 234
Referent-level code, 294, *294*
Reflection–impulsivity, 66
Reflective reasoning, 460
Regression in service of ego, 68
Rehearsal
covert, *394*
and memory, 83, 84
Reinforcement, *87,* 370 (*see also* Behaviorism)
covert negative, 303
and depression, 367
and free association, 242
schedules for, 495
Relaxation, 262, 273, 294–303, *302,* 395
Relevance in conversation, 104
Reliability, 315, 382, 414, 447
in coding, 171, 172, 178
coefficients, 355
and global judgments, 252
of observational data, 354, 355
predictive, 65
of projective methods, 139, 145
in rating scales, 260, 261
split-half, 331, 332
test–retest, 331, 376
in thought-listing, 331, 332
Repertory grid, 193, 195, 204, 207

Reportable subjective reactions, 314
Repression, 234, 333
Reptest Interaction Technique (RIT), 211
Reptest techniques, 193, 200, 209, 211
Resistance-to-change grid, 210, 211
Restructuring, cognitive, 391, 393, *394,* 395,
395, 396
Retrieval of information, 97–99
Retrospective accounts, 19, 242, 247, 248
Rigidity and cognitive structure, 261, 262
Rod-and-Frame Test, 65
Rokeach dogmatism scale, 70
Role Construct Repertory Test, *60,* 65, 193
Role playing, 142, 241, 243, 395, 396, 402,
407, 414, 422, 424
Rorschach test, 55, 62, 67, 68, 72, 73, 129,
480

San Jose State College, 441
Schizophrenia, 65, 66, 68, 69, 89–92, 195,
201, 209, 217–219, 367, 376, 379,
380, 498
"Science friction," 77
Scientific revolutions, 77, 78, 82 (*see also*
Information-processing paradigm)
Self-assessments, 482, 497
Self-characterization, 213, 214
Self-coaching, *392*
Self-concept, 314, 376
Self-control of bodily processes (*see also*
Biofeedback)
Self-deception, 446, 480
Self-disclosure, 211
Self-efficacy, 143, 445, 489
assessment of, 417–420, *418*
expectations of, 492
and self-reports, 246, 247
Self-estimates, 481
Self-evaluations, viii, 337, 389, 390, 423–425,
423, 448
Self-expectations, 482
Self-instructions, 397, 440, 495
and projective methods, 134, 141, 143
training in, 390, *393, 394*
Self-monitoring, 236, 256, 257, 485
Self-observation, 21, 24
Self-operations control, 298 (*see also* Relax-
ation)
Self-perception, negative, 364
Self-predictions, 481
Self-ratings
grid, *199*
of imagery, 152

Self-ratings (*continued*)
    validity of, 481, 482
Self-referent encoding, 368
Self-regulation, 493
    and metacognition, 114, 115
    systems of, 484, 490–496
Self-reinforcement, 364, *395*, 430, 493
    (*see also* Reinforcement)
Self-Rep Inventory, 211, 212
Self-reports, 5–9, 42, 237, 239, 242, 254,
        310, 315, 420, 443, 482 (*see also*
        Self-statements)
    and anxiety, 401
    appropriateness of, 239, 240
    data in, 247
    and depression, 361, 362
    direct, described, 479–483
    of fear, 156
    guidelines for, 6–9
    for imagery assessment, 155–158
    questionnaire, 152
    scales for, 4
    strategies of, 234–237
    validity of, 8
Self-role personality, 212
Self-statements, viii, 337, *392, 393*, 410, 411,
        483, 491–494, 496 (*see also* Self-
        reports)
    and anxiety, 404–417, *405–407*
    assessment of, 404–417, *405–407*
    modification of, 391, *394*, 395, *395*, 396
    negative, 389, 390, 397
    positive/negative, 253, 262, 345, 408, 415,
        416
    subjective meaning of, 429
    test of, *405*
Self-sufficiency, capacity for, 201
Self-theory, negative, 376
Semantic differential technique, *60*
Semantic interpretations, 277
Sensation
    and experience, 22
    and introspection, 25, 26
    kinesthetic, 27
Sensitization, 234
    covert, 303
Sensors, electrical, 281, *282*
Sensory saturation, 154
Sentence completion tests, 62
Sequential dependency in cognitive per-
        formance data, 343–356, 429
    data types, 343–345

methodological considerations for, 354,
        355
    sequence description, 345–352, *346, 347,
        349, 351*
    stability of event sequences, 352–354, *353*
    summary on, 355, 356
Sequential method of cognitive–behavioral
        projective tests, 135
Serial invalidation model, 217, 218
Serial rotation of dyadic interactions, 220
Sets of information, 105
Sexuality
    deviation in, 4
    fantasy of, 70
    performance of, 53
SFORM 1, 108
Sigma waves, *279*
Signal stopping technique, 310
Silent speech, 272
Similarity–attraction hypothesis, 219
Singer's Imaginal Processes Inventory (IPI),
        152, 155, 158
Situational Irrational Cognitions Inventory
        (SICI), *400, 403*
Sleep, research on, 254
Smith Sequence of Mental Events, 87, *88*, 89
Social Avoidance and Distress Scale, 409
Social competence research (*see* Problem
        solving)
Social evaluative anxiety (*see* Anxiety)
Social Interaction Self-Statement Test
        (SISST), 409, 426
Socialization, 484
    scale of, 69
Social learning theory (*see* Learning theory,
        social)
Social loafing, 333
Social problem situation analysis measure
        (SPSAM), 457–459
Social problem solving (SPS) (*see* Problem
        solving)
Social Readjustment Rating Questionnaire,
        364
Social skills
    observational indexes for, 461
    training for, 395
Sociobiology, 454
Socioeconomic status, 467
Sociometric status, 459
"Sources of Behavioral Variance . . . "
        (Endler & Hunt), *61*
Soviet Union

standardized psychological testing in, *59*
testing ban in, 56
Spatial reasoning tests, 159
Speech anxiety (*see* Anxiety)
Sport Competition Anxiety Test (SCAT),
446, 447
Sport psychology, 439 (*see also* Athletes)
S-R Inventory of General Trait Anxiousness,
61, 402
S-R psychology, 29, 30, 34, 35, 85, *87,* 96,
316, 317 (*see also* Behaviorism;
Conditioning)
*Standards for Educational and Psychological
Tests and Manuals* (APA), *61*
Stanford Achievement Test, *58*
Stanford–Binet intelligence test, *58, 62*
State transition diagram, 348, *349*
Stereotyping, 329–331, 487
Storage in computers, 81
Storage oscilloscope, *282*
Story completion test, 373
Strategy in cognition, 114
Stream of consciousness, 248
Stress, 420
inoculation, *392, 393,* 420
Strong–Campbell Interest Inventory, 70
Strong Vocational Interest Blank, *58,* 481
Stroop test, 313
Structure, 22–28
as basis of cognitive responses, 328, 329
of intelligence/intellect, *60, 63*
and latency, 28
and scoring of grids, 201
structuralism, 18, 22–28, 34
data in, 24, 25
issues in, 25–28
and think-aloud approaches, 261–263
Studies in Deceit (Hartshorne & May), *58*
Stuttering, 209, 210, 221
Style, cognitive, 62, 65, 66, 372–375, 397
Sub-delta waves, *279*
Subjective behavior rating scale, 402
Subjective Probability of Consequences
Scale, 408, 418, *418,* 419, 422
Subjective utility, *394*
subjective expected utility (SEU), 417–419
Subjectivity
and cognitive–social learning, 490
rating scale, 402
and self-statement, 429
utility, *394,* 417–419
and values, 490

Subordinate constructs, 209, 210
Subvocalization, 272
audio measures of, 276, *276*
Suicidal behavior/ideation, 241, 367
Superordinate constructs, 202, 209, 210, 221,
226
Survey of Heterosocial Interaction for
Females, 409
Susceptibility to hypnosis, 262
System architecture, 81
System differentiation, 225
Systems in science, 28, 29

Tachistoscope, 26, 34
Tacit construing, 221
Tactile imagery, 150, 156
Task variables in information, 114
Tension, 296–298
Test anxiety (*see* Anxiety)
Test of Attentional and Interpersonal Skills
(TAIS), 447
Test-taking skills, 389
Thematic Apperception Test (TAT), *59, 62,*
69, 135, 142, 170, 445, 446, 480, 481
Theory of Mental Tests, The (Gulliksen), *60*
Theta waves, *279*
Think-aloud approaches, 19, 30, 35, 233–263,
406, 416
and cognitive antecedents of behavior,
237–246
and cognitive processes, 245, 247, 248
conclusion on, 263
and continuous monologues, 248–258
and event recording, 256–258
problem solving, 10, 253
random sampling of thoughts, 254–256
rating scales, 258–260
reconstruction procedures for, 260, 261
and self-reports, 234–240, 242–258
and structure, 261–263
validity of, 238
verbal reports, 238, 239, 241–247, 255
Thought dubbing, 413
Thought-listing technique, viii, 4, 215,
309–337, 344, *405, 406,* 412, 413,
425, 429
and dimensions of cognitive response,
319–324
and electrophysiology, 311–314
as independent variable, 336, 337
and individual differences, 334, 335
instructions in, 315, 316

Thought-listing technique (*continued*)
    interval in, 316–318
    judging/combining of, 324–326
    procedures in, 345, 346, *346, 347,* 348
    reliability in, 331, 332
    and role of cognitive responses, 335, 336
    scoring of, 318, 319
    spoken/written assessment, 314
    and stereotypy of cognitive responses, 329–331
    and stream of cognitive responses, 326–328
    and structural bases of cognitive responses, 328, 329
Thought-sampling approach, 4, 234, 236, 254–258, 448
Thoughts–feelings ratings, *405*
Threat Index, 212
Tightening of constructs, 217
Timing and think-aloud approaches, 247, 248
Tomography, 66
Torrance test, 65
Torres Straits Expedition, *57*
"Toward a Cognitive Social Learning . . ." (Mischel), *61*
Traits, 486
    athletic, 441–444, 446, 449
    in psychology, 440, 441
    ratings of, 485
Transducers, 283
Two-factor theory of intelligence, *58*

Ulcers, 301
Ulysses (Joyce), 248
Uncertainty
    and global ratings, 252
    mathematical representation of, 80
Unclassifiable thoughts, 323
Unconscious processes, 248, 446, 488 (*see also* Psychoanalysis)
Uniqueness in conversation, 104
U.S. Army Air Force psychology section, *59*
U.S. Public Law 94–142, *61*
Unity of cognitive responses, 328
University of Illinois, 439
University of Wisconsin, 161
Utilizing in think-aloud approaches, 253

Validity, 315, 331*n.,* 382, 414, 426
    construct, *60,* 447
    discriminant, *60*
    ecological, 9

and global judgments, 252
of hypothetical–reflective method, 458–462
of observational data, 354, 355
predictive, 65, 447
of projective methods, 139, 145
in rating scales, 260, 261
of self-ratings, 481, 482
and self-reports, 246
of thinking aloud, 238
Variance in individual differences, 63
Verbal Behavior (Skinner), 85
Verbalization, 30, 250
    concurrent, 19
    and creativity, 254
    productive thinking, 63
    spontaneous, 417
    verbal coding, *294*
    verbal reports, 255
        accuracy of, 239–241
        usefulness of, 238, 239, 241–246
Videotapes, 4, 7, 115, 116, 236, 253, 260, 261, 311, 396, *405,* 413, 414, *421,* 424, 448
Videotape thought reconstruction (VTR), *406*
Visceral phenomena and cognitive processes, 270
Visual imagery, 150, 156
Visual systems and mental acts, 270
Vividness, sensory, 154, 156
Vividness of Visual Imagery Questionnaire, 156
Voting behavior, 209

Watson–Glaser Critical Thinking Appraisal, 64
Wechsler Adult Intelligence Scale (WAIS), 62, 249, 364
Wechsler Intelligence Scale for Children (WISC), *59, 62*
Wechsler Memory Scale, 66
Western Electric, 280
Whispering, involuntary, *276*
Wishful thinking, 324
Word association, *58,* 67, 244, 313, 364
Word listing technique, 70
Worry–Emotionality Inventory, 389

X rays, 135

Z index, 348, 350
Z score, 67